Routledge Revivals

Economics of Natural & Environmental Resources

I0891179

First written in 1977, *Economics of Natural and Environmental Resources* presents a collection of articles written in exploration of the economic, social, and ecological problems peculiar to natural and environmental resources. Whilst focusing on the economic theory of natural resources, the contributions also consider geological, technological, and institutional features of particular resources. Policy implications and considerations are central to the text and although the book was published over thirty years ago, the issues discussed remain relevant to today's society.

Routledge Revivals

Economics of Natural & Environmental Resources

Economics of Natural & Environmental Resources

Edited by
Vernon L. Smith

Routledge
Taylor & Francis Group

First published in 1977
by Gordon and Breach

This edition first published in 2013 by Routledge
2 Park Square, Milton Park, Abingdon, Oxon, OX14 4RN

Simultaneously published in the USA and Canada
by Routledge
711 Third Avenue, New York, NY 10017

Routledge is an imprint of the Taylor & Francis Group, an informa business

Publisher's Note
The publisher has gone to great lengths to ensure the quality of this reprint but points out that some imperfections in the original copies may be apparent.

Disclaimer
The publisher has made every effort to trace copyright holders and welcomes correspondence from those they have been unable to contact.

A Library of Congress record exists under ISBN: 73093135

ISBN 13: 978-0-415-84220-4 (hbk)
ISBN 13: 978-0-203-76066-6 (ebk)
ISBN 13: 978-0-415-84228-0 (pbk)

ECONOMICS OF NATURAL & ENVIRONMENTAL RESOURCES

Edited by
Vernon L. Smith

University of Arizona

GORDON AND BREACH
New York London Paris

Gordon and Breach Science Publishers Inc.
One Park Avenue
New York, N.Y. 10016

Editorial office for the United Kingdom

Gordon and Breach Science Publishers Ltd.
41/42 William IV Street
London W.C.2

Editorial office for France

Gordon & Breach
7-9 rue Emile Dubois
Paris 75014

Library of Congress Cataloging in Publication Data
Main entry under title:

Economics of natural & environmental resources.

1. Natural resources--Addresses, essays, lectures.
I. Smith, Vernon L. II. Title.
HC55.E357 333.7 73-93135
ISBN 0-677-15040-7

Library of Congress catalog card number 73-93135
ISBN 0 677 15040 7

Printed in Great Britain.

TABLE OF CONTENTS

PREFACE

This book has its origin in the growing interest in the economic, social, and ecological problems peculiar to natural and environmental resources. Production and consumption from such sources is characterized by (1) the possibility of exhaustion for fixed stock resources and of irreversible changes, including exhaustion, for replenishable and environmental resources, (2) externalities that arise primarily because of the common property features of some natural resources, (3) fundamental biophysical constraints expressing the laws of species growth, and (4) macrophysical constraints expressing the laws of conservation of energy and mass that directly link the quality of the environment with all forms of waste and energy discharge from production and consumption activities. The papers in this collection touch in some way upon these distinguishing characteristics.

The major guiding principle in selecting the papers has been to create a volume in the economic theory of natural resources. An attempt has also been made to include papers dealing with the geological, technological, and institutional features of particular resources. Such background material provides an essential input to the theoretical work in this book and to future extensions in theory. Policy implications and considerations are an important element in all of the papers, and for that matter is a motivating element in most of the papers. Research scholars interested in natural resources usually have an interest in public policies concerning such resources.

Individual chapters vary considerably in the mix of formal theory and technological-institutional materials that are presented.

For various reasons two or three important early articles, cited frequently in this volume, could not be included in the collection. I am particularly happy to acknowledge reprint permissions for the following, with original places of publication and copyrights holders as indicated:

Chapter 1. R. Cummings, "Some Extensions of the Economic Theory of Exhaustible Resources," *Western Economic Journal*, September 1969, 7, 201-210.

Chapter 2. N. Vousden, "The Theory of Exhaustible Resource Use: A Basic Model," a revision and extension of "Basic Theoretical Issues of Resource Depletion," *Journal of Economic Theory*, April 1973, 6, 126-143. Copyright held by Academic Press.

Chapter 3. V. Smith, "An Optimistic Theory of Exhaustible Resources," *Journal of Economic Theory*, December 1974, 9, 384-396. Copyright held by Academic Press.

Chapter 4. P. Dasgupta and G. Heal, "The Optimal Depletion of Exhaustible Resources," *Review of Economic Studies Symposium*, 1974, 3-28.

Chapter 5. J. McKie and S. McDonald, "Petroleum Conservation in Theory and Practice," *Quarterly Journal of Economics*, February 1962, 76, 98-121.

Chapter 6. P. Davidson, "Public Policy Problems of the Domestic Crude Oil Industry," *American Economic Review*, March 1963, 53, 85-108.

Chapter 7. R. Kuller and R. Cummings, "An Economic Model of Production and Investment for Petroleum Reservoirs," *American Economic Review,* March 1974, 64, 66-79.

Chapter 8. H. Wan, "A Generalized Wicksellian Capital Model--An Application to Forestry," *Economic Papers,* Economic Institute, Academia Sinica, Taipei, 1965, 1-13.

Chapter 9. A. Scott, "Optimal Utilization and Control of Fisheries," in Turvey and J. Wiseman, eds. *The Economics of Fisheries,* Round Table sponsored by the International Economic Association (Rome: FAO, 1957).

Chapter 10. R. Turvey, "Optimization in Fishery Regulation," *American Economic Review,* March 1964, 54, 64-76.

Chapter 11. J. Boyd, "Optimization in Fishery Regulation: Comment," *American Economic Review,* June 1966, 56, 511-517.

Chapter 12. V. Smith, "General Equilibrium with a Replenishable Natural Resource," *Review of Economic Studies Symposium,* 1974, 105-115.

Chapter 13. J. Crutchfield and A. Zellner, "Mathematical Formulations," Appendix 1, pp. 112-117 in "Economic Aspects of the Pacific Halibut Fishery," Fisheries Industrial Research I, Bureau of Commercial Fisheries, U.S. Department of the Interior, Washington, D.C. (On October 3, 1970, The Bureau of Commercial Fisheries was transferred to the Department of Commerce. It is now the National Oceanic and Atmospheric Administration from whom permission for reprinting was granted.)

Chapter 14. C. Plourde, "Exploitation of Common-Property Replenishable Natural Resources," *Western Economic Journal,* September 1971, 9, 256-266.

Chapter 15. V. Smith, "The Primitive Hunter Culture, Pleistocene Extinction, and the Rise of Agriculture," *Journal of Political Economy,* August 1975, 83, 727-755.

Chapter 16. O. Burt, "Optimal Resource Use Over Time With an Application to Ground Water," *Management Science,* September 1964, 11, 80-93.

Chapter 17. O. Burt, "Temporal Allocation of Ground Water," *Water Resources Research,* 1st Quarter 1967, 3, 45-56. (Permission for reprinting granted by the American Geophysical Union as primary publisher.)

Chapter 18. G. Brown and C. McGuire,"A Socially Optimal Pricing Policy for a Public Water Agency," *Water Resources Research,* 1st Quarter 1967, 3, 33-43. (Permission for reprinting granted by the American Geophysical Union.)

Chapter 19. V. Smith, "Economics of Production from Natural Resources," *American Economic Review,* June 1968, 58, 409-431.

Chapter 20. O. Burt and R. Cummings, "Production and Investment in Natural Resource Industries," *American Economic Review,* September 1970, 60, 576-590.

Chapter 21. R. Ayres and A. Kneese, "Production, Consumption, and Externalities," *American Economic Review,* June 1969, 59, 282-297.

Chapter 22. V. Smith, "Littering, Derelicts and the Pricing System," Previously unpublished.

Chapter 23. Published without the Appendix in V. Smith, "Dynamics of Waste Accumulation: Disposal versus Recycling," *Quarterly Journal of Economics*, November 1972, 86, 600-616.

Chapter 24. E. Keeler, M. Spence and R. Zeckhauser, "The Optimal Control of Pollution," *Journal of Economic Theory*, February 1972, 4, 19-34. Copyright held by Academic Press.

Chapter 25. W. Brock, "A Polluted Golden Age." Previously unpublished.

Chapter 26. A.Fisher, J. Krutilla and C. Cicchetti, "The Economics of Environmental Preservation: A Theoretical and Empirical Analysis," *American Economic Review*, September 1972, 62, 605-619.

Chapter 27. K. Arrow and A. Fisher, "Environmental Preservation, Uncertainty, and Irreversibility," *Quarterly Journal of Economics*, May 1974, 88, 312-319.

Chapter 28. V. Smith, "Economics of Wilderness Resources." *Intermountain Economic Review*, Fall 1976, 7.

I am indebted to the National Science Foundation for research support in natural resource economics.

Monticello, Utah
August 1971
Revised, Tucson, Arizona
May 1976

CHAPTER 1

SOME EXTENSIONS OF THE ECONOMIC THEORY OF EXHAUSTIBLE RESOURCES

RONALD G. CUMMINGS*
MONTANA STATE UNIVERSITY

This paper represents an attempt to extend that body of theory referred to in the literature as the "Economic Theory of Exhaustible Resources." An analytical model is presented that describes the optimal time-path of production for a decision-making unit exploiting an exhaustible natural resource under two differing sets of assumptions vis-a-vis conditions of resource-supply. In Case 1, centralized management of production from a common property resource is considered [14]. In Case 2, the decision-making unit is the firm, which is assumed to be the sole owner of a given resource-stock as in the theory of the mine [2], [6], [9], [13].

The results extend those derived in earlier works primarily in three ways: (1) With reference to the "theory of the mine," the analytical description of the firm's optimal time-path of exploitation, under conditions where costs are affected by cumulative production, is expanded and clarified. (2) The optimum time-path of production from a "common property" resource under central management is considered in contrast to the industry model presented by Smith [14]. (3) An effort is made to suggest the possible Pareto Optimal ramifications associated with the centrally-managed common property resource. A discussion is also provided concerning the possibility of boundary solutions, i.e., where the firm produces at a maximum or zero rate.

In Section I a model of production from exhaustible resources is presented. In Sections II and III, interpretative results from the model relating to two sets of assumptions regarding conditions of resource-supply are presented. A summary follows in Section IV.

I. A MODEL OF RESOURCE EXTRACTION FROM EXHAUSTIBLE SUPPLIES

We begin the formulation of our problem by defining an "exhaustible resource" as a natural resource the supply of which is not naturally replenished. This definition would include as exhaustible resources petroleum, coal, and other minerals, and groundwater in some basins and would exclude forests, fisheries, surface water, etc.[1] The model is that of n firms extracting an exhaustible natural resource. Each firm is assumed to be a "price-taker" in the market in which the resource is sold and is assumed to

*This paper draws heavily upon the author's Ph.D. dissertation submitted to the University of Kansas entitled "The Economic Theory of Exhaustible Resources: Some Extensions." The author wishes to acknowledge valuable assistance given by Richard W. Ruppert and Oscar Burt. Also, he is deeply indebted to R. L. Gordon for many helpful comments.

[1]This definition is admittedly arbitrary in that, given a sufficiently long time-horizon, even coal and petroleum supplies may be replenished. We are concerned with a time-horizon that excludes this possibility. Also, our framework of analysis focuses on a geographically specific resource-stock; thus, we do not consider ramifications of increased supplies through discoveries of new stocks.

behave in such a way as to maximize the present value of profits. We assume that firms know with certainty the time-path of prices between $t = 0$, the beginning of the decision unit's time horizon, and $t = T$, the end of the time horizon.

The optimum time-path of production from the exhaustible resource is considered under two differing assumptions vis-a-vis conditions of resource supply. In the Case 1 model, we posit the existence of n independent firms that share a common resource stock. Thus, each individual firm can claim as "its own" only that amount of the resource stock which it actually extracts. These conditions characterize in large part groundwater mining in the Texas "High Plains" area, where each firm accounts for only a small part of total groundwater mining. Under these conditions, it is generally accepted (see, e.g., [11]) that users of groundwater push the rate of use to the point where marginal profits associated with water are zero. In this model, we shall assume that each of these n firms assigns its right of resource-use to a central authority. The central authority then determines that rate of resource-use for each firm, at each t, which maximizes the present value of profits for the resource area as a whole.

In our Case 2 model we consider the case where each decision-making unit, the firm, has secure tenure in a particular resource stock. These conditions generally characterize the mine, where the firm owns a given quantity of land and the mineral rights to all minerals lying thereunder. The essential characteristic that distinguishes the Case 2 firm from the Case 1 firm is that the firm's costs and future revenues are independent from actions of other firms in the industry (given that each firm is a "price-taker"). Thus, our Case 2 model is simply a special case of the first model where $n = 1$.

Define $x(t)$ as the amount of the resource in stock at t,[2] and $q_i(t)$ as the quantity of the resource to be extracted by firm i at t. It is assumed that the initial resource stock, $x(0)$, is known and constant. Thus, the amount of the resource in stock at any t is given by

$$(1) \qquad x(t) = x(0) - \int_0^t \sum_{i=1}^{n} q_i(s)ds \qquad i = 1, \ldots, n, \text{ Case 1}; \quad n = 1, \text{ Case 2}$$

and the time rate of change in the resource stock is

$$(2) \qquad \frac{dx}{dt} = - \sum_{i=1}^{n} q_i(t) \qquad i = 1, \ldots, n, \text{ Case 1}; \quad n = 1, \text{ Case 2}$$

Since the resource is assumed *fixed* in supply, it must be true that total resource-use during the interval $0 \leq t \leq T$ may not exceed the initial resource stock, i.e.,

[2]The state variable $x(t)$ is defined in earlier works [6] [9], as *cumulative* production at t, rather than the undepleted stock as used here. Given the nature of the decision rules discussed below, we need to describe the state of the system at any particular t—thus the present definition of $x(t)$.

(3) $$\int_0^T \sum_{i=1}^{n} q_i(t)dt \leq x(0) \qquad i = 1, \ldots, n, \text{ Case 1} \quad n = 1, \text{ Case 2}$$

Our control $q_i(t)$ is assumed non-negative for all $0 \leq t \leq T$. Further, it is assumed that there exists an upper bound $h_i(x)$ on the rate of production for each firm, which becomes increasingly restrictive as resource-stocks fall. Assuming that each firm's capital stock is fixed over the interval $0 \leq t \leq T$,[3] the imposition of $h(x)$ is a simple application of the law of diminishing returns. These constraints are expressed by the inequalities

(4) $$-q_i(t) \leq 0$$

(5) $$q_i(t) \leq h_i(x), \qquad h_i(x) > 0$$

(6) $$\frac{\partial h_i}{\partial x} > 0 \qquad i = 1, \ldots, n, \text{ Case 1} \quad n = 1, \text{ Case 2}$$

Let the profit function for each firm be of the form

(7) $$\pi_i(t) = \pi_i[q_i(t), x(t)]$$

where $\pi_i(t)$ is an increasing concave[4] function of $q_i(t)$ and a monotonically increasing function of $x(t)$. Then the optimum rate of resource extraction is given by the arcs $u_i^0(t), x^0(t)$ which maximize

(8) $$\text{Max.} \int_0^T \sum_{i=1}^{n} \pi_i[q_i(t), x(t)]e^{-rt}dt \qquad n = 1 \text{ for Case 2}$$

subject to the constraints (2) – (5), where $x(0)$ and T are given constants.

Problems of the type stated above are best treated within the context of Optimal Control Theory [8]. Optimal Control Theory may be viewed essentially as an extension of the canonical form of the Euler Equations used in the classical calculus of variations [5, Ch. 4].[5] The most interesting feature of this extension, in terms of the interpretative richness of the results, is the addition of an auxillary arc $\beta(t)$ associated with the differential form of the exhaustion constraint (2).[6] At any time-period t^*, $0 \leq t^* < T$, $\beta(t^*)$ turns out to be the effect on the criteria function (7) evaluated at all $t > t^*$ of an incremental change in our state variable $x(t^*)$. Thus, for example, problems associated with cumulative production may be treated explicitly, while the

[3]Examination of the optimum time-path of exploitation in the case where capital stocks vary is made in [2] and [14].

[4]The assumption of concavity is used to avoid the problem of an indeterminate solution for $q(t)$. This is one of the basic difficulties in Hotelling's treatment of the competitive firm [9, pp. 140-41]—that if $P(0) = P(t)e^{-rt}$, $0 < t \leq T$, where P is *net* price, the rate of output for the individual firm is generally indeterminate (also, see [6, p. 281]).

[5]The extension of the classical calculus of variations by Optimal Control Theory is, in this writer's view, analogous to the extension of the classical calculus by Kuhn-Trucker theory.

[6]The author is particularly grateful for R. L. Gordon's review of this paper. His penetrating remarks concerning the relationship between Optimal Control Theory and the calculus of variations have proven invaluable.

form of the solutions given by the classical calculus of variations prohibited such a treatment.[7] A detailed discussion of the cumulative production problem is given in Section III.

The maximization of (8) subject to the constraints (2) – (5) is a special case of the general control problem of Bolza, to which a theorem developed by Hestenes may be applied [8, pp. 346-48]. If our system is appropriately differentiable, then at each t, $0 \leq t \leq T$, there exists a Hamiltonian function

$$H(t) = \sum_{i=1}^{n} \pi_i[q_i(t), x(t)]e^{-rt} - \beta(t)\sum_{i=1}^{n} q_i(t) - \lambda \sum_{i=1}^{n} q_i(t) - \sum_{i=1}^{n} \mu_i(t)[q_i(t) - h_i(x)] + \sum_{i=1}^{n} \varepsilon(t)q_i(t) \tag{9}$$

such that the following conditions hold

$$\frac{\partial \pi_i}{\partial q_i}(t)e^{-rt} - \beta(t) - \lambda - \varepsilon_i(t) + \mu_i(t) = 0 \qquad i = 1, \ldots, n \tag{10}$$

$$q_i(t) - h_i(x) \leq 0 \tag{11}$$

$$\mu_i(t)[q_i(t) - h_i(x)] \leq 0 \quad \mu_i(t) \geq 0 \qquad i = 1, \ldots, n$$

$$q_i(t) \leq 0 \tag{12}$$

$$\varepsilon_i(t)q_i(t) = 0 \quad \varepsilon_i(t) \geq 0 \qquad i = 1, \ldots, n$$

$$\int_0^T \sum_{i=1}^{n} q_i(t)dt - x(0) \leq 0 \tag{13}$$

$$\lambda[\int_0^T \sum_{i=1}^{n} q_i(t)dt - x(0)] = 0 \qquad \lambda \geq 0$$

$$\frac{d\beta}{dt} = -\{\sum_{i=1}^{n} [\frac{\partial \pi_i}{\partial x}(t)e^{-rt} + \mu_i(t)\frac{\partial h_i}{\partial x}(t)]\} \tag{14}$$

The reader familiar with Lagrangian and Kuhn-Tucker techniques will recognize the similarity between (10) – (13) and the necessary conditions for constrained maximization. The terms $\mu_i(t)$, $\varepsilon_i(t)$, and λ are, respectively, the shadow prices associated with the constraints (11), (12), and (13) and may be positive only if strict equality holds. Thus, in what follows, $\mu_i t$ and $\varepsilon_i(t)$ are referred to as "boundary costs."

The optimum arc for $q_i(t)$, i.e., the optimum time-path of production, is described by the following theorems which are stated without proof.[8] For notational simplicity, the following definitions are used.

[7] An interesting application of Control Theory to optimal investment policy is given in [4].

[8] The omission of formal proofs, which were included in an appendix to an earlier draft, is at the request of the Editor. The outline of the proofs is straightforward, however. Evaluate (10) at 0 and t. Substitute the solution for $\beta(t)$ derived by integration of (14), and Theorems 1 and 2 are the result. Corollaries 1 and 2 follow directly from (19). Proofs are available from the author upon request.

(15) $\frac{\partial \pi_i}{\partial q_i}(t) \equiv M\pi_i(t)$ is marginal profits at t for firm i.

(16) $\frac{\partial C_i}{\partial q_i}(t) \equiv MC_i(t)$ is marginal costs at t for firm i.

(17) $P(t) \equiv$ the market price of the resource at t.

THEOREM 1: Let Case 2 assumptions hold ($n = 1$); then at $t = 0$ the optimum rate of production for the firm is that rate such that

$$M\pi(0) - \mu(0) + \varepsilon(0) = M\pi(t)e^{-rt} - \mu(t) + \varepsilon(t) + \int_0^t [\frac{\partial \pi}{\partial x}(s)e^{-rs} + \mu(s)\frac{\partial h}{\partial x}]ds \tag{18}$$

for all t, $0 < t < T$.

THEOREM 2: Let Case 1 assumptions hold. Then the central authority optimally directs each firm i ($i = 1, \ldots, n$) to produce at a rate such that

$$MC_i(t) + \mu_i(t)e^{rt} - \varepsilon_i(t)e^{rt} = P(t) - [\beta(t) + \lambda]e^{rt} \tag{19}$$

for all t, $0 \leq t \leq T$.

COROLLARY 1: If (19) holds, then the central authority has equated the sum of marginal production costs plus "boundary costs" ($\mu_i(t) - \varepsilon_i(t)$) among all firms, i.e.,

$$\begin{aligned} MC_1(t) + [\mu_1(t) - \varepsilon_1(t)]e^{rt} &= MC_n(t) + [\mu_n(t) - \varepsilon_n(t)]e^{rt} \\ &= P(t) - [\beta(t) - \lambda]e^{rt} \end{aligned} \tag{20}$$

COROLLARY 2: Let Case 1 assumptions hold and choose two time-periods t and τ such that $0 \leq t < \tau \leq T$. Then the following relation holds:

$$\begin{aligned} [\lambda + \beta(t)]e^{rt} = {} & M\pi_i(\tau)e^{-r(\tau-t)} - (\mu_i(\tau) - \varepsilon(\tau))e^{rt} \\ & + e^{rt}\int_t^\tau [\sum_{i=1}^n \frac{\partial \pi_i}{\partial x}(s)e^{-rs} + \sum_{i=1}^n \mu_i(s)\frac{\partial h_i}{\partial x}]ds \end{aligned} \tag{21}$$

for all $i = 1, \ldots, n$.

Attention is now focused on an economic interpretation of the results (18) – (21).

II. THE OPTIMUM TIME-PATH OF EXPLOITATION: CASE 1

We now wish to examine the properties of the optimal decision rules given by a central authority to each of n firms exploiting a common property resource. By Theorem 2 and Corollary 1, the present value of profits associated with the entire resource-stock is maximized if, at each t, the central authority equates marginal production costs (plus "boundary costs") among all producing firms, i.e.,

$$MC_i(t) + \mu_i(t)e^{rt} - \varepsilon_i(t)e^{rt} = P(t) - [\beta(t) + \lambda]e^{rt} \tag{22}$$

On the left-hand side of (22) is the i-th firm's marginal production costs plus the terms $\mu_i(t)$, the cost to firm i at t of an *effective* upper bound on its rate of production $h_i(x)$, and $\varepsilon_i(t)$, the cost to firm i of producing at a zero rate at t.

On the right-hand side of (22) is an area-wide term that is a given constant to each firm. $P(t)$ is the market price of the resource at t. The term $[\beta(t) + \lambda]e^{rt}$ may be interpreted as a measure of the user costs to the entire resource area of an increment of resource use by firm i at t [see (21)]. This user cost includes (1) the present value of firm i's profits foregone in future periods associated with an increment in resource-use at t, and (2) the increased costs to *all* firms in the resource area which are "pushed forward" to future periods as a result of an increment in resource use by firm i at t. The entire right-hand side of (22) is then the "net" value of an increment of the resource to be used by firm i at t.

Equation (22) essentially represents Gordon's requirement for (socially) efficient industry behavior when his argument is extended to the common property resource. For example, Gordon argues that ". . . the [efficient] socialist managers can be expected to minimize production costs in a given period by equating marginal production costs among operating mines . . ." [6, p. 282], a requirement that is satisfied by (22).

Of further interest is Gordon's discussion of the probable difference between rates of extraction (and therefore income-streams) chosen by private and centralized decision-making units exploiting mineral deposits. Gordon argues that ". . . when user costs are involved, the (social) efficiency requirement becomes that the sum of social marginal production and user costs equal price; . . . [but, under private exploitation] each firm equates the sum of *its* marginal production and user costs to price and the issue is whether this sum is the same thing as the sum of social costs?" [6, p. 282]. This question is particularly relevant when private exploitation of the common property resource is considered. As was mentioned earlier, it has been rather convincingly argued in the literature that private exploitation of the common property resource is generally characterized by production at rates where marginal profits are zero.[9] Thus, the sum of marginal production and user costs (which are zero) for each firm i equals marginal revenue, i.e.,

$$MC_i(t) = MR(t) \tag{23}$$

If, however, production is centrally controlled, each firm i equates marginal production costs plus an area-wide user-cost to marginal revenues.

[9] See, for example, Milliman [11, p. 429] with reference to groundwater stocks, Davidson [3] on crude oil production, and Smith [14] for a general treatment of production from natural resources.

$$MC_i(t) + [\beta(t) + \lambda]e^{rt} = MR(t) \tag{24}$$

and there is indeed a difference in these sums.[10]

One might regard Gordon's view as that of arguing that centralized management of the resource results in a time-path of exploitation that is Pareto Optimal in a narrowly defined sense.[11] But this is precisely what is shown in this paper: that when firms operate at rates dictated by (22), in which case marginal costs are equated among all firms, the present value of area-profits are maximized and any alternative time-path of production must yield a value for area-profits that is no greater than (8).

The results of this paper suggest a method for using taxes to bring about alternative production rates by private firms exploiting a common property resource such that the present value of the time-stream of profits is increased. For example, a tax in the amount of $[\lambda + \beta(t)]e^{rt}$ would force private producers to operate at the optimal rate (24). The tax collections may be returned (in such a way as to avoid affecting the firm's choice of $q_i(t)$) in such a manner as to yield in present value terms an income stream for *all* firms that would be no lower than that generated by producing where $M\pi(t) = 0$ (for all t), and could increase the value of the income-stream for some (if not all) producers. This tax, then, would bring about a time-path of resource-extraction that would be Pareto Optimal in this narrowly defined sense.

III. THE OPTIMAL TIME-PATH OF EXTRACTION: CASE 2

In the instance where the firm has secure tenure in a given resource-stock the results from Theorem 1 apply. In the discussion that follows, our analysis is much less cumbersome if we make the simplifying assumption that $q(0)$ lies in the open interval $0 < q(0) < h(x)$. Boundary solutions will be discussed below.

From Theorem 1, the optimum rate of production for the firm is that rate at which

$$M\pi(0) = M\pi(t)e^{-rt} + \int_0^t \left[\frac{\partial \pi}{\partial x}(s)e^{-rs} + \mu(s)\frac{\partial h}{\partial x}\right]ds \tag{25}$$

for all $0 < t \leq T$.

The term on the left-hand side of (25) is marginal profits at $t = 0$. The first term on the right-hand side of (25) is the present value of the profits that an increment of the resource might earn in any future period $t > 0$. The second term is the integral of discounted costs that accrue to the firm at all $t > 0$ as a result of an incremental change in production at $t = 0$. This cost has two components: (1) the increase in costs at all future periods

[10] Boundary terms $\mu_i(t)$ and $\varepsilon_i(t)$ are not included in (24) so that our argument may parallel that of Gordon's. Gordon's model [6] does not explicitly consider bounded production rates.

[11] Particularly, in the sense that any alternative time-path of extraction would decrease the present value of basin profits.

attributable to an incremental fall in resource-stocks $[\frac{\partial \pi}{\partial x}(s)]$; (2) the incremental increase in the effectiveness of the upper bound $h(x)$ in all future periods in which the bound would be effective.

The entire right-hand side of (25) satisfies Scott's definition of a "user cost": ". . . the present value of the future profit foregone by a decision to produce a unit of output today [at $t = 0$]" [13, p. 42].

Decision rule (25) is tantamount to the rule: continue production at $t = 0$ until the marginal value of an increment in production at $t = 0$ equals its user cost.

In the case where production is unaffected by cumulative production, equation (25) becomes identical to the results derived in earlier works by Hotelling [9], Scott [12] [13], and Gordon [6]. Allowing $\frac{\partial \pi}{\partial x} = 0$, and implicitly, $\frac{\partial h}{\partial x} = 0$, (25) becomes

$$(26) \qquad M\pi(0) = M\pi(t)e^{-rt}$$

for all $0 \leq t \leq T$ which is the result derived by these writers.

If production is affected by cumulative production, however, the form of the decision rule given by (25) differs markedly from those derived by the above writers. It must be pointed out, however, that this difference is primarily the result of the mathematical tools employed rather than differences in assumptions. In particular, Hotelling and Gordon simply did not have the benefits of the relatively recent extensions of the classical calculus of variations represented by Optimal Control Theory. Thus, the mathematical tool used in this paper allows us to come to grips with a problem for which an interpretative solution eluded Hotelling, Gordon, and Scott, and we were able to identify explicitly the effect on the optimum time-path of exploitation of allowing costs to be affected by cumulative production.

Scott, for example, argues that ". . . deterioration [of the resource-stock] probably leads to a stretching-out of the removal process in excess of the time that would be required if the same amount of material were available under constant cost conditions" [13, p. 42]. To evaluate this argument, we observe that (25) must hold for all t, $0 \leq t \leq T$, in which case the following conditions hold for all τ, $t < \tau \leq T$

$$(27) \qquad M\pi(t)e^{-rt} = M\pi(\tau)e^{-r\tau} + \int_t^\tau [\frac{\partial \pi}{\partial x}(s)e^{-rs} + \mu(s)\frac{\partial h}{\partial x}(s)]ds.$$

Now, from (25) it is clear that marginal profits at $t = 0$ are larger (the rate of production is less) the greater the integral term. This same conclusion holds for all $t > 0$ by (27). Thus, costs and production rates that are affected by cumulative production do indeed "stretch-out" the production process and Scott's argument is verified. This conclusion follows, of course, directly from the argument that user-costs restrict the rate of production at any t. If $\frac{\partial\pi}{\partial x} > 0$, then an increment of production at any t "pushes forward" higher costs which constitute a user cost at t, thus further restricting the rate of output.

Also, it is interesting to note the effect on the "r percent profits growth rule" of costs that are affected by cumulative production [6, p. 283]. As Hotelling, Gordon, and Scott have observed, if $\frac{\partial\pi}{\partial x} = 0$, marginal profits increase at a rate of r percent (cf. (26)). If $\frac{\partial\pi}{\partial x} > 0$, and $\mu(t) = \epsilon(t) = 0$, it can be shown (10) that

$$M\pi(t) = [\lambda + \beta(t)]e^{rt} \qquad (28)$$

for all t, $0 < t \leq T$, in which case

$$\left[\frac{d}{dt}M\pi(t)\right]/M\pi(t) = r + e^{rt}\left(\frac{d\beta}{dt}\right)/M\pi(t) \qquad (29)$$

The term $\frac{d\beta}{dt}$ is negative by (14), and costs affected by cumulative production have the effect of slowing down the percentage rate of increase in marginal profits.

It is plausible to expect that at some t, say $t = 0$, relative prices may be such that production at the maximum rate $h(x)$ is warranted. In this case, by (18) we have

$$M\pi(0) - \mu(0) = M\pi(t)e^{-rt} + \int_0^t \left[\frac{\partial\pi}{\partial x}(s)e^{-rs} + \mu(s)\frac{\partial h}{x}\right]ds \qquad (30)$$

for all t, $0 < t \leq T$. We now have an additional cost in our solution: the opportunity cost of an *effective* upper bound $h(x)$. The term $\mu(0)$ measures the increment to profits at $t = 0$ should the upper bound $h(x)$ be varied incrementally ($\mu(0)$ could then be the return to investment at $t = 0$).

The other possibility, suggested by Gordon [6, p. 278], is that relative prices may be such that it does not pay to produce at some t, say $t = 0$. In this case (25) becomes

$$M\pi(0) + \epsilon(0) = M\pi(t)e^{-rt} + \int_0^t \left[\frac{\partial\pi}{\partial x}(s)e^{-rs} + \mu(s)\frac{\partial h}{\partial x}\right]ds \qquad (18)$$

for all t, $0 < t \leq T$. The term $\epsilon(0)$ is the cost to firm of the effective constraint $q(0) = 0$. The term $\epsilon(0)$ measures the difference (which is positive) between marginal profits that could be earned at $t = 0$ and the user cost associated with such use. $\epsilon(0)$ then measures the value of an increment in negative production, or the value of an increment of the resource stored for future use.

IV. SUMMARY AND CONCLUSIONS

An attempt has been made to bring together and formalize some of the problems that seem to exist in the "Pure Theory of Exhaustion." In the case of the common property resource, it is shown that profits in the resource area are maximized by equating marginal production costs plus an area-wide user cost among all producing firms. This requirement is very similar to Gordon's requirement for social efficiency in the production from mines.

With reference to the appropriated exhaustible resource, it has been shown that where costs increase due to cumulative production, the rate of extraction is reduced and the production period stretched out—a conclusion suggested by Scott, and that the percentage rate of growth in marginal profits is reduced. Also, the ramifications associated with the boundary solutions are made explicit.

REFERENCES

1. K. Arrow and M. Kurtz, *Public Investment, The Rate of Return and Optimal Fiscal Policy*, Institute for Mathematical Studies in the Social Sciences. Stanford 1968.
2. R. Cummings and O. Burt, "On the Economics of Production from Exhaustible Resources," *Am. Econ Rev.* (forthcoming).
3. P. Davidson, "Public Policy Problems of the Domestic Crude Oil Industry," *Am. Econ. Rev.*, Mar. 1963, *53*, 85-108.
4. A. Dobell and Y. Ho, "Optimal Investment Policy; An Example of a Control Problem in Economic Theory," *Instit. of Electronical and Electronics Eng., Trans. on Auto. Control*, Feb. 1967, AC-12, No. 1, 4-14.
5. I. Gelfond and S. Fomin, *Calculus of Variations*. New Jersey 1963.
6. R. L. Gordon, "A Reinterpretation of the Pure Theory of Exhaustion," *Jour. Pol. Econ.*, June 1967, *75*, 274-86.
7. L. C. Gray, "Rent Under the Assumption of Exhaustibility," *Quart. Jour. Econ.*, May 1914, *28*, 66-89.
8. M. R. Hestenes, *Calculus of Variations and Optimal Control Theory*. New York 1966.
9. H. Hotelling, "The Economics of Exhaustible Resources," *Jour. Pol. Econ.*, Apr. 1931, *39*, 137-75.
10. S. L. McDonald, *Federal Tax Treatment of Income from Oil and Gas*. Washington, D. C. 1963.
11. J. W. Milliman, "Commonality, The Price System, and Use of Water Supplies," *So. Econ. Jour.*, Apr. 1956, 22, 426-37.
12. A. Scott, "Notes on User Costs," *Econ. Jour.*. June 1953, *63*, 368-84.
13. ———, "The Theory of the Mine Under Conditions of Certainty," in *Extraction Resources and Taxation*, ed., Mason Gaffney. Madison 1967.
14. V. Smith, "Economics of Production from Natural Resources," *Am. Econ. Rev.*, June 1968, *58*, 409-31.
15. D. Todd, *Ground Water Hydrology*. New York 1966.

CHAPTER 2

THE THEORY OF EXHAUSTIBLE RESOURCE USE: A BASIC MODEL*

NEIL VOUSDEN, *Australian National University*

In this paper a relatively simple basic model of resource exploitation is developed both as a framework for subsequent analysis and as a means of directly answering some basic questions associated with resource scarcity. In the model presented the only factors of production explicitly acknowledged are natural resources. This simplification is justified on two grounds: (i) the gain in mathematical simplicity achieved by ignoring the roles of capital and labour makes it possible to encompass more problems than otherwise; and (ii) the essential features of these problems are most conveniently isolated when natural resources are the only inputs.

The central issues to be discussed here will be

(i) when will a community find it optimal to use up all of a scarce depletable asset?

(ii) for what duration of time should exploitation of such an asset continue?

(iii) what is the optimal intertemporal pattern of exploitation of the resource?

(iv) how are the decisions implicit in (i) - (iii) affected by the community's set of preferences and the physical constraints to which the economy is subject?

(v) how is the optimal use pattern of the resource affected by
(a) the length of the economy's planning horizon and
(b) the size of the initial stock of the resource?

The paper is divided into three sections. In Section I the basic model will be presented and the forms of the functions of the model discussed. Section II will examine the problem of exploiting a non-renewable resource so as to maximize the present value of utility derived from the future

*This paper is a generalized version of another paper by the author [4]. The author wishes to thank John Pitchford and Ngo Van Long for comments.

stream of consumption produced by using the resource. In Section III we will extend the analysis of Section II to incorporate an explicit conservation motive on the part of consumers and/or a depletion effect in production.

I. THE BASIC MODEL

In this section we shall formulate the problem of how to distribute exploitation of a fixed stock of an exhaustible asset over time in an optimal fashion. In establishing the foundations of the model it will be necessary to examine closely the properties of the main functions involved.

For the time being we will only discuss the functions relevant to Section II; those relevant to Section III will be discussed there.

To begin let us simply note that social welfare (W) is a strictly concave function of total consumption (C):

$$(1) \qquad W = v(C); \quad v'(C) > 0 \quad v''(C) < 0 \qquad v \in C^2$$

So that total consumption for the economy will never be zero (even when all of the resource has been used up) we assume that there is an alternative source of consumption in the economy which is not produced from the resource and which is permanently at a constant level, $\bar{C}$. This allows us to abstract from the question of what the community should do after the resource has been exhausted, a question which itself raises a whole range of other issues and lies beyond our present scope. Assuming this alternative source of consumption also provides us with a convenient simplification of the relevance of the rest of the economy to the resource-use decision.[1]

Production of consumption goods from resources (C_x) is assumed to be function of the amount of the resource extracted (E), so that:

$$C_x = \phi(E).$$

Thus total consumption is given by:

$$C = C_x + \bar{C} = \phi(E) + \bar{C},$$

and it is possible to regard the utility function simply as a function of E, which we shall denote u(E). Before we proceed we would like to know how the form of u is affected by the form of ϕ. We see that

$$u' = v'\phi'$$

$$u'' = v''(\phi')^2 + v'\phi''.$$

For all the functions we shall consider it is assumed that $\phi'(E) \geq 0$ so that $u'(E) \geq 0$. Also for the standard concave production function with $\phi'' < 0$ we have $u'' < 0$ in which case u has the same curvature properties as v. When ϕ is smoothly convex for low values of E and concave for higher values (Fig. 1(a)) then for all but low values of E u will be concave, but it may be convex for low E. While there is the slight possibility that u may in this case have more than one point of inflexion we shall ignore this contingency here.

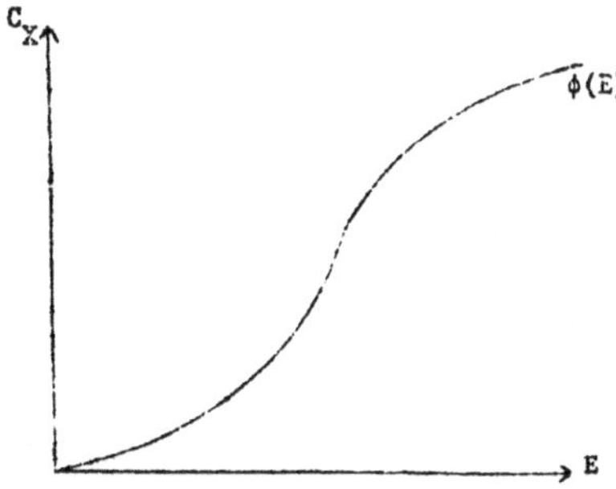

Figure 1(a)

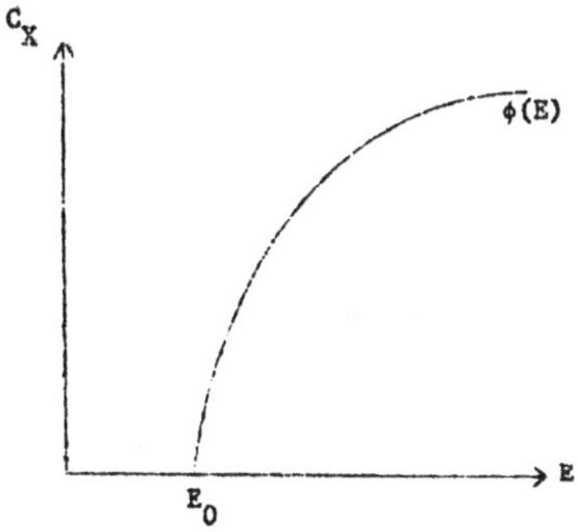

Figure 1(b)

It is also possible to envisage a production function of the form illustrated in Fig. 1(b) and defined formally by:

$$(2) \quad \begin{cases} E > E_0 \Rightarrow u(E) > 0; \quad u'(E) > 0; \quad u''(E) < 0; \\ 0 \leq E < E_0 \Rightarrow u(E) = 0 \\ \text{for some } E_0 > 0 \end{cases}$$

This form of production function would be relevant in a situation where a certain minimum level of extraction (E_0) is needed before any consumption goods can be produced. In this case the u function will have the same general form as ϕ (although the horizontal segment may correspond to negative values of u). For our purposes it will be convenient to distinguish three classes of u-function. They are illustrated in Fig. 2 below.

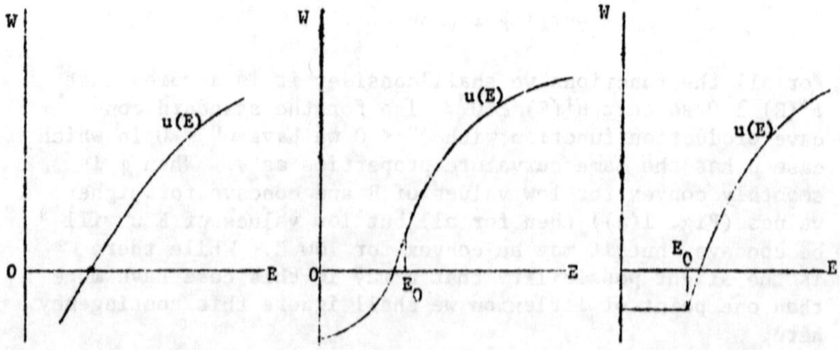

Figure 2(a) Figure 2(b) Figure 2(c)

(a) A class I u-function is defined by:

$$u'(E) > 0 \quad u''(E) < 0 \quad \forall_E \geq 0 \qquad \text{(Figure 2(a))}$$

(b) A class II u-function is defined by

$$\left.\begin{array}{lll} u'(E) > 0 & & \forall_E \geq 0 \\ u''(E) > 0 & & 0 \leq E < E_0 \\ & < 0 & E > E_0 \end{array}\right\} \qquad \text{(Figure 2(b))}$$

(c) A class III u-function is defined by:

$$\left.\begin{array}{l} u'(E) \equiv 0 \quad 0 \leq E < E_0 \\ u'(E) > 0; \quad u''(E) < 0; \quad \text{for } E > E_0 \end{array}\right\}$$

This completes our specification of the functions involved. Before examining the workings of the model it remains to specify the dynamic equation for the system and state the optimization problem.

If the stock of the resource in the ground at time t is X(t) and extraction at time t is E(t), then the depletion of X proceeds according to

(3) $\dot{X}(t) = -E(t) \quad X(0) = X_0.$

We are concerned with the problem of selecting a time path for E(t) and a value for X(T) which will maximize the present value of the stream of consumption from time 0 to time T. Formulated mathematically the problem is to find E(t) and X(T) to

(4) $$\max_{E(t),X(T)} \int_0^T u(E)e^{-\delta t}dt \qquad \delta \geq 0, \text{ constant}$$

$$\text{s.t.} \quad \dot{X}(t) = -E(t) \quad X(0) = X_0$$
$$X(t) \geq 0$$
$$E(t) \geq 0$$
$$\dot{X}(t) = 0 \text{ when } X(t) = 0.$$[2]

Applying Pontryagin's Maximum Principle (see Athans and Falb [3], Theorems 5.9 and 5.11, and Arrow and Kurz [2], Chapter 2, Propositions 4 and 7) the necessary conditions which must be satisfied by a solution to this problem are:

∃ a continuous function, ψ, such that (omitting time where it appears as an argument):

$$\mathcal{L} = u(E) - \psi E + \lambda_1\dot{X} + \lambda_2 E,$$

(5) $$\psi\delta - \frac{\partial \mathcal{L}}{\partial X} = \dot{\psi} = \psi\delta,$$

(6) $$\frac{\partial \mathcal{L}}{\partial E} = 0 \Longleftrightarrow \psi = u'(E) + \lambda_2 - \lambda_1,$$

(7) $$\psi(T)\, X(T) = 0,$$[3]

(8) $$\begin{cases} \lambda_1 \geq 0, & \lambda_1\dot{X} = \lambda_1 X = 0, \quad X \geq 0 \\ \lambda_2 \geq 0, & \lambda_2 E = 0, \quad\quad\quad\quad E \geq 0 \end{cases}$$

II. ANALYSIS OF THE MODEL

As we proceed it will become clear that there is a dichotomy of results between the model with class I u-functions on the one hand and the model with class II and III u-functions on the other. We will begin by looking at the most basic case, that of a zero discount rate

Case I: $\delta = 0$:

(a) *Class I u-function*:

It follows from (5) and (6) that the rate of exploitation is constant throughout the programme. Because of the necessary continuity of ψ we can easily deduce from (6) that it is never optimal to jump from a strictly positive E to E = 0 for X > 0 (it would lead to an upward jump in ψ). For X = 0 however such a jump in the E variable is permissible since the multiplier λ_1 can become positive and preserve the continuity of ψ (see Arrow [1] p.9, discussion prior to statement of Proposition 4). (7) tells us that when T is finite X(T) = 0 (since $\psi(t) > 0 \forall_t$). All of this gives us a clear picture of the optimal plan when T is any finite number. E will be set at some constant positive level until the resource is exhausted when it will fall to zero. What will be the optimal level of E? This may be determined by inspecting the present value integral:

$$P \equiv \int_0^T u(E)dt$$

$$= \int_0^{T'} u(E)dt + \int_{T'}^{T} u(0)dt,$$

where T' is the time at which X is exhausted and therefore equals $\frac{X(0)}{E}$.

$$Tu(0) + X(0)\left(\frac{u(E) - u(0)}{E}\right),$$

and so maximizing P entails choosing E to maximize $\frac{u(E) - u(0)}{E}$. But for a class I function the relevant value of E is zero.

Accordingly P will be maximized by choosing E to have as small a value as is consistent with resource exhaustion within the time available — this will be the value of E which spreads exploitation of the resource over the whole planning period from time 0 to time T, just exhausting the resource at time T. As the planning period, T, is lengthened, the optimal value of E will fall (see Fig.3) and as $T \to \infty$ optimal $E \to 0$. So that in the limiting case, $T = \infty$, there is no optimal solution. Any positive extraction path is dominated by a path with lower extraction while a zero extraction path (the limiting case) is dominated by *any* positive extraction path.

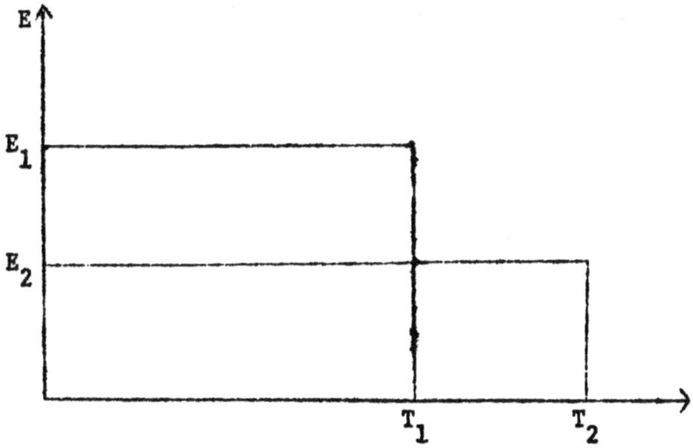

Figure 3

(b) *Class II and III u-functions*:

As before, when T is finite $X(T) = 0$. Now, we define $\hat{E}$ to be the value of E which maximizes

$$\frac{u(E) - u(0)}{E}$$

(in particular $\hat{E}$ will satisfy $u'(E) = \frac{u(E) - u(0)}{E}$). Because the Hamiltonian is non-concave for some values of E in this case the Pontryagin necessary condition that the constrained Hamiltonian be maximized at each point in time must be approached from first principles. Simply, we wish to

$$\max_{E} H(E) = u(E) - \psi E$$

$$\text{s.t.} \quad E \geq 0,$$

It is easily shown[4] that when $\psi < u'(\hat{E})$, optimal E will be the solution to $\psi = u'(E)$ with $E > \hat{E}$ (it can be seen diagrammatically with the aid of Fig. 4 drawn for a class II u-function: in the diagram

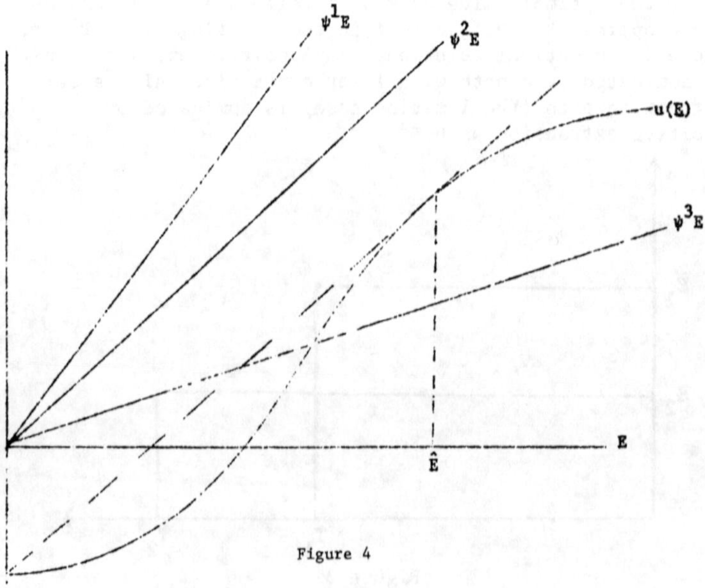

Figure 4

$\psi^1 > u'(\hat{E})$, $\psi^2 = u'(\hat{E})$ and $\psi^3 < u'(\hat{E})$). When $\psi > u'(\hat{E})$, $H(E) < u(0) \forall_E > 0$, $H(0) = u(0)$, and $E = 0$ consequently maximizes H. When $\psi = u'(\hat{E})$ the maximum value of H is u(0) and this is attained when either $E = 0$ or $E = \hat{E}$. Thus it is clearly never optimal to operate in the interval $0 < E < \hat{E}$. Moreover E cannot jump from a value greater than $\hat{E}$ to zero for $X > 0$ for this would require a jump in ψ, so for paths which involve $E > \hat{E}$ at some stage, E will be constant at that level until $X = 0$. It may be shown[5] that for $E \geq \hat{E}$ paths associated with lower values of E have a higher present value integral than paths for which E is high. Since X(T) is necessarily zero, for low values of T $(T < X(0)/\hat{E})$ the optimal path will entail E being set at that constant level consistent with exhausting the resource at time T. When $T = X(0)/\hat{E}$, then E will be set at $\hat{E}$ for the whole programme just running X to zero at time T. For longer planning horizons $(T > X(0)/\hat{E})$ clearly the appropriate positive level of extraction is $\hat{E}$ (since $\hat{E}$ dominates all higher values of E when it is feasible, and lower values of E have already been shown to be non-optimal). This will mean however, that for some of the programme $\hat{E}$ should be zero. Moreover since when $\psi = u'(\hat{E})$, $H(0) = H(\hat{E}) = u(0)$ both $E = 0$ and $E = \hat{E}$ will maximize H and there is therefore, nothing to stop E jumping to zero before X is exhausted, later jumping back up to $\hat{E}$, etc. until $X = 0$. Clearly all such paths (and there are an infinite number of them) yield the same present value for the stream of utility and are all optimal solutions to (4). There is no unique optimal path. However the path for which $E = \hat{E}$ until exhaustion will do as well as any.

Before proceeding to the case of a positive discount rate let us briefly assess the results obtained above:

The non-existence of an optimal solution for a Class I u-function when $T = \infty$ is the result of two factors:

(i) The type of u-function involved prevents us from finding a positive E which maximizes

$$\frac{u(E) - u(0)}{E} .$$

Because this expression, which we will term "excess average utility" (EAU)[6], is always greater than marginal utility, it is a decreasing function of E so that the same number of total units of extraction would yield more "total excess utility"

$$\left(TEU \equiv \int_0^T (u(E) - u(0))dt \right)$$

if spread as thinly as possible over the given time than if concentrated in a shorter interval of time (the EAU being higher in the former case). The TEU is therefore seen to rise as E moves closer to the E which maximizes EAU($E \to 0$). When a positive E can be found to maximize EAU (as in the case of class II and III u-functions) it constitutes the optimal extraction level for long time horizons.

(ii) The absence of a discount rate with the present generation wanting the same benefits for all future generations as for itself means that when a class I u-function is involved the TEU over all periods will be greater the lower the level of extraction at any point in time to the point where extraction is zero in all periods. Given the scarcity of the resource, a positive discount rate may well be needed to help ration the limited stock of the resource among generations.

The absence of discounting is also responsible for the indeterminacy arising in the case of class II and III functions. Quite simply, without a discount rate we have no criterion for choosing between points in time and therefore no criterion for establishing one policy as uniquely optimal. We now turn to the case of a positive discount rate.

Case 2: $\delta > 0$:

As we would expect we again find that the class I and class II-III functions yield results which are superficially different but which are nevertheless related. In case 1 above, because a community faced with a class I function was prevented from attaining an interior maximum for average excess utility, in the infinite horizon case it attempted to approach that ideal situation by running the level of extraction to zero (a boundary maximum for EAU) and there was no optimal solution. For a different reason there were an infinite number of optimal solutions for class II-III functions. Naturally the introduction of a positive discount rate changes this situation.

(a) *Class I u-function*

The interior solution to (5), (6) and (8) is characterized by the following relationships:

$$E > 0 \Rightarrow \lambda_1 = \lambda_2 \; 0$$

$$\dot{\psi} = \psi\delta$$

$$\text{and } \psi = u'(E).$$

Hence

$$E = \frac{u'(E)\delta}{u''(E)} < 0 \text{ for } \delta > 0 \tag{9}$$

Thus E falls over time as the resource is depleted. For all finite T $X(T) = 0$. It turns out to be optimal for large T to run $E(t)$ continuously to zero so that it reaches zero at the time at which X is exhausted. In the ψ-X phase-plane (Fig. 5(a) shows some of the paths satisfying the necessary conditions in ψ-X space) the optimal trajectory is the highest feasible path on or below path α in Fig. 5(a). Optimality is established using the following comparison of integrals proof:

Let asterisk superscripts denote the path claimed to be optimal (viz. the longest exhaustion path feasible in the time available). Then we compare the present value integral along this path (P*) with the present value along any other feasible Pontryagin path (i.e. some lower path in Fig. 5(a)).

$$P^* - P \equiv \int_0^T [u(E^*) - u(E)]e^{-\delta t}dt$$

$$> \int_0^T u'(E^*)(E^* - E)e^{-\delta t}dt$$

(since u is stricly concave in E)

$$= \int_0^{T^*} u'(E^*)(E^* - E)e^{-\delta t}dt$$

(where T* is the time at which X is exhausted along the path claimed to be optimal; since this is the longest feasible exhaustion path $E^*(t) = E(t) = 0 \ \forall_t \in (T^*, T]$)

$$= \int_0^T \psi^*(t)e^{-\delta t}(E^* - E)dt$$

$$= \Big[\psi_0^*(X - X^*) \Big]_0^{T^*} = 0 \text{ since } X(T) = X^*(T) = 0 \text{ and } X(0) = X^*(0) = 0.$$

Thus, in terms of Fig. 5(a) the optimal trajectory will be the highest feasible path on or below path α. For a time horizon of T_1 say, (Fig. 5(b)) path γ will be optimal. For a longer time horizon, say T_2 it will be feasible to spread extraction more over time so that path β is optimal. For time horizons greater than or equal to T_3, path α is optimal. In particular as $T \to \infty$ path α remains optimal. Provided

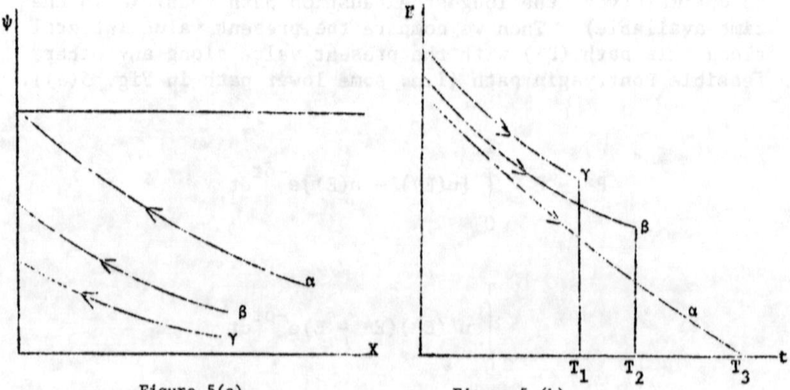

Figure 5(a) Figure 5 (b)

Provided $u'(0) < \infty$ (which is the likely situation when $\bar{C} > 0$) the resource will be exhausted in a finite time. This follows because

$$\psi(t) = \psi_0 e^{\delta t} = u'(E) + \lambda_2 - \lambda_1$$

and when $E > 0$ $\psi_0 e^{\delta t} = u'(E)$;

therefore E cannot be positive for an infinite period of time since

$$\lim_{t \to \infty} \psi(t) = \infty.^7$$

Finally it is noted again that for long time horizons optimal E will fall continuously to zero reaching zero at the time (finite) at which X reaches zero. For the remainder of the programme the economy will gain all its consumption from $\bar{C}$, the alternative source. In the case where $\bar{C} = 0$ and $u'(0) = \infty$ the exploitation of the resource will be spread over an infinite time period with E going asymptotically to zero. As an intuitively appealing conjecture it would seem that as the alternative source of consumption, $\bar{C}$, falls the period of exploitation should increase.

(b) *Class II and III u-functions*

Certain results proven for the case $\delta = 0$ carry over automatically here. In particular regardless of the magnitude of the discount rate it is still true that:

(i) when $\psi < u'(\hat{E})$ optimal E is the solution to $\psi = u'(E)$ with $E > \hat{E}$;

(ii) when $\psi > u'(\hat{E})$, $E = 0$ maximizes H;

(iii) when $\psi = u'(\hat{E})$ the maximum value of H is u(0), attained when $E = 0$ or $E = \hat{E}$;

(iv) it is never optimal to operate in the interval $(0,\hat{E})$.

When $\delta > 0$ for long time horizons the optimal path is the one for which E declines steadily to $\hat{E}$ reaching $\hat{E}$ at the time at which the resource is exhausted (path α in Fig. 6). E then jumps to zero and consumption is $\bar{C}$ until the end of the plan. For shorter time horizons (when there is insufficient time for exhaustion of the resource along

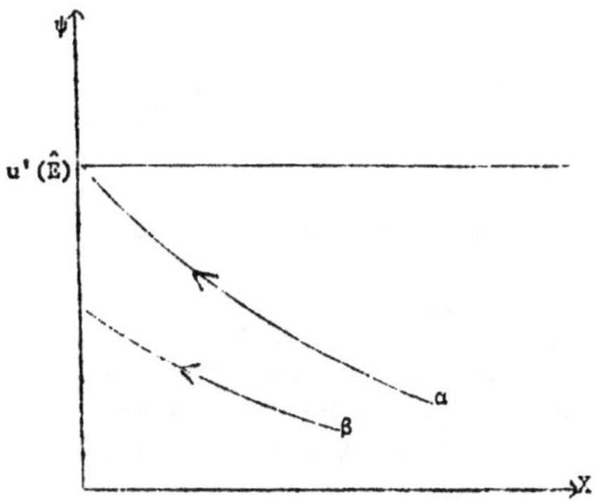

Figure 6(a)

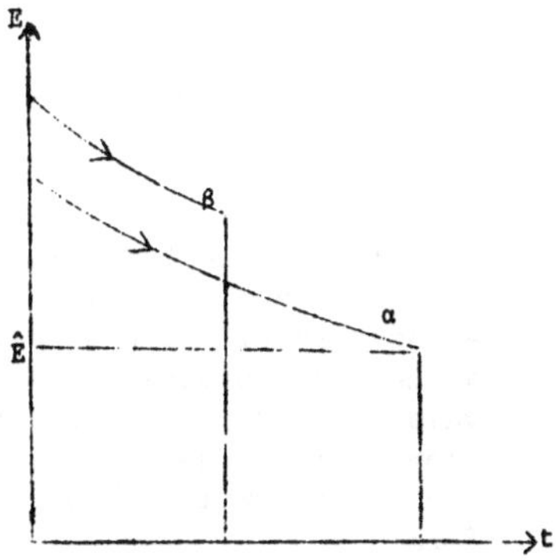

Figure 6(b)

path α) the longest feasible exhaustion path will be optimal (this will be the highest path - say path ∞ - below path α in Fig. 6(a)).

Optimality is established as follows. Let asterisks denote the path claimed to be optimal (the longest feasible exhaustion path on or below α in Fig. 6(a)) and let T^* denote the exhaustion time along the said optimal path and $T°$ the exhaustion time along some other arbitrarily chosen path. Then comparing present values:

$$P^* - P \equiv \int_0^T [u(E^*) - u(E)]e^{-\delta t}dt$$

$$> \int_0^T u'(E^*)(E^* - E)e^{-\delta t}dt$$

$$= \int_0^{T°} \psi_0^*(E^* - E)dt + \int_{T°}^{T^*} \psi_0^* E^* dt$$

$$= 0 \qquad \text{Q.E.D.}$$

III DEPLETION OF A NON-RENEWABLE ASSET: UTILITY FUNCTION INCORPORATING A CONSERVATION MOTIVE AND/OR DEPLETION EFFECT

The simple form of utility function assumed, in section II ignores an important phenomenon which is often associated with the depletion of a resource - a tendency to value the resource for its own sake independently of its value as a source of future consumption. Such a "conservation motive" (as we will refer to it) may be taken into account by employing a utility function of the following form:

$$
(10) \qquad \begin{array}{lll} u = v(C, X) & v_C > 0 & v_{CC} < 0 \\ & v_X > 0 & v_{XX} < 0 \\ v \, \varepsilon \, C^2 & v_{XC} \gtrless 0 & v_{CX} \gtrless 0 \end{array}
$$

Formulation (10) for the utility function is of relevance to a wide range of cases where externalities are present. Where the resource is associated with leisure its depletion may cause existing consumption (produced by depleting it) to be valued less highly (e.g. rutile mining and the defacing of beaches). Alternatively, the independent X in the utility function may be a dummy variable reflecting the uncertainty which the community feels about the feasibility of finding a substitute resource for producing its consumption goods when the present resource has been exhausted.

In addition there is the possibility of incorporating a *depletion effect* into the production function to reflect the increasing difficulty of extraction and/or the recourse to lower grades of the resource as it is depleted. This may be achieved by defining the production from resources as:

$$
\begin{array}{ll} C_X = \phi(E, X) & \phi_X \quad 0, \quad \phi_{XX} < 0 \quad \forall_E > 0 \\ \phi \, \varepsilon \, C^2 & \phi_{EE} < 0, \\ & \phi_{EX} = \phi_{XE} > 0, \\ & \phi_X(0, X) = \phi_{XX}(0, X) = 0 \end{array}
$$ [8]

It is possible to subsume this depletion effect in the utility function and treat it in much the same way as the conservation motive. This is done as follows:

Let $u = v(\phi(E, X) + \bar{C}, X) \equiv u(E, X)$.

It is easily checked that $\operatorname{sgn} u_E = \operatorname{sgn} \phi_E$, $u_X > 0$, $u_{EE} < 0$ and $u_{XX} < 0$.

However because:

$$
u_{EX} = u_{XE} = v_{CC}\phi_E\phi_X + v_{CX}\phi_E + v_C\phi_{EX}
$$

the cross partials may be either positive or negative.

Certainly, in the absence of a depletion effect we can say that sgn u_{EX} = sgn ϕ_E, and, if we follow the not unreasonable assumption of section II that $\phi_E > 0$, then $u_{EX} = u_{XE} \geq 0$. Moreover, in such a case, $u_{EX} = u_{XE} = 0$ if and only if $v_{CX} = v_{XC} = 0$, so that if there is no depletion effect then the u-function is additively separable if and only if the v-function is additively separable. We will initially confine our attention to this case in order to understand the basic structure of the problem. The optimization problem here is simply stated as that of selecting E(t) and X(T) to:

$$\text{(11)} \qquad \underset{E(t),X(T)}{\text{Max}} \int_0^T u(E, X)e^{-\delta t}dt \qquad \delta > 0 \text{ constant}$$

$$\text{s.t.} \quad \dot{X}(t) = -E(t) \qquad X(0) = X_0$$

$$X(t) \geq 0$$

$$E(t) \geq 0$$

$$\dot{X}(t) = 0 \text{ when } X(t) = 0.$$

The necessary conditions to be satisfied by a solution to this problem are:

E a continuous function, ψ, such that:

$$\text{(12)} \qquad \dot{\psi} = \psi\delta - u_X$$

$$\text{(13)} \qquad \psi = u_E(E, X) + \lambda_2 - \lambda_1,$$

$$\text{(14)} \qquad \psi(T)X(T) = 0 \quad \text{for } T < \infty,$$

$$\text{(15)} \qquad \begin{cases} \lambda_1 \geq 0 & \lambda_1\dot{X} = \lambda_1 X = 0, & X \geq 0, \\ \lambda_2 \geq 0 & \lambda_2 E = 0, & E \geq 0. \end{cases}$$

(12) and (13) imply that when E > 0:

$$\text{(16)} \qquad \dot{E} = \frac{u_E}{u_{EE}}\left(\delta - \frac{u_X}{u_E} + \frac{u_{EX}E}{u_E} \right)$$

and when u is additively separable in E and X:

$$\dot{E} = \frac{-u_E}{u_{EE}} \left[\frac{u_X}{u_E} - \delta \right]; \qquad \text{and} \tag{17}$$

$$\operatorname{sgn} \dot{E} = \operatorname{sgn} \left[\frac{u_X}{u_E} - \delta \right] \tag{18}$$

Equation (18) simply states that E will tend to rise over time if the conservation motive is stronger than the preference for current consumption over future consumption (the discount motive) $[u_X > \delta u_E]$ and E will tend to fall if the discount motive predominates.

We consider two cases:

Case 1: $u_X(0) \leqq \delta u_E(0)$:

This case may be thought of as that of a relatively weak conservation motive (weak relative to the discount motive). The graph of $\dot{E} = 0$[9] is shown in Fig. 7(a) for $u_X(0) < \delta u_E(0)$ in the E-X phase plane together with the paths which satisfy conditions (12) - (15). Figure 7(b) shows these paths in

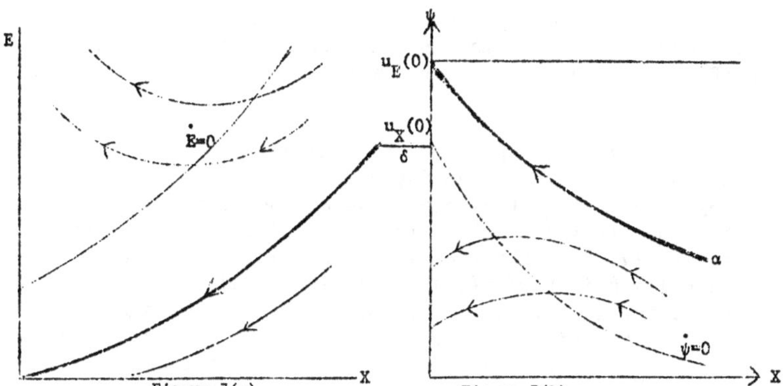

Figure 7(a) Figure 7(b)

the ψ-X phase plane. As in section II, it is also optimal here to exhaust the resource when the planning horizon is finite (via (14) - along non-exhaustion paths, in particular, $\psi(T) > 0$ and so (14) would be violated if $X(T)$ were not zero) and it may be shown that in Fig. 7(b) the highest feasible path on or below path α (in terms of Fig. 7(a) the lowest path on or above α) yields a higher present value of the stream of utility than all other feasible[10] paths satisfying the necessary conditions and is therefore optimal (see the Appendix for proof). For sufficiently large T, path α is optimal. Thus for long planning periods the optimal course is to exhaust the resource, running the level of extraction continuously to zero, E reaching zero at the same time as X. This solution will be less likely to be feasible the smaller is $\delta u_E(0) - u_X(0)$. In the limiting case where $\delta u_E(0) = u_X(0)$, along path α the relative strength of the conservation motive postpones exhaustion indefinitely meaning that exhaustion would take an infinite time if this path were followed, a fact which may be verified by noting that in this case the endpoint is the stationary solution for ψ and X. In such a case a more rapid exhaustion path will have to be followed for a finite horizon plan, although α would still be optimal if T were infinite. Clearly the stronger the conservation motive, the longer will be the optimal period of exploitation (assuming T is large enough to permit such flexibility of choice).

Case 2: $u_X(0) > \delta u_E(0)$:

With a strong conservation motive the $\dot{E} = 0$ locus will cut the X-axis to the right of the origin (Fig. 8(a)). The path here which is comparable to path α for Case 1 will be β (Figs 8(a) and 8(b) which leads to the equilibrium point P.

Obviously path β cannot be optimal for a finite horizon since it will take an infinite time even to reach P along it and for T finite we have already observed that $X(T) = 0$. It may be shown (see Appendix) that the lowest path in Fig. 8(a) above β will be optimal (i.e. the highest path below β in Fig. 8(b)) for T finite and path β will be optimal for T infinite. This means that although for all finite time horizons it is optimal to exhaust the resource, when the planning period is infinite it is optimal to leave a stock, $\bar{X}$, of the resource unexploited. The apparent paradox embodied in this result is resolved when the nature of the optimal path for a finite horizon is examined more closely. For a particular finite horizon the optimal path

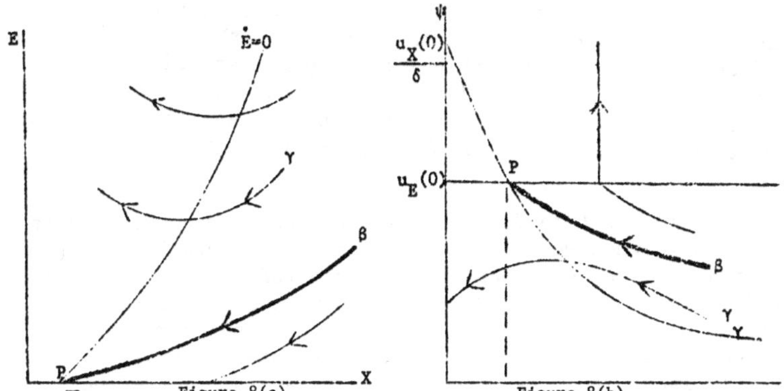

Figure 8(a) Figure 8(b)

may be path γ (Fig. 8). Along this trajectory extraction will initially decline (in the earlier stages of the programme the discount motive is naturally stronger than the conservation motive) but will eventually rise. The ultimate rise in E is attributable to a combination of:

(a) as time goes on the conservation motive increases in importance ($u_X(X)$ rises) relative to the discount motive - this tends to make it attractive to defer extraction into the future;

(b) because the programme is finite there is no incentive for leaving a positive stock of the resource unexploited at the end of the plan - on the contrary there is a definite incentive to run X to zero.

(b) and (a) together imply that as time T is approached, E will rise so as to meet the exhaustion requirement as well as the conservation motive.

As T is increased the date of exhaustion is naturally moved on into the future so that the time at which E will have to start increasing in order to exhaust X is deferred (this is seen by noticing that for longer time horizons E will necessarily have to be spread more thinly over time; this will increase the valuation placed on an extra unit of current consumption relative to future consumption, $\delta u_E(E)$, and so X will be smaller by the time $u_X(X)$ becomes sufficiently large to cause E to rise over time). As $T \rightarrow \infty$ the exhaustion date for X is deferred indefinitely - there is thus no constraint on E to increase in the "final" stages of the programme. The thin intertemporal spread of E combined with the conservation motive, slows extraction down to the extent that E asymptotes to 0 over an infinite period of time and leaves an unexploited stock $\bar{X} > 0$ at $T = \infty$.

It is now time for us to see whether the above results still hold when we allow for u to be non-separable either because v is non-separable or because there is a depletion effect in production. We shall continue our taxonomic approach here and look initially at the case where there is no depletion effect but v is non-separable and then we shall discuss the case where there is a depletion effect in production.

(a) *v non-separable* ($v_{CX} = v_{XC} > 0$), *no depletion effect* ($\phi_X \equiv 0$)

Now that the cross derivatives u_{EX} enter the picture the behaviour of paths in the equivalent diagrams to Figs. 7(a), 8(a) in the E-X plane is difficult to determine. However, we can be fairly explicit about the behaviour of the system in the ψ-X phase plane. The two main loci are $\dot{\psi} = 0$ and $\dot{E} = 0$. The $\dot{E} = 0$ locus is $\psi = u_E(0,X)$ and clearly has a positive slope. For the $\dot{\psi} = 0$ locus:

$$\frac{\partial\dot{\psi}}{\partial\psi} = \delta - \frac{u_{XE}}{u_{EE}} > 0$$

$$\frac{\partial\dot{\psi}}{\partial X} = \frac{u_{EE}u_{XX} - u_{XE}u_{EX}}{-u_{EE}} > 0$$

(if u is concave in E and X).

Thus $\left.\frac{d\psi}{dX}\right|_{\dot{\psi}=0} < 0.$

As for the separable cases we consider two alternatives:

Case 1: $u_X(0, 0) \leq \delta u_E(0, 0)$:

In this case (see Fig. 9), $\dot{\psi} = 0$ lies completely below $E = 0$[11] the only possible point of intersection of the two loci being on the vertical axis (and this is only possible in the limiting case, $u_X(0, 0) = \delta u_E(0, 0)$).

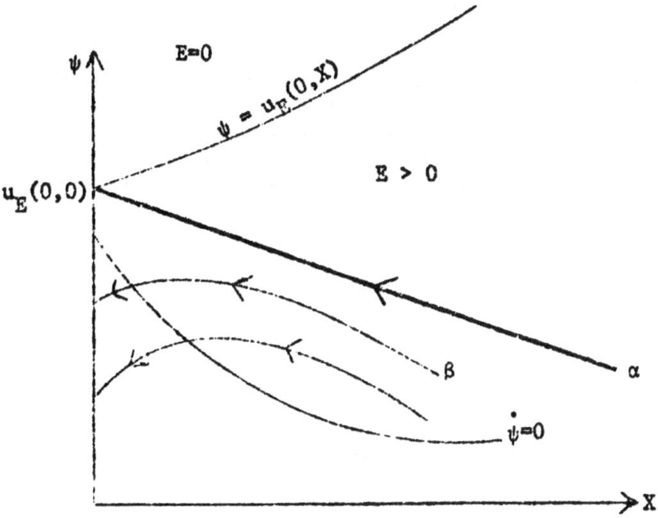

Figure 9

It is proven in the Appendix that the optimal path here is the highest path on or below path α in Fig. 9.

For long time horizons it will be optimal to follow trajectory α exhausting the resource in a finite time (except when $u_X(0, 0) = \delta u_E(0, 0)$ when an infinite time is required) and consuming $\bar{C}$ for the last stage of the programme when the path moves up the vertical axis. Along path α

$$\text{sgn}\ \dot{E} = \text{sgn}\left(\frac{u_X}{u_E} - \delta - \frac{u_{EX}E}{u_E}\right) .$$

But along α, $\dot{\psi} > 0$ so that using (12) and (13) $\frac{u_X}{u_E} - \delta < 0$ and so $\dot{E} < 0$.

Thus for long time horizons E will decline continuously to zero reaching zero at the time X = 0. For shorter time horizons (along, say, path β in Fig. 9) E will decline initially and for more of the programme than when u was separable, but its subsequent behaviour is indeterminate without more information.

Case 2: $u_X(0, 0) > \delta u_E(0, 0)$:

Here $\dot{\psi} = 0$ cuts the vertical axis above E = 0 (Fig. 10).[12] The point of intersection (P) is an equilibrium for the system. As for a separable u-function, the path leading to it (β in Fig. 10) is optimal for an infinite horizon plan, while the highest path below it which is feasible for a given finite horizon is optimal for that horizon.

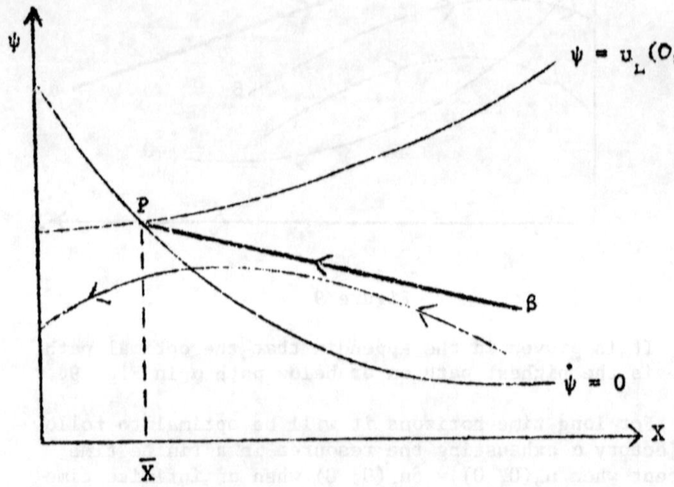

Figure 10

As in case 1, E declines continuously to zero along β and a positive stock $\bar{X}$ remains at T = ∞. Along the optimal path for a finite period plan, X(T) = 0. Thus the results for a separable v-function carry over when v is non-separable and there is no depletion effect in production.

(b) *No conservation motive, depletion effect in production:*

If we assume that $u_E(0,X^*) = 0$ for some $X^* > 0$, (it is likely that as X is severely depleted costs will rise to the point where the marginal cost of production exceeds the marginal product of the resource) then the boundary of the region $E = 0$ (namely $\psi = u_E(0, X)$ will cut the X-axis at $X^* > 0$ (Fig. 11). The exact form of $\dot{\psi} = 0$ is not immediately clear. However as $E \to 0$ $u_X(E, X) \to 0$ and $\dot{\psi} \to \psi\delta$, so that $\dot{\psi} = 0 \to$ the X-axis. For $E > 0$, $\dot{\psi} = 0$ if and only if $\psi\delta = u_X(E, X) > 0$. In addition it is reasonable to suppose that $\psi_X(E, X) \to 0$ as $X \to \infty$ (i.e. the depletion effect is irrelevant when the resource is not scarce). Thus the $\dot{\psi} = 0$ locus will have the form shown in Fig. 11. There is clearly

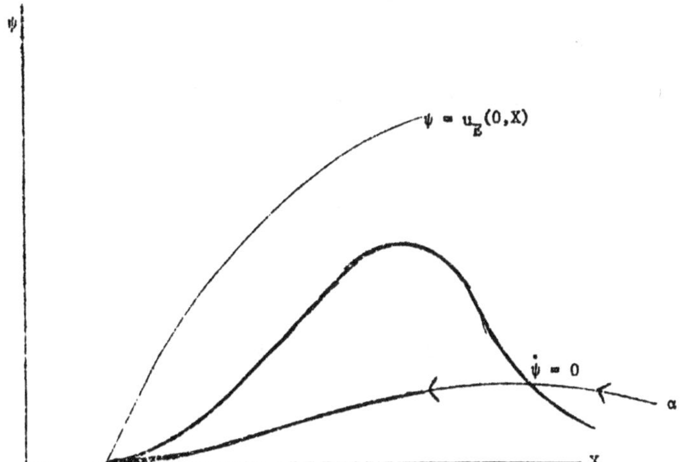

Figure 11

a unique equilibrium for the system of differential equations in ψ and X. This is not especially surprising since $u_X(0, 0) = 0$ and is greater than $\delta u_E(0, 0)$ which is negative. Thus the sufficient condition for a unique equilibrium established for (a) above is satisfied here and similar results are obtained. In this case there is no possibility of exhaustion being optimal since it is impossible to cross the locus $\psi = u_E(0, X)$. The resource becomes increasingly costly to extract until a point is reached where it is not worth continuing to extract it. Thus for a finite time horizon, the transversality condition (14) implies that $\psi(T) = 0$, and the optimal path is therefore that for which ψ reaches zero at time T. As $T \to \infty$, the optimal path tends to path α (Fig. 11). The larger is T the lower will be the terminal stock of X, however there will always remain a terminal stock of at least X*. Throughout the programme a positive shadow price is attached to the resource - however this social valuation eventually declines over time until the end of the programme at which point the resource is deemed worthless.

APPENDIX

Optimality in Section III

(a) *Conservation motive, no depletion effect:*

$$P^* - P = \int_0^T [u(E^*,X^*) - u(E,X)]e^{-\delta t}dt$$

$$= \int_0^T [u(E^*,X^*(- u(E,X^*) + u(E,X^*) - u(E,X)]e^{-\delta t}dt$$

$$> \int_0^T [u_E(E^*,X^*).(E^* - E) + u_X(E,X^*).(X^* - X)]e^{-\delta t}dt$$

$$\geq \int_0^T u_E(E^*,X^*).(E^* - E) + u_X(E^*,X^*).(X^* - X)]e^{-\delta t}dt$$

(since $X^*(t) \geq X(t)$, $E^*(t) \leq E(t)\ \forall_t$ and $u_{EX} = u_{XE} \geq 0$, without a depletion effect).

$$= \int_0^T \{[\psi^* - \lambda_2^* + \lambda_1^*](E^* - E) + [\psi^*\delta - \dot{\psi}^*](X^* - X)\}e^{-\delta t}dt$$

$$\geq \int_0^T \psi^*(E^* - E)e^{-\delta t}dt - [\psi^* e^{-\delta t}(X^* - X)]_0^T$$

$$+ \int_0^T \psi^*(E - E^*)e^{-\delta t}dt$$

$$- \int_0^T \lambda_1^* Ee^{-\delta t}dt$$

$$= \psi^*(T)e^{-\delta T}[X^*(T) - X(T)] - \int_0^T \lambda_1^* Ee^{-\delta t}dt$$

$$= \psi^*(0)[X^*(T) - X(T)] - \int_0^T \lambda_1^* Ee^{-\delta t}dt$$

(i) When T is finite $X^*(T) = X(T) = 0$ and $\lambda_1^* = 0$ along the longest feasible exhaustion path. Hence $P^* - P > 0$.

(ii) When T is infinite, either $X^*(T) = X(T) = 0$ and $\lambda_1^* = 0(\delta u_E(0, 0) > u_X(0, 0))$, or $\delta u_E(0, 0) < u_X(0, 0)$, in which case there is an equilibrium in ψ-X space and $\psi^*(T)e^{-\delta T} \to 0$ as $T \to \infty$. Also, in such a case $\lambda_1^* = 0$ for the entire programme, so $P^* - P > 0$.

(b) *No conservation motive, depletion effect in production*

Because only one path satisfies all of the necessary conditions, Proposition 5 in [1] may be invoked to establish optimality.

FOOTNOTES

[1] The questions of (a) the economy's behaviour after a resource ceases to be economical to extract and (b) disaggregation of the economy into resource production and resource-use sectors, are discussed in [5], Chapters 4 and 5 respectively.

[2] See Arrow and Kurz [2], Proposition 5, part (g) and preceding discussion.

[3] Condition (7) is only a necessary condition when optimal T turns out to be finite. If T is infinite then we cannot use (7) as a necessary condition (see Arrow and Kurz [2], p. 46).

[4] If $\psi < u'(\hat{E})$, and $H(E) - u(E) - \psi E$, then $E \neq 0$, since if it were:

$$H(E) > u(\hat{E}) - u'(\hat{E}).\ \hat{E} = u(\hat{E}) - (u(\hat{E}) - u(0)) = u(0) = H(0).$$

Also, for $E \in (0, \hat{E})$,

$$\begin{aligned} H(\hat{E}) - H(E) &= (u(\hat{E}) - u(0)) - (u(E) - u(0)) - \psi(\hat{E} - E) \\ &> (u(\hat{E}) - u(0)) - (u(E) - u(0)) - u'(\hat{E})(\hat{E} - E) \\ &< (u(\hat{E}) - u(0)) - \frac{E}{\hat{E}}(u(\hat{E}) - u(0)) - u'(\hat{E})(\hat{E} - E) \\ &= \frac{\hat{E} - E}{\hat{E}}[(u(\hat{E}) - u(0)) - \hat{E}.u'(\hat{E})] = 0. \end{aligned}$$

So we can assume an interior solution and differentiate H to obtain $u'(E) = \psi < u'(\hat{E})$ and $E > \hat{E}$ (since $H'(E) = u'(E) - \psi > 0$ in some neighbourhood of $\hat{E}$).

[5] For $E > \hat{E}$, $[u(E) - u(0)]/E$ is a decreasing function of E. Since the present value integral equals

$$Tu(0) + X(0)\left(\frac{u(E) - u(0)}{E}\right)$$

[6] This concept of excess average utility has significance here for two reasons:

(i) We are interested in the excess of utility from extraction over the utility derived when all consumption is derived from the alternative source ($\bar{C}$);

(ii) Because we are trying to find the intertemporal allocation of resource extraction which gives us the highest total utility summed over all periods and because all periods are valued equally, we would like to know whether *each unit* of extraction is yielding as much excess utility as possible - i.e. is $\frac{u(E) - u(0)}{E}$ being maximized?

[7] After X = 0, if any of the programme remains, the multipliers λ_1 and λ_2 can change in such a way that ψ continues to grow exponentially over time.

[8] Note that, unlike the utility function, the production function is not allowed to be additively separable. Additive separability may be justified for a utility function but does not seem reasonable for a production function. Hence the assumption $\phi_{EX} = \phi_{XE} > 0$.

[9] Let $L(E, X) = \frac{u_X}{u_E} - \delta$. Then $L_E = \frac{-u_X u_{EE}}{(u_E)^2} > 0$, and

$$L_X = \frac{u_E u_{XX}}{(u_E)^2} < 0 \text{ so that } \left.\frac{dE}{dX}\right|_{\dot{E}=0} = \frac{-L_X}{L_E} > 0.$$

[10] As before some of the paths satisfying the necessary conditions may not exhaust the resource in the time.

[11] Suppose this is not the case and $\dot{\psi} = 0$ intersects E = 0. Then above the E = 0 locus by definition E = 0 and $\dot{\psi} = \psi\delta - u_X(0, X)$. Then $\dot{\psi} = 0$ cuts the vertical axis at $\frac{u_X(0,0)}{\delta}$ and so $u_X(0,0) > \delta u_E(0,0)$ which is a contradiction.

[12] Suppose $\dot{\psi} = 0$ does not pass above e = 0 then $\exists E > 0$: $\frac{u_X(E,0)}{\delta} \leq u_E(0,0)$. But $u_X(E,0) > u_X(0,0)$. Thus $\delta u_E(0,0) > \delta u_X(0,0)$ which is a contradiction.

REFERENCES

[1] K.J.ARROW, "Applications of Control Theory to Economic Growth", *Stanford Institute for Mathematical Studies in the Social Sciences, Technical Report No.2* (1967) Stanford, California

[2] K.J. ARROW and M. KURZ, *Public Investment, the Rate of Return and Optimal Fiscal Policy*, Johns Hopkins, Baltimore, 1970.

[3] M. ATHANS and P.L. FALB, *Optimal Control*, McGraw-Hill, New York, 1966.

[4] N. VOUSDEN, "Basic Theoretical Issues of Resource Depletion", *Journal of Economic Theory, VI* (April 1973), pp. 126-143.

[5] N. VOUSDEN, *The Economics of Exhaustible Resources: A Theoretical Contribution*, Ph.D. dissertation to be submitted at the Australian National University.

CHAPTER 3

An Optimistic Theory of Exhaustible Resources

VERNON L. SMITH*

Division of the Humanities and Social Sciences, California Institute of Technology, Pasadena, California 91109

Received February 13, 1974

1. INTRODUCTION

The economic theory of exhaustible resources going back to Hotelling (e.g., Vousden [9], Koopmans [6], Anderson [1], Cummings [3], Hotelling [5]) has considered exhaustibility to imply that the products made possible by such resources would eventually become unavailable. It is clear that this assumption is unrealistically strong. It is more reasonable to assume that, as such resources become less plentiful, society will find substitutes for them (Nordhaus [7]; Solow [8]; Heal and Dasgupta [4]). Two examples of substitutes for broad classes of exhaustible natural resources will provide the motivation and technological basis for the model to be studied in this paper. The case of fossil and nuclear energy resources from earth deposits provides a class of natural resources that deplete with use and are clearly exhaustible within some finite historical epoch. Society may move from primary dependence on petroleum to coal to nuclear ores and to geothermal steam, but in 200, 500, perhaps 1000 years such resources appear to be due for exhaustion. Solar radiation is the most obvious substitute source of energy and this source appears to be inexhaustible, at least in historical time. The case is one of exhaustible, relatively low-cost sources of energy with an inexhaustible high-cost alternative.

A second case, formally equivalent to the first, is recycling, since numerous if not all material products of mines such as iron, copper, gold, zinc, gravel, and so on can be recycled from previously fabricated products at some cost. Furthermore, recycling provides a potentially inexhaustible source of such materials if one assumes that the deterioration or loss of such materials from previously fabricated products is negligible, and the demand for new material never exceeds the stock of recoverable or reclaimable material. Theoretically, the law of the conservation of mass

* I am indebted to the National Science Foundation for research support and to James Quirk and my referees for valuable comments.

guarantees that such materials will not disappear, but of course recovery costs may be high.

These two cases merge into the following paradigm: A homogeneous product can be produced either from an exhaustible natural resource at low initial cost, or from an inexhaustible alternative at high initial cost. Society begins by mining the low-cost exhaustible resource, but, as such recovery costs increase, society eventually supplements this output and ultimately produces entirely from the high-cost inexhaustible alternative.

2. A Resource Model with a High-Cost Inexhaustible Substitute

Let q_2 be the output of energy from fossil fuels or of iron from earth ores, and let q_1 be the output of usable energy from the sun or of iron from recycled scrap metal. Assume that there is a single variable resource such as labor or land, fixed in total amount $\bar{L}$, that can be employed to produce either q_1 or q_2, according to the concave production functions[1] $q_1 = f_1(\bar{L} - L)$, $q_2 = f_2(L, Q)$, where Q is the remaining unrecovered reserve of petroleum, coal, iron ore, etc. The production technologies will be assumed initally to exhibit constant returns to scale, i.e., $f_1(\bar{L} - L) = \gamma(\bar{L} - L)$, $f_2(L, Q) = Q\phi(L/Q)$, where γ is a constant, with $\phi'(0) \leqslant \infty$, $L \geqslant 0$, $Q \geqslant 0$.

The problem for society will be posed as one of maximizing discounted output,

$$\int_0^\infty (q_1 + q_2)\, e^{-\delta t}\, dt = \int_0^\infty [\gamma(\bar{L} - L) + Q\phi(L/Q)]\, e^{-\delta t}\, dt,$$

subject to the differential equation $\dot{Q} = -q_2 = -Q\phi(L/Q)$, $L \geqslant 0$, $Q \geqslant 0$. The current value Hamilton–Lagrange (Arrow [2]) criterion is

$$H = \gamma(\bar{L} - L) + Q\phi(L/Q) + \xi[-Q\phi(L/Q)]$$

[1] In the case of recycling this is a particularly simple representation. It assumes that the output from recycling activity is independent of the floating stock of recyclable material. If there are stock dependent costs of collecting and assembling metallic junk for recycling, then the model must be modified. For example, if Q_1 is the stock of metal embodied in discarded products, and Q_2 the stock of metal in earth ores, then $q_1 = f_1(L_1, Q_1)$, $q_2 = f_2(L_2, Q_2)$, with $Q_1 + Q_2 = \bar{Q}$, if $\bar{Q}$ is initial, endowed natural stock. Thus, if $L_1 + L_2 = \bar{L}$, we could write $q_1 = f_1(\bar{L} - L_2, \bar{Q} - Q_2)$, and the model can be expressed in terms of the single control, L_2, and a single state variable Q_2, since $-\dot{Q}_1 = \dot{Q}_2 = -q_2 = -f_2(L_2, Q_2)$. In a model of this type the question of how much of the existing stock of refined material should be recycled is itself an economic question. The recovery fraction from recycling is not in general a physical law, but rather a matter of effort. This effort will increase under prodding by the pricing system as primary sources are depleted and become more expensive.

for solutions $Q > 0$, where L is the control variable, Q the state variable, and ξ the auxiliary state variable. H is concave in L and a maximizing trajectory must satisfy the following conditions:

$$\text{If } \frac{\partial H}{\partial L} = (1-\xi)\,\phi'\left(\frac{L}{Q}\right) - \gamma \begin{cases} < 0, & L = 0 \\ = 0, & 0 \leqslant L \leqslant \bar{L} \\ > 0, & L = \bar{L} \end{cases} \tag{1}$$

$$\dot{\xi} = \delta\xi - \frac{\partial H}{\partial Q} = \delta\xi - (1-\xi)\left[\phi\left(\frac{L}{Q}\right) - \left(\frac{L}{Q}\right)\phi'\left(\frac{L}{Q}\right)\right]; \tag{2}$$

$$\dot{Q} = -Q\phi(L/Q); \tag{3}$$

$$\lim_{t\to\infty} e^{-\delta t}\xi(t) \geqslant 0, \qquad \lim_{t\to\infty} e^{-\delta t}\xi(t)\,Q(t) = 0. \tag{4}$$

Sufficient conditions for a maximum are satisfied (by Propositions 7 or 9, Arrow [2]) if (4) holds and if, for the maximizing value of L, H is concave in Q for given ξ, t. Substituting from (1) into the Hamilton–Lagrange criterion,

$$H = \begin{cases} \gamma\bar{L}, & \text{if } L = 0 \\ \gamma\left[\bar{L} - Q\phi'^{(-1)}\left(\frac{\gamma}{1-\xi}\right)\right] + (1-\xi)\,Q\phi\left[\phi'^{(-1)}\left(\frac{\gamma}{1-\xi}\right)\right], & \text{if } 0 < L < \bar{L} \\ (1-\xi)\,Q\phi(\bar{L}/Q), & \text{if } L = \bar{L}, \end{cases}$$

and H is concave in Q if $\xi \leqslant 1$. As will be seen shortly, the condition $\xi \leqslant 1$ will be satisfied everywhere along an equilibrium path.

Condition (1) is the familiar marginal productivity rule: Society places a consumption value of 1 on a unit of refined product or energy. The unit price of the reserve capital stock of the natural resource is ξ. Therefore $1-\xi$ is unit consumption value net of reserve value, where reserve value represents the opportunity cost associated with future consumption and future production alternatives. $(1-\xi)\,\phi'(L/Q)$ is the value of the marginal product of labor, and γ is the wage of labor measured in output units, ($1/\gamma$ is the opportunity cost of mining).

Condition (1) partitions the state space (ξ, Q) into three parts (see Fig. 1).

(i) Region I is the set of states

$$\begin{aligned} R_1 &= \{(\xi, Q) \mid (1-\xi)\,\phi_0' \leqslant \gamma, Q \geqslant 0\} \\ &= \{(\xi, Q) \mid \xi \geqslant \xi_0 = 1 - \gamma/\phi_0', Q \geqslant 0\}, \quad \text{where } \phi_0' = \phi'(0) \leqslant \infty, \end{aligned}$$

in which the economy depends exclusively on solar energy (or recycling).

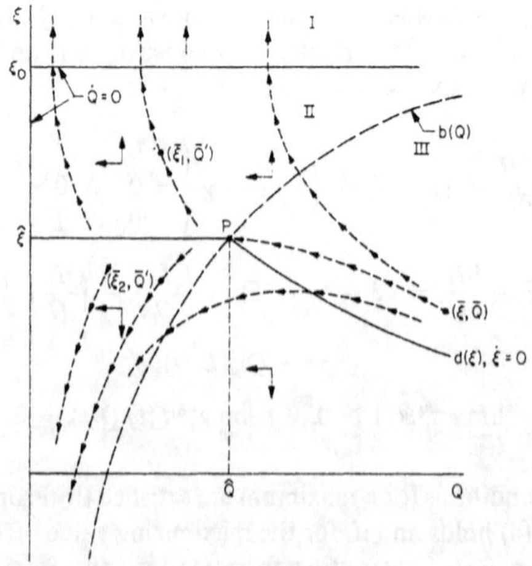

FIGURE 1

(ii) Region II is the set of transitional states

$$R_2 = \{(\xi, Q) \mid (1 - \xi)\, \phi'(L/Q) = \gamma,\ 0 < L < \bar{L},\ Q \geqslant 0\}$$

in which the economy uses both solar energy and fossil fuels (or recycling and mining).

(iii) Region III is the set of states

$$\begin{aligned} R_3 &= \{(\xi, Q \mid (1 - \xi)\, \phi'(\bar{L}/Q) \geqslant \gamma,\ Q \geqslant 0\} \\ &= \{(\xi, Q) \mid \xi \leqslant 1 - \gamma/\phi'(\bar{L}/Q),\ Q \geqslant 0\} \end{aligned}$$

in which the economy relies entirely upon primary earth products and fossil fuels. Throughout regions II and III, $\xi < \xi_0 \leqslant 1$, and the concavity condition on H is satisfied.

Substituting from (1) into (2) and (3), and letting $\xi = b(Q) \equiv 1 - \gamma/\phi'(\bar{L}/Q)$ be the separating boundary between regions II and III,[2]

$$\dot{\xi} = \begin{cases} \delta\xi, \quad \text{if } \xi \geqslant \xi_0 = 1 - \gamma/\phi_0'. & \text{(5a)} \\ \delta\xi - (1 - \xi)\left\{\phi\left[\phi'^{(-1)}\left(\dfrac{\gamma}{1 - \xi}\right)\right] - \left(\dfrac{\gamma}{1 - \xi}\right)\phi'^{(-1)}\left(\dfrac{\gamma}{1 - \xi}\right)\right\}, & \\ \qquad\qquad \text{if } \xi_0 > \xi > b(Q). & \text{(5b)} \\ \delta\xi - (1 - \xi)\{\phi(\bar{L}/Q) - (\bar{L}/Q)\, \phi'(\bar{L}/Q)\}, \quad \text{if } b(Q) \geqslant \xi. & \text{(5c)} \end{cases}$$

[2] In order to treat the case $Q = 0$, the Hamiltonian must have the added term μQ, where μ and Q are in a complementary slack relationship, $\mu \geqslant 0$, $Q \geqslant 0$, $\mu Q = 0$. (See, e.g., [4], or [2], [9]). Then the right sides of (5a) and (5b) will have $-\mu$ added. This allows $\dot{\xi} = 0$, when $Q = 0$, while preserving the continuity of $\xi(t)$.

$$\dot{Q} = \begin{cases} 0, \quad \text{if} \quad \xi \geqslant \xi_0 . & \text{(6a)} \\ -Q\phi\left[\phi'^{(-1)}\left(\frac{\gamma}{1-\xi}\right)\right], \quad \text{if} \quad \xi_0 > \xi > b(Q). & \text{(6b)} \\ -Q\phi(\bar{L}/Q), \quad \text{if} \quad b(Q) \geqslant \xi. & \text{(6c)} \end{cases}$$

Equation (5) is the usual intertemporal efficiency condition for capital markets. Thus (5b) and (5c) require the value of the marginal product of the reserve stock (quasirent net of depletion) to equal interest on invested capital net of capital gains, $\delta\xi - \dot{\xi}$. In competitive markets equilibrium requires extractive firms to expect capital gains at a percentage rate equal to the interest rate less the percentage scarcity rent of the depleting resource. Capital gains in excess of this level will induce firms to over-conserve the resource while a smaller rate of capital gains will induce too rapid depletion.

Consider the set of points $\{(\xi, Q) \mid \dot{\xi} = 0\}$ which defines the stationary state asset demand for nature's capital, Q. For $\xi_0 > \xi > b(Q)$, this set is the line $\xi = \hat{\xi}$, defined by

$$\delta\hat{\xi} - (1-\hat{\xi})\left\{\phi\left[\phi'^{(-1)}\left(\frac{\gamma}{1-\hat{\xi}}\right)\right] - \left(\frac{\gamma}{1-\hat{\xi}}\right)\phi'^{(-1)}\left(\frac{\gamma}{1-\hat{\xi}}\right)\right\} = 0.$$

For $\xi \leqslant b(Q)$, the set is a demand function $Q = d(\xi)$, defined implicitly by

$$\delta\xi - (1-\xi)\{\phi(\bar{L}/Q) - (\bar{L}/Q)\,\phi'(\bar{L}/Q\} = 0.$$

$d(\xi)$ is monotone decreasing,

$$d'(\xi) = +\frac{\delta + \phi - (\bar{L}/Q)\,\phi'}{(1-\xi)[(L^2/Q^3)\,\phi'']} < 0,$$

with range $Q \geqslant \hat{Q}$, where $\hat{\xi} = b(\hat{Q})$. Thus the capital market is in stationary equilibrium anywhere on $Q = d(\xi)$, $0 < \xi < b(Q)$, or on $\xi = \hat{\xi}, 0 \leqslant Q \leqslant \hat{Q}$, as shown in Fig. 1.

Next consider the set $\{(\xi, Q) \mid \dot{Q} = 0\}$. From (6) we have $\dot{Q} = 0$ for all $\xi \geqslant \xi_0$, $Q \geqslant 0$, and $\dot{Q} = 0$ if and only if $Q = 0$ for all $\xi < \xi_0$. Consequently, the stationary state "supply" of capital is the ξ axis boundary as indicated in Fig. 1.

Differentiating (5) and (6),

$$\frac{\partial\dot{\xi}}{\partial\xi} = \begin{cases} \delta > 0, \quad \text{if} \quad \xi \geqslant \xi_0 \\ \delta + \phi > 0, \quad \text{if} \quad \xi_0 > \xi > b(Q) \\ \delta + \phi - (\bar{L}/Q)\,\phi' > 0, \quad \text{if} \quad b(Q) \geqslant \xi \end{cases} \tag{7}$$

$$\frac{\partial\dot{Q}}{\partial Q} = \begin{cases} 0, \quad \text{if} \quad \xi \geqslant \xi_0 \\ -\phi < 0, \quad \text{if} \quad \xi_0 > \xi > b(Q) \\ -[\phi - (\bar{L}/Q)\,\phi'] < 0, \quad \text{if} \quad b(Q) \geqslant \xi. \end{cases} \tag{8}$$

For points above (below) $d(\xi)$, ξ must be increasing (decreasing), while Q is decreasing everywhere to the right of $Q = 0$ for $\xi < \xi_0$, as shown by the arrows in Fig. 1.

In Fig. 1, the path beginning at $(\bar{\xi}, \bar{Q})$ entering region II at point P and proceeding along the line $\xi = \hat{\xi}$ until $Q = 0$ satisfies the concavity conditions and the transversality conditions. By Proposition 9 (Arrow [2, p. 97]) this path is optimal. However, in general there may be other paths that are optimal and an optimal path may not converge. What can we say, in this model, about trajectories which do not terminate at $(\hat{\xi}, 0)$? No generality is sacrificed by considering paths that begin in region II. We first compute the value of the maximand, for initial $\bar{Q}' < \hat{Q}$, along the optimal path $\xi^*(t) = \hat{\xi}$, $L^* = \hat{x}Q^*$, $\hat{x} = (\bar{L}/\hat{Q})$, $\dot{\xi} = \delta\hat{\xi} - (1 - \hat{\xi}) \times [\phi(\hat{x}) - \hat{x}\phi'(\hat{x})] = 0$, $(1 - \hat{\xi})\,\phi'(\hat{x}) = \gamma$:

$$P^* = \int_0^\infty [\gamma(\bar{L} - L^*) + Q^*\phi(\hat{x})]\, e^{-\delta t}\, dt$$

$$= \frac{\gamma\bar{L}}{\delta} + [\phi(\hat{x}) - \gamma\hat{x}] \int_0^\infty Q^* e^{-\delta t}\, dt.$$

Since

$$\dot{Q}^* = -Q^*\phi(\hat{x}), \qquad Q^*(t) = \bar{Q}' e^{-\phi(\hat{x})t},$$

$$P^* = \frac{\gamma\bar{L}}{\delta} - \left[\frac{\phi(\hat{x}) - \gamma\hat{x}}{\delta + \phi(\hat{x})}\right] \bar{Q}' e^{-[\delta + \phi(\hat{x})]t} \Big|_0^\infty = \frac{\gamma\bar{L}}{\delta} + \hat{\xi}\bar{Q}'.$$

Consider a path that begins at $\bar{\xi}_1 > \hat{\xi}$, $\bar{Q}' < \hat{Q}$, and satisfies (5) and (6). If mining terminates at $T_1 \leqslant \infty$, then letting $x_1 = L_1/Q_1$, substituting from (5b) and (6b), and integrating by parts,

$$P_1 = \frac{\gamma\bar{L}}{\delta} + \int_0^\infty Q_1[\phi(x_1) - \gamma x_1]\, e^{-\delta t}\, dt$$

$$= \frac{\gamma\bar{L}}{\delta} + \int_0^\infty Q_1\{[\delta + \phi(x_1)]\,\xi_1 - \dot{\xi}_1\}\, e^{-\delta t}\, dt$$

$$= \frac{\gamma\bar{L}}{\delta} + \bar{\xi}_1\bar{Q}' - \lim_{t\to\infty} Q_1(T_1)\,\xi_1(t)\, e^{-\delta t}$$

$$= P^* + (\bar{\xi}_1 - \hat{\xi})\,\bar{Q}' - \lim_{t\to\infty} Q_1(T_1)\,\xi_1(t)\, e^{-\delta t}.$$

Since P^* is the value of an optimal path, P_1 cannot be better, i.e., $P_1 \leqslant P^*$, which implies

$$\lim_{t\to\infty} Q_1(T_1)\,\xi_1(t)\, e^{-\delta t} \geqslant (\bar{\xi}_1 - \hat{\xi})\,\bar{Q}' > 0.$$

But from (5a), $\xi_1(t) \sim e^{\delta t}$, $\lim_{t\to\infty} \xi_1(t)\, e^{-\delta t} > 0$, and therefore $Q_1(T_1) > 0$. Clearly, under constant returns to mining it cannot be optimal to leave some resource in the ground. For all $Q_1(T_1) > 0$, there exists a transfer $\epsilon(Q_1)$ of labor back into mining that increases output by

$$\phi'(\epsilon/Q_1(T_1)) - \gamma > 0.$$

Consequently, all paths entering region II at some $\xi > \hat{\xi}$ will eventually diverge across the boundary at ξ_0 into region I and will be nonoptimal. This is illustrated by a Cobb–Douglas production function in the next section.

Now consider a path that begins at $\bar{\xi}_2 < \hat{\xi}, \bar{Q}' < \hat{Q}$. If mining terminates at $T_2 \leqslant \infty$, then by the same reduction as before

$$\begin{aligned} P_2 &= \frac{\gamma \bar{L}}{\delta} + \int_0^\infty Q_2[\phi(x_2) - \gamma x_2]\, e^{-\delta t}\, dt \\ &= P^* + (\bar{\xi}_2 - \hat{\xi})\, \bar{Q}' - \lim_{t\to\infty} Q_2(T_2)\, \xi_2(t)\, e^{-\delta t}. \end{aligned}$$

If $\xi_2(t)$ remains positive, then $P_2 < P^*$. If $\xi(t)$ becomes negative (see the example in Section 3), then $\phi'(x_2) = \gamma/(1 - \xi_2) < \gamma$ and the path can be improved by reducing mining labor.

Referring to Fig. 1, along the optimal path starting at $(\bar{\xi}, \bar{Q})$, the economy at first specializes exclusively in the recovery of earth materials (region III) to satisfy its need for energy or metals. $\bar{Q}$ is society's initial endowment of the natural resource, and $\bar{\xi}$ is chosen so as to start the system on an optimal path. From (6c), since

$$\dot{Q} < 0 \qquad \text{and} \qquad \ddot{Q} = -\dot{Q}[\phi - (\bar{L}/Q)\, \phi'] > 0,$$

the extraction rate of the resource is highest initially and declines throughout region III. Hence, output $q_2 = -\dot{Q}$ is largest initially and declines during this phase. As the reserve stock falls, its value steadily increases, reflecting this increasing scarcity. The rising reserve price ξ reduces the unit net value of finished product $(1 - \xi)$, while the declining stock increases the labor-resource stock ratio and reduces the marginal physical productivity of mining labor, $\phi'(\bar{L}/Q)$. Both effects operate to reduce the net value marginal productivity of mining labor (see Fig. 2), until $\xi = \hat{\xi}$, $Q = \hat{Q}$ (point P in Fig. 1, R in Fig. 2). As the resource stock declines and the marginal productivity of mining labor is reduced, there will not be a corresponding decrease in mining effort since profit is maximized when all labor is employed in mining.

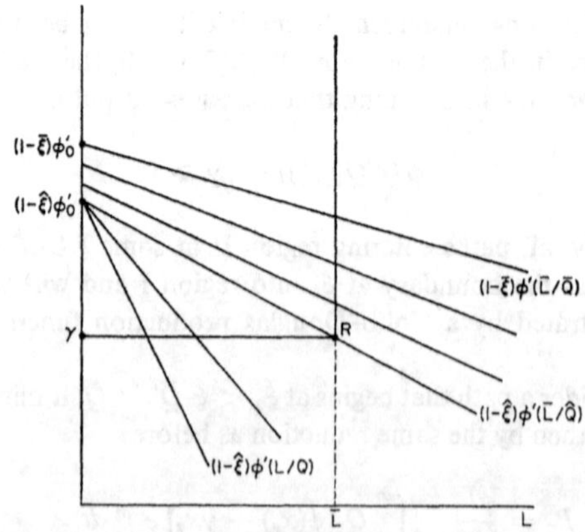

FIGURE 2

At turning point P, solar energy, or recycling, becomes competitive, and as the new technology (Nordhaus [7] calls this a "backstop" technology) comes onstream, labor is transferred out of mining into the new production process. Since the new technology is inexhaustible, once its employment is economical the resource price cannot continue to increase. Because mining is a constant cost process, labor is withdrawn at the same rate that the resource stock declines. Marginal physical product is therefore constant, and at the price $1 - \hat{\xi}$ marginal value product is constant and equal to labor opportunity cost γ. Resource owners are now indifferent between mining and employing the new technology, and, with zero capital gains, the only incentive for resource conservation is that due to diminishing returns to labor in extraction. Hence the mixed economy (region II) moves along the segment $\xi = \hat{\xi}$, with $\dot{\xi} = 0$, until the resource is exhausted. Along this path (Fig. 2) labor is transferred out of mining at a rate proportional to the declining stock of the resource, i.e., $L = \hat{x}Q$, and total output decays exponentially as

$$q = q_1 + q_2 = \gamma(\bar{L} - \hat{x}Q) + Q\phi(\hat{x}) = \gamma\bar{L} + \hat{Q}[\phi(\hat{x}) - \gamma\hat{x}]\, e^{-\phi(\hat{x})(t-\hat{T})},$$

approaching $\gamma\bar{L}$ as time passes. In Fig. 1 the economy approaches $(\hat{\xi}, 0)$ on the left boundary of region II—the golden specialized age of solar energy, or the recycling of product wastes, but this state is not reached in finite time.

3. A Cobb–Douglas Production Case

Some results of the previous sections will be illustrated using the Cobb–Douglas example, $\phi(x) \equiv x^{1/2}$. Consider first solutions in region II defined by $1 > \xi > 1 - 2\gamma(\bar{L}/Q)^{1/2}$ for this example. (5b) and (6b) become

$$\dot{\xi} = \delta\xi - \frac{(1-\xi)^2}{2\gamma}, \tag{9}$$

$$\dot{Q} = -\frac{Q(1-\xi)}{2\gamma}. \tag{10}$$

Solutions to (9) can be expressed as

$$\xi_i(t) = 1 + 2\gamma \left\{\frac{(\delta + s) + (s - \delta)\, k_i e^{-st}}{1 - k_i e^{-st}}\right\}, \qquad i = 1, 2 \tag{11}$$

where

$$k_i = \frac{(1 - \bar{\xi}_i) + 2\gamma(\delta + s)}{(1 - \bar{\xi}_i) + 2\gamma(\delta - s)}, \qquad s = \left[\frac{\delta(1 + \gamma\delta)}{\gamma}\right]^{1/2}.$$

There are two branches to the solution—one for $\xi_1(t) > \hat{\xi}$, and one for $\xi_2(t) < \hat{\xi}$. For this example, $\dot{\xi} = 0$ implies $\hat{\xi} = 1 + 2\gamma(\delta - s)$. Hence $k_1 < 0$ for a path that begins at $\bar{\xi}_1 > \hat{\xi}$ and $\xi_1(t)$ will be increasing. For a path beginning at $\bar{\xi}_2 < \hat{\xi}$, $k_2 > 1$, and $\xi_2(t)$ will be decreasing.

Solutions to (10), given (11), are

$$Q_1(t) = \bar{Q}_1(1 - k_1)^{-2}(-k_1)^{(\delta+s)/s}(1 - k_1e^{-st})^2(-k_1e^{-st})^{-(\delta+s)/s}, \tag{12a}$$

$$Q_2(t) = \bar{Q}_2(k_2 - 1)^{-2}(k_2)^{(\delta+s)/s}(k_2e^{-st} - 1)^2(k_2e^{-st})^{-(\delta+s)/s}, \tag{12b}$$

where

$$\bar{Q}_1, \bar{Q}_2 < \hat{Q} = \bar{L}\{\delta - [\delta(1 + \gamma\delta)/\gamma]^{1/2}\}^{-2}.$$

Several characteristics of these solutions should be noted:

(i) All paths $\xi_1(t) > \hat{\xi}$ reach $\xi = 1$, where mining ceases, in a finite time T_1 such that

$$(\delta + s) + (s - \delta)\, k_1 e^{-sT_1} = 0$$

in (11); i.e.,

$$T_1 = \left(\frac{1}{s}\right) \ln \frac{(s - \delta)(-k_1)}{\delta + s}.$$

(ii) From (12a) this occurs before the resource is exhausted for all initial conditions $(\bar{\xi}_1, \bar{Q}_1)$, i.e., $Q_1(T_1) > 0$.

iii All paths $\xi_2(t) < \bar{\xi}$ diverge, and the resource is exhausted in a finite time T_2. From (12b), $Q_2(T_2) = 0$ if and only if $k_2 e^{-sT_2} - 1 = 0$. Hence, $T_2 = (1/s) \ln k_2$. From (11),

$$\lim_{t \to T_2} \xi_2(t) = -\infty.$$

Region III is defined by $\xi \leqslant 1 - 2\gamma(\bar{L}/Q)^{1/2}$, and the equations of motion (5c) and (6c) become

$$\dot{\xi} = \delta\xi - \left(\frac{1-\xi}{2}\right)\left(\frac{\bar{L}}{Q}\right)^{1/2}, \tag{13}$$

$$\dot{Q} = -(\bar{L}Q)^{1/2}, \tag{14}$$

with solutions

$$\xi(t) = -\left(\frac{1}{2\bar{Q}^{1/2} - \bar{L}^{1/2}t}\right)\left[\frac{\bar{L}^{1/2}}{\delta} - \left(2\bar{Q}^{1/2}\bar{\xi} + \frac{\bar{L}^{1/2}}{\delta}\right)e^{\delta t}\right], \tag{15}$$

$$Q(t) = (\bar{Q}^{1/2} - \bar{L}^{1/2}t/2)^2. \tag{16}$$

The time until the supplemental technology is introduced, $\hat{T}$, can be computed from (16) by substituting the expression for $\hat{Q}$, giving

$$\hat{T} = \frac{2\bar{Q}^{1/2}}{\bar{L}^{1/2}} - \frac{2}{[\delta(1+\gamma\delta)/\gamma]^{1/2} - \delta}.$$

The period of dependence on the exhaustible resource is greater the higher the rate of interest; the higher is production cost $(1/\gamma)$ in the alternate technology, the greater the initial resource stock, and the smaller the labor supply.

4. Extensions: More General Technical and Utility Considerations

Heal and Dasgupta [4] have considered a model of exhaustible resources in which substitution is possible between a reproducible capital resource and an exhaustible natural resource. Vousden [9] has treated the case of an exhaustible resource that has asset value in society's utility function or can be directly consumed as a flow, but not as a productive input to any process. Both these models use discounted utility criteria for the maximand.

The assumptions of the present model are not easily weakened in any of these directions without sacrificing some of the exactness provided in the above calculations. However, in what follows we will consider briefly the effects of assuming (a) diminishing returns to the backstop technology, (b) maximization of discounted utility, and (c) decreasing returns to scale in mining.

A. *Diminishing Returns to the Backstop Technology*

In the original model we have $q_1 = f_1(\bar{L} - L)$, $f_1'' < 0$, and the motion of a point in region II is governed by

$$(1 - \xi)\,\phi' = f_1'(\bar{L} - L),$$
$$\dot{\xi} = \delta\phi - (1 - \xi)(\phi - x\phi'),$$
$$\dot{Q} = -Q\phi.$$

The demand function defined by $\dot{\xi} = 0$ is no longer constant at $\xi = \hat{\xi}$. We now have $d'(\xi) < 0$ in region II as well as III, as shown in Fig. 3. The reader may verify this by differentiating the first two of the above equations. After the alternative technology comes on stream, its labor productivity falls as output increases to replace mining output. This increase in the opportunity cost of mining requires the value of reserve stocks to rise by contrast with the previous case in which opportunity cost was constant. Figure 3 illustrates an optimal path terminating at ξ_0, in which resource capital gains continue throughout region II.

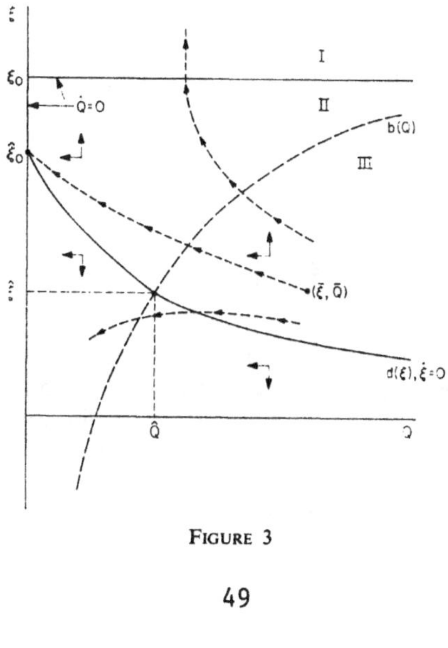

FIGURE 3

B. *Maximization of Discounted Utility*

In this case let the criterion be to maximize $\int_0^\infty u(q_1 + q_2)\, e^{-\delta t}\, dt$ where $u' > 0$, $u'' < 0$. The first-order conditions are now

$$(u' - \xi)\, \phi' = \gamma,$$
$$\dot{\xi} = \delta\xi - (u' - \xi)(\phi - x\phi'),$$
$$\dot{Q} = -Q\phi.$$

Again in region II, $\dot{\xi} = 0$ no longer implies a constant price for the resource stock. Now we can expect ξ to rise as Q falls because the price of output, u', increases as resource stocks become less plentiful, the backstop technology is relied upon, and output falls. Consequently, increased product scarcity value will cause an increase in the shadow price of resource stocks in region II to induce the right amount of conservation. An optimal path might be illustrated by the one shown in Fig. 3.

C. *Decreasing Returns to Scale in Mining*

As mines and oil wells get deeper, recovery becomes more costly. If we assume that the production function is homogeneous of degree $r < 1$, then $q_2 = Q^r\ \phi(x)$, and the equations of motion in region II become

$$(1 - \xi)\, Q^{r-1}\phi' = \gamma,$$
$$\dot{\xi} = \delta\xi - (1 - \xi)\, Q^{r-1}(r\phi - x\phi'),$$
$$\dot{Q} = -Q^r\phi.$$

This case is difficult. Region II is now defined by the inequalities

$$1 - \frac{\gamma Q^{1-r}}{Q_0'} < \xi < 1 - \frac{\gamma Q^{1-r}}{\phi'(\bar{L}/Q)},$$

and the expression on the right is not monotone. The set of stationary equilibrium points, $\dot{\xi} = 0$, do not imply a constant price. As Q declines, ξ increases due to rising extraction cost. The stationary demand function $d\{\xi)$ may now intersect region I at some positive stock level, and optimality may require mining to stop short of complete depletion. But an exact characterization of such solution possibilities does not appear to be easily specified.

References

1. K. Anderson, Optimal growth when the stock of resources is finite and depletable, *J. Econ. Theory* (April 1972), 256–267.
2. K. Arrow, Applications of control theory to economic growth, in "Mathematics of the Decision Sciences" (G. B. Dantzig and A. F. Veinott, Jr., Eds.), Part 2, pp. 85–119. American Mathematical Monthly, Providence, RI, 1968.
3. R. Cummings, Some extensions of the economic theory of exhaustible resources, *West. Econ. J.* (September 1969), 201–10.
4. G. Heal and P. Dasqupta, The optimal depletion of exhaustible resources, *Rev. Econ. Stud.*, to be published.
5. H. Hotelling, The economics of exhaustible resources, *J. Polit. Econ.* (April 1931), 137–75.
6. T. C. Koopmans, Some observations on "optimal" economic growth and exhaustible resources, in "Economic Structure and Development" (H. C. Bos, Ed.), pp. 239–256. North-Holland, Amsterdam 1973.
7. W. Nordhaus, The allocation of energy resources, in "Brooking Papers on Economic Activity 3" (A. M. Okun and G. L. Perry, Eds.). Brookings Institution, Washington, DC, 1974.
8. R. W. Solow, The economics of resources, *Amer. Econ. Rev.* **64** (1974).
9. N. Vousden, Basic theoretical issues of resource depletion, *J. Econ. Theory* **6** (1973), 126–143

CHAPTER 4

The Optimal Depletion of Exhaustible Resources [1, 2]

PARTHA DASGUPTA
LSE and Stanford University

and

GEOFFREY HEAL
University of Sussex

0. INTRODUCTION

0.1. In any given economy there must be a number of commodities that enter into production and which are used up, and whose available stock cannot be increased. Examples like fossil fuels come readily to mind. It would seem reasonable to argue that in the long run the limited availability of these commodities, together with their technological importance, would begin to act as a constraint on the economy's growth potential. In fact several recent studies have laid great emphasis on this possibility.[3] Although the point is an obvious one, most economic studies of the properties of long-run plans neglect it.[4] In this paper, therefore, we explore in a rather preliminary way the problems that appear to arise naturally when the existence of exhaustible resources is incorporated into the study of intertemporal plans.

It appears that questions in this area are hard to answer. For even in the simplest of environments where it is supposed that there is perfect foresight, one is concerned not merely with the optimal depletion of exhaustible resources but with the optimal rate of investment as well. The two must plainly be interrelated. The latter problem on its own is hard, and the combined problem is very complex. In fact it will appear in the course of the arguments that follow that intuition is not a very good guide for this joint problem. In any case, the assumption of perfect foresight is particularly dubious here since it would appear almost immediate that an investigation of intertemporal plans in the presence of exhaustible resources readily invites consideration of the possibilities of large-scale alterations in technology at dates in the future that are inherently uncertain. Moreover, it is clear that such extensive technological changes would not be achievable costlessly. In this paper, therefore, we attempt to demonstrate how one might, in a relatively simple manner, bring such considerations as these to bear on a set of questions that have generated a considerable amount of interest in recent years.

0.2. It is plain of course that the mere *existence* of a resource that is exhaustible is not a

[1] *First version received April* 1973; *final version accepted February* 1974 (*Eds.*).

[2] Among the many to whom acknowledgement is due for their comments we would like to mention Christopher Bliss, Steve Glaister, Terence Gorman, Frank Hahn, Tjalling Koopmans, Bill Nordhaus, Robert Solow, Joseph Stiglitz, Niel Vousden and, in particular, Harl Ryder.

[3] We have in mind the works of Forrester [8] and Meadows *et al.* [20]. But see also Cole *et al.* [4] for a penetrating commentary on the Forrester analysis; as well as the lively comments of Beckerman [3].

[4] Thus the extensive literature on optimal planning is clearly concerned with horizons long enough for such constraints to become effective, and yet it rarely mentions them. Exceptions are Anderson [1], Ingham and Simmonds [15], Vousden [27], and the seminal and rather neglected work of Hotelling [14]. Professors Koopmans [18], Solow [25], and Stiglitz [26] have recently, and independently of us, explored different aspects of the question under review here. Their findings are complementary to ours and, in what follows, we shall have occasion to refer to the tasks that they have undertaken in their contributions. For a detailed survey of recent modelling experiences in the area of exhaustible resources, see Dasgupta [7].

sufficient basis for apocalyptic visions. Even if we assumed away the possibility of technological change, exhaustible resources would pose a " problem " only if they are, in some sense, essential in production. Intuition suggests that one regards a resource as being *essential* if output of final consumption goods is nil in the absence of the resource. Otherwise, call the resource inessential.[1] It is then natural to ask whether feasible output must eventually decline to zero in an economy that possesses an essential exhaustible resource. Rather surprisingly, perhaps, the answer turns out to be " no ", and this even if there is no technological progress.[2] The point, of course, is that the possibilities open to such an economy depend crucially on the ease with which reproducible inputs can be substituted for the exhaustible resources. It follows, then, that the effect that the existence of an exhaustible resource will have on the characteristics of an *optimal* plan will depend on the extent of such substitution possibilities. In particular we demonstrate below that the *elasticity of substitution* between reproducible inputs and exhaustible resources plays an important and a rather direct role in the properties of an optimal plan. A related question that arises is whether one should, as intuition suggests, deplete an *essential* exhaustible resource slowly over the planning horizon, or whether one should exhaust it in finite time, closing down and living off the existing capital stock. In the same way one wants to know whether it is optimal to deplete an *inessential* exhaustible resource in finite time and, subsequently, rely solely on reproducible capital to continue production. In Section 1 we investigate this range of issues under the assumption that future technology is known with certainty to be the same as that available at present. As one would expect, the analysis will give an indication of the structure of relative prices that would sustain an optimal policy.

While intuition suggests that the elasticity of substitution will be an important parameter, it also suggests that it would be inappropriate to regard the technology of the economy as unchanging over time. Even if under present technological knowledge an exhaustible resource is judged essential it would be unwise to rule out the possibility of substitutes being discovered in the future. In one sense this is at the core of the controversy between Forrester and his critics. In their critiques of the results published by Forrester [8], both Maddox [19] and Nordhaus [21] argue that as an essential exhaustible resource is depleted its market price will rise, forcing entrepreneurs to search for cheaper substitutes. This argument clearly has force, though in the absence of a well-articulated intertemporal plan or a satisfactory set of forward markets it is not at all plain that market prices will be providing the correct signals.[3] Moreover, there are some additional problems that arise in this context, for many of the difficulties that are involved in making policy recommendations about the rate of depletion of exhaustible resources stem from the fact that crucial aspects of this problem are inherently uncertain, and it is not clear that an adequate class of contingent markets exists. There is, of course, some uncertainty about the amounts of resources actually available at any given date, but one would be inclined to feel that this is not the most interesting source of uncertainty. Rather, it would seem plausible that the really important source of uncertainty is connected with future technology. There is, for example, a chance that the discovery of substitutes will render previously essential resources inessential. This has happened a number of times in the past, and one would expect that the best policy towards resource depletion would depend on the probability of such an occurrence. In Section 2 we attempt to analyse this aspect of the problem. We assume in particular that technical change is costlessly attained and that we know in advance the form of the technical change (i.e. the nature of future technology and resource availability) but that the date of its appearance is random.

[1] Later we shall note that this method of partitioning resources that are exhaustible is not as helpful as might appear at first sight.

[2] See Solow [25] for a demonstration of this.

[3] Stiglitz [26] and Dasgupta [7] have investigated the properties of a competitive system where futures markets do not exist and where expectations are not necessarily fulfilled. As would be suspected, it is very easy in such an economy to have a systematic over or under utilization of the resource: for an analysis of the manner in which they have actually allocated resources over time see Heal [10, 12].

In point of fact, of course, substitutes are not obtained at zero cost. One would like (finally) to analyse a problem where resources are deployed in the search for substitutes and where, at the same time, there is no guarantee that the search will be successful. In such a situation the problem is not merely one of obtaining the optimal depletion rate for the exhaustible resources; it also involves finding the correct allocation of the resources used between the production of goods and expenditure on research. In a subsequent paper we shall analyse this aspect of the problem.

The problems that we are considering in this paper arise from the implications that a finite earth has for intertemporal planning. In this context the treatment of population poses considerable difficulties. It would clearly be unreasonable to consider an exogenously given rate of population increase, because the very factors that we are attempting to allow for must eventually force a voluntary or involuntary reduction in rates of population growth on society. There is thus, in principle, a clear need for an optimal population policy, together with an optimum consumption and depletion policy. Professor Koopmans [18] has recently investigated a special form of this problem which consists in assuming a *constant* and *given* population size, with the interesting twist that the planning horizon is regarded as choice variable. The Koopmans problem in effect consists of locating an optimal depletion policy and the optimal survival period for an economy that contains a given and fixed population. It looks as though the population problem in its general setting is particularly complex and we have, so far, been able to obtain some preliminary results only.[1] In this paper, therefore, we assume a constant level of population through time. We are, then, analysing a world in which the objective of zero population growth has been acccepted and achieved. Such a device poses its own interpretive problems, since one has to assume away the existence of a level of consumption below which life cannot be sustained. We can, of course, by suitable assumptions, avoid *zero* consumption along the optimum programme. But in effect we shall be supposing that the subsistence level of consumption is nil.

0.3. In order to clarify ideas it will prove convenient to review briefly the simplest of the models that attempt to capture the presence of exhaustible resources. What we review here is a slight generalization of the well-known "cake-eating" problem analysed first by Hotelling [14] and later by Gale [9]. It would seem plausible that the "cake-eating" problem would be a basic building block of any production model that is to catch the issues that we are concerned with in this paper. In subsequent sections of this paper we shall establish the precise sense in which this claim is true.

But for the moment assume that there is no production. The economy possesses, to begin with, a finite stock (inventory), S_0, of a homogeneous consumption good. By an absence of production in this economy we mean that the social rate of return to investment is zero. Our simple generalization consists of the supposition that a substitute for the resource is already available, in the sense that there is a steady flow of the consumption good that is fed into the economy at the rate M. Denote by C_t the rate of consumption at time t, and by $U(C_t)$ the instantaneous utility of consuming C_t. We assume, as is usual, that $U(\cdot)$ is monotonically increasing, strictly concave, and twice differentiable everywhere. We also suppose, as seems natural, that

$$\operatorname*{lt}_{C\to 0} U'(C) = +\infty.^2 \qquad \text{...(0.1)}$$

Write $\eta(C) = -CU''(C)/U'(C)$, for the *elasticity of marginal utility*. We take it that

$$+\infty > \operatorname*{lt}_{C\to 0} \eta(C) = \eta > 0. \qquad \text{...(0.2)}$$

[1] For an analysis of optimum population policies in the presence of a fixed factor (land), and external diseconomies through large population sizes, see Dasgupta [5].

[2] We follow the by now standard notation: $\dot{x}_t = dx_t/dt$ and $f'(x) = df/dx$. In what follows we shall often drop the time subscript. This should not cause any confusion.

Social welfare over the interval $[0, T]$ will be taken to be of a utilitarian form, yielding an amount

$$\int_0^T e^{-\delta t}U(C_t)dt, \qquad \ldots(0.3)$$

where δ is strictly positive.

One is therefore concerned with obtaining that consumption profile, C_t, which will maximize

$$\left.\begin{aligned}&\int_0^\infty e^{-\delta t}U(C_t)dt \text{ subject to}\\&\dot{S}_t = M - C_t,\\&\text{where } C_t, S_t \geqq 0, M \geqq 0, \text{ and where } S_0 \text{ is given}\end{aligned}\right\}. \qquad \ldots(0.4)$$

In exploring the problem as presented in (0.4) the natural thing to do is to introduce multipliers for the various constraints and write down the Hamiltonian of the system as

$$\mu = e^{-\delta t}U(C_t) + e^{-\delta t}p_t(M - C_t) + e^{-\delta t}q_tS_t \qquad \ldots(0.5)$$

where

$$q_t \geqq 0 \text{ and } q_tS_t = 0. \qquad \ldots(0.6)$$

We have not explicitly introduced the multiplier associated with the non-negativity of C_t simply because we know in advance that given (0·1) the multiplier will throughout be zero. It is then immediate that for a programme to be optimal it is necessary that

$$p_t = U'(C_t) \qquad \ldots(0.7)$$

and also that p_t, the spot price of consumption, should satisfy the differential equation

$$\dot{p}_t = -q_t + \delta p_t. \qquad \ldots(0.8)$$

Using (0.7) in (0.8) one obtains

$$\frac{\dot{C}}{C} = -\frac{\delta}{\eta(C)} + \frac{q_t}{\eta(C)U'(C)}. \qquad \ldots(0.9)$$

From (0.6) and (0.9) it is clear that there are two (possibly repeated) phases, namely: *Phase A*. During which $S_t > 0$ and hence

$$\frac{\dot{C}}{C} = -\frac{\delta}{\eta(C)} < 0 \qquad \ldots(0.10)$$

and *Phase B*. During which equation (0.9) holds with $q_t > 0$, so that $S_t = 0$.

The solution to problem (0.4) for the case $M = 0$ is well known (see e.g. Heal [11]). Consequently we sketch the argument for the case $M > 0$. One begins by noting from equation (0.9) that phase A cannot continue for all $t \geqq 0$ along an optimal policy. For then by (0.2) and (0.10), given any $\varepsilon > 0$ and C_0 there will exist a T such that $C_t \leqq \varepsilon$ for $t \geqq T$, and this would imply that $S_t \to \infty$, which is plainly inefficient. From (0.4) it is clearly feasible to have $C_t \geqq M$ for $t \geqq 0$. This suggests a policy of following phase A for an initial period $[0, T]$ followed by phase B for $t \geqq T$. During phase A equation (0.10) holds. Both C_0 and T are determined by the requirements

$$\int_0^T C_tdt = S_0 + MT \text{ and } \lim_{t \to T^-} C_t = C_T = M.$$

For $t \geqq T$ (i.e. during phase B) we have $C_t = M$. Thus one sets $q_t = 0$ for $0 \leqq t < T$ and

$$q_t = \frac{\delta}{U'(M)} \text{ for } t \geqq T.$$

The proposal satisfies the necessary conditions for an optimal policy. The Hamiltonian (0.5) is concave. It is also the case that along the proposed policy

$$\underset{t \to \infty}{\text{lt}} \; e^{-\delta t} p_t S_t = 0.$$

It follows that we have

Proposition 1. *An optimal policy for the problem* (0.4) *exists and it is uniquely given.*

Proposition 2. *If $M > 0$ the optimal policy consists of precisely two phases. It consists initially of phase A until a time T at which the stock, S_t, is nil. From T onwards the policy consists of phase B during which $C_t = M$.* (Figure 1 illustrates the policy described in Proposition 2.)

The following proposition is well known.

Proposition 3. *If $M = 0$, the optimal policy consists of only one phase, namely phase A. The initial consumption rate, C_0, is so chosen that*

$$\underset{t \to \infty}{\text{lt}} \; S_t = 0. \quad \text{(See Figure 1.)}$$

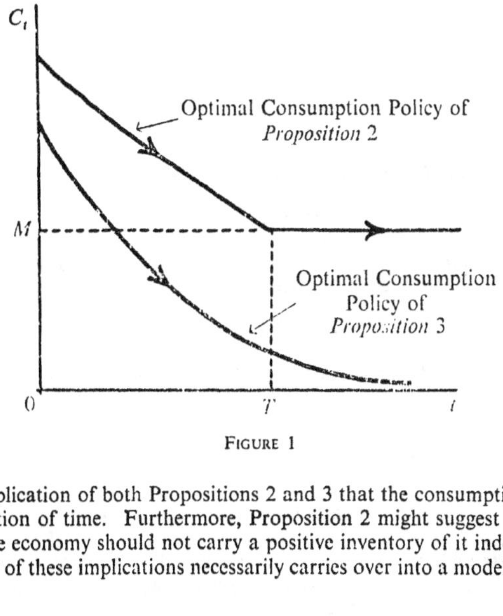

FIGURE 1

It is an implication of both Propositions 2 and 3 that the consumption rate is a non-increasing function of time. Furthermore, Proposition 2 might suggest that if a resource is inessential the economy should not carry a positive inventory of it indefinitely. It turns out that neither of these implications necessarily carries over into a model with production.

1. PRODUCTION

1.1. The economy introduced in Section 0.3 was instrumental merely in fixing ideas and was in itself of limited interest, as there was no production. Consequently we introduce production now. But before introducing exhaustible resources into a production model in a fully-fledged way we present, in this sub-section, a quick review of a production model that incorporates one aspect of the economy discussed in the previous section—namely that a steady stream of a resource that enters in production is fed into the economy from outside. By this device we are, of course, assuming away the essence of the problem.

There are, nevertheless, two reasons why we shall wish to review such a model here. First, it will allow one to see the sharp differences in the properties of an optimal path in an economy that has no exhaustible resources, and one in which such a resource constraint bites in the long run. Second, we shall use the model presented in this sub-section in our discussion of the specific issues that arise when one considers technological change.

We suppose now that there is a single non-deteriorating consumption good which, in conjunction with the service provided by a perfectly durable commodity (e.g. an energy source), can reproduce itself. The quantity of the durable commodity providing service is given and cannot be augmented. It is assumed to provide service at the constant rate M. We can, if we like, assume that the flow of service from the durable good can be stored costlessly, but we shall wish to suppose here that at the start of the planning period there is no inventory of the service.

Denote by K_t the stock of the reproducible composite commodity and by Z_t the rate of utilization of the service at time t. Efficient output possibilities are represented by the production function $G(K, Z)$. It is supposed that G is increasing, twice differentiable, strictly concave and that

$$G(0, Z) \geqq 0 \qquad \text{...(1.1a)}$$

$$\lim_{K\to\infty} \frac{\partial G}{\partial K}(K, M) < \delta \qquad \text{...(1.1b)}$$

$$\lim_{K\to 0} \frac{\partial G}{\partial K}(K, M) > \delta. \qquad \text{...(1.1c)}$$

It follows that consumption possibilities can be predicted by the equation

$$\dot{K} = G(K, Z) - C. \qquad \text{...(1.2)}$$

Denote by V_t the inventory of the service of the durable commodity at t. It follows that the rate, Z_t, at which one utilizes the service can be predicted by the equation

$$\dot{V}_t = M - Z_t, \text{ where } V_t \geqq 0 \text{ all } t \geqq 0. \qquad \text{...(1.3)}$$

The problem we are interested in is one of obtaining time profiles of $\tilde{C}_t$ and $\tilde{Z}_t$ which will maximize

$$\left.\begin{array}{l}\displaystyle\int_0^\infty e^{-\delta t}U(C_t)dt \text{ subject to equations (1.2), (1.3) and the constraints} \\ C_t, Z_t, V_t, K_y \geqq 0, \text{ and where } K_0(>0) \text{ is given and } V_0 = 0.\end{array}\right\} \qquad \text{...(1.4)}$$

The problem, though cast here in a rather unusual form, is a familiar one. Consequently we merely state the results and furnish no proofs. Write $g(K) = G(K, M)$ and define $\bar{K}$ as the solution of $g'(K) = \delta$. One has then

Proposition 4. *Problem* (1.4) *possesses a unique solution. Along the optimal policy* $Z_t = M$ *for all* $t \geqq 0$ (*i.e.* $V_t = 0$ *for all* $t \geqq 0$), *and the economy tends in the long run to the stationary-state consumption rate* $\bar{C} = g(\bar{K})$, *and therefore the capital stock level* $\bar{K}$. *If* $K_0 < \bar{K}$, *then along the optimal path* $\dot{C} > 0$ *and* $\dot{K} > 0$. *If* $K_0 > \bar{K}$ *then along the optimal path* $\dot{C} < 0$ *and* $\dot{K} < 0$.

(Figure 2 presents a typical consumption profile of Proposition 4 for the more plausible case of $K_0 < \bar{K}$.)

Consider now a special case of the model just discussed. Assume that the production function G satisfies (1.1b)-(1.1c) but now strengthen (1.1a) to the form

$$G(0, Z)>0 \text{ for } Z>0. \qquad \ldots(1.1a')$$

Consider problem (1.4) for this economy, but with the difference that now $K_0 = 0$ as well. That is, the economy begins with no capital stock and no inventory of the service. For completeness we express this special case of Proposition 4 as

Proposition 4′. *If G satisfies* (1.1a') *in addition to its other properties and if $K_0 = V_0 = 0$, then Problem* (1.4) *possesses a unique solution. Along the optimal path $Z_t = M$ for all $t \geqq 0$, (i.e. $V_t = 0$ for all $t \geqq 0$), and the economy tends, in the long run, to the stationary state consumption rate $\bar{C} = g(\bar{K})$, and therefore, to the capital stock level $\bar{K}$. Along the optimal path $\dot{C}>0$ and $\dot{K}>0$.*

(Figure 2 presents a typical consumption profile of Proposition 4′.)

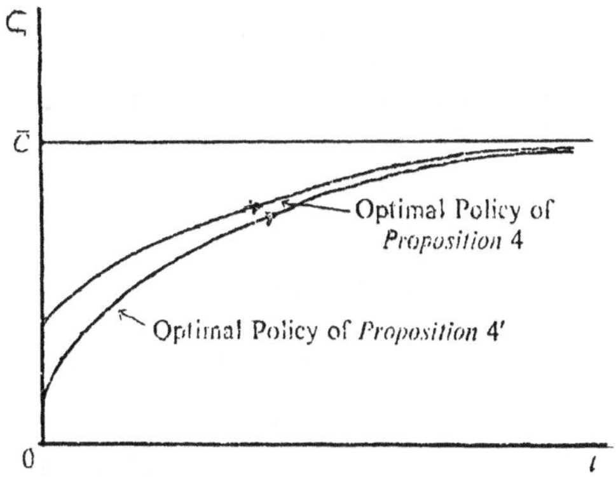

FIGURE 2

1.2. The economy discussed in the previous sub-section possessed no resource that was exhaustible. But it was suggestive, in that the technical possibilities in it were, albeit in a pristine form, the kind that one might be inclined to contemplate when reflecting on the circumstance that would prevail if, to take an example, some totally different source of energy (e.g. the sun) is harnessed. But presumably these are not the conditions that prevail as yet. Consequently we introduce exhaustible resources explicitly into production.

We suppose now that there is a non-deteriorating composite consumption good which, in conjunction with an exhaustible resource in production, can reproduce itself. We continue to denote by K_t the stock of the reproducible composite commodity at time t, but by R_t the flow of the exhaustible resource into production at t. Efficient output possibilities are, therefore, represented by a production function $F(K, R)$. It will be supposed that F is increasing, *strictly* concave, twice differentiable, and homogeneous of degree unity. Consumption possibilities are thus predicted by the condition

$$\dot{K}_t = F(K_t, R_t) - C_t. \qquad \ldots(1.5)$$

One assumes that the economy begins with a stock, S_0, of the exhaustible resource, and a stock, K_0, of the composite commodity. The planning problem then can be represented as being one of

$$\left.\begin{array}{l}\text{maximizing } \int_0^\infty e^{-\delta t}U(C_t)dt \text{ subject to equation (1.5) and the constraint}^{1} \\ \int_0^\infty R_t dt \leqq S_0, \text{ where} \\ C_t,\ K_t,\ R_t \geqq 0 \text{ and } K_0(>0) \text{ is given}\end{array}\right\}. \quad \text{...(1.6)}$$

As before, it would be pointless to introduce the multipliers associated with the non-negativity of C and K, since we have supposed (0.1). Consequently we express the Hamiltonian associated with problem (1.6) as

$$H = e^{-\delta t}U(C_t) + e^{-\delta t}p_t(F(K_t, R_t) - C_t) - \lambda R_t + e^{-\delta t}\mu_t R_t, \quad \text{...(1.7)}$$

where

$$\mu_t \geqq 0 \text{ and } \mu_t R_t = 0 \quad \text{...(1.8)}$$

and

$$\lambda \geqq 0 \text{ and } \lambda\left(S_0 - \int_0^\infty R_t dt\right) = 0. \quad \text{...(1.9)}$$

One expects (and this will be confirmed) that $\lambda > 0$. It should be noted that λ is independent of time. Maximizing (1.7) with respect to C yields the condition

$$p_t = U'(C_t). \quad \text{...(1.10)}$$

Likewise, maximizing (1.7) with respect to R_t yields the condition

$$\lambda = e^{-\delta t}\left(\mu_t + p_t \frac{\partial F}{\partial R_t}\right). \quad \text{...(1.11)}$$

Write $F_R = \partial F/\partial R$, $F_K = \partial F/\partial K$, etc. Equations (1.8) and (1.11) imply that when $R_t > 0$ along an optimal policy

$$\lambda = e^{-\delta t}p_t F_{R_t}. \quad \text{...(1.12)}$$

But when $R_t > 0$, λ denotes the present value shadow price of the exhaustible resource in utility numeraire. It follows that during an interval along an optimal path when $R_t > 0$ this present value shadow price remains constant. However, during this interval the price of the resource relative to the composite commodity numeraire is not, of course, constant, but equal to the marginal product of the resource. A question of importance is the behaviour of this relative price along an optimal programme.[2]

[1] We are thus supposing that extraction of the exhaustible resource is costless. Extraction costs do not appear to introduce any great problem, provided that we assume away non-convexities. One might for example, wish to assume that to extract the resource at a rate R when the remaining stock is of size S requires $E(R, S)$ units of the composite good. One might suppose that E is a convex function and that, in particular, $E(0, S) = 0$, $\partial E/\partial R > 0$ and $\partial E/\partial S \leqq 0$, the last inequality indicating that one is, as it were, digging deeper when the stock has shrunk. To have an interesting problem one would, in addition, need to assume that $\lim_{R\to 0} \partial F/\partial R > \lim_{R\to 0} \partial E/\partial R$. The planning problem (1.6) would in this event be modified only to the extent that equation (1.5) would be replaced by the equation,

$$\dot{K} = F(K, R) - C - E(R, S).$$

[2] If extraction costs were introduced (see previous footnote) equation (1.12) would be replaced by the condition

$$\lambda = e^{-\delta t}p_t[F_R - E_R].$$

Thus, in fact, during an interval when $R_t > 0$ the shadow price of the unextracted exhaustible resource relative to the composite commodity is the *difference* between the marginal product of the resource and its marginal extraction cost. But the price of the extracted resource relative to the composite commodity is of course its marginal product. The extraction cost could be regarded as a pure transport cost. We have found that even amongst professional economists there is often the belief that the price of an exhaustible resource should be its marginal extraction cost. It is, of course, rather obvious why this belief is false.

A related question is whether or not the exhaustible resource ought to be depleted in *finite* time. Towards this consider an economy for which

$$\operatorname*{lt}_{R\to 0} F_R = \infty. \qquad ...(1.13)$$

It is an immediate implication of equation (1.11) that we shall have

Proposition 5. *If* $F(K, R)$ *satisfies* (1.13), *then along an optimal policy, if one exists,* $R_t>0$ *for all* $t \geqq 0$.

The sufficient condition (1.13) in Proposition 5 is, of course, unduly restrictive. One can relatively easily, as we shall presently, weaken it. But it is suggestive in that a condition that prohibits the depletion of the stock of the exhaustible resource in finite time rests not so much on whether the resource is essential (in the sense of output being nil in its absence), but rather on the behaviour of the marginal product of the resource for low rates of usage of the resource. To an economist this is very intuitive.

Proposition 5 is analogous to Proposition 3 of the " cake-eating " problem. It is tempting to construct an analogue of Proposition 2. Towards this we complete the set of conditions necessary for optimality by noting that one must have as well that

$$\frac{d}{dt}(e^{-\delta t}p) = -e^{-\delta t}pF_K, \qquad ...(1.14)$$

or

$$-\dot{p}/p = F_K - \delta. \qquad ...(1.15)$$

Now, equation (1.15), which is the familiar Ramsey condition can, in turn, be re-expressed on using (1.10) as

$$\frac{\dot{C}}{C} = (F_K - \delta)/\eta(C). \qquad ...(1.16)$$

Consider now a time interval of positive measure, if one exists, during which it is optimal to set $R_t>0$. During this interval equation (1.12) is operative. It follows that on differentiating (1.12) with respect to time one obtains the condition

$$\frac{\partial(F_R)}{\partial t}\frac{1}{F_R} = \frac{-\dot{p}}{p} + \delta,$$

which, on using equation (1.15) reduces to the form

$$\frac{\partial(F_R)}{\partial t}\frac{1}{F_R} = F_K. \qquad ...(1.17)$$

Condition (1.17) is really rather obvious, for it is a statement concerning the equality of the rates of return on the two assets (the exhaustible resource and reproducible capital).

Write $x \equiv K/R$ and $f(x) \equiv F(K/R, 1)$. It follows from our assumptions on F that $F_K = f'(x)>0$, $F_R = f(x) - xf'(x)<0$, and $f''(x)<0$. Thus one has as well that $d(F_R)/dx>0$, for $x>0$. Write

$$\sigma = \frac{-f'(x)(f(x)-xf'(x))}{xf(x)f''(x)}, \quad (\infty>\sigma>0)$$

for the elasticity of substitution between K and R. It is then immediate that equation (1.17) reduces to the form

$$\frac{\dot{x}}{x} = \sigma\frac{f(x)}{x}. \qquad ...(1.18)$$

Equations (1.16) and (1.18) govern an optimal programme, if one exists, during an interval when $R_t>0$. Moreover, we have already established (Proposition 5) that if F satisfies (1.13) then equations (1.16) and (1.18) govern an optimal programme for all $t \geqq 0$.

It is remarkable that the conditions governing an optimal programme of aggregate consumption and resource depletion should be so simple in form. In particular, equation (1.18) makes the role of the elasticity of substitution very clear. The capital-resource ratio changes at a percentage rate equal to the product of the elasticity of substitution and the average product per unit of fixed capital. The former gives an indication of the ease with which substitution can be carried out, and the latter can be regarded as an index of the importance of fixed capital in production. Thus, the easier it is to substitute, and the more important is the reproducible input, the more one wants to substitute the reproducible resource for the exhaustible one.

We have already established that if F satisfies (1.13) then along an optimal policy, if one exists, $R_t>0$ for all $t \geqq 0$. The following Lemma yields considerable information regarding the broad characteristics of an optimal depletion policy.

Lemma. *Along an optimal programme, if one exists, an interval during which $R = 0$ cannot be followed by an interval during which $R>0$.*

Proof. Recall that $d(F_R)/dx>0$. Assume that $\sup (f(x)-xf'(x))$ is finite (for if not, the Lemma is trivially true in view of Proposition 5). Suppose then the contrary and let there be a change in phase at T. Assume first that the interval during which $R = 0$ is non-degenerate and that $R_T>0$. Then since K_t is continuous one has

$$\operatorname*{lt}_{t\to T^-} (f(x_t)-x_tf'(x_t)) = \sup (f(x)-xf'(x))>(f(x_T)-x_Tf'(x_T)).$$

But $\operatorname*{lt}_{t\to T^-} e^{-\delta t}p_t = e^{-\delta T}p_T$. Such a phase change, therefore, is impossible since, given equations (1.11) and (1.12), one must have

$$\operatorname*{lt}_{t\to T^-} e^{-\delta t}(\mu_t+p_t(f(x_t)-x_tf'(x_t))) = e^{-\delta T}p_T(f(x_T)-x_Tf'(x_T)),$$

with $\mu_t \geqq 0$.

The other possibility is that $R_T = 0$ but that during an interval (T, T_1) one sets $R_t>0$. But if this is so then during (T, T_1) equation (1.18) holds, and in order for (1.18) to hold it must be the case that $\operatorname*{lt}_{t\to T^+} R_t>0$. In other words, there must be a discontinuity in R at T. Thus $f(x_T)-x_Tf'(x_T)> \operatorname*{lt}_{t\to T^+} (f(x_t)-x_tf'(x_t))$. One argues now, as earlier, that such a phase change is impossible since equations (1.11) and (1.12) dictate that

$$e^{-\delta T}(\mu_T+p_T(f(x_T)-x_Tf'(x_T))) = \operatorname*{lt}_{t\to T^+} e^{-\delta t}p_t(f(x_t)-x_tf'(x_t))$$

and $\mu_T \geqq 0$. ||

The Lemma is powerful in its implications, for we can now assert

Proposition 6. *Along an optimal policy, if one exists, R_t is a continuous function of time. Furthermore, either $R_t>0$ for all $t \geqq 0$ or there exists a finite $T(>0)$ such that $R_t>0$ for $0 \leqq t<T$ and $R_t = 0$ for $t \geqq T$.*

Proof. The second part (with the exception of the demonstration that $T>0$) of the proposition is a direct implication of the Lemma, and a simple argument (as in the proof of the Lemma) showing that we cannot have $R_t=0$ for $0 \leqq t \leqq T$ and $R_t > 0$ for $t>T$. Therefore we begin by proving that R_t must be continuous if $T>0$. Thus if $R_t>0$ for all $t \geqq 0$ then the continuity of R_t is trivially true since x_t must satisfy (1.18) for all $t \geqq 0$ and since K_t must be a continuous function. Suppose then that there exists a finite $T(>0)$ at which there is a phase change from $R>0$ to $R = 0$. During the interval $[0, T)$ equation (1.18) holds. Since $\dot{x}>0$ during $[0, T)$, $\operatorname*{lt}_{t\to T^-} x_t$ exists. But it cannot be finite. For suppose it is. By hypothesis $x_T = \infty$. This implies that we would violate the condition necessary at the switch point, namely that

$$\underset{t\to T^-}{\text{lt}}\ e^{-\delta t}p_t(f(x_t)-x_t f'(x_t)) = e^{-\delta T}\{\mu_T + p_T[f(x_T)-x_T f'(x_T)]\},$$

where $\mu_T \geqq 0$.

It follows that during $[0, T)$, x_t increases continuously to ∞. That is $\underset{t\to T^-}{\text{lt}}\ x_t = x_T = \infty$. Since $K_t > 0$ for all $t \geqq 0$ this implies that $\underset{t\to T^-}{\text{lt}}\ R_t = R_T = 0$.

What remains to be proved is that $T > 0$. So suppose on the contrary that the phase change occurs at $t = 0$. That is, assume $T = 0$ (i.e. that R_t is a δ-function). Once again we appeal to the assumption that $\frac{d}{dx}(f(x)-xf'(x)) > 0$ and note that if there is a singularity at $t = 0$ one would violate a condition necessary at this switch point, which is

$$p_0\{f(x_0)-x_0 f'(x_0)\} = \underset{t\to 0^+}{\text{lt}}\ e^{-\delta t}p_t\{f(x_t)-x_t f'(x_t)\} + \mu_t,$$

where $\mu_t \geqq 0$, $x_0 = 0$ and $\underset{t\to 0^+}{\text{lt}}\ x_t = \infty$.

We are now in a position to construct a proposition analogous to Proposition 2 of the previous section. Towards this consider an economy for which

$$\underset{x\to\infty}{\text{lt}}\ (f(x)-xf'(x)) = \gamma < \infty$$

and ...(1.19)

$$F(K, 0) > 0 \text{ for } K > 0.$$

It is then simple to confirm that it cannot be optimal to maintain $R_t > 0$ for all $t \geqq 0$ in an economy that satisfies (1.19). For suppose the contrary. From (1.18) one has $x_t \to \infty$. Furthermore, from the second part of (1.19) it follows that

$$\underset{x\to\infty}{\text{lt}}\ f(x)/x = \underset{x\to\infty}{\text{lt}}\ f'(x) = \rho > 0.$$

Therefore, from (1.14) one has that the present value price of consumption $(e^{-\delta t}p_t)$ goes to zero, and from the first part of (1.19) the fact that the marginal product of the exhaustible resource is bounded above by γ. But these would contradict the requirement that the economy satisfies (1.12). Thus one has

Proposition 7. *If $F(K, R)$ satisfies* (1.19) *then along an optimal policy, if one exists, $R_t > 0$ for $0 \leqq t < T$ where T is finite and $R_t = 0$ for $t \geqq T$. Moreover R_t is continuous for all $t \geqq 0$.*[1]

1.3. The arguments of the previous sub-section were fairly general, and were concerned with glancing at the conditions that an optimal programme must necessarily satisfy. In particular, we noted the rather direct way in which the elasticity of substitution enters into the characterization of an optimal programme during a phase when $R_t > 0$. In this section we parametrize the economy somewhat further to obtain some definite answers to questions that one would like to ask. One would, for example, like to know under what circumstances an optimal programme exists, and whether the rate of consumption along an optimal policy necessarily falls if the resource is essential and indeed, whether the rate of consumption necessarily rises if the resource is inessential. Furthermore, one

[1] An example of an economy, satisfying (1.19) is one where $f(x) = \rho(1+x+\phi(x))$ with $\rho > 0$, $\phi(0) = 0$, $\phi'(x) > 0$, $\phi''(x) < 0$ and $\underset{x\to\infty}{\text{lt}}\ \phi(x) < \infty$. One should note that we have avoided the case $f(x) = \rho(1+x)$ (i.e. $F(K, R) = (K+R)\ \rho$, $\sigma = \infty$) by our assumption of strict concavity of $F(K, R)$. We shall have occasion to comment on this case in Section 1.4.

would like to know if the optimal utilization rate of the resource is non-increasing over time, as well as conditions under which the capital stock ought to be built up over time.

Towards this we turn to the simplest laboratory that might provide answers, namely the class of production functions for which the elasticity of substitution is constant. It might seem plausible that the class of CES production functions captures the variety of the issues under review. In fact, the CES production functions (with the exception of those for which $\sigma = 1$ and ∞) have rather unusual properties at the " corners ". Consequently some of the characteristics of an optimal policy in a CES world are, at first blush, counter-intuitive. It will be plain that one can establish rather easily conditions under which an optimal programme exists for a much larger environment than the CES world provides. Since the arguments turn out to be rather similar to the ones that we shall provide for the CES case, we do not elaborate on them here.

Recall that the CES production functions is of the form

$$F(K, R) = [\beta K^{(\sigma-1)/\sigma}+(1-\beta)R^{(\sigma-1)/\sigma}]^{\sigma/(\sigma-1)},$$

where $0<\beta<1$ and $\infty \geqq \sigma \geqq 0$.

The analysis of the previous sub-section implied that one is particularly interested in the properties of the production function for $R = 0$. It is convenient, then, to catalogue the following properties:

If $\sigma = 1$ (i.e. the Cobb-Douglas form)

$$F(K, 0) = 0 \qquad \text{...(1.20}a\text{)}$$

$$\underset{x\to\infty}{\text{lt}}\ f'(x) = \underset{x\to\infty}{\text{lt}}\ \frac{f(x)}{x} = 0 \qquad \text{...(1.20}b\text{)}$$

$$\underset{x\to\infty}{\text{lt}}\ (f(x)-xf'(x)) = \underset{x\to\infty}{\text{lt}}\ f(x) = \infty. \qquad \text{...(1.20}c\text{)}$$

If $0 \leqq \sigma<1$ then

$$F(K, 0) = 0 \qquad \text{...(1.2}a\text{)}$$

$$\underset{x\to\infty}{\text{lt}}\ f'(x) = \underset{x\to\infty}{\text{lt}}\ \frac{f(x)}{x} = 0 \qquad \text{...(1.21}b\text{)}$$

$$\underset{x\to\infty}{\text{lt}}\ (f(x)-xf'(x)) = \underset{x\to\infty}{\text{lt}}\ f(x) = (1-\beta)^{\sigma/(\sigma-1)}. \qquad \text{...(1.21}c\text{)}$$

If $\infty>\sigma>1$ then

$$F(K, 0) = \beta^{\sigma/(\sigma-1)}K \qquad \text{...(1.22}a\text{)}$$

$$\underset{x\to\infty}{\text{lt}}\ f'(x) = \underset{x\to\infty}{\text{lt}}\ \frac{f(x)}{x} = \beta^{\sigma/(\sigma-1)}>0 \qquad \text{...(1.22}b\text{)}$$

$$\underset{x\to\infty}{\text{lt}}\ (f(x)-xf'(x)) = \underset{x\to\infty}{\text{lt}}\ f(x) = \infty. \qquad \text{...(1.22}c\text{)}$$

An exhaustible resource is essential to production only when $\sigma \leqq 1$. Otherwise it is inessential. The pair (1.22*c*) and (1.21*c*) are curious: an inessential resource is infinitely valuable and an essential resource is finitely valuable at the margin when the rate of utilization of the resource is zero. Only the Cobb-Douglas form may be said to have properties that are reasonable at the corner.

From (1.20*c*) and (1.22*c*) and Proposition 5 it is immediate that when $\infty>\sigma \geqq 1$, along an optimal policy, if one exists, $R_t>0$ for all $t \geqq 0$. We demonstrate now that this must be true for the case $0<\sigma<1$ as well. Recall Proposition 6. Assume that there exists a finite $T(>0)$ such that $R_t=0$ for $t \geqq T$. During the interval $[0, T)$ equation (1.18) must be satisfied. Moreover R_t must be continuous at T. But this is impossible, for the constancy of σ and condition (1.21c) imply that x cannot increase to infinity via equation (1.18) in finite time.[1]

We have yet to demonstrate that an optimal programme exists. To keep the *presentation* simple we restrict ourselves to the case of utility functions that are iso-elastic. That is, assume $\eta(c) = \eta > 0$. Write

$$\rho = \operatorname*{lt}_{x\to\infty} f'(x) = \operatorname*{lt}_{x\to\infty} \frac{f(x)}{x} \text{ and } S_t = S_0 - \int_0^t R_\tau d\tau.$$

We can then establish

Proposition 8. *If* $\sigma(\infty > \sigma > 0)$ *is constant,* $\eta(>0)$ *is constant, and* $\delta > \rho(1-\eta)$, *a unique optimal policy exists and it satisfies equations* (1.5), (1.16) *and* (1.18)*for all* $t \geqq 0$. *Moreover, the optimal programme* $(\tilde{C}_t, \tilde{R}_t, \tilde{K}_t, \tilde{x}_t, \tilde{S}_t)$ *satisfies the following asymptotic properties:*

$$\operatorname*{lt}_{t\to\infty} \tilde{x} = \infty \quad \text{...(1.23)}$$

$$\operatorname*{lt}_{t\to\infty} \tilde{C} = \operatorname*{lt}_{t\to\infty} \tilde{K} = \infty \text{ if } \rho > \delta \quad \text{...(1.24)}$$

$$\operatorname*{lt}_{t\to\infty} \tilde{C} = \operatorname*{lt}_{\to\infty} \tilde{K} = 0 \text{ if } \rho < \delta \quad \text{...(1.25)}$$

$$\operatorname*{lt}_{t\to\infty} \frac{\dot{\tilde{C}}}{\tilde{C}} = \operatorname*{lt}_{t\to\infty} \frac{\dot{\tilde{K}}}{\tilde{K}} = \frac{\rho-\delta}{\eta} \quad \text{...(1.26)}$$

$$\operatorname*{lt}_{t\to\infty} \frac{\tilde{C}}{\tilde{K}} = \rho + \frac{\delta-\rho}{\eta} \quad \text{...(1.27)}$$

$$\operatorname*{lt}_{t\to\infty} \frac{\dot{\tilde{R}}}{\tilde{R}} = \operatorname*{lt}_{t\to\infty} \frac{\dot{\tilde{S}}}{\tilde{S}} = \frac{\rho-\delta}{\eta} - \sigma\rho < 0 \quad \text{...(1.28)}$$

$$\operatorname*{lt}_{\to\infty} \frac{\tilde{R}}{\tilde{S}} = \sigma\rho + \frac{\delta-\rho}{\eta} > 0. \quad \text{...(1.29)}$$

Proof. It has already been established that the conditions necessary for optimality are that equations (1.16) and (1.18) must hold for all $t \geqq 0$. Condition (1.23) is then immediate from (1.18). From equation (1.18) one recognizes as well that for any pair of paths $x_t^{(1)}$ and $x_t^{(2)}$ one has $x_t^{(1)} > x_t^{(2)}$ for all $t > 0$ if $x_0^{(1)} > x_0^{(2)}$. From (1.16) it follows that $C_0^{(1)} > C_0^{(2)}$ if, and only if, $C_t^{(1)}(C_0^{(1)}, x_0) > C_t^{(2)}(C_0^{(2)}, x_0)$. Now write equation (1.5) as

$$\frac{\dot{K}}{K} = \frac{f(x)}{x} - \frac{C}{K}. \quad \text{...(1.30)}$$

It follows from (1.30) that $K_t^{(1)}(C_0^{(1)}, x_0) < K_t^{(2)}(C_0^{(2)}, x_0)$ if, and only if, $C_0^{(1)} > C_0^{(2)}$.

Write $y = C/K$, and use equations (1.16) and (1.30) to obtain

$$\frac{\dot{y}}{y} = y - \frac{\delta}{\eta} + \frac{f'(x)}{\eta} - \frac{f(x)}{x}. \quad \text{...(1.31)}$$

Recall that K_0 and S_0 are given and that we are to choose optimally C_0 (i.e. y_0) and R_0(i.e. x_0). The point is to observe that these choices can, in principle, be separated out

[1] It is now immediate that Proposition 5 can be generalized to

Proposition 5′. *Along an optimal policy, if one exists,* $R_t > 0$ *for all* $t \geqq 0$ *if either* $F(K, R)$ *satisfies* (1.13) *or* $F(K, 0) = 0$.

Since the sufficiency conditions in Propositions 5′ and 7 are not merely mutually exclusive but exhaustive as well, it follows that these two Propositions cover all the cases.

conveniently. We have, of course, assumed $\sigma>0$. Then, using (1.23) it follows from (1.31) that for large t

$$\frac{\dot{y}}{y} \simeq y - \frac{(\delta-\rho)}{\eta} - \rho. \qquad \text{...(1.32)}$$

It follows from (1.31) and (1.32) that *given* x_0, if C_0 (i.e. y_0) is chosen large enough, then $y_t(x_0)\to\infty$ as $t\to\infty$. But this entails from (1.30) that the feasibility requirement, $K_t \geqq 0$, is violated in finite time. It follows as well from (1.31) and (1.32) that *given* x_0, if C_0 (i.e. y_0) is chosen positive, but low enough, then $y_t(x_0)\to 0$ as $t\to\infty$.

Thus let $\tilde{C}_0(x_0) = \sup\,[C_0 \mid y_t(C_0, x_0) \geqq 0 \text{ for } t \geqq 0]$. From (1.32) it is immediate that

$$\underset{t\to\infty}{\text{lt}}\; y_t(\tilde{C}_0(x_0), x_0) = \rho + (\delta-\rho)/\eta > 0,$$

confirming (1.27). From (1.16) and (1.30) condition (1.26) follows directly.

One can now verify that

$$\underset{t\to\infty}{\text{lt}}\; \frac{d(e^{-\delta t}p_t\tilde{K}_t)/dt}{e^{-\delta t}p_t\tilde{K}_t} = \frac{\rho-\delta}{\eta} - \rho < 0, \text{ and thus that } \underset{t\to\infty}{\text{lt}}\; e^{-\delta t}p_tK_t = 0. \qquad \text{...(1.33)}$$

But $\dot{R}/R = \dot{K}/K - \dot{x}/x$. On using (1.26) and (1.18) it is immediate that

$$\underset{t\to\infty}{\text{lt}}\; \frac{\dot{R}}{R} = \frac{\rho-\delta}{\eta} - \sigma\rho < 0. \qquad \text{...(1.34)}$$

It follows from (1.34) that $S(x_0) \equiv \int_0^\infty R_t(\tilde{C}_0(x_0), x_0)dt$ is well defined. It follows as well that we can choose x_0 large enough (i.e. R_0 small enough) so that $S(x_0) < S_0$, and x_0 small enough (i.e. R_0 large enough), so that $S(x_0) > S_0$. The former would be inefficient and the latter choice unfeasible. Thus write

$$\tilde{x}_0 \equiv \sup\,\{x_0 \mid S(x_0) \leqq S_0\}.$$

Then

$$S_t = \int_t^\infty \tilde{R}_\tau(\tilde{C}_0(\tilde{x}_0), \tilde{x}_0)d\tau \text{ and } \underset{t\to\infty}{\text{lt}}\; \tilde{S}_t = 0.$$

But $\dot{S}/S = -R/S$. Hence

$$\underset{t\to\infty}{\text{lt}}\; \dot{\tilde{S}}/\tilde{S} = \underset{t\to\infty}{\text{lt}}\; -\tilde{R}/\tilde{S} = \underset{t\to\infty}{\text{lt}}\; \dot{\tilde{R}}/\tilde{R} = (\rho-\delta)\eta - \sigma\rho < 0,$$

and conditions (1.28) and (1.29) are confirmed. Plainly

$$\underset{t\to\infty}{\text{lt}}\; \lambda\tilde{S}_t = 0. \qquad \text{...(1.35)}$$

Conditions (1.24) and (1.25) are implied immediately by (1.26).

Finally, the Hamiltonian (1.7) is strictly concave. The two transversality conditions (1.33) and (1.35) have been verified. The proposition is thus established. ‖.

Having established the main proposition of this section we present some specific commentaries in the following sub-section.

1.4. The case $0<\sigma<1$ is at once the simplest and the most pessimistic of all.[1] As total output is bounded if $\sigma<1$, it is plain that *feasibility* dictates that $C_t\to 0$ as $t\to\infty$. Since $\rho = 0$ it is clear that an optimum exists if $\delta>0$. This is so, even if $U(\cdot)$ is unbounded above (i.e. $0<\eta<1$). Given (1.23), the shadow price of the exhaustible resource relative to the composite is monotonically increasing. Given (1.21*c*) in addition, it is clear that

[1] We have, of course, assumed away the case $\sigma = 0$ by our assumptions on F. It is not a case that presents any special problems of analysis but as its analysis calls for some extra notation, we do not discuss it here.

this shadow price tends in the long run to the value $(1-\rho)^{\sigma/(\sigma-1)}$ (see equation (1.12)). This is mildly surprising, given that the resource is essential.

The Cobb-Douglas case is particularly interesting since the analysis can relatively easily be taken further. To begin with, since $\rho = 0$, an optimum exists if $\delta > 0$. Furthermore, given (1.20*c*) and (1.23), the price of the exhaustible resource relative to fixed capital is increasing and tends to infinity with time. Let $f(x) = x^{\alpha}$ with $0 < \alpha < 1$. Professor Solow [25] has demonstrated that consumption can be unbounded if $\alpha > 1/2$, but that feasible consumption must tend to zero if $\alpha < 1/2$. But from (1.25) we have that for all α, $0 < \alpha < 1$, $\tilde{C}_t \to 0$.

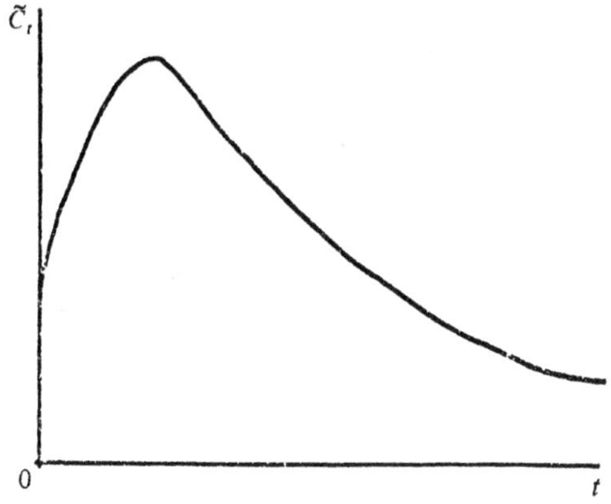

FIGURE 3

Now integrate (1.18) to obtain

$$\tilde{x}_t = [(1-\alpha)t + x_0^{(1-\alpha)}]^{1/(1-\alpha)}, \qquad \ldots(1.36)$$

and thus that in the long run the price of the exhaustible resource relative to the composite commodity should be approximately

$$(1-\alpha)^{1/(1-\alpha)} t^{\alpha/(1-\alpha)}.$$

It is also the case that in the long run the percentage rate of change in the rate of depletion of the exhaustible is approximately equal to $-\delta/\eta$ (see (1.28)) and, in particular, the rate of depletion, as a fraction of the then existing stock of the resource, is δ/η (see (1.29)).

Using (1.36) in equation (1.16) and integrating, the optimal consumption profile is

$$\tilde{C}_t = \tilde{C}_0 \tilde{x}_0^{-\alpha/\eta} [(1-\alpha)t + \tilde{x}_0^{(1-\alpha)}]^{\alpha/\eta(1-\alpha)} e^{(-\delta/\eta)t}. \qquad (\ldots 1.37)$$

From (1.37) it would appear that if the initial stocks K_0 and S_0 are " large " the optimal rate of consumption will, during an initial period, be rising, and will in fact be single peaked, with a maximum at T where [1]

$$T = \frac{\alpha}{\delta(1-\alpha)} - \frac{\tilde{x}_0^{1-\alpha}}{(1-\alpha)}.$$

A typical consumption profile is presented in Figure 3. It is routine to show that

$$\dot{\tilde{R}}_t = \tilde{C}_0 \tilde{x}_0^{-\alpha/\eta} [(1-\alpha)t + \tilde{x}_0^{1-\alpha}]^{\alpha/\eta} e^{(-\delta/\eta)t},$$

[1] It should, of course, be evident that T is not independent of η, since $\tilde{X}_0$ is dependent on η. Professor Solow ([25], appendix) considers the case where $\alpha > 1/2$ and $\delta = 0$. This last ensures that our existence theorem is not applicable to his case. He shows, in effect, that if η is large enough, then $T = \infty$. For this limiting case of $\delta = 0$ he assumes, therefore, that $\alpha > 1/2$ to ensure that consumption can be unbounded and large enough η to ensure the existence of an optimal policy.

from which

$$\text{sign}\,(\ddot{\tilde{R}}_t) = \text{sign}\left[\delta - \frac{\alpha(1-\alpha)}{(1-\alpha)t + \tilde{x}_0^{1-\alpha}}\right].$$

It follows that while $\dot{\tilde{R}}<0$ for all $t \geqq 0$ and $\ddot{\tilde{R}}_t>0$ for large enough t, one would have $\ddot{\tilde{R}}_t<0$ for an initial period for large values of K_0 and S_0, yielding a time profile of resource utilization as in Figure 4.

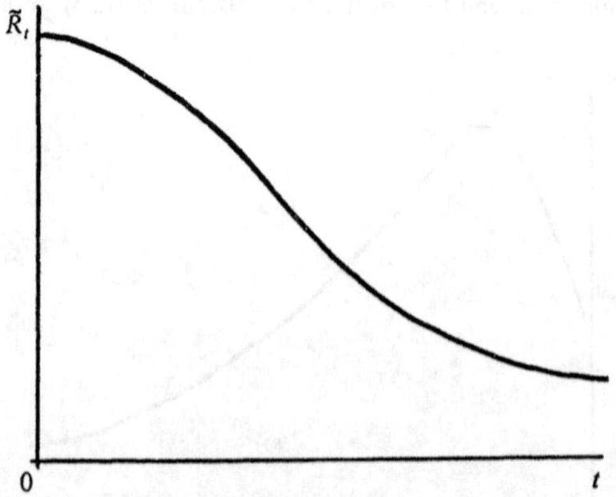

FIGURE 4

The case $\sigma>1$ is one in which exhaustible resources are not a fundamental problem, since they are inessential in production. Given (1.23) the shadow price of the exhaustible resource relative to fixed capital is monotonically increasing, but given (1.22*c*) one does have the surprising result that this price tends to infinity with time. Since $\rho>0$ it is plain that $\delta>0$ is not sufficient for the existence of an optimum policy. But if $U(\cdot)$ is bounded above (i.e. $\eta>1$) an optimum exists for $\delta \geqq 0$. As conditions (1.24) and (1.25) make clear, whether or not it is optimal to have a growing economy in the long run depends on whether ρ is greater than, or less than δ, a condition that is intuitively plain.

The case, $\sigma = \infty$, though silly, merits a brief glance, though we have so far assumed it away. Assume then that $f(x) = \rho(1+x)$, where $\rho>0$. It satisfies (1.19). But since f is linear, Proposition 7 is not strictly operative. Nevertheless, it is an easy matter to confirm that if $\delta>(1-\eta)\rho$ an optimal programme exists and that the optimal depletion rate, $\tilde{R}_t$, is a Dirac-δ-function with the singularity at $t = 0$. The point is that since the marginal product of the resource is constant, it does not pay to leave the resource lying idle. As we have imposed no costs of extraction one can, in principle, use up the entire initial stock, S_0, instantaneously to build up the capital stock, which is, in fact, the optimal strategy.[1]

2. TECHNICAL CHANGE AND UNCERTAINTY

2.1. Technological progress is, as usual, hard to model. We are concerned now with those situations where technical change causes a resource that was previously essential to become inessential. In practice this is most likely to be due to the discovery of a synthetic substitute (for example, being able to harness solar energy or nuclear fusion), and it is this type of alteration in the technological possibilities that provides the motivation

[1] The reader can easily check that if $\delta>(1-\eta)\rho$ then a unique optimum exists if the production function $f(\cdot)$ is of the form given in the footnote to Proposition 7. Given Proposition 7, the optimal depletion function, $\tilde{R}_t$, is continuous for this case, but the entire stock is exhausted in *finite* time.

for the discussion that follows. In such situations, although one may not know in advance exactly what the substitute will be like, there will probably be general information about its likely characteristics. Industrial research directed towards innovation is, after all, not carried out aimlessly. A more important source of uncertainty seems to be the exact *timing* of the availability of the substitute. It would seem reasonable to argue that we are much more uncertain about when, if ever, such an event will occur, than we are about the characteristics it will have if it does occur, and we shall focus attention on this aspect of the problem. Consequently we suppose that we know exactly the nature of the technical change that will occur, but we treat the date at which the event occurs as a random variable. In this paper, however, we suppose that the distribution of the random variable is exogenously given.

The basic framework that we shall present appears to us to be fairly robust in that it can accommodate quite diverse characterizations of the technological breakthrough. Furthermore, it would seem that one could, in principle, extend the analysis quite directly to allow for the possibility of a *finite* sequence of such events in the future. But it seems most interesting to conceive of the event as being the discovery of a substitute for an exhaustible resource which releases the economy from the resource constraints. Moreover, for the sake of simplicity we take it that only one such event is to be considered. Towards this we amalgamate the production model considered in Sections 1.1 and 1.2 in a sequential manner.

Assume that the economy is endowed initially with a stock, K_0, of the composite consumption good, and a stock, S_0, of an exhaustible resource. Production possibilities until the date of the technological breakthrough are represented, as in Section 1.2, by the production function $F(K_t, R_t)$, where, as before, R_t is the flow of resources into production at t. Suppose the technological breakthrough occurs at date $T>0$. Then the constraints that limit the choice of consumption till T can be denoted by the conditions

$$\dot{K}_t = F(K_t, R_t) - C_t,\ 0 \leqq t \leqq T;\ \int_0^T R_t dt \leqq S_0 \text{ and } K_0 \text{ and } S_0 \text{ are given.} \qquad \ldots(2.1)$$

We characterize the technological innovation as being the discovery of a perfectly durable commodity which provides a flow of service at the constant rate M. But it would seem hard to think that the production possibilities after the event would remain the same as those before. It is here that we revert to the economy discussed in Section 1.1, and suppose that the production function after the innovation can be regarded as being $G(K_t, Z_t)$, where Z_t is the rate of utilization of the service at date t. Now, there is of course nothing to suggest that the service provided by the durable commodity is a perfect substitute for the exhaustible resource in the production function, G. In fact there is every reason to suppose that it is not. Nevertheless, for the moment, to keep the presentation simple we suppose that they are perfect substitutes. It follows that the constraints that limit the choice of a consumption profile for the period *beyond* T are represented by the conditions

$$\left.\begin{array}{l} \dot{K} = G(K, Z) - C \\ \dot{V} = M - Z \\ \text{where } Z_t, K_t, C_t, V_t \geqq 0 \text{ and } V_T = S_0 - \int_0^T R_t dt \\ \text{and } K_T \text{ given} \end{array}\right\} . \qquad \ldots(2.2)$$

The date T, is assumed unknown. In fact suppose that T is random number with a probability density function ω_t. Thus we suppose that

$$\omega_t > 0 \text{ and } \int_0^\infty \omega_t dt = 1. \qquad \ldots(2.3)$$

The second condition in (2.3) supposes that the substitute source will certainly be discovered *sometime* in the future. One might wish to allow for the possibility of it *never* being discovered. Nothing substantial seems to emerge by supposing so. Therefore we suppose (2.3).[1]

We take it that the valuation function for planning is $E\int_0^\infty e^{-\delta t}U(C)dt$, where E is the expectation operator. An important question then arises as to what penalty one would wish to attach to depleting completely the exhaustible resource *before* the substitute is discovered. It would seem most interesting to formulate the problem in such a way as to make the penalty infinite. Thus we impose the restriction that along a feasible strategy the probability of being caught short with none of the exhaustible resource before the substitute is discovered, is nil.

Define $W(K_T, V_T)$ = maximum value of $\int_T^\infty e^{-\delta(t-T)}U(C_t)dt$ subject to (2.2). It follows that

$$E\int_0^\infty e^{-\delta t}U(C)dt = \int_0^\infty \omega_T\left\{\int_0^T e^{-\delta t}U(C)dt + W(K_T, V_T)e^{-\delta t}\right\}dT. \quad \text{...(2.4)}$$

Write $\Omega_t = \int_t^\infty \omega_\tau d\tau$, and integrate the RHS of (2.4) by parts to obtain

$$E\int_0^\infty e^{-\delta t}U(C)dt = \int_0^\infty e^{-\delta t}\{U(C)\Omega_t + \omega_t W(K_t, V_t)\}dt. \quad \text{...(2.5)}$$

The problem then reduces to one of

$$\left.\begin{array}{l}\text{maximizing expression (2.5) subject to the constraints}\\ \dot{K} = F(K, R) - C\\ \dot{S} = -R\\ \text{where } V_t = S_t \text{ and } K_t, C_t, R_t, S_t \geqq 0\end{array}\right\}. \quad \text{...(2.6)}$$

It is as well to point out that the optimal policy is to pursue the solution path of problem (2.6) only until the substitute is discovered. At the date the substitute is discovered there is a switch in regime and the optimal policy from then on is to follow the policy which yields $W(K_T, V_T)$.[2]

In order to analyse (2.6) it is convenient to express the Hamiltonian of the system as

$$H = e^{-\delta t}\{U(C)\Omega_t + \omega_t W(K_t, V_t)\} + e^{-\delta t}p_t\{F(K, R) - C\} - e^{-\delta t}q_t R_t + e^{-\delta t}\pi_t R_t + e^{-\delta t}\gamma_t S_t, \quad \text{...(2.7)}$$

where

$$\left.\begin{array}{l}\pi_t \geqq 0 \text{ and } \pi_t R_t = 0\\ \gamma_t \geqq 0 \text{ and } \gamma_t S_t = 0\end{array}\right\}, \quad \text{...(2.8)}$$

and

We shall assume $W(K_t, V_t)$ to be bounded and differentiable. The former can be justified if we assume that $U(\cdot)$ is bounded above, and we shall assume that this is so. The concavity of W follows from assumptions that we have already made. From (2.1) it is plain that $e^{-\delta t}p_t$ is the present value price of the composite consumption good and that $e^{-\delta t}q_t$ is the present value price of the exhaustible resource. One notes as well from (2.8) that $\gamma_t > 0$ implies that $\pi_t > 0$.

[1] For simplicity of exposition we shall take it, in fact, that $\omega_t > 0$ for $t \geqq 0$, though this is not at all essential.

[2] The solution to (2.6) is thus a conditional strategy, conditional upon the substitute not having been discovered.

For a programme to be optimal it is then necessary that it satisfies the following conditions

$$p = \Omega_t U'(C) \qquad \text{...(2.9)}$$

$$pF_R = q - \pi_t \qquad \text{...(2.10)}$$

$$\dot{p} = \delta p - \omega_t W_K - pF_K \qquad \text{...(2.11)}$$

and

$$\dot{q} = \delta q - \omega_t W_V - \gamma_t, \qquad \text{...(2.12)}$$

where

$$W_K = \frac{\partial W}{\partial K}, \text{ etc.}$$

Now $W_V \geqq 0$ and $W_K \geqq 0$. It follows from (2.10) to (2.12) that if F satisfies (1.13) then we shall have $R_t > 0$ for all $t \geqq 0$ along an optimal policy. We suppose, therefore, that this is so. Consequently $\gamma_t = \pi_t = 0$ for all $t \geqq 0$.

Write $\Psi_t = \omega_t/\Omega_t$, for the conditional probability of the substitute being discovered at t given that it has not been discovered earlier. From equations (2.9) and (2.11) one has [1]

$$\frac{\dot{C}}{C} = \frac{F_K - \delta + \Psi_t\{(W_K - U'(C))/U'(C)\}}{\eta(C)}. \qquad \text{...(2.13)}$$

Differentiate (2.10) with respect to time and use equations (2.12), (2.13) and the production constraint in (2.6) to obtain

$$\dot{x} = \sigma f(x)\left\{1 + \frac{W_K \Psi_t}{U'(C)f'(x)}\right\} + \frac{W_V \Psi_t}{xf''(x)U'(C)}, \qquad \text{...(2.14)}$$

where x, σ and $f(\cdot)$ are as in Section 1.2.[2] Equations (2.13) and (2.14) govern the solution to the problem expressed in (2.6). The nature of the path they define is far from obvious except in some special cases. We turn to these. Now the technology G subsequent to the technological breakthrough is likely to be considerably different from that prior to T. The simplification that we introduce lies in the supposition that at T (the date of the discovery), the then existing stocks of capital and the exhaustible resource come to have no economic value. This is, of course, a terribly strong assumption, but not totally unreasonable. It seems, for example, very likely that if fusion reactors ever become a commercial proposition, turning water into an abundantly available substitute for fossil fuel, then power stations generating electricity from fossil fuels will be rapidly phased out. Both the capital equipment that they comprise and the remaining fossil fuel stocks will have little economic value as sources of energy, although of course fuels would have value as sources of organic chemicals. This assumption implies

$$W_K = W_V = 0. \qquad \text{...(2.15)}$$

Given (2.15) we shall certainly have to suppose that $G(0, Z) > 0$ for $Z > 0$ (see condition (1.1a')). Using (2.15) we note that equations (2.13) and (2.14). reduce to the forms

$$\frac{\dot{C}}{C} = \frac{f'(x) - (\delta + \Psi)}{\eta(C)} \qquad \text{...(2.16)}$$

and

$$\dot{x} = \sigma f(x). \qquad \text{...(2.17)}$$

Assume that the utility function is iso-elastic. Having already assumed that $U(\cdot)$ is bounded above, this implies that $\eta > 1$. But the conditions (2.16) and (2.17) which an

[1] As one would expect, equation (2.13) reduces to equation (1.16) when $\Psi_t = 0$.

[2] As would be expected, (2.14) reduces to (1.18) if $\Psi_t = 0$.

optimal policy must satisfy differ from (1.16) and (1.24) only by the addition of an amount Ψ_t to the discount rate. Thus the optimal policy is to suppose that the substitute will *never* be discovered and to pursue the solution described in Section 1.4 with the single proviso that it be assumed that the utility rate of discount is not merely δ but $\delta+\Psi_t$. Since $\Psi_t>0$, one is in effect discounting at a higher rate in this uncertain problem than in the problem of Section 1.3. This is intuitively very reasonable. If, at T, the substitute appears, the economy switches regime and the optimal policy is to pursue the programme

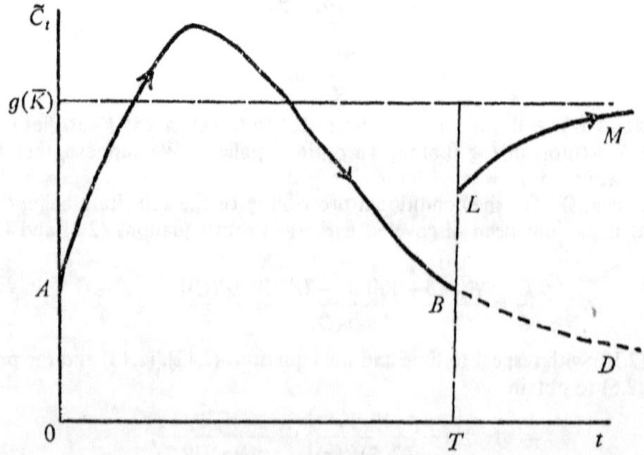

FIGURE 5

described in Proposition 4′. In fact Proposition 4′ is precisely what is required since assumption (2.15) entails a total break with the past at T. At T the economy is totally new, with no existing capital stock and no inventory of the resource. The break with the past is complete.[1] In Figure 5 we present the optimal consumption profile for this economy. *ABD* describes in broad terms the consumption profile of Figure 3. Throughout, however, the rate of discount is higher than δ by an amount Ψ_t. *LM* is the optimal consumption policy described in Proposition 4′.[2] We have then

Proposition 9. *Consider the two following problems:*

$$\left.\begin{aligned} &\textit{maximize} && \int_0^\infty [U(C)\Omega_t+\omega_t W(K_t, S_t)]e^{-\delta t}dt \\ &\textit{subject to} && \dot{K}=F(K, R)-C \\ & && \dot{S}=-R \\ & && C_t, K_t, R_t, S_t \geqq 0 \textit{ and } K_0, S_0 \textit{ given} \end{aligned}\right\} \quad \ldots(2.18)$$

and

$$\left.\begin{aligned} &\textit{maximize} && \int_0^\infty e^{-\gamma_t t}U(C)dt \\ &\textit{subject to the same constraints as in (2.18),} \end{aligned}\right\} \quad \ldots(2.19)$$

where γ is a discount rate which is independent of the path followed by the economy.

[1] In effect, then, condition (2.15) reduces the model to one where the economy faces an uncertain terminal date, a case that has been explored in another context by Yaari [28].

[2] As would be expected, there is generally a discontinuity in consumption at T. By assumption (2.15) the height TL is independent of the value taken by T.

Then, necessary and sufficient conditions for Problems (2.18) *and* (2.19) *to have identical solutions are*

(i) $W_K = W_S = 0$ *for all* K, S.

(ii) $\gamma_t = \delta t + \int_0^t \Psi_\tau d\tau.$

Proof. Sufficiency is obvious. To establish necessity note that the conditions that a solution of problem (2.19) must satisfy are

$$\frac{\dot{C}}{C} = \frac{(F_K - \gamma)}{\eta(C)} \qquad \text{...(2.20)}$$

and that

$$\dot{x} = \sigma f(x). \qquad \text{...(2.21)}$$

It follows that if equation (2.13) is identical to equation (2.20) we must have $W_K = 0$. But if (2.14) is identical to (2.21) we must have

$$\frac{\sigma f(x) W_K \Psi}{U'(C) f'(x)} + \frac{W_V \Psi}{x f''(x) U'(C)} = 0.$$

But since $W_K = 0$ it follows that $W_V = 0$. ‖

What is interesting about Proposition 9 is that it gives a precise statement of a set of conditions under which we can allow for uncertainty merely by solving a certain problem with a suitably chosen discount factor depending only on the nature of the uncertainty (a kind of certainty equivalent result), *and* where the equivalent certain problem is independent of the expected supply of the substitute. The amount Ψ_t that has to be added to the utility discount rate, δ, is of course generally time variant and equals the conditional probability of the substitute arriving at t, given no previous occurrence. We need hardly point out that non-constancy of Ψ_t, does *not* imply that the optimal policy is intertemporally inconsistent. In general one suspects that the conditional probability distribution is complex, but possibly single peaked. For example, it has been suggested that the conditional probability of harnessing nuclear fusion will rise to a peak at about the end of this century but will then fall, the argument being that expectations, though rising over the near future, will diminish if the discovery is not made by the turn of the century. A conditional distribution having such attributes would result if ω_t were log normally distributed. For the simple case where $\omega_t = \pi e^{-\pi t}$ (i.e. ω_t, is a Poisson distribution) Ψ_t is constant and equal to π and the planning problem becomes still easier.

Proposition 9 yielded a sufficient *and* necessary set of conditions under which the optimal depletion problem could be solved by pretending that the substitute will never appear and solving for the optimal depletion problem by a simple increase in the utility discount rate. Raising the utility discount rate to handle uncertainty has much intuitive appeal. Proposition 9 implies that an error will be committed in doing this if the conditions do not hold. It is then, naturally interesting to ask whether we have any reasons for believing that the error is as likely to go one way as the other. In fact, it is possible to establish the following proposition about the nature of the errors introduced if the " certainty equivalent " problem is used as a guide to decision-making when it should not be.

Proposition 10. *If we suppose* $W_K = W_V = 0$ *and solve the certainty equivalent problem, when in fact* $W_K = 0$ *but* $W_V > 0$, *then the values of* R_0 *and* C_0 *thus chosen will be greater than or equal to their correct values, and at least one will be strictly greater.*

2.3. The results established in the previous sub-section may seem to be dependent upon some of the unpalatable simplifying assumptions used there—a one-sector economy, a homogeneous capital stock, etc. The point of this section is to observe that in fact similar results hold in a far more general situation. In order to see this point, it is helpful to consider an economy whose evolution is characterized by three functions of time, $\underline{C}$, $\underline{K}$ and $\underline{S}$, which are respectively mappings to R^1, R^m and R^n: $\underline{C}_t$ is the consumption vector at t; $\underline{K}_t$ the vector of capital stocks, and $\underline{S}_t$ the vector of remaining resource stocks. Over any finite period $[0, T]$, and given the initial values $\underline{K}_0$ and $\underline{S}_0$, there exists a set $\mathscr{E}_T$ of triples $(\underline{C}_t, \underline{K}_t, \underline{S}_t)$ such that a triple is in $\mathscr{E}_T$ if and only if it describes an evolution of the economy from 0 to T which is feasible given the technology and initial conditions. Associated with each such path over $[0, T]$ is another triple $(\underline{C}_T, \underline{K}_T, \underline{S}_T)$ giving the terminal values of consumption, stocks of capital and resources. For such an economy, we consider the following finite-horizon problem:

$$\text{maximize} \quad \int_0^T U(\underline{C})e^{-\delta t} + e^{-\delta T}W(\underline{K}_T, \underline{S}_T)$$

$$\text{subject to} \quad (\underline{C}_t, \underline{K}_t, \underline{S}_t) \in \mathscr{E}_T.$$

This involves maximizing a utility integral and a terminal stock valuation function, subject to the usual technological constraints. It is assumed that a solution to this problem exists for each T.

Now suppose that the horizon T is a random variable with density function ω_T, and that planners seek a path of the economy which will maximize the expected value of the utility integral plus stock valuation function over this random horizon—i.e. they seek to

$$\text{maximize} \quad \int_0^\infty \omega_T \left\{ \int_0^T U(\underline{C})e^{-\delta t}dt + e^{-\delta T}W(\underline{K}_T, \underline{S}_T) \right\} dT.$$

To make this a well-defined maximization problem, it is necessary to specify the operative constraints. A reasonable formulation would be to require the programme adopted to be feasible whatever the horizon should turn out to be: if $\omega_T > 0$ for all t, this gives as a constraint

$$(\underline{C}_T, \underline{K}_T, \underline{S}_T) \in \mathscr{E}_\infty$$

where $\mathscr{E}_\infty$ is the set of programmes feasible *ad infinitum*, given the technology and initial conditions. We can now prove the following simple but useful result:

Proposition 11. *The solution to the problem.*

$$\textit{Maximize} \quad \int_0^\infty \omega_T \left\{ \int_0^T U(C)e^{-\delta t}dt + e^{-\delta T}W(K_T, S_T) \right\} dT$$

$$\textit{subject to} \quad (C_t, K_t, S_t) \in \mathscr{E}_\infty$$

is identical to the solution to

$$\textit{maximize} \quad \int_0^\infty U(C)e^{-\delta t - \int_0^t \Psi_\tau d\tau} dt + \int_0^\infty \omega_t e^{-\delta t} W(K_t, S_t)dt$$

subject to the same constraint, where

$$\Psi_\tau = \omega_\tau \Big/ \int_\tau^\infty \omega_t dt.$$

Proof. Consider the term

$$\int_0^\infty \omega_T \left(\int_0^T U(C)e^{-\delta t}dt \right) dT.$$

Defining $\Omega_t = \int_t^\infty \omega_\tau d\tau$ and integrating by parts, this equals

$$\int_0^\infty U(C)\Omega_t e^{-\delta t}dt.$$

Now $\dot{\Omega}_t = -\omega_t$ so that $\dot{\Omega}_t/\Omega_t = -\omega_t/\Omega_t = -\Psi_t$. Hence on integration

$$\Omega_t = e^{-\int_0^t \Psi_\tau d\tau}. \|$$

An immediate corollary of this is the following

Proposition 12. *Consider the problems*

maximize $$\int_0^\infty \omega_T \left\{ \int_0^T U(C)e^{-\delta t}dt + e^{-\delta T}W(K_T, S_T) \right\} dT$$

subject to $(C_t, K_t, S_t) \in \mathscr{E}_\infty$ *and*

maximize $\int_0^\infty U(C)e^{-\alpha_t t}dt$ *subject to the same constraint.*

Then a sufficient condition for these two problems to have the same solution is that

(i) $W(K_T, S_T)$ *should be independent of* K_T *and* S_T *for all values of these variables, and*

(ii) $\alpha_t = \delta t + \int_0^t \Psi_\tau d\tau.$

Proposition 12 is clearly a generalisation of Proposition 9, in that it states a set of conditions under which it is possible to replace an uncertain problem (which is clearly a generalisation of the problem of the previous sub-section), by a certain problem derived from it by a modification of the discount rate that makes use solely of the probability function.[1]

3. CONCLUDING REMARKS

In this paper we have attempted to answer some questions that appear to arise rather naturally when one thinks of intertemporal planning in the presence of exhaustible resources. Since many of these questions are, in fact, independent of one's exact notion of intergenerational equity we have posed them within the context of the, by now standard, utilitarian framework.[2] In Section 1.2 we presented a simple production model with no uncertainty. While it is plain that the characteristics of an optimal *depletion policy* depend crucially on whether or not the resource is essential to the production of final goods, it is not *a priori* plain as to what constitutes essentiality. The analysis led rather naturally to a simple articulation of this notion, namely the sufficiency conditions in Proposition 5 (see footnote 1, p. 15): that is, that *either* the marginal product of the resource is unbounded *or* that ouput of final goods is nil in the absence of the resource. It is intuitively clear that the elasticity of substitution between reproducible capital and exhaustible resources is an important determinant of the characteristics of an optimal

[1] The "certainty equivalent" problem that we have discussed here should not be confused with the problem of determining the optimal depletion rate where it is supposed that the substitute *will* become available at its *expected date* of arrival. That the latter problem may, in some case, yield a bias towards excessive depletion rates is intuitively clear, and it is this issue that is discussed by Henry [13]. In spite of its shortcomings the certainty equivalent approach (of either variety) is adopted explicitly or implicitly in much of the more empirically oriented literature in this type of problem. On this see Posner [24].

[2] Dasgupta [6] and Solow [25] have explored some of these questions within the context of alternative notions of intergenerational equity.

policy. It turned out that the parameter enters in a natural and in fact strikingly simple way in the intertemporal plan (viz. equation (1.18)). One would judge that for the near future at least, one will have to resort to simple production models (such as, say, the class of CES functions) to obtain numerical results. It is partly for this reason (and partly also for pedagogic ones) that we have presented our existence theorem (Proposition 8) for a world that has a production function that is of the CES form, and a utility function that is iso-elastic. It is in fact relatively simple to extend Proposition 8 to cover the case of production functions that are not of the CES variety as well as utility functions that are not iso-elastic. We need hardly point out that one would need to make appropriate assumptions (such as (0.2)) about the behaviour of the elasticity of marginal utility for low and high rates of consumption and that it is these asymptotic values of the elasticity of marginal utility that would enter into the condition that guarantees the existence of an optimal policy, namely that $\delta > \rho\ (1-\eta)$. If, in particular $\delta > \rho$, then we would be interested in the value of the elasticity of marginal utility as consumption tends to zero. Likewise, if $\rho > \delta$ then we would be interested in the value of the elasticity of marginal utility as consumption tends to infinity.

The main novelty that exhaustible resources introduce in a planning exercise is that one has to be particularly conscious about the properties of production functions at the " corners ". The banality of this observation is matched only by the problems this poses in obtaining empirical estimates. Certainly it is possible that we live in a world where for " moderate " values of the capital-resource ratio, the elasticity of substitution between capital and the resource exceeds one.[1] The point of concern, of course, is its behaviour for large values of the capital-resource ratio, given that large values cannot be avoided in the long run.[2] For the purposes of planning one is particularly interested in the conditions under which it is optimal to spread the exhaustible resource thinly over the distant future and thereby never to exhaust it completely. In a *very* general sense the analysis of Section 1.2 has been re-assuring to intutition in that the conditions under which it is optimal to exhaust the resource in finite time are really rather stringent (see Proposition 7). Certainly, if we wish to rely on the working hypothesis that the elasticity of substitution is constant then irrespective of its value (except for the case where it is infinite, which is, of course, just silly) we should not exhaust the resource in finite time. But the analysis does suggest that if $\sigma \geqq 1$ but σ is not unduly large, the price of the exhaustible resource relative to output ought to be rising rather rapidly. Experience does not suggest that this has been the case.[3]

In Section 2 we presented a model incorporating technical progress under uncertainty. It seems entirely reasonable to suppose that the important uncertainty concerns the date of arrival of new knowledge. Furthermore, it seemed to us that for the kind of problem that we have in mind here, it would not be very appropriate to make use of the law of large numbers (as say, would be implicitly the case for models such as those of Arrow [2] and Kaldor and Mirrlees [16]) to generate technical progress in a continuous fashion. Rather, we are here trying to envisage it as coming in a discrete manner. The event (or perhaps we should say " Event "!) can, of course, be quite anything. It can, for instance, be the discovery of a new stock of the same resource (e.g. new beds of oil or natural gas). But in this event exhaustible resources would remain a fundamental problem if they were initially so. Certainly the discussions that are currently conducted amongst energy experts suggest that what they have in mind is the possibility of discovering a source that will provide, for all practical purposes, an unlimited flow of energy. It is for such reasons that we have explored the problems that arise if technological change consists in the economy being provided by a steady stream of an alternative resource which can replace

1 The important work by Nordhaus and Tobin [22] suggests that this may be true.
2 Either this or one runs down capital sufficiently rapidly as well, in which event consumption trivially goes to zero in the absence of technical progress.
3 For an analysis of the behaviour of oil prices in particular, see Heal [12].

a resource that was previously essential. The date of the discovery we have supposed uncertain, but in this paper we have supposed that the random variable is uninfluenced by policy; that is, that the acquisition of knowledge is costless.

While it appears to be customary in practice to cope with uncertainty by raising the rate of discount by an amount that merely reflects the uncertainty, it is generally recognized that it leads to errors. In Section 2.2 we explored the conditions under which no such error will in fact be committed. It emerged that this is so only when both the existing stock of capital and the stock of the exhaustible resource is judged totally devoid of value at the date of the technical change (Proposition 9). It appeared, not surprisingly perhaps, that in this instance the model bears a strong resemblance to one where the economy faces an uncertain terminal date; a case that has been explored at some length by Yaari [28]. That one will, in general, commit an error by this simple method of coping with uncertainty is not surprising. But it is not plain that there will be a bias. In fact, one can say something specific about such biases, and we have presented the result in the form of Proposition 10.

Finally, and at a more primitive level, while one can take the view (reflected in the model economy of Section 2) that even though exhaustible resources may be essential currently they will not remain so over the indefinite future, it is not plain that it is a particularly comforting view. The model of uncertainty that we have presented here certainly articulates the view that the probability of the new source being discovered *sometime* over the indefinite future is precisely one. But it may well be a long while coming. If in fact major discoveries occur only at a great distance in the future, the intervening generations will naturally be that much worse off. In particular, one can argue that one's conception of intergenerational justice ought to be influenced by the likelihood of the arrival of technological change. This may well be an appropriate view. In this paper we have not attempted to face this set of difficult questions. Our purpose has been to explore some of the immediate implications of the existence of exhaustible resources.

REFERENCES

[1] Anderson, K. P. " Optimal Growth when the Stock of Resources is Finite and Depletable ", *Journal of Economic Theory* (1972).

[2] Arrow, K. J. " The Economic Implications of Learning by Doing ", *Review of Economic Studies* (1962).

[3] Beckerman, W. " Economists, Scientists and Environmental Catastrophe ", *Oxford Economic Papers* (1972).

[4] Cole, H. S. D. *et al. Thinking about the Future: A Critique of the Limits to Growth* (Chatto and Windus, for Sussex University Press, 1973).

[5] Dasgupta, P. " On the Concept of Optimum Population ", *Review of Economic Studies* (1969).

[6] Dasgupta, P. " Some Alternative Criteria for Justice Between Generations ", Paper presented at the ISPE Conference on the Demand for Public Goods, Siena (1973).

[7] Dasgupta, P. " Some Theoretical Explorations in the Economics of Exhaustible Resources ", Paper presented at the Bayerisch Academy Symposium on Systems Analysis, Reisenburg (1973).

[8] Forrester, J. W. *World Dynamics* (Wright-Allen Press Inc., Cambridge, Mass., 1971).

[9] Gale, D. " Optimal Development in a Multi-Sector Economy ", *Review of Economic Studies* (1967).

[10] Heal, G. M. " The Depletion of Exhaustible Resources: Some Theoretical Issues ", in M. Parkin and R. Nobay (eds.) *Issues in Contemporary Economics*, (Manchester University Press, 1974).

[11] Heal, G. M. *The Theory of Planning* (North Holland, 1973).

[12] Heal, G. M. " Economic Aspects of Natural Resource Depletion ", in D. Pearce (ed.) *Economics of Natural Resource Depletion*, (Macmillan, London, 1975).

[13] Henry, C. " Irreversible Investment Decisions Under Uncertainty ", *American Economic Review*, forthcoming.

[14] Hotelling, H. " The Economics of Exhaustible Resources ", *Journal of Political Economy* (1931).

[15] Ingham, A. and Simmonds, P. " The Optimal Use of Natural Resources ", *Review of Economic Studies*, forthcoming.

[16] Kaldor, N. and Mirrlees, J. A. " A New Model of Economic Growth ", *Review of Economic Studies* (1962).

[17] Koopmans, T. C. " A Proof for the Case where Discounting Advances the Doomsday". *Review of Economic Studies* (this issue).

[18] Koopmans, T. C. " Some Observations on ' Optimal ' Economic Growth and Exhaustible Resources ", Cowles Foundation Discussion Paper, No. 356 (1973).

[19] Maddox, J. *The Doomsday Syndrome* (Macmillan, London, 1971).

[20] Meadows, D. H. *et al. The Limits to Growth* (Universe Books, New York, 1972).

[21] Nordhaus, W. D. " World Dynamics: Measurement without Data ", Cowles Foundation Discussion Paper (1972).

[22] Nordhaus, W. D. and Tobin, J. " Is Economic Growth Obsolete ", in *Economic Growth* (Fiftieth Anniversary Colloquium, V), National Bureau of Economic Research (1972).

[23] Pontryagin, L. S. *et al. The Mathematical Theory of Optimal Processes* (Interscience, New York, 1972).

[24] Posner, M. V. *Fuel Policy: A Study in Applied Economics* (MacMillan, London, 1972).

[25] Solow, R. M. " Intergenerational Equity and Exhaustible Resources ", *Review of Economic Studies* (this issue).

[26] Stiglitz, J. E. " Growth with Exhaustible Natural Resources ", *Review of Economic Studies* (this issue).

[27] Vousden, N, " Basic Theoretical Issues in Resource Depletion ", *Journal of Economic Theory* (1973).

[28] Yaari, M. E. " Uncertain Lifetime, Life Insurance, and the Theory of the Consumer ", *Review of Economic Studies* (1965).

CHAPTER 5

PETROLEUM CONSERVATION IN THEORY AND PRACTICE

JAMES W. MCKIE AND STEPHEN L. MCDONALD

The imposition of mandatory federal import controls on oil in 1959 focused public attention on the weakening markets, the unused capacity, and the high relative costs of the domestic oil industry. Even before that event, the application of production controls in the United States and their relation to conservation policy had frequently been called into question; the growing volume of this criticism, from sources both within and without the petroleum industry, indicates a need for constructive economic analysis and evaluation of petroleum conservation.

The waste of oil resources which led, thirty-odd years ago, to the imposition of conservation controls was the result of the rule of capture. The owners of the surface rights above oil pools would drill wells in a dense pattern along the edges of their properties and produce as rapidly as possible in order to drain the oil or gas from under neighboring tracts. The resulting exploitation was unrestrained by any consideration of long-run price, demand or cost. The frantic production of oil severely depleted the natural energy of the reservoirs, and much oil had to be left in the ground that could otherwise eventually have been produced with wiser reservoir management. The physical wastes of excessive production also led to an economic crisis, as the flood of oil drove prices down to and below the direct costs of production. From the beginning, avoidance of waste has gone hand in hand with price stabilization. This story is well known. One unfortunate result of the industry crisis of 1930 was that the ends of conservation became confused with the price-stabilization purposes of production control. Another was that the industry has been prone to think of the chaos of pre-control days as the only alternative to the kind of conservation policy that now prevails.

The Economic Meaning of Conservation

Recent economic analysis has shown that "conservation" has at least two different meanings. One relates to the "wise" use of the nation's endowment of national resources in general. It is concerned largely with the rate of growth of production and population and the pressure that this growth exerts upon limited resources. In its strictly economic aspects it involves a problem of dynamic general equilibrium: growth, substitution of resources, limitational factors and long-run changes in income, prices, factor returns, costs and outputs of the economic system in all its phases. This problem is scarcely separable from the economic problem as a whole.[1]

Another, narrower, meaning of "conservation" relates to the use of a single resource under assumed conditions of economic growth, relative prices, demand, cost and substitutability. Even this definition of conservation does not confine its application to some factors of production identifiable as "natural resources." The theory of conservation is largely the theory of capital stated in other words.[2] Conservation of a resource is an aspect of the theory of ideal output: it simply means an optimum time-rate of use of the resource. Conservation as a special problem of private or public policy arises, then, whenever the time-rate of use of some resource is at issue. The objective of conservation policy is " . . . the avoidance of wastes associated with a faulty time distribution of the use of resources."[3]

Resources possess "stock" and "flow" characteristics in varying proportions. A stock of the resource exists which tends to diminish as the resource is consumed (the stock aspect), while the flow can be perpetuated in some degree by renewal of the stock (the flow aspect). A conservation problem is the more likely to arise the more prominent the stock characteristic of a resource. Resources consisting of nonrenewable stocks, or having a long period of renewal during which stocks can become exhausted, are the most likely to exhibit a faulty time-distribution of use. A "pure" flow resource, lacking any stock characteristic, might be defined as one whose future supply cannot be affected by changes in the present rate of use. Only free goods like

1. Harold J. Barnett has identified this aspect of conservation as the "doctrine of resource scarcity." As he points out, it is a problem in ecological balance and ecological interdependence. "Population Change and Resources," in National Bureau of Economic Research, *Demographic and Economic Change in Developed Countries* (Princeton University Press, 1960), pp. 423ff.

2. For a persuasive analysis of this point, see Anthony Scott, *Natural Resources: The Economics of Conservation* (Toronto University Press, 1955).

3. E. S. Mason, "The Political Economy of Resource Use," in *Perspectives on Conservation*, ed. H. Jarrett (Baltimore: Johns Hopkins Press, 1958), p. 162.

sunshine meet this test, although there are economically scarce resources, such as labor,[4] whose future availability is little affected by present use. Such resources correspondingly present little or no problem of conservation. At the other end of the spectrum of possibilities are resources which consist of a finite stock already in existence, which cannot be increased by any known human means and whose uses are already fully developed. Here the economic problem is to find the optimum rate of use of the resource over time until it is finally exhausted. This is a "pure" case of conservation in that the time-rate of use is the only problem.

Probably no actual resource perfectly illustrates the "pure" conservation of a known and irreplaceable stock. Although the stock of any grain crop, for example, is fixed once the harvest is in and must be conserved over an extended period of use, the stock is eventually renewable, and the rate of use will be influenced by expectations concerning the size of the next crop. When the period of renewal of any resource or good is long, two decisions must be made with respect to conservation: first, the rate of use of the existing stock, and second, the amount of investment in renewal. Obviously the two decisions are mutually dependent. The combined production-investment decision involves the marginal adjustment of intensive exploitation of existing supplies to extensive investment in new supplies. In this respect the investment criteria are qualitatively no different from those in any process of production over time; it is only the large ratio of stock to flow and the possibility of substantial discontinuities in the production process that may create a special problem.

The total quantity of minerals like lead, mica, or oil and gas in the earth's crust is fixed. But this does not mean that economical utilization of these minerals consists simply of choosing an optimum rate of depletion of a known fixed stock.[5] The amount in the earth's crust is not the amount available for use. The total quantity that may ultimately become available is unknown. Finding what remains to be discovered and extracting it require investment, and new

4. Scott Gordon, "Economics and the Conservation Question," *The Journal of Law and Economics*, I (Oct. 1958), 110–21.

5. We do not use the words "conservation" and "depletion" as *opposites*, as Ciriacy-Wantrup and Gordon do. Conservation does not necessarily involve a relative postponement of utilization of resources; to define it in this relative sense seems to lessen its usefulness. Conservation includes the concept of an optimum rate of depletion. We use the term "conservation" in the same sense as Ciriacy-Wantrup's "optimum state of conservation." See S. v. Ciriacy-Wantrup, "Private Enterprise and Conservation," *Journal of Farm Economics*, XXIV (Feb. 1942), 79.

discovery and preparation for extraction are analogous to renewal. The optimum rate of depletion of known stocks is mixed with the economics of an investment cycle.

To reach an ideal decision on the rate of permissible production (i.e., ideal conservation) in the light of expected future demands, costs, prices and discoveries would doubtless be beyond the capacity of any public control agency, even if the uncertainties of future discovery were less than they actually are. But if the public authority is indeed trying to optimize the time-rate of use, it should begin with an economic concept of the most efficient use of existing supplies. In oil and gas production, the basic criterion of efficient production has come to be known as the Maximum Efficient Rate.

The Maximum Efficient Rate and Well Spacing

Any conservation policy must be adapted to the special technical characteristics of the industry producing the resource. The concept of the Maximum Efficient Rate (MER) is a reflection of certain technical peculiarities of petroleum production. In explaining the concept and its role in an appropriate approach to petroleum conservation, we shall make use, therefore, of some basic definitions and relationships derived from reservoir engineering.

The volume of oil and gas ultimately recoverable from most reservoirs depends on the rate of production over time, among other things.[6] Efficient rates of production are those which involve no waste, i.e., no loss of output whose value would be greater than the cost of avoiding the loss. The Maximum Efficient Rate for a reservoir is not a purely physical measure. While some engineers treat the MER as a physical maximum, the following authoritative quotation clearly indicates the economic content of the MER concept:

> Operation of a reservoir at an infinitesimally low rate of oil production would not in itself assure efficient recovery unless other necessary conditions were met. However, if all other conditions are fulfilled, the ultimate oil recovery from most pools is directly dependent on the rate of production. The nature of this dependence is such that for each reservoir there is for the chosen dominant mechanism a maximum rate of production that will permit reasonable fulfillment of the basic requirements for efficient recovery. *Rates lower than such maximum may permit still higher ultimate oil recovery, but once the rate is sufficiently low to permit the basic requirements to be met the incremental ultimate recovery obtainable through further reduction of the rate of production may be insufficient to warrant the additional deferment of a return and the additional operating expenses that would result from a prolongation of the operation. A rate of production so low as to yield no return*

6. Ultimate recovery also depends upon the structure of the oilbearing rock and the qualities of the oil itself.

would obviously be uneconomic, of no advantage to the operators, and of no ultimate benefit. However, increase of the rate of production beyond the maximum commensurate with efficient recovery will usually lead to rapidly increasing loss of ultimate recovery. From these considerations there has developed the concept of the maximum efficient rate of production, often referred to as the M.E.R. For each particular reservoir it is the rate which if exceeded would lead to avoidable underground waste through loss of ultimate oil recovery.[7]

The dependence of ultimate physical recovery upon rate of production is related to the type of drive in operation. The present discussion is confined to natural drives only, and takes no account of production by pumping or secondary recovery. Under natural drives, reservoir pressure brings the oil to the surface. Reservoir pressure may be created by (a) gas dissolved in the oil; (b) free gas associated with the oil as a pressurized "cap," which expands to force oil out of the rock formation; and (c) water entering the reservoir and sweeping the oil before it.[8] Some reservoirs have only one of these pressure agents, though many initially have two or all three. Each type of drive presents a different problem of reservoir mechanics. In the pools with dissolved-gas drive only, the total recovery does not vary much within a wide range of production rates.[9] When gas-cap and water drives are present, on the other hand, the physical efficiency of the drive falls as rates of production rise. Gas may escape prematurely from the cap or bypass oil in the formation as it moves with relative rapidity through the formation from high to low pressure points. Since water moves more freely than oil through the tiny pores and interstices of oil-bearing rock, too-rapid production of oil, with consequent sharp reduction of pressure around the well itself, may allow water to surround and bypass oil in place, which usually means permanent loss. Proper rates of production allow a relatively uniform advance of the water (or gas) face and a more thorough flushing of the rock formation.[1] With these two types of drive, lower rates of production generally mean a higher percentage of recovery of the total oil in a reservoir, up to some theoretical physical limit for a given type or combination of types.

7. S. E. Buckley (ed.), *Petroleum Conservation*, American Institute of Mining and Metallurgical Engineers, 1951, pp. 151–52. Emphasis added.

8. Erich W. Zimmermann, *Conservation in the Production of Petroleum* (Yale University Press, 1957), pp. 60–65.

9. "It has not been conclusively demonstrated that reduction in the rate of production can bring about any improvement in the recovery efficiency in a pool that has no free gas cap and no potential water drive and that has physical conditions that prevent any segregation of fluids by gravity." Buckley, *op. cit.*, p. 158.

1. Zimmerman, *op. cit.*, p. 63. Efficient utilization of a gas cap or water drive may, of course, involve pressure maintenance through reinjection of gas or water.

A very much simplified picture of cumulative production from an oil reservoir under one of these types of drive is shown in Figure I. To simplify the analysis we make the artificial assumption that the rate of production is constant over time until the drive is effectively exhausted, and that no rejuvenation through secondary recovery takes place. Figure I also assumes a given pattern of well spacing

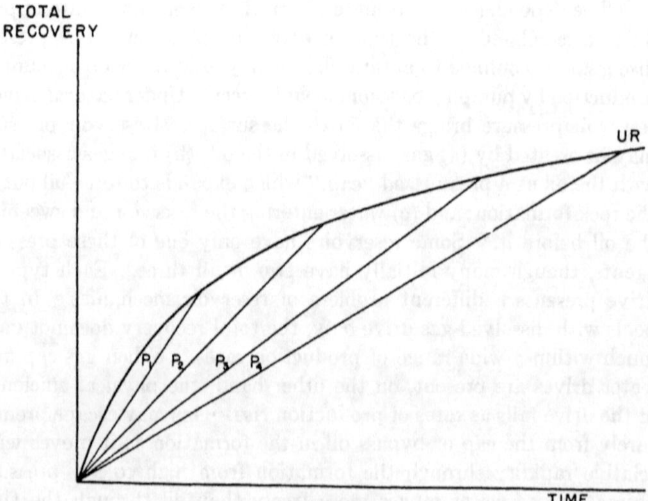

FIGURE I

and an unchanging technique of recovery. Curve UR, showing total ultimate recovery, is the locus of the termini of the alternative cumulative production lines P_1, P_2, etc. The lower the rate of production, the larger is the fraction of the total oil in the reservoir recovered and the longer the period of recovery. The curve UR approaches some theoretical limit at very long periods of production.

Any firm owning rights to the whole pool would estimate future prices, apply them to the alternative production schedules and discount to the present the alternative time-streams of gross income for purposes of determining the optimum rate of production. Under competitive market conditions, it would apply a rate of discount equal to the rate of return on capital available in alternative uses, which, after allowance for risk and uncertainty, should equal the market rate of earnings for the representative competitive firm. In any case, the present values of alternative discounted gross income streams take a form represented by curve DVR in Figure II. This curve has a maximum, but since it is not a net income curve its maximum does not indicate the maximum efficient rate of production. We must first allow for two kinds of cost: lifting or production costs, including maintenance of production equipment, and the costs of drilling and equipping the field. The latter involve the choice of well spacing, which is a major determinant of the costs of access to the oil.

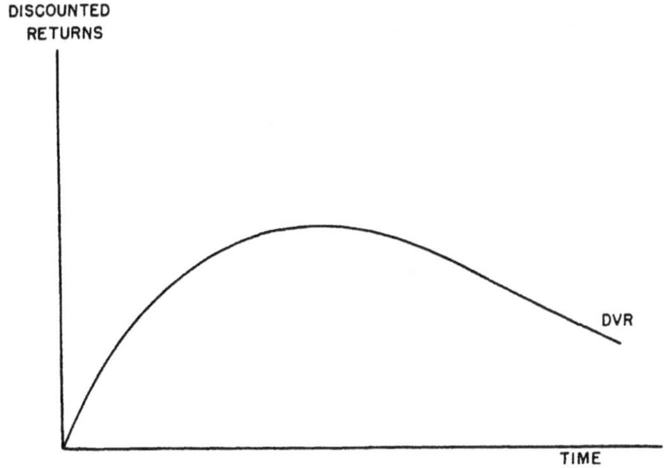

FIGURE II

Well spacing, rate of production and ultimate recovery are interdependent variables. Given a specified ultimate recovery, the rate of production of the pool varies directly with the number of wells, at least within very wide limits. A given ultimate recovery can be obtained with very few wells if a sufficiently long period of time is allowed to produce the oil;[2] and up to a point, the same ultimate recovery can be obtained in a shorter time if more wells are drilled. Similarly, given a specified production rate for the pool as a whole, ultimate recovery varies directly with the number of wells up to a point. Thus, production of 250 barrels per day from each of four wells may lead to greater ultimate recovery than production of 500 barrels per day from each of two wells. This effect tends to diminish as more wells are added, and eventually becomes negligible. Hence

2. "It is the consensus of many investigators that the ultimate oil recovery is independent of well-spacing — that the distances between wells is, in itself, not one of the pertinent physical factors that affect the recovery of the oil from the reservoir. . . . It has been demonstrated that reservoir fluids can move through intercommunicating and continuous porous media over great distances, distances comparable with gross reservoir dimension." R. C. Craze and J. W. Glanville, *Well Spacing* (Humble Oil and Refining Company, 1955), p. 47.

curves *UR* and *DVR* in Figures I and II are each one of a family of curves that depend upon well spacing. The physical relationship is different for every reservoir, but its general form is indicated in Figure III. In this diagram, each *U* curve represents a different ultimate recovery and indicates the combinations of production rate and number of wells consistent with that ultimate recovery. The production rate consistent with any given ultimate recovery can

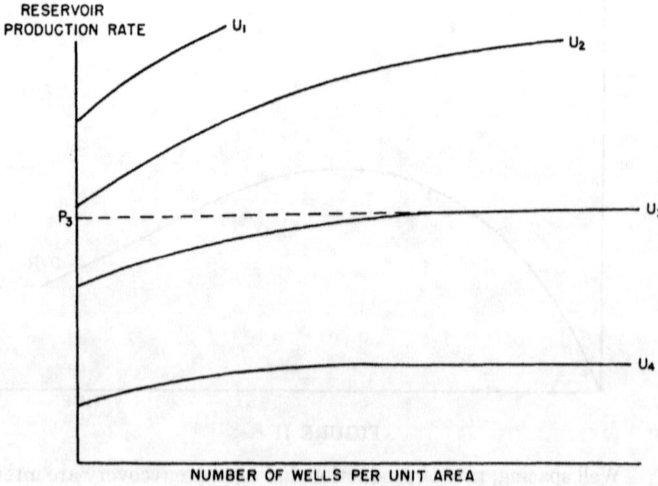

FIGURE III

rise up to a point as the number of wells is increased, thereafter remaining constant. (Increasing ultimate recovery is signified by shifts from U_1 to U_2, etc.)

Of course, the relevant problem is not the physical relationship but the economic relationship. If wells cost nothing, a firm having exclusive control of a reservoir would always drill enough wells to achieve the highest production rate consistent with its desired ultimate recovery, such as P_3 in Figure III if U_3 were the goal. Alternatively, an abundance of wells would give the highest ultimate recovery consistent with any given production rate such as P_3. Under such circumstances, we could construct a *UR* curve for Figure I unconstrained by well spacing. But the operator must in fact compare marginal costs and returns for different numbers of wells or different spacing patterns. Determination of the optimum production rate and optimum number of wells is illustrated in Figures IV and V. For each number of wells on the reservoir there is a corresponding

UR (hence *DVR*) curve. Plotting all the possible *DVR* curves in three dimensions gives us a "relief map" of present values of gross incomes (Figure IV).[3] As the reservoir production rate rises with given well spacing, the present values at first rise because of a shift of income toward the present, but eventually fall because of the adverse effects of higher production rates on ultimate physical recovery.

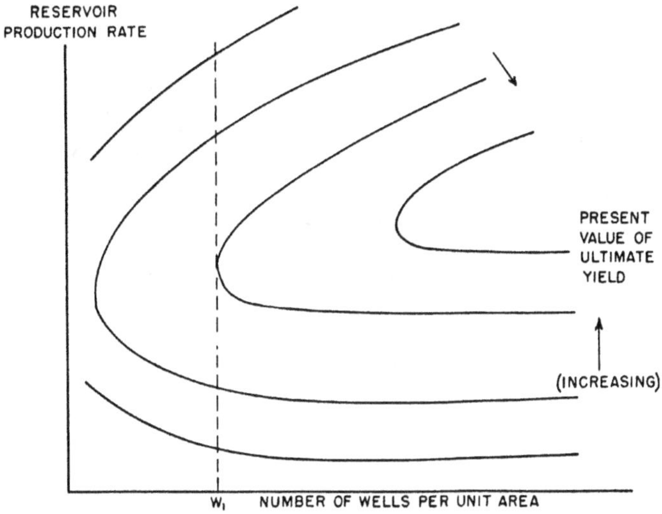

FIGURE IV

Because a change of a given per cent in the production rate typically has a much stronger effect on ultimate yield than similar percentage variations in well numbers, the present value contours are shown considerably elongated in the horizontal direction.

The well-cost surface is a plane inclined upward from the production-rate axis. The difference between the present value of well and production costs and the present value of ultimate yields forms the net value contours of Figure V. Because the beneficial effects of additional wells on ultimate recovery quickly diminish while the total cost increases arithmetically, the contours of net present value close to form a summit at point *M*. The corresponding production rate is the optimum (ideally the *MER*), and the corresponding number of wells is the optimum.

A representation of the mutual adjustment of MER and well numbers (hence well spacing) is given from another perspective in

3. The *DVR* curve of Figure II is a profile of this surface on an ordinate plane.

Figure VI. We assume that the firm develops the reservoir as a unit, and that it makes all outlays for access and development at or very near the beginning of the period of production. Curves C_1 through C_3 are typical discounted cost curves, which rise with time owing to the accumulation of lifting and maintenance costs. The different cost curves represent different numbers of wells.

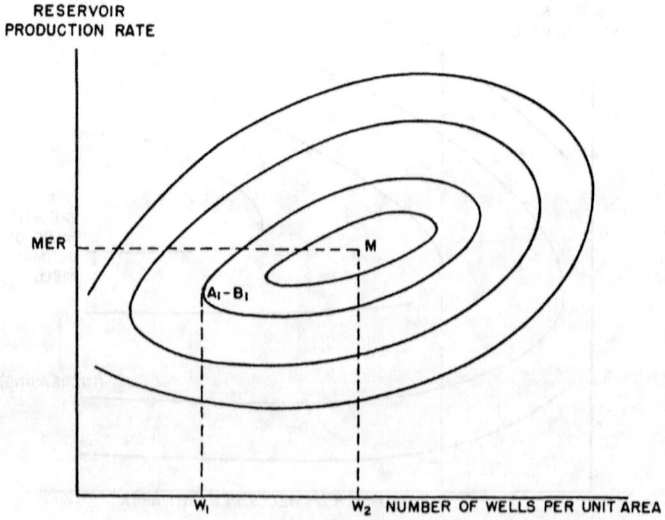

FIGURE V

If the operating firm could develop the reservoir without obligation to landowners to drill offset wells, or to drill in certain patterns or by specified dates, it presumably would begin with a cautiously wide spacing pattern. It is always possible to increase well density through infill drilling. Such a wide spacing pattern might yield the cost curve C_1 with well costs OW_1 in Figure VI. The maximum net present value of production with this spacing pattern would be A_1B_1. (The corresponding points are shown on Figures IV and V.) As the firm accumulated more information about the field, however, it would choose to shift to a denser spacing pattern and thus would never reach point A_1; instead, both discounted cost curve and discounted revenue curve would shift upward, and the net present value would now become A_2B_2, which is larger than A_1B_1.[4] As Figure IV

4. Owing to the geometry of reservoir development, the choices might well be discontinuous as shown. A field already developed on an 80-acres-per-well pattern cannot be redeveloped on a *regular* 75-acres-per-well pattern by infill drilling.

indicates, the upward shift of the *DVR* curve with increasing well density must eventually become negligible; hence the *AB* segment must reach a maximum, here assumed to be A_2B_2 with a corresponding production rate P_2 (not shown). Further increase in well density would raise the *C* curve more than the *DVR* curve. The point A_2 corresponds to the summit *M* in Figure V and locates both MER and optimum well spacing.

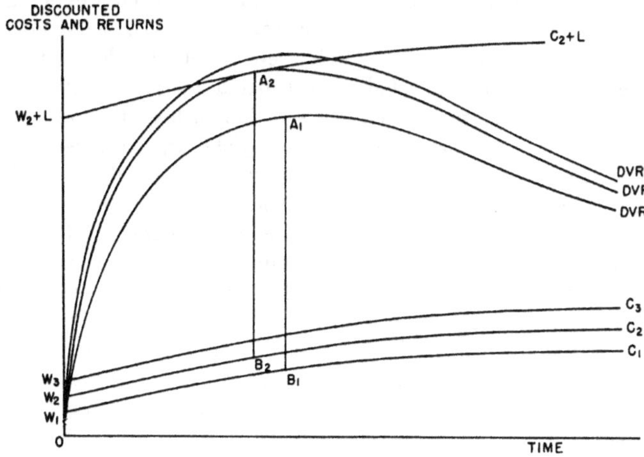

FIGURE VI

The well costs OW_2 are not the only fixed costs to the developing firms. The access costs include discovery costs and lease bonuses paid to landowners. (A constant proportion of the gross revenues is also ordinarily paid to landowners as royalties.) But the discovery costs and lease bonuses are "sunk" before drilling begins, so they do not affect the decisions concerning optimum production rates and spacing patterns. If the reservoir yields a net revenue of A_2B_2, this amount would, of course, be rent; and if everyone concerned had perfect foreknowledge of the existence, size and properties of the oil pool, implying zero discovery costs, the landowners could exact this rent from the developing firm in the form of lease bonuses. In this case the development costs plus landowners' bonuses, $OW_2 + L$, would be tangent to the *DVR* curve at A_2, the point of maximum net present value.[5]

5. We assume the discounted *DVR* curves to be net of landowners' royalty. It is an institutional fact that competition for oil rights almost always focuses on the lease bonus, which is highly flexible, and not on the royalty rates, which are extraordinarily rigid.

Neither landowners nor operators, however, have perfect foreknowledge. Each pool must be discovered, and the characteristics of a pool reveal themselves only slowly and imperfectly with development. The parties are typically committed to some level of rents before the pool is discovered. For the individual pool, therefore, no perfect tangency between present value of returns and present value of costs and contractual rents can be expected. Of course, in bargaining over rent, oil companies and landowners make use of whatever information is available on the rock formations, characteristics of known reservoirs in the vicinity, etc. Thus the level of rents agreed upon is not unaffected by anticipated margins of return over development and production costs. Nonetheless, the relation is highly uncertain. Some reservoirs will yield large surpluses above total costs to operators; others will not yield enough above development and production costs to cover lease bonuses and discovery outlays. (And some ventures, resulting in no commercial discovery, yield nothing whatever.) Operators can only expect that, taking all developed reservoirs together, surpluses will counterbalance deficits, leaving a satisfactory mean return.[6] A higher average return would lead to increased exploration effort, higher rents and lower prices for oil; poorer returns to the opposite. In this manner under the assumed competitive conditions the margin of extensive investment in oil resource renewal would be continually adjusted to the margin of intensive exploitation of existing supplies.

Aside from the problem of rents, another effect of uncertainty in evaluation is that operators may make mistakes in the early stages of reservoir development, such as spacing wells too closely, that are difficult or impossible to rectify later. Furthermore, the zone of uncertainty surrounding estimates of reservoir characteristics may compel them to rely on rules of thumb based on straightforward engineering criteria — such as maintenance of reservoir pressure above the saturation point — before attempting to make a nice calculation of present values and costs of exploitation. Determination of MER and optimum well spacing requires some preliminary development of the pool and study of the characteristics discovered in the process.

Changes in the basic variables, of course, affect the determination of MER and optimum well spacing. To give a few illustrations: If production costs were expected to rise relatively in the future,

6. The risk-income preferences of exploring firms and the distribution of probabilities and uncertainties in pure exploratory ventures are beyond the scope of this paper.

C curves would assume a steeper slope and shift the optimum depletion time toward the present. A rise in drilling costs would not affect rates of production in existing pools, but would reduce optimum well densities in fields developed in the future. A rise in drilling and exploration costs would squeeze down prospective net returns on properties being considered for lease and exploration, and would cause firms to discard some areas previously considered eligible for development. More intensive exploitation of existing supplies would be encouraged at the expense of new discovery effort. Conversely, a fall in discovery and development costs would encourage exploration for new deposits, which if successful would cause some abandonment of marginal pools. An expected rise in prices in the future, such as would result from an increasing cost trend, would prolong the rise in the *DVR* curves in existing reservoirs and shift production toward the future, resulting in more intensive exploitation of deposits.

If firms in the industry developed each oil reservoir as a unit and chose optimum production rates and spacing patterns under conditions of perfect foresight, as assumed above, it is doubtful that oil production would create an important problem of conservation policy. The actual conditions in the industry, of course, are quite different. Faced with wasteful competitive underground drainage by owners of divided surface rights over oil and gas pools, the conservation commissions in various states have been obliged to interfere with private exploitation and set up rules to govern development and extraction. We now turn to a consideration of whether the conservation policies of these regulatory authorities produce an approximate simulation of economically optimum oil-pool management.

State Regulation

The conservation policies of the several producing states vary widely. However, the approaches of Texas, Louisiana and Oklahoma are basically similar; and since these states account for about 60 per cent of total output, a description of their policies should be sufficient to illustrate the contrast between theory and practice in the conservation of oil.

Texas, with over one-third of total U. S. production, is in a sense the balance wheel of the domestic industry. The Texas Railroad Commission has been regulating the production of oil and gas since the early 1930's. Its practice developed slowly. After the economic crisis that originally provoked the imposition of production controls had passed, the Commission began rather cautiously to curb offset drilling[7] and dense well spacing, and to move toward a determination of the conditions affecting ultimate recovery under various withdrawal rates in individual fields. After 1940 it began to apply some elements of the MER concept in setting maximum field production rates. But its approach fell short of the ideal in several ways. In the first place, the available data were inadequate to permit accurate estimates of MER for many reservoirs, and the scientific theory of reservoir management was still maturing. Second, the Texas Commission seldom considered the economic factors affecting MER at all, and if it applied a discount factor it must have used only an implicit and intuitive one. Third, the Commission did not attempt as a rule to make a simultaneous determination of MER and well spacing; it tended to treat well spacing as a parallel but separate problem rather than as a joint determining factor. As a result of these difficulties the Commission usually relied on crude engineering data such as the appearance of a pronounced and persistent pressure drop or uneven water encroachment, looking chiefly for evidence of an unsustainable rate of withdrawal.[8]

The application of an MER standard even on such a limited basis was a distinct advance over the chaos that existed before production controls were instituted. Since 1948, however, when a rudimentary MER principle was barely established, the concept of MER has tended to lose significance to a point almost approaching disuse as the basis of oil conservation. The dominant consideration in regulatory policy has become the allocation of a restricted "market demand."

Though the Commission has often made an effort to determine the MER of large and important fields, and since 1957 has held

7. Offset wells are drilled along the boundary of a lease in order to drain the oil from under a neighboring lease, whose operator will naturally do the same. The Commission has imposed minimum distances between wells and lease boundaries.

8. As de Chazeau and Kahn point out, the Commission has tended to use an MER concept that is "... an engineering-geological determination of the theoretically maximum rate of flow of crude oil from the well that will not endanger ultimate recovery from the pool by a too rapid release of underground pressures." We have argued that this "maximum" necessarily depends on some kind of discount concept to give meaning to "too rapid." De Chazeau and Kahn go on to say that "... [MER] will generally be guided by mechanical indices like the pressure at the bottom of the well ... or the ratio of gas to oil in the crude produced. ... While the proper determination of MER involves the application of the best scientific knowledge available, at best the range of competent judgment is broad, so that MER may represent little more than an informal guess." *Integration and Competition in the Petroleum Industry* (Yale University Press, 1959), p. 123 n.

hearings on all newly-discovered fields before setting field rules, most oil fields in Texas are under a uniform formula that the Commission worked out in 1947. This "1947 Yardstick" is shown in Table I. It clearly has no relation to any scientific determination of MER.

TABLE I

THE "1947 YARDSTICK" OF THE TEXAS RAILROAD COMMISSION

	Daily Allowable Per Well for Spacing Patterns of:					
Depth	10 Acres	20 Acres	40 Acres	80 Acres	160 Acres	Incremental Depth Change for All Spacing Patterns
0–1,000	18	28	—	—	—	—
1,000–1,500	27	37	57	97	177	9[1]
1,500–2,000	36	46	66	106	186	9[1]
2,000–3,000	45	55	75	115	195	9
3,000–4,000	54	64	84	124	204	9
4,000–5,000	63	73	93	133	213	9
5,000–6,000	72	82	102	142	222	9
6,000–7,000	81	91	111	151	231	9
7,000–8,000	91	101	121	161	241	10
8,000–8,500	103	113	133	173	253	12[1]
8,500–9,000	112	122	142	182	262	9[1]
9,000–9,500	127	137	157	197	277	15[1]
9,500–10,000	152	162	182	222	302	25[1]
10,000–10,500	190	210	230	270	350	48[1]
10,500–11,000		225	245	285	365	15[1]
11,000–11,500		255	275	315	395	30[1]
11,500–12,000		290	310	350	430	35[1]
12,000–12,500		330	350	390	470	40[1]
12,500–13,000		375	395	435	515	45[1]
13,000–13,500		425	445	485	565	50[1]
13,500–14,000		480	500	540	620	55[1]
14,000–14,500		540	560	600	680	60[1]

Source: *Oil and Gas Journal*, January 18, 1960, p. 42.
1. Increases for 500-foot intervals.

Instead it reflects the dominance of two factors: A *"fair"* allocation of production, i.e., an equal allocation among producers regardless of differences in reservoir characteristics; and the dominance of the individual well, not the reservoir, as the unit of production in the proration formula.

The fields in Texas number 7,000 or so, but in 1961 only 153 fields had MER's in excess of the 1947 Yardstick. These produced upwards of 10 per cent of the state's output. (This does not include the giant East Texas field, which is also subject to special rules.) All of them were old fields, whose MER's for the most part were determined years ago when demand was high relative to supply. Few if any pools have been granted an MER "higher than Yardstick" in recent years.[9] It is not hard to understand the reasons for this disuse of the MER concept. There seems to be little point in careful determination of MER when production would be restricted to perhaps one-third of it.[1] Under such circumstances MER becomes simply the unit of division of a restricted output, not a conservation limit. The political pressure on the regulatory authority from a host of competing producers to equalize the benefits and sacrifices is very strong.

Producers — especially the numerous holders of small tracts — tend to think of the well, rather than the oil pool as a whole, as the unit of productive capacity. Overdrilling was one of the reasons for the imposition of controls in the first place, but the regulatory authority apparently has found that proper restraint of drilling is a very difficult problem. If the authority could freely manipulate well density, it could at least distantly approximate the MER standard for many fields, even under a rigid formula like the 1947 Yardstick. The Texas Railroad Commission, handling well spacing as a factor separate from MER, has made slow progress. It adopted a spacing rule in 1940 setting a state-wide minimum of 20 acres per well for the first time (the standard before that had been two-acre spacing). Since 1957 the Commission has imposed wider spacing on

9. *Oil and Gas Journal*, June 27, 1960, p. 75. We have no information on how many fields have MER's less than Yardstick. The Commission has been under severe pressure to "equalize" the share of these high-MER fields by cutting them back to Yardstick allowables. Some wells are exempt from the usual production restrictions. The principal classes of exempt wells are (1) wells in newly-discovered fields, which have special discovery allowables until the sixth well is drilled or eighteen months have elapsed, whereupon the Commission sets development rules; (2) marginal wells on the pump, incapable of producing more than a specified amount dependent on depth (these are called "stripper wells"); (3) wells producing oil from secondary water-flood projects.

1. The formal allocation of the statewide production quota in Texas has always been expressed in terms of per-well allowables. In the simplest form, a field under the 1947 Yardstick with 5,200 foot wells on 20-acre spacing would be given an allowable per well of 82 barrels. If there were 20 wells in the field, the total allowable for the field (one should hardly call it "MER") would be 1,640 barrels per day. This allowable would total 49,200 in a 30-day month. If the Commission decided to restrict Texas production in nonexempt fields to 50 per cent of total allowable capacity, it would express the order as a restriction to "15 days' production" — for this field, 15 x 82 or 1,230 barrels for each well during the month. (This would total 24,600 barrels for the field, but each well has its own allowable and its own prorated share of production.) The operator of each well in this field would restrict production to 1,230 barrels during the month but would not actually shut down production for 15 days. Each field would be under a similar restriction to 50 per cent of its total allowable or MER, except for certain special cases.

many new fields, but most are still on 20 acres and under. Of 20,767 wells drilled in Texas in 1958, 15,829 or 76 per cent were on 20-acre spacing or less.[2] A great many were drilled on very small plots, under one exemption or another. The Commission grants exemptions from minimum spacing rules for two major reasons. One is the unusual physical conditions of recovery in certain types of oil-bearing structures, such as piercement salt domes. The other is ownership of surface rights in less than 20-acre plots (or whatever the standard spacing plot may be). In Texas, at least, anyone who owns a lease on any plot of land can drill a well on it, even though the land may be subdivided into town lots.[3] Since lease blocks smaller than the minimum are very common, the result has been drilling far in excess of the optimum density in many fields, new as well as old. And under the per-well proration formulas that are typically used, the operator of such a small lease is able to drain oil from under neighboring large leases that are not exempt from minimum spacing rules.

But exemptions are only one of the defects of well-spacing regulation. Another, perhaps equally important, is the weight that proration formulas give to the individual well. The effect is to encourage the drilling of unnecessary wells. The leases on most fields are divided and subdivided among many owners, including both large and small oil companies and individuals. Small operators are typically unwilling to pool their leases with others to permit operation of the field as a unit, at least while flush production continues. Because they regard the individual well as the source of income, they usually want to drill a number of wells on their property, and the prevailing mode of production controls creates a strong motive to do so. Even the operators of large lease blocks, who are more aware of the importance of proper management of the reservoir as a whole and who have more of a long-run interest in its economical development, may find that the allocation formula drives them to drill unnecessary wells. If the regulatory authority, under pressure from small operators and following historic precedent, decrees a 20-acre pattern under some allocation system like the 1947 Yardstick, a leaseholder will drill up to a 20-acre pattern even though he may believe that an 80-acre pattern would be economically superior. As Table I shows, the Yardstick gives an extra allowable of only one barrel per day for every extra acre per well. An operator with an 80-acre plot on a 5,500 foot pool would get a total daily allowable of

2. *Oil and Gas Journal*, January 18, 1960, p. 43.

3. Subdivision *after* discovery does not create any additional claims to exemption.

328 barrels with four wells on 20-acre spacing, 204 barrels with 40-acre spacing, and 142 barrels with one well on 80-acre spacing. The additional quota would usually more than repay the cost of the extra wells even if the producing days per month were cut to 10 over the life of the field. In self-defense every operator usually must drill up to the maximum. Individual allocation formulas in fields not under the Yardstick ordinarily produce the same effect. The result is wasteful overdrilling and unnecessarily high unit costs of production.

It would be unfair to compare the spacing patterns prevalent in the Middle East, where drainage areas are sometimes measured in square miles rather than in acres, with the drilling pattern on U. S. oil reservoirs, which are much smaller than the Middle Eastern pools and have quite different conditions of communicability, pressure and conformation.[4] Yet it cannot escape notice that the oil companies are able to develop and operate the Middle Eastern fields as *units*, free of the conflicting interests and pressures that arise when a multitude of small producers share in the control of oil reservoirs. Lacking information on the relative physical conditions prevailing in domestic fields, we do not know how far the well-spacing patterns in Texas and elsewhere depart from the optimum; but we are left with a strong impression that the regulatory authorities have not even distantly achieved an adequate framework for economical development of petroleum deposits.

Fragments of information from industry sources support this impression. "Texas follows up this initial incentive [in the 1947 Yardstick] for drilling unneeded wells in its MER system of allocation by giving heavy weight to the well factor in the bulk of the individual field allocation formulas it approves. . . . The over-all effect is to stimulate the drilling of thousands of unneeded wells.[5] R. E. Hardwicke estimated in 1952 that ". . . the economic waste (money, labor, materials) resulting from drilling, equipping, and operating unnecessary wells in Texas is tremendous, amounting on

4. The average producing well in the United States has an oil reserve of about 60,000 barrels and produces 13 barrels per day (though there is considerable dispersion about the average). In Venezuela, the average well has 1 million barrels reserve and produces 200 barrels per day. In the Middle East, the average well has 270 million barrels reserve and produces over 5,000 barrels per day. At the end of 1958 there were only 1,104 producing wells in the entire Middle East. Many single pools in the United States have more than 1,000 wells. *World Oil*, November 1959, pp. 105–6; August 15, 1959, p. 102.

5. *Oil and Gas Journal*, January 18, 1960, p. 42. The *Journal* went on to point out that in the previous four years the total number of wells in Texas had increased from 159,000 to 193,000 while Texas petroleum reserves had not increased at all.

an average to much more than $100,000,000 each year of the last five and a half years. The figure is a conservative one."[6] It seems very conservative. Some estimates of possible saving in development well drilling run over 50 per cent. If similar conditions prevailed in other states, this would imply excess development costs approximating one billion dollars per annum for the nation as a whole in recent years.[7]

The Texas Commission has been more inclined to order wide spacing in fields where the operators themselves offer no opposition. It has approved 100-acre spacing in fields where there was no opposition to the major companies' requests for such an order, and in 1959 for the first time approved allocation of allowables by formulas based entirely on acreage.[8] But the problem of reconciling divergent interests is not easy to solve.[9]

Conservation practice in other oil-producing states is not identical with Texas practice, but there are many points of resemblance. The Louisiana Department of Conservation has never attempted to estimate and use MER's as the basis of production controls in individual pools. The Louisiana state-wide yardstick for many years was based entirely on depth and gave no weight at all to well spacing. If an operator drilled two wells on 20-acre spacing he got twice the allowable for one well on the same tract. This formula still holds for

6. R. E. Hardwicke, "Oil-Well Spacing Regulations and Protection of Property Rights in Texas," 31 *Texas Law Review* 111 (1952).

7. Annual expenditure for the drilling and completion of producing wells in the United States is now in the neighborhood of $2,000,000,000. C. C. Anderson (Chief Petroleum Engineer, U. S. Bureau of Mines), "Petroleum and Natural Gas in the United States — Relation of Economics and Technological Trends," paper presented to the World Power Conference, Montreal, Sept. 1958. See also the findings of the joint association survey of drilling costs, reported in *World Oil*, July 1959, p. 120.

8. *Oil and Gas Journal*, August 31, 1959, p. 38. In the fall of 1961 the Commission began to approve such formulas, with solid major-company support, even though opposed by small operators.

9. One of the Commissioners opposed the 160-acre spacing approved by the Commission in the Spraberry and Dune Wolfcamp fields, asserting that the large operators would use it " . . . as the vehicle to freeze out the owner of the small tract who does not see fit to yield to high pressure to unitize his property." He also favored denser drilling because " . . . the only truly accurate means of determining the amount of oil underlying any part of the earth's surface is the drill bit." These remarks more or less epitomize the attitude of the small operator.

Another Commissioner remarked that " . . . broader spacing of wells can be achieved if the operators will set the patterns of spacing when the discovery is made. . . . It is not proper to drill a cluster of wells and then expect the Commission to extend the spacing out from this cluster . . ." *Oil and Gas Journal*, January 26, 1959, p. 106. This remark obviously reflects paramount concern with the equitable rights of other operators, assuming that the well, rather than acreage, is the proper basis for production allocation.

pools developed before 1960. But in 1960 the law was changed to require an acreage factor in the allocation formula for new pools. For development patterns under 40-acre spacing, the allowable per well is cut down proportionally, so that a 20-acre well gets only half as much as a 40-acre well. For patterns over 40-acre spacing, the well gets a schedule allowable exceeding the standard 40-acre depth-bracket allowable by a factor equal to one-half the difference in acres per well. Thus an 80-acre well would get 50 per cent more than a 40-acre well. (Some sample figures are given in Table II.) The

TABLE II

LOUISIANA ONSHORE SCHEDULE ALLOWABLES FOR 2,000–10,000 FOOT BRACKETS: STANDARD DEPTH-BRACKET AND 30- AND 60- ACRE SPACING

	Schedule Allowable per Well (bbls/day)		
Well Depth (feet)	A 30-Acre Spacing (Col. B × 30/40)	B 40-Acre Spacing (Depth-bracket Allowable)	C 60-Acre Spacing (Col. B + [½ × 20/40 × Col. B])
2,000–3,000	71	95	119
3,000–4,000	86	114	143
4,000–5,000	101	134	168
5,000–6,000	119	159	199
6,000–7,000	140	186	233
7,000–8,000	161	214	268
8,000–9,000	179	239	299
9,000–10,000	206	274	343

Source: Louisiana Department of Conservation

Louisiana authority then cuts this schedule allowable back to a production allowable month by month if slack demand requires it, not by reducing the "producing days" as in Texas, but by applying a percentage reduction across the board. In January and February, 1961 the allowable production was one-third the amount shown in Table II. This would correspond roughly to "10 producing days" in Texas.

The Louisiana formula will certainly discourage overly-dense drilling. The effects of Louisiana's previous depth-bracket formula, which gave no weight at all to acreage, were actually modified in practice by a much tougher policy than Texas followed on well spacing, including a policy of forcing pooling of acreage to make up minimum drilling units instead of granting exceptions on small lease holdings as in Texas. But the Louisiana formula does not especially encourage drilling on a wider pattern than 40 acres, which now becomes a virtual standard. There is no scientific or economic basis whatever for supposing that a standard state-wide pattern of 40-acre spacing is an optimum, or that the Louisiana formula yields an approximation of the Maximum Efficient Rate for each and every pool.

In Oklahoma, an extremely haphazard system of control prevailed up to 1954. In that year the state introduced a new "yardstick" based on the following formula:

$$Y = DCe^{mx}$$

where Y = daily allowable per well
D = the market demand percentage factor
C = a constant based on market demand
x = a depth factor
m = a constant based on the depth-cost ratio.

This formula too is not based on MER nor does it take into account the scientific aspects of reservoir dynamics or well spacing, though it does take account of one cost factor. However, we are told that it has not been very effective. During 1955 and 1956 the wells subject to the formula were in fact given allowables ranging from 39 per cent to 65 per cent of the formula allowables, while the majority of Oklahoma wells were entirely exempt.[1] It was not until 1959 that Oklahoma got around to passage of a minimum-spacing statute, which provided for 40-acre spacing at a minimum and compulsory integration of tracts into minimum-size drilling units.[2]

It is clear from the foregoing that conservation in leading oil-producing states is dominated far more by principles of equity than by principles of economic efficiency. Divided control and the political pressures arising from the large number of producing interests have caused the regulatory authorities to impose regulations that in general lead to inefficient methods of exploitation and wasteful expenditure on drilling. The result is "conservation" only in the sense that it is less wasteful than the results of unrestrained drilling and production under the rule of capture.

The Intensive and the Extensive Margin

The determination of equitable rights in a restricted marketable output may collide with economic efficiency not only through its encouragement of excess costs of capacity but also through its short-

1. Pools have been switched between the allocated category and the unallocated category just to give producers bigger allowables, and "dead" wells have remained on the books to raise the quota of the remaining wells on the lease. *Oil and Gas Journal*, January 7, 1957, p. 73.

2. *Oil and Gas Journal*, August 31, 1959, p. 37.

run division of quotas among high-and low-cost producers. Costs of production vary considerably among the known and proven pools, and even among wells in a pool. Generally speaking, low-cost petroleum comes from wells in flush production, especially in large fields, while high-cost production comes from "stripper" wells which produce small amounts of oil by pumping from reservoirs, or segments of reservoirs, that are no longer capable of flush production.

If we think of "conservation" in absolute physical terms, loss of marginal oil through abandonment of stripper deposits would appear to be wasteful. But if conservation is based on economics, then relative costs and values should determine the choice. The regulatory authorities apparently incline more toward the former view, though it might be more accurate to say that the practical exigencies rather than any theory of conservation dictate their actions. Texas again will serve as the dominant example. The Commission first estimates the "market demand" at the existing price, using the U. S. Bureau of Mines forecast as well as other information. Translating this into production estimates by adjustment for stock changes and imports, the Commission then estimates the probable share of Texas in this total output. The "nominations" or purchasing estimates by major oil companies assist it to make these estimates. Then from this projected total of Texas output the Commission subtracts the expected output of the exempt fields and wells, including waterflood projects and stripper wells, and allocates the remainder among the wells subject to proration in the manner described above (see footnote 1, p. 113).

Now it is obvious that this system creates a kind of leverage effect against the flush reservoirs subject to proration, which becomes greater the more production is restricted below the total rated productive capacity of the state. These inequities can arise in a system based on equity because the major oil companies' primary interests are in the large, efficient, low-cost, flush reservoirs, whereas the home-based and numerous independent interests are concentrated more in the small or high-cost pools and the stripper-well output. We do not know, of course, how much weight the Commission gives to physical conservation of every known barrel of oil regardless of cost, but the two considerations add up to the same result. In recent times the distortions have become quite striking.

At the end of 1960 there were about 7,000 oil fields in Texas. Most are small and a substantial number are stripper fields. On the other hand 80 giant fields contain 65 per cent of the Texas oil reserves. In recent years they have produced about 40 per cent of the Texas output. Of the state's nearly 200,000 wells, about 100,000 are exempt from prorationing, most of these being stripper wells on smaller fields or in depleted segments of the giant fields. Stripper wells themselves have a maximum allowable, and it is their inability to produce more than this maximum which causes them to be classified as stripper wells, exempting them from the producing-days restriction. For shallow wells this maximum is 10 barrels per day, but because most stripper wells cannot produce their maximum, the statewide average of actual daily stripper well production is 7.5 barrels. In 1959 about 43 per cent of the total production came from stripper wells and others in the exempt category, while 57 per cent came from flush wells producing at an average equivalent of 10 days per month.[3]

It is readily apparent that the effect of restricting production to "market demand" — the quantity demanded at the going price — is to lend support to the going price.[4] Historically, the going price has been high enough to cover the costs of operating "marginal wells" exempt from the controls that restrain the production of efficient, low-cost oil properties primarily operated by the major companies. The production controls have prevented a flood of low-cost oil from undermining this price. In effect, the inefficiencies forced upon operators of flush properties have sustained the operation of the unrestricted marginal wells. The allocative system, however, has failed to control two variable elements in crude oil availability. One is the number of wells, which has increased out of proportion to oil reserves owing to the encouragement of unnecessary drilling in the per-well proration formulas. As a result more and more wells are drilled in both efficient and inefficient pools whose sole purpose is to obtain an extra allowable, which in turn causes a further cutback in the production quota allowed each well. The second is the availability of oil elsewhere. This has increasingly cut into the share of Texas, the market leader,[5] but conservation practices in other states have

3. *Oil and Gas Journal*, March 21, 1960, pp. 100–102. It can be seen from Table I that an exempt stripper well may actually produce more in total than a shallow flush well if the latter is restricted to 8 or 10 days' production of its allowable. As one operator in the East Texas field put it, "The marginal cut-off point in East Texas is 20 barrels a day. But the top allowable for the better wells in the field also is only slightly over 20 barrels daily — and these are subject to shutdown days. The ridiculous upshot of this is that the marginal well, the least efficient well in the field, gets to produce up to 620 barrels of oil this month. Meanwhile, the top-allowable well, the field's most efficient, is restricted to only 200 barrels for the month." (The East Texas field is subject to special rules.) *Oil and Gas Journal*, January 25, 1960, p. 126.

4. We should emphasize that the Texas Commission does not actively control or fix prices. It acts passively to support the going price by restricting output to "market demand."

not done much to keep the costs of domestic oil down to competitive levels on world markets.

Until recently, the relatively high prices which encouraged "conservation" of marginal oil in known deposits also encouraged discovery of new deposits. In the last few years the growth of imports and the increasing cut-backs of production in relatively new domestic pools have combined to discourage new exploration. But we cannot here discuss the very complex problem of exploratory incentives, which are affected by the depletion allowance and other special tax provisions as well as by relative movements in the prices of other energy sources. Nor can we extend the scope of this discussion to consider whether or not a policy of price stabilization is desirable, even though all these matters affect the determination of the optimum rate of depletion. It seems clear that the present policies fail to meet more rudimentary tests of conservation in that they encourage the waste of "other" resources — labor and capital — in the name of oil conservation.

5. For example, if we compare production rates in January–June 1956 with rates in March, 1958 — before compulsory import quotas were imposed — we find that production in the United States declined from 7,166,000 barrels per day average in the former period to 6,290,000 barrels in the latter. Of this cut of 876,000 barrels daily, Texas alone accounted for 739,000 leaving 137,000 for the rest of the United States, though Texas produces less than 40 per cent of the total. Meanwhile production in Louisiana, the Rocky Mountain province and New Mexico actually increased. (To some extent, of course, this reflected a natural long-run shift in supply sources rather than the effect of restriction.) *Oil and Gas Journal*, April 7, 1958, p. 103.

Vanderbilt University

The University of Texas

CHAPTER 6

PUBLIC POLICY PROBLEMS OF THE DOMESTIC CRUDE OIL INDUSTRY

By PAUL DAVIDSON*

The domestic crude oil industry has been the object of much legislation and presently operates under (a) state production restrictions (prorationing), (b) federal controls (the Connally Hot Oil Act prohibits interstate commerce in oil and oil products that have been produced in violation of state prorationing laws), and (c) special tax considerations (percentage depletion). Prorationing and the Connally Act are expressions of a public policy which has emerged because the free competitive market has been unable to perform its primary function of husbanding existing oil reserves; while percentage depletion is often justified by arguing that in the absence of this tax provision, the free market would not allocate sufficient resources to exploration for new oil reserves.

For most of its history, the domestic crude oil industry has been characterized by wasteful production practices. Many members of the industry, who are normally among the most outspoken advocates of freely competitive markets, as well as many disinterested observers agree on the desirability of a public conservation policy. Investigators have, however, differed on what form this policy should take. Some observers have argued for some type of voluntary or mandatory production restrictions (prorationing) which would limit supply to demand at the going price, while others have advocated voluntary or mandatory field unitization, that is, a policy by which all the producers who draw crude oil from a single underground pool would form a unified management for the specific purpose of operating the wells in the field as a single production unit.

The state of the debate on the proper public policy for the domestic crude oil industry has been justly criticized in an important recent study as follows [3, p. 58]:

> Despite an abundance of statistical and historical information about the oil industry, dismayingly little will be found to have direct relevance to the public policy issues posed by the inquiry, and conclusions must be

* The author is assistant professor of economics at the University of Pennsylvania. He is indebted to S. Weintraub, F. G. Adams, and E. Smolensky for helpful comments on an earlier draft.

based on an informed judgment in which the intuition of different observers may lead them to widely different views.

In view of the analytical inadequacy of so much of the discussion, the purpose of this paper is to provide a complete model of the domestic crude oil industry. This model casts considerable light on the short-run question of the optimum level of production from existing facilities, as well as on the long-run question of incentives to add capacity by exploring presently nonproductive oil lands.

The first half of the paper uses a short-run model which takes the stock of production facilities as given. Under this assumption it is possible to show why the free competitive market improperly allocates oil production over time. It is also possible to derive simple economic criteria which can be used to formulate a public policy which will assure the optimum output of crude oil through time.

The second half of the paper deals with the longer-run question of the incentives to increase capacity by exploring presently nonproductive oil land. It is this long-run view which is relevant for the appraisal of the desirability of granting a tax concession in the form of percentage depletion to the crude oil industry. The major conclusion of this section is that percentage depletion primarily increases the income of landowners rather than encouraging exploration of nonproducing oil lands.

I. *Short-Term Expectations and Production Decisions*

We begin by examining the factors determining entrepreneurial decisions in the crude oil industry. The decisions can be classified as based on either short-term or long-term expectations. Decisions based on short-term expectations involve matters affecting daily output from existing wells; decisions to explore and drill new wells are associated with long-term expectations.

In analyzing the factors bearing on the decision process of the independent producers (who operate two-thirds of the oil wells in the United States[1]) we first assume no prorationing or percentage depletion. Then the effects of depletion and/or state production restrictions can be examined.

A. *Posted Prices*

Originally crude oil was traded on an organized exchange. By the turn of the century, however, most buyers of crude, following the action

[1] There are at least 7000 companies operating 563,000 crude oil wells in 30 states [3, p. 12]. Some of these firms are integrated through all the stages of production, transportation, refining, and marketing, while others confine their activities to one or two stages. The overwhelming majority are not integrated at all.

of the Standard Oil Company, purchased crude in the field under a posted price policy. Thus, when a purchasing company decided upon the price it was willing to pay, this price was posted on a board in the field where it could be seen by all who were interested. More recently, a few large integrated companies (who are also large crude producers) have announced through the press the posted price for crude oil in each field in which they purchase [3, p. 132].[2] When a price is posted in a field, all the producers of that field receive the same price for the same grade,[3] regardless of the volume purchased. This price is F.O.B. well-head and does not include gathering and transportation costs.

The posted price expresses the buyer's judgment regarding the derived value of a complex raw material [3, p. 132]. The independent producer accepts the price as a datum. Analytically, the independent producer is in the same position as a seller in a purely competitive market, i.e., he faces a perfectly elastic demand curve.[4] Since the producer who maximizes profits will equate marginal prime cost to posted price, we must examine the nature of the cost function for crude oil production.

B. *The Cost of Crude Oil Production*

The total cost of crude oil production may be divided into supplementary costs which are here defined as all costs not directly associated with production, and prime costs, regarded as all costs associated with output changes.

For crude oil production, supplementary costs (really investment expenditures) consist mainly of (1) intangible exploration and development costs, (2) tangible exploration and development costs, and (3) leasehold costs.[5]

[2] The posted price is also used as the accounting price for valuing the shipments of the integrated refiner's production department.

[3] Although crude oil is not a homogeneous commodity (it varies with sulphur content and specific gravity), we will assume for analytical convenience that only a single quality of domestic crude is produced.

[4] Cassady has emphasized the fact that posted prices are sometimes shaded and consequently actual price changes often precede posted price changes [2, pp. 119-20]. Cf. the *tatonnements* of the Walrasian system.

[5] Intangible exploration and development costs cover the expenses of drilling, providing roads to the well, the use of chemicals, etc.; these outlays which have no salvage value, may be, for tax purposes, treated as expenses during the year they are incurred [14, p. 1021]; but while following this practice for tax purposes, many firms capitalize these costs and subject them to depreciation charges on their financial statements and for managerial purposes. Tangible exploration and development costs, such as the cost of equipment and structures, approximate 30 per cent of total finding and development costs. They are always capitalized and subject to depreciation. Leasehold costs are subject to cost depletion on financial records.

Oil producing companies treat both depreciation and leasehold cost depletion charges

The prime costs of crude oil production consist mainly of: (1) operating costs, including factor costs of lifting the crude and special lifting costs for nonfree-flowing wells (e.g., gas or water injection), (2) royalties, and (3) user costs.

1. *Operating costs.* Approximately 20 per cent of total annual expenditures of the petroleum production industry are operating costs [3, p. 67, n. 13]. The variable costs of lifting oil from an underground pool vary with the type of well. Over 10 per cent of the wells in the United States are flowing under natural gas or water pressure [4, p. 284]. Another 20 per cent require pumping or some form of artificial aid to augment the outflow of crude. Finally, about ⅔ of all U.S. wells are "strippers,"[6] which barely cover production costs at prevailing prices [4, p. 284], and produce only about ⅙ of total U.S. production [3, p. 68]. Because state production restrictions affect only nonstrippers, however, this overestimates the importance of strippers in the potential output of the industry.

For the nonstripper wells factor costs are small relative to sunk costs. Under secondary recovery methods (i.e., the injection of either water or dry gas into the reservoir to increase crude flow), unit variable costs will be higher than on wells under natural drive, but investment in durable equipment will rise by even a greater proportion, so that the ratio of sunk to out-of-pocket costs is still high [3, p. 67]. Lifting costs are rather large per barrel of output only for stripper wells.

Thus, for most nonstrippers, total operating costs are generally small until capacity is approached. Empirical evidence suggests that marginal operating costs tend to decline in low ranges of output and are then small and nearly constant over a wide range.[7] As capacity is approached the marginal operating cost curve becomes very steep [4, p. 284].

To fix ideas and represent the estimated facts, Figure 1 shows an elongated U-shaped marginal operating cost curve (s_1) for a typical well. The ordinate distance (cd) between the X-axis and the minimum marginal operating cost will vary with each well and will depend on

---

on a unit-of-recovery basis. This accounting practice has created some confusion as to whether these charges are fixed or variable costs. For example, DeChazeau and Kahn declare that "such charges are clearly variable" [3, p. 72, n. 23]. Nevertheless, it is our contention that exploration, development, and leasehold costs are sunk rather than prime costs, and they do not affect short-run production decisions. If producers expected the present price to continue into the future, it would pay them to produce even if marginal revenue did not cover book depreciation and depletion charges. DeChazeau and Kahn have confused book depreciation and depletion charges with the user cost inherent in all raw materials. This latter concept is developed in the following analysis.

[6] "Strippers" are old, marginal wells which require a good deal of mechanical pumping to bring oil to the surface.

[7] For a comprehensive discussion of the economies and diseconomies associated with output changes, see [13, Ch. 10], and for some cost data, see [13, pp. 495-96].

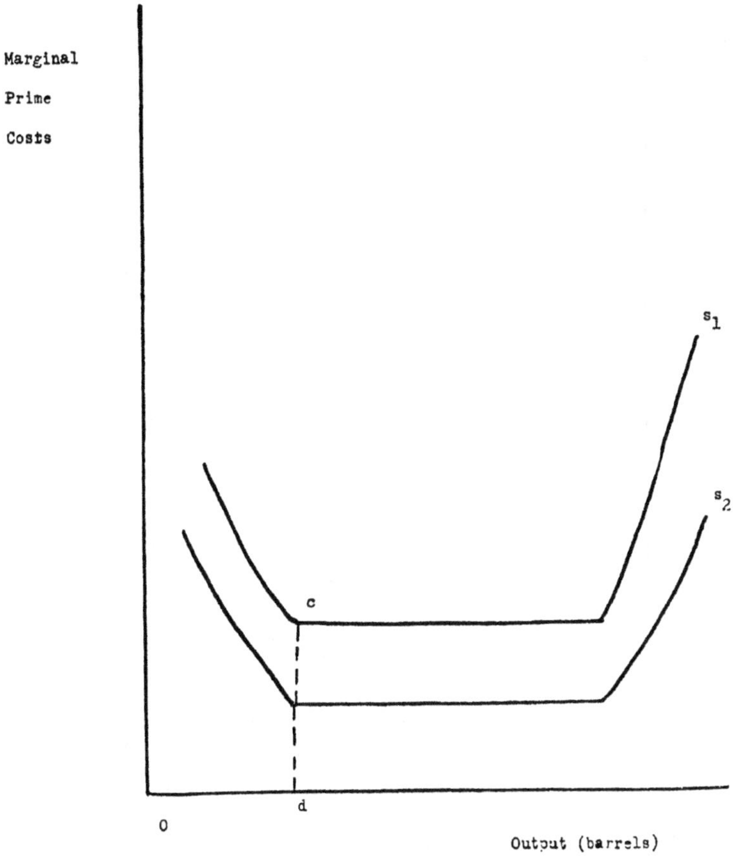

FIGURE 1. TYPICAL MARGINAL PRIME COST FUNCTIONS

the geological conditions in the reservoir, the age of the well, etc. For a young, highly productive, free-flowing well, for example, the distance, *cd,* may represent only a few cents per barrel.

Average and marginal operating costs of stripper wells are much higher than those of nonstrippers. In the short run, the marginal operating cost curve of a stripper will be U-shaped, but it will start from a much higher level than the nonstripper's curve, and it will tend to rise rapidly. At present prices, most stripper wells can profitably produce only four or five barrels per day [4, p. 284].

Assuming the industry draws upon output from the lowest-cost wells first, then the industry marginal operating cost curve, the lateral summation of the individual well curves, would tend to be relatively flat at

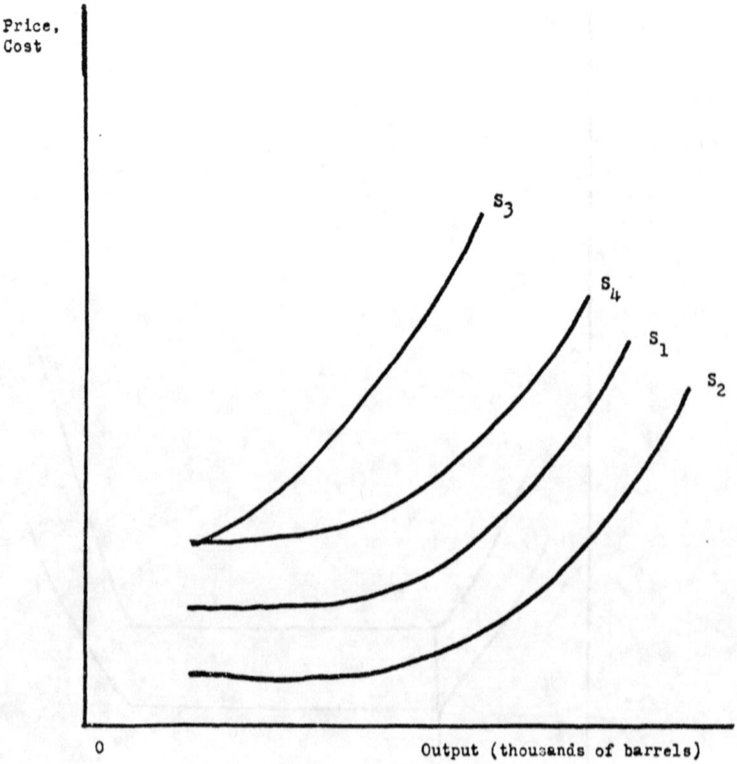

FIGURE 2. ALTERNATIVE INDUSTRY SUPPLY CURVES

low levels of production and rise rapidly as more costly wells are brought into production (S_1 in Figure 2).

2. *Royalties.* Royalty payments to the mineral rights owner are usually fixed by contract before development is begun.[8] Normally a fixed proportion of gross revenue obtained from the well (typically 12½ per cent) is paid out in royalties, i.e.,

$$R = 1/8PQ \tag{1}$$

where R represents total royalty payments per period, P is the short-run supply price of crude, and Q denotes the barrels of output per period from a well. The marginal royalty cost is simply ⅛ of the supply price.

[8] Royalties are an important component of the short-run supply function. Nevertheless, since royalties provisions are fixed at the outset and depend upon expectations of the future income stream from the well, royalties are, in the long run, price-determined rather than price-determining (see Section II below).

If marginal royalty and marginal operating costs were the only marginal prime costs, and since short-run profit maximization would require the firm to equate the sum of these marginal costs to price, then the short-run supply function for the firm would be obtained by elevating the marginal operating cost curve by $\frac{8}{7}$, or $14\frac{2}{7}$ per cent, so as to include marginal royalty costs in the supply price.

3. *User costs.*[9] If user cost phenomena are ignored, then the industry marginal operating cost curve (S_1 in Figure 2), elevated by $14\frac{2}{7}$ per cent to cover marginal royalty costs, would be the short-run supply curve for the industry. But in fact marginal user cost dominates supply decisions in the crude oil industry.

User costs have been defined as "the change in the value of facilities of the firms due to operating as opposed to not operating during the week" [9, p. 58]. In the crude oil industry, one can identify three types of user costs: (a) user cost inherent in all raw materials (U_m); (b) user cost relating to ultimate recovery (U_u); and (c) user cost due to the rule of capture (U_c).

a. User cost inherent in all raw materials. For any particular producer oil in the ground is a stock. The more used today, *ceteris paribus*, the less there will be available tomorrow. Consequently, for production to occur under conditions of profit maximization, marginal revenue must not only cover marginal operating and royalty costs, but must also cover the highest present value of marginal profits given up by producing this week rather than later. Hence,

$$U_m = \beta Q \tag{2}$$

where β is the present value of the greatest potential profit per barrel because of an expected future price (or cost) change. Since

$$\frac{dU_m}{dQ} = \beta, \tag{3}$$

if prices are expected to rise substantially in the future ($\beta > 0$), the marginal user cost due to this factor will be positive and will tend to restrict present production. On the other hand, the expectation of a price decline will make user cost due to this factor negative, and hence expand present production. Thus, dU_m/dQ is the basic economic conservation guideline for deciding whether or not to substitute future consumption of oil for present use, i.e., for evaluating future benefits against the present costs of a slower rate of use.

b. User cost of ultimate recovery. Given the technology and the costs of production, only a fraction of the total volume of crude oil trapped

[9] In the typical theoretical analysis of supply price, user cost has often been neglected despite Keynes' warning that user cost phenomena should not be ignored in the analysis of the firm [6, p. 55, n. 1].

in an underground pool can be brought to the surface during the productive life of the reservoir. Moreover, for any given set of geological conditions the quantity of crude that can ultimately be recovered from the pool will depend on the rate at which the oil is brought to the surface. In general after some point, the faster the rate of production, the lower the volume of crude that can ultimately be recovered.

Public discussions about the conservation of crude oil have usually centered on the question of the quantity of crude that can ultimately be recovered from an oil pool. The economic criterion for conserving oil is different from the geological rule to avoid waste. The geologist desires that production plan which yields the maximum total volume of output over the life of the reservoir. The geologist has therefore developed the concept of MER (the Maximum Efficient Rate of Production). MER is a rate of output (determined by engineering and geological factors) which will maximize the ultimate recovery from the reservoir. The geologist desires a daily production rate which is equal to, or less than MER.[10] The economist, in contrast, seeks to ascertain the oil production plan which maximizes benefits relative to costs over time. If the economist's plan tends to abandon oil in the ground which might, under a slower rate of output, be ultimately recovered, there is no economic waste, only geological waste.[11]

Assuming equality between (1) the social and private rates of time discounting, and (2) social and private costs of production, it will be shown that unitization of oil fields and competition between sellers will promote economic conservation and will tend to result in the optimum allocation of resources over time.[12]

[10] In their recent analysis of oil conservation, McKie and McDonald have defined MER as that rate which maximizes the difference between discounted future returns and discounted future costs of production, or the rate of production which maximizes profits [8, pp. 107-8]. While the concept of MER appears prominently in the jargon of the petroleum industry, it should be stressed, in contrast to the position of McKie and McDonald, that MER is not an economic concept. As one well-known authority in petroleum engineering noted:

> . . . [MER] is that rate which will realize the most efficient use of reservoir energy . . . the oil producer should strive to maintain this most efficient rate of production as nearly as possible, but it should be recognized that this is not necessarily the most profitable rate [13, p. 474].

For further discussion of MER, see [1, pp. 836-37] [3, p. 123, n. 2] [10, p. 30] [12, pp. 125-26].

[11] During the Second World War, for example, because of the scarcity of certain grades of crude, some oil fields in the United States produced at rates in excess of MER [1, p. 1147] [13, p. 577]. It was taken for granted that the social benefits of more production at that critical period greatly exceeded the social costs of lower ultimate recovery.

[12] Because of uncertainty in estimating future demands and costs there are many practical difficulties in assessing the maximum income stream of an oil property. DeChazeau and Kahn argue that "the mere statement of the problem . . . serves to support a general disposition to leave these complicated calculations to the self-interest of businessmen in competitive markets" [3, p. 236].

Let T be the total number of barrels of oil in an underground pool, while S_r is the amount that can ultimately be recovered from the pool for any given production rate. Given the state of technology and the geological conditions, there will be a maximum ultimate recovery of S_0 barrels of crude (where $T > S_0$), if the well is always operated at MER.

Empirical engineering studies have shown that if the crude oil is brought to the surface at a rate of flow that is less than MER, the gas pressure is dissipated as the tubing in the well acts as an oil-and-gas separator; hence, " 'dead' oil is left in the reservoir" [11, p. 66], i.e., ultimate recovery is reduced [13, p. 577]. Nevertheless, if a daily output level is desired which is lower than that which would be obtained by operating the well continuously at MER, it is possible to achieve this desired level without reducing ultimate recovery. The well can be operated at the maximum efficiency rate of flow until the desired number of barrels is obtained; then the flow from the well can be shut off

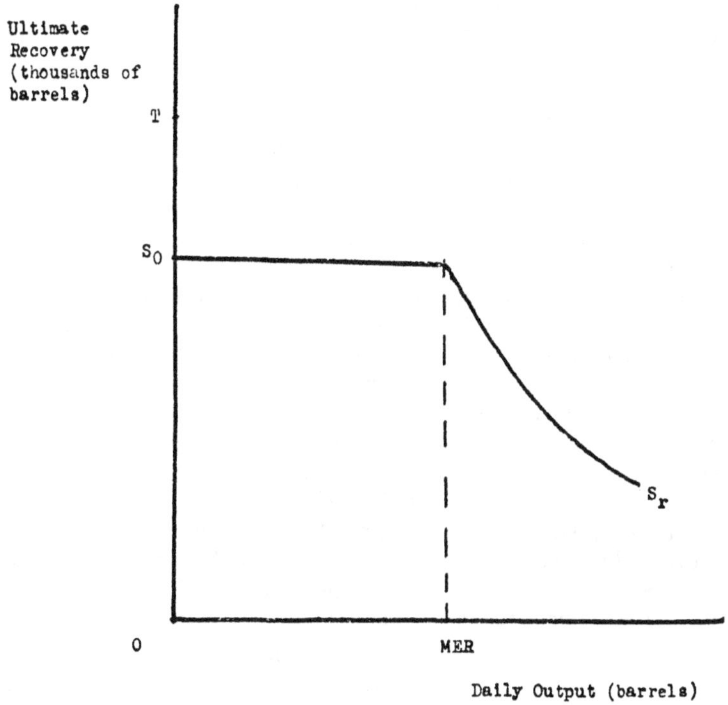

FIGURE 3. THE ULTIMATE RECOVERY FUNCTION

for the remainder of the day. Accordingly, for any output level less than MER, $S_r = S_0$.

If the rate of production exceeds MER, then S_r is a decreasing function of the rate of production. (Schematically this can be represented by the S_r curve in Figure 3.) Hence, $(S_0 - S_r)$ is equal to the number of barrels which ultimately would be sacrificed if the rate of production exceeds MER. The user cost of ultimate recovery is:

$$U_u = \gamma(S_0 - S_r) \tag{4}$$

where γ is the discounted net value of a barrel of oil which could have been produced in the future. The marginal user cost of producing above MER is:

$$\frac{dU_u}{dQ} = -\gamma \frac{dS_r}{dQ}. \tag{5}$$

If production exceeds MER, then $dS_r/dQ < 0$, and under conditions of profit maximization, marginal revenue will have to cover the net value of the barrels of oil that are sacrificed. Thus, dU_u/dQ is the basic economic conservation criterion for assessing the cost of reducing the total crude available over the life of the reservoir relative to the benefits of having more crude for present consumption.

c. User cost of the rule of capture. It is the common law of the rule of capture that makes the supply function of oil unique by including in it a large *negative* marginal user cost. Moreover, it is the rule of capture which prevents dU_m/dQ and dU_u/dQ from acting as the regulators of economic conservation in the market place.

Under the rule of capture, whatever a landowner can withdraw from an underground oil pool (which transcends surface property lines) is his to take and keep, irrespective of its effects on his neighbor. If there is more than one producer from a common pool, then adjacent producers are in danger of losing all "their" oil to their neighbors. Hence, it is in the self-interest of each producer to attempt to bring to the surface as much crude oil as quickly as possible, before his neighbor draws off more oil. In terms of marginal user costs, each additional barrel of oil produced reduces the possible loss of the value of a barrel of output to one's neighbor as the underground inventory is depleted.[13] If S_r is the number of barrels of oil which can ultimately be recovered from a given pool, while Q is the number of barrels of crude which the individual producer brings to the surface, then $(S_r - Q)$ represents the total possible barrels of oil that could be lost to the neighbor. Thus, the user cost due to the rule of capture is:

$$U_c = \gamma(S_r - Q). \tag{6}$$

[13] Here is a classic example where marginal private costs are less than marginal social costs.

The marginal user cost is:

$$\frac{dU_c}{dQ} = \gamma \frac{dS_r}{dQ} - \gamma. \tag{7}$$

Since dS_r/dQ is either equal to zero (at or below MER), or less than zero (above MER), therefore $dU_c/dQ < 0$.

From equations (3), (5), and (7) we obtain the total marginal user cost curve as:

$$\frac{dU}{dQ} = \frac{dU_m}{dQ} + \frac{dU_u}{dQ} + \frac{dU_c}{dQ},$$

or

$$\frac{dU}{dQ} = \beta - \gamma \frac{dS_r}{dQ} + \gamma \frac{dS_r}{dQ} - \gamma = \beta - \gamma. \tag{8}$$

Thus the marginal user cost associated with the rule of capture not only tends to offset any positive costs associated with the marginal user cost inherent in all raw materials, but it also completely nullifies any positive marginal user cost associated with sacrificed ultimate recovery. Accordingly, under the rule of capture, producers will ignore the economic conservation criteria implied in dU_u/dQ and dU_m/dQ, and hence resources will not be optimally allocated over time by the market.

Moreover, the rule of capture makes the crude oil market inherently unstable with respect to new discoveries since there may be no positive price which can bring supply into equilibrium with demand in the short run. For example, assuming that initially the current price is expected to continue into the future so that $\beta = 0$, then equation (8) becomes

$$dU/dQ = -\gamma. \tag{9}$$

Consequently the inclusion of marginal user costs in the marginal prime cost curve will tend to pull the latter down (s_2 in Figure 1); and the industry supply curve will also be lower (S_2 in Figure 2). Thus, when a large new field is discovered, the number of gushers and high-producing free-flowing wells in the industry will increase and depress the supply curve. If the demand for crude is relatively price-inelastic, there may be a precipitous price decline. Expectations of further price declines could then develop (i.e., $dU_m/dQ < 0$) and the supply curve would be further depressed. Under such circumstances there may not be any crude price above zero which would restore equilibrium.[14]

Even though under such circumstances the energy-consuming industries may, in the short run, be able to buy their energy supply at "bargain" prices, the long-run supply situation is obscured. The chaotic

[14] With the discovery of the huge East Texas field in 1931, crude prices toppled from a level of over $1.00 a barrel to a recorded price of 10 cents per barrel in the field [3, p. 67]. Even at this low price, the market was not cleared.

price situation after a large discovery may lead to incorrect planning decisions in the consuming industries regarding their future energy supply costs. Such a situation is socially undesirable and would require governmental interference in the market to restore order.

C. *Regulation to Assert the Public Interest*

Basically, two different types of proposals have been advanced for altering short-term production decisions. They are (1) state-enforced production controls limiting production either to (a) market demand, or (b) MER; or (2) compulsory field unitization.

1. *Market demand prorationing.* The production control scheme presently used in most large oil producing states is some variant of market prorationing. Its stated purpose is to avoid waste, which is defined as production in excess of market demand (at the going price).

In Texas, for example, the state regulatory commission estimates market demand for crude oil and then subtracts (1) estimated production not under its authority (imports and production from other states) and (2) production that cannot be curtailed for economic and political reasons (mainly stripper wells and wells using secondary recovery methods). The residual is the total which will be prorated among fields and among wells within each field "in a manner calculated to preserve equity among producers and to prevent any well from producing beyond its Maximum Efficient Rate (MER)" [3, p. 123].

Thus the production path is altered so that the most efficient wells are not used intensively. Accordingly, the industry's marginal operating cost curve is shifted to the left, while the elastic portion of the curve bears the brunt of the production restraints (S_3 in Figure 2). Furthermore, the impact of the rule of capture is attenuated, for each landowner is restricted either by technology and costs (in the case of strippers) or by the state regulatory commission as to how much oil he can draw off the common pool. Thus, under market prorationing where $\beta = 0$ and $S_0 - S_r = 0$, we are entitled to infer that the relevant marginal user cost function is given by equation (9). Nevertheless, since producers of low-cost wells are not permitted to maximize profits, supply is determined by administrative decree within the constraint that each well produces at a point where marginal revenue is either equal to or exceeds marginal prime cost.

2. *MER prorationing.* If production prorationing limited wells only to MER, the low-cost wells would expand production and would supply a much larger proportion of the output than they would under market prorationing. Equation (8) would be the relevant marginal user cost function, although many low-cost producers might still be operating at

a point where marginal revenue exceeded marginal prime cost (at MER).

From an economic standpoint, it should be apparent that prorationing does not provide a scheme for optimally allocating crude oil resources over time. Market prorationing does diminish the effects of the rule of capture, but the social costs of using the inefficient wells to capacity while limiting the output from efficient operations is obviously uneconomic. Market prorationing is but a sop to practicality for it avoids the regimentation of a host of small enterprises. This, in fact, may be its best defense. One might argue that if the administrative costs outweigh the benefits of the MER prorationing scheme, then the present arrangements are tolerable.

Nevertheless, even if prorationing merely limited well production to MER, resources would not necessarily be optimally allocated over time, even though geological waste were to be prevented. The rule of capture would lead all producers to operate at MER and, when β is positive but less than γ, it would force producers to sell at a price below the value to them of holding oil underground for future sale [3, p. 239, n. 17]. On the other hand, governmental regulation would prevent producers from exceeding MER, even when the social benefits of such action exceeded the social costs. Thus, prorationing provides insufficient guidelines for the economic conservation of crude oil.

3. *Compulsory field unitization.* Some investigators have suggested compulsory field unitization as a way of avoiding the socially undesirable effects of the rule of capture. Unitization would "require the organization of companies or cooperatives in which all surface owners would share on an equitable basis" [10, p. 45]. The advantage of such an operation would be to void the rule of capture and allow the flow from the individual wells to be determined by other economic criteria. Under unitization $dU_c/dQ = 0$; consequently the marginal user cost function becomes:

$$\frac{dU}{dQ} = \beta - \gamma \frac{dS_r}{dQ} \cdot \qquad (10)$$

Assuming constant price and cost expectations, when unitized field production is equal to, or is less than MER, marginal user cost would be zero. Thus, for profit maximization, marginal revenue would have to equal marginal operating plus marginal royalty costs. If production exceeds MER, dS_r/dQ is negative and therefore the second term in equation (10) is positive, implying that there is a positive cost involving lower ultimate recovery for these output levels. Nevertheless, under unitization, production could be pushed past MER in arriving at a profit-maximizing decision if the existing market conditions indicated that the marginal revenue would cover the marginal costs of the resulting geological waste.

On the other hand, if future prices are expected to differ from present prices, then under unitization a current price in excess of marginal operating plus marginal royalty costs at or below MER may not provide a sufficient incentive to produce at that level if there is reason to believe that the price tomorrow will be sufficiently higher to compensate for limiting the amount sold today. Under these circumstances, some oil reserves would be conserved for more valuable uses tomorrow at the cost of less valuable uses today.

Unitization completely eliminates the negative marginal user cost due to the rule of capture, and allows the two economic conservation criteria, the marginal user cost inherent in all raw materials (dU_m/dQ) and the marginal user cost of ultimate recovery (dU_u/dQ), to govern production decisions. Moreover, unitization would ensure that the lowest-cost wells were used intensively. Under unitization, the industry supply curve might be represented as S_4 in Figure 2. (The ordinate difference between S_4 and S_1 reflects marginal royalty costs and any marginal user costs that are associated with the present price and a given set of expectations.)

Nevertheless, supply price will fluctuate with discoveries, technological break-throughs, and cost conditions. Barring adverse price expectations, however, a short-run stable equilibrium at a positive crude price is possible.

D. *The Crude Oil Buyer*

Normally buyers have a vested interest in obtaining a commodity at the lowest price possible. Because of the depletion tax provision and the fact that many integrated refiners are large buyers[15] of domestic crude as well as producers and hence sellers of crude, some purchasers may have a desire for a high rather than a low price of crude.[16]

[15] Most integrated refiners are not completely self-sufficient in regard to their supply of crude oil but must buy some crude in the field. The largest refiners are usually more nearly self-sufficient than the average. The top 20 "major" oil companies (18 of which are fully integrated) controlled about 55 per cent of U.S. production in 1955, and had over 80 per cent of domestic refining capacity [3, p. 18]. Hence, they accounted for over half of total crude sales (not including royalty sales) and over four-fifths of domestic crude purchased in 1955.

[16] DeChazeau and Kahn note that "there are at least four important considerations that incline large vertically integrated companies toward higher crude oil prices, even though they produce only about one-half of their domestic needs. . . . (1) . . . our tax laws make a dollar of earnings from the production of crude oil, *at home or abroad,* more valuable than a dollar earned from the sale of products. (2) World crude oil prices are geared to the American level, and price policies must take into account self-sufficiency ratios world-wide. (3) Production is the stratum of the industry most effec-

An integrated oil firm's after-tax profits are substantially affected by the balance between production of crude oil and refinery operation. Percentage depletion accords a preferential tax treatment to profits from production of crude oil which is not enjoyed by refining, marketing, or transportation profits. With an effective depletion rate of 27½ per cent, profits from the production of crude oil are taxed at an effective rate of 37.7 per cent, whereas profits earned in the other processes are taxed at the ordinary 52 per cent rate under existing tax laws [3, p. 222, n. 49].

Thus, as DeChazeau and Kahn have shown, a rise in the price of crude unaccompanied by a rise in the prices of petroleum products would increase the after-tax profits of any integrated oil company whose net self-sufficiency ratio[17] was greater than 77 per cent [3, p. 222]. Considering only domestic production, in 1956 there were eight firms who would benefit from a crude price rise without any increase in product prices. Despite the fact that the number of firms that would benefit from a rise in the crude price is small, it is just these firms that are typically the posted price leaders in many of the major producing fields. Thus, in regional markets where there is a good deal of oligopsony power, the oligopsonists may have a vested interest in a high crude price.

Moreover, if at least a part of the crude price increment can be passed on in higher product prices, then the breakeven self-sufficiency ratio is reduced. For example, if 50 per cent of the price increment is passed on, then all refiners with a net self-sufficiency ratio of more than 38½ per cent (in 1959, 27 out of the largest 34 refiners) would show an after-tax gain [3, p. 222]. Assuming that one-half of a barrel of crude can be refined into gasoline, then if the crude price increases by $.25 per barrel, the price of gasoline at the pump would have to rise by less than $.0075 per gallon for these 27 enterprises to obtain an increase in after-tax income per barrel of crude.

Price-movement data show that the typical pattern is for the crude oil price to follow product price increases much more promptly than product price declines [3, pp. 414-22]. It appears, therefore, that increased earnings due to product price increases are quickly passed down the integrated chain to the tax-sheltered production segment, as even oil companies with low self-sufficiency ratios tend to benefit from such action.

tively controlled in global terms. . . . (4) Production is the stratum that *must* be controlled if final product prices are to be stabilized above costs" [3, p. 442, n. 37]. Thus, Cassady is incorrect when he argues that *all* refiners stand to gain from a drop in domestic crude prices [2, p. 127].

[17] The net self-sufficiency ratio is defined as the ratio of the firm's domestic crude production (net of royalty payments) to the amount of crude used in the firm's refineries.

The reaction to a product price decline is, however, different. If this decline in income is passed back to the production department, firms with high self-sufficiency ratios will tend to lose after-tax earnings. These companies can, however, resist downward pressures on crude prices that might be exerted by less self-sufficient refiners, because the former enterprises are usually the largest buyers in many of the domestic oil fields. Given the desire of the independent producer to obtain the highest price for his product, posted price oligopsony leadership rather than buyers competition will prevail in the crude market during the periods of slack demand.

Even the refiner with a relatively low net self-sufficiency ratio, however, may desire to maintain crude prices because of the ubiquitous phenomenon known as crude oil trading. A crude oil trade is a reciprocal agreement between two or more companies, in which one company agrees to deliver a given quantity and quality of crude oil to another refiner in return for a similar accommodation by the latter. Although the number of barrels exchanged in a given period may be the same, the number of dollars involved is almost never identical, because of quality differences in the crudes that are traded. Many refiners engage in a volume of trading transactions which exceed their own needs in order to obtain exactly what the refinery requires.

Besides eliminating costly cross-hauling from distant fields to a particular firm's refinery, crude oil trading provides the refiner with an exchangeable supply of crude as a hedge against price fluctuations. It is in the self-interest of each refiner to prevent the price of crude which he controls from declining, so that he may be able to trade at advantageous terms. Since refiners are usually the posted price leaders in the fields where they are the important producers as well as buyers, there is a built-in downward rigidity in crude oil prices.

Thus, most integrated refiners even if they are not completely self-sufficient have a vested interest in a high rather than a low crude price (cf. [3, p. 225]).

E. *Short-run Production Decisions—Summary*

Assuming that private and social rates of discount, and private and social costs of production are equal, compulsory field unitization will solve the problem of economic conservation on the supply side of the market. Unitization may, however, increase the oligopsonist strength of the large integrated refiners who are usually the large producers in each field. Thus, public policy would be required to assure that the price that refiners were willing to pay for crude accurately reflected the demand of consumers of petroleum products. Such a policy might involve either the divestiture of production departments by integrated refiners [10, pp. 119-123], or the removal of the depletion allowance, or both.

The incentive to move the profits of integrated firms to their tax-sheltered production departments by raising the posted price would be removed by eliminating the percentage depletion of the tax law. In view of the emotional reactions aroused by this issue, it is important to analyze the economic effects of the current depletion allowance and its reduction.

II. *Long-Term Expectations and the Decision to Explore*

Percentage depletion is a deduction from taxable income available to all producers of mineral resources. For petroleum, percentage depletion is computed as 27½ per cent of gross revenue from the property, but the deduction may not exceed 50 per cent of net income in any one year.[18] Hence, except for the net income restraint, percentage depletion is merely a negative ad valorem excise tax; and the effects of changes in the rate can be analyzed with the usual tools of tax incidence.

The usual belief of most advocates, as well as opponents, of the present depletion allowance is that it tends to raise after-tax profits in crude oil production vis-à-vis other industries, and therefore it encourages entrepreneurial decisions to explore and drill for oil on presently nonproductive oil land. Industry spokesmen maintain that national security requires an increased allocation of resources to domestic exploration and development [14, pp. 986-87] and that percentage depletion has been essential in encouraging such exploration.[19]

Actually, there are two alternative effects that can be attributed to the depletion allowance. These are: (1) to encourage additional exploratory activity, and (2) to increase the value of mineral holdings. Although most investigators have been quick to emphasize the link between percentage depletion and exploratory activity, the effect on the value of mineral holdings have typically been given short shrift. Consequently, it is important to indicate the conditions under which effect (1) and/or effect (2) will be significant.

[18] The ability to charge off intangible exploration and development costs as expenses in the year they are incurred helps the producer to avoid the 50 per cent net income constraint. Most of these intangible costs are incurred before any oil is produced. These costs, therefore, may be used to offset other taxable income. Once the well is producing, since most of the costs have already been written off, the difference between net and gross income is quite small. If intangibles had to be capitalized and written off over the producing life of the well, the net income in any production period would be much smaller and might severely limit the tax deduction from the depletion allowance.

[19] For example, the preamble of the American Petroleum Institute's Statement of Policy on Percentage Depletion (November 1961) states that "this provision has been a key factor in maintaining high-risk exploration for new oil and gas reserves."

A. *Percentage Depletion, the Value of Undeveloped Oil Land, and the Incentive to Explore*

The effect of percentage depletion on reallocating resources and raising property values can be analyzed with the help of a simplified model. Assume that all income is taxed proportionately and that initially there is no depletion allowance. If two assets, A and B, have equivalent present costs and net income streams, then an individual will be indifferent as to purchasing either A or B. If the tax law is then changed so that a specific proportion of the future income stream of asset A is made tax exempt, then asset A will have a higher present value than before, while the present value of B remains unchanged. The individual will now be willing to incur greater costs to obtain A than before.

Two extreme situations may result. If, in the first case, asset A is in perfectly elastic supply, resources will be diverted towards the production of A, there will be an expansion in the output of the industry, and the product price will decline until the rate of return on A would equal the rate of return on B [15, p. 379]. If, in the second case, asset A is in perfectly inelastic supply then the willingness of individuals to pay more for asset A will, in a competitive environment, merely lead them to bid up the price of A until the expected rate of return on A is the same as can be earned on B. The original owner of A receives a windfall in the form of a higher economic rent for the use of his asset. The individual investor will receive the same rate of return on A or B; therefore, he will obtain the same rate of return as he would have received before the depletion allowance was instituted. Since the original owner receives the windfall while no benefits accrue to the individual operator, there is no incentive to move resources.

In reality, most capital assets fall somewhere between the two extreme cases. Given the depletion allowance, the more nearly perfect is the elasticity of supply of mineral lands, the greater will be the stimulus to reallocate resources, and the smaller will be the effect on the value of mineral holdings. On the other hand, the more inelastic the supply of mineral lands, then the greater will be the landowners' windfalls, while the additional exploratory activity will be minor. In the case of the domestic oil industry, therefore, the significance of percentage depletion will depend on the elasticity of supply of oil lands, i.e., on the supply conditions of those properties from which producers expect to be able to obtain crude oil.[20]

[20] Although many have argued that percentage depletion has encouraged exploration in the domestic oil industry, none has given a more lucid analysis of this position than Harberger, who argues that the depletion allowance misallocates resources in the oil industry. In his careful study, however, Harberger clearly recognizes that in certain

B. *Leasehold Costs and Royalties*

In the domestic oil industry, leasehold costs approximate 30 per cent of exploration costs [7, p. 155], while royalties represent 12½ per cent of total revenue. In the long run both of these costs are price-determined rather than price-determining (Cf. [3, p. 175]), and therefore the major costs in oil exploration and development are economic rents.

A brief description of the institutional arrangements for paying for the use of oil lands will be helpful in understanding the supply conditions of oil lands and in indicating why the rent payments take the dual form of lease bonuses and royalty payments. In the typical oil lease, the surface rights remain in the possession of the owner, who may use the land for agriculture or other purposes. The lessee is only granted the right to enter upon the land and explore, and to produce and sell oil if possible. In return for this privilege, the lessee pays the landowner a royalty, consisting of an agreed percentage of the oil produced or its gross value, plus an initial bonus, and an annual rental as long as the property is nonproductive. Once oil is discovered in profitable quantities, the lease remains in force as long as oil is produced.

Although the typical royalty is 12½ per cent, both the royalty percentage and the lease bonus are open to negotiation. Royalties as high as 50 per cent and bonuses of $1000 an acre have been offered on property where production is assured by surrounding development [13, p. 170]. Typically, the lease bonus depends on "how promising the prospect looks to the lessee, and on competition from other parties"

---

mineral-producing industries, percentage depletion will encourage little or no additional exploration and that its main effect may be merely to increase the value of mineral holdings [5, p. 444]. Nevertheless, Harberger interprets the conditions in the domestic oil industry to be such that oil lands clearly are assets of the elastic-supply case [15, p. 379]. The fact that the annual volume of domestic oil exploration is large leads Harberger to conclude that the reason for all this exploratory activity is percentage depletion [5, p. 443].

My own acquaintance with the crude oil industry leads me to interpret the facts differently. In any discussion of the effects of percentage depletion, the emphasis must be on the encouragement of *additional* exploratory activities and not on the total volume of exploration. Since exploration has always been relatively large in the domestic industry, while the precursor to the present depletion allowance was not enacted until 1916, and since many foreign oil companies have done a good deal of foreign exploration over the years even though in many foreign countries there is no depletion allowance, it would appear that the large annual volume of domestic oil exploration cannot be used as prima facie evidence that percentage depletion has significantly encouraged exploration of oil lands.

Testifying several months after his study was published, Harberger comes closer to my own position when he hints at the inelasticity of supply of oil lands. For example, he states, in ". . . some real sense our reserves are the amount that is underground in this country and . . . the faster we try to use them up, the worse shape we are going to be in in the future," i.e., the long-run supply of crude is perfectly inelastic [15, p. 379], and crude oil "is a wasting asset," i.e., oil is not reproducible [15, p. 400].

[7, p. 545], while, it is often claimed, the royalty rate appears to be "extraordinarily rigid" [8, p. 108, n. 5].

McKie and McDonald have indicated that with perfect competition and perfect foreknowledge, landowners could extract, in the form of rents, all the after-tax profits of the producing firms [8, p. 108]. In the absence of uncertainty, the lease bonus would equal the present value of the net income stream and there would be no need for royalty payments. Given uncertainty and large dispersions around the expected present value of an oil property, the lease bonus is only a partial measure of the expected mean value; the royalty payment allows the producer and the landowner to share the risks inherent in the wide dispersion about the mean value.

Lease bonuses and royalty percentages on producing properties have been fixed by a contract and reflect the producer's and landowner's estimates of the capitalized value of oil in the ground (taking into account the after-tax value of the depletion deduction) at the time of the signing of the contract.[21] These costs are essentially fixed for the life of the contract even if the depletion allowance is changed. Existing contracts on nonproducing properties, on the other hand, can, at the option of the lessee, always be renegotiated to reflect the expected capitalized value of oil in the ground at some future time.

The landowner of any undeveloped oil property exhibits a perfectly inelastic supply function for his mineral rights—there is no alternative use. Thus, the lease bonus and royalty payments are, as McKie and McDonald intimate, Ricardian rent payments. Since a reduction in percentage depletion is equivalent to the levying of an ad valorem excise tax, it follows that if the depletion allowance is reduced, (1) the after-tax capitalized value of all oil properties would decline proportionately; (2) producers would lower their bids for all nonproductive acreage; and (3) the tax could be passed back completely to those landowners who were not protected by existing contracts.

Thus, a reduction in the depletion allowance would not, in itself, change the expected future income stream, net of lease bonuses and royalty payments, on undeveloped oil properties; consequently, in the long run, there should be no reduction in the incentives to explore nonproductive oil lands.[22] The future relative distribution of income be-

[21] As an illustration, assume perfect foreknowledge in a competitive economy having initially no depletion allowance and a 50 per cent corporate profits tax. If a 25 per cent depletion rate is then established, the after-tax value of this tax deduction would be equal to 12½ per cent of the expected income. Consequently, the producers would, under competitive conditions, bid up the price of nonproductive acreage by 12½ per cent. Is it coincidental that the typical royalty in the midcontinent area is ⅛th?

[22] Of course those producers who presently have leases on nonproductive acreage would

tween producers and landowners would be altered. On presently undeveloped properties, the landowners' potential income share would be reduced.

C. *Depletion and Production from Existing Facilities*

Although a change in the depletion allowance will not significantly affect decisions to explore based on long-run expectations of the net income stream of presently nonproductive acreage, there will be some short-run effects.

Landowners of presently producing properties are protected by contracts so that the additional tax cannot be pushed back on them. Industry spokesmen argue therefore, that any increase in taxes due to a reduction in the depletion allowance would be passed forward to the consumer. Basically the industry spokesmen are claiming that, given production techniques and factor prices, a reduction in the depletion allowance will cause the short-run supply curve to shift upwards. The ultimate incidence of this rise in the supply function will depend on the price elasticities of supply and demand. Industry representatives (in and out of Congress) believe that the supply schedule is highly elastic, while the demand for all petroleum products except gasoline is elastic. Owing to the lack of substitutes, the price elasticity of demand for gasoline is normally considered to be rather low. Thus it is argued that the gasoline consumer will bear the full brunt of the rise in the supply schedule; the pump price would rise by as much as 5 cents per gallon; and the industry would recoup the additional tax payments via higher product prices [14, p. 1004].

This analysis assumes that there would be no change in crude oil import quotas or state production restrictions as the domestic industry supply curve shifted upward. These suppositions are questionable on both political and economic grounds. Certainly any attempt to raise the pump price of gasoline by 5 cents a gallon would induce a public demand for a removal of import quotas.

Moreover, if the tax increase were not passed forward, many of the high-cost stripper wells would have to be abandoned. As a consequence, even under the present prorationing scheme, production from the more

have to write off the original lease bonus as a loss if they wanted to renegotiate the contract for the property. If a producer decides to terminate his lease, then he will have to compete with all other producers for a new lease for the property. He will have to pay the new market price which, after a reduction in percentage depletion, will be, *ceteris paribus,* less than the original price (in terms of bonus plus royalties) by an amount equal to the discounted value of the reduction in the depletion allowance. Since the expected net income stream will not have changed, there will be no reduction in the incentive to explore for the industry even though some producers suffer losses because of previously paid lease bonuses.

efficient wells would increase. Thus, the short-run supply curve of the industry could shift outwards rather than upwards.

Of course, if a policy of compulsory field unitization were adopted, then removal of percentage depletion would assure that the resultant industry supply curve (S_4 in Figure 2) would be based on rational conservation principles. The resulting product prices cannot be determined a priori, but they are not likely to exceed current market prices.

To summarize, the major proposition emanating from this long-run analysis is that, given the inelastic supply conditions of nonproductive oil properties, percentage depletion tends mainly to increase the value of mineral holdings. As a consequence, the depletion allowance is primarily an ad valorem subsidy to mineral rights owners who have no alternative use for their resource.[23] Moreover, we have shown in Section I that, in the short run, percentage depletion gives many integrated refiners a vested interest in higher crude oil prices. Thus, it would appear that there is ample justification based on both short-run and long-run considerations for the reduction or elimination of percentage depletion from the tax structure. Only on the basis of equity considerations could a continuation of percentage depletion be defended.[24]

If the depletion provision were altered, it might be desirable to mitigate the possible adverse effects on production income on producing properties. This may be accomplished by either (a) maintaining exist-

[23] In the absence of prorationing and percentage depletion, the short-run supply curve for the firm would be the sum of the marginal operating and marginal user cost curves elevated by 14⅔ per cent to cover marginal royalty costs. Introduction of an effective depletion rate of 27½ per cent with a corporate tax rate of 52 per cent would induce a downward shift in the firm's supply curve of 14.3 per cent, since the depletion allowance is an ad valorem subsidy with an after-tax value to corporations of 14.3 per cent of the supply price. (If the firm is unincorporated and the owners face a marginal personal income tax rate which exceeds 52 per cent, then the depletion allowance would be worth more than 14.3 per cent.) Hence, the marginal royalty cost (which shifts the supply schedule upwards) and the depletion allowance (which shifts the supply schedule downwards) tend to offset each other. The present marginal royalty payment closely reflects the present marginal value of the tax deduction due to depletion. As a result, most of the subsidy to the producer is passed on to the landowner.

[24] Despite the steady stream of propaganda on the need for the depletion tax concession in order to stimulate exploration, it is unquestionably recognized even by the proponents of this special doctrine that they are protecting their income position. Their intuition here has been keener than the reams of apologetic "scholarly" support for the allowance.

These proponents have often used equity arguments to justify percentage depletion. Those equity considerations most often emphasized are: (1) after-tax rewards should be greater in oil production than in other business operations because crude oil production is a more risky undertaking than other business ventures, and (2) oil is a wasting asset, i.e., the industry is selling its "capital assets on an installment basis" and therefore its net revenue should not be looked upon entirely as taxable income [14, p. 988-91].

It is not the intent of this paper to make any value judgment on these equity considerations. Harberger has, however, argued "It cannot have been the intent of Congress to make owners of mineral deposits richer at the expense of the rest of the community" [5, p. 444].

ing depletion allowances on presently producing wells, or (b) reducing the depletion rate slowly on such wells.

Alternative (a) would, in effect, hold an umbrella over producers who would otherwise suffer losses because of unexpected changes in the tax laws. Since percentage depletion has been under attack by Treasury officials and members of Congress for more than a decade, producers must have been well aware of the risks involved when they entered into lease agreements. With alternative (b), if the average life of an oil well is about ten years [14, p. 963], then a partial shelter for producers may be provided by scheduling reductions in the depletion rate over a ten-year period, with small reductions occurring in the early years and larger ones in later years.

III. *Conclusions*

Our analysis has shown that proper guidelines for the economic conservation of oil reserves can be formulated in terms of the marginal user cost inherent in all raw materials plus the marginal user cost of ultimate recovery. Unfortunately, the marginal user cost associated with the rule of capture prevents these other user costs from performing their allocative function, and as a result the free competitive market cannot properly husband oil reserves. Conservation policy must (1) eliminate the user cost associated with the rule of capture and (2) assure a free competitive market between crude oil buyers and sellers. Adoption of such a policy would promote industry operations more nearly consistent with the optimum allocation of resources over time than ensues from present legal and institutional practices.

Furthermore, our analysis has indicated that, in the long run, percentage depletion does not significantly encourage the allocation of additional real resources to exploring presently nonproductive oil lands. The depletion allowance is primarily an ad valorem subsidy to mineral rights owners. A reduction in the depletion allowance will not reduce the incentives to explore undeveloped oil lands. Hence, except perhaps on equity grounds, it is hard to sustain a defense of this favored tax treatment in our tax laws.

References

1. American Petroleum Institute, *History of Petroleum Engineering*. New York 1961.
2. R. Cassady, *Price Making and Price Behavior in the Petroleum Industry*. New Haven 1954.
3. M. G. DeChazeau and A. E. Kahn, *Integration and Competition in the Petroleum Industry*. New Haven 1959.
4. J. B. Dirlam, "The Petroleum Industry," in W. Adams, ed., *The Structure of American Industry*, 3rd ed. New York 1961.

5. A. Harberger, "The Taxation of Mineral Industries," in *Federal Tax Policy for Economic Growth and Stability*, Washington 1955, pp. 439-49.
6. J. M. Keynes, *The General Theory of Employment, Interest and Money*. New York 1936.
7. J. W. McKie, "Market Structure and Uncertainty in Oil and Gas Exploration," *Quart. Jour. Econ.*, Nov. 1960, *74*, 543-71.
8. ——— and S. L. McDonald, "Petroleum Conservation in Theory and Practice," *Quart. Jour. Econ.*, Feb. 1962, *76*, 98-121.
9. A. C. Neal, *Industrial Concentration and Price Inflexibility*. Washington 1942.
10. E. Rostow, *A National Policy for the Oil Industry*. New Haven 1948.
11. T. P. Saunders, "Low Producing Rates Waste Reservoir Pressures," *Oil and Gas Jour.*, July 11, 1940, *39*, p. 66.
12. L. C. Uren, *Petroleum Production Engineering—Oil Field Exploitation*, 3rd ed. New York 1953.
13. ———, *Petroleum Production Engineering—Petroleum Production Economics*. New York 1950.
14. U. S. Congress, Committee on Ways and Means, *Compendium of Papers on Broadening the Tax Base*. Washington 1959.
15. U. S. Congress, Joint Committee on the Economic Report, *Hearings on Federal Tax Policy for Economic Growth and Stability*. Washington 1956.

An Economic Model of Production and Investment for Petroleum Reservoirs

By ROBERT G. KULLER AND RONALD G. CUMMINGS*

Economists have long been concerned with problems associated with petroleum production. However, efforts to develop an analytical framework for the study of such problems have been impeded by the morass of technological and socioeconomic problems peculiar to this decision environment. Analytical models suggested in earlier works do not consider certain processes which are basic to the technology of petroleum production. For example, Paul Davidson, James McKie and Stephen McDonald, and Vernon Smith, fail to provide an analytical model for petroleum production which includes interaction among (a) current production rates, (b) the role of investment (both in terms of pressure maintenance, and present and/or future use of artificial lifting methods), and perhaps most important, (c) the possible dependence of recoverable stocks on the time-path of production. Further, earlier works, with the exception of those by Smith and Kuller, rely on linear production paths, and only the latter attempts to develop explicitly both the economic and physical nature of the user costs involved in petroleum production.

The purpose of this paper is to present an economic model for petroleum reservoir management which includes the above described characteristics of petroleum production. The model, essentially a specific application of the general resource model developed by Oscar Burt and Cummings, represents our attempt to characterize production relations in a manner consistent with current procedures used by petroleum engineers for predicting reservoir performance. The model is designed with a combination water-gas drive reservoir in mind, yet is adaptable for application to other types of reservoirs.

In Section I below, the arguments begin with a physical description of a petroleum reservoir, in which an attempt is made to find a middle ground for exposition that is sufficiently technical to satisfy readers familiar with petroleum technology and yet is comprehensible to other readers.

In Section II, the management model is presented; the mathematical development for this model is included in the Appendix. An economic interpretation of the resulting decision rules for production and investment is given in Section III, and an extended discussion of the implications of such rules for policy, as well as a comparison of results from earlier works, is the topic of Section IV. Concluding remarks are given in Section V, along with suggestions concerning the possible extension of this management model for the purpose of determining optimal expenditures for exploration.

I. Petroleum Reservoir Mechanics

A petroleum reservoir is a body of porous and permeable rock saturated with a solution of oil, gas, and ordinarily, water. An untapped reservoir exists under very

* Assistant professor of economics, University of Wyoming, and professor of resource economics, University of Rhode Island, respectively. We wish to express our appreciation to Resources for the Future, Inc., The Division of Business and Economic Research, University of Wyoming, and the Rhode Island Agricultural Experiment Station (Contribution #1510) for their generous support of this work.

high pressure, imposed on the reservoir by, for example, confining layers of impermeable rock, an aquifer which surrounds the reservoir, a gas cap or pocket, or some combination of the preceding.

When the reservoir is tapped by a well, an immediate pressure differential results. The pressure in the well-hole is considerably less than the pressure in the reservoir. As a result, the tightly compressed molecules of oil and gas expand and move in the direction of the well. Similarly, it is the pressure differential between the bottom and top of the well which, if great enough, gives rise to the continued "natural" flow of the oil-gas solution to the surface. Production of oil and gas by means of this phenomenon is referred to as production from the reservoir's "natural drive."

The amount of pressure which exists in the reservoir, and particularly, the time-path of pressure depletion, are crucial in terms of two important dimensions of petroleum production, viz., the production rate and the amount of oil recoverable from the reservoir. In terms of production, the relevance of sufficient pressure to provide production from natural drive is immediately obvious. Such production is virtually costless in terms of direct variable costs (that such production is not costless, in terms of *user* costs, is developed in the following two sections). Even when natural drive forces alone are no longer capable of sustaining production, the extent of artificial lift production (for example, pumping) is affected by the rate at which oil moves through the reservoir into the well by natural forces. This rate depends upon the amount of dissolved gas in the solution, which in turn is dependent upon the previous time-path of pressure.

The recoverable portion of the total volume of oil in the reservoir depends upon a number of factors. A primary determinant is the source of the reservoir's natural drive: dissolved gas drive (production derives solely from the expansion of oil and gas), gas cap drive (the expansion of a free gas "pocket" forces the oil toward the well), water drive (water displaces the oil and maintains pressure), or combination drive which results from a combination of the preceding forces. The portion of the initial oil stock that is recoverable by natural drive will vary from 15 to 30 percent in dissolved gas reservoirs to as high as 80 percent in gas cap, water and combination drive reservoirs (see N. Clark, Part 1, p. 160).[1]

Of particular importance in this paper is the fact that the recoverable stock may be *rate dependent*; i.e., the recoverable stock may depend upon the time-path of production. Following Benjamin Craft and Murray Hawkins, " . . . many reservoirs are clearly *rate sensitive* and there is a *maximum efficient rate* (MER) above which there will be a significant reduction in the practical ultimate oil recovery" (p. 197). Such dependence is particularly relevant for water drive and combination drive reservoirs.

Consider, for example, the mechanics of a water drive reservoir. As pressure in the reservoir is reduced by production, water displaces the oil ahead of it, essentially maintaining an interface, or juxtaposition, with the body of oil (i.e., the body of water continues to "push against" the body of oil). Thus, pressure is maintained, and " . . . provided that water moves through all segments of the reservoir sand and all areas over which the reservoir occurs" (Clark, Part 1, p. 160), only small amounts of oil are lost in isolated pockets and in mixture with water, so that a large portion of oil is gleaned from the saturated reservoir rock.

[1] The relatively low percentage recovery by dissolved gas drive follows from the fact that production by this method implies the simultaneous production of the reservoir's principle source of pressure—not necessarily the case for production by the other mechanisms.

The rate at which water will displace the oil, and thereby maintain pressure, is in turn determined by a number of factors, for example, the relative size of the aquifer and amount of its pressure, and the permeability and porosity of the reservoir rock. If oil is extracted at a greater rate than that at which water displaces the oil, reservoir pressure is reduced. Also, "since water moves more freely than oil through the tiny pores and interstices of oil-bearing rock, too rapid production of oil . . . may allow water to surround and bypass oil in place, which usually means permanent loss" (McKie and McDonald, p. 102).[2] For example, suppose 5 million barrels of oil are to be extracted over a 5-year period. A uniform production rate of 1 million barrels per year might have a considerably different effect on the ultimate recoverable stock than a sequence of rates of 4 million barrels the first year and 250,000 barrels each of the following 4 years. Thus, the essence of rate dependence is that total recovery, as well as annual production rates from natural drive, may depend not only on cumulative production, but also on the rate at which such production has taken, and will take place (see Clark, Part 1, p. 160; Robert Gordon, p. 278, n. 8; McKie and McDonald, pp. 102–03; S. J. Pirson, pp. 708–10; and Smith, p. 414, n. 6).

From the above discussion it is obvious that pressure is a key element in petroleum production. While the discussion thus far has been focused on "natural" pressure in the reservoir, it should be noted that in many cases pressure may be maintained or increased artificially through investment activities. Water, gas, steam, or other fluids may be pumped into the reservoir (see Pirson, pp. 539–42). Thus, the recoverable stock, as well as production rates, generally will depend strongly on investment. Such dependence is not only on cumulative investment (i.e., the capital stock), but also on the time-path of investment (i.e., there is rate dependence with reference to investment). The rate dependence of recoverable stocks on investment follows directly from the above argument concerning production rates. Thus, the impact of rapid production rates on total recovery may be offset to some extent by investments for pressure maintenance.

The evaluation and prediction of reservoir performance requires considerable data concerning reservoir pressure, geological properties of the reservoir rock, fluid properties, and production history (for example, see A. Baca, p. 1; Clark, Part 1, p. 157; and Pirson, p. 533). These data are then used by engineers to develop "reservoir performance curves" similar to those depicted in Figure 1. Given an annual rate of extraction, for simplicity some constant value u', an estimate is made of the future time-path of pressure maintained in the reservoir. In this manner the "production life," and therefore the recoverable stock from the reservoir with reference to natural drive is obtained. In many cases, a faster annual extraction rate, u'' in Figure 1, may result in a leftward movement in the cumulative production curve, reflecting as discussed above, the "rate dependence" of recoverable stocks. If ultimate recovery is rate dependent, the faster rate u'' may not result in lower recovery given some annual investment, v', for pressure maintenance activities.

Thus, for some planning horizon of T periods,[3] $t=1, 2, \ldots, T$, let:

[2] It is of interest to note that water drive *gas* reservoirs may behave in an opposite fashion, i.e., too slow production of gas may result in the loss of a significant quantity of the initial gas stock (see R. G. Agarwal, R. Al-Hussainy and H. J. Ramey).

[3] Comments on the choice of T are given in Section V below.

u_t = the total volume of petroleum extracted from the reservoir during period t

$U_t = (u_1, u_2, \ldots, u_t)$

v_t = gross investment for all capital components during period t

$V_t = (v_1, v_2, \ldots, v_t)$

X = the total recoverable quantity of petroleum in the reservoir

K_t = capital stocks at the beginning of t

F_t = an upper (physical) bound on the capacity to produce petroleum from the reservoir during period t

C_t = the generalized cost function for production in period t

The following general relations may then be postulated as conceptually determinable from the reservoir performance curve methodology used by petroleum engineers:[4]

(1) $$\sum_{\tau=1}^{T} u_\tau \leqq X(U_T, V_T),$$

$$\frac{\partial X}{\partial u_\tau} \leqq 0, \quad \frac{\partial X}{\partial v_\tau} \geqq 0$$

(2) $$u_t \leqq F_t(U_t, V_t, K_t), \quad \frac{\partial F_t}{\partial u_t} \leqq 0,$$

$$\frac{\partial F_t}{\partial v_t} \geqq 0, \quad \frac{\partial F_t}{\partial K_t} \geqq 0$$

(3) $$C_t(U_t, V_t, K_t), \quad \frac{\partial C_t}{\partial u_\tau} \geqq 0,$$

$$\frac{\partial C_t}{\partial v_t} \geqq 0, \quad \underset{(\tau \neq t)}{\frac{\partial C_t}{\partial v_\tau}} \leqq 0, \quad \frac{\partial C_t}{\partial K_t} \leqq 0$$

[4] We gratefully acknowledge comments on an earlier draft of this paper by Oscar Burt. He suggests an alternative statement of the relations below which might be most useful in terms of empirical applications with dynamic programming, viz., the use of X_{1t}, reservoir pressure at t, and X_{2t}, maximum recoverable stock at t, as state variables, along with K_t, in a recursive programming format. We have experimented with this system and find that for analytical purposes the resulting decisions rules are almost identical. However, Burt's method may be preferred for empirical applications.

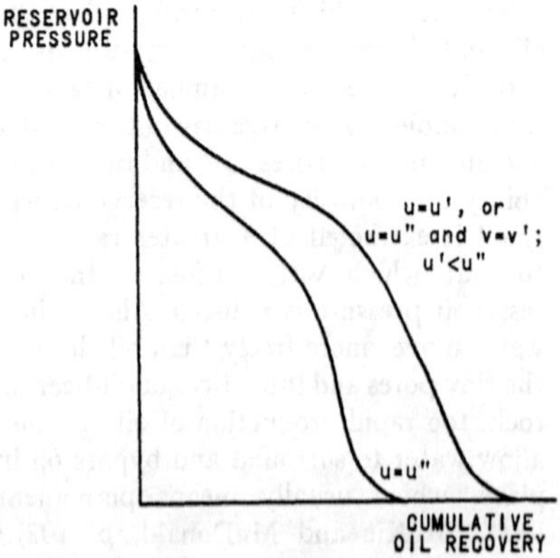

FIGURE 1

Equation (1) states that total petroleum production over the T period horizon may not exceed the recoverable stock X, where X is determined by the time-path of production and investment over the entire period $1 \leqq t \leqq T$. Since the dissolved gas content of the reservoir solution, as described above, affects the natural forces driving petroleum toward the well (for production by artificial lift), X is viewed here as recoverable stock from natural drive as well as from artificial lift.

Equation (2) imposes an upper bound, F_t, on annual production from the reservoir. This value of F_t is determined by reservoir pressure at t which is in turn determined by the previous and current values of u and v, and by capital stocks (for example, size and number of wells, and artificial lift equipment, in the case of artificial lift).

Equation (3) is a generalized cost function. Variable production costs in t may be (essentially) zero,[5] if sufficient pressure

[5] Reference here is to the individual firm. This assumption may or may not reconcile James Griffin's recent arguments, but is of no concern at this point. The arguments, as shown below, are unaffected by rising marginal costs.

exists for production via natural drive, thus the dependence of C_t on the previous paths of u and v (reference to V_t here is to $v_1, \ldots, v_{t-1}$, where v_t is viewed as a current investment charge, i.e., $\partial C_t/\partial v_t \geqq 0$). If u_t and v_t are such that pumping is required in t, u_t results in current direct costs; i.e., $\partial C_t/\partial u_t > 0$. Capital stocks, reflecting the efficiency of the production system, are assumed to decrease unit costs.

Having specified the above relations, (1) through (3), a production and investment model for the reservoir may now be suggested. The notation used above is expanded as follows:

- u_{jt} = the volume of petroleum extracted by firm j, $j=1, \ldots, n$ during period t
- U_t = annual production rates by *all* firms during all periods, $1, \ldots, t$; i.e., $(u_{11}, u_{21}, \ldots, u_{n1}, \ldots, u_{1,t-1}, \ldots, u_{n,t-1}, u_{1t}, \ldots, u_{nt})$
- v_{jkt} = gross investment by firm j in capital component k, $k=1, \ldots, q$, during period t
- $v_{jt} = (v_{j1t}, \ldots, v_{jqt})$
- V_t = gross investment for all capital components by all firms during the periods $1, \ldots, t$
- K_{jkt} = firm j's stock of capital component k at the beginning of period t
- $K_{jt} = (K_{j1t}, \ldots, K_{jqt})$
- D_{jkt} = net depreciation of firm j's stock of capital component k during period t
- F_{jt} = an upper (physical) bound on firm j's capacity to produce petroleum during period t
- C_{jt} = firm j's cost function during period t
- β_t = a discount factor, $(1+r)^{-t}$, where r is the appropriate discount rate
- p_t = unit price of petroleum during period t

II. A Management Model for the Reservoir

The existence of n firms exploiting a given petroleum reservoir is postulated. Production from the reservoir is assumed to be a sufficiently small part of total (national) petroleum production such that the n firms may be viewed as price takers. For a T period horizon, $t=1, \ldots, T$, it is assumed that all prices are known.

Each firm j is assumed to maximize the value of a stream of discounted profits from the sale of petroleum over the planning horizon, which is equivalent to maximizing the following relation:

$$(4) \qquad \sum_{t=1}^{T} [p_t u_{jt} - C_{jt}(U_t, V_t, K_{jt})]\beta_t$$

In the above, $p_t u_{jt}$ represents gross revenues to the firm; C_{jt} is the firm's cost function, the nature of which was detailed above in Section I.

The following relations and restrictions are assumed to apply to the production process:

$$(5) \qquad K_{jk,t+1} = K_{jkt} - D_{jkt}(u_{jt}, v_{jkt}, K_{jkt})$$

and

$$(6) \qquad u_{jt} \leqq F_{jt}(U_t, V_t, K_{jt}), \quad \text{for all } j, k, \text{ and t}$$

Equation (5) states that the stock of capital component k at the end of period t (i.e., the beginning of period t+1) equals the initial stock minus *net* depreciation. Net depreciation is assumed to decrease with gross investment and to increase with u and K. In most applications, either u, implying a consumptive-use notion of depreciation, or K, implying a capital-decay notion of depreciation, will be used. In either case, the following conditions hold:

$$(7) \qquad \frac{\partial D_{jkt}}{\partial v_{jkt}} \leqq 0, \quad \frac{\partial D_{jkt}}{\partial u_{jt}} \geqq 0, \quad \frac{\partial D_{jkt}}{\partial K_{jkt}} \geqq 0$$

In (6) the generalized upper bound on current production rates (in t) discussed above in equation (2) is imposed on the individual firm j. It should be noted that this bound relevant for firm j depends upon past and current production and investment rates from all firms producing from the reservoir (inasmuch as reservoir pressure is determined by total production from the reservoir, as well as from aggregate investment activities for pressure maintenance). Thus,

$$\frac{\partial F_{jt}}{\partial u_{i\tau}} \leqq 0 \tag{8.1}$$

$$\frac{\partial F_{jt}}{\partial v_{i\tau}} \geqq 0 \tag{8.2}$$

$$\frac{\partial F_{jt}}{\partial K_{jt}} \geqq 0, \tag{8.3}$$

for all i, j, k, and t; $\tau = 1, \ldots, t$

Finally, for the reservoir as a whole, the following form of equation (1) discussed above is required in order to determine the recoverable stock:

$$\sum_{\tau=1}^{T} \sum_{j=1}^{n} u_{j\tau} \leqq X(U_T, V_T) \tag{9}$$

Concern in this paper is with centralized control or management of the reservoir.[6] Thus, the relevant optimization problem is expressed by the following:

Maximize:

$$\sum_{t=1}^{T} \sum_{j=1}^{n} \{p_t u_{jt} - C_{jt}(U_t, V_t, K_{jt})\}\beta_t \tag{10}$$

subject to the conditions

$$K_{jk,t+1} = K_{jkt} - D_{jkt}(u_{jt}, v_{jkt}, K_{jkt}) \tag{11}$$

$$u_{jt} \leqq F_{jt}(U_t, V_t, K_{jt}) \tag{12}$$

$$\sum_{\tau=1}^{T} \sum_{j=1}^{n} u_{j\tau} \leqq X(U_T, V_T) \tag{13}$$

$$u_{jt} \geqq 0, \quad v_{jkt} \geqq 0, \quad \text{for all } j, k, \text{ and t} \tag{14}$$

Necessary conditions for a maximum in the system (10) through (14) are developed in the Appendix. Discussion here continues with an economic interpretation of the decision rules implied by the conditions (A2) and (A3) in the Appendix.

III. Optimal Paths for Production and Investment

Rearrangement of terms in Appendix equations (A2) and (A3) yields the following relations which characterize optimal paths for production and investment for the reservoir during all periods t, $1 \leqq t \leqq T$, for which u_{jt} and v_{jt} are positive.

$$\begin{aligned} \left(p_t - \frac{\partial C_{jt}}{\partial u_{jt}}\right)\beta_t &= \lambda\beta_T\left(1 - \frac{\partial X}{\partial u_{jt}}\right) + \Psi_{jt}\beta_t \\ &- \sum_{\tau=t}^{T} \sum_{i=1}^{n} \Psi_{i\tau} \frac{\partial F_{i\tau}}{\partial u_{jt}} \beta_\tau \\ &+ \sum_{k=1}^{q} \Delta_{jk,t+1}\beta_{t+1} \frac{\partial D_{jkt}}{\partial u_{jt}} \\ &+ \sum_{\tau=t+1}^{T} \frac{\partial C_{j\tau}}{\partial u_{jt}} \beta_\tau + \sum_{\tau=t}^{T} \sum_{\substack{i=1 \\ i \neq j}}^{n} \frac{\partial C_{i\tau}}{\partial u_{jt}} \beta_\tau \end{aligned} \tag{15}$$

$i, j = 1, \ldots, n; \; 1 \leqq t \leqq T$

$$\begin{aligned} \frac{\partial C_{jt}}{\partial v_{jkt}} \beta_t &= -\Delta_{jk,t+1}\beta_{t+1} \frac{\partial D_{jkt}}{\partial v_{jkt}} + \lambda\beta_T \frac{\partial X}{\partial v_{jkt}} \\ &+ \sum_{\tau=t}^{T} \sum_{i=1}^{n} \Psi_{i\tau}\beta_\tau \frac{\partial F_{i\tau}}{\partial v_{jkt}} \end{aligned} \tag{16}$$

[6] As suggested to us by the referee, the objective function of this paper may be limited in terms of social control over reservoir production. More general treatments are implied in Burt and Cummings, and Smith.

$$-\sum_{\substack{i=1\\i\neq j}}^{n}\frac{\partial C_{it}}{\partial v_{jkt}}\beta_t-\sum_{\tau=t+1}^{T}\sum_{i=1}^{n}\frac{\partial C_{i\tau}}{\partial v_{jkt}}\beta_\tau$$

$$i,j=1,\ldots,n;k=1,\ldots,q;1\leqq t\leqq T$$

Characteristics of Optimum Production Rates

At any t, $1 \leqq t \leqq T$, any firm j produces at the rate described by (15), assuming that $u_{jt}>0$; conditions for a zero production rate are discussed below. The left-hand side of (15) is, of course, the present value of marginal net income to j during period t. On the right-hand side of (15) are six terms which may be interpreted as the "user costs" of an increment in production during t by firm j. User costs are defined by Anthony Scott as "... the present value of future profit foregone by a decision to produce a unit of output today" (1967, p. 34). In the present context, "future profit" corresponds to future net incomes to the reservoir. Given the major role and peculiarities of user costs in petroleum production, it will be useful to develop in some detail the elements of such costs.

Stock User Costs

The term $\lambda\beta_T$ may be interpreted as the marginal scarcity value of petroleum to the reservoir as a whole for the entire period $t=1,\ldots,$ T. From Appendix equation (A7), λ may be nonzero only in the case where equality holds in the relation (13); i.e., the endogenously determined recoverable stock X is exhausted at or before T. The coefficient λ then measures the increase in net incomes from the the reservoir associated with an incremental change in the endogenously determined stock. This value is weighted by the term $(1-\partial X/\partial u_{jt})$ which is no less than one, since by equation (1) $\partial X/\partial u \leqq 0$ which reflects the impact on the total recoverable reservoir stock (through for example, pressure reduction) of an increment in production by firm j in t. Thus, the term $\lambda\beta_T(1-\partial X/\partial u_{jt})$ may be thought of as j's "stock user cost" during t.

Boundary User Costs

The Lagrangian multiplier Ψ_{it}, $i=1,\ldots,n$, is associated with the above restriction set (12) which imposes an upper bound F_{it} on each firm i's production rate during any period $t=1,\ldots,$ T. Then for any period τ, $t\leqq\tau\leqq T$, during which $F_{i\tau}$ is effective—equality holds in (12)—for any firm i, $\Psi_{i\tau}$ measures the increase in net incomes which would result from an incremental relaxation of the restriction, and $\partial F_{i\tau}/\partial u_{jt}$ measures the "relaxation" obtained from an incremental change (lowering) of the firm j's production in t. Thus, the second and third terms on the right-hand side of (15) are interpreted as "boundary user costs."

User Costs of Capital Consumption

The multiplier $\Delta_{jk,t+1}$, for which an expanded expression is developed in Appendix equation (A11), measures the marginal productivity of capital-type k used by firm j in all future periods $t+1$, $t+2,\ldots,T$. The term $\partial D_{jkt}/\partial u_{jt}$ measures the capital consumed in t (and therefore not available, *ceteris paribus*, in all future periods) by an increment in production by j in t. Thus, $\Delta_{jk,t+1}\beta_{t+1}\partial D_{jkt}/\partial u_{jt}$ measures the user cost of capital consumption by firm j.

Production User Costs

As discussed in Section I above, given a set of investment rates, current production may affect natural drive pressures as well as the characteristics (for example, viscosity) of the oil-gas solution for artificial lift purposes in current and/or future years. The resulting impacts of current production (for example, movement from natural drive to pump production, lower pump efficiencies from high viscosity solutions) on j's (as well as all other firms') future variable costs are the measures given by the last two terms on the right-hand side of (15), and thus, their interpretation as production user costs. These user costs reflect the stock value of oil and gas to the firm, contributing to output as natural factors of production (see for example, James Quirk and Smith, p. 9, for a discussion of the effects of resource stocks on output).

In summary, the rate characterized by (15) is that which follows the rule: produce at a rate where marginal net income to firm j equals the user cost associated with firm j's production. The user cost reflects not only the impact of u_{jt} on future costs internal to j, but also all external effects which result from j's production, viz., effects on the aggregate recoverable stock (λ), effects on other firms' maximum rates of production (Ψ), and impacts on all firms' direct production costs ($\partial C_i/\partial u_j$, $i=1, \ldots, n$). Of course, at any t during which inequality holds in (15), (i.e., marginal net income for j is less than j's user costs for all possible values of u_{jt}), $u_{jt}=0$ by Appendix equation (A2′), (i.e., firm j does not produce during t).

A further development of the ramifications of (15) for reservoir management requires a discussion of the characteristics of optimal investment rates, given the "offsetting" role in terms of pressure maintenance which investment activities vis-à-vis current production may play. This development is given in Section IV.

Characteristics of Optimum Investment Rates

Equation (16) dictates the optimal level of firm j's investment in capital-type k during any t, $1 \leqq t \leqq T$, for which such investment is positive. On the left-hand side of (16) is the present value of the marginal costs of such investment to firm j. On the right-hand side of (16) are aggregate benefits to the reservoir as a whole associated with such investment, and these benefits include the following elements. The first term is $\Delta_{jk,t+1}\beta_{t+1}$ weighted by $\partial D_{jkt}/\partial v_{jkt}$, the latter of which may be viewed as equal to -1. The term Δ_{jkt} is expanded in Appendix equation (A11) and repeated here, adjusted to t+1.

$$(17)\quad \Delta_{jk,t+1}\beta_{t+1} = \sum_{\tau=t+1}^{T}\left(-\frac{\partial C_{j\tau}}{\partial K_{jk\tau}} + \Psi_{j\tau}\frac{\partial F_{j\tau}}{\partial K_{jk\tau}}\right)\beta_\tau \prod_{s=t+1}^{\tau-1}\left(1-\frac{\partial D_{jks}}{\partial K_{jks}}\right) + \prod_{s=t+1}^{T}\left(1-\frac{\partial D_{jks}}{\partial K_{jks}}\right)\Delta_{jk,T+1}\beta_{T+1}$$

In (17), the $\partial C_j/\partial K_{jk}$, nonpositive by (3), are direct effects on j's extraction costs of larger capital stocks; $\Psi_j(\partial F_j/\partial K_{jkt})$ is the imputed value of capital by way of relaxing the bound F (see equation (2)). Then the sum is the present value of the stream of benefits to j of an increment in v_{jk} in t, discounted by a capital survival factor $(1-\partial D/\partial K)$. The last term in (17) may be viewed as the marginal value of current investment in terms of terminal capital stocks, which in most applications will be zero. Equation (17) may thus be interpreted as the present value of the future stream of direct benefits (the marginal productivity) from an increment in investment during t.

The second term in (16) measures external impacts of an increment in j's investment in t. Thus $\lambda\beta_T$ is the marginal scarcity value of recoverable stocks, and $\partial X/\partial v_{jkt}$ is the impact on such stocks of an increment in j's investment in capital-type k in t. The third term measures for all firms, the above impact (pressure maintenance) vis-à-vis the upper bound F. The fourth and fifth terms measure, for firm j and all other firms, the marginal impact of investment in capital-type k with reference to pressure maintenance and therefore, operating (variable) costs, for all periods $\tau \geqq t$.

The rule (16) then has the interpretation: equate the marginal cost of investment (to firm j for capital-type k) with the marginal present value of the reservoir-wide benefits associated with such investment, where the latter includes not only direct impacts on the marginal productivity of j's capital and j's future variable and boundary costs, but also external impacts on other firms' variable and boundary costs as well as on the recoverable stock.

Of course, for many types of capital (elements of $k=1, \ldots, q$), several elements in (16) will not apply. For investment in pressure maintenance activities, all terms will probably be included. For later investments in, for example, pumping equipment, it may be that only the first term will appear.

With the above characterizations for optimum production and investment rates, attention may now be turned to a brief discussion of the ramifications of such rates for reservoir management policies.

IV. Policy Ramifications

Consider the decision environment for petroleum extraction during the early "rule of capture" period in the United States (see McKie and McDonald, p. 98). Under such highly competitive production conditions (for a single reservoir), each firm is concerned only with the cost-benefit items directly affecting it. Efforts by a firm j to restrain production and/or to incur investment costs for pressure maintenance, for the purpose of increasing recoverable stocks and lowering future production costs (by maintaining natural drive forces), may be negated by the lack of such restraint on the part of other firms resulting in losses accruing to j. These potential losses imply, among other things, a very high discount rate, which in turn implies relatively low values for those terms in (15) and (16) with values depending on future flows. To clarify the point under discussion, suppose that firm j ignores all externalities. The relevant optimization problem is given in Appendix equations (A12) and (A13). Conditions which correspond to those given in (15) and (16) are as follows:

$$(18)\quad \left(p_t-\frac{\partial C_{jt}}{\partial u_{jt}}\right)-\sum_{k=1}^{q}\Delta_{jk,t+1}\frac{\partial D_{jkt}}{\partial u_{jt}}\beta_{t+1}=\Psi_{jt}$$

and

$$(19)\quad -\frac{\partial C_{jt}}{\partial v_{jkt}}=\Delta_{jk,t+1}\frac{\partial D_{jkt}}{\partial v_{jkt}}\beta_{t+1}$$

$$\text{for some } j=1,\ldots,n;\ 1\leqq t\leqq T$$

Firm j is thus seen to be producing "rationally" at that rate where $u=F$ (see equation (2)), in which case marginal profit (which is essentially the unit price of petroleum under natural drive conditions) less capital consumption costs equals the marginal imputed cost of the upper bound F, which in this case depends solely on K_{jt}. This bound may be relaxed by investment, for example, new wells (which is obviously limited by physical restrictions not included in this model). Production is thus at the maximum rate (F) allowed by producing facilities (wells), and as long as the marginal costs of expanding such facilities are less than the marginal future value of larger future production facilities, such facilities are expanded to their physical limit.

The impact of such production patterns in terms of losses, for example, in recoverable stocks, is self-evident. Central management of the reservoir must increase the present value of the income stream attributable to reservoir production. Such control may take the form of production "rules" based on the rates implied by (15) and (16), or the form of unit-taxes which capture all user cost items on the right-hand sides of (15) and (16).

In terms of taxes, it has been argued that depletion allowances have the effect of increasing not only production, but also investment rates (see for example, Agria, pp. 92–100; Harberger, p. 444; McDonald (1967), p. 280; and Steiner, p. 951, n. 6). Setting aside questions regarding the desirability of such increases, the effects may be demonstrated quite easily by (15) and (16). Let UC denote all user cost elements on the right-hand side of (15), and let MP denote all future productivity effects of investment v_{jkt} on the right-hand side of (16), excluding in both cases, the terms involving $\lambda\beta_T$. Solving (16) for $\lambda\beta_T$ and substituting into (15), results in the following expression:

$$(15') \quad \frac{\left(p_t - \frac{\partial C_{jt}}{\partial u_{jt}}\right)\beta_t - UC}{\left(1 - \frac{\partial X}{\partial u_{jt}}\right)} = \frac{\frac{\partial C_{jt}}{\partial v_{jkt}}\beta_t - MP}{\frac{\partial X}{\partial v_{jkt}}}$$

If $(p_t - \partial C_{jt}/\partial u_{jt})$ is viewed as "after-tax" marginal profits, equality holds in (15′) for some value $\bar{u}_{jt}$ and $\bar{v}_{jkt}$. A depletion allowance increases the value of marginal profits at $\bar{u}_{jt}$, in which case inequality results in (15′). By Appendix equation (A2), this inequality implies an increase in u_{jt} to some value $\bar{\bar{u}}_{jt} \geq \bar{u}_{jt}$. As u_{jt} rises, elements in the MP term may rise, in which case inequality would hold in (16), and by Appendix equation (A3), equality would be restored only by an increase in v_{jkt} to some value $\bar{\bar{v}}_{jkt} \geq \bar{v}_{jkt}$. Thus, depletion allowances may indeed result in increases in production and investment rates (for some capital items k). This analysis suggests that tax provisions which tend to increase marginal after-tax profits (for example, the unit of production method of depreciating tangible exploration and development costs) may lead to a similar result (see McDonald (1967), p. 279). However, policies which tend to reduce marginal after-tax profits (for example, the imposition of a severance tax) may be expected to reduce production and investment rates (see Agria, pp. 101–04).

The results from this work may be compared with those from earlier works as follows. The present model extends the work of McKie and McDonald by (a) allowing many firms to produce from a reservoir; (b) allowing optimal production and investment rates to vary over the economic life of the reservoir; (c) allowing investment in artificial lift, pressure maintenance and secondary recovery methods; and (d) offering characterizations of both the optimal path of production (15), and the optimal path of investment (16), which include explicit statements of user costs.

The model presented in this work allows the analytical development of arguments suggested in the works of both Davidson and McDonald (1971).[7] In addition, the work of Davidson is extended by allowing variation in production and investment rates over time.

[7] Davidson defines three kinds of user costs associated with oil recovery. The first is the user cost associated with all raw materials; i.e., "the more used today, *ceteris paribus*, the less will be available tomorrow" (p. 91). Using the notation of the present paper, this user cost is simply $\lambda\beta_T$ of (15). Davidson's second user cost is associated with rate sensitivity of oil reservoirs, which is captured in (15) by $-\lambda\beta_T(\partial X/\partial u_{jt})$ and by the next to the last term in the right-hand side of (15). Finally, Davidson observes that if a reservoir is controlled by more than one firm, a "cost of the rule of capture" will be incurred (p. 94), which in the present model is essentially measured by the last term in the right-hand side of (15). McDonald (1971, p. 84) states a marginal condition for the optimum rate of unrestrained production by a firm, and identifies terms in his equation as marginal user costs (pp. 98 and 99). These user costs correspond to those defined by Davidson.

Smith discusses crude oil production within the context of a general model which attempts to provide "... a unified theory of production from natural resources" (p. 409). The present work extends that of Smith by providing simultaneously determined characterizations of the optimal paths of production and investment, and by allowing both the path dependence of ultimate recovery, and the use of artificial lift and pressure maintenance.[8]

Kuller presents an optimal control model of oil production for a firm. This analysis is extended in the present model by the explicit treatment of investment.

V. Final Observations

In the above sections an attempt has been made to provide a model for petroleum reservoir management based, as closely as possible, upon a characterization of variables which allows empirical applications using (for physical relations) the current estimation techniques of petroleum engineers. The following two observations are made in conclusion.

First, various writers have been concerned with the problem of determining optimal expenditures for exploration in the petroleum industry (see for example, Orris Herfindahl, pp. 133–38; and McDonald (1971), pp. 86–91). While such a topic is beyond the scope of this paper, some possible extensions of this work may be suggested which might provide interesting insights concerning exploration.

Applying the model developed above in Section II to N reservoirs, an estimate of the nation's (optimally determined) petroleum stock χ_t could be derived for any time t, where

$$\chi_t = \sum_{n=1}^{N} X_n(U_n, V_n) \tag{20}$$

The X_n's are the endogenously determined stocks for each reservoir $n=1, \ldots, N$ as defined above in (9). Let E_t be expenditures for exploration in t, and $\Gamma(E_t)$ be the expected value of oil reserves discovered as a result of exploration expenditures E_t. If, for the simplest of examples, national benefits from petroleum production are viewed as the simple sum of net incomes from each reservoir—i.e., the sum of equation (10) over N reservoirs—the appropriate criterion function will include the term $-E_t\beta_t$, and the national stock (ignoring exports and imports) will be expressed by

$$\chi_t = \sum_{n=1}^{N} X_n(U_n, V_n) + \Gamma(E_t) \tag{21}$$

Differentiating such a model with respect to E_t, if E_t is nonzero, a term of the following form appears:

$$\beta_t = \Lambda\theta_t \frac{\partial\Gamma}{\partial E_t} \tag{22}$$

In (22), Λ is the marginal scarcity value of the nation's known petroleum reserves (again, optimally determined, see the above development of λ for the individual reservoir); $\partial\Gamma/\partial E_t$ is the expected increase in known reserves from an increment in E. The term β_t, of course, is the present value of a one dollar marginal expenditure for exploration. Optimum expenditures for exploration are thus the level at which marginal costs of exploration expenditures equal the present value of the expected increase in reserves resulting from the marginal expenditure.

This result is intuitively obvious on a priori grounds; not immediately obvious is a method by which the present value of expected stock-increases might be esti-

[8] The Smith model considers production solely by natural drive. However, a method for including artificial lift and pressure maintenance in the analysis is suggested (p. 414, n. 6). The possible rate dependence of ultimate recovery is recognized, although not incorporated in the model.

mated. Two recent works relate to this problem, however. Maurice Allais has suggested a method for providing a "... reasonable forecast of the economic prospects of mining exploration ..." (p. 285).[9] More recently, Russell Uhler and Paul Bradley suggest a model which may be used for "... determining the economic prospects of petroleum exploration ..." (p. 623).

Second, in the discussions above, reference has been made to the problem of choosing T, the planning horizon, and some comments are required. In terms of analytical "neatness," this problem is discussed in some detail in other works (see for example, Burt and Cummings, Appendix). In most empirical applications, a convergence of optimal policies to some fixed path u^* is generally expected (see R. Bellman and Burt). If, for whatever reason, recursive techniques are not used, it will generally be necessary to run a sensitivity analysis on an arbitrarily chosen T, and to continue with increasingly larger values of T until the impact of changes in T, vis-à-vis the resulting solution, is sufficiently small to be regarded as "negligible."

Appendix

The optimization problem expressed above by equations (10) through (14) may be treated within the framework of Kuhn-Tucker theory (see G. Hadley, pp. 188, 192, 193). Assuming that the functions in (10) through (13) are continuous, and possess first partial derivatives with respect to each argument, the following Lagrangian expression may be formed, where the Lagrangian multipliers are explicitly discounted for the purpose of economic interpretation.

$$\text{(A1)}\quad L = \sum_{t=1}^{T}\sum_{j=1}^{n}\{p_t u_{jt} - C_{jt}(U_t, V_t, K_{jt})\}\beta_t$$

$$- \sum_{j=1}^{n}\sum_{k=1}^{q}\Delta_{jk,t+1}\beta_{t+1}\{K_{jk,t+1} - K_{jkt} + D_{jkt}(u_{jt}, v_{jkt}, K_{jkt})\}$$

$$- \sum_{j=1}^{n}\Psi_{jt}\beta_t\{u_{jt} - F_{jt}(U_t, V_t, K_{jt})\}$$

$$- \lambda\beta_T\left\{\sum_{\tau=1}^{T}\sum_{j=1}^{n}u_{j\tau} - X(U_T, V_T)\right\}$$

$$+ \sum_{j=1}^{n}\xi_{jt}\beta_t u_{jt} + \sum_{j=1}^{n}\sum_{k=1}^{q}\sigma_{jkt}\beta_t v_{jkt}$$

Necessary and sufficient conditions for a maximum in (A1) include the following (given in Hadley, pp. 192–93):

$$\text{(A2)}\quad \frac{\partial L}{\partial u_{jt}} = \left(p_t\beta_t - \sum_{\tau=t}^{T}\sum_{i=1}^{n}\frac{\partial C_{i\tau}}{\partial u_{jt}}\beta_\tau\right) - \sum_{k=1}^{q}\Delta_{jk,t+1}\beta_{t+1}\frac{\partial D_{jkt}}{\partial u_{jt}} - \Psi_{jt}\beta_t + \sum_{\tau=t}^{T}\sum_{i=1}^{n}\Psi_{i\tau}\beta_\tau\frac{\partial F_{i\tau}}{\partial u_{jt}} - \lambda\beta_T\left(1 - \frac{\partial X}{\partial u_{jt}}\right) + \xi_{jt}\beta_t \leqq 0$$

$$\text{(A2}'\text{)}\quad \left(\frac{\partial L}{\partial u_{jt}}\right)u_{jt} = 0$$

$$j = 1, \ldots, n;\ t = 1, \ldots, T$$

$$\text{(A3)}\quad \frac{\partial L}{\partial v_{jkt}} = \left(-\frac{\partial C_{jt}}{\partial v_{jkt}}\beta_t - \sum_{\substack{i=1\\ i\neq j}}^{n}\frac{\partial C_{it}}{\partial v_{jkt}}\beta_t - \sum_{\tau=t+1}^{T}\sum_{i=1}^{n}\frac{\partial C_{i\tau}}{\partial v_{jkt}}\beta_\tau\right) - \Delta_{jk,t+1}\beta_{t+1}\frac{\partial D_{jkt}}{\partial v_{jkt}} + \sum_{\tau=t}^{T}\sum_{i=1}^{n}\Psi_{i\tau}\beta_\tau\frac{\partial F_{i\tau}}{\partial v_{jkt}} + \lambda\beta_T\frac{\partial X}{\partial v_{jkt}} + \sigma_{jkt}\beta_t \leqq 0$$

$$\text{(A3}'\text{)}\quad \left(\frac{\partial L}{\partial v_{jkt}}\right)v_{jkt} = 0$$

[9] Although fuels are not included in Allais' study, he asserts that his method is applicable to the search for coal and oil.

$j = 1, \ldots, n; k = 1, \ldots, q; t = 1, \ldots, T$

$$\text{(A4)} \quad \frac{\partial L}{\partial K_{jkt}} = -\frac{\partial C_{jt}}{\partial K_{jkt}}\beta_t - \Delta_{jkt}\beta_t + \Delta_{jk,t+1}\beta_{t+1}\left(1 - \frac{\partial D_{jkt}}{\partial K_{jkt}}\right) + \Psi_{jt}\beta_t\frac{\partial F_{jt}}{\partial K_{jkt}} \leqq 0$$

$$\text{(A4')} \quad \left(\frac{\partial L}{\partial K_{jkt}}\right)K_{jkt} = 0$$

$j = 1, \ldots, n; k = 1, \ldots, q; t = 1, \ldots, T$

$$\text{(A5)} \quad \frac{\partial L}{\partial \Delta_{jk,t+1}} = -\left\{K_{jk,t+1} - K_{jkt} + D_{jkt}(u_{jt}, v_{jkt}, K_{jkt})\right\} \geqq 0$$

$$\text{(A5')} \quad \left(\frac{\partial L}{\partial \Delta_{jk,t+1}}\right)\Delta_{jk,t+1} = 0, \qquad \Delta_{jk,t+1} \gtreqless 0$$

$j = 1, \ldots, n; k = 1, \ldots, q; t = 1, \ldots, T$

$$\text{(A6)} \quad \frac{\partial L}{\partial \Psi_{jt}} = -\left\{u_{jt} - F_{jt}(U_t, V_t, K_{jt})\right\} \geqq 0$$

$$\text{(A6')} \quad \left(\frac{\partial L}{\partial \Psi_{jt}}\right)\Psi_{jt} = 0, \qquad \Psi_{jt} \geqq 0$$

$j = 1, \ldots, n; t = 1, \ldots, T$

$$\text{(A7)} \quad \frac{\partial L}{\partial \lambda} = -\left\{\sum_{\tau=1}^{T}\sum_{j=1}^{n} u_{j\tau} - X(U_T, V_T)\right\} \geqq 0$$

$$\text{(A7')} \quad \left(\frac{\partial L}{\partial \lambda}\right)\lambda = 0, \qquad \lambda \geqq 0$$

$$\text{(A8)} \quad u_{jt} \geqq 0, \qquad u_{jt}\xi_{jt} = 0, \qquad \xi_{jt} \geqq 0,$$

$j = 1, \ldots, n; t = 1, \ldots, T$

$$\text{(A9)} \quad v_{jkt} \geqq 0, \qquad v_{jkt}\sigma_{jkt} = 0, \qquad \sigma_{jkt} \geqq 0,$$

$j = 1, \ldots, n; k = 1, \ldots, q; t = 1, \ldots, T$

Let capital stocks K_{jkt} be positive for all t, $1 \leqq t \leqq t^*$, $t^* \leqq T$. From (A4′) it follows that:

$$\text{(A10)} \quad \Delta_{jkt}\beta_t = -\frac{\partial C_{jt}}{\partial K_{jkt}}\beta_t + \Psi_{jt}\beta_t\frac{\partial F_{jt}}{\partial K_{jkt}} + \left(1 - \frac{\partial D_{jkt}}{\partial K_{jkt}}\right)\Delta_{jk,t+1}\beta_{t+1},$$

for all t, $1 \leqq t \leqq t^*$

Solving (A10) for $\Delta_{jk,t+1}$, then $\Delta_{jk,t+2}, \ldots, \Delta_{jkt^*}$, and substituting these terms into (A10) results in the following expression:[10]

$$\text{(A11)} \quad \Delta_{jkt}\beta_t = \sum_{\tau=t}^{t^*}\left(-\frac{\partial C_{j\tau}}{\partial K_{jk\tau}} + \Psi_{j\tau}\frac{\partial F_{j\tau}}{\partial K_{jk\tau}}\right)\beta_\tau \prod_{s=t}^{\tau-1}\left(1 - \frac{\partial D_{jks}}{\partial K_{jks}}\right) + \prod_{s=t}^{t^*}\left(1 - \frac{\partial D_{jks}}{\partial K_{jks}}\right)\Delta_{jk,t^*+1}\beta_{t^*+1}$$

It is useful for discussions in the text to note that Δ_{jkt} is positive, given[11] $\partial C_j/\partial K_{jk} \leqq 0$, by (3); $\Psi_j \geqq 0$, by (A6′), and $\partial F_j/\partial K_{jk} \geqq 0$, by (2).

For the case where firm j ignores all externalities, discussed in the text, the relevant optimization problem is that of maximizing:

$$\text{(A12)} \quad \text{Max} \sum_{t=1}^{T}\left\{p_t u_{jt} - C_{jt}(u_{jt}, v_{jt}, K_{jt})\right\}\beta_t$$

subject to:

$$\text{(A13)} \quad K_{jk,t+1} = K_{jkt} - D_{jkt}(u_{jt}, v_{jkt}, K_{jkt}), \quad u_{jt} \leqq F_{jt}(K_{jt}), \quad u_{jt} \geqq 0$$

[10] In (A11) let b_s denote $(1 - \partial D_{jks}/\partial K_{jks})$, then

$$\prod_{s=t}^{t-1} b_s \equiv 1$$

$$\prod_{s=t}^{t} b_s = b_t,$$

$$\prod_{s=t}^{t+1} b_s = b_t b_{t+1}, \text{ etc.}$$

[11] A possible exception would arise with $\partial D/\partial K > 1$, a circumstance which would be expected only in a most pathological case.

REFERENCES

R. G. Agarwal, R. Al-Hussainy, and H. J. Ramey, "The Importance of Water Influx in Gas Reservoirs," *Transactions*, AIME, Nov. 1965, *234*, 1336–42.

S. R. Agria, "Special Tax Treatment of Mineral Industries," in A. C. Harberger and M. J. Bailey, eds., *The Taxation of Income from Capital,* Washington 1969.

M. Allais, "Method of Appraising Economic Prospects of Mining Exploration Over Large Territories," *Management Sci.,* July 1957, *3,* 285–345.

A. Baca, *Prediction of the Performance of a Solution Gas Drive Reservoir by Muskat's Equation,* Computer Contribution 8, State Geological Survey, Univ. Kansas, Lawrence 1967.

R. E. Bellman, *Dynamic Programming,* Princeton 1957.

O. R. Burt, "The Economics of Conjunctive Use of Ground and Surface Water," *Hilgardia,* 1964, *32,* 31–111.

——— **and R. G. Cummings,** "Production and Investment in Natural Resource Industries," *Amer. Econ. Rev.,* Sept. 1970, *60,* 576–90.

N. J. Clark, "A Review of Reservoir Engineering," *World Oil,* May 1951, Part 1, and June 1951, Part 2.

B. C. Craft and M. F. Hawkins, Jr., *Applied Petroleum Reservoir Engineering,* Englewood Cliffs 1959.

R. G. Cummings, "Some Extensions of the Economic Theory of Exhaustible Resources," *Western Econ. J.,* Sept. 1969, *7,* 201–10.

P. Davidson, "Public Policy Problems of the Domestic Crude Oil Industry," *Amer. Econ. Rev.,* Mar. 1963, *53,* 85–108.

R. L. Gordon, "A Reinterpretation of the Pure Theory of Exhaustion," *J. Polit. Econ.,* June 1967, *75,* 274–86.

J. M. Griffin, "The Process Analysis Alternative to Statistical Cost Functions: An Application to Petroleum Refining," *Amer. Econ. Rev.,* Mar. 1972, *62,* 46–56.

G. Hadley, *Nonlinear and Dynamic Programming,* Reading 1964.

A. C. Harberger, "The Taxation of Mineral Industries," in *Federal Tax Policy for Economic Growth and Stability,* Joint Committee on the Economic Report, 84 Cong., 1st sess., Washington 1955, 439–49.

O. C. Herfindahl, "Some Fundamentals of Mineral Economics," *Land Econ.,* May 1955, *31,* 131–38.

A. E. Kahn, "The Depletion Allowance in the Context of Cartelization," *Amer. Econ. Rev.,* June 1964, *54,* 286–314.

R. G. Kuller, "Optimal Exploitation of Resources: The Case of Petroleum," res. pap. no. 43, Univ. Kansas, Lawrence 1972.

S. L. McDonald, *Petroleum Conservation in the United States: An Economic Analysis,* Baltimore 1971.

———, "Percentage Depletion, Expensing of Intangibles, and Petroleum Conservation," in M. Gaffney, ed., *Extractive Resources and Taxation,* Madison 1967.

J. W. McKie and S. L. McDonald, "Petroleum Conservation in Theory and Practice," *Quart. J. Econ.,* Feb. 1962, *76,* 98–121.

T. E. W. Nind, *Principles of Oil Well Production,* New York 1964.

S. J. Pirson, *Oil Reservoir Engineering,* New York 1958.

J. Quirk and V. Smith, "Dynamic Economic Models of Fishing," in A. Scott, ed., *Proceedings of the H. R. MacMillan Fisheries Economics Symposium,* Vancouver 1969.

A. Scott, "Notes on User Costs," *Econ. J.,* June 1953, *63,* 368–84.

———, "The Theory of the Mine Under Conditions of Certainty," in M. Gaffney, ed., *Extractive Resources and Taxation,* Madison 1967.

V. Smith, "The Economics of Production from Natural Resources," *Amer. Econ. Rev.,* June 1968, *58,* 409–31.

P. O. Steiner, "Percentage Depletion and Resource Allocation," in *Tax Revision Compendium,* House Committee on Ways and Means, 86 Cong., 1st sess., Washington, 1959, *2,* 949–66.

R. S. Uhler and P. G. Bradley, "A Stochastic Model for Determining the Economic Prospects of Petroleum Exploration Over Large Regions," *J. Amer. Statist. Assn.,* June 1970, *65,* 623–30.

L. C. Uren, *Petroleum Production Engineering —Oil Field Exploitation,* New York 1953.

CHAPTER 8

A GENERALIZED WICKSELLIAN CAPITAL MODEL —AN APPLICATION TO FORESTRY—

By HENRY Y. WAN JR.

One of the most popular examples in capital theory is the tree model. Its pedigree can be traced at least to the Part III of von Thunen's *Der Isolierte Staat*,[1] while its modern version[2] is an exact paraphrase of the Wicksellian wine model.[3] In such a "pure aging" process (according to Haavelmo's classification),[4] the Jevons formula[5] can be derived at a single stroke. Perhaps it seems rather paradoxical that while most economists are exploiting the pedagogical simplicity of the tree model, specialists in forestry economics are left without any usable model for operational purposes.

The present study includes: (1) a restatement of the lumbering problem; (2) a brief review of the received model; (3) successive steps of generalization of the classical model and (4) a suggested pragmatical approach for deriving optimal policies.

I. A GENERAL FORMULATION

Let A be the total acreage in question

$a(v,t)$ be the distribution of acreage covered by vintage-v trees at time t.

$b(v,t)$ be the distribution of acreage of vintage-v trees cut at time t.

$f(v,t)$ be the amount of lumber obtainable by cutting one acre of vintage-v trees at time t.

$R[q(v,t)]$ be the revenue obtained at time t if the vintage-distribution of the lumber sold at time t is $q(v,t)=b(v,t)f(v,t)$

L be the amount of labor needed to plant trees over one acre.

$w(t)$ be the wage rate at time t.

$\rho(t)$ be the instantaneous interest rate at time t.

The optimization problem for the lumbering operation can then be formulated in most general terms:

(1) $$\text{Max } Z_o = \int_t \{R[q(v,t)] - wLa(t,t)\} e^{-\int_0^t \rho(\tau)d\tau} dt$$

Subject to:

$$\left.\begin{array}{l} q(v,t) = b(v,t)f(v,t) \\ \int_v^t b(v,t)dt \leq a(v,v) - a(v,t) \\ \int_v a(v,t)dv \leq A \end{array}\right\} \text{for all } v, t$$

$$\begin{array}{ll} a(v,t) = 0 & \text{for all } t < v \\ a(v,t) \geq 0 & \text{for all } t \geq v \\ b(v,t) = 0 & \text{for all } t < v \\ b(v,t) \geq 0 & \text{for all } t \geq v \end{array}$$

(1) shows that the present worth of the operation is to be maximized. All the constraints are self-evident.

Note that $a(v,t)$ and $b(v,t)$ are distributions rather than ordinary functions. They can assume the form of the Dirac operator. Hence it is possible to have $\int_v a(v,0)dv = A$ while $a(v,0) = 0$ for all $v > 0$.

From the mathematical point of view this is a formulation even more general than the functional analysis model of Loüis Court.[6] There are many thorny problems hidden in this model. The very existence of an optimum is not guaranteed, nor are the necessary conditions for optimization easy to enumerate. Further restrictions on R, a, b, f etc. are necessary before one can deduce useful results from such a formulation. However, it is believed that such restrictions should be explicitly introduced so that implicit theorizing can be reduced to the minimum.

II. THE RECEIVED THEORY REVISITED

Cast rigorously as a specialization of the above said general problem, the classical formulation stipulates:

1. No reforestation is contemplated so that $a(v,t) = 0 = b(v,t)$ for $v > 0$
2. No standing timber exists at the initial date. Therefore $a(v,0) = 0$ for all $v < 0$.
3. Lumbering operation is viable in the long run so that $\text{Max } Z_0 \geq 0$.

4. The interest rate is constant over time so that $\rho(t)=r$.

5. The present firm is a price taker, so that $R[q(v,t)]=\int_v p(v,t)q(v,t)dv$ where $p(v,t)$ is the market price for vintage-v timber at time t.

The problem is simplified to the following form:

$$\text{(2)} \qquad \text{Max } Z_1=\int_t p(0,t)b(0,t)f(0,t)e^{-rt}dt-wL\int_t b(0,t)dt$$

subject to:

$$\int_t b(0,t)dt \leq A$$

$$b(0,t)\geq 0 \qquad \text{for all } t$$

The optimality conditions take the form:

1. $b(0,t^*)=A\delta(t-t^*)$ where δ is the Dirac operator
2. $p(0,t^*)f(0,t^*)e^{-rt*}\geq p(0,t)f(0,t)e^{-rt}$, for all $t\geq 0$

The first condition implies that: (a) all the acreage will be planted with trees, and (b) all trees are to be cut at a given age t^*. The second condition implies that the discounted revenue for an acre of age t^* trees should be no less than the same of age t trees for all admissible values of t. The necessity of both conditions can be directly verified. It should be noted that, in general, t^* need not be unique. If so, condition 1 should be modified accordingly.

Setting $F(t)=p(0.t)f(0,t)$ and assuming its differentiability, one can derive from condition 2, the Jevons formula:

$$\frac{dF}{dt}\Big/F=r$$

by differentiation.

It turns out that lumber of and only of age-t^* will be produced by the firm.

Note that from the distribution point of view, the classical theory represents a "boundary" solution or "corner" solution. It is precisely because of this simple but important case, one has to formulate the problem in such general terms in section I.

III. SIMPLE EXTENSIONS OF THE RECEIVED MODEL

In this section, the assumptions 1–4 of last section will be relaxed.

(1) Suppose the firm decides to reforest its land immediately after the falling of the timber, and also suppose the price for lumber of a given age stays the same over the indefinite future, i, e., $p(v,t)=p(t-v)$ then the maximand will will take the form:

$$\text{Max } Z_2 = \int_t \Big[\int_v p(t-v) b(v,t) f(v,t) dv - w\text{L}a(t,t) \Big] e^{-rt} dt$$

The side conditions remain the same as in (1).

It can be deduced that the optimality conditions take the form:

1. $b(v,t) = \begin{cases} 0 & \text{for } v \neq kt^* \quad k \text{ is any non-negative integer.} \\ \text{A}\delta(t-v-t^*) & \text{for } v = kt^* \end{cases}$

2. $\dfrac{-w\text{L}+p(t^*)f(t^*)e^{-rt^*}}{1-e^{-rt^*}} \geqq \dfrac{-w\text{L}+p(t)f(t)e^{-rt}}{1-e^{-rt}}$ for all admissible t

The first condition again stipulates that all land should be planted with trees according to a t^*-period reforestation cycle. The second condition implies that a reforestation cycle of t^* periods should give rise to a present worth not lower than any other alternative reforestation period. Again t^* may not be unique.

Several observationscan be noted here:

1. As in the last section, the price-taker postulate leads to the result: *Although under an optimal strategy, alternative but equally-profitable tree lives may co-exist side by side, one can always achieve optimality by concentrating on one economic life.*
2. The optimal tree life is constant over time. This property can be derived from the recursive functional equation.

   $$\text{Max } Z_2 = \underset{t}{\text{Max}} \{-w\text{L}+e^{-rt}[\text{P}(t)f(t)+(\text{Max } Z_2)]\}$$

Since the imbedded second stage problem (Max Z_2) is identical to the original problem, the optimal initial tree life for the latter problem should also be optimal for the former problem. But then the optimal life of the secend generation trees need not differ from that of the first generation ones. By iteratively applying such reasoning, the above property is proved.

3. As in the case of machinery noted by Preineich,[8] the optimal life for an investment chain is not shorter than that for a simple-account investment. A differential calculus rendition of the second optimality condition yields a modified Jevons formula:

$$\frac{F'}{F+(Fe^{-rt*}-wL)/(1-e^{-rt*})}=r$$

or
$$\frac{F'}{F}=r\left[1+\frac{e^{-rt*}-\frac{wL}{F}}{1-e^{-rt*}}\right]$$

The first version shows that in computing the own rate of interest, capitalized future profit $\left[\frac{Fe^{-rt*}-wL}{1-e^{-rt*}}\right]$ should also be added to the investment value. The second version implies that the initial proportional growth rate of tree value should be set at a level usually higher than the interest rate. The second order condition for maximization implies that a shorter economic life will usually be chosen. Of course under the classical assumption of free entry—hence zero profit— (i. e. $Fe^{-rt*}=wL$) whether there is reforestation or not does not make any difference.

(2) It turns out that the initial age distribution of trees presents little complication. Let t^* be the optimal life for trees (both in the case of reforestation and no reforestation), and $a(v,0)$ be the initial age distribution, the optimal condition can be modified to:

$$\begin{cases}\text{For } v<-t^* & \text{set } b(v,t)=a(v,0)\,\delta(0)\\ \text{For } v\geq -t^* & \text{set } b(v,t)=a(v,0)\,\delta(t^*-v)\end{cases}$$

In other words, for trees which have passed their optimal lives, immediate cutting is desirable. Otherwise, wait until the normal optimal period arrives.

(3) In case that no $t^*\geq 0$ can be found such that $Fe^{-rt*}\geq wL$, then shut down will be the best possible solution.

(4) A variable interest rate can be easily handled in the no-reforestation case. In the second optimality condition for problem (2) in section II, one can simply substitute the factor $e^{-\int_0^t \rho(\tau)d\tau}$ for e^{-rt}. The most important effect is that the optimal life of trees will no longer be constant

over time. In that case, little can be said without further specifications of the estimated form of $\rho(t)$ over time.

IV. AN ADDITIVE, NEGATIVELY-SLOPED DEMAND WITHOUT REFORESTATION

A really significant modification of the classical model occurs when the fifth assumption (price-taker) in section II is relaxed. To make the problem solvable, it is tentatively assumed that the demand for vintage-v lumber at time t is independent of the demand for lumber of other vintages and at other points in time.

Taking up the no reforestation case first, one can formulate the problem as:

$$\text{(4)} \quad \text{Max } Z_3 = \int_t R[b(0,t)f(0,t);\, t]e^{-rt}dt - wL\int_t b(0,t)\,dt$$

Subject to:

$$\int_t b(0,t)\,dt \leq A$$

and $b(0,t) \geq 0$

where R is a one-parameter family of ordinary functions, with t as the parameter and $R' > 0 > R''$.

It is not certain that problem (4) admits an optimum solution. For instance, the value of lumber may increase so fast over time that postponement of tree cutting is always profitable. Assuming that an optimal policy does exist, one may attempt to characterize it by means of the Lagrangian form:

$$\int_t R[b(0,t)f(0,t);\, t]e^{-rt}dt - wL\int_t b(0,t)\,dt + \lambda[A - \int_t b(0,t)\,dt]$$

with $b(0,t) \geq 0, \quad \lambda \geq 0 \qquad A \geq \int_t b(0,t)\,dt$

A pair of necessary conditions for optimization can be stated as:

$b(0,t)\{f(0,t)R'e^{-rt} - wL - \lambda\} = 0$ for all $t \geq 0$ also $f(0,t)\ R'e^{-rt} \geq wL + \lambda$

and $\quad \lambda\{A - \int_t b(0,t)\,dt\} = 0$

These Kuhn-Tucker conditions of complementary slackness[9] can also be written as:

1. $b(0,t)>0$ implies $f(0,t)R'e^{-rt}-wL-\lambda=0$
2. $f(0,t)R'e^{-rt}-(wL+\lambda)<0$ implies $b(0,t)=0$
3. $\lambda>0$ implies $A-\int_t b(0,t)dt=0$
4. $A-\int_t b(0,t)dt>0$ implies $\lambda=0$

Identifying λ as the imputed rent one has the following economic interpretations:

1. If some trees are cut at age t, the discounted marginal revenue over current cost for trees of that age must equal to the imputed rent.
2. If the discounted marginal revenue is less than the sum of current cost for trees of age t and the imputed rent, then trees should never be cut at that age.
3. If the inputed rent is positive, all available land should be fully utilized.
4. If there is unutilized land even under the optimal policy, then the imputed rent must be zero.

This is in sharp contrast with the received theory where the optimizing firm need not cut trees at two different ages. Here optimality usually demands that trees be cut according to an optimal spectrum of age distribution.

If one so chooses one can carry out a logarithmic differentiation for the condition, $f(0,t)R'e^{-rt}-(wL+\lambda)=0$, thus,

$$\left\{\frac{d}{dt}[fR']\right\}\Big/fR'=r$$

However, since R′ is a function of not only t but also $q(0,t)$, the formal resemblance the above equation bears to the Jevons Formula is perhaps more misleading than illuminating.

After replacing the classical first order conditions with the more general complementary slackness conditions, one may carry out a comparative static analysis. The derivation of such conclusions become less mechanical and more ad hoc. Nonetheless as it will be shown in the following, with some algebraic manipulation, one can still deduce those results parallel to what exist in the Wicksellian theory.

With both the imputed rent, λ, and the total forest acreage $\int_t b(0,t)dt$, positive, then:

1. The variation of total available acreage will be negatively associated with the variation of λ and semi-positively associated with that of $b(0,t)$

   Proof.

   For given values of r and t if $\lambda^0 < \lambda^1$ then

   $$R'[fb^0;t] = \frac{wL+\lambda^0}{fe^{-rt}} < \frac{wL+\lambda^1}{fe^{-rt}} = R'[fb^1;t] \text{ for all } t \text{ where } b(0,t) \geq 0$$

   Since $R'' < 0$, this implies
   $b^0(0,t) \geq b^1(0,t)$ for all $t \geq 0$
   If $\lambda^0 = \lambda^1$, one can similarly deduce that
   $b^0(0,t) = b^1(0,t)$
   Hence if
   $\int_t b^0(0,t)dt = A^0 < A^1 = \int_t b^1(0,t)dt$
   one must have

   $$\lambda^0 > \lambda^1$$

   This must imply that:
   $b^0(0,t) \leq b^1(0,t)$ for all $t \geq 0$
   $b^0(0,t) < b^1(0,t)$ for some $t \geq 0$

   Q. E. D.

2. The variation of interest rate r is negatively associated with that of the imputed rent λ. It is positively (negatively) associated with the variation of $b(0,t)$ for all $b(0,t) > 0$ and $t < \bar{t}$ $(t > \bar{t})$ for some $\bar{t} > 0$

   Proof. If $r^0 < r^1$ and $\lambda^0 \leq \lambda^1$ then
   $R'[fb^0;t] < R'[fb^1;t]$ for all t where $b^0(0,t) \geq 0$
   Hence $(b^1 - b^0)$ is semi-negative. This contradicts the fact that

   $$\int_t b^0(0,t)dt = A = \int_t b^1(0,t)dt$$

Therefore $r^0 < r^1$ implies $\lambda^0 > \lambda^1$

Consider two points in time, t_1 and t_2, $t_1 < t_2$ with $b^0(0, t_1) > 0$, $b^0(0, t_2) > 0$, $b^1(0, t_1) > 0$, $b^1(0, t_2) > 0$

$$\frac{f(t_2)\mathrm{R}'[fb^0;\, t_2]}{f(t_1)\mathrm{R}'[fb^0;\, t_1]} = e^{r^0(t_2-t_1)} < e^{r^1(t_2-t_1)} = \frac{f(t_2)\mathrm{R}'[fb^1;\, t_2]}{f(t_1)\mathrm{R}'[fb^1;\, t_1]}$$

Hence

$$\frac{\mathrm{R}'[fb^0;\, t_2]}{\mathrm{R}'[fb^1;\, t_2]} < \frac{\mathrm{R}'[fb^0;\, t_1]}{\mathrm{R}'[fb^1;\, t_1]}$$

since $\mathrm{R}'' < 0$, if $b^0(0, \bar{t}) \geq b^1(0, \bar{t})$, $\mathrm{R}'[fb^0;\, \bar{t}] \leq \mathrm{R}'[fb^1, \bar{t}]$. Thus,

$$\frac{\mathrm{R}'[fb^0; t]}{\mathrm{R}'[fb^1; t]} < \frac{\mathrm{R}'[fb^0; \bar{t}]}{\mathrm{R}'[fb^1; \bar{t}]} \leq 1 \text{ for all } t > \bar{t} \text{ and } b^1(0, t) > 0$$

Hence,

$b^0(0, t) > b^1(0, t)$ for all such t

Similarly, if $b^0(0, \bar{t}) \leq b^0(0, \bar{t})$, then for all $t < \bar{t}$, and $b^0(0, t) > 0$, $b^0(0, t) < b^1(0, t)$. Moreover, unless $b^0(0, t) = \mathrm{A}\delta(t - \bar{t}) = b^1(0, t)$ there must be t_1 and t_2, $t_1 < t_2$ such that $b^0(0, t_1) > b^1(0, t_1)$ and $b^0(0, t_2) < b^1(0, t_2)$. Otherwise, it can be shown that the relation $\int_t b^0(0, t)\,dt = \mathrm{A} = \int_t b^1(0, t)\,dt$ will be contradicted. $\bar{t}$ can be chosen as: $\mathrm{Sup}\,\{t \mid b^0(0, t) > b^1(0, t)\}$ where $\bar{t} \leq t_2$. Q. E. D.

3. The variation of the wage rate w (or the labor requirement per acre of tree planting L) is negatively associated with that of the imputed rent. For small variations there will be no effect on $b(0, t)$.

   Proof. From the first equilibrium condition, it is obvious that a small variation of w or L will be exactly absorbed by a compensating variation of λ so that $(w\mathrm{L} + \lambda)$ will remain a constant and nothing else will be affected. Q. E. D.

V. INDEPENDENT, NEGATIVELY SLOPED DEMAND WITH REFORESTATION

Once the reforestation aspect is taken into account, the model in the last section becomes most complicated. Two simplifying assumptions will be introduced here to make the problem more manageable:

1. The revenue function for vintage-v lumber at time t depends only on the age of the tree, $s=t-v$. So does the physical growth of trees.
2. The total acreage will be fully utilized throughout the indefinite future.

Now the problem can be stated as:

$$\text{Max } Z_6=\int_0^{\infty}\left\{\int_v \mathrm{R}[f(t-v)b(v,t)\,;\,(t-v)]dv-w\mathrm{L}\int_u b(t,u)du\right\}e^{-rt}dt$$

Subject to:

$$\int_v b(v,t)dv=\int_u b(t,u)du \qquad \text{for all } t\geqq 0$$

$$\int_{t\geqq 0} b(v,t)dt=a(v,0) \qquad \text{for all } v\leqq 0$$

$$\int_v a(v,0)dv=\mathrm{A}$$

$$a(v,0)\geqq 0 \qquad \text{for all } v$$

$$b(v,t)\geqq 0 \qquad \text{for all } v,t$$

A Lagrangian form can be set up as:

$$\int_0^{\infty}\left\{\int_v \mathrm{R}[f(t-v)b(v,t)\,;\,(t-v)]dv-w\mathrm{L}\int_u b(t,u)du\right\}e^{-rt}dt$$

$$-\int_0^{\infty}\lambda_t\Big[\int_u b(t,u)du-\int_v b(v,t)dv\Big]dt$$

$$-\int_{v\leqq 0}\lambda_v\Big[\int_{t\geqq 0} b(v,t)dt-a(v,0)\Big]dv$$

$$-\lambda_0\Big[\int_v a(v,0)dv-\mathrm{A}\Big]$$

Differentiation with respect to $a(v,0)$, $v\leqq 0$ and $a(v,0)>0$ yields:

$$\lambda_v=\lambda_0 \qquad \text{for } v<0$$

Differentiation with respect to $b(v,t)$, $v\leqq 0\leqq t$ and $b(v,t)>0$ yields:

$$\{f(t-v)\mathrm{R}'[fb;\,(t-v)]\}e^{-rt}+\lambda_t=\lambda_v$$

Differentiation with respect to $b(v,t)$, $t\geqq v\geqq 0$ yields:

$$\{f(t-v)\mathrm{R}'[fb;\,(t-v)]\}e^{-rt}+\lambda_t=\lambda_v+w\mathrm{L}e^{-rv}$$

The economic implication can be summarized as follows:

1. Under the optimal policy, one can derive a system of imputed land values λ_v for all $v \geqq 0$
2. For trees of vintage-v to be cut at time t, it is necessary that the discounted marginal revenue product per acre $\{fR'e^{-rt}\}$ plus the imputed value of vacated land λ_t must equal to either (a) the sum of discounted tree planting cost wLe^{-rv} plus the imputed value of land used at time v, λ_v for $v \geqq 0$ or (b) the imputed value of land at the initial date $t=0$, λ_0, for $v<0$.
3. The system of imputed land value λ_v must be such that at all times the forest acreage is fully utilized.

This completes the description of the equilibrium conditions.
Little can be said, a priori, about λ_v except that:

1. For $b(v,t)>0$ and $t>v>0$, $\lambda_v \geqq \lambda_t$. This follows from the fact that the discounted marginal revenue product of timber land should never fall short of the discounted cost of tree-planting. Hence

$$\lambda_v - \lambda_t = fR'e^{-rt} - wLe^{-rv} \geqq 0$$

2. For all $t>0$, $\lambda_0 \geqq \lambda_t$. This follows from: (i) the discounted marginal revenue product of timber land at time 0 should not be negative, hence $fR'e^{-rt} = \lambda_0 - \lambda_t \geqq 0$ and (ii) result 1, listed above.

VI. REALISM VERSUS FRUITFULNESS

To be completely realistic, the marginal revenue of vintage-v trees at time t cannot be entirely independent of the sales of timber of other vintages and/or at different instants. But without carrying out a further step of generalization, one may take inventory of what has been discussed so far.

The Jevons formula can be used to derive the optimal tree-life with the assistance of a piece of semilog paper. In the no-reforestation case, the generalized model provides qualitative insights through a comparative static analysis. In the reforestation case, however, all that can be conveniently achieved is a pair of equilibrium conditions which contain an undetermined parametric function $\lambda_v, v \geqq 0$. Additional generality is achieved at an increasingly expensive cost of vagueness. Hence it can be safely concluded that further generalizations along the present approach can hardly lead to any useful results.

One alternative is to recast the problem into the dynamic programming form:

$$\text{Max } Z_6 = \sum_{t=0}^{\infty} \delta^t \{R(\beta_t) - wLb_t\}$$

Subject to: $\alpha_t - \beta_t + \varepsilon_{t+1} b_t = \alpha_{t+1}$ for $t=0, 1, \cdots\cdots$

and α_t, β_t are non-negative infinite sequences,

where $\alpha_t = \{a(\underline{v}, t), a(\underline{v}+1, t), \cdots\cdots, a(0, t), a(1, t), \cdots\cdots\}$

$\beta_t = \{b(\underline{v}, t), b(\underline{v}+1, t), \cdots\cdots, b(0, t), b(1, t), \cdots\cdots\}$

$$b_t = \sum_{v=\underline{v}}^{\infty} b(v, t)$$

$\varepsilon_{t+1} = \{0, 0 \cdots\cdots, 1, 0, 0, \cdots\cdots\}$ with the unity placed at the place, $\underline{v}$ is defined as:

$$(-f) \text{ Max} \begin{cases} \text{the age of oldest tree at } t=0 \\ \text{the longest period one can possibly keep} \\ \text{a tree standing} \end{cases}$$

Here α_0 is the initial condition to be given.

Set $\wedge(\alpha)$ = the maximized value of Z_6 subject to the initial condition $\alpha = \alpha_0$ then one can derive the recurrence relation:

$$\wedge(\alpha) = \text{Max}_{\beta} \{\Pi(\beta) + \delta \wedge [E^{-1}(\alpha - \beta) + \varepsilon_0 b]\}$$

where $\Pi(\beta) = R(\beta) - wLb$

and E^{-1} is the forward shift operator.

The relationship between b and β are similar to what is explained before.

The solution of the above functional equation yields the optimal strategy one should follow, since for every initial condition vector α one can associate an immediate action vector, β, which transforms the initial condition vector into another vector. The iteration goes on.

The following remarks can be made:

1. The dynamic programming approach can take account of the inter-variety dependence among the markets for timber of different age. The price for this is one has to be content with a discrete model so far as the output unit is concerned.
2. Through the functional equation, computations for an optimal strategy can be carried out, *in principle*. Qualitative results, however, are harder to obtain along this approach.
3. The computational work involved in such an approach may still be formidable, yet it seems that the combination of suitably devised shortcuts and high-speed computors offers good promise to solve the practical problems of lumbering operations. However, detailed discussions of this nature clearly lies beside the scope of the present study.

REFERENCES

(1) J. H. VON THÜNEN; *Der Isolierte Staat* in *Beziehung auf Landwirtschaft und National ökonomie*, Jena, 1930.

(2) F. LUTZ & V. LUTZ; *The Theory of Investment of the Firm*, Princeton, 1951, pp. 27 ff.

(3) KNUT WICKSELL, *Lectures on Political Economy*, Vol. I, London, 1934.

(4) T. HAAVELMO, *A Study in the Theory of Investment*, Chicago, 1960.

(5) W. S. JEVONS, *The Theory of Political Economy*, Kelley & Millman, New York, 1957.

(6) LOUIS M. COURT, Entrepreneural and Consumer Demand Theories for Commodity Spectra, *Econometrica*, 1941.

(7) R. BELLMAN, *Dynamic Programming*, Princeton, 1957.

(8) G. A. D. PREINREICH, The Economic Life of Industrial Equipment, *Econometrica*, 1941.

(9) H. W. KUHN & A. W. TUCKER, Nonlinear Programming in J. Neyman (ed.), *Proceedings of the 2nd Berkeley Symposium on Mathematical Statistics and Probability*, Berkeley, 1951.

CHAPTER 9

OPTIMAL UTILIZATION AND THE CONTROL OF FISHERIES

ANTHONY SCOTT

1. INTRODUCTION

The outlines preparing the participants in this Round Table were (with respect to this paper) unintentionally ambiguous: one of them ambitiously directed me to consider "further" the optimal allocation of resources between types of fish, fishing grounds, methods of fishing and over time; the other more prudently advised me to hope less to answer problems than to raise new questions. I have gratefully taken refuge in the shelter of the second directive, for while the answering of the problems of allocation of resources does not easily yield to the pressure of concentrated study, it may reveal further problems that complicate the previous methods by which the problem may be considered.

2. ALLOCATION AMONG INDUSTRIES

Professor Scott Gordon was, probably, the first economist to raise within a coherent theoretical framework the allocation problems posed by the fishery as a type of common-property resource.[1] He contrasted the fishery with the more familiar private property industry such as farming. In his paper Professor Gordon first reminded us that the sole-owner of a farm will attempt to maximize the rent on his farm. If the owners of all other fixed resources attempt to do likewise, and if the owners of labour and other variable inputs seek out the best return, they will all achieve in a final static equilibrium, the optimum allocation of factors among the various uses (or fixed resources). This final equilibrium may be

[1]H. Scott Gordon, "The Economic Theory of a Common-Property Resource: The Fishery", *Journal of Political Economy*, April 1954, pp. 124-42. See also Anthony Scott, "The Fishery: The Objectives of Sole Ownership", *Journal of Political Economy*, April 1955, pp. 116-24.

described in a literary way by saying that when it has been achieved, no owner of a factor can better his position by changing the employment of the factor; no resource owner can better his rent by changing the amount of each factor that he employs; and no resource or part of one could produce a higher net return than with the quantity of factors now exploiting it.

The same equilibrium is described more precisely (for labour) by saying that in it, the return to similar units of labour is the same in every employment (labour cannot better itself), that every owner pays for each worker a price equal to its marginal product (he maximizes his rent) and that therefore throughout the economy the marginal product of labour (of uniform quality) is the same.

Professor Scott Gordon has demonstrated that since fishing grounds are not private property, there is no proprietor to limit the employment of labour when the rent on the ground is maximized. Instead of finding a level where the price of labour equals its marginal product, employment finds a higher level where the price equals the average product. On each ground an equilibrium is reached where in comparison with private ownership the total catch is higher, total employment is higher, and rent is lower (possibly zero). In the rest of the economy, if labour is mobile, the marginal product of labour is the same as the average product in fishing.

The first thing to ask is whether this is really a bad thing. What effect has it on the fishery? Professor Scott Gordon answered this question by writing: "This is why fishermen are not wealthy, despite the fact that the fishery resources of the sea are the richest and most indestructible known to man. By and large, the only fisherman who becomes rich is one who makes a lucky catch or one who participates in a fishery that is put under a form of social control that turns the open resource into property rights".[2]

Now this, I feel, is not quite correct. The rice lands of China and South-East Asia are also of fabulous fertility and durability. The peasants who work them are also very poor, and their mobility between occupations and their

[2] loc. cit., p. 132

opportunity costs are low. So far there is no difference between the fishery and the rice farm. The difference arises first when we observe that in such countries high rent incomes are appropriated by the landholding class. Because they hold the land as their own, they are able in effect to act as employers who hire only enough farmers to maximize the rent of land. Hence the fact of private property does not bring wealth to the workers on a rich resource, but only to the rentier, who may be an absentee.

The lowness of the fisherman's income then, is due first to his low opportunity costs, which are low because he is geographically or industrially unadaptable.[3]

Secondly, his poverty relative to the rest of the economy might be argued to be due to the fact that most Western farmers are (unlike the peasants in a rice economy who only earn the equivalent of wages) also the recipients of quasi-rent on their capital goods. But the boat-owner also gets a return on capital as far as the share system will allow it, so it is not the quasi-rent that makes the difference. Fishing analyses include nets and boats in the factor "effort", but (apart from the working of the share system) there is no reason arising from common property why there should not be interest and profit to be made from having the right type of equipment at the right time.

We are left, then, with the conclusion that the low incomes in fishing relative to those in farming arise from the fact that the typical farmer of the Western world receives a return that is a mixture of rent, interest, profit and wage; while the return of the fisherman (a) omits rent - indeed there is none to receive, (b) includes a wage - but this may be lower than the farmers' wage because of immobility (low opportunity cost) and (c) includes some profit and interest - but these too may be low both because the share system gives capital a low return and the immobility of capital may give it a low opportunity cost.

Hence we see that the allocation of resources to the fishery may be too generous for three reasons: the share system, low mobility, and common-property. If the economy is to put the fisherman and the farmer on the same bases, methods must be found for adjusting all three of these matters. Common-property is certainly not a good thing, but neither is

---

[3]See Professor Scott Gordon, op. cit., on this, however, at p. 132.

it the only factor making for poverty. To put it another way, the fisherman is much like the farmer's hired man, who receives only his labour opportunity costs; he is not much like the prosperous farmer who receives rent and profit as well.

In the second place, for the purposes of discussion at least, I am tempted to go farther in this examination of the ill-effects of common-property and to suggest that when one takes the distribution of income into account, the mis-allocation of society's resources that results from having too many fishermen is not, from the rest of society's point of view, a bad thing. The sufferers are the fishermen. This proposition may be examined by asking: If fishermen were employed by proprietors of detached fishing grounds, so that many were displaced and moved eventually to other jobs, would the gain to the *rest* of society be over-balanced by

(a) the higher incomes of the remaining fishermen, *plus*

(b) the higher incomes to be paid to displaced fishermen in their new jobs, *plus*

(c) the probable increase in the price of fish (in the absence of innovation in catching methods)?

I am inclined to think that most of the gain would accrue to those still in fishing. There would still be a gain for the

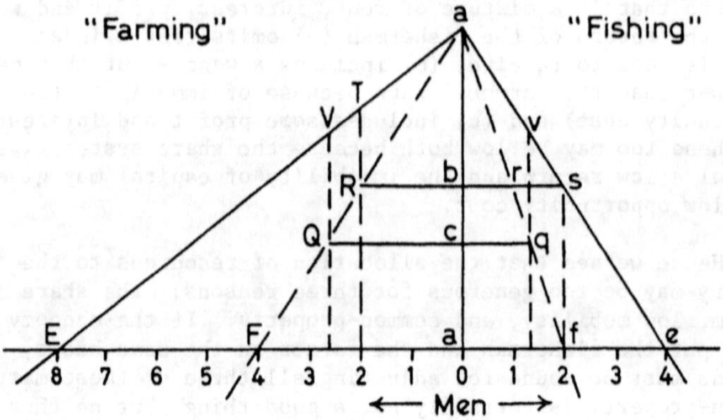

Diagram III.1

rest of the world as long as the "terms of trade" for fish did not rise, but if the price of fish rose a great deal, it is not impossible that the rest of society would long for the good old days when they exploited the fisherman.

Diagram III.1. may illustrate the point. The right-hand side shows the average and marginal productivity curves for "fishing" effort (all fishing in the economy) and the left-hand side shows, with horizontal scale reversed, the average and marginal productivity curves for "farming" (representing the alternative use for fishing labour). Labour is assumed to get the same return in either sector - there is no immobility. We start with four units of labour, applying two in each industry. In fishing we have effort over-applied so that there is no rent and (by accident) zero marginal product. In farming the return to labour is equal to its marginal product. Then farmers will receive rent equal to *aRb*. In the entire economy the wage or price of labour will be equal to *db*.

Now let us assume that the fisheries all become private property. There will be decreased employment there,[4] and since the men are assumed to be mobile, more of the total of four units will have to be employed in farming. First, taken as a unit, the whole economy is better off because the total product (the area under both the marginal curves) is larger. If income were redistributed equally in both situations, everyone would have more. If we examine the actual distribution of gains we see that throughout the economy, with four units and with the return of labour equal in both industries, the equilibrium wage will be equal to *cd*. Wages go down by *bc* and the rent of land and fisheries rise to *aQc* and *aqc* respectively.

To make our point, we must neglect the difference between wages and rent in the new situation and assume that the fishing grounds are communally owned by the fishermen, and that every farmer owns his land. Then the average productivity in each industry tells us how well an average individual in each sector is making out. In farming, inevitably, the farmer is worse off (though the new arrivals in the industry may take the poorer land and the old farmers stay comfortably off). In fishing, the fishermen are better off since the average product has jumped from the level of *s* to *v*. On this basis, fishermen gain and farmers do not

[4]If the fishery was being over-utilized. See below for a fuller statement.

lose much. (If they confined the new recruits to labouring or to marginal land, they would not lose at all.) But on the average the farming world has not reaped the gain of the change. If, in addition, the terms of trade for fish improve so that curve *ae* rises vertically relatively to *aE*, there may be an absolute loss to the farming world.

These outcomes depend upon the elasticity of marginal product - that is upon the position and the slope of the two curves. With different slopes and positions - and with curved functions - a variety of outcomes could be obtained. I have only suggested one, to illustrate my point. This point is that even if political economists and their audiences may accept the point that there is misallocation of labour in the fisheries under common-property resource ownership, the economist must also demonstrate that society has much to gain by remedying the situation. As things develop in the above model, a fisheries tenure reform would benefit fishermen a good deal more than the rest of the world.

3. FOUR FORCES AFFECTING LANDINGS

Our next task (though the last is far from finished) is to review the forces affecting the return from a particular fishery. What is meant, for example, by the assertion that as more effort is applied the average and marginal products fall? Unfortunately, four distinct phenomena may be mixed together here.

(a) *Diminishing returns*. Within a given fishing vessel, the application of more labour time may mean that the most efficient proportion of labour, leisure and capital is passed. The cost per unit of fishing-effort may rise. It may become increasingly difficult to maintain the ship and its equipment; the hold of the ship may be inadequate for the amount caught so that frequent wasteful returns for unloading are required; the crew may become tired and inefficient.

This is the kind of diminishing returns that would be experienced if an inexhaustible fishery, exploited by a single crew, attempted to increase its weekly catch without changing the capital equipment or the techniques employed. It is the same kind of diminishing returns as in the classical law of variable proportions, showing the profitability of keeping some optimum proportion between labour and capital.

Because there are so many fishing vessels and so many men

in each fishery, this kind of diminishing return is rarely to be observed. But it would certainly exist in the short run if the fishery was on a private-property basis, and if a sole-owner attempted to increase his landings.

(b) *External diseconomies*. Beyond the scope of any vessel, but within a fishery, there may be interference with the efficiency of fishing, built up by the number of vessels. Many coastal fisheries afford relatively few good fishing spots, depending as they do upon advantageous reefs, banks, bays, narrows, shallows, flats or rapids. Since such natural advantages for fishing are often scarce, the more vessels there are fishing, the less the efficiency of each vessel. (Against this, however, we must offset the greater efficiency of *finding* fish when there are more vessels out. Indeed, the greater difficulty in *catching* fish when the fish population is low (as opposed to the likelihood of decimating the population) is a diseconomy of scale). The point has nothing to do with fish population. While there may be an inexhaustible stock of fish, there may be a scarcity of locations to fish from. The point has much in common with the external diseconomies found in other resources, such as petroleum, ground water and game. It is also to be found in connection with the use of (common-property) highways where it is properly referred to as "congestion".

In the petroleum industry, quite apart from the question of the limited amount of oil in a pool being drilled for by competing producers, there is a question about the optimum number of wells drilled. More than this optimum will mean that all drillers together have higher costs, without an equal or proportionate gain in the number of barrels pumped. Each new driller deprives his neighbours of the gas pressure that drives oil up to the surface. In the case of water underground, an increase in the number of users means a fall in the water table, so that the pumping costs of all users rise. In the case of wild animals, an increase in the number of hunters may alarm the game, so that the task of each hunter is more difficult. And on highways, increase in the number of vehicles may imply that each moves more expensively. In each case, then, there is no question of the "population" or stock that is available to be used. The stock may be unchanged, or inexhaustible. What changes is not the physical population (or in the case of highways, the amount of highway) but the cost that each user experiences in attempting to capture a portion of the population.

Diseconomies (a) and (b) are not independent. In one

fishery, exploited mainly by small fishermen, there may be little internal diseconomy: a man and his boat can with equal average ease cast twenty or forty lines. Yet another fishery may be dominated by large vessel owners or charterers who themselves experience the losses that their own attempts to increase effort impose upon vessels already in use. Further, both the internal and external economy effects outlined above may be swamped by the effect of local shortages that falsify our assumption that factors are homogeneous by necessitating the use of unsuitable or exhausted labour, obsolete vessels, or worn equipment.

If we are, as in the following pages, interested in the long-run equilibrium of the fishery, most of these internal and external economies cancel out. Only a shortage of natural fishing places, or a permanent local shortage of labour, skill or capital are likely to cause the cost of effort to be other than a linear function of labour input. On the other hand, if we are interested in the short run, all the causes of increasing costs, both internal or external, are likely to be relevant for finding the year-to-year position of the fishery.

(c) *Population*. This point differs from (b) above. Admittedly, it requires considerable refinement of definition to distinguish in economic language the shortage of fishing places from a shortage of fish. If more effort is applied to a fishery, the achievement of that extra effort may be a source of extra expense or inconvenience to every competitor in the fishery. If it is, it is here classified in (b) above. If, in addition, the extra effort may reduce the stock of fish so that the equilibrium catch is permanently reduced, we classify it as a "population" effect (c).

This is something that can only happen to a population or biological resource with its own internal principles of reproduction and survival. With other resources, the population effect occurs only once, not as a permanently available principle of management. A coal resource, for example, may cost more to mine as the shaft is deepened. But since the mine cannot be replenished, little use can be made of the principle by the manager in reaching an "equilibrium". The economy may switch from coal to a substitute, but this is of no comfort to the coal mine operators. A ground water resource, on the other hand, is replenished by nature, so that its managers could decide upon a rate of use which they could maintain indefinitely at a certain cost per gallon. A forest, too, is replaced slowly by nature, so that forest owners can decide upon a rate of cutting that will give them the best combination of timber, cost and timing.

So it is with the fishery. The stock of fish at any time is in process of growing. Its growth (caused by its own reproductive force, which exceeds its natural death rate) would be indefinite if it were not that food shortages, physical habitat limitations and predators slow down the absolute time rate of growth as total population increases; eventually they prevent further growth. If any of these limiting factors increases in intensity, the population is depleted, then begins to grow more vigorously toward its previous size.

One of the "predators" is the fisherman. His efforts can reduce the population to such a low level that fish are literally scarce. If he maintains this effort, the population and the catch will remain small. On the other hand natural predators that depend upon a certain fishery for food will themselves suffer and shrink in numbers if their predacity reduces the fishery to the point of real scarcity. The fish population can then grow back toward a maximum level, though predators may also increase in number, and inhibit the rate of growth. Clearly we must know the ecology of the whole ocean to know how far any population may grow.

Thus *at any level*, there is an absolute time rate of increase in the population. (dP/dT, where P is population and T is time.) If the population is very small, the breeding stock is too small to achieve a large time rate of increase. If it is very large, the force of outside predators, etc., will be so great that the time rate of increase in the stock will not be great. Thus at any level of population there is one rate of catching fish that will keep the population at just that size: the time rate of increase that would exist in the absence of the fishing effort. And the proposition works the other way: if a rate of catching is begun and continued, there is a level to which the population will move which will increase at just the rate required to keep the landings stable indefinitely (*ceteris paribus* in the ecological world).[5]

---

[5]This is my understanding of the idea of "equilibrium catch" implied in Professor Scott Gordon's paper, loc. cit., p. 137, and expounded in greater detail in "Some Aspects of the Dynamics of Populations Important to the Management of the Commercial Marine Fisheries", by Milner B. Schaefer, *Bulletin of the Inter-American Tropical Tuna Commission*, Vol. 1, No.2, La Jolla, California, 1954. Mr. Schaefer has very kindly shown

As our third type of diminishing return, then, we are faced with the opinion that (i) the greater the sustained effort, the smaller will be the population and the smaller the catch that can be permanently produced by that small permanent population. (ii) At the other extreme, the smaller the effort, the greater the population, and the *smaller* again the catch that can be permanently drawn from a population of that large size. (iii) In between, there will be other levels of effort that, if continued indefinitely, would result in intermediate-sized populations that will have natural rates of growth compatible with larger annual catches.

This is shown in a revised version of the diagram which, originally adapted from work by Professor Scott Gordon, I published in the *Journal of Political Economy* in June, 1955. (Diagram III.2.)

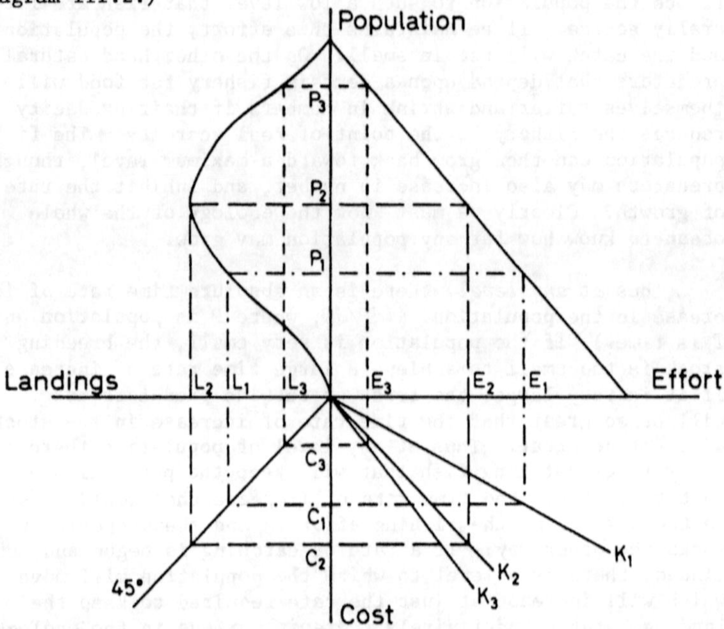

Diagram III.2.

me a further paper on this subject which he will shortly publish. It appears to me that while one need not accept the specific shapes of curves that he suggests, one cannot but be impressed with this way of putting the basic idea that a rate of landings that is in equilibrium with a certain population is the same as the natural time rate of increase of that population in the absence of the fishing effort.

The only change in the structure of this diagram from that previously published is that the population curve has been shown as double-valued with respect to landings. This is the graphic counterpart of the discussion above.

It should be emphasized that this is an equilibrium picture of a competitive fishery. It shows things as they would look if an equilibrium in the economic system coincided with a biological - and ecological - equilibrium.[6] The outcome is partly what one would expect from common sense, but it has a curious characteristic.

As the diagram is drawn, the operative variable is the cost function (K). Conforming to what has become conventional, the function has been drawn as a straight line, but it is possible to relax this assumption considerably without substantially changing the outcome. If the fishery experienced permanent internal or external diseconomies (or economies) of scale, the straight line in the north-east quadrant would be appropriately curved. Diseconomies would cause a curvature concave to the origin. It will be seen that for each line K there is a unique equilibrium for the whole system, given that cost, C, is to equal L, the value of landings. Generally speaking, these solutions conform to intuition: the higher the cost of effort, the less effort is purchased, and the greater the population that therefore survives fishing. This is an economically satisfying situation since a steep cost curve presumably symbolizes a high opportunity cost for fishermen, perhaps reflecting a stronger demand for industrial goods than for fish.

The curious result is that the level of landings does not rise monotonically. Because of the population principle outlined earlier, the low cost curve K_1 is in long-run equilibrium with high effort and low landings ("overfishing"); higher costs K_2 with less effort and more landings ("maximum yield"); and the really high costs of fishing effort of curve K_3 are in equilibrium with very little effort and landings which are less than the maximum. (In the original papers by Professor Scott Gordon and myself, the range from P_2 to origin O was omitted). If one sought the "maximum yield" L_2, as a long run equilibrium of a competitive fishery, it would be necessary to make the effort E_2.

[6]In Mr. Schaefer's article there is a discussion of the route by which the population might approach a given equilibrium level.

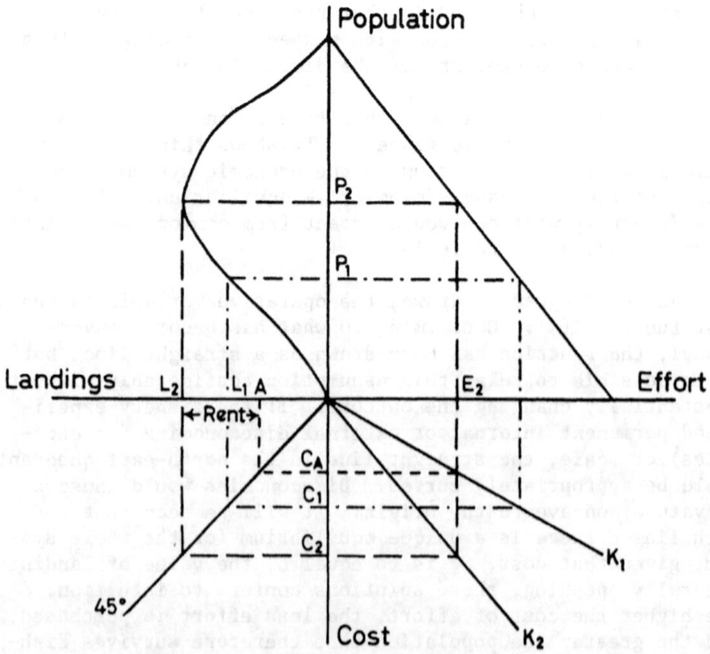

Diagram III.3.

Diagram III.3. presents the same set of curves and the same cost curves. It is now assumed that there is a desire to manage this fishery as a sole-ownership ("monopoly", but not a sole seller of fish). We may imagine either that one proprietor has been given title to the fishery, or else that a communal group or the government is running it to maximize rent as a sole-owner would.

The competitively exploited fishery discussed above had an equilibrium in which total cost is equal to total landings. A sole-ownership on the other hand, is run so that rent is maximized, that is, so that on the diagram there is the greatest difference possible between L and C (both in value terms). Two situations present themselves, distinguished by costs relative to the cost curve that would give maximum landings under pure competition.

(i) If the cost curve is less than K_2 (e.g., K_1), we can say at once that the owner will never hire more effort than E_2. For if he did, his labour bill would increase beyond E_2 but his landings would fall below L_2, and his rent would fall. This solution, with the maximized rent, is shown in diagram III.3.

Would he (with costs less than shown by K_1) hire less effort than E_2? It is unlikely. Only if the decline in his landings (represented by the combined slopes of the two population curves: population-landings function and population effort) was less than the decline in his costs would he find it advantageous to hire effort other than E_2. Apart from this special case, we may conclude that a sole-owner would, when the cost curve is lower than K_2, hire effort equal to the amount that would be used in equilibrium of a competitive fishery when the cost curve is equal to K_2.

(ii) When the cost curve is above K_2, the solution suggested in my original paper stands. It is shown in diagram III.4., (although this diagram cannot demonstrate that the rent *DB* is the maximum rent, which requires either algebra or a very large-scale diagram for its trial-and-error location). It will be seen that in the particular situation covered by the diagram, the sole-owner would find it profitable to reduce his effort purchases. His landings would also fall, but less than his costs.

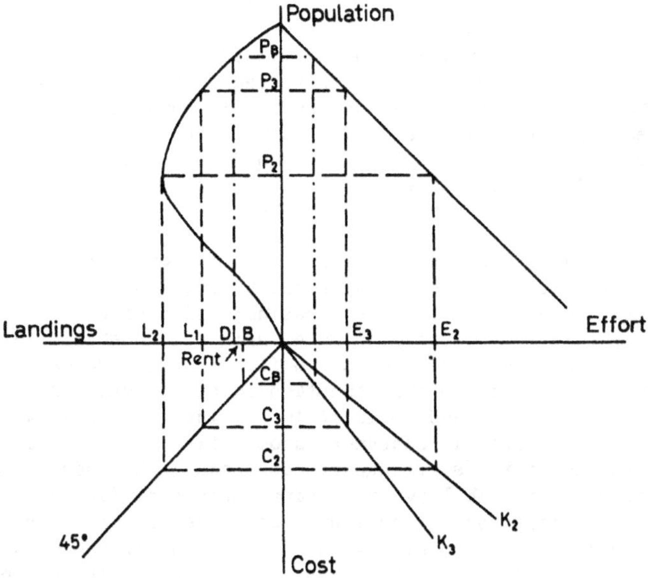

Diagram III.4.

We have here another approach to the original proposition that an increase in effort will dissipate rent. In both situations there is an original situation in which a small number of fishermen earn a rent. In both situations the rent attracts workers from other industries till the effort increases and the population decreases so far that there is no rent. With respect to landings, however, competition gives a smaller catch than sole-ownership would in the first case; but in the second, competition actually gives a higher catch than the rent-maximizing ownership would yield. (Presumably those who prefer the maximum catch to the maximum economic efficiency of the industry should advocate sole-ownership in the first situation, but unrestricted fishing in the second, if the choice of controls is restricted to two methods of management).

There is a good deal more to be said about population (c), the third force operating on landings, than we have discussed above, particularly with respect to methods of control. But to complete the list, let us turn first to the fourth type:

(d) *Allocation over time*. By this phrase I refer to the fact that static equilibrium is not an end in itself. The life span of commercial fish, I am told, runs from perhaps two years for some species up to fifty years for others, and a generation is therefore a long period in human terms. To get a fish population into equilibrium with the economic system may take many fish generations, even if the economic system is otherwise in equilibrium. If it too is growing and changing, equilibrium may be centuries in arriving.

Meantime, demands for labour and fish will alter. The demand for protein, about which the biologists so often warn us, may suddenly become more pressing; fish prices may rise. This is likely to occur much more rapidly than the leisurely equilibrium process can adjust to it. In other words, the wages implicit in the cost function in our diagram are not fixed; and the demand implicit in the landings curve will alter with changes in consumer income, fish sticks' flavour, war, famine, tariffs, transport costs and techniques. What is needed is the ability to operate a fishery with respect to this anticipated alteration in cost and demand. Why work the population toward biological equilibrium if the demand is disappearing? - why not exhaust the stock? (There are undoubtedly some good reasons why not, but a move in that direction may be rational). Why not flood the market with cheap fish, caught by drawing down stocks for a while, so as to change the pattern of demand over the long run? (This would require monopoly, but sole-ownership would help). Why now allow the stock to build up toward the range of maximum landings while labour costs are high and demand low, or at least demand is smaller than it is expected to be later?

In other words, why not encourage disinvestment and investment in the fishery as year-to-year adjustments dictate? The rents described earlier are achievable only through investment or disinvestment in the stock. Such actions will provide an eventual equilibrium. But equilibrium is much less an end than the ability to manage the fishery flexibly: to anticipate yields if planned horizons become foreshortened, and the contrary if expectations are disappointed.

Such actions, which are a part of efficiency of the economy, are impossible unless unified control of each fishery is achieved. The best parallel is seen in the actions of government authorities over oil fields, who cut down the allowable yield of a field when the price falls below what is believed to be "normal". I believe that there is also a suspicion that the Pacific herring control paid more attention to the market for its product than purely biological objectives would require; which is what one would wish it to do, if its forecasting studies are reliable.

4. METHODS OF REGULATION

Though in the outline of the Round Table, I am asked to deal with methods of regulation, I do so with some misgiving, since the practical aspects of such methods are largely unknown to me.

It has been suggested in the discussion so far that the magnitude of internal and external economies or diseconomies in competitive fisheries discussed in (a) and (b) in section 3 are unknown but are suspected of not being large. This may be true, but I suspect that if such fisheries were privately owned they would be rapidly developed with new and perhaps labour-saving techniques. This would certainly occur in the West coast salmon and halibut fisheries. If there are such economies to be earned, it would follow that the method of regulation would be better if it gave an incentive to economise on effort rather than giving an incentive to circumvent quota restrictions, taxes, or subsidies.

To be specific, it might be argued that other fisheries should follow the leadership of those that are now governed by fishing regulations as to time, place or size. Such regulations are from the present point of view less than ideal since they force the competitive members of the industry to build larger ships, buy heavier gear, and spend longer at sea to catch what may after all be only a slightly different amount than would be caught under unrestricted fishing conditions.

On the other hand, such regulations may force the industry under the pressure to catch as many fish as possible during an open season, to adopt better methods or invent new techniques. Such innovations may actually reduce the social cost of bringing in a certain catch. Whatever cost reduction is achieved is likely to be offset by the increasingly shortened season resulting from using better methods to land a catch of predetermined size.

As regards (c) in section 3, the rent of a fishery is likely to be competed away by too much effort applied to a given population. The theoretical optimum population, catch and effort are suggested in the diagrams. How are such optima to be achieved?

In the first place, it should be possible to work with a competitive fishery and move along the effort axis on the diagram so that the optimum-rent solution is reached. I say it should be, because although it is easy to determine the best course of action when all the biological and cost facts are known, the shape of the population-landings curve makes it very difficult to know how far to move.

The general rule appears to be complicated: When the cost curve is K_2, reduce the competitively determined effort till it is just sufficient to bring in the maximum equilibrium catch, that is, to E_2; but when it is above K_2 reduce it rather less (so as to obtain the outcome of diagram III.4.). It would be pleasant to be able to advocate that the amount of effort to be used should always be E_2, but when labour has high opportunity costs relative to this catch, an input of effort such as E_2 would mean expanding the fishery and running it at a social loss.

Assume, however, that the best amount of effort has been determined. How is the input to be reduced? One proposal is a limit on the number of fishermen, or, in order to avoid wasteful expansion of the fleet, on the number of men and ships

In other words, the state might assume a property right of the kind the owner of a toll-road or of a common carrier does, and charge for the "privilege" of fishing. Those who bought a "privilege" would of course attempt, once again, to catch as many fish as possible, and catches per ship would rise. The number of privileged fishermen might have to be further reduced, but eventually a number would be reached which would be the equivalent of a sole-owner's maximum-rent use of effort.

One efficiency-maximizing aspect of this arrangement is that the rent of the fishery would accrue to the fishermen. Those who were the most efficient would be able to offer the most rent, stated either as a percentage share of the catch, or as an absolute sum of money. The less efficient fishermen would be eliminated from the industry. The government would accept the highest bids until the right number of privileges had been granted. In order to keep some incentive going, bidding for privileges would have to be allowed at wide intervals, related to the willingness of men to move into and out of the industry.

A large amount of the rent would be recaptured by the government, in bids for privileges: in perfect competition all the rent would be recaptured. It does not matter here what is done with these funds. At the outset they might be used to resettle displaced and disappointed fishermen, or merely to compensate them, over a given period, for the loss of their traditional livelihood. In later years, and generations, the money could be redistributed among the privileged fishermen, if this procedure would not appreciably change the number that would bid under given circumstances. Or, the state could keep the rent, as landlord. I know of no ethical reason why either of these courses should be preferred, but if it is desired to put fishermen as much as possible in the same position as farmers, the redistribution among the privileged few would be the preferred course. This method would keep the rent of fishing among fishermen, just as the rent of agricultural land is responsible for making many farmers wealthy. Finally, in view of the tremendous scientific complexity of deciding upon the sole-ownership scale of the industry, a good deal of the money would be required for communal purposes such as administration and policing, research, and, not least, paying subsidies for the destruction of predators on the administered fishery.

Police would be necessary to keep the members of other fisheries on their grounds, and to help the research staff keep track of the amount and type of effort being used.

Research would be necessary to revise estimates of the population, the optimum catch, and the optimum effort. Further, if point (d) of the previous section is relevant, it would be useful to keep track of markets and price and cost trends, so that the users of the fishery could invest or disinvest in their stock. Since fisheries are not independent of one another, it would be necessary to determine the best balance between the sizes of adjoining fisheries which prey on one another or compete for the same oceanic environment of food and location. It would be possible to use the price system to decide which of two competing fisheries was to prevail.

It seems to be quite obvious that this solution is a mere variant of the sole-ownership solution in all its stark simplicty.

The sole-owner might be a co-operative association of all the fishermen using the fishery at a certain date, but it is difficult to imagine such a group decisively reducing the amount of effort in a short period. To succeed, it would have to charge a fee for admission to the association, so that many of the problems and features of the government "privilege" organization would appear here as well.

The sole-owner might also be a capitalist in the usual sense, who buys his charter for the whole fishery from the state and runs it as a business thereafter, just as a farmer does who buys land from the state. He would presumably hire the boats on the fishery, rather than chartering them. Indeed, in the limiting case, he would own them and would hire the crews just as a farmer employs hired men. If he was a strong bargainer, the fishermen would, just as now, receive only their opportunity cost, and would not necessarily benefit from the change in arrangement. But if the bargaining power of the fishermen was stronger, they could argue themselves into a position where much of the rent of the fishery accrued to them.

Since in most parts of the world fishermen and ships participate during the year in several fisheries, not confining themselves to a single fish population, the situation would in fact arise where a "privilege" system would find a boat and crew holding privileges in several fisheries at once. A market in such "privileges" might arise as men retired, ships were damaged, or individuals decided upon changing combinations of activity throughout the year. If there were no need periodically to change the number of "privileges", the government could allow this market to allocate them, and no re-bidding would be necessary in successive years. Indeed, once the number is determined and granted, there is no need from the point of view of allocation to collect bids.

Similarly, under sole-ownership, fishermen would probably belong to several co-operatives; and individual proprietors would hire men and ships working in a different fishery each season.

In the second place, it might be possible to fix the catch rather than the amount of effort.

I am personally dubious that in the conditions of my model this would be efficient. Fixing the amount of the catch in absolute terms has been shown to *increase* the misallocation of effort by inducing more investment and labour effort, in seasonal peaks, without increasing the catch or return per worker.

What about subsidies and taxes? A tax on the catch, that increased in rate as the amount caught in a season cumulated, would have much the same bad effect as a quota system. The incentive to build up effort in the earlier part of the season would be increased. Similarly, a tax on catch at the rate which depended upon the amount each boat landed would merely build up the incentive to add to the number of boats.

It seems that the best tax would be one levied on the fishermen or on total outfits. It should be levied at a rate which kept their number down to the required effort input; obviously, in equilibrium it would be much like the "privilege" system. (A subsidy could also be paid for not fishing, but it would be difficult to know how to administer this once the system got under way: who should receive it?) Such a tax system would not differentiate among those who were most keen to fish or were the best fishermen, and might have some unfortunate allocational effects. It seems to me therefore less useful than a practice of charging for fishing "privileges" or for sole (or co-operative) ownership.

CHAPTER 10

OPTIMIZATION AND SUBOPTIMIZATION IN FISHERY REGULATION

By RALPH TURVEY*

The purpose of this article is to show that fishery regulation is one of those spheres of economic policy where what is the best thing to do depends on what can be done. This is usually illustrated by the analogy that, if one wants to climb as high as possible but cannot climb all the way up the highest mountain, the best thing to do may be to walk in the opposite direction and climb to the top of a lower one. If the ***optimum optimorum*** is to be reached (the highest mountain scaled), then regulation must extend not only to the scale but also to the mode of operation.

That this rather general point has an important application in fisheries management became apparent to me during a conference in Ottawa of economists, biologists, and administrators organized by the Food and Agricultural Organization in 1961. The proceedings of this conference have now been published [8]. The two general survey papers by Professor Scott and Dr. Dickie at the beginning of this volume afford an admirable survey of the whole subject, including a review of the literature. I shall therefore not attempt to summarize their contributions, and what follows is a self-contained argument which may, however, incidentally serve to introduce readers to a fascinating subject where economists and biologists are clearly complements and only talk as though they were substitutes when they misunderstand one another.

What follows is a static (i.e., steady state) analysis of a single-trawl fishery where there is only one fish stock, fished from ports which supply a common market and which are equidistant from the fishing ground. It is assumed that the port market is competitive and that there are no restrictions on entry into the fishery. These assumptions serve to make the exposition reasonably simple; their removal would not destroy the essential argument of the paper.

* The author is reader in economics at the London School of Economics. He is much indebted to R. J. H. Beverton, L. M. Dickie, B. B. Parrish, F. A. Popper, and A. D. Scott for their constructive comments on an earlier draft of this paper.

I. *Catch*

The determinants of the weight of catch, under these assumptions, are twofold,[1] given constant natural population parameters. The first is the rate of capture (the fishing mortality rate) of the fish liable to capture, which is proportionate to the amount of fishing effort. This is defined as the product of the number of hours' fishing (or some other index of fishing time) and of fishing power, where the fishing power of any particular ship is defined by reference to a standard vessel by comparing their catches when fishing at the same time and place. In practice, the fishing power of trawlers is broadly related to the gross tonnages, so that fishing effort in a given time interval may be measured as the average gross tonnage of the fishing fleet multiplied by the total number of hours' fishing. The relevance of fishing effort is simply that, if it is decreased, the stock of fish will grow and the average age, weight, and size of the fish will increase, making fishing easier, i.e., increasing catch per unit of fishing effort.

The second determinant of the weight of catch is the size (age) at which the fish become liable to capture, i.e., are "recruited" to the fishery. In a trawl fishery, which is the example we take here, this is regulated by the mesh size of the cod-ends of the trawls used. This determines the minimum size of fish caught; the larger the mesh, the older, larger, and heavier will be the fish liable to capture. Thus, other things remaining the same, an increase in mesh size will initially reduce the catch but may ultimately raise it by increasing the stock. Here, since the analysis is static, it is only this ultimate effect which concerns us.

Biologists have formulated a number of models which provide a function relating the weight of catch to the two variables, mesh size and fishing effort. These models deal with the rates of natural mortality, growth, and recruitment, each of which is a function of the size of the stock and its age distribution. As in economics, metrics is several steps behind theory, however, so that not all the parameters of the more complicated models can at present be estimated, owing to lack of data. Things which are known to be relevant, such as the spatial distribution of fishing effort, just have to be ignored. If we confine ourselves to the operational models used for most fishery assessments, the simplified biological interrelationships that have been introduced are the following: (a) natural mortality a function of age; (b) growth of the fish, by weight and length, a function of its age; (c) recruitment to the fish stock, i.e., the number of fish reaching catchable size, treated as exogenous; and (d) fishing mortality rate proportional to fishing effort.

[1] The standard work on all this is by R. J. H. Beverton and S. J. Holt [1]. On the measurement of "fishing effort" see also J. A. Gulland [3]. A useful survey article, of which Dr. Parrish has kindly lent me a translation, is by G. Hempel and D. Sahrhage [4].

The steady-state catch in weight from a fish stock is then determined by the interaction between the rates of these natural processes and the fishing mortality rate. The relationship between weight of catch and age of recruitment (mesh size) and fishing mortality rate (fishing effort), estimated from a simple, dynamic model in which the rates of the natural processes are assumed constant, takes the form shown in Figure 1, where fishing effort is measured horizontally and weight of catch is measured vertically. Each yield curve shows catch as a function of fishing effort for a given age of recruitment to the fished stock. (The dotted line will be explained later.)

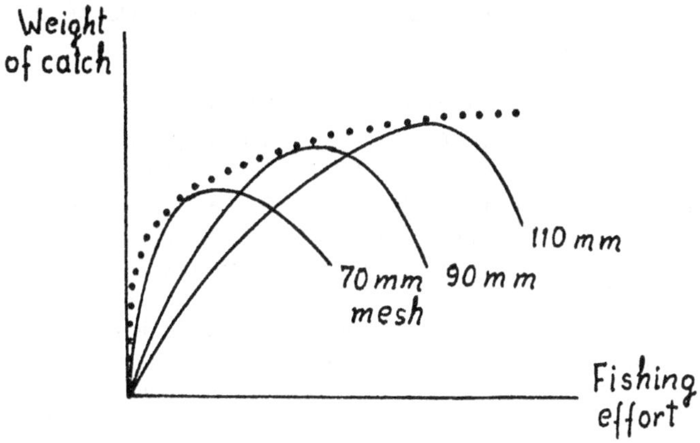

FIGURE 1

II. *Costs*

The study of fishing costs is a complicated matter. To illustrate, a large part of fishermen's remuneration is a share in profits rather than a wage.[2] Such matters are not relevant to the argument of the present paper, however, so I shall exclude them by simply assuming that over the relevant range of catch, the total cost of fishing effort rises more than proportionately to the amount of fishing effort because the minimum earnings necessary to attract and retain labor and capital at the margin rise as more of these resources are employed in fishing. Total cost is defined to include the "rents" of the intramarginal factors, i.e., the excess of their actual earnings over the minimum required to retain them in the industry. This is the only aspect of costs that we require in the present argument, so I need not discuss whether few ships fish

[2] See Zouteweij, "Fishermen's Remuneration" in [7]. Economies of scale in shore installations constitute another example.

many hours or vice versa, since fishing effort as defined above is the independent variable of the cost function. What is significant in this formulation is the implicit assumption that mesh size has no noticeable effect upon the costs of fishing effort. This is probably true within the range of mesh size that is relevant in practice.

III. *Revenue*

The price of fish, given income levels and the prices of other foods, depends not only upon the total weight of the catch but also upon its size distribution and upon its freshness. Here we shall assume that there is some given minimum marketable size of fish; otherwise I neglect these points.[3] Thus I postulate a given function relating total revenue to weight of catch.

IV. *Steady-State Bionomic Equilibrium*

Let us postulate that: (1) any fluctuations in the natural processes are small and have no trend; and (2) there is free entry of resources to the fishery. Then, given all the various functions discussed above, the long-run equilibrium position can be deduced.

On the economic side, the equilibrium condition is that total revenue equals total cost including the rent of intramarginal factors. We put it this way rather than in terms of average revenue and long-run marginal cost because average revenue is related to weight of catch and marginal cost to fishing effort. In order to relate average revenue to marginal cost, we would have to convert catch into effort, and write the condition as:

Price × Catch per unit effort = Marginal cost of fishing effort excluding rent

i.e., Average revenue × Catch per unit effort = Average cost including rent

which gives us:

Price × Catch = Average cost including rent × No. of units of effort

i.e., Total revenue = Total cost including rent.

If total revenue exceeds total costs, resources not in the industry will find that it is worth while to move into it, while in the reverse case some resources at the margin will be earning less than is required to retain them in the industry, and they will leave it.

Each fisherman will want to maximize the marketable value of his catch at any given level of costs. This means, on our assumptions, that

[3] The way in which price depends upon size and freshness can, of course, be observed but it would probably be extremely difficult to estimate how the price pattern would change following alterations in these variables. Note that freshness is related to length of stay at sea, which in turn is related to the size of ship and hence affects costs.

he will wish to maximize the weight of his catch of fish above the minimum marketable size for any given level of costs. Thus for the present argument we will assume that he will choose a mesh which limits his catch to fish above that size. If he used a smaller mesh, he would have to throw part of his catch back into the sea, which would involve unnecessary trouble.

We can now describe the equilibrium position. The minimum marketable size of fish determines mesh size. This, in conjunction with fishing effort, determines the weight of catch. This, in turn, determines total revenue which must equal the total costs of the amount of fishing involved. All this is shown in Figure 2 whose N.E. quadrant corresponds to Figure 1 and where the equality of total revenue and total costs is shown by using a 45° line in the S.W. quadrant.

As Figure 2 is drawn, either a general fall in cost or a rise in the demand for fish will cause an increase in the equilibrium catch. But if fishing effort has been carried beyond the point of maximum yield this standard conclusion does not follow, as Figure 3 shows. Here the dashed line shows one equilibrium position and the dotted line shows another; the latter corresponds to a higher level of demand, represented by the dotted total revenue curve. In this case the higher level

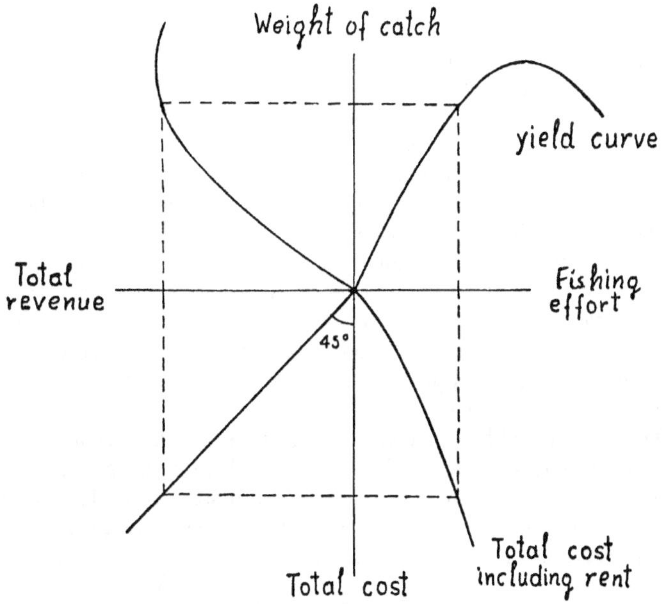

FIGURE 2

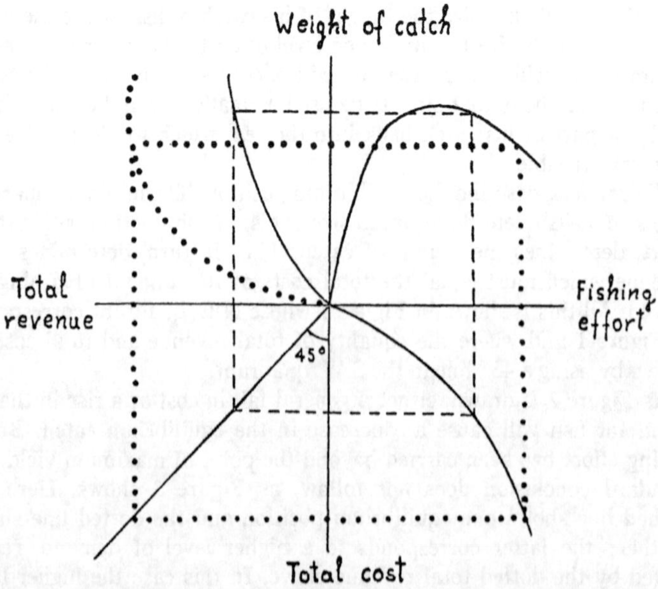

FIGURE 3

of demand means a greater employment of resources in the industry but a smaller total product!

V. *External Diseconomies*

Such a peculiar result indicates that there is something special about the industry. There is indeed. But from what has been said it should be apparent that two problems are involved, not one. The first is that while the catch of the individual fisherman is proportionate to his own fishing effort, the same is not true of all fishermen together; i.e., the yield curves for all fishermen in Figure 1 are not straight lines through the origin.[4] Each fisherman imposes an external diseconomy upon his brethren; the marginal private product of his fishing effort exceeds the marginal social product.

The second problem involves mesh size. By catching small fish, fishermen are reducing the number of large fish to be caught later. If an individual fisherman were to raise his mesh size he would lose by increasing the number of hauls necessary to achieve any given weight of catch. Yet in the long run, his use of a larger mesh may lower the costs

[4] They are straight lines in an underdeveloped fishery where natural mortality is infinite relative to fishing mortality.

of all fishermen together and, if all of them used larger meshes, all would benefit. Here again, social and private product diverge.

VI. *The Optimum Optimorum*

When external economies are involved both in the level of fishing effort and in the choice of mesh size, it is clear that to achieve the optimum resource allocation requires regulation of *both* these variables.

Let us assume for the present that the conditions for optimal resource allocation are fulfilled in the rest of the economy, so that no problems of "second best" arise. Let us further assume, first, that the effect of changes in the price of fish upon the distribution of real income between fish consumers and others is unimportant and, second, that a level of earnings in the industry which is equal (at the margin) to the earnings those resources could obtain elsewhere is socially acceptable. Finally, let us consider only those cases where the fishery is a very small part of the economy.

Under these conditions, the *optimum optimorum* is reached when G is maximized, G being the excess of the value of the catch to consumers over the value to them of the alternative goods and services sacrificed by devoting resources to fishing. Now the value of the catch to consumers is the maximum they would pay rather than go without it, i.e., what they do pay (total revenue) *plus* consumer surplus: $TR + S$, the area under the demand curve. The value of goods and services sacrificed is equal to the contribution to production that the resources used in fishing would make if they were not so used and this, on our assumptions, is what they could earn elsewhere. It is therefore measured by the total costs of the fishery *less* the rents of the intramarginal resources, $TC - R$. Thus the *optimum optimorum* is to be reached by maximiziing:

$$G = (TR + S) - (TC - R).$$

A necessary, but insufficient, condition for maximization is that mesh size be such as to maximize the catch for the actual level of fishing effort. In terms of Figure 1 this means that the fishery must be "on" the dotted envelope curve, known as the "eumetric yield curve" (Beverton and Holt [1]). It is a property of this curve that, unlike the individual yield curves for given mesh sizes, it is asymptotic to the horizontal, thus rising throughout its length.

Figure 4 shows the determination of the optimum. The level of fishing effort, OF, must be so chosen as to maximize G. This is achieved when the slope of the $TR + S$ curve (i.e., price per unit catch) multiplied by the slope of the eumetric yield curve (i.e., marginal social yield of fishing effort) equals the slope of $TC - R$ (i.e., the marginal cost of

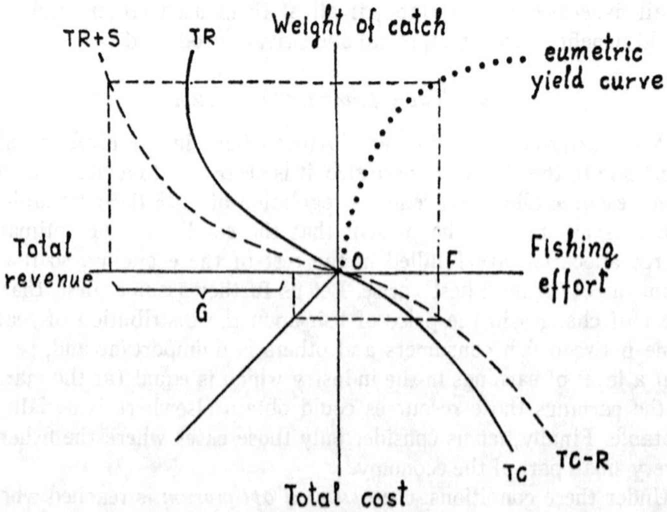

FIGURE 4

fishing effort). When this is the case, i.e., when:

Price × Marginal social yield = Marginal cost of fishing effort excluding rent

i.e., Price × Marginal social yield = Average cost of fishing effort including rent

it must be true that:

Price × Average yield > Average cost of fishing effort including rent

(since the average yield of fishing effort *exceeds* the marginal social yield),[5] which means that total revenue exceeds total costs including rent. $G = S + R + (TR - TC)$, the maximum gain, is the sum of consumers' surplus, producers' surplus (the rents of intramarginal labor and capital), and the rent of that other scarce resource, the fish stock.[6]

In an unregulated fishery, where resource allocation is nonoptimal, free entry means that total revenue will equal total costs so that no rent of the fish stock is achieved. Under these circumstances, the total gain from the fishery $G = S + R$.[7] Whether a shift from this situation to the *optimum optimorum* will raise or lower the total catch (and hence

[5] I.e., the eumetric curve is concave from below.

[6] Cf. H. S. Gordon [2]. Note that if capital and fishermen of equal skill are both in infinitely elastic supply and if the fishery meets a very small part of the total demand, *R* and *S* respectively will be zero. Nevertheless, the *optimum optimorum* still requires regulation of both effort and mesh size.

[7] Which will equal zero in the special case of the previous footnote!

S) and whether it will raise or lower the amount of fishing effort (and hence R) cannot be determined a priori.

VII. *Suboptimization of Mesh Size*

In order to show this it is convenient to consider the regulation of mesh size and the regulation of fishing effort separately and to show that in some circumstances these may have opposite effects. It is of great importance to consider the suboptima that can be reached by regulating only one or the other of these variables since, in practice, political and administrative considerations frequently make one or the other type of regulation impossible to introduce. This is the case, for example, with the regulation of international trawl fisheries, where agreement upon mesh size is much easier to attain than agreement about the share of fishing effort (and hence catch) to be apportioned to each nation.

When mesh size alone can be regulated, it is obvious that the fishery ought to move on to the eumetric curve, since this is the boundary of the production function. At the original level of fishing effort and costs this will raise the weight of catch but may either lower total revenue (elasticity of demand less than unity) or raise it (elasticity greater than unity). In the first case resources will leave the industry, so that fishing effort is reduced; conversely in the second case. Even in the first case, however, catch will be greater in the new suboptimum equilibrium than it was in the initial nonoptimum equilibrium. If it were not greater, total revenue would be higher or the same as before while fishing effort and total costs would be lower, so that total revenue would exceed total costs—a state of affairs incompatible with equilibrium when entry of resources is unrestricted.

Suboptimization with respect to mesh size thus involves maximizing:

$$G = S + R$$

subject to the constraint $TR = TC$. Moving to the suboptimum, equilibrium must raise S, since catch rises, but may either raise or lower R. If R falls, the rise in S must exceed the fall.[8] But if there were constant costs (R always zero) and an infinitely elastic demand (S always zero), there would be no point in regulating mesh size.

VIII. *Suboptimization of Fishing Effort*

While, as we have just seen, suboptimizing mesh size must raise catch but may either raise or lower fishing effort and costs, suboptimizing

[8] Because TR and TC fall equally (by assumption); R must fall less than TC (when the supply curves of factors are rising); S must rise more than TR falls (since $TR + S$ rises with movement down any downward-sloping demand curve).

fishing effort will always lower fishing effort and costs but may either raise or lower catch. The analysis of this case follows the same lines as that of the *optimum optimorum* (see Figure 4), save that the yield curve is not the eumetric curve but a constant-mesh yield curve. Now such a curve, as shown in Figure 1, has a maximum. If the initial non-optimum equilibrium is to the left of this maximum, suboptimizing with respect to fishing effort will *reduce* both fishing effort and catch. But if the initial equilibrium is to the right of this maximum, so that the marginal social product of fishing effort is actually *negative,* sub-optimization will increase the catch. North Sea plaice and haddock are examples of trawl fisheries where fishing effort is to the right of the maximum for the mesh size in use. The classic case of this is not a trawl fishery but is said to be the Pacific halibut fishery.

How can fishing effort be regulated? The answer is surely to charge fishermen a rent for fishing, so that they economize in the use of the scarce resource. This rent would take the form of a charge per unit of weight of catch proportionate to the difference between marginal private yield (catch per unit of effort) and marginal social yield (the slope of the yield curve). The effect of this would be to raise the marginal private cost of catching fish to equal the marginal social cost.

An alternative method would be to impose quantitative restriction upon the amount of fishing effort. In practice, such restriction would produce an inferior suboptimum, unless it were so all-embracing as to amount to the institution of a sole-owner of the fishery. The reason is that any restriction must be framed in terms of a limit upon one or more of the resources used in the industry. But to ration the supply of any resource is to invite the substitution of other resources for it. Thus if the number of boats were limited, larger engines would be installed, bigger crews carried, and more resources devoted to securing a rapid turn-around in port. None of this would be efficient, in terms of resource allocation; it would simply increase the total costs of all alternative levels of fishing effort. Furthermore, it would concentrate the rent to be had from fishing economically, i.e., the gain from suboptimizing fishing effort, in the hands of the owners of the boats. In some circumstances this would be less desirable from the point of view of income distribution than a charge that placed the rent in the hands of the government which could dispose of it in a variety of ways. Thus a tax on catch is generally necessary for suboptimization. To reach the *optimum optimorum,* however, such a tax is necessary but not sufficient.

There is a great deal more that can be said about the effects of restricting entry to a fishery in ways that lead to economic inefficiency, but I shall not pursue the matter here. My purpose is merely to assert the fundamental principle that either mesh regulation or the control of fishing effort is better than nothing but that regulation of both is still better.

IX. *Second Best*

If the assumptions listed at the beginning of the section on the *optimum optimorum* are not met, allowance must be made for this fact in deciding policy. I do not believe that the distributional effects of changes in fish prices are worth bothering about, but there might well be circumstances in which regulation adversely affected the earnings of fishermen to an undesirable extent. Where this resulted from the creation of an excess of total revenue over total costs, the government would acquire more than sufficient funds to compensate the displaced fishermen. Where mesh regulation alone was involved, however, no such funds would be available, and the problem acquires important political elements.

Leaving these distributional questions aside, the recommendation to optimize or, if that is impossible, to suboptimize depends crucially upon the assumptions that the costs of fishing effort do reflect the value of resources in alternative uses and that the price of fish does measure the marginal contribution of fish to consumer welfare. The economist who is concerned to help formulate policy rather than to maintain his theoretical purity will, however, seek to make rough corrections for all the imperfections that he can think of in closely related markets and will then go on to make his recommendations. Thus the level of unemployment in fishing ports and subsidies or tariffs on meat and eggs are likely to draw his attention. He will, on the other hand, remain indifferent to the effects upon fishing costs of restrictive practices among suppliers of marine paint or to the effect upon the demand for fish of resale price maintenance in the confectionery trades.[9]

Even the purists, however, will agree that on resource-allocation grounds there are two things that can be recommended unreservedly. One is a shift to the eumetric curve and the other, as an alternative, is a reduction in fishing effort whenever the fishery is on a falling yield curve. Either of these will raise the catch and/or reduce costs, providing that "something for nothing" which alone appears to gladden the hearts of our erudite welfare economists.

There are complications, however, Even when cost, demand, and natural conditions remain constant through time so that steady state equilibrium can be achieved, the introduction of the regulation of mesh size or fishing effort will initially reduce the catch. This initial, tempo-

[9] Cf. E. J. Mishan [5].

rary loss clearly has to be weighed against the eventual, permanent gain. A rate of social time discount is required to make such weighing-up possible. All this complicates matters, but introduces no interesting new principles.

X. *Alternative Methods of Regulation*

There is probably no fishery conforming to our simplifying assumptions. It is not worth while removing them one by one in a general discussion such as this, however, since the particular assumptions that should replace them will vary from one fishery to another. Thus, instead of going on to complicate the analysis,[10] I shall conclude by mentioning other forms of regulation than those dealt with so far. The main alternatives that have been applied in practice are: limitation of total catch, closed seasons, closed areas, minimum size limits, and the prescription of particular types of gear. These have in common that they involve no restraint on entry to the industry so that, taken alone, none of them results in the creation of a rent of the fishery. Despite this imperfection, such measures may often be better than no regulation at all, so that if one of them is all that is politically or administratively practicable there is a suboptimum to be found.[11] In some fisheries, two of these measures, size limits and the closure of nursery grounds, are fairly close substitutes for the regulation of mesh size, so that the type of analysis presented above can be applied. With any of them, however, total revenue and total costs will be equal in equilibrium so that the social gain to be had from the fishery is limited to the sum of consumers' and producers' surpluses: $G = S + R$.[12]

An important conclusion follows from this, as it did in the case of suboptimizing mesh size. Any measure that raises weight of catch without affecting the total cost curve will raise G. This is not unambiguously an improvement in a second-best world if resources are drawn into the industry; but if demand has an elasticity of less than unity, so that the increased catch lowers total revenue, resources will leave the industry, and the matter is simpler. Unless the immediate loss outweighs the long-run gain, the only possible objection to getting more fish at a lower cost would be that the resources in the industry deserved the rents they would lose.

[10] For an example, see Beverton and Holt's discussion of fisheries based on two species caught by the same gear but having different eumetric yield curves [1, pp. 388, 421, ff.].

[11] Furthermore, existing measures have initiated cooperation and involved a start on some of the necessary research, without either of which there is no hope of further developments.

[12] We are still assuming that the fishery is only a small part of the economy.

XI. *Conclusion*

I have not attempted any general survey of the economics of fishery conservation, though I hope that this article may serve as an introduction to Professor Scott's paper on the subject and Professor Crutchfield's case study of the Pacific halibut fishery, both in the proceedings of the Ottawa conference [8]. Although my exposition is mainly in terms of trawl fisheries, it can be applied more generally to other fisheries when selectivity is controllable. My purpose has been to provide an interesting and important example of the notions of optimization and suboptimization and of the proposition that coping with external diseconomies will sometimes involve interfering with the nature as well as the scale of private productive activities [6].

References

1. R. J. H. Beverton and S. J. Holt, *On the Dynamics of Exploited Fish Populations.* London 1957.
2. H. S. Gordon, "The Economic Theory of a Common Property Resource," *Jour. Pol. Econ.*, April 1954, *62*, 124-42.
3. J. A. Gulland, *On the Fishing Effort in English Demersal Fisheries.* London 1956.
4. G. Hempel and D. Sahrhage, "Recent Model Concepts on the Dynamics of Demersal Fish Stocks," *Ber. Deutsche Wiss. Komm. für Meeresforschung*, XVI:2.
5. E. J. Mishan, "Second Thoughts on Second Best," *Oxford Econ. Papers*, Oct. 1963, *14*, 205-17.
6. Ralph Turvey, "On Divergences between Social Cost and Private Cost," *Economica*, Aug. 1963, *30*, 309-13.
7. ——— and J. Wiseman, ed., *The Economics of Fisheries.* Rome 1956.
8. F. A. O. Fisheries Reports No. 5, *Economic Effects of Fishery Regulation.* Rome 1962.

CHAPTER 11

Optimization and Suboptimization in Fishery Regulation: Comment

In the March 1964 issue of this journal, Ralph Turvey states that "if the *optimum optimorum* is to be reached, . . . then (fishery) regulation must extend not only to the scale but also to the mode of operation" [1, p. 64]. He recommends both a toll or charge per pound of fish caught (scale regulation) and the imposition of a legal minimum mesh size (mode regulation) in order to achieve a Pareto-optimum.

If certain implicit assumptions in his argument are made explicit, however, it becomes clear that the necessity for either or both of these regulations is hardly an immutable law of nature. The chief fault in Turvey's otherwise excellent paper is that he does not clearly state the relation between these critical assumptions and his conclusions for public policy. It should be useful to examine in more detail exactly which conditions must be present for one or the other of these regulations to in fact be necessary for a Pareto-optimum.

It is well known that if institutions are such that technological externalities are present, competitive equilibrium will not be Pareto-optimal. Turvey states that two kinds of external diseconomies are present in the kind of competitively organized, single-trawl fishery which he considers. In the first place, a fish caught by fisherman A reduces the stock of fish available to other fishermen, increasing the amount of resources which these others must use to land a given catch. Secondly, a fish caught today by fisherman A will not be around tomorrow as a larger, more valuable fish, again imposing additional costs upon the industry as a whole.

Let the set of all fish in the banks be divided into two subsets: fish that have reached catchable size (called the "fish stock") and fish which have not yet reached that size. The size of the smallest fish in the fish stock is determined by the size of the mesh in nets used by the fishermen. Turvey states [1, p. 65] that operational models used by biologists to assess fisheries commonly make the following assumptions: (a) growth of fish and natural mortality are functions of age, (b) fishing mortality rate (catch) is proportional to "effort," and (c) recruitment into the fish stock, i.e., the number of fish reaching catchable size, is exogenous.

If assumption (c) is taken literally, then "weight recruitment," or *pounds* of fish reaching catchable size per time period, would depend only on mesh size, since larger mesh would lead to recruitment at a heavier weight. Specifically, the number of fish in the fish stock or the size of the catch would not affect recruitment. It seems reasonable to assume that the number of fish eggs laid per year is proportional to the number of fish in the banks, and that the number of fish hatching is proportional to the number of eggs laid. If recruitment is to be exogenous, then, mortality in the set of fish which have not reached catchable size must be inversely proportional to the number of fish of egg-laying age, which contradicts assumption (a). It would seem somewhat less fishy to assume that mortality is an increasing function of the number and size of fish competing for food.

The simplest recruitment assumption consistent with (a) and (b) seems to be that natural mortality is a function only of the age of the fish, and that the number of eggs laid per year is determined exogenously. (We will examine the consequences of relaxing this assumption below.) Let the growth

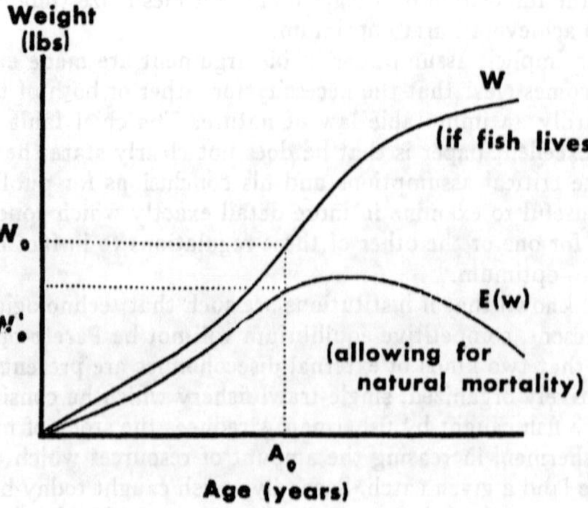

FIGURE 1. GROWTH OF A TYPICAL FISH

of a typical fish be depcited in Figure 1. The solid upper curve shows the growth of the fish as a function of its age, provided the fish lives. The probability that a given fish, once hatched, will have died can be expected to increase as the time elapsed since his hatching grows longer. The bottom dashed curve gives his expected weight (in the statistical sense) when natural mortality has been allowed for.

The size in pounds of the fish as it reaches catchable size is proportional to the cube root of mesh size: thus, the larger the mesh, the older the youngest fish in the fish stock. Given a mesh size of m_0 inches, a fish will be recruited into the fish stock at the corresponding weight w_0, at age a_0. The total "weight recruitment" into the fish stock is given by:

$$r = n \cdot w_0' \tag{1}$$

where r=recruitment into the fish stock (lbs./yr.), n=number of eggs hatching per year, and w_0' =expected weight of typical fish at age of recruitment (lbs.). Given our assumptions, w_0' is a function only of mesh size, so that equation (1) becomes:

$$(1') \qquad r = r(m) \qquad \text{(recruitment function)}$$

$$m = \text{mesh size} \qquad \text{(inches)}.$$

For the individual fisherman, catch (and hence revenue) is a function of mesh size, size of fish stock, and of the resources he expends. Turvey defines an aggregated input called "fishing effort," defined in such a fashion that the fisherman's catch, measured in pounds, is proportional to effort. Effort, then, appears as the argument in the fisherman's cost function. His production function exhibits constant returns to scale if doubling of all inputs results in a doubling of effort as defined. If, in addition, all inputs are available to the industry in perfectly elastic supplies, average cost, *ceteris paribus* (fish stock and mesh size constant), per pound of fish will be constant. If, on the other hand, factor supply curves are not all perfectly elastic, then average cost (again, *ceteris paribus*) will be a rising function of industry output. For the industry as a whole, then, we have:

$$(2) \qquad f = g(F, E, m) \qquad \text{(industry production function)}$$

$$(3) \qquad C = C(E) \qquad \text{(total industry cost)}$$

where f = total fish catch (lbs. yr.), F = size of fish stock (lbs.), C = total cost of catching fish (\$), and E = fishing effort (units).

Biological steady-state equilibrium of the fish stock, given the biological envrionment, depends both on the quantity of fish entering the fish stock (recruitment) and on the quantity of fish removed from the fish stock (catch) each year:

$$(4) \qquad F = B(f, r) \qquad \text{(biological equilibrium)}.$$

Substituting (4) into (2), we have:

$$f = g(B(f, r(m)), E, m)$$

$$(5) \qquad f = h(E, m) \qquad \text{(sustained-yield production)}.$$

Equation (5) represents sustained-yield production as a function of mesh size and fishing effort. In other words, it represents a steady-state equilibrium level of catch compatible both with fishing technology and with the biological productivity of the fishing banks.

Turvey assumes that the price of fish depends only on the weight of the industry catch, subject to the condition that all fish be at least of a given "minimum marketable size" [1, p. 67]. Thus, rounding out our model, we have:

$$(6) \qquad P = P(f) \qquad \text{(industry demand)}$$

$$P = \text{price of fish (\$/lb.)}.$$

Variations in mesh size can be assumed to be costless. Hence, for any given level of fishing effort, Pareto-optimality requires that mesh size be such as to maximize sustained-yield production. Given our assumptions, however, a fisherman, left to his own devices, will choose a mesh size such that the smallest fish caught is also the minimum-marketable-size fish [1, p. 68]. In Figure 2a, this minimum marketable size is w_{min}, and the corresponding recruitment is as indicated. Legislating a larger mesh size in this case would increase, *ceteris paribus*, costs for the individual fisherman. Since recruitment would be reduced (shown by the downward-sloping $E(w)$ curve), size of the fish stock would actually be reduced, further increasing costs.

In Figure 2b, increasing mesh size would increase recruitment, and thus the fisherman's parameter F. Only if the decreased costs associated with

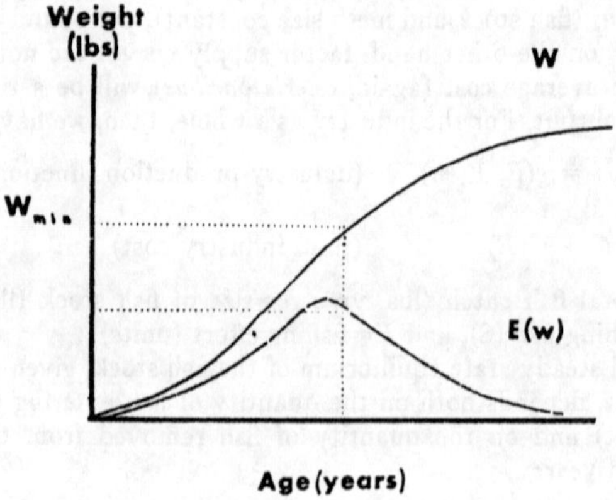

FIGURE 2a. GROWTH OF TYPICAL FISH: NO MESH-SIZE REGULATION NEEDED

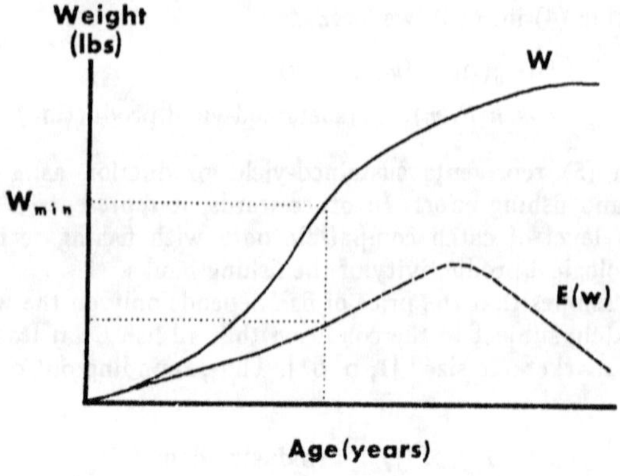

FIGURE 2b. GROWTH OF TYPICAL FISH: MESH-SIZE REGULATION POSSIBLY NEEDED

the increased steady-state fish stock at least offset the increased production costs due to the larger mesh size, however, will a larger mesh size be Pareto-superior. If, and only if, this is indeed the case will external diseconomies of the second type mentioned above exist, and then, and only then, will some sort of regulation of mesh size be necessary for a Pareto-optimum.

Let us now examine the consequences of altering the assumptions that natural mortality is a function only of the age of the fish, and that the number of eggs laid per year is determined exogenously. If both are made functions of the size of the fish stock (F), no new variables are introduced, and the model is not significantly altered. Let the natural mortality (at a given age) and the number of eggs laid per year both vary directly with F. Then equation (1) becomes:

$$r = n(F) \cdot w_0'(F). \tag{1a}$$

$$r = r(m, F) = r(m, B(f, r)) = r'(m, f). \tag{1a'}$$

Stated in words, steady-state recruitment now depends both on mesh size and on the size of annual catch. Equation (5) becomes simply:

$$f = g[B(f, r'(m, f)), E, m]$$

$$f = h'(E, m). \tag{5a}$$

As before, sustained-yield catch depends on industry effort and mesh size, although in general the functional form will be different and perhaps more complex. Moreover, the same conclusions hold. If, and only if, increasing mesh size will lower total (steady-state) industry costs will mesh size regulation be necessary for a Pareto-optimum.

More formally, the assumption that variations in mesh size are costless implies:

$$\left.\frac{\partial h}{\partial M}\right|_{\Delta E = 0} \leq 0. \tag{7}$$

The strict inequality holds for the case where m is such as to catch fish of minimum marketable size. When equation (7) holds, suboptimization with respect to mesh size has been achieved, and then industry catch can be written as a function solely of industry effort:

(8) $f = S(E)$ (industry sustained-yield catch, given suboptimum mesh size).

Equation (8) describes the "eumetric yield curve" [1, p. 70; p. 66, Fig. 1]. Alternatively, effort expended can be written as a function of fish caught:

$$E = t(f). \tag{9}$$

Since at sufficiently high levels of effort, sustained-yield catch may actually decline (negative industry returns to effort), t may be double-valued.

Benefits derived from the fish stock may be written:

$$G = \int_0^f P(f)df - C(E)$$

$$= \int_0^f P(f)df - C[t(f)].$$

Maximizing G, we have:

$$\frac{\partial G}{\partial f} = P(f) - \frac{\partial C}{\partial E}\frac{\partial t}{\partial f} = 0$$

$$P = \frac{\partial C}{\partial E}\frac{\partial t}{\partial f} = \frac{\partial C}{\partial f}\,. \tag{10}$$

In words, additional fish ought to be caught up to the point where the increment in costs associated with an additional pound of fish just equals the value the market places on that additional pound of fish. In the absence of a toll or charge for the use of the fish stock, long-run competitive equilibrium will be achieved when $P=C/f$, the average cost to the fishing industry.

Now, average cost equals marginal cost only when the former is a constant. If this is the case, additional industry output will be proportional to the extra fishing effort expended. This is equivalent to stating that increases in *industry* output have a negligible effect on the fish stock, and, hence, that the marginal product of the fishing banks is zero. If, however, increases in industry output decrease the fish stock, the marginal product of the fishing banks will be positive. Average cost will be less than marginal cost as defined, and external diseconomies of the first type will be present. If a toll, T, per pound of fish caught is levied, then $P=T+C/f$ is the condition for long-run competitive equilibrium. Hence, from equation (10), optimum utilization of the fishing banks requires that:

$$T = \frac{\partial C}{\partial f} - C/f. \tag{11}$$

In words, a toll should be levied on each pound of fish caught equal to the difference between the marginal social cost ($=\partial c/\partial f$) and the marginal private cost ($=C/f$, the average industry cost in long-run competititve equilibrium). This toll is completely analogous to a rent on any fixed facility, and is exactly equal to the toll that would be collected by a profit-maximizing, perfectly competitive fishing-banks operator, if, indeed, fishing banks were owned by individuals.

It is interesting to note that if the marginal product of the fishing banks is zero, then "type 2" externalities are not present either. For if increasing the industry output has no effect on the fish stock, then fishing mortality is a negligible fraction of total mortality. Increasing mesh size from the minimum would also have a negligible effect on the size of the fish stock. The converse is not true; it is conceivable that "type 1" diseconomies could exist without "type 2" diseconomies. Thus, (a) no regulation, (b) toll only, and (c) toll plus mesh-size regulation, are three possible optimizing prescriptions, depending on conditions actually encountered.

In the special case where Pareto-optimality does require both scale and mode regulation (case (c)), there is still no necessity to institute regulation by fiat to control mesh size. A penalty toll on all fish in a catch smaller than the size corresponding to the optimum mesh size would accomplish the same end. This fact hints that Turvey's dual recommendation, when valid, is a product of the peculiar technology involved in fisheries. Suppose that fishermen could choose whatever size distribution of catch they wanted, instead of being limited to choosing only the minimum size of fish in the catch. Then, regulation only of the minimum-size fish and of fishing effort would probably not be sufficient for a Pareto-optimum.

In terms of Figure 1, fishermen ought to be penalized for catching fish younger than the maximum expected weight age, and encouraged to devote relatively more effort to older age classes. A variable toll, either continuous or by size class, would be necessary. The actual form of the toll would also depend on the relative costs of landing different-size fish and upon the effects of the fishing activity on the shape of the $E(W)$ curve and on the number of eggs hatching. But, in general, it would not be infinity for fish smaller than a certain size and contant for larger fish.

J. Hayden Boyd*

* The author, instructor in economics at the University of Minnesota, is grateful to Herbert Mohring for several helpful comments.

Reference

1. Ralph Turvey, "Optimization and Suboptimization in Fishery Regulation," *Am. Econ. Rev.*, March 1964, *54*, 64–76.

CHAPTER 12

GENERAL EQUILIBRIUM WITH A REPLENISHABLE NATURAL RESOURCE

VERNON L. SMITH

This essay provides an exposition of stationary general equilibrium in a two-commodity world where one of the commodities is produced from a common property replenishable resource such as an ocean fishery, hunting ground, or groundwater supply. The principal emphasis is on the derivation of the production transformation set and its properties since this is where the effect of common tenure is manifest. Two-commodity models have been employed by Scott and Southy (1970) in a static context and by Quirk and Smith (1970) and Plourde (1971) using a control theory formulation, but these studies do not provide a detailed examination of the production transformation set. Also, the present essay will treat the determination of the number of firms in each industry allowing an extension of partial equilibrium concepts to general equilibrium.

1. THE COMPETITIVE ECONOMY

(a) *Consumption and Production*

Assume that there are two commodities consumed: an amount q_1 produced from a common property natural resource (fish); and amount q_2 of a "normal" good (corn). There are n consumers each with the same differentiable, concave, strictly increasing utility function $u(q_1, q_2)$. By assuming identical consumers, the graphical exposition and discussion of Pareto Optimality is greatly facilitated, and permits exclusive concentration on the issues peculiar to the replenishable resource. Each consumer receives factor income wL from his ownership of L units of an appropriated resource (labour or capital) whose price is w, and income $(n_1\pi_1 + n_2\pi_2)/n$ from his per capita share of the profit (π_i) of each of n_i producers of good i, i = 1, 2. The consumer budget equation is then $p_1q_1 + q_2 = wL + (n_1\pi_1 + n_2\pi_2)/n$ where p_1 is the price of good 1, and the price of good 2 has been set equal to 1.

Necessary and sufficient conditions for an interior maximum of $u(q_1, q_2)$ subject to the budget constraint are then

$$p_1 = u_1/u_2 \tag{1}$$

$$p_1 q_1 + q_2 = wL + (n_1\pi_1 \; n_2\pi_2)/n. \tag{2}$$

In (1) and in what follows, subscripts on functions will refer to derivatives, for example $u_1 = \partial u(q_1,q_2)/\partial q_1$.

Production occurs in two industries. The first is a fishing industry consisting of n_1 fishing units or firms with production function $f^1(L_1, X)$, increasing and concave in its arguments with $f^1(0, X) = f^1(L_1, 0) = 0$. L_1 is the amount of labour devoted to harvesting fish, and X is the biomass of fish contained in a free-access ocean fishery. The biomass of fish enters each fisherman's production function because a given labour input rate produces a greater catch rate, the greater the stock of fish. But the biomass of fish is perceived by each fisherman as a free capital resource beyond his control. Each fishing firm is then motivated to choose $L_1 \geq 0$ so as to maximize $\pi_1 = p_1 f^1(L_1, X) - wL$, for given X. Labour is applied until, for an interior solution,

$$p_1 f^1_1(L_1, X) = w \tag{3}$$

Industry number 2 consists of n_2 firms with production function $f^2(L_2)$, increasing and concave in the amount of labour, L_2, applied, and with $f^2(0) = 0$. These firms also choose L_2 so as to maximize $\pi_2 = f^2(L_2) - wL_2$ giving the condition,

$$f^2_1(L_2) = w \tag{4}$$

In addition to (1) - (4) there are the market clearing conditions:

$$nq_1 = n_1 f^1(L_1, X), \tag{5}$$

$$nq_2 = n_2 f^2(L_2), \tag{6}$$

$$n_1 L_1 + n_2 L_2 = nL. \tag{7}$$

Finally, the growth rate of the biomass of fish is assumed to be determined by a growth law, or "recruitment rate" function (Lotka, 1956; Smith, 1968) F(X), where $F(0) = F(\bar{X}) = 0$, $F'(\hat{X}) = 0$, $F''(X) < 0$, $X \geq 0$. Since there are n_1 firms in the predator fishing industry, society's total catch rate is $n_1 f^1(L_1, X)$. It is assumed that the catch is just an additive loss from the biomass of fish which does not interact with the growth properties of the resource so that the rate of change of the biomass net of harvest is $\dot{X} = F(X) - n_1 f^1 L_1, X)$. Biomass equilibrium occurs when it is stationary, giving the equilibrium condition,

$$\dot{X} = F(X) - n_1 f^1(L_1, X) = 0 \tag{8}$$

Equations (1) - (8) define a competitive bionomic (Gordon, 1954) equilibrium for the economy and its single natural resource environment. In the development of sections 1 and 2 it will be assumed that the numbers of firms in each industry (n_1, n_2) are given. Without loss of generality, in what follows, we will set $n_1 = n_2 = n$. Modifications to deal explicitly with the determination of industry size will be treated in section 5.

(b) *Production Transformations*

(i) *Definition*: P, the *production equilibrium* transformation is the set of points (q_1, q_2) that satisfies (5) - (7) for given (L, X), or

$$P(L,X) = \{(q_1, q_2) \mid q_1 = f^1(L_1,X),\ q_2 = f^2(L_2),\ L_1 + L_2 = L,\ X\}$$

Thus P is just the usual production transformation of general equilibrium theory which is determined for given resource endowments of an economy. Since $dq_1 = f^1_1 dL_1$, $dq_2 = f^2_1 dL_2$, $dL_1 = -dL_2$, the marginal rate of transformation of fish into corn in the set P (marginal private cost) is:

$$\left.\frac{dq_2}{dq_1}\right|_P = \frac{f^2_1 dL_2}{f^1_1 dL_1} = -\frac{f^2_1}{f^1_1} < 0. \tag{9}$$

Since $f^1_2 > 0$, the transformation P must increase in the q_1 direction with increases in X, i.e.,

$$\left.\frac{dq_1}{dX}\right|_{q_2 = \text{constant}} = f^1_1 \frac{dL_1}{dX} + f^1_2 = f^1_2 > 0.$$

This is seen in Fig. 1 by comparing P** and P*, where X** > X*.

(ii) *Definition*: B, the *bionomic equilibrium* transformation, is the set (q_1, q_2) which satisfies (5) - (8)

for given L,

$$B(L) = \{(q_1, q_2) \mid q_1 = f^1(L_1, X), q_2 = f^2(L_2), L_1 + L_2 = L, F(X) = nf^1(L_1, X)\}$$

We now prove that B defines a double-valued relation of q_1 to q_2.

Note first that for $X = 0$, and $X = \bar{X}$,

$$\{(0, \bar{q}_2) \mid 0 = f^1(0,0), \bar{q}_2 = f^2(L), F(0) = nf^1(0,0) = 0\} =$$

$$\{(0, \bar{q}_2) \mid 0 = f^1(0,\bar{X}), \bar{q}_2 = f^2(L), F(\bar{X}) = nf^1(0,\bar{X}) = 0\}$$

That is, the point $(0, \bar{q}_2) \in B$ corresponds to two fish stock, 0, and $\bar{X}$.

Consider any (X^*, X^{**}), where $0 < X^* < \hat{X} < X^{**} < \bar{X}$, and $F(X^*) = F(X^{**})$. Let L_1^* satisfy $(F(X^*) = nf^1(L_1^*,X^*) = nq_1^*$, and L_1^{**} satisfy $F(X^{**}) = nf^1(L_1^{**}, X^{**}) = nq_1^{**}$. Then $q_1^* = q_1^{**}$, and since $-f_1^1/f_2^1 < 0$ (L_1 and X are substitutes), $L_1^* > L_1^{**}$. Let $L_2^* = L - L_1^*$, $L_2^{**} = L - L_1^{**}$. Then $L_2^* < L_2^{**}$, and $q_2^* = f^2(L_2^*) < q_2^{**} = f^2(L_2^{**})$, since f^2 is increasing.

Finally, at $X = \hat{X}$ let $\hat{L}_1$ satisfy $F(\hat{X}) = nf^1(\hat{L}_1, \hat{X})$, and $\hat{L}_2 = L - \hat{L}_1$. Then the corresponding outputs, $\hat{q}_1 = f^1(\hat{L}_1, \hat{X})$, $\hat{q}_2 = f^2(\hat{L}_2)$ are unique.

It follows that the set B can be partitioned into two subsets B^*, B^{**}, where $B^*(L) = \{(q_1, q_2) \mid q_1 = f^1(L_1, X), q_2 = f^2(L_2), L_1 + L_2 = L, F(X) = nf^1(L_1, X), 0 \leq X < \hat{X}\}$

$$B^{**}(L) = \{(q_1, q_2) \mid q_1 = f^1(L_1, X), q_2 = f^2(L_2), L_1 + L_2 = L, F(X) = nf^1(L_1, X), \hat{X} \leq X < \bar{X}\}$$

The sets B^* corresponding to $F'(X) > 0$, and B^{**} corresponding to $F'(X) < 0$, are shown in Fig. 1.

Differentiating (5) - (8), $dq_1 = f_1^1 dL_1 + f_2^1 dX$, $dq_2 = f_1^2 dL_2$, $dL_1 = -dL_2$, $(F' - nf_2^1)\, dX = nf_1^1 dL_1$, we can compute the marginal rate of transformation of fish into corn in the set B (marginal social cost):

$$\left.\frac{dq_2}{dq_1}\right|_B = -(f_1^2/f_1^1) + (nf_1^2 f_2^1/f_1^1 F') \tag{10}$$

From (9) and (10),

$$\frac{dq_2}{dq_1}\bigg|_B = \frac{dq_2}{dq_1}\bigg|_P + nf_1^2 f_2^1 / f_1^1 F' \tag{11}$$

Let $P^* = P(L, X^*)$ for any $0 \leq X^* < \hat{X}$, and $P^{**} = P(L, X^{**})$ for any $\hat{X} \leq X^{**} < \bar{X}$. Then, since $F'(X^*) > 0$

$$\frac{dq_2}{dq_1}\bigg|_{P^*} = -\frac{f_1^2(L_2^*)}{f_1^1(L_1^*, X^*)} < -\frac{f_1^2(L_2^*)}{f_1^1(L_1^*, X^*)}\left[1 - \frac{nf_2^1(L_1^*, X^*)}{F'(X^*)}\right]$$

$$= \frac{dq_2}{dq_1}\bigg|_{B^*} \gtrless 0,$$

where $\frac{dq_2}{dq_1}\Big|_{B^*} \gtrless 0$ as $nf_2^1(L_1^*, X^*) \gtrless F'(X^*)$. Consequently for all $0 \leq X^* \leq \hat{X}$, the marginal rate of transformation in P is less than it is in B, or marginal private cost is less than marginal social cost at any such point of bionomic equilibrium. This is illustrated in Fig. 1, at (q_1^*, q_2^*). Figure 1 is drawn on the assumption that $\frac{dq_2}{dq_1}\Big|_{B^*}$ is zero at some $q_1 = q_1'$, and negative below q_1'. Clearly $\frac{dq_2}{dq_1}\Big|_{B^*} > 0$ at points near $(\hat{q}_1, \hat{q}_2)$, for then $F'(X^*)$ is near zero and we must have $nf_2^1(L_1^*, X^*) > F'(X^*)$. The quantity $nf_2^1(L_1^*, X)$ is the *marginal technological productivity* of X, i.e. the increase in the harvest rate with increases in the fish stock, while $F'(X^*)$ is the *marginal biological productivity* of X. For points in B* where $nf_2^1 > F'$ an increase in the output of corn q_2 by transfering labour from fishing to corn production reduces fishing pressure and increases the stock of fish. But with $nf_2^1 > F'$ at the new equilibrium stock the harvest is larger. That is, the increase in X more than compensates for the decrease in L_1 with the result that q_1 and q_2 both increase. For points in B* where the harvest is less responsive than biological yield to increases in $X(nf_2^1 < F')$, we have $\frac{dq_2}{dq_1}\Big|_{B^*} < 0$. In this case an attempt to increase q_1 causes the stock of fish to fall. This decreases biological yield more than it does the harvest with the result that at the new harvest equilibrium labor is released to produce more corn.

The marginal rates of transformation in P* and P** will now be compared for any X* and X** such that $F(X^*) = F(X^{**})$. Since $L_2^* < L_2^{**}$, $f_1^2(L_2^*) > f_1^2(L_2^{**})$. If we assume that $f_{12}^1 > 0$, then since $L_1^* > L_1^{**}$, $X^* < X^{**}$, it follows that $f_1^1(L_1^*, X^*) < f_1^1(L_1^*, X^{**}) < f_1^1(L_1^{**}, X^{**})$. Therefore

$$\frac{dq_2}{dq_1}\bigg|_{P^*} = -\frac{f_1^2(L_2^*)}{f_1^1(L_1^*, X^*)} < -\frac{f_1^2(L_2^{**})}{f_1^1(L_1^{**}, X^{**})} = \frac{dq_2}{dq_1}\bigg|_{P^{**}} .$$

This is illustrated in Fig. 1, where the marginal rate of transformation in P** at a point (q_1^*, q_2^{**}) is greater than in P* at a point (q_1^*, q_2^*) directly below. The two points correspond to equal total harvest rates but different fish populations.

Finally since $F'(X^{**}) < 0$,

$$\frac{dq_2}{dq_1}\bigg|_{P^{**}} = -\frac{f_1^2(L_2^{**})}{f_1^1(L_1^{**}, X^{**})} > -\frac{f_1^2(L_2^{**})}{f_1^1(L_1^{**}, X^{**})} + \frac{nf_1^2(L_2^{**})f_2^1(L_1^{**},X^{**})}{f_1^1(L_1^{**}, X^{**})F'(X^{**})} = \frac{dq_2}{dq_1}\bigg|_{B^{**}} ,$$

as shown at (q_1^*, q_2^{**}) in Fig. 1.

(c) *Competitive General Equilibrium*

From (1), (3) and (4) at a competitive equilibrium (C.E.),

$$p_1 = u_1/u_2 = f_1^2/f_1^1 , \tag{12}$$

where the production equilibrium transformation is tangent to an indifference curve. f_1^2/f_1^1 measures the private marginal cost of the fish harvest as observed by competitive firms to whom the stock of fish is a free resource. Such an equilibrium is illustrated by the point C in Fig. 2. There may be many such equilibria. If at a point such as C′, $p_1 = u_1/u_2 < f_1^2/f_1^1$, as shown, fishing firms can increase profits (reduce losses) by reducing the employment of fishing labor, which is absorbed by corn producers who can increase profit by expansion. Thus q_1 falls and q_2 increases along B** until the equilibrium at C is reached.

A C.E. need not occur in the set B**. Thus in Fig. 3 the C.E. has depressed the biomass of fish to some X* where $F'(X^*) > 0$. The boundary case of such "overfishing" is illustrated in Fig. 4 where the C.E. is at $(0, \bar{q}_2)$ with extinction of the fish species, i.e. $q_1 = 0 = f^1(0, 0)$, $\bar{q}_2 = f^2(L)$, $F(0) = 0$ and $-f_1^2(0,0)/f_2^1(L) \geq -u_1(0, \bar{q}_2)/u_2(0, \bar{q}_2)$. This is in contrast to another boundary C.E. also at $(0,\bar{q}_2)$, but with $q_1 = 0 = f^1(0, \bar{X})$, $\bar{q}_2 = f^2(L)$, $F(\bar{X}) = 0$ and $-f_1^2(0, \bar{X})/f_1^1(L_2) \leq -u_1(0, \bar{q}_2)/u_2(0, \bar{q}_2)$. In this latter case production from the fishery is not profitable at any level of output, as indicated in Fig. 5.

2. PARETO OPTIMALITY

In the above model, welfare is unambiguously measured by the (per capita) utility function $u(q_1, q_2)$. The Pareto Optimal solution for the economy is obtained by maximizing u subject to the technological and biological constraints (5) through (8), so as to determine the biomass of fish, X, as well as L_1 and L_2. Hence, the social objective is to

$$\max_{L_1, L_2, X} \{u[f^1(L_1, X), f^2(L_2)] + \lambda(L - L_1 - L_2) + \mu[F(X) - nf^1(L_1, X)]\}$$

Eliminating λ and μ from the first order conditions, gives the marginal social condition

$$\frac{u_1}{u_2} = \frac{f_1^2}{f_1^1} - \left[\frac{nf_2^1}{F'}\right]\frac{f_1^2}{f_1^1} \tag{13}$$

which, along with constraints (5) - (8), must be satisfied by any socially optimal vector (q_1, q_2, L_1, L_2, X).

Comparing (10) and (13) it is seen that the right side of (13) is simply the marginal rate of transformation in the bionomic equilibrium set B, or the marginal social cost of the fish harvest.

It should be noted that conditions (5) - (8) and (13) are only necessary for an interior P.O. Thus in the Lagrange expression above, u, f^1, f^2 and $L - L_1 - L_2$ are concave in (L_1, L_2, X) but $nf^1(L_1, X) - F(X)$ is not (the difference between two concave functions is not concave). However, it is well-known from partial equilibrium analysis (Smith, 1968) that a P.O. can only occur at a biomass stock at which the biological rate of growth of the resource is declining.[1] This easily-proved result will be extended for the present general equilibrium model.

Theorem. At a Pareto Optimum $(q_1^\circ, q_2^\circ, L_1^\circ, L_2^\circ X^\circ), F'(X^\circ) < 0$.

Assume the contrary, that there exists a P.O. $(q_1^*, q_2^*, L_1^*, L_2^*, X^*)$ satisfying (13) and the constraints (5) - (8), but with $F'(X^*) > 0$. Then there exists X^{**}, with $F(X^*) = F(X^{**})$ and $F'(X^{**}) < 0$, such that $q_1^{**} = f^1(L_1^{**}, X^{**}) = q_1^* = f^1(L_1^*, X^*)$, $L_1^{**} < L_1^*$. The resulting labour saved $(L_1^* - L_1^{**})$ could then be used to increase q_2 to $q_2^{**} > q_2^*$. Hence, $u(q_1^*, q_2^*) < u(q_1^*, q_2^{**})$, and the initial point cannot have yielded maximum utility. The result is transparent in Fig. 6, where the point (q_1^*, q_2^*) satisfies (5) - (8) and (13), but is subject to the indicated Pareto improvement to (q_1^*, q_2^{**}).

For an interior P.O., (13) and the constraints must be satisfied with $nf_2^1/F' < 0$. It follows that $u_1/u_2 > f_1^2/f_1^1$ whereas $u_1/u_2 = f_1^2/f_1^1$ at any competitive equilibria. The point (q_1°, q_2°) in Fig. 6 illustrates a P.O. At such a point $p_1 = u_1/u_2 > f_1^2/f_1^1$ and competitive firms will find it profitable to expand fishing pressure along B** to a C.E. point such as (q_1^c, q_2^c). In the case illustrated the C.E. requires more fishing labour and produces more fish than at the P.O. allocation. Figure 3 illustrates a case in which the C.E. uses less fishing labour and produces less fish than with a P.O. allocation for the economy. One might expect the C.E. to be characterized by a larger fishing effort and a larger catch than is socially optimal, but this need not be the case unless more restrictive assumptions are imposed on the production and utility functions.

3. USER CHARGES, FISHING QUOTAS AND PARETO OPTIMALITY

The classical prescription of applying "taxes", or in this case a charge for using the social capital represented by the common property stock of fish, can in principle be used to internalize the external production costs in the fishery. Thus if a charge c is put on each unit of fish caught, each firm maximizes $(p_1 - c) f^1(L_1, X) - wL_1$, giving

$$(p_1 - c)\ f_1^1 = w \tag{3'}$$

in place of (3) above.

The tangency condition for C.E. is now

$$p_1 = \frac{u_1}{u_2} = \frac{f_1^2}{f_1^1} + c$$

which is identical to the condition (13) for P.O. if the authorities set $c = -\left[\frac{nf_2^1}{F'}\right]\frac{f_1^2}{f_1^1} > 0$. This means that given a P.O. allocation for the economy, this allocation can be maintained by a competitive fishing industry subjected to the catch charge c.

A quota on the fish catch can serve an equivalent function. But a P.O. quota, say q_1°, will have a shadow price equal to c for profit maximizing firms. This dualism is seen by noting that fishing firms under a quota system are subjected to the constraint $q_1^\circ \geq f^1(L_1, X)$. If θ is the Lagrange multiplier for this constraint, firms maximize

$$p_1 f^1(L_1, X) - wL_1 + \theta[q_1^\circ - f^1(L_1, X)]$$

giving

$$(p_1 - \theta)\ f_1^1 = w \tag{3''}$$

which is identical to (3′) when $c = \theta$.

4. STABILITY

The stability of general competitive equilibrium requires $d\dot{X}/dX = F'(X) - nf_1^1(dL_1/d_X) - nf_2^1 < 0$, or $F'(X)/n < f_1^1(dL_1/dX) + f_2^1$, which states that a change in the biomass of fish must change biological product less than the economy's harvest (= consumption) of fish after adjusting fishing labour to the new fish stock. Hence, for stocks X such that $F'(X) < 0$, a sufficient condition for stability is for $q_1 = f^1$ to be production-consumption superior with respect to X. That is, increases in X, cause an increase in the value of q_1 that satisfies equation (1) - (7), as illustrated in Fig. 7. More generally, what the stability condition states is that if $F'(X) < 0$, then q_1 must not fall with X at a rate faster than $F'(X)/n$, i.e. not be too production-consumption inferior. For stocks X such that $F'(X) > 0$, we have instability if q_1 is production-consumption inferior.

5. THE ALLOCATION OF FIRMS BETWEEN INDUSTRIES

The simplifying assumption that there are a given, unexplained, number of firms in each industry will now be relaxed. This extension is of particular substance in the present model because the biological constraint (8) depends nontrivially on the number of fishing firms, while the other equations determining a C.E. are not affected by a proportional increase in firms and households.

Suppose the economy consists of n households who supply labour to the two types of firms as before. In addition the creation and maintenance of a firm is assumed to require the expenditure of a fixed amount of labour C_i, $i = 1, 2$, per period. Total cost for firm i is then composed of variable cost wL_i, and fixed cost wC_i. The number of firms n_i, is now a variable.

The consumer, firm, market clearing and biological growth conditions for a C.E. with catch charge c are now

$$p_1 = u_1/u_2 \tag{14}$$

$$p_1 = (f_1^2/f_1^1) + c \tag{15}$$

$$w = f_1^2 \tag{16}$$

$$nq_1 = n_1 f^1(L_1, X) \tag{17}$$

$$nq_2 = n_2 f^2(L_2) \tag{18}$$

$$n_1(L_1 + C_1) + n_2(L_2 + C_2) = nL \tag{19}$$

$$\dot{X} = F(X) - n_1 f^1 = 0 \tag{20}$$

$$\pi_1 = (p_1 - c)f^1 - w(L_1 + C_1) = 0 \tag{21}$$

$$\pi_2 = f^2 - w(L_2 + C_2) = 0 \tag{22}$$

The familiar partial equilibrium conditions (21), (22) for expressing "long-run" equilibrium permit the determination of (n_1, n_2) in the present general equilibrium system. Thus, if $\pi_1 > 0$, the cost of creating a new firm, wC_1, would be less than the return to such a new firm, $(p_1 - c) f^1 - wL_1$. Assuming perfect divisibility, it would then pay to continue "producing" firms until $\pi_1 = 0$.

Given (n, L) a C.E. allocation, $Q^c = (q_1^c, q_2^c, L_1^c, L_2^c, X^c, n_1^c, n_2^c, p_1^c, w^c)$ must satisfy the nine equations (14) - (22).

If a catch charge $c = -\left[\frac{n_1 f_2^1}{F'}\right] \frac{f_1^2}{f_1^1} > 0$, $F' < 0$, is

levied, a C.E. allocation Q^c will be P.O. Thus, for a P.O. allocation of labour within firms, *and* to the creation of firms, the objective is to

$$\max_{L_1, L_2, X, n_1, n_2} \{u(n_1 f^1/n, n_2 f^2/n) + \lambda(nL - n_1 L_1 - n_1 C_1 - n_2 L_2 - n_2 C_2) + \mu[F(X) - n_1 f^1]\}$$

giving

$$\frac{u_1}{u_2} = \frac{f_1^2}{f_1^1} - \left[\frac{n_1 f_2^1}{F'}\right] \frac{f_1^2}{f_1^1}, \tag{23}$$

as in section 2, and, from the vanishing of derivatives with respect to n_i,

$$\left[\frac{n_1}{u_2} + \frac{n_1 f_2^1 f_1^2}{f_1^1 F'}\right] f^1 - f_1^2(L_1 + C_1) = 0 \tag{24}$$

$$f^2 - f_1^2(L_2 + C_2) = 0 \tag{25}$$

From the C.E. model we have $p_1 = u_1/u_2$, $w = f_1^2$, and (24) is just the condition (21) that $\pi_1 = 0$, while (25) is the condition $\pi_2 = 0$.[2]

REFERENCES

GORDON, H. SCOTT "The Economic Theory of a Common-Property Resource: The Fishery," *Journal of Political Economy*, April 1954, 62, 124-142.

PLOURDE, C. "Exploitation of Common Property Replenishable Natural Resources," *Western Economic Journal*, September 1971, Vol. 9, 256-266.

QUIRK, J. and V. SMITH "Dynamic Economic Models of Fishing," *Economics of Fisheries Management: A Symposium* (Ed. A. Scott). Vancouver: University of British Columbia, Institute of Animal Resource Ecology, 1970, 3-32.

SCOTT, A. and C. SOUTHY, "The Problem of Achieving Efficient Regulation of a Fishery," *Economics of Fisheries Management: A Symposium* (Ed. A. Scott). Vancouver: University of British Columbia, Institute of Animal Resource Ecology, 1970, 47-59.

SMITH, V. "Economics of Production from Natural Resources," *American Economic Review*, June 1968, 58, 409-431.

FOOTNOTES

[1] This result does not necessarily follow in models of maximization over time (See Quirk and Smith, 1970).

[2] In a model of maximization over time it is natural to assume that the fixed labour cost of a firm C_i is a *lump sum* capital cost. If we let $I_i = \dot{n}_i$ $i = 1, 2$ be control variables representing the rates of investment in (= production of) firms, the control problem is to choose $L_1(t)$, $L_2(t)$, $I_1(t)$, $I_2(t)$ so as to maximize

$$\int_0^\infty u\left[\frac{n_1 f^1}{n}, \frac{n_2 f^2}{n}\right] e^{-rt} dt$$

subject to

$$n_1 L_1 + n_2 L_2 + I_1 C_1 + I_2 C_2 = nL$$

$$\dot{n}_1 = I_1$$

$$\dot{n}_2 = I_2$$

$$\dot{X} = F - n_1 f^1$$

The resulting Euler-Hamilton conditions lead to the same zero profit conditions in the stationary state except that now the return to a firm must equal the interest on the investment in a firm. For example, instead of (25) we would have

$$f^2 - f_1^2 L_2 - r f_1^2 C_2 = 0,$$

where $r f_1^2 C_2$ is the interest on the capital cost of creating a firm.

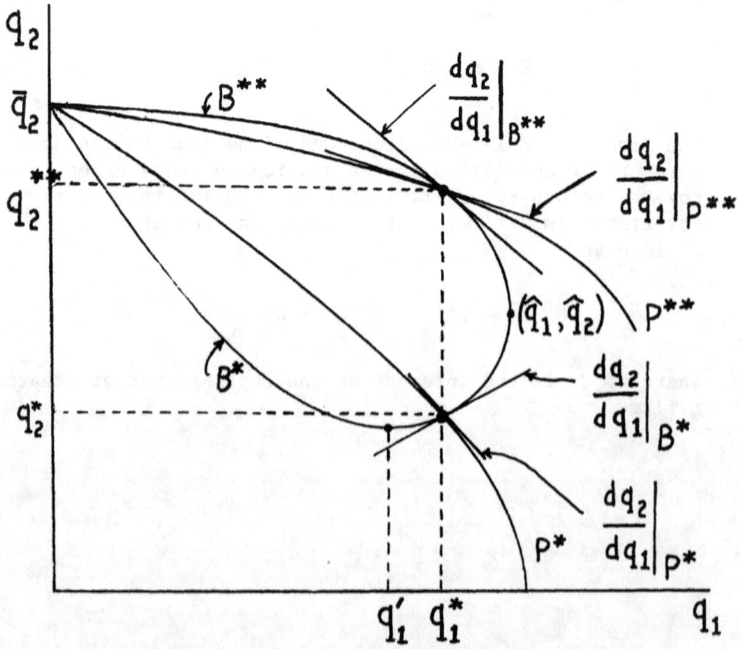

FIGURE 1

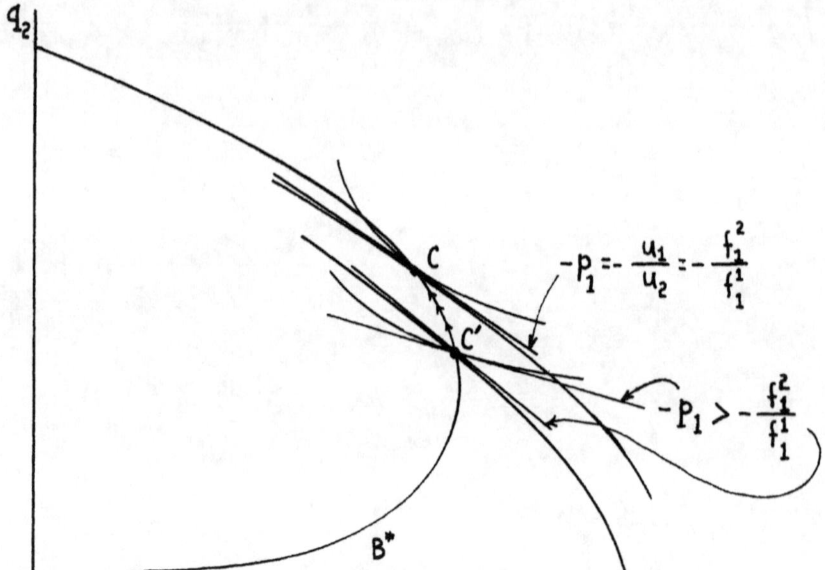

FIGURE 2

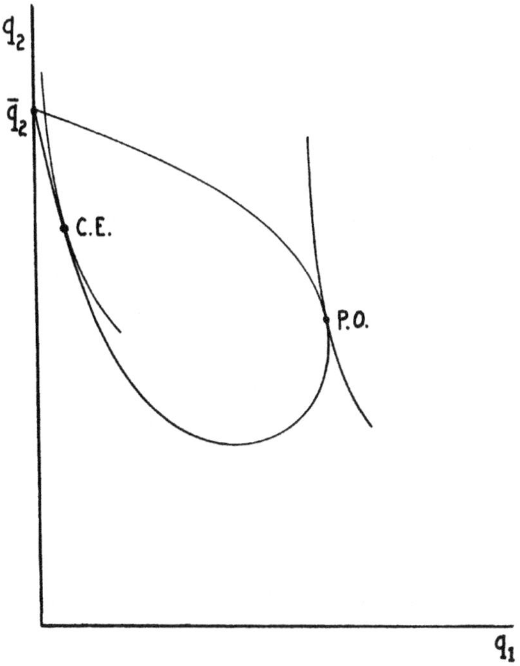

FIGURE 3

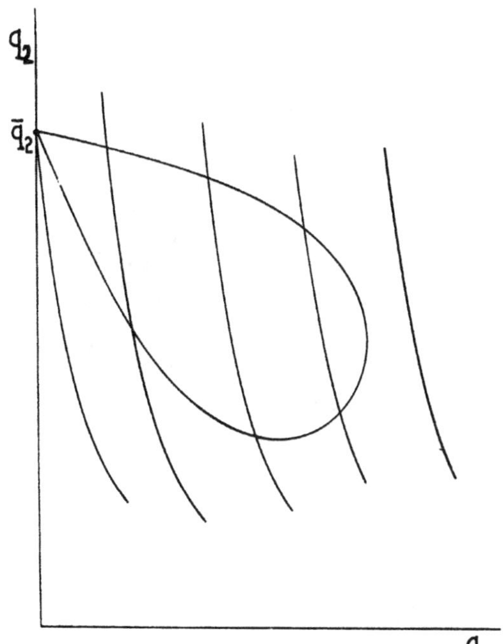

FIGURE 4

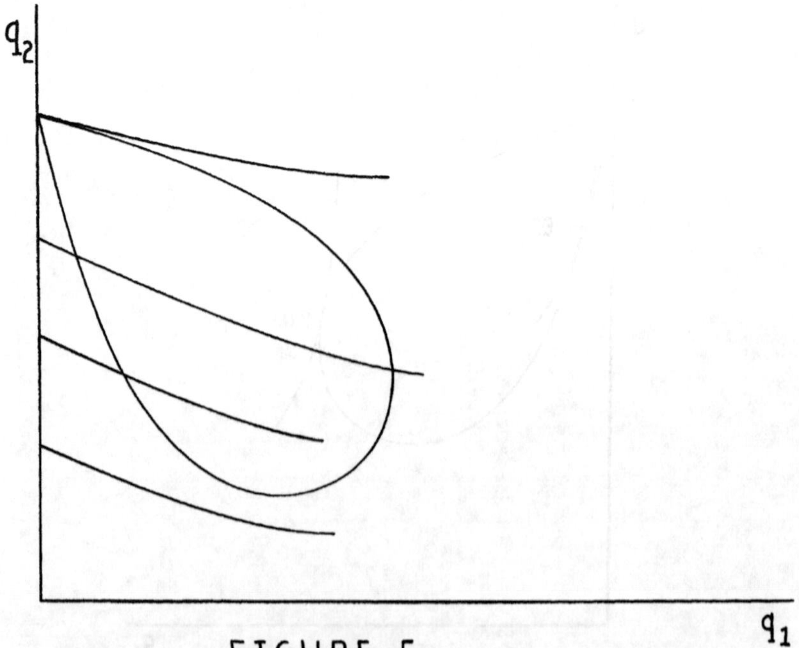

FIGURE 5

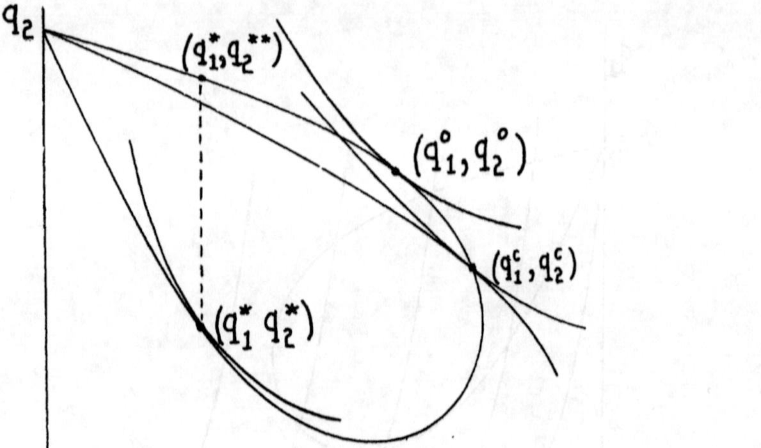

FIGURE 6

FIGURE 7

CHAPTER 13

MATHEMATICAL MODELS OF A FISHERY

James Crutchfield and A. Zellner

In this essay the properties of a model of the population dynamics of an unexploited fishery will be explored. Then the model will be expanded to take into consideration the effects of economic exploitation of the fishery resource by man. Finally, a "micro" analysis of the management of a privately owned fish resource will be presented.

A MODEL OF AN UNEXPLOITED FISHERY

The basic relationship in this approach [1] to the behavior of an unexploited fish population is the following one:

$$\frac{dN}{dt} = rN(1 - N/Ns), \qquad (1)$$

where $\frac{dN}{dt}$ is the instantaneous rate of change of the fish population, N is the population at time t, and r and N_s are parameters, or fixed quantities.

Equation 1 states that the dependence of the natural growth rate, $\frac{dN}{dt}$, on the population, N, is such that it is zero when $N = O$ and when $N = N_s$, positive when $O < N < N_s$ and negative when $N > N_s$. When $N = \frac{1}{2} N_s$, the natural rate of increase attains a maximum. Further, over the range of positive growth rates, the relation is symmetrical about $N = \frac{1}{2} N_s$. As Beverton and Holt pointed out (p. 330), the few experimental studies supporting equation 1 refer to increase in numbers, not in weight. To assume that growth in population weight is also a symmetrical sigmoid involves some difficulties of which the assumption that "the increase of the population depends solely on its total weight and is independent of the age- and size-composition of the individuals comprising them" appears to be the most serious. They remark, however, that this approach "seems to describe well enough the essential features of the growth towards stationary states of the very few natural populations for which suitable data are available." For this reason it will be adopted in what follows.

The solution to the differential equation in (1) is the well-known logistic growth curve.

$$N = \frac{N_s}{1-(1-N_s/N_0)\,e^{-rt}} \tag{2}$$

in which t is time, e is the natural logarithm base, and N_0 is the population at time zero or the initial population. The solution in equation 2 indicates that as time progresses the population will change from its initial value, N_0, and will finally reach the value N_s, the final stationary value. As equation 1 is written, this development of the population will take place without oscillations.

[Cunningham (1958:234) states that experimental studies with biological populations "almost invariably show a variation much like this (that shown by equation 2). However, instead of approaching the ultimate value (N_s) monotonically, there are usually overshoots and decaying oscillations about this value. Sometimes, even violent oscillations about this value are ob-

[1] According to Beverton and Holt (1957), the approach pursued in this section, the "sigmoid curve" theory, was developed by Hjort, Jahn, Ottestad, and Graham, and subsequently adopted in essence by a number of other authors in discussing problems of fishery exploitation (for example, Sette; Baerends; and Schaefer). For additional references, see the bibliography in Beverton and Holt's work. Some shortcomings of this approach are noted by Beverton and Holt. They, however, do state: "the sigmoid curve theory, by making the simplest reasonable assumption about the dynamics of a population, is valuable as a means of obtaining a rough appreciation from the minimum of data." It is hoped that fishery biologists will be interested enough in the models presented in this appendix to make improvements in the biological aspects of the analysis.

served." He discusses the following modification of equation 1, a mixed difference-differential equation, the solution to which may exhibit such oscillations:

$$\frac{dN}{dt}=rN\left(1-N_{t-n}/_{ns}\right)$$

in which N_{t-n} is the population lagged n time periods. If such a model is applicable to the halibut case and if the parameters in the model assume appropriate values, perhaps a case could be made for natural fluctuations in the halibut population as Burkenroad suggests; however, as far as the authors are aware, there are no empirical studies that have been carried through to test the validity of this modified form of equation 1.]

A MODEL OF AN EXPLOITED FISHERY

To take account of man's exploitation of the fish population, a model incorporating traditional economic considerations, as well as the biological considerations presented above, must be constructed. The elements of one such model are shown below:

Demand relationship: $X^d=a_1p+a_0 \quad a_1<0, a_0>0$ (3)
Supply relationship: $X^s=b_1p+b_2N \quad b_1 \text{ and } b_2>0$ (4)
Market—clearing: $X^d=X^s=X$ (5)

Biological constraint: $\frac{dN}{dt}=r\,N(1-N/N_s)-X$ (6)

The demand and supply relationships indicate the quantity of halibut demanded per unit time, X^d, and the quantity supplied per unit time, X^s as functions of the price per pound and of the price per pound and the fish population, respectively. Since a_1 is negative, a negative dependence of X^d on price exists: the higher the price, the smaller the quantity demanded. With b_1 and b_2 positive, a positive dependence of quantity supplied on price and population exists: the higher the price with a given population the larger the quantity supplied to the market by fishing enterprises; also, the larger the population with a given price, the larger the quantity supplied. (In brief, it is assumed that $\frac{\delta X^d}{\delta p} < 0$, $\frac{\delta X^s}{\delta p} > 0$ and $\frac{\delta X^s}{\delta N} > 0$.) The market-clearing equation states that the variables in the model, price, and population adjust to equate quantity supplied to quantity demanded. Lastly, the biological constraint indicates that the net rate of change in the population is the natural rate of increase, given by $rN\ (1-N/N_s)$ minus the amount taken by man per unit time, denoted by X.

To study the characteristics of the solutions to the model presented above, one finds it convenient to substitute X for X^d and X^s in the first two relations to obtain:

$$X = a_1 p + a_0,$$

and

$$X = b_1 p + b_2 N$$

Then upon multiplying the first of these last two equations by b_1 and the second by a_1 and subtracting the second from the first, it is possible to eliminate p and to obtain X in terms of N; that is

$$X = \frac{1}{b_1 - a_1}(b_1 a_0 - a_1 b_2 N)$$

This expression for X may then be substituted in the biological constraint (6) to yield

$$\frac{dN}{dt} = rN(1 - N/N_s) - \frac{1}{(b_1 - a_1)}(b_1 a_0 - a_1 b_2 N)$$

or

$$\frac{dN}{dt} + \frac{r}{N_s}N^2 - \left(r + \frac{a_1 b_2}{b_1 - a_1}\right)N + \frac{b_1 a_0}{b_1 - a_1} = 0. \quad (7)$$

This, then, is the fundamental equation for the population implied by the model. For convenience, it may be written as follows:

$$\frac{dN}{dt} + k_1 N^2 - (r - c)N + k_0 = 0 \quad (7')$$

where

$$k_1 \equiv \frac{r}{N_s}, c \equiv -\frac{a_1 b_2}{b_1 - a_1} \text{ and } k_0 \equiv \frac{b_1 a_0}{b_1 - a_1}.$$

Before obtaining an explicit solution to (7′), it is possible to infer some properties of the steady state solutions from phase-diagram considerations. That is, in a plot of $\frac{dN}{dt}$ against N, there will be two values of N for which $\frac{dN}{dt}=0$ as shown in the figure below:

Phase Diagram for Equation (7′)

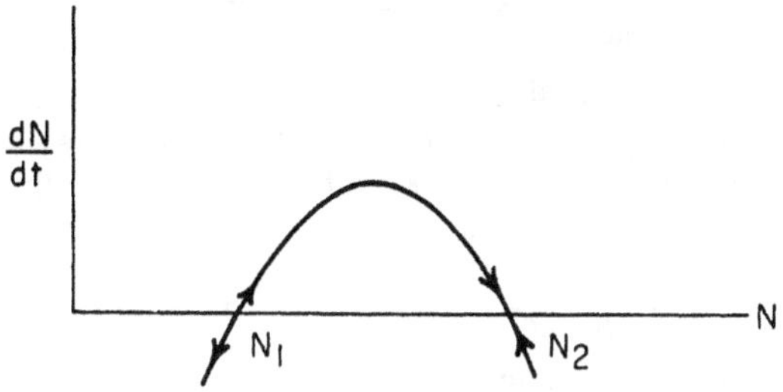

The phase diagram reveals that there are two values of the population, N_1 and N_2, for which the rate of change, $\frac{dN}{dt}=0$; however, one of these, N_1 is an unstable solution since a slight change in the population produces a movement away from N_1. At a population equal to N_2, $\frac{dN}{dt}=0$ and the solution is stable in the sense that with small disturbances the population will tend to reestablish at the level N_2. Explicitly,

$$N_2=1/2\,N_s\left[(1-c/r)+\sqrt{(1-c/r)^2-\frac{4\,k_0}{r\,N_s}}\right] \quad (8)$$

is the value of the population associated with the stable solution. Graphically the solution corresponds to the intersection of the demand curve, supply curve, and sustained yield curve (see fig. . . in the text.) In general, the stationary equilibrium will involve a stable equilibrium population, N_2, which is smaller than the steady-state population, N_s, associated with the unexploited fishery.

The general solution to (7′) may be obtained as follows, given that two particular solutions, N_1 and N_2, are known. Insert the particular solutions in (7′) to obtain:

$$k_1N_1^2-(r-c)N_1+k_0=0$$

and

$$b_1N_2^2-(r-c)N_2+k_0=0$$

Subtract each of these equations from (7′) to obtain:

$$\frac{dN}{dt}+k_1(N^2-N_1^2)-(r-c)\ (N-N_1)=0$$

and

$$\frac{dN}{dt}+k_1(N^2-N_2^2)-(r-c)\ (N-N_2)=0$$

Divide both sides of the first of these two last equations by $(N-N_1)$ and both sides of the second by $(N-N_2)$; then subtraction of the first from the second yields:

$$\frac{1}{N-N_2}\frac{dN}{dt}-\frac{1}{N-N_1}\frac{dN}{dt}+k_1(N_2-N_1)=0$$

Now integration yields:

$$\log(N-N_2)-\log(N-N_1)+k_1(N_2-N_1)t+K_1=0$$

or

$$\frac{N-N_2}{N-N_1}=Ke^{-k_1(N_2-N_1)t}$$

where K is a constant of integration. Finally, this last expression may be put in the following form:

$$N=\frac{N_2-N_1Ke^{-k_1(N_2-N_1)t}}{1-Ke^{-k_1(N_2-N_1)t}} \qquad (9)$$

Since $N_2>N_1$ and $k_1=\frac{r}{N_e}>O$, it is seen that as time progresses, N approaches N_2 the stable equilibrium solution.

While the model presented in equations (3)–(6) is an excellent starting point for the analysis of economic and biological changes in an exploited fishery, it suffers from at least one deficiency which is extremely important, namely, no allowance has been made for the effects of changes in income and technology, two factors which played a vital role in the halibut case. Consumer income, Y, should be included in the demand relationship and a technological improvement factor, T, should be included in the supply relationship. These two relationships now become:

$$X^d = a_1 p + a_2 Y + a_0, \tag{3'}$$

and,

$$X^s = b_1 p + b_2 N + b_3 T. \tag{4'}$$

Both a_2 and b_3 should be positive indicating that the higher the level of income, all other things constant, the greater the quantity of halibut demanded, and the higher the level of technique or technology, the larger the quantity of halibut supplied, all other things constant. Both Y and T are viewed as exogenously determined factors. The simplest assumption that can be made regarding Y and T is that they are trend factors obeying the following relationships:

$$Y = \alpha_0 + \alpha_1 t \tag{10}$$

and

$$T = \beta_0 + \beta_1 t \tag{11}$$

where the α's and β's are parameters and t represents time.

If these modifications are introduced, the differential equation for N, equation (7) above, now becomes:

$$\frac{dN}{dt} + \frac{r}{N_s} N^2 - \left(r + \frac{a_1 b_2}{b_1 - a_1}\right) N + \frac{1}{b_1 - a_1} [b_1 a_0 - b_1 a_2 Y - a_1 b_3 T] = 0 \tag{12}$$

Remembering that $a_1 < 0$, it is seen that both Y and T have positive coefficients in (12). Thus the differential equation for N may be written as follows (a modification of (7′) which takes account of (10) and (11) above):

$$\frac{dN}{dt} + k_1 N^2 - k_2 N + \delta_0 + \delta_1 t = 0 \tag{13}$$

with k_1, k_2, and c as defined above, and

$$\delta_0 \equiv \frac{1}{b_1 - a_1} (b_1 a_0 + b_1 a_2 \alpha_0 - a_1 b_3 \beta_0),$$

and

$$\delta_1 \equiv \frac{1}{b_1 - a_1} (b_1 a_2 \alpha_1 - a_1 b_3 \beta_1).$$

The quantity δ_0 will be larger than zero and, with Y and T growing, δ_1 will also be positive.

The following method of obtaining an approximate solution to (13) is described by Cunningham (1958:250–253). Let

$$Z = \exp\left(k_1 \int_0^t N dt\right).$$

Then equation (13) can be written in terms of Z as follows:

$$\frac{d^2Z}{dt^2} - k_2 \frac{dZ}{dt} + k_1(\delta_0 + \delta_1 t)Z = 0.$$

Letting

$$Z = Y \exp\left(\int \frac{k_2}{2} dt\right) \text{ or } Y = Z \exp\left(-\int \frac{k_2}{2} dt\right),$$

this last equation becomes:

$$\frac{d^2y}{dt^2} + \left[k_1(\delta_0 + \delta_1 t) - \left(\frac{k_2}{2}\right)^2\right]Y = 0$$

or

$$\frac{d^2y}{dt^2} + G(t)^2 Y = 0 \tag{14}$$

where

$$[G(t)]^2 = k_1(\delta_0 + \delta_1 t) - \left(\frac{k_2}{2}\right)^2.$$

An approximate solution to (14), the so-called WKBJ approximation, is

$$Y = \frac{1}{\sqrt{G}}[A \cos \phi(t) + B \sin \phi(t)],$$

where

$$\phi(t) \equiv \int G(t) \, \mathrm{dt}.$$

Then, from above,

$$Z = Y \exp\left(\int \frac{k_2}{2} dt\right) = \frac{\exp\left(\int \frac{k_2}{2} dt\right)}{\sqrt{G}} [A \cos \phi(t) + B \sin \phi(t)].$$

Since

$$N = \frac{1}{k_1 Z} \frac{dZ}{dt} = \frac{1}{k_1} \frac{d}{dt} 1n\, Z,$$

where $1n\, Z$ is the natural logarithm of Z, and

$$1n\, Z = \int \frac{k_2}{2} dt + 1n [A \cos \phi(t) + B \sin \phi(t)] - \frac{1}{4} 1n\, G^2.$$

Then,

$$N=\frac{1}{k_1}\left[\frac{k_2}{2}+\frac{(B\cos\phi(t)-A\sin\phi(t))\frac{d\phi}{dt}}{A\cos\phi(t)+B\sin\phi(t)}-\frac{1}{4}\frac{\frac{dG^2}{dt}}{G^2}\right].$$

From the expression for G^2, given above,

$$\frac{dG^2}{dt}=k_1\delta_1 .$$

Thus

$$N=\frac{k_2}{2k_1}-\frac{1}{4k_1}\frac{\delta_1}{\delta_0+\delta_1 t-\frac{k_2^2}{4k_1}}+$$

$$\frac{1}{k_1}\frac{B\cos\phi(t)-A\sin\phi(t)}{A\cos\phi(t)+B\sin\phi(t)}\frac{d\phi}{dt},$$

or

$$N=\frac{1}{2}N_*(1-\frac{c}{r})+\frac{N_*}{r}\frac{\delta_1}{(r-c)^2-4(\delta_0+\delta_1 t)}+$$

$$\frac{N_*}{r}\frac{B\cos\phi(t)-A\sin\phi(t)d\phi}{A\cos\phi(t)+B\sin\phi(t)dt} \qquad (15)$$

wherein use has been made of the definitions of k_1 and k_2. It is seen that as time progresses the second term in (15) approaches zero. The third term can give rise to oscillations. It is indeed interesting to observe that in a model without logarithms and with no oscillatory impressed force the approximate solution is characterized by an oscillatory component the characteristics of which, unfortunately, can not be specified precisely, given present inadequate knowledge of the values of parameters in the model.

MANAGEMENT OF A PRIVATELY OWNED FISH RESOURCE

In line with traditional economic theory, it is assumed that the owner of a fish resource will maximize discounted profits. Profits at time t are given by total revenue, pX, minus total costs, C; profits at time τ will then be given by:

$$\pi(\tau)=\int_{\tau}^{\infty}(pX-C)e^{-\delta t}dt \qquad (16)$$

in which δ is the discount rate employed by the owner of the fish resource. It is necessary to find the time paths of output, input, and fish population which maximize $\pi(\tau)$. (In the present case price, p, is assumed constant.) This is the problem of management as viewed by the private owner of a fish resource. (It is assumed that this resource owner is one of many so that variations in his output rate do not influence market price, p.)

In maximizing (16), the owner of the fish resource is subject to three constraints: (a) a technological production function relating fishing effort E and population to output, (b) a cost function for inputs, and (c) a biological constraint. These are set forth below:

Production function: $X = aE^{\alpha}N^{\beta}$ (17)

Cost function: $C = bE$ (18)

Biological constraint: $\frac{dN}{dt} = \tau N\left(1 - \frac{N}{N_{*}}\right) - X.$ (19)

Except for the parameters, α, β and b, the only new quantity introduced is E, input of fishing effort per unit time. The production function resembles one used by Schaefer except for the fact that his condition that $\alpha = \beta = 1$ has not been adopted. To conform with the law of diminishing returns, it is assumed herein that α and β lie between 0 and 1. The cost function, precisely similar to that employed by Gordon and others, states that units of fishing effort are available at a constant cost per unit. Finally, the biological constraint is the same one employed in the previous section.

The problem of the private resource owner is then to maximize discounted profits subject to the constraints, (17) – (19), that is to determine the time paths for X, N and E consistent with the constraints which make discounted profits a maximum. In addition to a different specification of the production function, the approach outlined above differs fundamentally from that employed by all other workers in that the private owner is not assumed to take a sustained yield. He may do so if this is consistent with profit maximization; however, this is not a requirement of the present approach.

To show the importance of this latter modification, results flowing from former analyses will be contrasted with those given by the present approach. Formerly, Gordon, Schaefer, and others have employed models very similar if not identical to that shown below:

Production function:	$X = aEN$
Sustained yield restriction:	$X = rN(1 - N/N_{*})$
Cost function:	$C = bE$
Profit equation:	$\pi = pX - C$

Note that the interest rate is ignored in this model. Now on substituting in the profit equation,

$$\pi = prN(1 - N/N_{*}) - \frac{br}{a}(1 - N/N_{*}).$$

The necessary condition for profit maximization, $\frac{d\pi}{dN} = 0$, yields the following stationary profit-maximizing population, N_m;

$$N_m = \frac{1}{2}\left(N_{*} + \frac{b}{ap}\right). \tag{20}$$

Since $\frac{N_{*}}{2}$ is the population compatible with a "maximum sustained physical yield," it is clear that the private resource owner takes less than a maximum sustained physical yield. Further, this formulation leads to the conclusion that the private resource owner will, in the process of profit maximization, operate with a fish population *larger* than that consistent with maximum sustained physical yield.

It is very interesting to note that introduction of a positive interest rate has no effect on N_m. This is obviously the case since the resource owner is assumed to take a sustained yield. That is, the sustained yield which maximizes profits in any period will also maximize discounted profits. Formally, the resource owner is now assumed to maximize discounted profits, $\pi(\tau)$, given by:

$$\pi(\tau) = \int_{\tau}^{\infty} (pX - C)\, e^{-\delta t} dt,$$

where δ is the interest rate. Maximization of the integral via an application of Euler's condition leads to the result given in (20). Thus within this model, the interest rate has no effect on the profit maximizing values of N, X, and E. This, it should be emphasized, is due to the ill-advised assumption that the resource owner is constrained to take a sustained yield.

If the sustained yield restriction in the above model is replaced by the biological constraint in (19), the profit-maximizing solution does depend on the interest rate. In fact (20) is the profit-maximizing population only if the interest rate is zero. In the present formulation, discounted profits are given by:

$$\pi(\tau) = \int_{\tau}^{\infty} (pX - C)\, e^{-\delta t} dt$$

$$= \int_{\tau}^{\infty} \left\{ p[rN(1 - N/N_s) - \dot{N}] - bE \right\} e^{-\delta t} dt$$

where $\dot{N} = dN/dt$. Since E can be expressed in terms of N and X and since $X = rN(1 - N/N_s) - \dot{N}$, from the biological constraint, the integrand is a function of N, $\dot{N}$ and t, say $I(N, N, t)$. That is,

$$\pi(\tau) = \int_{\tau}^{\infty} [rN(1 - N/N_s) - \dot{N}] \left[p - \frac{b}{aN} \right] e^{-\delta t} dt,$$

or

$$\pi(\tau) = \int_{\tau}^{\infty} I(N, \dot{N}, t)\, dt.$$

Application of the Euler necessary condition for an extremum, $\frac{\delta I}{\delta N} - \frac{d}{dt} \frac{\delta I}{\delta \dot{N}} = 0$, leads to the following value for the profit-maximizing population, N'_m:

$$N'_m = \frac{N_s}{4arp}\left[ap(r-\delta)+\frac{br}{N_s}+\right.$$

$$\left.\sqrt{\left[ap(r-\delta+\frac{br}{N_s}\right]^2+\frac{8apbr\,\delta'}{N_s}}\right]. \qquad (21)$$

It is interesting that once again a stationary population is a solution. Note too that in (21) there is a negative dependence of N'_m on the interest rate δ except for the second term under the square root sign which is small compared with other terms involving δ. Thus a rise in the interest rate leads the resource owner to reduce the fish population toward that compatible with a maximum sustained yield, thereby raising output. This can easily be seen by noting that the profit-maximizing value of output, X_m, may be obtained by substituting N'_m in the biological constraint given in (19).

Finally if the production function in (17) with α and β not necessarily equal to one is employed, the solution to the maximization problem is indeed complicated. In general it will involve both stationary and nonstationary solutions. In the particular case, $\alpha=\beta=\frac{1}{2}$ and $\delta=0$ which was chosen since it leads to the following relatively simple necessary condition for maximization:

$$\frac{d^2N}{dt^2}+\frac{1}{N}\left(\frac{dN}{dt}\right)^2+\left(\frac{2r}{N_s}N^2-\frac{2r}{N_s}N-r-\frac{2}{N}\right)\frac{dN}{dt}-\frac{3r^2}{N_s}N3$$

$$+\left(\frac{4r^2}{N_s}-\frac{2a^2pr}{b}\right)N^2+\left(\frac{a^2pr}{b}-r^2-\frac{2r}{N_s}\right)N+2r=0$$

Even under simplifying conditions, it is seen that the condition on N is complex. Particular stationary solutions may be obtained by solving the following equation:

$$\frac{3r^2}{N_s}N^3-\left(\frac{4r^2}{N_s}-\frac{2a^2pr}{b}\right)N^2+\left(\frac{a^2pr}{b}-r^2-\frac{2r}{N_s}\right)N+2r=0$$

The solutions to this cubic equation represent particular stationary solutions to the generalized problem under the special assumptions $\alpha=\beta=\frac{1}{2}$ and $\delta=0$.

LITERATURE CITED

BEVERTON, R. J. H., and S. J. HOLT.
1957. On the dynamics of exploited fishery populations. Her Majesty's Stationery Office, London, 533 p.

CUNNINGHAM, WALTER J.
1958. Introduction to non-linear analysis. McGraw, Hill Book Co., Inc., New York, 349 p.

CHAPTER 14

EXPLOITATION OF COMMON-PROPERTY REPLENISHABLE NATURAL RESOURCES

C. G. PLOURDE*
University of Western Ontario

This paper will expand the theory of common-property resources as developed for a commercial fishing industry by S. Gordon [4], C. Plourde [9] and J. Quirk and V. Smith [12]. A general equilibrium model of a two-good economy is developed. In this economy one of the two consumption goods is produced using a common-property natural resource. As in Quirk and Smith [12], the problem of optimal exploitation of this common-property natural resource is expressed as a control problem. This paper is able to achieve specific results by assuming restrictive properties on the functions describing biological growth, production of resource product and social utility.

I. A GENERAL EQUILIBRIUM MODEL

Assume an economy in which there are two consumer goods Y_1 and Y_2 and one variable input of production L, fixed in total supply and fully employed. Production of resource product Y_2 is summarized by the function $G(L_2,N)$ where N is the available natural resource mass and L_2 is the amount of L allocated to the resource sector. For convenience G will be specified as Cobb-Douglas. Hence G is continuous with continuous second partial derivatives, has positive marginal products for all positive amounts of inputs, $G_{ii}<0$ and L_2 and N are indispensable. Production of the other consumption good Y_1 is summarized by specification of $F(L_1)$ where $F'>0$, $F''<0$ and $F(0)=0$. Input L may be interpreted as efficiency units of labor, or a mixture of many variable inputs.

Assume human population is constant over time, and that there exists a social discount rate $\delta>0$. Denote the amount of Y_i consumed by C_i. It is required that the welfare functional

(1) $\int_0^\infty W(C_1,C_2)e^{-\delta t}dt$ be maximized subject to the constraints

(2) $$G(L_2,N) - C_2 \geqslant 0$$

(3) $$F(L_1) - C_1 \geqslant 0$$

(4) $$L_1 + L_2 = L$$

(5) $$dN/dt = \lambda N - \epsilon N^2 - G(L_2,N)$$

*This paper is taken in part from my doctoral dissertation [9]. I wish to thank my adviser, Professor Edward Foster, for helpful comments. All errors are the responsibility of the author.

Equation (5) represents the biological growth rate of the resource mass[1] after human extraction of amount $G(L_2,N)$. Assume an additive utility function, i.e., that $W(C_1, C_2) \equiv U(C_1) + V(C_2)$. Assume further that:

$$U'(*)>0,\ U''(*)<0,\ U'(C_1) \rightarrow \infty \text{ as } C_1 \rightarrow 0$$

$$V'(*)>0,\ V''(*)<0,\ V'(C_2) \rightarrow \infty \text{ as } C_2 \rightarrow 0$$

Necessary conditions for maximization of (1) subject to (2) through (5) and initial conditions $N(0) = N_0 > 0$ are[2] that there exist an auxiliary variable p_t and Lagrangian multipliers q_1, q_2, w such that controls, L_1, L_2, C_1, C_2, instantaneously maximize H, the current-value Hamiltonian (for all values of N_t) where

(6) $$H = U(C_1) + V(C_2) + p[\lambda N - \epsilon N^2 - G(L_2,N)] \text{ and}$$

(7) $$\Psi = U(C_1) + V(C_2) + p[\lambda N - \epsilon N^2 - G(L_2,N)] + q_1[F(L_1) - C_1] + q_2[G(L_2,N) - C_2] + w(L - L_1 - L_2)$$

and such that

(8) $$dp/dt = \delta p - p(\lambda - 2\epsilon N - \partial G/\partial N) - q_2 \partial G/\partial N$$

(5) $$dN/dt = \lambda N - \epsilon N^2 - G(L_2,N)$$

evaluated at the optimal values of the controls. Thus

a) $$U'(C_1) = q_1$$

b) $$V'(C_2) = q_2$$

c) $$(q_2 - p)G_1 = w = q_1 F'$$

These conditions which are necessary for an interior maximum can be interpreted as follows: q_1, q_2 and p are dynamic prices of goods Y_1, Y_2 and N respectively where N has an imputed price as an investment good. For example, a unit of fish in the ocean if not harvested at time t can be thought of as accumulating "interest" because of the natural growth of the biomass. Conditions (a) and (b) state that prices should equal mar-

1. See Plourde [10] or Smith [15] for details. Essentially N represents the biomass of a natural resource where λ and ϵ represent parameters and the resource is called replenishable if $\lambda > 0$. Fish extraction by man has the effect of a predator; thus $G(L_2,N)$ is subtracted from the natural growth function $\lambda N - \epsilon N^2$ to form (5).

2. Subscripts of t will be dropped except where their inclusion is instructive.

ginal utilities at each time t.[3] Condition (c) states that marginal revenue products (for society) should always be equal in both production sectors. This is a condition of social efficiency.

Equations (5) and (8) state the dynamic changes in resource mass N and its implicit price p as N varies due to its natural growth and human exploitation. In this model the biomass N_t is the only "state" variable. It is the endowment which is passed on from generation to generation. It will be convenient to express all other variables in terms of N and its price p.

L_1 and L_2 as functions of N and p. For any given values (N_0, p_0) of the state and auxiliary variables, condition (c) states that

$$(q_2 - p_0) G_1(L_2, N_0) = q_1 F'(L_1)$$

Using (a) and (b), condition (c) becomes

$$\{V'[G(L_2, N_0)] - p_0\} G_1(L_2, N_0) = \{U'[F(L_1)]\} F'(L_1)$$

This relationship implicitly defines L_1 and L_2 as functions of N and p. Define

$$(9)\quad M \equiv \{V'[G(L_2, N)] - p\} G_1(L_2, N) - \{U'[F(L - L_2)]\} F'(L - L_2)$$

Now

$$M(N, p, L_2) = 0 \text{ and } M_3 = D$$

where

$$(10)\qquad D = V''G_1^2 + (V' - p)G_{11} + U''(F'F') + U'F''$$

But V'', G_{11}, U'', and F'' are negative and G_1^2, $V' - p$, F', and U' are nonnegative. Unless no production takes place at all, $D < 0$.[4] So for (N, p) satisfying the necessary conditions for maximizing H one may write[5]

$$L_2 = f(N, p)$$

where f is continuous at (N, p) and has continuous first partials given by

$$(11)\qquad f_1 = -M_1/D = -[V''G_1G_2 + (V' - p)G_{12}]/D$$

3. It is at this point that specification of a (separable) additive utility function is convenient. For the interesting case where resource product is desired, $q_2 > 0$, therefore $C_2 = G(L_2, N)$. It is instructive to write q_2 as a function of L_2 and N, i.e., $q_2 = V'(C_2) = V'[G(L_2, N]$ in order to show L_2 as a function of N and p. For the complications that arise when the utility function is not separable, see Uzawa [18].

4. If $(q_2 - p)$ and q_1 were given market prices, and if condition (c) were the first-order condition for profit maximization for a competitive firm, then $D < 0$ would be the second-order condition that profits be maximized, or, equivalently, that variable inputs be used efficiently.

5. See Taylor [17, p. 241].

(12) $f_2 = -M_2/D = G_1/D < 0$ since $G_1 > 0$ and $D < 0$

These derivatives represent the changes in allocation of L to production of Y_1 and Y_2 that are necessary for efficiency when the biomass N or the implicit price p change. From (12) $\partial L_2/\partial p < 0$, so as the price of uncaught fish goes up, that is, as fish in the ocean as an investment becomes more socially valuable, less effort should be used in extraction. The more society wishes to "save" the resource for the future, the less it should fish today.

A crucial question in this analysis concerns the sign of f_1 in (11). As the biomass N increases, is it socially efficient and desirable to increase fishing effort or to decrease it? If $\partial L_2/\partial N > 0$, more L may be allocated to Sector 2 because, combined with more N, L is more productive in this sector. Or L might move out of Sector 2, if, for example, no more of C_2 is wanted and N is substituted for L_2 in production. In this case $\partial L_2/\partial N < 0$.

The sign of $\partial L_2/\partial N$ depends jointly upon the substitutability of factors L and N, which can be represented through the elasticity of substitution $e = (G_1 G_2)/(G G_{12})$, and the desire of society for products Y_1 and Y_2, which can be expressed through the elasticity of marginal utility $m = -C_2(V''/V')$.[6] In equilibrium $q_2 > 0$ and $C_2 = G$, so $me = -C_2(V''/V')(G_1 G_2/G G_{12})$.

Sign f_1 = sign $\{V''G_1 G_2 + V'G_{12}\} \gtreqless 0$ as $1 \gtreqless me + p/q_2$ and hence as $1 - em \gtreqless p/q_2$. For $G(L_2,N)$ Cobb-Douglas $e = 1$. Assume $G_{12} > 0$. Hence the sign of f_1 is the same as the sign of $(1 - m - p/q_2)$. From condition (c), $(q_2 - p) > 0$ and $(1 - p/q_2) > 0$. For $m = 0$ clearly $f_1 > 0$. However, generally the values of m, p and q_2 must be known before it can be decided whether $f_1 \gtreqless 0$. In this paper the case where $f_1 > 0$ will be treated in full. The $f_1 = 0$ case is quite trivial, and the $f_1 < 0$ case can be developed in the same way as for $f_1 > 0$.[7]

II. STEADY-STATE EQUILIBRIUM FOR INTERIOR SOLUTIONS

The system of differential equations (5) and (8) along with the initial

6. For $V(C_2) = C_2^a$, $m = 1 - a$. For $V(C_2)$ linear, $m = 0$, and quadratic $m = 1$. A. K. Sen [14] shows that in a primitive, one-factor economy, m constant and less than unity is the only case that leads to intuitively appealing results.

Green [5] and Hicks [7, p. 252] conclude that if utility functions are to be stationary, homogeneous and independent over time, then m should exceed unity and be constant. Upon integrating one can show this condition requires there exist a Bliss state, as Ramsey employed.

7. Plourde [9] contains a full derivation of the case when $f_1 \leqslant 0$.

state value for the biomass N_0 describe the way the variables N_t and p_t should vary optimally over time. The steady-state equilibrium will now be analyzed. For notational convenience call

(13) $$G(L_2(N,p),N) = Q(N,p), \text{ so}$$

(14) $$Q_N = G_1(\partial L_2/\partial N) + G_2$$

(15) $$Q_p = G_1(\partial L_2/\partial p)$$

The differential equations that describe flows of points (N_t,p_t) in phase space are

(5) $$dN_t/dt = \lambda N_t - \epsilon N_t^2 - Q(N,p)$$

(8) $$dp_t/dt = p_t(\delta - \lambda + 2\epsilon N_t + G_2) - V'[Q(N,p)]G_2$$

where $G_2 = \partial G/\partial N$.[8]

For this autonomous system an equilibrium is the steady-state defined by (N^*,p^*) such that $dN/dt = dp/dt = 0$ at (N^*,p^*).

Slopes of dp/dt and dN/dt curves in Phase Space $N \times p$. The following analysis will determine the slopes dp/dN for $dp/dt = 0$ and $dN/dt = 0$. Consider the graph of $dN/dt = 0$ in Figure 2. $dN/dt = 0$ if and only if $\lambda N - \epsilon N^2 = Q(N,p)$, or $\gamma(N,p) = 0$ where $\gamma = \lambda N - \epsilon N^2 - Q(N,p)$. $\gamma_2 = -Q_p = -G_1(\partial L_2/\partial p) > 0$ so implicit differentiation is valid. Therefore

(16) $$dp/dN = -(\partial\gamma/\partial N)/(\partial\gamma/\partial p) = \{\lambda - 2\epsilon N - Q_N\}/G_1(\partial L_2/\partial p)$$

The denominator of (16) is $(-\gamma_2)$ which is negative. If $Q_N \geqslant \lambda - 2\epsilon N$, then the denominator of (16) is non-positive and $dp/dN \geqslant 0$. If $Q_N < \lambda - 2\epsilon N$, then $dp/dN < 0$. Both cases are possible and will be considered later in Figure 1.

Consider next the graph of $dp/dt = 0$. Define

(17) $$R(N,p) = p[\delta - \lambda + 2\epsilon N + G_2] - q_2 G_2 = 0$$

where

$$q_2 = q_2(N,p) = V'[Q(N,p)] \text{ and}$$

$$G_2(L_2,N) = G_2[L_2(N,p),N]$$

8. Equation (8) results from expanding $dp/dt = \delta p - (\partial\psi/\partial N)$ evaluated at (N_t,p_t,L_2^*) where $L_2^* = L_2^*(N,p)$ and $\psi = W(C_1,C_2) + p(\lambda N - \epsilon N^2 - G(L_2,N)) + q_2[G(L_2,N) - C_2] + q_1[F(L_1) - C_1] + w(L - L_1 - L_2)$.

Figure 1

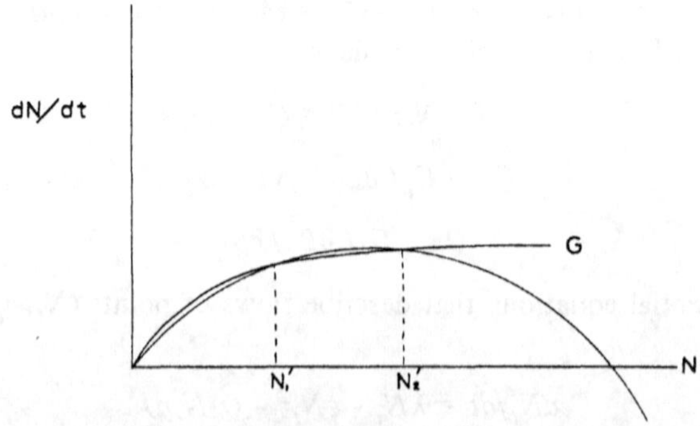

Figure 2

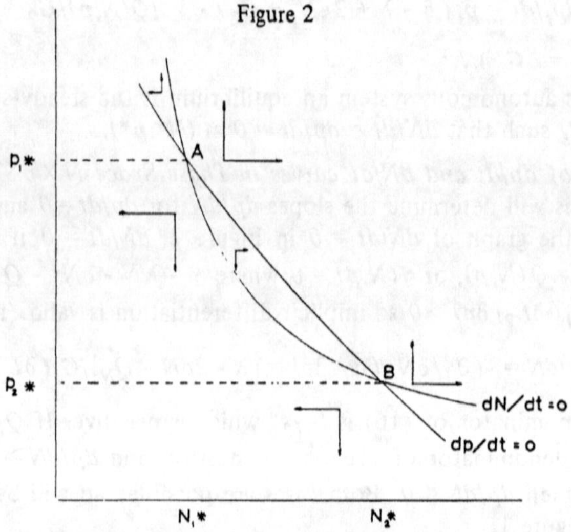

From (15) and (12)

$$(18) \qquad \partial q_2/\partial p = V''[G_1(\partial L_2/\partial p)] = +V''G_1(G_1)/D$$

where from (10) $D = V''G_1^2 + (V' - p)G_{11} + U''(F'F') + U'(F'')$. Therefore $D < V''G_1^2 < 0$ and

$$(19) \qquad 0 < \partial q_2/\partial p < 1$$

Condition (19) states that a rise in the imputed demand price of investment (in terms of the utility of present consumption foregone) will be accompanied by a rise (smaller in size) of the imputed demand price of resource product; i.e., the more one desires to have fish product in the future, the higher will be his present imputed price of fish product.

Since $q_2 > 0$, then $R(N,p) = 0$ implies $p \neq 0$. Interpret p as the imputed price of the unharvested resource. This study is interested only in commercially exploitable natural resources, not in such resource questions as lamprey control, so only the case where $p > 0$ will be of interest. Hence

$$\delta - \lambda + 2\epsilon N + G_2 = (q_2/p)G_2 \tag{20}$$

and in order to satisfy $dp/dt = 0$, values of N will be defined by

$$N^{**} = \{\lambda - \delta + [(q_2 - p)/p]G_2\}/2\epsilon \tag{21}$$

Since

$$(q_2 - p)G_1 = w = q_1 F' > 0 \text{ and } G_1 > 0 \text{ from condition (c)} \tag{22}$$

Therefore $(q_2 - p) > 0$ and $N^{**} > (\lambda - \delta)/2\epsilon$.

Heuristically, the condition $(q_2 - p) > 0$ states that the imputed demand price of the resource product exceeds the imputed demand price of the unharvested resource. In my earlier model on fishing [10] these prices were equal. The difference revealed in the present model is caused by the existence of production costs. The equilibrium value of N here must exceed the value $(\lambda - \delta)/2\epsilon$ which was the equilibrium value of the simplified model.

Whenever there are costs of production, the optimal steady-state population will exceed the modified maximum sustained yield population. This conclusion was reached earlier by Crutchfield and Zellner [3].

Along the curve $dp/dt = 0$

$$dp/dN = -(\partial R/\partial N)/(\partial R/\partial p) \text{ if } \partial R/\partial p \neq 0 \text{ where} \tag{23}$$

$$\partial R/\partial p = [(p - q_2)G_{21}(\partial L_2/\partial p) + G_2(1 - \partial q_2/\partial p) + \delta - \lambda + 2\epsilon N]$$

However $(1 - \partial q_2/\partial p) > 0$. $\partial L_2/\partial p < 0$ and $N^{**} > (\lambda - \delta)/2\epsilon$, and so $\delta - \lambda + 2\epsilon N > 0$. Hence $\partial R/\partial p > 0$. The sign of $\partial R/\partial N$ will be positive for $\partial L_2/\partial N > 0$ as illustrated below.

$$\partial R/\partial N = 2\epsilon p + (p - q_2)[G_{22} + G_{21}\partial L_2/\partial N] - G_2 \partial q_2/\partial N \tag{24}$$

where $\partial q_2/\partial N = Q_N(V'') = V''[G_2 + G_1(\partial L_2/\partial N)]$. So $\partial q_2/\partial N < 0$ and

$G_{22} + G_{21}(\partial L_2/\partial N)<0$.[9] It follows that $\partial R/\partial N>0$ and $dp/dN<0$.

Phase Space. It was just shown that the slope of the curve $dp/dt = 0$ in phase space is negative. The $dN/dt = 0$ curve may have any slope and will intersect the $dp/dt = 0$ curve in zero, one or two points as illustrated in Figure 1. Since it is the intention of this analysis to study properties of steady-state equilibria, attention will be directed to the last two cases. If the number of intersections is one, it will be shown that the slope of the $dN/dt = 0$ curve will be positive and the resulting equilibrium will be a saddle-point. If there are two intersections (see Figure 2) then it will be shown that one is unstable, the other is a saddle-point.

Consider again the curve $dN/dt = 0$. For each $p>0$ there may be two positive values of N as in Figure 1. Label them N_1' and N_2' for a cross-section of $Q(N,p)$ at $p = p'$. Assume $N_1'<N_2'$. At (N_2',p'), $Q_N>\lambda-2\epsilon N$, and therefore $dp/dN>0$. At (N_1',p') assume $Q_N<\lambda - 2\epsilon N$, and therefore $dp/dN<0$. If $N_2'=N_1'$, then $Q_N = \lambda - 2\epsilon N$ and $dp/dN = 0$.

The phase diagram for the case of two intersections depicted in Figure 1 is given in Figure 2. In it there are two possible steady-state equilibria labelled A and B. It will be shown later that A is an unstable equilibrium and that B is a saddle-point.

If $N_0<N_1^*$ in Figure 2, the resource mass should be reduced to zero; if $N_0 = N_1^*$ it should (perhaps) stay there, and for $N_0>N_1^*$ there exists an optimal trajectory that the economy should follow to approach the long-run biomass level of N_2^*.

Trajectories in Phase Space. In Figure 2, $dN/dt = \lambda N - \epsilon N^2 - Q(N,p)$. It is easily verified that above the line $dN/dt = 0$ it is true that $dN/dt>0$, and below it $dN/dt<0$ since $G[L_2(N_0,p),N_0]$ is a decreasing function of p. Since $dp/dt = p(\delta - \lambda + 2\epsilon N) - (q_2 - p)G_2$ is an increasing function of N, therefore above and to the right of $dp/dt = 0$ it follows that $dp/dt>0$ and to the left $dp/dt<0$. Arrows in Figure 2 indicate direction of movements of points in Phase Space.

To Show (N_2^*, p^*) is a Saddle-Point. Expand dp/dt and dN/dt about

9. To show $G_{22} + G_{21}(\partial L_2/\partial N)<0$ for $G(L_2,N)$ Cobb-Douglas of degree $\gamma<1$ employ Euler's theorem to get $NG_2 + L_2G_1 = \gamma G$ and

$$N[G_{22} + G_{21}(\partial L_2/\partial N)] = (\gamma - 1)[G_1\partial L_2/\partial N + G_2] - L_2[G_{12} + G_{11}(\partial L_2/\partial N)] \tag{26}$$

But $\partial L_2/\partial N = -\{G_2 + [(V' - p)G_{12}]/V''G_1\}/G_1 + [(V' - p)G_{11}]\, V''G_1 + P$ where P represents the positive term $\{[U''(F'F') + U'F'']/V''G_1\}$. Subtracting the positive term $[\partial L_2/\partial N)G_1 + G_2]$ from (26) yields $(V' - p)[G_{11}(\partial L_2/\partial N) + G_{12}]/V'' + G_1P<0$. Hence $G_{12} + G_{11}(\partial L_2/\partial N)>0$ and since $(\gamma - 1)<0$ from (26), the desired result is obtained.

(N_2^*, p^*) as a Taylor series, taking only linear terms.

$$\begin{bmatrix} dp/dt \\ \\ dN/dt \end{bmatrix} = A \begin{bmatrix} p - p^* \\ \\ N - N_2^* \end{bmatrix}$$

where A is a constant 2×2 matrix. It can be shown that the eigenvalues of A are real and of opposite sign. Alternatively, using L'Hospital's Rule and evaluating derivatives at (N_2^*, p^*),

$$dp/dN = (d(dp/dt)/dN)/(d(dN/dt)/dN) \tag{25}$$

This results in a quadratic equation in (dp/dN). The product of the roots is $(Qp)(\partial R/\partial N)$ which is negative. Hence the roots are of opposite sign and real, so (N_2^*, p^*) or B is a saddle-point. The same analysis will give two positive eigenvalues for A and hence show it is unstable. The optimal trajectory to B will correspond to the negative root.[10]

III. RELATION OF N^* TO OTHER STEADY-STATE VALUES

In this model the steady-state biomass is $N^* = [(\lambda - \delta)/2\epsilon] + [(q_2 - p)/2\epsilon p]$. Clearly $(q_2 - p)/2\epsilon p$ is non-negative, and the larger is q_2 relative to p the larger is N^*. When production is costless $q_2 = p$ and the steady-state value is that given in Plourde [10] which is less than the maximum sustained yield biomass $\lambda/2\epsilon$. Rewriting N^* as $N^* = \lambda/2\epsilon + [q_2 - p(1 + \delta)]/2\epsilon$, it is noticed that there is no a priori reason to suspect N^* will be either larger or less than $\lambda/2\epsilon$.

As δ increases, N^* decreases. This is intuitively appealing since one expects it is generally socially advisable to harvest less resource the higher society weights the consumption of future generations. If in fact $q_2 - p(1 + \delta) \geqslant \lambda$, the resource would not be harvested at all. In this case costs of harvesting are prohibitively high and all variable input should be allocated to production of Y_1. Changes in tastes or technology may cause shifts in optimal steady-state resource biomasses. Interesting examples at the present time are swordfish and tuna, which require increased costs in processing, and seals or whales where public concern over possible extinction has caused a shift in tastes.

IV. REGULATION OF THE INDUSTRY: TAXES VS. QUOTAS

Typically, regulation of fishing has been done by means of seasonal quotas as for example in the case of halibut. As much of the literature[11]

10. Since $p_t e^{-\delta t} \to 0$ and $N_t \to N^*$ as $t \to \infty$ it follows that the transversality conditions are met. Sufficient conditions are not easily found. See [8].

11. For examples see [3] [4] [10] [12] and [16].

has pointed out, if quotas are set equal to the maximum sustained yield, there is no a priori reason for such conservation programs to be optimal because the prescription gives no direction as to how to correctly achieve a desired steady-state, and the steady-state chosen is probably nonoptimal. The model above clearly specifies a desired steady-state and how to achieve it from any initial point.

Control may take the form of quotas, but it is easy to devise dynamic tax rates that are equivalent in effect[12] and have the added advantage of providing signals to the controller if changes in parameters take place. The tax has the effect of internalizing the common-property externality through appropriation. It may be the case that auctioning of fishing rights is preferred to per unit taxes.

The popular concern for expanding the future role of economic resources and the common-property nature of these resources suggest the need for international control. In fact OECD has proved to be an important source of data, and there is hope that international control will result for currently uncontrolled species.

Difficult measurement problems are inevitable. One is the measurement of the present biomass. Another is estimation of the growth function. Current research suggests the curve may not be a logistic. With slight modification the analysis above can be applied to any functional form of the growth law that achieves a maximum and for which $dN/dt = 0$ for N sufficiently large.

12. Such taxing schemes are derived in [9] and [12].

REFERENCES

1. K. Arrow, "Applications of Control Theory to Optimal Growth," Institute for Mathematical Studies in the Social Sciences, Stanford Univ., 1967.
2. F. Christy and A. Scott, *The Common Wealth of Ocean Fisheries*. Baltimore 1965.
3. J. Crutchfield and A. Zellner, "Economic Aspects of the Pacific Halibut Fishery," *Fishery Industrial Research*, *1*, No. 1, Department of the Interior, Washington, Apr. 1962.
4. H. S. Gordon, "The Economic Theory of a Common-Property Resource: The Fishery," *Jour. Pol. Econ.*, Apr. 1954, *62*, 124-42.
5. H. A. J. Green, "Intertemporal Utility and Consumption," *Oxford Econ. Papers*, Mar. 1967, New Series *19*, 111-15.
6. M. Hestenes, *Calculus of Variations and Optimal Control Theory*. New York 1966.
7. J. R. Hicks, *Capital and Growth*. Oxford 1965.
8. O. L. Mangasarian, "Sufficient Conditions for the Optimal Growth of Nonlinear Systems," *SIAM Journal of Control*, 1966, *4*, 139-52.
9. C. G. Plourde, *Optimal Exploitation of a Replenishable Natural Resource*. Unpublished doctoral dissertation, Univ. of Minnesota, 1970.

10. ———, "A Simple Model of Replenishable Natural Resource Exploitation," *Am. Econ. Rev.*, June 1970, *60*, 518-22.

11. L. S. Pontryagin, et al. (translation), *The Mathematical Theory of Optimal Processes*. New York 1962.

12. J. Quirk and V. Smith, "Dynamic Economic Models of Fishing," *Research Paper 22*, Department of Economics, Univ. of Kansas, June 1969.

13. A. Scott, "The Fishery: The Objectives of Sole Ownership," *Jour. Pol. Econ.*, Apr. 1955, *63*, 116-24.

14. A. K. Sen, "Peasants and Dualism With or Without Surplus Labor," *Jour. Pol. Econ.*, Oct. 1966, *74*, 425-50.

15. V. Smith, "Economics of Production from Natural Resources," *Am. Econ. Rev.*, June 1968, *58*, 409-31.

16. ———, "On Models of Commercial Fishing," *Jour. Pol. Econ.*, Mar./Apr. 1969, *77*, 181-98.

17. A. Taylor, *Advanced Calculus*. Boston 1955.

18. H. Uzawa, "An Optimum Fiscal Policy in an Aggregative Model of Economic Growth," in *The Theory and Design of Economic Development*, eds., I. Adelman and E. Thorbecke, Baltimore, 1966.

CHAPTER 15

The Primitive Hunter Culture, Pleistocene Extinction, and the Rise of Agriculture

Vernon L. Smith

University of Southern California and California Institute of Technology

The hypothesis that megafauna extinction some 10,000 years ago was due to "overkill" by Paleolithic hunters is examined using an economic model of a replenishable resource. The large herding animals that became extinct, such as mammoth, bison, camel, and mastodon, presented low hunting cost and high kill value. The absence of appropriation provided incentives for the wastage killing evident in some kill sites, while the slow growth, long lives, and long maturation of large animals increased their vulnerability to extinction. Free-access hunting is compared with socially optimal hunting and used to interpret the development of conservationist ethics, and controls, in more recent primitive cultures.

1. Introduction

Many archaeologists and other scientists believe that the available evidence supports the hypothesis—startling to nonspecialists—that the unusual incidence of large-animal extinctions throughout the world during the late Pleistocene period was caused, to an important extent, by Paleolithic hunters. Even if true, the extinction of large animals is but one of the more dramatic examples of the very substantial impact that primitive as well as modern man has had on his "natural" environment (Heizer 1955). The purpose of this essay is threefold: (1) to acquaint

Support from the National Science Foundation, the Center for Advanced Study in the Behavioral Sciences, and the Fairchild Distinguished Scholar program at Caltech is gratefully acknowledged. I wish also to express my debt to Robert F. Heizer for a great deal of help and encouragement in the course of many discussions on the topic of this paper and for providing me with a guide to the relevant archaeological literature. If I have been a poor student, he bears no responsibility for the final product.

economists with some of the evidence and hypotheses from other sciences concerning the role of primitive man as hunter par excellence, (2) to parameterize some important features of these observations and hypotheses in the context of a model of the primitive hunter culture which, in the face of animal extinctions, turns increasingly to agriculture, and (3) to attempt to demonstrate to archaeologists and other scientists the potential that economic analysis may have in unifying and integrating this body of evidence and conjecture. In what follows, the reader should bear in mind that much of the "evidence" to which reference will be made is subject to dispute; certainly the interpretation of that evidence is controversial.

It is my belief, in reading the archaeological literature in this area, that there is a natural economic rationale for "overkill" as a possible explanation for the large-animal extinctions which has not been adequately or fully articulated. Briefly stated, the large extinct herbivores hunted by primitive men, such as the mammoth and bison, were gregarious herd animals, easily located, and apparently easily approached and struck with crude missile weapons or stampeded into "jumps." Multiple kills were therefore likely, but because of their large size, even a single kill represented high value. The combination of low hunting cost and high value would make large animals the most economical prey. Furthermore, in the absence of appropriation or other incentives for the individual hunter to attach value to the live animal stock, wastage killing was possibly commonplace. Biologically, the larger genera of animals are characterized by slow growth, long lives, and long periods of maturation, and are therefore the most vulnerable to hunting pressure. That is, the hunter harvest is more likely to exceed net biological growth, causing a decline in biomass.

In Section 2, some of the facts, conjectures, and interpretations of late Pleistocene extinctions are summarized. In Section 3, a particularly simple form of existing models of production from common-property replenishable resources is used to stylize the hunter-agrarian economy. This permits a comparative-statics treatment of the effect of prey size, vulnerability, and value, and of predator technology and population, on prey biomass and extinction potential (Section 4). Socially optimal hunting is modeled in Sections 5 and 6 and the Appendix, on the assumption that institutional mechanisms of control (property-right systems or cultural or legal constraints that internalize the social costs of individual hunter actions) are adequate to support the optimal sustained-yield harvesting of prey. These optimal patterns are compared with free-access hunting. This analysis is used to develop the conditions under which it may be optimal to "conserve" or, alternatively, to destroy a hunted species and to compare such cases with the corresponding free-access solutions.

2. The Hypotheses of Pleistocene Extinction

One of the great scientific puzzles studied extensively by archaeologists, paleontologists, and geologists is the cause and process of the unprecedented wave of large-animal extinction in the late Pleistocene period. Martin (1967, pp. 75, 82–86) suggests the loss of over 200 genera worldwide and lists 80 late Pleistocene extinct animals in continental North America of which 49 had an average adult body weight in excess of 110 pounds (the "megafauna"). These megafauna included camels, horses, bison, mastodons, llamas, ground sloths (including a giant the size of an elephant), mammoths (the largest, *Mammuthus imperator*, was 13 feet tall and considerably larger than the African elephant), beavers, short-faced bears, armadillos, several saber-tooth cats (including *Smilodon*, the tiger), shrub oxen, moose, tapirs, antelope, and many more. Of the 49 genera in the late Pleistocene, 33 became extinct at a time which could have roughly coincided with the arrival of the Paleo-Indians in North America. Of the 31 smaller extinct mammals listed by Martin, only one could have been associated with man. Those terminal Pleistocene megafauna apparently found in "direct association" with man include ground sloths, camels, mastodons, horses, mammoths, shrub oxen, tapirs, and the extinct bison. Evidence of human predation is clearest in the case of mammoth and extinct bison. That Clovis fluted-point hunters killed mammoth around 11,000 years ago is hardly open to question, and sometime later, perhaps after the sudden disappearance of the mammoth, the Folsom point was developed and used to kill now-extinct bison (Haynes 1964). The Clovis, Folsom, and subsequent Scottsbluff point projectile technologies seem specifically designed for big-game hunting.

Although accelerated extinctions had occurred in periods earlier than the late Pleistocene, they had affected marine organisms, plants, and the smaller mammals as well as the larger mammals. Furthermore, the pattern of worldwide extinction of the larger mammals seems suspiciously to correlate with the migration chronology of man. This has led Martin (also see Sauer 1944) to the hypothesis that Pleistocene extinction was due to overkill by Paleolithic hunters armed with the stone-tipped spear, fire, and the communal hunting party. Martin (1967, p. 75) states:

> Except on islands where smaller animals disappeared, extinction struck only the large terrestrial herbivores, their ecologically dependent carnivores, and their scavengers. Although it may have occurred during times of climatic change, the event is not clearly related to climatic change. One must seek another cause. Extinction closely follows the chronology of prehistoric man's spread and his development as a big-game hunter. No continents or islands are known in which accelerated extinction

> definitely predates man's arrival. The phenomenon of overkill alone explains the global extinction pattern.

A scenario built around this hypothesis goes as follows: For 200,000 years prior to the arrival of man, the large herbivores of North America were increasing in diversity and experienced no shrinkage of range. They evolved and survived over tens of millions of years in the presence of numerous environmental changes and predators. Several genera had emigrated over the Bering land bridge to the hospitable environment of North America. Consequently, the North America of 15,000 years ago was comparable to nineteenth-century Africa in terms of the huge, strange, "unlikely" beasts that grazed the plains and browsed the forests and brush. Then, approximately 12,000 years ago, the first Paleolithic men, ancestors of many of the present-day Indians, arrived across the exposed Bering land bridge. They were hunters, perhaps driven to wider migration by the dwindling herds of prey in Eurasia. They brought with them the culture, skill, and technology of big-game hunting—the spear, perhaps the atlatl (spear thrower), fire, and stone projectile points. At some time in this migration, they developed the Clovis fluted point—a work of craftsmanship in stone carefully adapted to the demands of killing large animals. These hunters preyed on gregarious herds of mammoth, bison, and perhaps mastodon, camels, tapirs, horses, and other animals which were easy to locate and probably showed little fear of the new predators. By 11,000 years ago, this efficient new predator had wiped out the mammoth and was concentrating on now-extinct species of bison. The bison may have been killed by jumps (as was common within historic times by Indians) and perhaps fire drives, and by this time the Clovis point was giving way to the Folsom projectile point. The population of Paleo-Indians expanded rapidly across North and South America, appearing at the southern tip of South America by 10,000 years ago, and, one may conjecture, lived affluently for as long as the game was plentiful. As the herds disappeared, their predators, the saber-toothed tiger, dire wolf, and hyena, became extinct. Hunting effort was directed at smaller, less vulnerable game which produced a relatively meager existence and was eventually replaced by an agricultural technology in which subsistence depended on crops of corn (and later beans and squash) supplemented with small game.

The scenario is plausible but is by no means an established fact. That man arrived about 12,000 years ago is probable, as there is no firm radiocarbon dating of any earlier evidence of man (Haynes 1967). That man hunted mammoth and, later, two species of now-extinct bison is surely a certainty based on documented kill sites (Haury, Antevs, and Lance 1953; Gross 1951; Agogino and Frankforter 1960; Leonhardy 1966).[1] Hester

[1] This is conjecture on my part, but it seems plausible that the Bering land bridge might have acted as a filter through which only the most able hunting tribes could have

and Wendorf (1962, pp. 166–67) report that the most common hunting pattern for both mammoth and bison was to stalk and kill animals while they were drinking in a pond or stream. Killing occurred by means of spears aimed at the thoracic region, although in one site, the presence of boulders suggests they were used to kill wounded mammoth. A second pattern was the stampede, probably present in three kill sites of early man. The animals (extinct bison) were driven into a stream or over a cliff, sometimes in numbers as high as several hundred. At the Olsen-Chubbuck site in Colorado, well-preserved and carefully excavated remains of bones and artifacts prove that about 8,500 years ago some 200 *Bison occidentalis* were stampeded into an arroyo only 5–7 feet deep. The injured animals were killed by projectile points generally of the Scottsbluff type. About 75 percent of the animals were then systematically butchered (Wheat 1967). The killing of bison in the sixteenth to eighteenth centuries by stampeding them over carefully selected "jumps" is quite well established (Kehoe 1967; Butler 1971).

Whether the early Americans stampeded animals by fire drives is not known, nor is it critical to the overkill hypothesis. The first account of the southwestern Indians, by Cabeza de Vaca, records that the inhabitants of what is now southwest Texas burned favorable animal ranges in order to deprive the animals of forage and force them to frequent areas where they could be more easily hunted (Covey 1961, p. 81; cited by Jelinek 1967, p. 197). Burning of this type (and there is abundant evidence for the occurrence of fires in association with man) could have been a more effective means by which man contributed to Pleistocene extinction than by the occasional fire drive. In the case of herd animals such as *Bison* that are easily stampeded, it is not clear that fire drives were even functional unless it was to ensure that the confused animals would not stampede in the wrong direction!

That the mammoth was gone by 10,000–11,000 years ago is also likely, based on radiocarbon dating. That there existed a big-game hunting tradition is also clearly established by the widespread occurrence of the Clovis projectile point type. It is found from Florida to Nova Scotia, in the high plains, the Southwest, across the Midwest, and in the South. It was a large projectile, 7–15 centimeters long and 3–4 centimeters wide. Bases were concave, and a fluting or channeling extended from the base up to one-half the length of the point. They were flaked by percussion and the base edges ground down to prevent cutting of the thongs that

---

passed. The bridge would not have been a suitable viaduct for a gatherer culture, "because no likely food sources but game existed for most of the year in the tundra areas they traversed" (Jelinek 1967, p. 195). Hence, the early North Americans may have been the product of a selection process that favored only the most mobile, skilled, and dedicated hunters. This could help explain why megafauna extinction in North America was more rapid than in Europe, Asia, and Africa.

secured them to the spear shaft.[2] Early American points were probably too heavy, large, and ill-designed for arrow tips. Spears, thrust or thrown as a javelin, or darts—perhaps propelled by the atlatl—were the main tool of the hunt. Clovis points date back to 12,000 years ago and apparently evolved into the Folsom. The Folsom point dates from about 10,000–11,000 years ago and is much less widely dispersed than the Clovis. The Folsom point is more delicately made, with fine-edge flaking, and is associated with the hunting of the extinct *Bison antiquus*. The Scottsbluff and several similar points date from about 9,000 years ago and are associated with the killing of the slightly smaller extinct *Bison occidentalis*. By 7,000–10,000 years ago, projectile points had been adapted to the killing of modern smaller game such as sheep, the so-called American bison, deer, and antelope. A primitive maize, perhaps in the early stages of domestication, has been dated by radiocarbon to around 5,000–6,000 years ago (Mangelsdorf and Smith 1949).

Until recently, the commonly accepted cause of late Pleistocene extinctions was climatic change and a reduction in grassland areas. This view probably still predominates. Thus, according to Guilday (1967, p. 121), "the fact that the late Pleistocene extinctions were so widespread and geographically almost simultaneous does call for a major overlying cause, however. I suggest that the prime mover was post-Pleistocene desiccation. Evidence for such an episode is present on all continents, and its effects would have been both swift and lethal. It may have been the spur to turn man from hunting to a life centered around animal husbandry and agriculture." This states the climatic as against the "overkill" extinction hypothesis. The desiccation referred to is associated with a drier climate following recession of the last great ice sheet.[3] A variant of the climate hypothesis attributes extinction to the effect of more severe seasonal fluctuations (colder winters, warmer summers) on those mammals with longer gestation periods (Slaughter 1967). But here we have an identification problem, for it is the mammals with longer gestation periods, longer periods of maternal care, and longer lives that are most vulnerable to hunting pressure.

[2] Jelinek (1967, p. 196) notes the significance of this design technology for the hypothesis of a vulnerable fauna (mammoth): "Grinding would prevent the edges of the point from cutting the lashing that bound it to a shaft if the point was subjected to repeated lateral stress" as would occur "in a point on a thrusting spear or lance whose shaft remained in the hand of the hunter after it penetrated the animal—a technique that would be most effective against a relatively easy quarry and of little use against a skittish and fearful prey."

[3] However, desiccation followed the three previous glaciation periods and in one instance was probably more severe. "Recent pollen evidence from western America seems to indicate that in at least some areas occupied by the extinct fauna the conditions following the retreat of an earlier glaciation (Illinoian) were probably more arid and as warm or warmer than at present. Thus conditions of temperature and aridity do not appear likely as direct causes of extinction" (Jelinek 1967, p. 194).

Finally, of course, there is the multiple-cause, or combination, hypothesis, here defined by Hester (1967, p. 170): "I take the view that Pleistocene man could not have caused the extinction of the North American megafauna until after natural causes had greatly reduced the population of each species." However, Hester's study of historical extinction (extinction or near extinction of species since European settlement) in North America lists (1) hunting by primitive man and (2) hunting by civilized man with firearms as the first and second major factors in order of frequency.

Much of the earlier skepticism surrounding the "overkill" hypothesis stems from a disbelief (to some extent perhaps a romantic disbelief) in the ability of primitive men to accomplish, with primitive instruments, the destruction of such huge creatures, already the prey of the formidable saber-toothed tiger and dire wolf. Yet these men were not genetically, in terms of intelligence and skill capacity, that different from modern man. Also, modern studies of predation by the timber wolf on Isle Royale indicate that moose stock may be strengthened by the killing of old, weak, and diseased animals (Mech 1970). The large kill sites of mammoth and bison suggest wastage—killing beyond immediate butchering requirements—so that there is some reason to believe that man was orders of magnitude more effective in predation than his animal competitors. Overfishing in historic times is well known. The demise of great whales (and recently the Alaskan king crab) is well known, and the capacity of man for wholesale rivalrous killing, even with the most primitive of weapons, is dramatically documented in the following *Palo Alto Times* (March 13, 1973) account:

> In the course of a few hours early Sunday a shoal of 637 pilot whales were driven into a narrow fjord on the island of Vaga (Faeroe Islands, Denmark) by stone-throwing islanders in an armada of small boats. Then they were slaughtered with long spears and knives in a gruesome spectacle that has been part of Faeroese life for centuries. The whales churned their tails furiously in shallow water . . . The shoal of whales was one of the biggest since more than 2000 pilot whales were killed in one day east of here 20 years ago.

Some time between 12,000 and 3,000 years ago the early Americans turned from an exclusively hunting and gathering culture to one based more and more on agriculture. I assume that men found it to their economic advantage to make this change. It is perhaps significant to the overkill hypothesis that man did not turn from big game to smaller game except as a supplement to agriculture, as a result of the large-animal extinctions. Even the plentiful American bison apparently was hunted only incidentally until after the introduction of riding horses by the

Spanish in historic times.[4] It may have been the case that only the largest herding animals were economical to hunt with the tools of Paleolithic man.

Perhaps the weakest element in the overkill hypothesis is the scant direct evidence that early North Americans hunted extensively any of the extinct animals other than mammoth and bison.[5] Extinct horse, camel, tapir, mastodon, and antelope have been found in mammoth and bison kill sites but not so as to clearly demonstrate death by the spear[6] (or other means attributable to paleohunters). At the Lehner Ranch site in Arizona (Haury, Sayles, and Wasley 1959) nine mammoths and at least one each of horse, bison, and tapir occur in a single bone bed. Directly associated with these bones was evidence of man's destruction of at least some of the animals. Thus, Clovis spear points were found in situ among ribs of a mammoth and a bison. However, Irwin-Williams (1967, p. 346) reports that at a kill site near Puebla, Mexico, "the character of the assemblage (bones and projectile points) indicates hunting and butchering activities involving mastodon, mammoth, horse, camel, four-horned antelope, etc." But the fact that such evidence is not firm or more widespread is puzzling in view of the fact that there is much evidence for the hunting of the horse as well as mammoth at an earlier date in Europe. Sites such as Solutré in France contain the remains of an estimated 100,000 horses (MacCurdy 1933, p. 173; cited by Jelinek 1967, p. 195). But for the purposes of this paper, it is enough to assume that the earliest Americans subsisted primarily on mammoth and bison, turning to gathering, agriculture, and supplemental game as these animals became extinct.

The abandonment of agriculture and the return to the hunting of

[4] When the horse was reintroduced to the New World by the Spanish in the sixteenth century, *Equus* had been extinct throughout the Americas for only about 8,000 years. In North America horse bones are among the most common Pleistocene fossils (Martin and Guilday 1967, pp. 41–42). Upon reintroduction, the horse reproduced and spread rapidly and thrives today in the wild, as does the burro, under extremely arid conditions in Nevada, Arizona, and Utah. This development makes it the more puzzling that late Pleistocene extinction of the horse would have been due to desiccation.

[5] The survival of African megafauna is often cited as negative evidence for the overkill hypothesis. But this view has been challenged by several writers. Martin (1967, pp. 110–11) notes that some 50 genera (about 30 percent) disappeared in Africa during the Pleistocene. Most of this extinction occurred before 40,000–50,000 years ago and "seems to coincide with the maximum development of the most advanced early Stone Age hunting cultures.... The case of Africa neither refutes the hypothesis of overkill nor supports the hypothesis of worldwide climatic change as a cause of extinction." Jelinek (1967, p. 194) also suggests that Africa is not comparable to those areas of the northern hemisphere where extinction occurred, because the African flora was more favorable for gathering. Thus, gathering may have been sufficiently economical to have reduced the hunting stress to which the African megafauna was exposed.

[6] Martin (1973, pp. 969–74) explained the absence of kill sites for horse, camel, and ground sloths by the hypothesis that they were killed too quickly and easily to leave extensive fossil traces. The idea is that vulnerability to overkill and archaeological visibility are inversely related.

bison by some American Indian groups in historic times (seventeenth and eighteenth centuries) is well established. According to Wedel (1936), "the introduction of the horse deeply affected the Pawnee, as it did most of the plains tribes... [leading to] the tendency toward a nomadic, bison-hunting mode of life made possible by the horse.... From a sedentary tribe the Pawnee became one in which the chase and maize culture shared almost equally."

The more revolutionary effect of the horse on the "fighting Cheyenne" of the northern plains is reported by Strong (1940, pp. 359, 370, 375–76). Wedel (1940, p. 327) reports that the Cheyenne and Arapahoe abandoned their villages, pottery arts, and horticulture to become bison hunters, while the Plains Apache (already subsisting on bison herds in 1541 as reported by the Spanish explorer Coronado) merely adapted the horse to a preexisting bison culture. Apparently, the vast encampments with large tepees of bison hide familiar to later European settlers depended on a substantial increase in the bison harvest made possible by the riding horse.

3. A Model of the Primitive Hunter-Agrarian Economy

I have characterized the Paleo-Indian as a big-game hunter who turned to agriculture as his chief prey became extinct but whose descendants returned to a more nomadic hunting economy after the introduction of the riding horse. This stark representation will be stylized in an economic model of subsistence based on free-access hunting and/or agriculture in which the biomass of game is determined by biological growth considerations that are autonomous but are affected by the harvest product of the hunt.

Consider an economy of population n, each member of which is free to engage in hunting or agriculture[7] as a productive activity. Hunting activity is applied to a single homogeneous species of biomass, M, such as mastodon, mammoth, or bison, and yields a per capita output of m per unit of time. Agricultural activity is applied to the production of a single homogeneous crop, such as corn or beans, and yields a per capita output of c per unit of time. Then H units of hunting labor per capita, and A units of agricultural labor per capita, are employed, with $L = H + A$, the total per capita labor available. The production function for corn is $c = g(\gamma A)$ and for meat $m = f(\beta H, M/n)$, in which it is assumed that increasing the stock of game and of hunters by the same proportion has no effect on the per capita output of meat. The parameters β and γ are efficiency parameters for labor in hunting and farming, respectively.

[7] I shall refer to the alternative to hunting as "agriculture," but it could just as well be gathering. To the early North Americans, the only viable alternative to hunting prior to 5,000–6,000 years ago would seem to have been gathering.

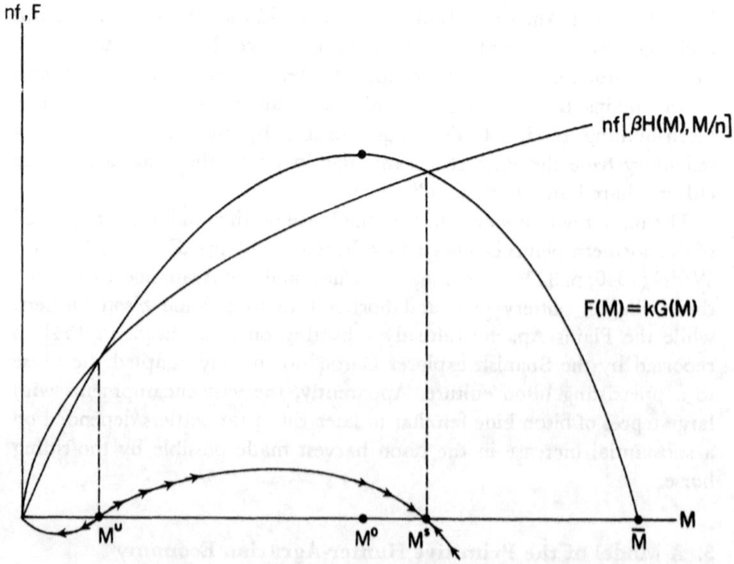

Fig. 1

Thus, an increase in β increases the hunting efficiency of labor. The effect of a technological change in weapons, or the introduction of the horse into the Plains Indian culture, is assumed to be captured by an appropriate increase in β.

It will be understood, without always making it explicit, that all of the variables are dated, that is, $M = M(t)$, $H = H(t)$, and so on with n, L, β, and γ given constants.

The hunted resource is assumed to be subject to a biological growth law (see, e.g., Lotka 1956; Smith 1968; Plourde 1971), which, in the absence of predation by man, is given by $M'(t) = F[M(t)]$. It will be assumed that $F(M)$ can be written in the form $F(M) = kG(M)$, $k > 0$, $G''(M) < 0$, $M \geq 0$; $G'(M^0) = 0$, $G(M) \geq 0$, $0 \leq M \leq \bar{M}$, where $\bar{M}$ is the maximum naturally sustainable stock of the hunted biomass (see fig. 1). The parameter k expresses the biotic growth potential and therefore the predator vulnerability of the species in the sense that an increase in k increases the growth rate of the stock for $0 < M < \bar{M}$ but does not increase the natural equilibrium stock, $\bar{M}$. It may be supposed that a great many factors influence k. A change in climate affecting reproduction, infection by disease, or a change in food availability would alter k for a given genus. Among different genera, k would vary with growth characteristics such as feeding habits, energy requirements, gestation period, age of maturation, life span, and efficiency of food conversion. Generally, the larger genera of mammals are slower growing, have longer gestation periods, require longer periods of maternal care, and live longer. These factors spell greater vulnerability to hunting pressure in that a given tonnage reduction in biomass will require longer to regenerate. In this regard, the modern forms of those extinct species hunted by or found in association with primitive man have relatively long lives (and gestation periods): llama, 20 years (10–11 months gestation); camel, 45 years (10–14 months); horse, 25–30 years (11–12 months); elephant, 60–80 years (22 months); and bison, 18–22 years (9 months). It is perhaps significant that the American bison (*Bison bison*) familiar to nineteenth-century European settlers dates no further back than Paleo-Indian times and is believed to represent a dwarfed form of the extinct *Bison occidentalis* (Edwards 1967). Also, mammoth kill sites commonly contain the remains of the giants of the species (*Mammuthus imperator*, 4.0 m high; *Mammuthus columbi*, 3.6 m high), both larger than the largest African elephant (3.52 m high) (Martin and Guilday 1967).

On the matter of size, age of maturity, and speed of growth, Hammond (1961, p. 321) observes that a considerable reduction in size has occurred over the last 50 years in the major beef breeds of cattle due to deliberate selection for early maturation in body proportions. Hence, under common-property conditions we have Paleolithic hunters selectively harvesting the larger, slower-growing mammals due to emphasis on consuming the stock. But under appropriation with domesticated animals and emphasis on sustained-yield harvesting, investment favors the smaller, earlier-maturing animals which provide a higher biomass growth rate.

When each member of a population of size n applies H units of labor to hunting, this yields a harvest of $nm = nf(\beta H, M/n)$ units of the replenishable resource, and the net growth rate of the resource is given by

$$M'(t) = F(M) - nf(\beta H, M/n). \tag{1}$$

Each of n individuals is assumed to choose (H, A) so as to maximize a utility function $u(c, m)$ subject to $L = H + A$ and the above production constraints. By substituting $c = g[\gamma(L - H)]$ and $m = f(\beta H, M/n)$, the problem can be expressed

$$\max_{H} u\{g[\gamma(L - H)], f(\beta H, M/n)\}.$$

If $u(g, f)$ is concave in H for given M, an interior maximum is defined by the condition

$$-u_1\gamma g' + u_2\beta f_1 = 0, \qquad 0 < H < L. \tag{2}$$

Equation (2), requiring the marginal rate of transformation between corn and meat to be equal to their marginal rate of substitution, can be regarded as determining an economic equilibrium between H and M.

That is, for each resource stock, M, there is a corresponding economical expenditure of hunting labor so that (1) and (2) together determine a differential equation in $M'(t)$ and $M(t)$ only. An illustrative solution to (1) and (2) is shown graphically in figure 1. The curve at the bottom of figure 1 represents growth in the biomass of the hunted resource net of harvested units. The equilibrium harvest function, $nf(\beta H, M/n)$, is shown intersecting the growth function, $F(M)$, at two points M^u and M^s, both of which satisfy (1) and (2) when $M'(t) = 0$. Stability in the neighborhood of a point M^s where $M'(t) = 0$ requires $dM'/dM < 0$. Differentiating (1) and (2), one can easily verify that the sign of dM'/dM is ambiguous, even where $F'(M) < 0$, given only the concavity of $u, f,$ and g. In the illustration of figure 1, point M^s is shown as locally stable while M^u is not.

More specific results will be derived and illustrated graphically, while those parameters essential to the subsequent applications of the model are retained, by introducing the following simplifying assumptions:

1. $u(c, m) = c + vm,\ u_1 = 1,\ u_2 = v$. Corn and meat are perfect substitutes, and value is measured in subjective corn-equivalent units. The parameter v is the society's subjective value of meat relative to corn. Thus, u is the per capita income (welfare) of the society.

2. $f(\beta H, M/n)$ and $g[\gamma(L - H)]$ are increasing, concave, and homogeneous of degree 1, with $f(0, M) = f(\beta H, 0) = g(0) = 0$. Hence, letting $x = \beta Hn/M$ be hunting intensity, that is, total hunting labor per unit biomass, we can write

$$f(\beta H, M/n) = (M/n)\phi(x),\ \phi' > 0,\ \phi'' < 0,\ \phi(0) = 0,$$

$$f_1 = \phi'(x) > 0,\ f_2 = \phi - x\phi' > 0,$$

$$g[\gamma(L - H)] = \gamma(L - H),\ g' = 1.$$

Applying these assumptions, (2) becomes $\beta v\phi'(x) = \gamma$, or

$$\frac{\beta Hn}{M} = \phi'^{(-1)}\left(\frac{\gamma/\beta}{v}\right) = \phi'^{(-1)}(r/v), \tag{3}$$

where r is a relative efficiency parameter, that is, the efficiency of labor in agriculture relative to hunting, and r/v is the real wage or the opportunity cost of hunting (the value of the corn forgone). Under these assumptions, (1) becomes

$$M'(t) = F(M) - M\phi[\phi'^{(-1)}(r/v)]. \tag{4}$$

At an equilibrium point, M^*,

$$M'(t) = F(M^*) - M^*\phi[\phi'^{(-1)}(r/v)] = 0, \tag{5}$$

and the stability condition, near M^*, is

$$\frac{dM'}{dM} = F'(M^*) - \phi[\phi'^{(-1)}(r/v)] < 0. \tag{6}$$

Equilibrium can also be expressed as occurring at M^* where the average biological growth rate, $a(M^*; k)$, is equal to the harvest intensity (output per unit biomass), ϕ. That is, rewriting (5) and substituting $F(M) = kG(M)$,

$$\frac{kG(M^*)}{M^*} \equiv a(M^*; k) = \phi[\phi'^{(-1)}(r/v)]. \tag{7}$$

4. Comparative Statics of Hunting

The marginal effect of any of the parameters k, v, n, and β on equilibrium hunting effort, H^*, and equilibrium biomass, M^*, can be deduced by differentiating (3) and (7). By differentiating $u^* = \gamma(L - H^*) + (vM^*/n)\phi(x^*)$, the effect of such parameters on equilibrium per capita income can also be ascertained. In determining such effects, any factor which reduces the equilibrium stock of the resource may also, in the limiting case, produce extinction (see Gould [1972] and Clarke [1973] for analyses of extinction). From (7), it is clear that extinction of a species due to hunting pressure will occur if $a(0; k) < \phi[\phi'^{(-1)}(r/v)]$, that is, if $r/v < \phi'\{\phi^{-1}[a(0; k)\}$. It follows that unless $\phi(x)$ has an upper bound below $a(0; k)$ there is always a real wage rate small enough (i.e., a return on agricultural labor that is small enough) to produce extinction.

The effect of changes in the indicated parameters on (M^*, H^*, u^*) is summarized below:

1. $$\frac{dM^*}{dk} = -\frac{a}{ka'} > 0, \qquad \frac{dH^*}{dk} = \frac{H^*}{M^*}\frac{dM^*}{dk} > 0,$$

$$\frac{du^*}{dk} = (v/n)(\phi - x\phi')\frac{dM^*}{dk} > 0,$$

where $a' = [\partial a(M^*; k)]/\partial M^* < 0$. Consequently, if larger animal species have a lower biotic growth potential (i.e., smaller k), this will tend to (i) reduce the equilibrium stock (and increase the possibility of extinction), (ii) encourage agricultural effort at the expense of hunting, and (iii) decrease per capita income.

2. $$\frac{dM^*}{d\beta} = -\frac{(\phi')^2}{a'\phi''\beta} < 0, \qquad \frac{dH^*}{d\beta} = \frac{H^*}{M^*}\frac{dM^*}{d\beta} - \frac{M^*\phi'}{n\beta^2\phi''} - \frac{H^*}{\beta} \gtrless 0,$$

$$\frac{du^*}{d\beta} = vH^*\phi' + \frac{v}{n}(\phi - x\phi')\frac{dM^*}{d\beta} \gtrless 0.$$

The greater the efficiency of hunting labor, the smaller the equilibrium stock of animals. One implication is that larger animals and/or gregarious animals that tend to congregate in herds, such as mammoth, bison, antelope, camels, and llamas (among the extinct genera), would have comparatively high visibility and low search cost, making them easier prey and increasing β. Thus, Edwards (1967, p. 149) argues that "human technology, including use of missile weapons, greatly reduces the counter-attacking defensive advantages of large size and emphasizes concealment and speed of flight. At this point . . . the genetically selected optimum body size of many forms declines sharply." Also, the introduction of the riding horse into the Plains Indians culture by the Spanish would have had the effect of increasing bison hunting efficiency and reducing the stock of bison. Armed with the horse and the bow, the Plains Indians in another 200 years could possibly have depleted the stock of bison as effectively as did Buffalo Bill and the U.S. cavalry.

However, changes in hunting efficiency could either increase or decrease hunting effort and per capita income ($dH^*/d\beta \gtreqless 0$, $du^*/d\beta \gtreqless 0$). Greater hunting efficiency could release labor for agricultural employment or so reduce the animal stock that the society is made poorer. It would appear that this was not the effect of the horse on the Plains Indians, many of whom were uprooted from their agrarian activities but who achieved greater affluence as bison hunters. This affluence could have been a temporary phenomenon; that is, in the short run, given the animal stock, we have $dM^*/d\beta = 0$ and $du^*/d\beta = vH^*\phi' > 0$. The short-run effect of an increase in hunting efficiency is always to increase per capita income.

$$3. \quad \frac{dM^*}{dv} = -\frac{(\phi')^2}{va'\phi''} < 0, \qquad \frac{dH^*}{dv} = -\frac{M^*\phi'}{\beta vn\phi''} + \frac{H^*}{M^*}\frac{dM^*}{dv} \gtreqless 0,$$

$$\frac{du^*}{dv} = \frac{M^*\phi}{n} + \frac{v}{n}(\phi - x\phi')\frac{dM^*}{dv} \gtreqless 0.$$

The greater the consumption value of the hunted resource, the smaller will be the equilibrium biomass. Hunting labor and per capita income could also be smaller depending on how much the biomass of animals is depleted (if the species becomes extinct, then, obviously, hunting will cease):

$$4. \quad \frac{dM^*}{dn} = 0, \qquad \frac{dH^*}{dn} = -\frac{H^*}{n} < 0,$$

$$\frac{du^*}{dn} = -(vM^*/n^2)(\phi - x\phi') < 0.$$

In a mixed economy, increasing the human population causes no change in the stock of animals but reduces hunting effort and per capita income. With constant returns in agriculture, equilibrium requires total hunting intensity to be constant. Consequently, any increase in population will be offset by a corresponding decrease in each individual's hunting labor. This is a very strong empirical implication of the model, for it asserts that (under our technological assumptions) once a hunting society diversifies into agriculture (or gathering), the pressure of increasing population on animal stocks disappears. Of course, the moment decreasing returns occur in agriculture, this result no longer holds.

It should be noted that the assumption of a mixed economy is presumed not to apply to the Paleo-Indians. For a pure hunter culture we have $H = L$, and the equilibrium animal stock is defined by $F(\hat{M}) - \hat{M}\phi(\beta Ln/\hat{M}) = 0$. Hence,

$$\frac{d\hat{M}}{dn} = \frac{(\beta L/M)\phi'}{D} < 0$$

if $D = a' + (\beta Ln/M^2)\phi' < 0$, which is required for stability.

5. Institutional and Analytical Aspects of Optimal versus Free-Access Hunting

Economists have long been familiar with the proposition that unconstrained nonpriced access to any common-property resource such as a fishing or hunting ground (Gordon 1954; Scott 1955; Smith 1968; Plourde 1971) leads to the inefficient use of such resources. This inefficiency takes the form of a reduction of the natural biological stock of the resource below the optimal stock required for sustained-yield harvesting. The phenomenon can be described as an instance of market (or price mechanism) failure after Bator (1958) or of property-right failure after Demsetz (1967). It is perhaps more accurately described as an instance of incentive failure caused by cultural or institutional inadequacies. What fails is the private incentive of the individual to harvest (and "conserve" the stock) at socially optimal levels over time. In principle, optimality can be achieved by (1) simulating the market that has failed, for example, by instituting a user charge—somewhat erroneously called a "tax"—for the resource, thereby inducing the individual to economize user payments by conserving his use of the resource; (2) instituting a property-right system which induces the individual to conserve his use of the resource as a means of maximizing the return on his property; (3) constraining individual hunting activity by social or legal restrictions such as quotas, sharing rules, licensing, or prohibitions; and (4) limiting the hunting harvest by enculturating voluntary conservationist values or behaviour.

Property rights, social or legal restrictions on individual harvesting, and the enculturation of conservationist behaviour have all been used extensively and ingeniously by primitive peoples at one time or another. However, the evidence is recent, for there appears to be no evidence to suppose that Paleolithic practices exhibited such sophistication. It is the hypothesis of this section that sometime after the extinction of the megafauna, human culture developed a sensitivity to the need to prevent overharvesting. Whether man as a superpredator was in fact the principal agent in the extinction of the large herbivores and their dependent carnivores and scavengers, it is plausible to assume that men saw parallels between hunting and the loss of the valued prey, from which arose oral and religious traditions, myths, and superstitions which had the effect and perhaps the intention of conserving common-property resources. At some point the ancestral message became a directive to "take sparingly of the bounty of nature."

Heizer (1955) provides pages of documented examples of primitive strictures on the harvesting of replenishable resources. One of the most common techniques was the private ownership of land—fishing holes, hunting grounds, nut-bearing trees, and grass seed areas (see Heizer [1955, p. 4] for numerous reference summaries on land ownership). Constraints on harvesting from common-property lands took many forms. Great Lakes Indians stripped only a portion of the fiber off basswood trees in order that the wound would heal and the tree live. Vancouver Island Indians "never fully strip the bark from a cedar tree lest the tree die and its spirit curse the man who peeled the bark and he die also" (Heizer 1955, p. 4). The Choctaw had laws regulating the game that could be killed by one family, with strict accounting by the captain of each band. The Kaska trap marten in a given area only every 2 or 3 years. The Iroquois spared the females of hunted species during the breeding season; the sparing of pregnant females was widespread. The Yurok had "game laws" the violation of which would cause loss of "hunting luck" (Heizer 1955, pp. 4–5). The Naskapi of Labrador are cited as typical of numerous tribes that believe animals and plants were created to help man (Heizer 1955, p. 6). In return for killing an animal, the hunter must protect it from profane treatment, such as wasting the animal or letting dogs gnaw its bones, lest the animal take offense and spoil the success of the hunter. Certain species may be hunted by some tribes but avoided by others in the belief that the tribe's ancestry traces to such species. Many tribes believe that game is watched over by supernatural authorities who become angry with men if too many deer are killed or if they merely wound the animals (Heizer 1955, p. 7).

Many more such examples could be cited, but evidence for conservationist ethics and institutions (defined as any set of strictures, laws, or practices which limit the harvesting of common-property resources) is widespread among primitive peoples in historic or near historic times. Such primitive practices may appear to be exceedingly crude rationing devices. But every efficient price system has its dual equivalent quota system, and modern legislators no less than primitive peoples find it more natural to think in terms of quota restrictions on external effects than in terms of prices.

Among primitive peoples who have invented property-right systems, there are instances of sophistication that would rival the modern property deed. Thus, among the Karok private ownership of a particular fishing ground did not mean owning the land along the river but owning the right to fish a given stretch of the river regardless of who owned the land (Kroeber and Barrett 1960, pp. 3–4). A fishing right might entitle the owner to use the spot every third night and day, with the right transferable by sale or inheritance. Similarly, the right to hunt or share in the hunting of sea lions on a particular rock was owned, and each person on a particular stretch of coast had rights to some cut of a beached whale, with residents of other areas denied such rights except by inheritance or purchase (Kroeber and Barrett 1960, p. 115).

The possibility of the existence of property rights or quota regulations governing hunted resources raises the issue of optimal versus free-access harvesting of species. In the following analysis, the assumptions of the previous simple model of production from a common-property hunted resource and an appropriated agricultural resource will be used to state an optimal control model. Primarily, the model will be used to study the conditions for optimal versus free-access species extinction.

If δ is the time preference discount rate for an individual and we assume that instantaneous utility, $u = c(t) + vm(t)$, is additive over time, then total welfare for the economy is

$$\lim_{T \to \infty} \int_0^T ue^{-\delta t} dt,$$

to be maximized subject to the production function and resource constraints and the resource growth equation (1). Making the substitutions $c = \gamma(L - H)$ and $m = (M/n)\phi(x)$, the current-value Hamilton-Lagrange criterion is (Arrow 1968)

$$\Psi = \gamma(L - H) + \left(\frac{vM}{n}\right)\phi\left(\frac{\beta Hn}{M}\right) + \mu M\left[a(M; k) - \phi\left(\frac{\beta Hn}{M}\right)\right]$$

to be maximized with respect to the control variable H, where $0 \leq H \leq L$. Necessary conditions, according to the maximum principle, are that

$$\text{if } \frac{\partial\psi}{\partial H}\begin{cases} < 0, \text{ then } H = 0, \\ = 0, \text{ then } 0 \leq H \leq L, \\ > 0, \text{ then } H = L, \end{cases} \tag{8}$$

$$\mu'(t) = \delta\mu - \frac{\partial\psi}{\partial M}, \tag{9}$$

$$M'(t) = M[a(M; k) - \phi(x)], \tag{10}$$

and the transversality conditions

$$\lim_{t\to\infty} e^{-\delta t}\mu(t)M(t) = 0, \ \lim_{t\to\infty} e^{-\delta t}\mu(t) \geq 0.$$

Letting $\xi = n\mu$, condition (8) implies the following:

$$\text{if } \frac{r}{v-\xi}\begin{cases} > \phi'\left(\frac{\beta Hn}{M}\right), \text{ then } H = 0, \\ = \phi'\left(\frac{\beta Hn}{M}\right), \text{ then } 0 \leq H \leq L, \\ < \phi'\left(\frac{\beta Hn}{M}\right), \text{ then } H = L. \end{cases} \tag{11}$$

Consequently, if we define $\phi'_0 = \phi'(0)$, $\xi_0 = (v - r/\phi'_0)$ if $\phi'_0 > r/v$, with $\xi_0 = 0$ otherwise, and let the separating boundary between a pure hunter economy and a hunter agrarian economy be $\xi(M) \equiv v - r/\phi'(\beta Ln/M)$, then (9) and (10) can be written[8]

$$\xi'(t) = \begin{cases} \xi[\delta - F'(M)], \text{ if } \phi'_0 < \frac{r}{v-\xi}, \text{ or } \xi > \xi_0; & \text{(12a)} \\ \xi[\delta - F'(M)] - (v-\xi) \\ \quad \times \left\{\phi\left[\phi'^{(-1)}\left(\frac{r}{v-\xi}\right)\right] - \left(\frac{r}{v-\xi}\right)\phi'^{(-1)}\left(\frac{r}{v-\xi}\right)\right\}, \\ \qquad \text{if } \xi(M) \leq \xi \leq \xi_0; & \text{(12b)} \\ \xi[\delta - F'(M)] - (v-\xi)\left[\phi\left(\frac{\beta Ln}{M}\right) - \left(\frac{\beta Ln}{M}\right)\phi'\left(\frac{\beta Ln}{M}\right)\right], \\ \qquad \text{if } \phi'\left(\frac{\beta Ln}{M}\right) > \frac{r}{v-\xi}, \text{ or } \xi < \xi(M); & \text{(12c)} \end{cases}$$

[8] These conditions are sufficient as well as necessary if Ψ is concave in M for given ξ and t and for H set at its maximizing level. Under the assumptions in the text, Ψ is concave in M for $v \geq \xi \geq 0$.

$$M'(t) = \begin{cases} Ma(M; k), \text{ if } \xi > \xi_0; & (13a) \\ M\left\{a(M; k) - \phi\left[\phi'^{(-1)}\left(\dfrac{r}{v - \xi}\right)\right]\right\}, & \\ \qquad\qquad \text{if } \xi(M) \le \xi \le \xi_0; & (13b) \\ M\left[a(M; k) - \phi\left(\dfrac{\beta L n}{M}\right)\right], \text{ if } \xi < \xi(M). & (13c) \end{cases}$$

Note that the equality condition in (11) reduces to (3) for free-access harvesting when $\xi = 0$. The ξ is interpreted as the market value of a live unit of the animal stock. Ordinarily we would think of ξ as being nonnegative. A negative value would correspond to animals that are a public nuisance requiring a bounty for optimal social control. This value is zero to the individual in the absence either of adequate property rights in live animals or of harvesting restrictions which impute value to live animals. Thus, enculturated limitations on free-access harvesting, such as lead hunters to believe they will receive supernatural punishment if they harvest too much game, impute a positive value, ξ, to live animals. One does not need to pass judgment on the merits of such devices for social control over the chase to appreciate their behavioral (and imputed price) effects.

Since ξ is the social marginal value of a live animal, the quantity $v - \xi$ in (11)–(13) is the net marginal value of a harvested animal. Since $\phi - (\beta Hn/M)\phi'$ for $H \le L$ is the marginal physical product of the biomass of game (biological capital), equations (12b) and (12c) require the net marginal value productivity of the game stock, $(v - \xi)[\phi - (\beta Hn/M)\phi']$ for $H \le L$, to equal net interest on investment in a live animal less capital gains, $\xi[\delta - F'(M)] - \xi'$, where the interest rate, $\delta - F'(M)$, is reckoned net of the biological "own" rate, $F'(M)$. The biological rate, $F'(M)$, is analogous to a capital depreciation rate when $F'(M) < 0$ and a capital appreciation rate when $F'(M) > 0$.

Equations (12) and (13) provide two first-order autonomous differential equations in $[\xi(t), M(t)]$ which, together with the transversality conditions and initial conditions, must be satisfied along an optimal bionomic development path. Paths satisfying (12) and (13) will be characterized by the usual phase diagram representation in (ξ, M) space.

In figures 2–4 the set of points $E(\xi)$ is defined by the condition $\xi'(t) = 0$ in (12) and represents the stationary state asset demand for the animal stock. The set of points $B(\xi)$ is defined by the condition $M'(t) = 0$ in (13) and represents the stationary state asset supply of animals. Properties of these functions and the phase diagrams in figures 2–4 are derived in the Appendix.

Along $E(\xi)$ the value of the marginal product of the game stock is

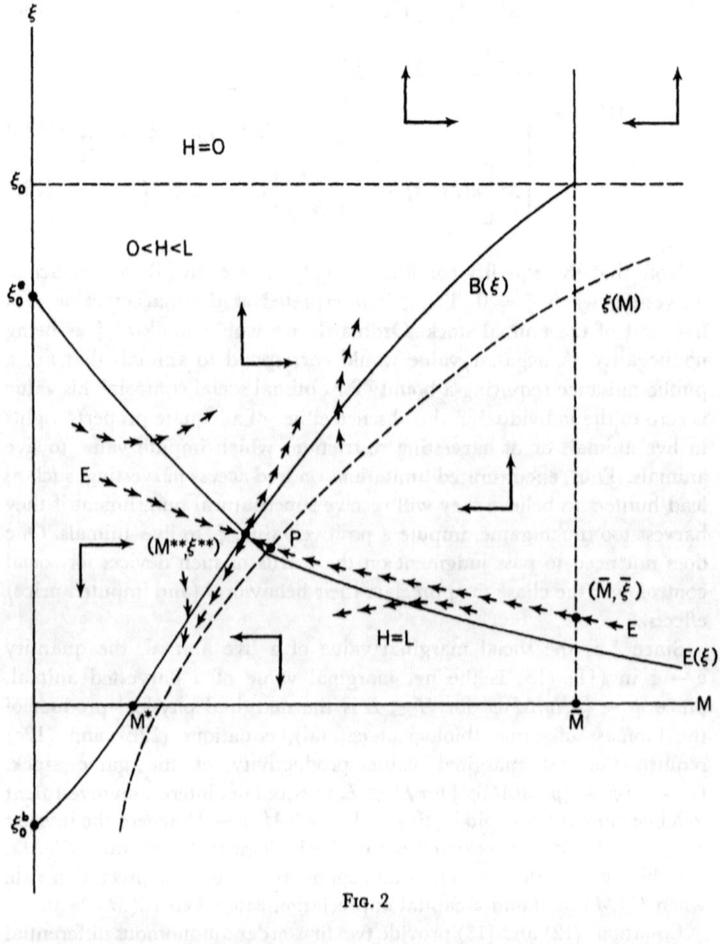

FIG. 2

equal to interest net of biological growth. Hence, an increase in the animal stock reduces biological growth, increases net interest, and reduces the price of live animals. Along $B(\xi)$, the harvest intensity is equal to average biological growth. For a mixed economy, increases in the live animal price reduce the harvest per unit of biomass and increase the game stock.

An optimal equilibrium path yielding a mixed economy in the stationary state is shown in figure 2. Starting with initial conditions $(\bar{M}, \bar{\xi})$, it is socially desirable for the culture to specialize in hunting. As the game stock is depleted and its value rises, optimality requires the economy eventually (beginning at P) to begin agricultural production. In long-run

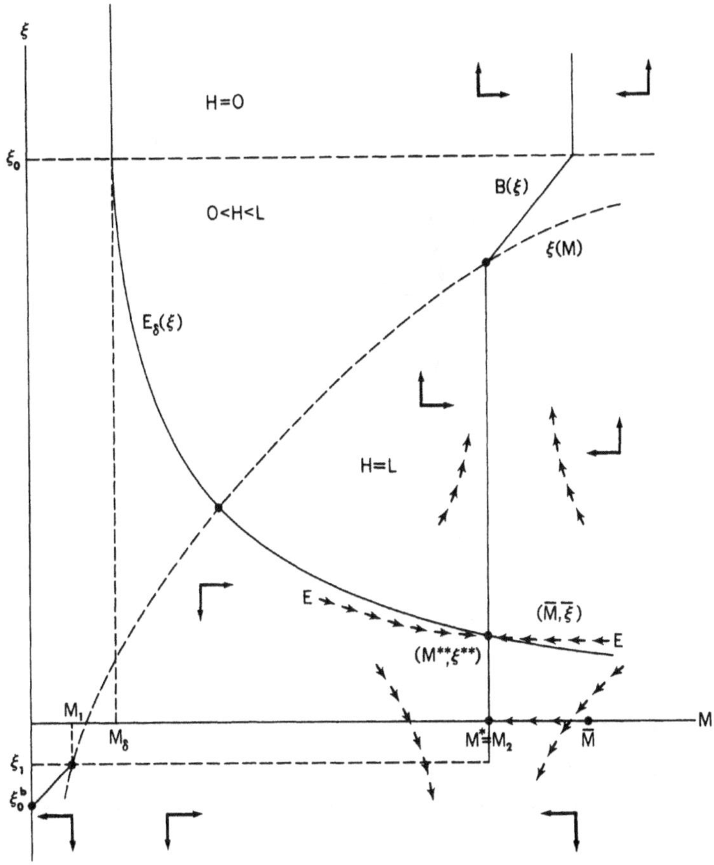

FIG. 3

equilibrium at (M^{**}, ξ^{**}), both hunting and agriculture reach stable levels of production. Figure 3 illustrates an optimal path for an economy that begins as, and remains to the end, a culture of specialized hunters. In this case, the free-access economy produces a socially optimal equilibrium.

Agricultural specialization may occur following a period of hunting that causes extinction. This is illustrated in figure 4 in which $\xi_0^b > \xi_0^e$, where $B(\xi_0^b) = E(\xi_0^e) = 0$. At all prices $\xi \leq \xi_0^b$, the harvest rate exceeds the growth rate for every live animal stock, causing extinction. At all prices $\xi \geq \xi_0^e$, interest on investment in animals exceeds the net value of the marginal product of live animals for every animal stock. Hence, $\xi_0^b \geq \xi_0^e$ implies that, along an optimal development path, the

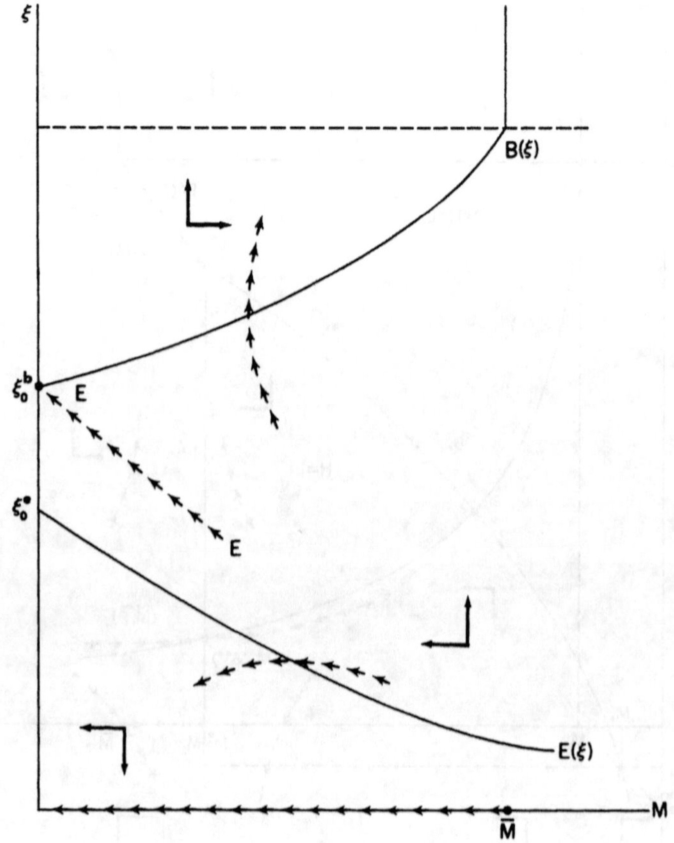

FIG. 4

economy perpetually consumes capital and must eventually wipe out the stock of live animals and specialize thereafter in agriculture. Along an optimal path beginning at $(\bar{M}, \bar{\xi})$ one would at first observe a pure hunter culture, then a mixed economy, and ultimately an agrarian economy.

The effect of free-access harvesting and its contrast with an optimal development path are obtained by setting $\xi = 0$ for all t. This condition replaces those stated in (12) and corresponds to the nonexistence of a market in live animals or of any equivalent valuation system for expressing the opportunity costs of the current harvest. In effect, the "demand" for biological capital is perfectly elastic at $\xi = 0$. If $\xi_0^b > 0$, the free-access economy eventually harvests to extinction as in figure 4. If $\xi_0^b < 0$, such an economy harvests short of extinction and conserves an animal stock $M^* = B(0) > 0$ as in figures 2 and 3.

Figures 2 and 4 apply to "high-impatience" economies, $\delta \geq F_0'$. For low-impatience economies, $\delta < F_0'$, extinction of an animal species will never be optimal since the net cost of biological capital $\delta - F'(M) \to 0$ as $M \to M_\delta$, making it optimal to stop biological capital consumption at $M = M_\delta$ for all capital prices $\xi \geq \xi_0$. This means that the static asset demand for biological capital becomes completely inelastic at $M = M_\delta$, $\xi \geq \xi_0$, as illustrated by $M = E_\delta(\xi)$ in figure 3. However, the concept of "high" or "low" impatience must be measured relative to the biotic growth potential of the hunted species. Using the simple parameterization $F(M) = kG(M)$, a relatively high (low) impatience economy is defined by $\delta/k \geq G_0'(\delta/k < G_0')$. If $F_0' = kG_0'$ is finite for any given species, it is clear that there always exists a cultural impatience rate, δ, high enough that it may be optimal to harvest the species to extinction.

6. Comparative Stationary States of Hunting

For interior solutions $0 < H < L$, the effect of the parameters (δ, r, v, k) on the optimal stationary-state level M^{**} is obtained by implicit differentiation of the following equations:

$$\xi[\delta - F'(M^{**})] - (v - \xi)(\phi - x\phi') = 0, \tag{14}$$

$$a(M^{**}; k) - \phi(x^*) = 0, \text{ where } x^* = \phi'^{(-1)}\left(\frac{r}{v - \xi^{**}}\right). \tag{15}$$

Since

$$D = \begin{vmatrix} \delta - F' + \phi & -\xi F'' \\ -\dfrac{(\phi')^2}{\phi''(v - \xi)} & a' \end{vmatrix} < 0,$$

we deduce

$$\frac{dM^{**}}{dk} = -\frac{(\delta - F' + \phi)a}{kD} > 0,$$

$$\frac{dM^{**}}{dr} = \frac{\phi'(\delta - F') + \phi'(\phi - x\phi')}{\phi''(v - n\xi)D} > 0,$$

$$\frac{dM^{**}}{dv} = \frac{(\phi')^2(\delta - F')}{\phi''(v - \xi)D} < 0,$$

$$\frac{dM^{**}}{d\delta} = -\frac{(\phi')^2\xi}{\phi''(v - \xi)D} < 0.$$

The optimal stationary-state animal stock is smaller (and the prospect of extinction greater) the lower the biotic potential of the species, the lower the efficiency of labor in agriculture relative to hunting, the higher the cultural value placed on meat, and the higher the culture's preference for present over future consumption. Certain features of the prey stock may affect both r and k. Thus, if larger animals have a lower biotic potential and are easier to hunt, this implies lower r and lower k, yielding a magnified decrease in M^{**}.

These results and the similar conclusions of Section 4 for free-access hunting do not provide any new evidence on the causes of Pleistocene extinction. They are offered in an attempt to demonstrate the use of a coherent economic framework for the study and evaluation of extinction or other hypotheses concerning the primitive hunter culture.[9] It is hoped that the framework of this paper will enhance the possibility of a more comprehensive evaluation of the limited qualitative cross-cultural, chronological, and regional data on hunting-gathering-agricultural activities in primitive societies.

Appendix

In this Appendix, properties of the differential equations (12) (13) and their phase diagram representation will be developed in greater detail. First consider (12):

1. From (12a) we have $\xi'(t) \gtreqless 0$ according as $\delta - F'(M) \gtreqless 0$ for $\xi > \xi_0$. Let $\delta - F'(M) \leq 0$ for $0 \leq M \leq M_\delta$, and $\delta - F'(M) > 0$ for $M > M_\delta$. Then $\xi'(t) \leq 0$ in the region $(\xi > \xi_0,\ 0 \leq M \leq M_\delta)$, and $\xi'(t) > 0$ in $(\xi > \xi_0, M > M_\delta)$. This is illustrated by the vertical arrow above ξ_0 in figure 2 for the case in which $M_\delta = 0$, that is, $\delta - F'(0) \geq 0$. It should be noted that $\xi_0 = 0$ in the event that $\phi_0' \leq r/v$, that is, hunting is uneconomical relative to agriculture at all hunting intensities even when live animals have zero value. This degenerate case leads to agricultural specialization from time zero, which must be distinguished from agricultural specialization following the hunting of prey to extinction.

2. From (12b)–(12c), let $M = E(\xi)$ be defined by the set of points $[(\xi, M) \mid \xi'(t) = 0, 0 \leq \xi \leq \xi_0, M \geq 0]$. The condition $\xi'(t) = 0$ requires

$$\delta - F'(M) = \begin{cases} \left(\dfrac{v-\xi}{\xi}\right)\left\{\phi\left[\phi'^{(-1)}\left(\dfrac{r}{v-\xi}\right)\right] - \left(\dfrac{r}{v-\xi}\right)\phi'^{(-1)}\left(\dfrac{r}{v-\xi}\right)\right\}, & \xi(M) \leq \xi \leq \xi_0, \quad (16a) \\[2ex] \left(\dfrac{v-\xi}{\xi}\right)\left[\phi\left(\dfrac{\beta Ln}{M}\right) - \left(\dfrac{\beta Ln}{M}\right)\phi'\left(\dfrac{\beta Ln}{M}\right)\right], & \xi < \xi(M), \quad (16b) \end{cases}$$

that is, the net rate of interest must equal the relative value marginal productivity of the biomass of prey. The function $E(\xi)$ implied by the interior solution (16a) is derived graphically in figure 5 for two distinguishing cases: (1) if $F_0' \leq \delta$, the curve labeled $E(\xi)$ is obtained; (2) if $F_0' > \delta$, the curve labeled $E_\delta(\xi)$ is the result. The curve in quadrant I of figure 5 is the relative value marginal productivity of the biomass. Quadrant II shows net interest as a function of the biomass of game. For each price of live game ξ such that net interest equals

[9] For example, if the environment was economically more favorable for gathering in Africa than it was in North America, then the overkill hypothesis is not inconsistent with the greater survival of megafauna in Africa.

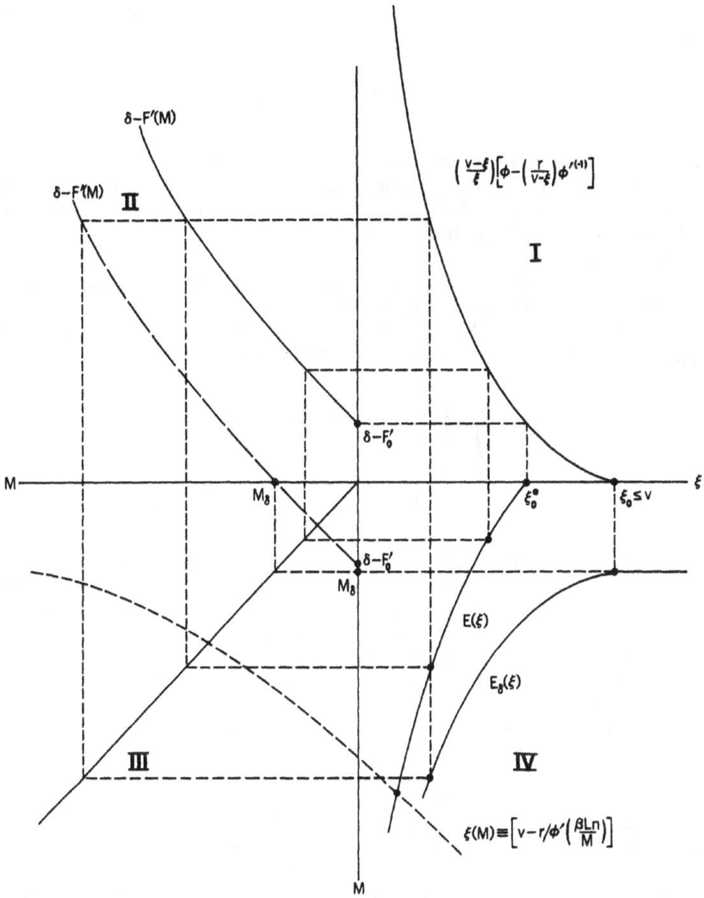

FIG. 5

relative value marginal productivity, we associate a biomass $M \geq 0$ in quadrant IV. Curve $E(\xi)$ or $E_\delta(\xi)$ represents economic equilibrium in the capital market where capital gains (losses) vanish. Quadrant IV also illustrates the boundary $\xi(M) \equiv [v - r/\phi'(\beta Ln/M)]$ separating the interior region $\xi(M) \leq \xi \leq \xi_0$, representing a mixed hunter-agrarian economy, from the region $\xi < \xi(M)$, representing the specialized hunter economy. This boundary is monotone increasing, $\xi'(M) = -(r\phi''\beta Ln)/[(\phi')^2 M^2] > 0$,

$$\text{with } \lim_{M \to 0} \xi(M) = -\infty \text{ if } \lim_{x \to \infty} \phi'(x) = 0, \text{ and } \lim_{M \to \infty} \xi(M) = \xi_0.$$

Some key properties of $E(\xi)$ are summarized below.

a) At $M = 0$, if $\delta - F_0' \geq 0$, then $\xi = \xi_0^e \leq \xi_0 \leq v$ satisfies (16a). At $M = M_\delta$, if $\delta - F_0' < 0$ and $\delta = F'(M_\delta)$, then $\xi = \xi_0$.

b)
$$\lim_{M \to \infty} E^{-1}(M) = 0,$$

since $\phi - (\beta Ln/M)\phi' \to 0$ in (16b) while $\delta - F' > 0$.

c) The function $E(\xi)$ is monotone decreasing; that is, differentiating (16a) and (16b), it can be verified that $dM/d\xi < 0$ and from (12b) and (12c) that $\partial\xi'(t)/\partial\xi > 0$, $\xi \leq \xi_0$, as illustrated by the vertical arrows in figure 2.

Now consider (13):

1. From (13a), $M'(t) \gtreqless 0$ according as $0 < M \lesseqgtr \bar{M}$, if $\xi > \xi_0$ as indicated by the horizontal arrows above ξ_0 in figure 2.

2. From (13b) and (13c), let $M = B(\xi)$ be defined by the set of points $[(\xi, M) \mid M'(t) = 0, \xi \leq \xi_0, M \geq 0]$. This implies

$$a(M; k) = \begin{cases} \phi\left(\dfrac{\beta Hn}{M}\right), & \text{if } \dfrac{\beta Hn}{M} = \phi'^{(-1)}\left(\dfrac{r}{v - \xi}\right), \\ \phi\left(\dfrac{\beta Ln}{M}\right), & \text{if } \dfrac{\beta Ln}{M} \leq \phi'^{(-1)}\left(\dfrac{r}{v - \xi}\right). \end{cases} \tag{17}$$

For each $\xi \leq \xi_0$, this equation provides a corresponding $M \geq 0$. Points on $M = B(\xi)$ represent biological equilibrium in the prey stock. In figure 6, let $k = k_1$, giving the monotone decreasing percentage average rate of biomass growth $a(M; k_1)$. Since this function is everywhere below the harvest per unit of biomass when the economy specializes in hunting, it follows that we have an interior maximum $0 < H < L$ for every ξ and a corresponding M determined by the intersection $a(M; k_1) = \phi\{\phi'^{(-1)}[r/(v - \xi)]\}$. At $\xi = \xi'''$ equilibrium is at Q''', while at $\xi = \xi'' < \xi'''$ equilibrium is at Q''. For this case the function $B(\xi)$ will be in the region $\xi(M) \leq \xi \leq \xi_0$ as shown in figure 2. But if $k = k_2$ the constraining boundary set defined by $\phi(\beta Ln/M)$ intersects $a(M; k_2)$ at two points corresponding to a biomass M_1 and M_2 as shown in figure 6. Consequently, for any ξ such that $\xi_1 < \xi < \xi_2$, where $M_1 = B(\xi_1)$, $M_2 = B(\xi_2)$ (e.g., $\xi = \xi''$ in fig. 6), hunting intensity is constrained at the level $\beta Ln/M$ and the harvest intensity is $\phi(\beta Ln/M) < a(M; k_2)$, with $M'(t) > 0$ for all $M_1 < M < M_2$. Thus, at ξ_1 an increase in the stock above M_1 reduces harvest intensity by more than growth intensity because hunting effort cannot be increased. The stock rises until M_2 is reached, where the growth rate is depressed to the level of the harvest. Hence, equilibrium on $M = B(\xi)$, just above ξ_1, is reached because of naturally occurring diminishing returns to biomass growth and cannot be influenced by the control H. In figure 3 this means that the function $B(\xi)$ intersects the boundary $\xi(M)$ and is discontinuous at $M_1 = B(\xi_1)$. This phenomenon is a property of labor-scarce economies, since for L large enough $B(\xi)$ will be entirely in the interior set for a mixed economy.

Some key properties of $B(\xi)$ in the interior $[\xi(M) < \xi < \xi_0, M \geq 0]$ are:

a) At $M = 0$, $\xi = \xi_0^b \gtreqless 0$ satisfies (17).

b) At $M = \bar{M}$ $a(\bar{M}; k) = 0$ and $\xi = \xi_0$.

c) The function $B(\xi)$ is monotone increasing, that is, from (17), $dM/d\xi > 0$.

From (13b) and (13c), referring to figures 3 and 6, if:

i) $\xi < \xi_1$, then (*a*) $M'(t) > 0$ if $M < B(\xi)$; (*b*) $M'(t) < 0$ if $B(\xi) < M < M_1$; (*c*) $M'(t) > 0$ if $M_1 < M < M_2$; and (*d*) $M'(t) < 0$ if $M > M_2$.

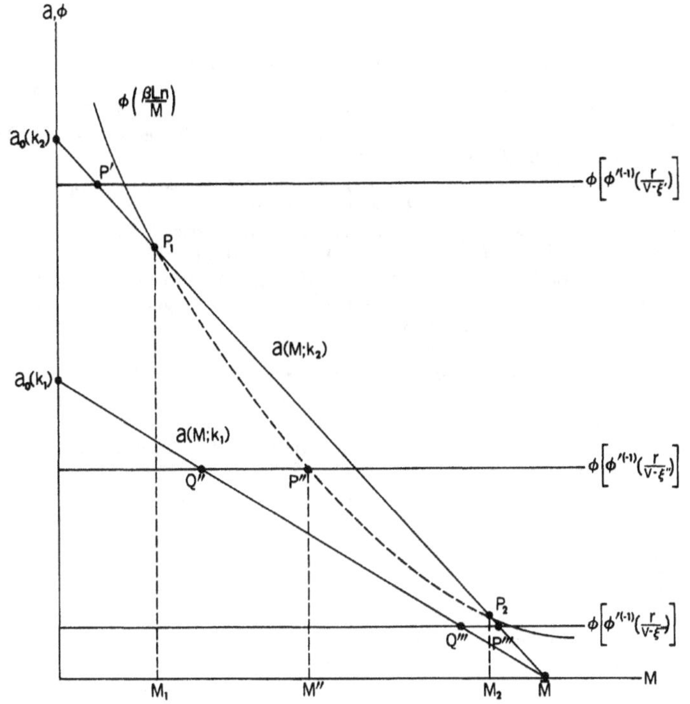

FIG. 6

ii) $\xi_1 < \xi \leq \xi_2$, then (*a*) $M'(t) > 0$ if $M < M_2$ and (*b*) $M'(t) < 0$ if $M > M_2$.

iii) $\xi_2 < \xi < \xi_0$, then (*a*) $M'(t) > 0$ if $M < B(\xi)$ and (*b*) $M'(t) < 0$ if $M > B(\xi)$. Each of these directions of motion is illustrated by the horizontal arrows in figure 3.

References

Agogino, G. A., and Frankforter, W. D. "A Paleo-Indian Bison-Kill in Northwestern Iowa." *American Antiquity* 25, no. 3 (January 1960): 414–15.

Arrow, K. J. "Applications of Control Theory to Economic Growth." In *Mathematics of the Decision Sciences*, pt. 2, edited by G. B. Dantzig and A. F. Veinott, Jr. Providence, R.I.: American Math. Soc., 1968.

Bator, F. "The Anatomy of Market Failure." *Q.J.E.* 72 (August 1958): 351–79.

Butler, B. R. "A Bison Jump in the Upper Salmon River Valley of Eastern Idaho." *Tebiwa*, vol. 14, no. 1 (1971).

Clarke, C. W. "Profit Maximization and the Extinction of Animal Species." *J.P.E.* 81, no. 4 (July/August 1973): 950–61.

Covey, C., ed. *Cabeza de Vaca's Adventures in the Unknown Interior of America*. New York: Collier, 1961.

Demsetz, H. "Toward a Theory of Property Rights." *A.E.R.* 57 (May 1967): 347–73.

Edwards, W. E. "The Late-Pleistocene Extinction and Diminution in Size of Many Mammalian Species." In *Pleistocene Extinctions*, edited by P. S. Martin and H. E. Wright, Jr. New Haven, Conn.: Yale Univ. Press, 1967.

Gordon, H. S. "The Economic Theory of a Common Property Resource: The Fishery." *J.P.E.* 62, no. 2 (April 1954): 439–51.

Gould, J. R. "Extinction of a Fishery by Commercial Exploitation: A Note." *J.P.E.* 80, no. 5 (September/October 1972): 1031–39.

Gross, Hugo. "Mastodon, Mammoth, and Man in America." *Bull. Texas Archeological and Paleontological Soc.*, no. 23 (October 1951): pp. 101–31.

Guilday, J. E. "Differential Extinction during Late-Pleistocene and Recent Times." In *Pleistocene Extinctions*, edited by P. S. Martin and H. E. Wright, Jr. New Haven, Conn.: Yale Univ. Press, 1967.

Hammond, J. "Growth in Size and Body Proportions in Farm Animals." In *Growth in Living Systems*, edited by M. X. Zarrow. New York: Basic Books, 1961.

Haury, E. W.; Antevs, E.; and Lance, J. F. "Artifacts with Mammoth Remains, Naco, Arizona." *American Antiquity* 19, no. 1 (July 1953): 1–24.

Haury, E. W.; Sayles, E. B.; and Wasley, W. W. "The Lehner Mammoth Site, Southeastern Arizona." *American Antiquity* 25, no. 1 (July 1959): 1–30.

Haynes, C. V. "Fluted Projectile Points: Their Age and Dispersion." *Science*, June 19, 1964, pp. 1408–13.

———. "Carbon-14 Dates and Early Man in the New World." In *Pleistocene Extinctions*, edited by P. S. Martin and H. E. Wright, Jr. New Haven, Conn.: Yale Univ. Press, 1967.

Heizer, R. F. *Primitive Man as an Ecologic Factor*. Kroeber Anthropological Society Papers no. 13. Berkeley: Univ. California Press, 1955.

Hester, J. J. "The Agency of Man in Animal Extinctions." In *Pleistocene Extinctions*, edited by P. S. Martin and H. E. Wright, Jr. New Haven, Conn.: Yale Univ. Press, 1967.

Hester, J. J., and Wendorf, F. "Early Man's Utilization of the Great Plains Environment." *American Antiquity* 28, no. 2 (October 1962): 159–71.

Irwin-Williams, C. "Associations of Early Man with Horse, Camel, and Mastodon at Hueyatlaco, Valsequillo (Puebla, Mexico)." In *Pleistocene Extinctions*, edited by P. S. Martin and H. E. Wright, Jr. New Haven, Conn.: Yale Univ. Press, 1967.

Jelinek, A. J. "Man's Role in Extinction of Pleistocene Faunas." In *Pleistocene Extinctions*, edited by P. S. Martin and H. E. Wright, Jr. New Haven, Conn.: Yale Univ. Press, 1967.

Kehoe, T. F. "The Boarding School Bison Drive Site." *Plains Anthropologist*, vol. 12, no. 35 (February 1967).

Kroeber, A. L., and Barrett, S. A. *Fishing among the Indians of Northwestern California*. Anthropological Records, vol. 21, no. 1. Berkeley: Univ. California Press, 1960.

Leonhardy, F. C., ed. *Domebo: A Paleo-Indian Mammoth Kill in the Prairie-Plains*. Lawton, Okla.: Great Plains Hist. Assoc., 1966.

Lotka, A. *Elements of Mathematical Biology*. New York: Dover, 1956.

MacCurdy, G. G. *Human Origins*. Vol. 1. New York: Appleton-Century, 1933.

Mangelsdorf, P. C., and Smith, C. E., Jr. "New Archaeological Evidence on Evolution in Maize." *Botanical Museum Leaflets*, vol. 13, no. 8 (1949).

Martin, P. S., and Guilday, J. E. "A Bestiary for Pleistocene Biologists." In *Pleistocene Extinctions*, edited by P. S. Martin and H. E. Wright, Jr. New Haven, Conn.: Yale Univ. Press, 1967.

Martin, Paul S. "Prehistoric Overkill." In *Pleistocene Extinctions*, edited by P. S. Martin and H. E. Wright, Jr. New Haven, Conn.: Yale Univ. Press, 1967.

———. "Discovery of America: Pleistocene Extinctions Following Migration to the Western Hemisphere." *Science*, March 9, 1973, pp. 969–74.

Mech, David L. *The Wolf*. Garden City, N.Y.: Nat. Hist. Press, 1970.

Plourde, C. "Exploitation of Common-Property Replenishable Natural Resources." *Western Econ. J.* 9 (September 1971): 256–66.

Sauer, Carl O. "A Geographical Sketch of Early Man in America." *Geographical Rev.* 34, no. 4 (1944): 529–73.

Scott, A. "The Fishery: The Objectives of Sole Ownership." *J.P.E.* 63, no. 2 (April 1955): 116–24.

Slaughter, B. H. "Animal Ranges as a Clue to Late-Pleistocene Extinction." In *Pleistocene Extinctions*, edited by P. S. Martin and H. E. Wright, Jr. New Haven, Conn.: Yale Univ. Press, 1967.

Smith, V. L. "Economics of Production from Natural Resources." *A.E.R.* 58 (June 1968): 409–31.

Strong, W. D. "From History to Prehistory in the Northern Great Plains." In *Essays in Historical Anthropology of North America*. Washington: Smithsonian Inst., 1940.

Wedel, W. R. *An Introduction to Pawnee Archeology*. Bureau of American Ethnology, bull. 112. Washington: Smithsonian Inst., 1936.

———. *Culture Sequences in the Central Great Plains*. Washington: Smithsonian Inst., 1940.

Wheat, J. B. "A Paleo-Indian Bison Kill." *Scientific American* 216 (January 1967): 44–51.

CHAPTER 16

OPTIMAL RESOURCE USE OVER TIME WITH AN APPLICATION TO GROUND WATER

OSCAR R. BURT

University of California, Davis

This paper is concerned with optimal allocation over time of a single resource which is either fixed in supply or only partially renewable at a point in time. Some resources which fall in this category are mineral deposits, ground water, petroleum, wildlife, and fish. A functional equation is obtained from a dynamic programming formulation of the problem. This functional equation is used to derive approximate decision rules for resource use as a function of current supply. The results are applied to ground water storage control and tested empirically by comparison with a decision rule obtained by detailed numerical methods.

We first derive approximate decision rules for a general resource allocation model and then examine some of the implications for ground water storage control. Then the model is further modified to permit carrying out an empirical analysis where ground water is used conjunctively with surface water.

The optimal rate at which a natural resource should be used is important to both private and public decision making units. We are not concerned here with problems of divergence between net private and social benefits from allocation of resources, but only with optimal temporal allocation from a specific point of view. The point of view might be that of a single firm, or it might be that of a public agency responsible to any particular group of citizens.

Needless to say, the objective function will vary from one decision unit to another, but a common decision model is relevant for all. The expected net output function per unit of time is the part of the model which will change, depending on the decision unit. In the case of private firms, it would appear that there are no serious conceptual problems in measurement, but the same cannot be said for public agencies. Problems involved in measurement of net social benefits have received a good deal of attention in economics [7], [8], [10], but are beyond the scope of this paper. For present purposes, the output or benefit function is taken as given and problems associated with its measurement are not considered.

The following notation is used:

s = quantity of resource in stock or reserve

x = quantity of resource used from stock per period

w = quantity of resource added to stock per period (not under the decision maker's control)

$G(x, s)$ = expected net output per period

$h(w, s)\,dw$ = probability density function for additions to stock

$\omega(s)$ = expectation of w for a given magnitude of s
β = $(1 + r)^{-1}$, where r is the periodic interest rate.

Typically, net output will be a function of the quantity of resource used per period, x, and the remaining stock of the resource, s, as exemplified by $G(x, s)$. The role of x in specifying net output is obvious while the influence of s stems from increasing costs which are usually experienced as stock of the resource declines. For example, mining costs can be expected to increase since the richest ore is utilized first and greater depths also increase costs; costs associated with ground water increase due to greater depths of pumping; and costs associated with consumption of fish increase due to reduced supplies and subsequent difficulties of capture.

The quantity of resource added to stock per period, w, is zero with probability one in the context of some applications such as optimal mining of a mineral deposit of known quantity. However, in many other applications a meaningful probability distribution will exist as in the case of ground water allocation where w would be the quantity of water recharged to the underground supply. In the case of a fishery it would be the amount of fish reproduced per period and therefore the probability distribution would be dependent on the parameter, s, the amount of fish in stock. In still other applications, such as temporal allocation of petroleum reserves, w might be the quantity of new discoveries of the stock of resource per period, in which case the probability distribution would not be known or even estimable with any confidence. The variable, w, could also be the increment to revised estimates of stocks as new information unfolds about previously discovered deposits (taking on either positive or negative magnitudes).

The following analysis is quite general in most respects, but there is one major restriction. Initial quantity of resource in reserve must be quite large relative to expected decline in reserve per time period under an optimal policy. This requirement is somewhat relaxed if the optimal rate of use as a function of resource reserve declines to the expected rate of renewal before the reserve is exhausted. The justification and implications of these assertions will be discussed later.

An alternative approach to optimal allocation of an exhaustible resource of known fixed supply is given by Hotelling [6], using the calculus of variations.

The Functional Equation

The methods of dynamic programming permit derivation of a functional equation for optimal resource allocation. When x units of resource are withdrawn from stock during a period in which initial stock was s units, stock at the beginning of the immediately following period is $s + w - x$ units. Decisions are made at the beginning of each period. Let $f_n(s)$ be present value of expected net output under an optimal policy from the last n periods of the planning horizon.

Applying Bellman's "principle of optimality" (see [1], p. 83) we obtain the recursive relation

$$f_n(s) = \operatorname*{Max}_x \left[G(x, s) + \beta \int f_{n-1}(s + w - x)h(w, s)\, dw \right]. \tag{1}$$

If the planning horizon is infinite (which is a reasonable approximation for long-run resource allocation), we will be interested in the limiting form of (1). In the limit as $n \to \infty$, $f_{n+1}(s) = f_n(s) = f(s)$, (see [1], p. 121) and we have

$$f(s) = \operatorname*{Max}_x \left[G(x, s) + \beta \int f(s + w - x) h(w, s)\, dw \right]. \tag{2}$$

This is the equation which will provide a means for obtaining approximate decision rules. Direct analytical solution of (2) is not possible, except for very simplified relationships.

In cases where it is not reasonable to assume a constant net output function over time—$G(x, s)$ is conditioned by the stage n—the relationship expressed by (2) is no longer valid. The convergence property does not necessarily hold. However, the relationship expressed by (2) where $G(x, s)$ is the net output function for current conditions may be a very useful approximation to the exact functional equation where $f_n(s) \neq f_{n-1}(s)$.

First Degree Approximation

If s is large relative to $w - x$, then $f(s + w - x)$ can be approximated by the first two terms of the Taylor's series evaluated at $f(s)$. That is

$$f(s + w - x) \approx f(s) + (w - x) f'(s), \tag{3}$$

where we neglect the higher order terms of the expansion. Using this approximation, relation (2) becomes

$$\begin{aligned} f(s) &= \operatorname*{Max}_x \left[G(x, s) + \beta \int \{f(s) + (w - x) f'(s)\} h(w, s)\, dw \right] \\ &= (1/(1 - \beta)) \operatorname*{Max}_x \left[G(x, s) + \beta\{\omega(s) - x\} f'(s) \right]. \end{aligned} \tag{4}$$

The maximization problem in relation (4) is solved implicitly by setting the first partial derivative of the quantity to be maximized equal to zero. Thus,

$$\partial G(x, s)/\partial x - \beta f'(s) = 0 \tag{5}$$

and second order conditions for a maximum require

$$\partial^2 G(x, s)/\partial x^2 < 0. \tag{6}$$

Relation (4) can be written as the two equations

$$f(s) = (1/(1 - \beta))[G(x, s) + \beta\{\omega(s) - x\} f'(s)], \tag{7}$$

and (5). However, we have no measure of $f'(s)$ and must use an approximation which we obtain by differentiating both sides of (7) with respect to s using the auxiliary relation (5) which implies x is a function of s. All derivatives of $f(s)$ higher than the first are neglected which gives an approximation for $f'(s)$ in the same order of magnitude as the original approximation of (3). Carrying out the differentiation,

$$(8)\quad \begin{aligned} f'(s) &= \frac{1}{1-\beta}\left[\frac{\partial G}{\partial s} + \frac{\partial G}{\partial x}\frac{\partial x}{\partial s} - \beta f'(s)\frac{\partial x}{\partial s} + \beta f'(s)\omega'(s)\right] \\ &= \frac{1}{1-\beta}\left[\frac{\partial G}{\partial s} + \frac{\partial x}{\partial s}\left\{\frac{\partial G}{\partial x} - \beta f'(s)\right\} + \beta f'(s)\omega'(s)\right]. \end{aligned}$$

Observe that the factor by which $\frac{\partial x}{\partial s}$ is multiplied is zero by (5). Therefore,

$$(9)\quad f'(s) = \frac{1}{1-\beta[1+\omega'(s)]}\frac{\partial G}{\partial s}$$

within the limits of our approximation.

Substitution of (9) into (5) gives the decision rule

$$(10)\quad \begin{aligned} \frac{\partial G}{\partial x} &= \frac{\beta}{1-\beta[1+\omega'(s)]}\frac{\partial G}{\partial s} \\ &= \frac{1}{r-\omega'(s)}\frac{\partial G}{\partial s}. \end{aligned}$$

In the case of many resources, $\omega'(s) = 0$, i.e., the probability distribution for w is independent of resource reserves. This situation exists for petroleum, mineral deposits, and ground water in many basins. In most cases, ground water recharges are affected by quantity in stock only if the underground reservoir is approaching maximum capacity.

If additions to resource reserves are independent of the reserve, relation (10) reduces to

$$(11)\quad \frac{\partial G}{\partial x} = \frac{1}{r}\frac{\partial G}{\partial s},$$

which is seen not to rely on w or its probability distribution in any way whatsoever. This simplified decision rule appears promising for such situations as allocation of mineral stocks, petroleum, and ground water, where information on additions to reserves is quite often limited or completely unknown.

The decision rule specified by (11) has the following interpretation:

> Expand production to the point where marginal net output with respect to current consumption of the resource is equal to present value of a perpetual annuity equal in value to marginal net output with respect to quantity of resource in stock.

Another relationship which is of interest is the change in optimal use rate with respect to quantity in stock, i.e., $\partial x/\partial s$. An approximation to this measure is obtained by differentiating (5) and disregarding $f''(s)$ as we did in obtaining the decision rule, which yields

$$(12)\quad \frac{\partial x}{\partial s} = -\frac{\partial^2 G}{\partial s \partial x}\bigg/\frac{\partial^2 G}{\partial x^2}.$$

However, an exact measure (exact for our approximate decision rule) can be derived by differentiation of (10). Little, in general, can be deduced about the sign of $\partial x/\partial s$ from differentiation of (10), but in the simpler case where (11) applies

$$\frac{\partial x}{\partial s} = \left(\frac{1}{r}\frac{\partial^2 G}{\partial s^2} - \frac{\partial^2 G}{\partial s \partial x}\right) \Big/ \left(\frac{\partial^2 G}{\partial x^2} - \frac{1}{r}\frac{\partial^2 G}{\partial x \partial s}\right). \tag{13}$$

If the approximation given by (12) is used, then the sign of $\partial x/\partial s$ is completely specified by the sign of the mixed derivative $\partial^2 G/\partial s \partial x$. This follows from the second order conditions for a maximum given in (6). From the previous discussion of various resources, we would expect $\partial^2 G/\partial s \partial x > 0$, implying $\partial x/\partial s > 0$ in relation (12). If in addition $\partial^2 G/\partial s^2 < 0$, then the same conclusion as to the sign of $\partial x/\partial s$ is reached using relation (13). Positivity of $\partial x/\partial s$ will be used later in the analysis of ground water storage control to show existence of a stable equilibrium.

The preceding approximations used to arrive at the decision rule expressed by (10) lean heavily on the assumption that s is large relative to $w - x$. The magnitude of error for situations where this assumption is questionable can be reduced by adding an additional term in the Taylor's series of (3), which is what is done in the following section. However, the success of this added refinement rests partially on whether s will be large relative to $w - x$ for a considerable time into the future under an optimal policy. If it will, then the discount factor will insure a good approximation to the optimal policy by our procedure.

On the other hand, if s does not remain large relative to $w - x$ for a "long enough" time into the future, discounting will not nullify the influence, and the approximate decision rule will be in serious error. In fact, the physical restriction that x must be less than or equal to s will become effective if s is no longer large relative to x at an optimal level, and the curvature of $f(s)$ might be reversed from that which is indicated by the following second degree approximation. If this situation exists the second degree approximation will be in greater error than the first degree approximation just derived. As will be seen, the empirical application to ground water control illustrates this very situation. Nevertheless, good results are obtained in the application for a decision rule to use immediately because the quantity of ground water currently in storage is very large.

Second Degree Approximation

In order to prevent the following analysis from becoming unwieldy, the probability distribution of w is specified independently of s. We use the operator, E, to denote mathematical expectation.

The approximation of (3) is improved by adding another term of the Taylor's series giving

$$f(s + w - x) \approx f(s) + (w - x)f'(s) + f''(s)(w - x)^2/2. \tag{14}$$

Following the same methods as in the last section except third and higher derivatives of $f(s)$ are neglected we obtain

$$(15)\quad f(s) = (1/(1-\beta))[G(x, s) + \beta E(w-x)f'(s) + (\beta/2)E(w-x)^2 f''(s)]$$

$$(16)\quad \partial G/\partial x = \beta[f'(s) + E(w-x)f''(s)]$$

provided the additional condition for a maximum,

$$(17)\quad \partial^2 G/\partial x^2 + \beta f''(s) < 0,$$

is met.

We approximate $f'(s)$ by differentiating both sides of (15) neglecting greater than second order derivatives of $f(s)$ and utilizing (16) implicitly for a relation between x and s. Differentiation of (15) gives

$$(18)\quad \begin{aligned} f'(s) &= \frac{1}{1-\beta}\left[\frac{\partial G}{\partial s} + \beta E(w-x)f''(s)\right. \\ &\qquad \left. + \frac{\partial x}{\partial s}\left\{\frac{\partial G}{\partial x} - \beta f'(s) - \beta E(w-x)f''(s)\right\}\right] \\ &= \frac{1}{1-\beta}\left[\frac{\partial G}{\partial s} + \beta E(w-x)f''(s)\right]. \end{aligned}$$

The last step of (18) utilizes (16) to show the last term is zero.

The second derivative $f''(s)$ is approximated by differentiation of (18) and neglecting higher order derivatives. Thus

$$(19)\quad f''(s) = \frac{1}{1-\beta}\left[\frac{\partial^2 G}{\partial s^2} - \beta f''(s)\frac{\partial x}{\partial s} + \frac{\partial^2 G}{\partial x \partial s}\frac{\partial x}{\partial s}\right].$$

An approximation to $\partial x/\partial s$ is obtained by differentiation of (16),

$$(20)\quad \frac{\partial x}{\partial s} = \left(-\frac{\partial^2 G}{\partial s \partial x} + \beta f''(s)\right)\bigg/\left(\frac{\partial^2 G}{\partial x^2} + \beta f''(s)\right).$$

Substitution of (20) into (19) gives a quadratic function in $f''(s)$,

$$(21)\quad \begin{aligned} &\beta[f''(s)]^2 + \left[(1-\beta)\frac{\partial^2 G}{\partial x^2} - 2\beta\frac{\partial^2 G}{\partial s \partial x} - \beta\frac{\partial^2 G}{\partial s^2}\right]f''(s) \\ &\qquad + \left[\frac{\partial^2 G}{\partial s \partial x}\right]^2 - \frac{\partial^2 G}{\partial s^2}\frac{\partial^2 G}{\partial x^2} = 0. \end{aligned}$$

We face the task of choosing between the two roots of (21). The two roots can be written from the quadratic formula as

$$f''(s) = \frac{-a_1 \pm \sqrt{a_1^2 - 4\beta a_0}}{2\beta}$$

where

$$(22)\quad \begin{aligned} a_1 &= (1-\beta)\frac{\partial^2 G}{\partial x^2} - 2\beta\frac{\partial^2 G}{\partial s \partial x} - \beta\frac{\partial^2 G}{\partial s^2} \\ a_0 &= \left[\frac{\partial^2 G}{\partial s \partial x}\right]^2 - \frac{\partial^2 G}{\partial s^2}\frac{\partial^2 G}{\partial x^2}. \end{aligned}$$

The smallest root is shown to be the appropriate solution to (22) under fairly general conditions. These conditions are that $f''(s)$ be a continuous function of the parameters $\partial^2G/\partial s\partial x$ and $\partial^2G/\partial s^2$ at magnitudes for x implied by an optimal policy.

The smallest root is shown to be the solution when $\partial^2G/\partial s\partial x = \partial^2G/\partial s^2 = 0$, and therefore, the solution in general under the above condition of continuity. The recurrence relation of (1) is utilized to obtain successive approximations and by induction it is shown that $f''(s) = 0$. Zero is the smallest root of (22) in this case. The derivation is relegated to Appendix A.

We are now in a position to obtain the optimal decision rule for temporal resource allocation within the limits of our second degree approximation. Substitution of (18) into (16) gives

$$\frac{\partial G}{\partial x} = \frac{1}{r}\left[\frac{\partial G}{\partial s} + E(w - x)f''(s)\right]. \tag{23}$$

Substitution of the smallest root of (22) for $f''(s)$ results in

$$\frac{\partial G}{\partial x} = \frac{1}{r}\left[\frac{\partial G}{\partial s} + E(w - x)\left(\frac{-a_1 - \sqrt{a_1^2 - 4\beta a_0}}{2\beta}\right)\right] \tag{24}$$

with

$$a_1 = (1 - \beta)\frac{\partial^2G}{\partial x^2} - 2\beta\frac{\partial^2G}{\partial s\partial x} - \beta\frac{\partial^2G}{\partial s^2}, \qquad a_0 = \left[\frac{\partial^2G}{\partial s\partial x}\right]^2 - \frac{\partial^2G}{\partial s^2}\frac{\partial^2G}{\partial x^2}.$$

This is the final decision rule from the second degree approximation of (2).

Equation (24) might be difficult to solve depending on the nature of $G(x, s)$. However, iterative methods can readily be applied using the solution from the first degree approximation as an initial magnitude for x.

The sign of $\partial x/\partial s$ is not so easily established as in the first degree approximation to the optimal policy. Due to the complexity of the situation, direct differentiation of (24) is not considered as a feasible alternative for establishing the sign. We rely entirely on the approximation expressed by (20). Observe that the denominator of the expression for $\partial x/\partial s$ in (20) is the left-hand side of inequality (17) and therefore negative. Consequently, $\partial x/\partial s$ is positive if and only if

$$\partial^2G/\partial s\partial x - \beta f''(s) > 0. \tag{25}$$

Only in the case $f''(s)$ is positive would we question (25).

In applications, the sign of $\partial^2G/\partial s^2$ would be expected negative or at most zero. Careful examination of the smallest root of (22) will show that it increases as $\partial^2G/\partial s^2$ increases. Therefore, if (25) holds for $\partial^2G/\partial s^2 = 0$, it also holds for negative magnitudes of $\partial^2G/\partial s^2$. The condition for (25) to hold when $\partial^2G/\partial s^2 = 0$ is derived in Appendix B. That condition is

$$\partial^2G/\partial x^2 + \partial^2G/\partial s\partial x < 0, \qquad \partial^2G/\partial s\partial x > 0, \tag{26}$$

which would be expected to hold in practical applications because of physical and economic relationships. A positive mixed derivative reflects increasing costs of utilizing stocks of the resource, and the first inequality of (26) implies marginal net output is more sensitive to level of current usage than level of resource reserves.

Ground Water Storage Control

Most of the work concerned with ground water management has concentrated on the economic inefficiency and misallocation of resources resulting from uncontrolled use of a common-property resource [4], [5]. Briefly, this problem arises when several firms exploit a resource which is owned jointly, and each firm optimizes his interests independently of the others. For example, in a large ground water basin with many firms, the quantity of water pumped by an individual firm has a negligible effect on future pumping costs, but for all firms as a group the current pumping rate has a very important effect on future pumping costs. Thus, firms acting individually will cause misallocation of the ground water over time from the point of view of all producers as a group; and most likely, from the point of view of the nation, state, or other regional unit in which the basin is contained.

The question of optimal use over time (in a quantitative sense) of a common-property resource in such a way that joint returns to all users (or net social benefits as viewed by a public agency responsible to a specific group of citizens) are maximized has been answered with very limited success [9]. The approximate results derived in the preceding sections provide a basis to help answer this question. For situations which do not meet the assumptions necessary for these approximate results to apply, another method is available (although much more laborious). Specifically, the alternative method is numerical solution of the functional equation by discrete approximation of the continuous variables [2]. For an application of this numerical method to ground water storage control see [3].

For most basins, the net output function can be written in two components as

$$G(x, s) = R(x) - c(s)x, \tag{27}$$

where $R(x)$ is net output before deduction of pumping costs and $c(s)$ is per unit pumping costs. Substitution of (27) into the decision rule expressed by (11) yields

$$(R'(x) - c(s))/x = -c'(s)/r. \tag{28}$$

The literal interpretation of (28) is:

> Production for the basin is expanded to the point where marginal net output per unit of water is equal to the negative of capitalized marginal pumping costs with respect to water in storage ($c'(s)$ being negative).

This statement is quite intuitive economically. The right-hand side of (28) is the opportunity cost of ground water in the sense that if the water is not used in current production its next best use is as storage which implies a saving in all future pumping costs. The future savings in pumping costs resulting from an increment to storage is in the form of a perpetual annuity reduced to present value.

Marginal value of water in storage is given by (9). Using (27) and specifying $\omega'(s)$ equal to zero,

$$(29)\qquad f'(s) = -c'(s)x/(1 - \beta) = (1 + r)[-c'(s)x/r]$$

which can be used as a base price for implementing an optimal storage policy under certain conditions. This aspect of storage control will be discussed later.

It is noted that $\partial^2 G/\partial s \partial x = -c'(s)$ when relation (27) prevails for the net output function. Since an inverse relationship between quantity in storage and pumping costs must exist, the mixed derivative for net output must be positive. The mixed derivative is marginal pumping cost per unit of water with respect to quantity of water in storage and is a small positive number. In the application presented later $\partial^2 G/\partial s \partial x = 0.2$ which would require $\partial^2 G/\partial x^2$ less than $-.2$ in order for (26) to hold which insures $\partial x/\partial s$ positive. However, in the application the second derivative is -116 which is a sizable margin.

Long-Run Equilibrium Storage

The question of when safe yield is optimal can be answered by solving equation (23) for s with x set equal to $E(w)$. Note that the term involving $f''(s)$ drops out for $x = E(w)$. In fact, the first degree approximation then equals the second. The value of s satisfying equation (23) with $x = E(w)$ is long-run equilibrium storage in the sense that an optimal policy will tend to move storage to this level from quantities above or below (assuming $\partial x/\partial s$ is positive). Denote this equilibrium magnitude of s by s^*.

Suppose $s = s^*$ and we experience a deviation from s^* in the following period. First let the deviation make s greater than s^*. When $s = s^*$, $x = E(w)$ and since $\partial x/\partial s$ is positive we have $x > E(w)$ if $s > s^*$. Therefore, there is a tendency to move back to s^* because annual withdrawals exceed expected annual recharges. The argument for storage moving below s^* is similar and confirms s^* as the stable long-run equilibrium storage level. However, the random nature of recharges makes the equilibrium storage level a magnitude that is approached but rarely experienced.

Differentiation of (23) at $x = E(w) = \omega$ and solving for $\partial s^*/\partial \omega$ yields

$$(30)\qquad \frac{\partial s^*}{\partial \omega} = \left(-\frac{\partial^2 G}{\partial \omega^2} + \frac{1}{r}\frac{\partial^2 G}{\partial s^* \partial \omega}\right) \Big/ \left(\frac{\partial^2 G}{\partial s^* \partial \omega} - \frac{1}{r}\frac{\partial^2 G}{\partial s^{*2}}\right)$$

where $G = G(x, s^*)$ at $x = \omega$. The sign of $\partial s^*/\partial \omega$ is most likely positive and is definitely positive if $\partial^2 G/\partial s^2$ is zero (linear pumping costs) or negative. An increase in mean recharge to ground water will in most situations increase the equilibrium ground water storage level.

An implication of this fact is that optimal consumption will not necessarily increase by the same amount as the addition to mean annual supply resulting from water resource development. Storage might be down to or below equilibrium for the old mean supply and after the increase in supply, storage will be built up toward the new equilibrium. This phenomenon would be expected with introduction of artificial recharge or surface water and associated incidental recharge to a previously developed basin.

The above discussion of an equilibrium storage level suggests a means of evaluating the approximate decision rules for an empirical application. If the equilibrium storage level is positive and sufficiently far from zero so that the chance of the inequality constraint, $x \leqq s$, being effective at any time is very small, then our approximate decision rules should give good results, particularly the second degree approximation. If the equilibrium level is negative or very close to zero, we cannot be confident of the approximate decision rules unless the quantity of water in storage is currently very large and then the decision rule is appriate only for the immediate future, i.e., only as long as the quantity in storage remains large. In other words, the approximate policies are most valid for conditions where increasing pumping costs are the ultimate limitation on utilization of ground water, as contrasted to physical supply of ground water being the limitation.

Implementing Storage Control

Control can be effected either by regulating total quantity used per period (that is x), or by charging producers a price per unit of water pumped which would augment variable costs per unit of water used. Quantity control requires allocation of total water used in the basin among producers, or equivalently, allocation among parcels of land. This problem will not be considered, but we shall go to the question of pricing.

The foregoing analysis provides an optimal price under certain conditions. The price is specifically $f'(s)$, i.e., the marginal value of water in storage and is given by relations (18) and (9) (or (29) as a simplified case) for the second and first degree approximations, respectively. This measure of marginal value of stored water is appropriate as a price to confront producers in order to ration water only if marginal value of water to an individual producer is equal to that for producers as a group at the equilibrium quantity x given by (24) (or (28) if using the first degree approximation in its simplified form).

The necessary conditions for $f'(s)$ to be the correct price are:

(1) identical production functions for all producers

(2) commodities produced in small enough quantities relative to the total market that production in the basin has a negligible effect on prices.

When these two conditions are nearly met, the methods of the preceding sections provide a basis for rationing water optimally by a per unit charge to producers. If these requirements are not met, the underlying relations in individual producing units must be examined in order to ascertain prices which will give the desired total withdrawal of water by the entire basin.

An Empirical Application

This application was worked previously using numerical methods to obtain the functional equation [3], thus giving us a comparison for the approximate analytical solution obtained here. The region of study is an area serviced by the Pine Flat Reservoir on the Kings River in parts of Kings, Fresno, and Tulare Counties, California. The ground water model is more complex than the preceding model, but modifications are easily made.

Recharge is not independent of total water used per period by the basin and part of the water is provided by surface water from Pine Flat Reservoir. The model requires the following revised notation:

x = total quantity of water used per period for current production (both surface and ground water delivered at the site where used)
w = quantity of water diverted into the surface distribution system, one-half of which is incidental recharge to ground water and the other half reaches the farm level for production
$c_0 - cs$ = per acre-foot pumping cost
$G(x, s) = R(x) - (c_0 - cs)(x - E(w)/2)$. Ground water pumped each year is a random variable, being the difference between total use and surface water used.

Due to the fact that surface water captured either goes to recharge or as a substitute for ground water, the functional equation of (2) remains essentially the same as under the original model. That is to say, if s units of water are in storage, then $s + w - x$ units will be in storage in the immediately following year. This is true regardless of the fixed proportion recharged.

The output function $R(x)$ was estimated using discrete methods and is approximated in the range in which a solution is almost certain to occur by the quadratic equation

$$R(x) = -641.0690 + 449.6900x - 58.3920x^2$$
$$3.50 \leqq x \leqq 4.00$$

with x in units of million acre-feet and output in million dollars. Pumping costs were estimated by the linear function

$$c_0 - cs = 14.58 - .2004s$$

with s in million acre-feet of storage and pumping costs in dollars per acre-foot. The mean supply of water $E(w)$ was estimated at 1.815 million acre-feet. An interest rate of six percent is used. Average pumping depth is about 50 feet corresponding to s = 54.78 million acre-feet when maximum pumping depth is 400 feet. Results from our approximate methods will be invariant with respect to specified maximum pumping depth as long as specific yield remains fairly uniform.

The optimization equation (23) for the empirical problem is

$$(31) \quad R'(x) - (c_0 - cs) = [c(x - E(w)/2) + E(w - x)f''(s)]/r.$$

Substitution of the above empirical measures into (31) gives the following equation in x

$$(32) \quad \begin{aligned} &449.6900 - 116.7840x - 14.58 + (.2004)(54.78) \\ &\qquad = [(.2004)(x - 1.815/2) + (1.815 - x)f''(s)]/.06. \end{aligned}$$

Since $f''(s)$ is constant, it is computed separately using (22) and is equal to

.00575. Simplification of (32) and solving, $x = 3.7402$ million acre-feet. Marginal value of stored water is computed from (18) and equals \$9.85.

Using the first degree approximation (setting $f''(s)$ equal to zero) does not alter results but slightly. This small change would be expected by observing the small value of $f''(s)$. The first degree approximation gives optimal annual use equal to 3.7388 million acre-feet and marginal value of stored water is \$10.03. The slight difference is a consequence of $\partial^2G/\partial s\partial x$ being very small relative to the absolute value of $\partial^2G/\partial x^2$ (.2004 compared to 116).

Numerical methods to obtain the functional equation [3] yielded an optimal annual use rate of 3.7181 million acre-feet and a marginal value of stored water equal to \$11.84. The functional equation computed was concave downward (the opposite of the approximate model) primarily because of the limit placed on underground storage and the high return per unit of water. Ground water storage would be exhausted long before pumping costs prevented economic pumping. If maximum depth of underground storage had been specified greater than 400 feet, we would have expected marginal value of stored water (and optimal rate of use) to more nearly approach the measures obtained in the approximate analytical model.

When it is suspected that the actual functional equation is likely to be concave downward due to physically limited pumping depths, the first degree approximation will give more accurate results. The correction offered by the use of $f''(s)$ is in the wrong direction when physical capacity limits pumping instead of pumping costs. The reason for the approximate model giving satisfactory results in this application is because quantity in storage is large relative to expected change in storage under an optimal policy. Discounting of future net output dwarfs the effects of the discontinuity in the net output function at the empty storage state and the effects of the inequality constraint $x \leqq s$.

Value of net output relative to pumping costs in this application is unusually high. Agricultural production is dominated by intensive crops such as grapes and tree crops which yield net returns to water and land in the neighborhood of 70 to 80 dollars per acre-foot of water. Therefore, good results from the approximate model under this adverse situation should be encouraging for its use in more appropriate circumstances. However, the rapidly diminishing marginal net output function in the region of solution which was experienced in the application is favorable to obtaining good results from the approximate model.

Appendix A

It is our task in this appendix to show that the smallest root of (22) is the appropriate solution when $\partial^2G/\partial s\partial x = \partial^2G/\partial s^2 = 0$. Since $\partial^2G/\partial s\partial x = \partial^2G/\partial s^2 = 0$, $\partial G/\partial s =$ a constant, k, for all x and s. Let $f_0(s)$ in (1) equal zero. Then

$$f_1(s) = \text{Max}_{x_1}\, G(x_1, s)$$

which can be written as the two equations

$$\text{(A-1)} \qquad \begin{aligned} f_1(s) &= G(x_1, s) \\ \partial G/\partial x_1 &= 0. \end{aligned}$$

Likewise, letting $n = 2$ in (1),

$$\text{(A-2)}\qquad \begin{aligned} f_2(s) &= G(x_2, s) + \beta E f_1(s + w - x_2) \\ \partial G(x_2, s)/\partial x_2 - \beta E f'_1(s + w - x_2) &= 0. \end{aligned}$$

Substituting (A-1) in (A-2),

$$\text{(A-3)}\qquad \begin{aligned} f_2(s) &= G(x_2, s) + \beta E G(x_1, s + w - x_2) \\ \partial G(x_1, s + w - x_2)/\partial x_1 &= 0 \end{aligned}$$

$$\partial G(x_2, s)/\partial x_2 - \beta k - \beta E(\partial G(x_1, s + w - x_2)/\partial x_1)(\partial x_1/\partial(s + w - x_2)) = 0.$$

Differentiating the second equation of (A-1) we obtain

$$\frac{\partial x_1}{\partial s} = -\frac{\partial^2 G}{\partial s \partial x_1} \Big/ \frac{\partial^2 G}{\partial x_1^2} = 0$$

since $\partial^2 G/\partial s \partial x = 0$ for all magnitudes of x and s. Therefore, the last equation of (A-3) reduces to

$$\text{(A-4)}\qquad \partial G(x_2, s)/\partial x_2 - \beta k = 0.$$

Differentiating (A-4) we obtain

$$\partial x_2/\partial s = 0.$$

Continuing in the same manner we obtain

$$\text{(A-5)}\qquad \begin{aligned} f_3(s) &= G(x_3, s) + \beta E f_2(s + w - x_3) \\ \partial G(x_3, s)/\partial x_3 - \beta k - \beta^2 k &= 0. \end{aligned}$$

By induction, the general recurrence relation is

$$\text{(A-6)}\qquad \begin{aligned} f_n(s) &= G(x_n, s) + \beta E f_{n-1}(s + w - x_n) \\ \partial G(x_n, s)/\partial x_n &= k(\beta + \beta^2 + \cdots + \beta^n). \end{aligned}$$

The limit of (A-6) is obviously

$$\text{(A-7)}\qquad \begin{aligned} f(s) &= G(x, s) + \beta E f(s + w - x) \\ \partial G(x, s)/\partial x &= k/r = (1/r)\partial G/\partial s. \end{aligned}$$

Since the second equation of (A-7) is the necessary condition for the right-hand side of the first equation to be a maximum with respect to x,

$$k/r = \beta E f'(s + w - x).$$

Therefore, $Ef''(s + w - x) = 0$ which implies $f''(s) = 0$ for all values of s. Thus our proof is complete.

The equilibrium condition expressed by (A-7) is identical to that of relation (11) obtained in the last section. Consequently, the first degree approximation is seen to be very good if the optimal use level x is not sensitive to quantity in storage s. This proposition follows from the fact that (A-7) implies that the optimal level of x is independent of quantity in storage.

Appendix B

Relation (26) is derived as the condition which must be met so that (25) holds. Inequality (25) can be written (using the smallest root of (22) and setting $\partial^2 G/\partial s^2 = 0$)

$$\frac{\partial^2 G}{\partial s \partial x} + \frac{1}{2}\left[(1-\beta)\frac{\partial^2 G}{\partial x^2} - 2\beta\frac{\partial^2 G}{\partial s \partial x}\right]$$

$$> -\frac{1}{2}\left[(1-\beta)^2\left(\frac{\partial^2 G}{\partial x^2}\right)^2 + 4\beta^2\left(\frac{\partial^2 G}{\partial s \partial x}\right)^2 - 4\beta(1-\beta)\frac{\partial^2 G}{\partial x^2}\frac{\partial^2 G}{\partial s \partial x} - 4\beta\left(\frac{\partial^2 G}{\partial s \partial x}\right)^2\right]^{1/2}. \tag{B-1}$$

Inequality (B-1) holds if the square of the left-hand side is less than the square of the right-hand side, or multiplying both sides by two and collecting some terms

$$\left[(1-\beta)\frac{\partial^2 G}{\partial x^2} + 2(1-\beta)\frac{\partial^2 G}{\partial s \partial x}\right]^2 < (1-\beta)^2\left(\frac{\partial^2 G}{\partial x^2}\right)^2 - 4\beta(1-\beta)\frac{\partial^2 G}{\partial x^2}\frac{\partial^2 G}{\partial s \partial x} - 4\beta(1-\beta)\left(\frac{\partial^2 G}{\partial s \partial x}\right)^2. \tag{B-2}$$

Squaring out the left side of (B-2) and collecting terms

$$4(1-\beta)^2\frac{\partial^2 G}{\partial s \partial x}\left[\frac{\partial^2 G}{\partial x^2} + \frac{\partial^2 G}{\partial s \partial x}\right] < -4\beta(1-\beta)\frac{\partial^2 G}{\partial s \partial x}\left[\frac{\partial^2 G}{\partial x^2} + \frac{\partial^2 G}{\partial s \partial x}\right]. \tag{B-3}$$

It is easily seen that (B-3) holds if and only if

$$\partial^2 G/\partial x^2 + \partial^2 G/\partial s \partial x < 0, \tag{B-4}$$

provided $\partial^2 G/\partial s \partial x$ is positive.

References

1. Bellman, Richard, *Dynamic Programming*, Princeton University Press, Princeton, 1957.
2. ——, *Adaptive Control Processes: A Guided Tour*, Princeton University Press, Princeton, 1961, Chapter 5.
3. Burt, Oscar R., "The Economics of Conjunctive Use of Ground and Surface Water," *Hilgardia* (publication of California Agricultural Experiment Station), forthcoming, 1964.
4. Gordon, H. Scott, "The Economic Theory of a Common-Property Resource: The Fishery," *Journal of Political Economy*, Vol. 62 (1950), pp. 124–42.
5. Hirshleifer, Jack, Dehaven, James C., and Milliman, Jerome W., *Water Supply*, University of Chicago Press, Chicago, 1960, pp. 59–60.
6. Hotelling, Harold, "The Economics of Exhaustible Resources," *Journal of Political Economy*, Vol. 39 (1931), pp. 137–75.
7. Lerner, A. P., *The Economics of Control*, Macmillan, New York, 1944.
8. Maass, Arthur, *et al.*, *Design of Water Resource Systems*, Harvard University Press, Cambridge, 1962, Chapter 2.
9. Renshaw, Edward F., "The Management of Ground Water Reservoirs," *Journal of Farm Economics*, Vol. 45 (1963), pp. 285–95.
10. Wantrup, S. V., *Resource Conservation Economics and Policies*, University of California Press, Berkeley, 1952.

CHAPTER 17

VOL. 3, NO. 1 WATER RESOURCES RESEARCH FIRST QUARTER 1967

Temporal Allocation of Groundwater[1]

OSCAR R. BURT

University of Missouri, Columbia

Abstract. A relatively simple economic model for allocation of groundwater in time is developed. The economic consequences of altering various parameters in the model are examined with respect to the effect on equilibrium stocks and rate of use. The concept of a conditional decision rule for stochastic groundwater recharge and the properties of the implied equilibrium are discussed. In its simplest form, the derived decision rule is to equate marginal net output with respect to rate of use to capitalized marginal net output with respect to water stocks. (Key words: Economics; groundwater; water management; water resources)

Groundwater basins are typically endowed with a stock of water that has built up over time from a relatively small flow or recharge to the stock. An important economic question is the optimal rate of use of this stock component of groundwater. Should the water be used very rapidly to give immediate production in large quantities; should only safe yield or rate of recharge be used and the initial stock left perpetually; or is optimal rate of use a compromise between these two extremes?

A general quantitative solution to this question would specify rate of use for all possible stocks at each date in the future. Under stable economic conditions there presumably exists an equilibrium storage level such that rate of use would exceed recharge if stocks were above the equilibrium, and rate of use would fall short of recharge if stocks were below the equilibrium. The equilibrium is brought about by increased pumping costs as groundwater stocks are depleted and increased value of the water reserves as a contingency in relation to uncertain future supplies. In many basins an equilibrium is assured even under certainty with respect to future water supplies, whereas in other basins the value of water is so high relative to pumping costs (at the marginal rate of use) that an equilibrium exists owing primarily to the contingency value of stocks. The equilibrium is not likely to be near full capacity of the underground reservoir, since delayed production has an associated cost reflected by the interest rate. An optimal policy for temporal allocation balances off the urgency of immediate production against (1) diminishing returns with respect to water used in a given period; (2) increasing pumping costs with depletion of stocks; and (3) the insurance value of stocks against uncertainty.

The decision rules obtained in this paper were first derived from the functional equation of a dynamic programming formulation [*Burt*, 1964*a*]. This paper is primarily expository, using intuitive economic reasoning and geometry, and much of the economic interpretation is new. For a review of the literature see *Burt* [1966], where a general model for temporal allocation of groundwater is presented. But that model requires an electronic computer to carry out the numerical analysis, and, of course, a suitable computer program which is quite specialized. The methodology in *Burt* [1966] has the virtue of generality and completeness for empirical estimation of optimal groundwater policies, but it is fairly demanding in the amount of resources required to obtain the estimated policies. The present approach to the problem has the advantage of simplicity and promotes an understanding of the economic forces involved.

AN APPROXIMATELY OPTIMAL DECISION RULE AND EQUILIBRIUM STORAGE

For the immediately following discussion, it is assumed that groundwater recharge is a constant (not subject to random variation), and that pumping depths ultimately limit economic utilization of groundwater stocks (as contrasted

[1] Contribution from the Missouri Agricultural Experiment Station. Approved by the director September 16, 1966. Journal series No. 4089.

to physical exhaustion). Also, it is temporarily assumed that the periodic net output relationship for the basin remains constant through time. Net output, as used here, is any appropriately defined economic measure of production per time period. Groundwater recharge is defined as the net additions to stock per period, which takes into consideration natural flows from the aquifer.

The net output relation is simplified to a function of two variables: (1) rate of use and (2) groundwater stocks. Implicitly, all other variables are specified at their most economic levels. That is, land, labor, and capital are assumed to be at optimal levels in relation to any specific storage level and rate of use for water. This assumption also implies an optimal allocation of water spatially within the basin.

It is assumed that pumping a given quantity of water from storage is accomplished without creating local overdrafts relative to basinwide stocks of water. This assumption can be met by a proper distribution of wells, although technical knowledge required for the spacing might be unavailable in many basins. The net output relation is denoted $G(x,s)$, with x defined as withdrawals of groundwater per period and s as groundwater stocks. The role of x in specifying net output is quite obvious, since it is the amount of water used per time period to carry on production. The influence of groundwater stocks stems primarily from increasing pumping costs as the stock is depleted and consequently pumping lift is increased, but near reservoir capacity a reduction in stocks can be beneficial if drainage is impaired by the high level of groundwater.

When we later drop the assumption of a constant recharge rate and let it become a random variable, the level of stocks will also reflect the contingency value of stocks. There are some conceptual and empirical problems associated with this generalization which are best discussed after the following developments under certainty. Additional discussion of the net output function under various circumstances is also given in *Burt* [1966].

To facilitate understanding of the method of analysis to be used, we begin with an artificial problem of water allocation. Imagine that the basin purchases water at a fixed price P, and the problem is to allocate the water between current use and stocks of groundwater. The net output function in this hypothetical situation is defined as the net of any costs necessary to get purchased water into storage, just as this function reflects pumping costs in the actual problem with which we are dealing, but it does not include any deduction of the purchase costs of water. We assume that net output is held constant perpetually, with rate of use and stocks each held at the same level year after year. Therefore, the annual cost per unit of water put in stock is rP, where r is the interest rate, and the cost of water allocated to direct production is P, because the water put in stock is an investment of infinite life, whereas that for direct production must be purchased each year.

For a fixed annual outlay used in the purchase of water, say C_0, water must be allocated between direct use and storage such that we remain on the line

$$Px + (rP)s = C_0$$

or

$$x + rs = C_0/P$$

Using a two-dimensional graph with x and s on the vertical and horizontal axes, respectively, the graph of the above line has a negative slope of $-r$ (line AA′ in Figure 1).

The graph of a constant net output for various levels of x and s is depicted in Figure 1 as curve 00′. The other curves convex to the origin and lying above 00′ are also iso-net-output curves implying successively higher levels of output. The curvature and slope assumptions for the iso-net-output curves in Figure 1 are discussed later.

An economically efficient allocation of water between direct use and storage implies attainment of the highest net output for a given outlay on water. Clearly, from Figure 1, we see that points of tangency between price lines parallel to AA′ and iso-net-ouput curves are the locus for efficient production, i.e., curve BC. An alternative, but equivalent, interpretation of curve BC is the locus of least cost purchases of water for given net outputs.

Now we return to the actual problem of allocating a stock of groundwater presently existing in the basin, where there is no opportunity for purchase of outside supplies. Water used in current production has an opportunity cost as a

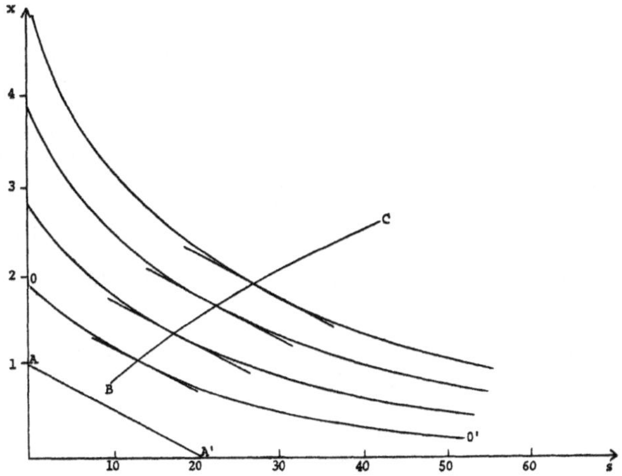

Fig. 1. Iso-net-output map and decision rule.

source of supply to the stock of groundwater. An increment to storage reduces present and future pumping costs, whereas an increment to the amount used in direct production makes its entire contribution immediately. Therefore, at any fixed net output, the rate of use x and stock s can be thought of as substitute inputs to produce that level of output, and each of these two inputs has a cost associated with it in an opportunity cost context.

The ratio of the opportunity cost of s to x is the interest rate if the same net output is to be produced perpetually. Water added to storage makes its contribution each year in the future, and if it adds one dollar to the first year's net output, the present value of all of its contributions is $1/r$, where r is the interest or discount rate. On the other hand, a dollar added to net output through an increment in x makes its entire contribution the first year and has present value equal to 1. Thus the price ratio of s to x in an opportunity cost sense is r when the two inputs are considered as substitutes in producing a fixed net output perpetually.

This is the price ratio that evolved from the artificial situation assumed where water was being purchased at a fixed price and allocated between storage and periodic use. The economic problem involved is the same in either situation, and curve BC traces out the points of efficient allocation for the appropriately defined net output function $G(x,s)$ and discount rate r. The so called artificial problem here could be an actual one in some basins with access to imported surface water, but our discussion focuses on the more common case of an isolated basin and its internal allocation problem with respect to time. The net output relation is therefore defined in this context, which implies that pumping costs have been deducted.

The economic theory is very similar to efficient combinations of factors in production economics. Curve BC is the counterpart of an 'expansion path' for efficient proportions among factors in producing various levels of *physical* output. The marginal rate of substitution of s for x in producing a given net output is given by the slope of the iso-net-output curve corresponding to that net output, just as the marginal rate of substitution of one factor for another in production economics is given by the slope of an isoquant.

The iso-net-output curves are convex to the origin if there exists a diminishing marginal rate of substitution of s for x throughout the entire range of s. A sufficient condition for convexity is diminishing marginal net output with respect to each x and s, and $\partial^2 G/\partial x \partial s > 0$. Quite obviously, the iso-net-output curves have negative slopes if marginal net output is positive with respect to each x and s.

The relative value of s to x, in the sense of opportunity costs, was established under the assumption that net output would be at the same level perpetually. (This relative value is the discount rate r.) When groundwater stocks reach their equilibrium under an optimal policy under certainty, they will remain at that equilibrium perpetually, making the constant net output assumption valid for equilibrium stocks. Clearly, rate of use x will be equal to rate of recharge when equilibrium storage is reached. Therefore, equilibrium storage is given by the point on curve BC where rate of use x equals rate of recharge. Suppose the unit of measure in Figure 1 is millions of acre-feet; a constant recharge of 1.5 million acre-feet would imply equilibrium storage at about 20 million acre-feet. However, recharge is sometimes dependent on stocks over some range; and if equilibrium were within that range, it would be at the intersection of the graph of recharge and curve BC in Figure 1. Usually recharge is constant except near maximum storage capacity, so that the equilibrium can be ascertained by only knowledge of the constant rate of recharge at relatively lower levels of storage.

Figure 1 provides a method to find equilibrium storage, equilibrium being determined by (1) the net output function $G(x,s)$ used to construct the iso-net-output curves; (2) the interest rate; and (3) recharge rate to groundwater stocks. However, we have said nothing about the optimal path of use rates to follow in getting to the equilibrium, although we would recognize it if we were there and optimize by maintaining it. The curve BC can be used as an *approximately optimal* decision rule for any quantity in stock. It is a conditional decision rule: for any quantity of groundwater in stock, we can read from the graph the quantity to withdraw for current production.

The decision rule is only approximately optimal, even under our assumptions of certainty and a constant net output relation over time, except at equilibrium storage, because both stocks s and rate of use x will be changing from year to year unless stocks are at equilibrium. The price line with slope $-r$ was justified only under the assumption that net output remained constant for all future periods. To understand the nature of the approximation, efficient points given by line BC are examined further. The negative of the slope of an iso-net-output curve is the ratio of marginal net output with respect to stocks s to marginal net output with respect to rate of use x. Denoting these two marginal relations by MNO_s and MNO_x, respectively, the curve BC tracing out tangency of the price line and iso-net-output is given by the equation

$$MNO_s/MNO_x = r \tag{1}$$

or

$$MNO_x = MNO_s/r \tag{2}$$

Mathematically relation 2 is

$$\partial G/\partial x = (\partial G/\partial s)/r$$

It is noted that in general MNO_x and MNO_s are each functions of both variables x and s.

Relation 2 is quite intuitive: marginal net output with respect to rate of use is equated with capitalized marginal net output with respect to stocks. The relationship is optimal at equilibrium storage, but we must examine the implications for other levels of storage. The influence of discounting on the approximation is made more apparent by writing the right-hand side of relation 2 as

$$MNO_s\ (1/(1 + r) + 1/(1 + r)^2 + \cdots)$$

which shows that MNO_s in distant years has relatively little influence on the size of MNO_s/r. To see the rate at which storage is likely to change through time, observe that storage in year $t + 1$ is equal to storage in year t, plus recharge, minus rate of use in year t. Thus, change in storage from year to year is the differential in rate of use and recharge. If this differential is small in relation to stocks s, stocks and consequently rate of use will change slowly through time. Therefore, MNO_s will be approximately constant for the immediate future where $1/(1 + r)^t$ is relatively large, and our approximate decision rule should give good results.

ANALYSIS OF THE POLICY AND EQUILIBRIUM

The objective in this section is to analyze various factors influencing optimal groundwater allocation in time. As mentioned earlier, equilibrium stocks are reached under a given policy when recharge rate is equal to rate of use specified by the policy. When curve BC in Figure 1 is used to determine a groundwater policy, equilibrium storage is implied for the level of stocks s at which rate of use x is equal to rate of recharge. Thus curve BC can be interpreted as the equilibrium storage relation for various rates of recharge measured on the vertical axis. The positive slope of BC lets us conclude that equilibrium storage increases with the recharge rate. Convexity of the iso-net-output curves to the origin assures a positive slope for BC.

The influence of the discount rate on optimal rate of use and equilibrium storage can be inferred from Figure 1. An increase in the interest rate makes line AA′ steeper (smaller algebraically), which shifts curve BC upward and to the left. Thus an increase in the interest rate increases rate of use at a given storage level and vice versa. It also follows that a greater interest rate decreases equilibrium storage for a given rate of recharge.

Slopes of the iso-net-output curves (in absolute value) are given by the left side of equation 1, namely, MNO_s/MNO_x. Thus a decrease in MNO_x, due to such things as decreased product prices or increased factor prices, increases the slope (absolute value) of the iso-net-output curve at any particular point. As a consequence, curve BC is shifted to the right, which implies lower rates of use at given storage levels and a higher equilibrium stock of groundwater for given recharge. Of course, the converse is true for an increase in MNO_x, *ceteris paribus*.

An improvement in pumping technology and the associated decrease in pumping costs increases MNO_x and decreases MNO_s. Both of these changes reduce the ratio MNO_s/MNO_x and shift BC to the left, which implies higher rates of use in relation to storage and a lower equilibrium for storage.

The effects of the above two structural changes on rates of use are clarified by Figure 2, where MNO_x and MNO_s/r are graphed as a function of x, with s taken at some constant level. The relations are drawn linearly for convenience. The slopes imply diminishing marginal productivity of water within a given period (MNO_x has negative slope) and complementarity between the two resources x and s (MNO_s has positive slope with respect to x). Complementarity between x and s is quite obvious since positive MNO_s stems primarily from the inverse relation between pumping costs and s, and x is the number of units of water pumped.

Marginal net output with respect to rate of use MNO_x is initially line ab, and capitalized marginal net output with respect to storage MNO_s/r is initially line cd. Optimal rate of use by our approximate decision rule (relation (2)) is given by intersection of these two lines at $x = A$. A shift of MNO_x from line ab to a″b″ as a result of increased factor prices or decreased product prices yields a new solution at $x = \mathrm{B}$, which is less than A. Improved pumping technology shifts MNO_x up to line a′b′ and MNO_s/r down to line c′d,′ yielding the new solution $x = C$, which exceeds A.

Effects of the preceding changes on equilibrium groundwater storage can be analyzed by Figure 3. The marginal relations in Figure 3

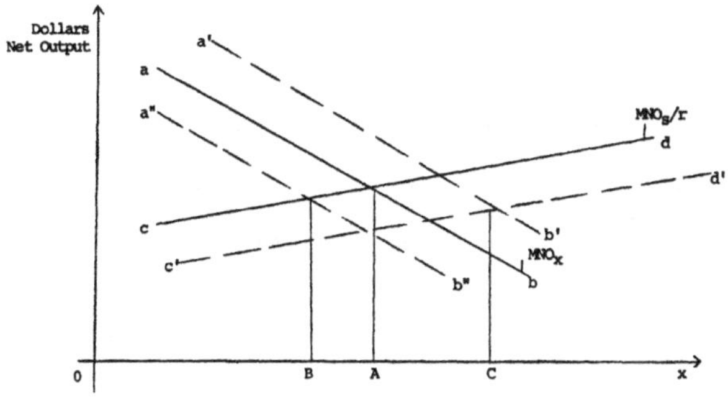

Fig. 2. Marginal net output relations with groundwater storage fixed.

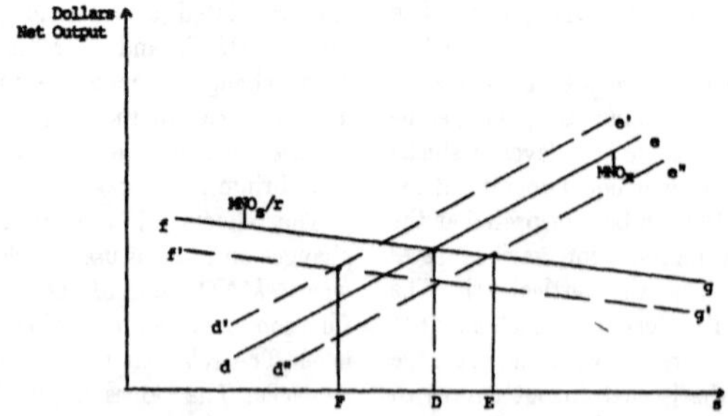

Fig. 3. Marginal net output with rate of use at rate of recharge.

implicitly assume that rate of use is equal to rate of recharge, and these marginal relations are functions of only storage. Again, linear relations are used for convenience, but some discussion of the slopes is probably in order. Positive slope on MNO_x is due to decreasing pumping costs per unit of water as groundwater storage increases (pumping depths decrease). Negative or zero slope is postulated for MNO_s under the assumption that pumping costs increase at an increasing rate with depth or at a constant rate. There is some empirical support for an approximately constant rate [*Calif. Dept. Water Resources,* 1958], and the physical relations would tend to support increasing costs. If specific yield (the proportion of soil volume that holds water that can be removed by pumping) of the underground strata in which water is held increases systematically with depth, the MNO_s relation could be an increasing function of s. Nevertheless, as long as the slope of MNO_s/r is less than that of MNO_x, equilibrium storage is stable. That is, the equilibrium is stable provided that MNO_s/r cuts MNO_x from above as we move from left to right in Figure 3.

Equilibrium storage is given by the intersection of MNO_x and MNO_s/r in Figure 3. This equilibrium is the solution of equation 2 in the variable s, with x set equal to rate of recharge. A shift of MNO_x downward from de to d″e″ results in a new equilibrium storage at $s = E$, which exceeds the old equilibrium D. An advance in pumping technology shifts MNO_x up to d′e′ from de and shifts MNO_s/r down from fg to f′g′, giving a new equilibrium at $s = F$, which is a decrease from the old equilibrium at $s = D$.

A change in the discount rate or rate of recharge can be analyzed using Figures 2 and 3, but the results obtained using Figure 1 were so obvious that we shall not belabor them further.

Although the decision rule has been analyzed with the rate of use as a function of groundwater storage thus far, we could transform the rule into one that specifies rate of use as a function of time for any initial stock of groundwater. Suppose that initial stocks are s_0 and rate of recharge is w. Our decision rule can be applied to obtain rate of use in the first period, which is denoted x_0. Storage at the beginning of the next period is $s_0 + w - x_0$, which we denote by s_1. Applying the decision rule again to s_1, the rate of use for the second period is obtained, denoted x_1. The general recursive relation for storage at year t is

$$s_t = s_{t-1} + w - x_{t-1} \tag{3}$$

and repeated application of our decision rule to s_t yields the sequence of use rates $x_0, x_1, x_2, \cdots$. This sequence is our decision rule, where rate of use is expressed with respect to time instead of storage.

RELAXATION OF ASSUMPTIONS

The decision rule expressed in regard to time is of only theoretical interest, because recharge is a random variable in reality. Thus, s_t in relation 3 is a random variable, since recharge rate w is random. Future storage cannot be predicted with certainty, and greater opportunity for optimization exists if withdrawals are not specified in the future. Instead, a conditional decision rule or strategy is applied. Groundwater stocks at the beginning of each period are used as a decision criterion, and rate of use is not specified until stocks are known at the beginning of the period in which the withdrawal takes place. In other words, the approximate decision rule, given by relation 2 or curve BC in Figure 1, is applied sequentially to whatever stock s exists at the beginning of the period.

Recognizing the uncertain nature of recharge makes equilibrium storage a stochastic equilibrium which is always approached but rarely experienced. We let $x(s)$ be the decision rule (curve BC in Figure 1) and let s^* represent equilibrium storage in the sense that $x(s^*) = \omega$, where ω is the mean of w. It is assumed that $x(s)$ is an increasing function of s (curve BC has positive slope), which implies that for $s > s^*$, $x > \omega$ and for $s < s^*$, $x < \omega$. Since rate of use exceeds mean recharge when storage is above equilibrium and is less when it is below, the tendency is to move toward equilibrium from either above or below.

Since groundwater stocks will have a high contingency value as they near depletion when recharge is a random variable, we can be confident that an equilibrium stock exists, which was not the case under certainty, where only pumping costs were the ultimate barrier to complete exhaustion of stocks. Under certainty, basins with very high returns to water relative to pumping costs would eventually remove the entire stock of groundwater. But with a stochastic supply of recharge, high returns relative to pumping costs would merely imply a relatively low equilibrium stock but never zero.

The insurance value of water stocks must be determined simultaneously with the optimal policy for temporal allocation by methods such as discussed in *Burt* [1964*b*; 1966]. Nevertheless, this contingency value can be approximated and incorporated into the net output function $G(x, s)$, thus permitting economic analysis in the framework in which our discussion has been set. The approximation is obtained by amortization of the present value of expected net output under an assumed policy for different initial storage conditions. The variation of amortized expected present value over initial stocks of water is a measure of the contingency value of stocks. The most obvious choice of an assumed policy is a constant rate of use equal to mean recharge. The method for incorporating an estimate of the contingency value of water from this assumed policy is given in the Appendix. For low levels of storage, one would expect this policy to exaggerate the value of stocks relative to their value under an optimal policy, because the optimal policy would specify a rate of use less than recharge, permitting stocks to build up in a probability sense.

The assumption that the net output function $G(x, s)$ is unchanging through time can be relaxed. Let $G_t(x, s)$ be the net output relation at time t, where t is the number of years into the future ($t = 0$ is the present). The decision rule is modified, and its new form is a generalization of equation 2

$$MNO_x^0 = MNO_s^1/(1 + r) + MNO_s^2/(1 + r)^2 + \cdots \qquad (4)$$

where MNO_x^t and MNO_s^t denote marginal net output in year t with respect to x and s, respectively. Clearly, relation 2 is a special case of (4) when $G_t(x, s)$ is invariant through time. When the beginning of the second year is reached (assuming that the net output projections are not revised), the decision rule is

$$MNO_x^1 = MNO_s^2/(1 + r) + MNO_s^3/(1 + r)^2 + \cdots$$

applied with s set equal to whatever quantity prevails in storage.

Variable interest rates, say $r_1, r_2, \cdots$, could be applied in relation 4 if economic projections for the future warranted a change from year to year. Of course, estimates of $G_t(x, s)$ and r_t for the future suffer all the problems associated with economic projections. Quite often uncertainty of future conditions encourages use of a single relation $G(x, s)$ and discount rate r. It is fairly obvious from the form of the decision rule, equation 2 for example, that the magnitude of the discount rate has a great deal of leverage on rate of use, and the utmost care should be used in its selection.

As groundwater storage approaches the surface, mean recharge may not be constant with regard to storage but a decreasing function of it. In fact, for some basins that are not completely isolated, mean recharge might be a decreasing function of storage throughout. We let $\omega(s)$ denote this mean recharge relationship and assume that its slope is nonpositive. Our decision rule can be modified to handle this additional complexity.

At the margin when substituting water between current production and storage, the incremental loss of water caused by an increment to storage must be evaluated. This incremental loss of water is the negative of the slope $\omega(s)$, which we denote by $-\omega'(s)$. Its periodic value per unit at the margin is MNO_s and its total value is $-\omega'(s)MNO_s$, but since the loss will occur perpetually, its present value is $-\omega'(s) MNO_s/r$. The above argument is in the context of our approximation device, where $G(x, s)$ is taken as constant perpetually. The decision rule given by (2) is generalized by subtracting the marginal cost with respect to storage, caused by lost recharge, from the right-hand side. The result is

$$MNO_x = MNO_s/r - (-\omega'(s)MNO_s/r)$$

and after simplification the decision rule is

$$MNO_x = MNO_s/[r - \omega'(s)] \qquad (5)$$

Relation 5 reduces to (2) when $\omega'(s)$ is zero, but near the surface $\omega'(s)$ is negative and has the same effect as an increased discount rate. Thus, near the surface there is an additional economic force tending to increase rate of use. If groundwater is so near the surface that drainage is severely impaired, MNO_s is negative and the decision rule would imply using water at a level where its marginal net output is negative. This situation can be construed to mean that drainage is suggested by the decision rule.

If groundwater storage is large relative to the differential between rate of use under an optimal policy and rate of recharge, the net output relationship need not reflect the insurance value of stocks for the approximate policy given by (5) to give good results, even if pumping costs alone would not guarantee an equilibrium. When storage is large relative to the difference between rate of use and recharge, physical exhaustion of groundwater reserves is so remote in the future that discounting makes the consequences of little economic significance, and capitalized marginal pumping cost with respect to storage is a good estimate of the marginal value of water as a stock resource. Therefore, an approximately optimal policy for many basins in the earlier periods of their development can be estimated with relative ease, although more elaborate procedures would be required as groundwater stocks are depleted.

The right-hand side of equation 5 [or equation 2 when $\omega'(s) = 0$] is an estimate of the marginal value of groundwater as a stock resource, and it can be used as a price with which to confront producers in the basin to implement a groundwater allocation policy. This aspect of groundwater management is developed in *Burt* [1966].

A NUMERICAL EXAMPLE

A numerical example may help to clarify the application of the approximately optimal decision rule. The following example is only illustrative but not completely divorced from reality. Pumping costs are those estimated for an area in the San Joaquin Valley in California [*Burt*, 1964*b*]. A more complete pumping cost function would partition costs into variable and amortized fixed costs, each as a function of groundwater storage. However, there are some conceptual problems even with this method of handling costs. These problems stem from (1) the fact that pumping lifts will vary from year to year; (2) there is a choice of the distribution and size of wells; and (3) depths to which wells are initially constructed are also a decision and not predetermined. A considerably more complicated model than that being used would be needed to make all of these decisions optimally, but good results can be anticipated without this complexity if pumping depths change slowly through time. Some evidence is given shortly that suggests that pumping lifts will change quite slowly from year to year.

The net output relation is artificial, but it was constructed so that a realistic equilibrium depth to groundwater exists and marginal values of water are reasonable for agricultural production in many areas. The net output function is

$$G(x, s) = -4x^2 + 35x - (25 - 0.2s)x + K$$

$$= -4x^2 + 10x + 0.2sx + K \qquad (6)$$

where K is net output for the basin with no groundwater withdrawals, $(25 - 0.2s)$ is the cost per acre-foot of water pumped when storage is at s, and net output is in units of million dollars and water in million acre-feet. If the smallest cost of water at any depth is around

2 dollars, maximum storage is 115 million acre-feet, found by setting the cost function equal to 2 and solving for s.

Since relation 6 is quadratic in x with s fixed, marginal net output with respect to rate of use is linear, that is

$$MNO_x = -8x + 10 + 0.2s$$

Groundwater storage enters the net output relation linearly with rate of use held constant; therefore, marginal net output with respect to stocks is constant over the variable s and is given by

$$MNO_s = 0.2x$$

Application of the decision rule as given in relation 2 yields

$$-8x + 10 + 0.2s = 0.2x/r \qquad (7)$$

The left-hand side of (7) is line ab in Figure 2 (storage s determines its intercept), and the right side of 7 is line cd, which does not shift with s in this case. In reference to Figure 3, mean recharge $\omega(s)$ is substituted for x in (7), and lines de and fg are the left- and right-hand sides of the equality, respectively. Note that line fg has zero slope for this particular net output relation if $\omega(s)$ is a constant rate irrespective of storage.

An equilibrium storage equation can be constructed from (7) by solving for s in terms of x and setting $x = \omega(s)$. The equilibrium storage equation so obtained is

$$s = (40 + 1/r)\omega(s) - 50 \qquad (8)$$

Suppose mean recharge is 2 million acre-feet regardless of storage and that the discount rate is 5%. Equilibrium storage obtained by solving (8) is $s^* = 70$ million acre-feet.

Specific yield and acreage of the basin imply a relationship between storage and depth to groundwater. In this example, the relationship is

$$L = 752 - 6.5s \qquad (9)$$

where L is pumping lift in feet. Relation 9 is implied for the basin used as a source of pumping costs, except that estimates of specific yield are extrapolated to greater depths than in the original study [*Burt*, 1964*b*].) Thus an equilibrium storage of $s^* = 70$ implies an equilibrium depth to groundwater of $L^* = 297$ feet.

As mean recharge declines, the equilibrium storage level declines. (We are simplifying the recharge relationship to a constant $\omega(s) = \omega$.) For example, at $\omega = 1$, equilibrium storage is 10 million acre-feet, and depth to water is 687 feet. If we were to assume unlimited pumping depths and no recharge to groundwater, equilibrium storage would be -50 million acre-feet by relation 8. Interpreting negative storage as merely a relatively low quantity compared with zero, its substitution into (9) yields an equilibrium depth to water of 1077 feet. Substitution of -50 for s in the left-hand side of relation 7 shows negative marginal net output for positive x and zero marginal net output at $x = 0$. An immediate conclusion is that water is mined until its marginal net output is zero only if mean recharge is also zero.

The decision rule given by curve BC in Figure 1 is the solution of equation 7 for x as an explicit function of s. At a 5% discount rate, the solution is

$$x = 5/6 + s/60 \qquad (10)$$

which is obviously linear. The decision rule is applied by waiting to observe groundwater storage at the beginning of the decision period and applying relation 10 to obtain x for the observed magnitude of s. To illustrate its application, full capacity at $s = 115$ implies $x = 2.75$, compared with $x = 2$ at $s = 70$ or $x = 1$ at $s = 10$ (all figures in million acre-feet).

Although the approximately optimal decision rule, such as (10), would be applied in a stochastic situation in reality, some indication of the rate at which groundwater storage approaches equilibrium is given by treating recharge as nonstochastic and forming a difference equation for storage. Letting the subscript t on x and s denote time measured from the present, storage in future years is given by equation 3, which is a first-order, linear difference equation when the linear decision rule given by (10) is substituted for x_{t-1}. The difference equation is

$$s_t - 59/60s_{t-1} = w - 5/6$$

with solution [*Allen*, 1957, p. 186]

$$s_t = 60(w - 5/6) + A(59/60)^t \qquad (11)$$

where A is an unknown parameter determined by specifying initial storage.

Taking $w = 2$ and $s_0 = 115$, the difference equation for storage is

$$s_t = 70 + 45(59/60)^t$$

Since the constant 59/60 taken to the power t is less than unity, the limit of s_t as t becomes infinite is 70, the same equilibrium found more directly by equation 8. Future storage starting from an initial level of 115 is given in Table 1 at 10-year intervals. It is clear from Table 1 that changes through time in rate of use under the decision rule are slow and not likely to cause adjustment problems. Admittedly, this conclusion was drawn from a mere illustration, but the general structure of equation 11 suggests that groundwater storage changes relatively slowly, which tends to cause small changes in rate of use from year to year.

ADDITIONAL REFINEMENTS

The decision rule given by (5) was derived by the author in an earlier article [*Burt*, 1964*a*] as a first-degree approximation to a functional equation arising from formulation of the groundwater allocation problem in a dynamic programming model. Thus the intuitive analysis above is supported by an approximation using formal mathematics. The same methods can be applied inductively to obtain equation 4, or the slightly more general relation

$$\partial G_0/\partial x = \sum_{t=1}^{\infty} (\partial G_t/\partial s)/ (1 + \omega'(s))^{t-1}(1 + r)^t \qquad (12)$$

Relation 12 can be thought of as a generalization of (5) to a net output function that is variable through time.

A second-degree approximation that yields a more nearly optimal decision rule is [see *Burt*, 1964*a*]

$$\frac{\partial G}{\partial x} = \frac{1}{r}\left[\frac{\partial G}{\partial s} + (\omega - x) \cdot\left(\frac{-a_1 - \sqrt{a_1^2 - 4a_0}}{2}\right)\right], \qquad (13)$$

where

$$a_1 = r\frac{\partial^2 G}{\partial x^2} - 2\frac{\partial^2 G}{\partial s\,\partial x} - \frac{\partial^2 G}{\partial s^2}$$

$$a_0 = (1 + r)\left[\left(\frac{\partial^2 G}{\partial s\,\partial x}\right)^2 - \frac{\partial^2 G}{\partial s^2}\frac{\partial^2 G}{\partial x^2}\right]$$

Relation 13 assumes that mean recharge is constant for all levels of storage, i.e., that $\omega(s)$ equals a constant ω, and the net output function is unchanging through time.

A slight variation in the right-hand side of (13) is an estimate of the marginal value of groundwater as a stock resource. The formula is [see *Burt*, 1964*a*]

$$\frac{1 + r}{r}\left[\frac{\partial G}{\partial S} + \frac{\omega - x}{1 + r} \cdot\left(\frac{-a_1 - \sqrt{a_1^2 - 4a_0}}{2}\right)\right] \qquad (14)$$

which is a function of x and s, but x is determined by (13). Therefore, relations 13 and 14 can be used to obtain an estimate of the marginal value of groundwater at any level of storage s. Except for $G(x, s)$ quadratic, (13) is a nonlinear equation in x for given s and must be solved by iterative methods. However, the first-degree approximation given by (2) is quite simple, and its solution first would give an excellent starting value for the iterative method used to solve (13).

Taking cognizance of the formulas for a_1 and a_0 in (13), it is very likely that the factor

TABLE 1. Future Storage for an Example Groundwater Basin, million acre-feet

Time t	0	10	20	30	40	50	60	As $t \to \infty$
Storage s	115	108	102	97	93	89	86	70
Rate of Use x	2.75	2.63	2.54	2.45	2.38	2.32	2.27	2

$$1/2[-a_1 - \sqrt{a_1^2 - 4a_0}] \qquad (15)$$

in (13) is positive. Actually, (15) is an estimate of the slope of the marginal value function for groundwater stocks. If either (15) or $\omega - x$ is zero, (13) reduces to the first-degree approximation of the optimal decision rule. Thus a positive value of (15) lets us conclude that for $x > \omega$ the decision rule given by (2) is overly conservative and not enough water is withdrawn for current production. We note that $x > \omega$ implies $s > s^*$, i.e., storage is above the equilibrium. When $x < \omega$ (or equivalently $s < s^*$) the converse is true of the bias in the rule given by (2), and too much water is used in relation to the optimum amount.

A comparison of decision rules for our example problem under relation 2 versus (13) may be of interest. The decision rule implied by (2) was given earlier, but it is repeated here in decimal numbers for comparison:

$$x = 0.8333 + 0.0167s \qquad (16)$$

The decision rule given by (13) is

$$x = 0.9200 - 0.1040\omega + 0.0184s \qquad (17)$$

Both relations are linear in s, but the slope is greater in (17) and the intercept is smaller for $\omega > 0.8337$. Let us take $s = 100$ and $\omega = 2$ for a specific comparison. The result is $x = 2.50$ and $x = 2.55$ for relations 16 and 17, respectively. Since our unit is millions of acre-feet, the difference is 50,000 acre-feet, which is the extra amount used under the more nearly optimal decision rule. This is less than a 2% error from using the simpler decision rule. The error becomes progressively less as equilibrium storage is approached, and at equilibrium 16 and 17 yield identical results.

APPENDIX

A procedure is outlined here for estimation of the value of groundwater stocks as a contingency against uncertain future supplies. The discussion assumes a policy that specifies mean recharge as the rate of use regardless of stocks, except at stocks lower than mean recharge, where the entire stock is used. The analysis would be essentially the same under any assumed policy, but the one used here is most likely to be used for empirical estimation owing to its simplicity.

We approximate the continuous storage variable by discrete intervals identified by the lower limits of the intervals: $s_1, s_2, \ldots s_n$ with $s_j < s_{j+1}, j = 1, 2, \cdots N$, and $s_1 = 0$. Given the ith stock in time period t, the probability of the jth stock in period $t + 1$ is

$$Pr[s_j < s_i + w - \omega \leq s_{j+1}]$$

where w is recharge (a random variable) and ω is the mean of w. This conditional probability of going to the jth storage level, given the ith level, is denoted P_{ij}; and the probability distribution for storage within our discrete variable framework is described by the matrix P, with elements P_{ij}, $i, j = 1, 2, \ldots N$. Thus the probability distribution for storage is a finite Markov chain.

The vector of net outputs that specifies expected periodic net output in the immediately ensuing period for each possible storage state has components $G(\omega, s_i)$, where G is the net output function defined in the text. This vector is denoted g. Expected present value of net output after t years of operation is given by the vector [*Burt*, 1964*b*, p. 41]

$$v(t) = [I + P/(1 + r) + P^2/(1 + r)^2 + \cdots + P^{t-1}/(1 + r)^{t-1}]g$$

where I is the identity matrix of dimension N, and

$$v = \lim_{t \to \infty} v(t) = [I - P/(1 + r)]^{-1} g$$

The ith component of v is expected present value of net output when initial storage at $t = 0$ was s_i, and amortized expected present value is rv. The costs of uncertainty of groundwater stocks can be measured by the difference $g - rv$.

If recharge were not a random variable, $g - rv$ would equal zero, since v in this case would be a vector with ith component $G(\omega, s_i)/r$. However, a random recharge rate implies a possibility of reaching zero storage and an associated penalty on net output. The lower the initial stocks are, the more likely is complete exhaustion of stocks. Therefore, the ith component of v decreases as i decreases, since $s_1 < s_2 < \cdots s_n$.

The costs due to stochastic recharge can be estimated as a continuous function of storage by fitting a curve to the points $(g_i - rv_i, s_i)$,

$i = 1, 2, \cdots N$. Let this fitted relation be $c(s)$; then the net output function incorporating the contingency value of groundwater stocks is $G(x, s) - c(s)$. We would expect $c(s)$ to have negative slope throughout its range and probably approach zero for very large stocks. If $c(s)$ has slope near zero for large stocks, we are justified in skipping its estimation to determine an approximately optimal policy for groundwater at relatively high levels of storage.

The case where mean recharge is a function of storage, defined by the functional relation $\omega(s)$, can be analyzed by the above method also. It merely complicates the notation.

REFERENCES

Allen, R. G. D., *Mathematical Economics*, Macmillan and Co. Ltd., London, 1957.

Burt, Oscar R., Optimal resource use over time with an application to groundwater, *Management Sci., 11*, 80–93, 1964*a*.

Burt, Oscar R., The economics of conjunctive use of ground and surface water, *Hilgardia, 36*(2), 31–111, California Agricultural Experiment Station, December 1964*b*.

Burt, Oscar R., Economic control of groundwater reserves, *J. Farm Econ., 48*, 632–647, 1966.

California Department of Water Resources, unpublished analysis of pumping costs in Kern County, 1958.

(Manuscript received August 17, 1966.)

CHAPTER 18

VOL. 3, NO. 1 WATER RESOURCES RESEARCH FIRST QUARTER 1967

A Socially Optimum Pricing Policy for a Public Water Agency

GARDNER BROWN, JR.

University of Washington, Seattle

C. B. McGUIRE

University of California, Berkeley

Abstract. A simple model is developed for determining the socially optimum price to charge locationally differentiated irrigation districts for both surface and groundwater supplies. Steady-state conditions are assumed for groundwater conditions and water demand functions. A divergence between social and private optimums arises from the existence of unadjudicated rights to groundwater supplies. The social optimum can be achieved by an appropriately conceived taxing policy. Water prices, tax rates, and optimum lift levels are estimated for seven irrigation districts, members of a master water agency. (Key words: Economics; water management; water resources)

INTRODUCTION

Throughout the arid west, the real cost of developing new water supplies has tended to increase through time, because the rate of technological change has not kept pace with the increasing inaccessibility of untapped water resources. Under these circumstances we may reasonably expect to observe increased efforts to manage existing sources of water more efficiently.

A difficulty often encountered in the search for better resource decision rules is the identification and estimation of externalities. The economic model developed in this paper diagnoses a classic externality in an environment where both surface and groundwater are available to some water districts over time, whereas only surface water is available to others. The individual water districts are members of a master water agency whose responsibility it is to find answers to the following set of questions: What annual quantity of surface water should the master agency purchase from a supplier of water? What annual quantities of groundwater should be pumped in each member district? What prices, if any, should be charged by the master water agency for district purchases of surface water? What control should be exerted by the master agency over groundwater pumping? How should the annual quantity of surface water be allocated among the member districts? To the extent that they can be influenced, what should be the levels of the various groundwater tables? These conditions and questions fairly describe the Kern County Water Agency (KCWA) in the early 1960's. This agency is one of the principal contractors for water in the first stage of the California water plan. Although the KCWA will sell water for both urban and agricultural use, the application of the model is limited to the derivation of pricing policies for the irrigation districts.

In this model it is assumed that a stable environment (the year 1990) has been reached. The build-up of surface water deliveries has reached its peak, and this delivery rate continues unchanged in each succeeding year. Farm and land development, it is assumed, have reached a similar steady state. Agricultural technology and farm prices remain constant. Groundwater tables have by this time either risen or declined to the level at which they will be maintained hereafter, or have declined forever beyond economic reach. Surface water distribution systems are assumed to be completed. Each succeeding year is like the last one in all respects. Since nothing in the environment changes, the decisions made each year concerning surface water use, groundwater use, crop selection, and other important factors remain the same. However, even in a steady-state situation a farmer might quite reasonably decide to rotate crops annually. The rotation plan, therefore, is a regular one.

Conceptualizing water planning problems in this context is not so far-fetched when it is realized that water projects are long-term experiments. In particular, the expiration date for the KCWA contract is 2035, so that the costs and benefits during the 1990–2035 period are important. Present decisions and plans for the intervening years will be influenced by future expectations, and some assumptions about future farm prices and technology must necessarily be made in the current planning period.

An indicator of welfare. If a correct pricing policy is to be found, there must be a measure of correctness, a success indicator defined explicitly enough to be stated in a formula that will yield numerical values. Various measures of welfare might be adopted. (a) Maximize gross revenue to KCWA. If this welfare indicator is chosen, that water policy that brings in the most revenue to the master agency will be selected. Most revenue might mean gross average annual revenue or gross revenue over the future discounted at some particular interest rate. This indicator places a heavy weight on the importance of the master agency's ability to meet its repayment obligations to the water supplier, without explicitly considering the cost of water. It appears to leave out the effect of the water policy on the farmer. Does he pay 'too much' for his water? Does he receive 'too small' an allocation? (b) Maximize profits to the master agency. This indicator is a simple modification of (a) and suffers from similar shortcomings. Total costs, both fixed and variable, are subtracted from total revenue. The first subtraction will have no effect on the ranking of different water policies. If a given number is subtracted from each element in a set of numbers, the original ranking is preserved. The second subtraction will affect the ranking, since those water policies that sometimes take less than the contracted allocation will result in smaller variable transportation charges. (c) Regarding the master agency and all the farmers within its political jurisdiction as a division and the employees, respectively, of a large hypothetical business firm, maximize total profits to the firm. There remains the question of good and bad ways to distribute the profit among the 'employees' (the farmers), but the issue of profit distribution can be separated from the total profit maximization and water pricing policy selection problem. Whatever view is held about fair distribution of profit, one can readily agree that total profit should be large. So long as profit distribution can be accomplished without affecting the implementation of the chosen water policy, then it is legitimate to break the whole problem into these two parts. The maximization of total profit to this hypothetical firm is the welfare indicator adopted in this model.

Allocative efficiency in the steady state. Three parts comprise the total profit to the hypothetical master water agency. First is the total gross benefits or savings accruing to farmers on being supplied with specific quantities of water. The second part (a negative one) is the total of purchase costs for surface water from the supplier plus the total of local distribution costs for this same water. The third part consists of total pumping and well costs for groundwater.

Clearly, one should not maximize total profit for a single year, because it is often possible to increase one year's profit at the expense of another, nor can annual profit be added over the years. Commonly, the present value of the stream of profit over future years is calculated by discounting at a chosen rate of interest each future year's profit to the present. Alternatively, we could discount to the beginning of the steady-state regime to yield a 1990 value. This study follows the last procedure, using a constant rate of interest of 6%. In the steady state, when each year's profit is the same, say π, then the present value of the stream of future profits is simply $\pi/0.06$.

THE MODEL, THE SOLUTION, AND SOME IMPLICATIONS FOR POLICY

Functions. Let us define

$h_i(x)$ = value of the marginal product of water in District i when x acre-feet of water are being applied. h is the long-run demand curve, with price expressed as a function of quantity demanded;

$F(x)$ = total annual cost to the agency of purchasing x acre-feet from the State;

$f_i(x)$ = total annual cost to District i of distributing x acre-feet of surface water;

$g_i(x, m)$ = total annual cost of pumping a total of x acre-feet at pumping lift in District i.

Parameters. Assume that the above functions have the following linear form:

$$h_i(x) = u_i - v_i x$$
$$F(x) = E + Dx$$
$$f_i(x) = e_i + d_i x$$
$$g_i(x, m) = a_i + b_i m + c_i mx$$

where u_i and v_i are the demand parameters price intercept and slope, respectively. E is the fixed annual bill from the State to the agency, and D represents those unit charges by the State that *do* depend on the amount of water purchased. e_i and d_i are the fixed and variable costs for distribution within districts. $(a_i + b_i m)$ is the fixed cost associated with the whole array of wells in District i when (the common) pumping lift is m. $c_i m$ represents the unit cost of pumping at lift m.

A_i and B_i are hydrological parameters in District i. A_i denotes the annual natural recharge of the aquifer underlying District i measured in feet of rise of the groundwater table; B_i denotes the decline of this groundwater table brought about by the pumping of 1 acre-foot of groundwater from this aquifer. 'Safe yield,' that quantity of groundwater that can be pumped without changing the level of the ground table, is therefore A_i/B_i.

Total surface water availability in year t will be denoted $\bar{Y}_t$; r will denote the interest rate, and we will write $R = 1/(1 + r)$.

Variables. Define

- Y_t = surface water (in acre-feet) purchased by the agency in year t;
- y_{it} = surface water (in acre-feet) consumed by District i in year t;
- z_{it} = groundwater (in acre-feet) consumed by District i in year t;
- m_{it} = the pumping lift (in acre-feet) in District i at the end of year t. The initial lifts m_{i0} are assumed to be given.
- T_i = tax charge per acre-foot of groundwater pumped in District i.
- p = internal price charged by the agency for delivering at a turnout one acre-foot to a district.

The welfare function and optimization. In year t when y_{it} and z_{it} are the amounts of water consumed in total by farmers in District i, $(i = 1, \cdots, N)$, the gross benefits to these farmers are

$$\int_0^{y_{it}+z_{it}} h_i(x)\, dx$$

Distribution costs in this district are $f_i(y_{it})$, and pumping and well-maintenance costs are $g_i(z_{it}, m_{i,t-1})$.

Summing over districts and adding in the cost to the agency of providing surface water, we have

$$W_t = \sum_{i=1}^{N} \left[\int_0^{y_{it}+z_{it}} h_i(x)\, dx - f_i(y_{it}) - g_i(z_{it}, m_{i,t-1}) \right] - F(Y_t) \qquad (1)$$

Consider now the period $t = 1, 2, 3, \cdots$ extending into the future. The present value (i.e., at the beginning of the period studied) of the stream of future years' welfare functions is then

$$W = \sum_{t=1}^{\infty} R^t W_t \qquad (2)$$

We wish to choose non-negative values for the variables Y_t, y_{it}, z_{it}, m_{it} $(i = 1, \cdots, N$ and $t = 1, \cdots)$ so as to maximize W subject only to

$$\sum_{i=1}^{N} y_{it} = Y_t \quad \text{for all} \quad t \qquad (3)$$

$$Y_t \leqq \bar{Y}_t \quad \text{for all} \quad t \qquad (4)$$

and

$$m_{it} = m_{i,t-1} - A_i + B_i z_{it} \quad \text{for all} \quad i, t \quad (5)$$

Assume that D, the *variable* cost to the agency of surface water, is so small compared with demand and with costs of alternative supplies that it is never found optimal to use less than the full amount of surface water made available by the State. It is always the case that $Y_t = \bar{Y}_t$. For constraints 3 and 4 we can substitute the single constraint

$$\sum_{i=1}^{N} y_{it} = \bar{Y}_t \quad \text{for all} \quad t \qquad (6)$$

By successive substitution of $m_{i,t-1}$ in the expression for m_{it}, we can also rewrite constraint 5 as

$$m_{it} = m_{i0} - tA_i + B_i \sum_{s=1}^{t} z_{is}$$

for all i, t (7)

Differentiating the 'Lagrangian' L of our problem with respect to y_{it}

$$\frac{\partial L}{\partial y_{it}} = R^t[h_i(y_{it} + z_{it}) - f_i'(y_{it})] - \lambda_t \quad (8)$$

where λ_t is the multiplier, or 'shadow price,' associated with constraint 6. For y_{it} to be greater than zero, this derivative must be zero.

Differentiating with respect to z_{it}

$$\frac{\partial L}{\partial z_{it}} = R^t\left[h_i(y_{it} + z_{it}) - \frac{\partial}{\partial z} g_i(z_{it}, m_{i,t-1})\right] - B_i \sum_{s=t}^{\infty} \theta_{is} \quad (9)$$

where θ_{is} is the Lagrange multiplier for constraint 7. If $z_{it} > 0$, then $\partial L/\partial z_{it} = 0$.

Finally, the derivative of L with respect to m_{it} is

$$\frac{\partial L}{\partial m_{it}} = -R^{t+1} \frac{\partial}{\partial m} g_i(z_{i,t+1}, m_{it}) + \theta_{it} \quad (10)$$

which must be zero if m_{it} is at any but its minimal level.

Derivatives 8, 9, and 10 then allow us to recognize an optimal solution. If positive y_{it}, z_{it}, m_{it}, λ_t, and θ_{it} ($i = 1, \cdots, N$ and $t = 1, 2, \cdots$) can be found for which constraints 6 and 7 hold, and for which all the partial derivatives 8, 9, 10 are equal to zero, then these values maximize the welfare function W. This roughly correct statement ignores the possibility of certain 'corner' solutions, where one or more of the variables are equal to zero. In such a case, the respective derivative need not vanish; it suffices that it be ≤ 0. The same revision holds if a variable is to be constrained from below by a value other than zero. For instance, suppose that m_{it} cannot have a value less than some number, say 100 feet. Either enter the constraint $m_{it} \geq 100$ explicitly into the problem or omit it, but check to see whether in the solution m_{it} is above or below 100. If it is above, the solution is correct; if it is below, m_{it} must be increased to 100 and it must be required that $\leq$ holds in constraint 10.

If the derivative 8 is to be zero

$$h_i(y_{it} + z_{it}) = f_i'(y_{it}) + R^{-t}\lambda_t$$

for all i, t (11)

The first term on the right is marginal distribution cost at current surface water use levels. The second term is a mathematical object used in testing for optimality. It is useful to interpret the multiplier λ_t as an 'internal' price (internal to the agency) that might be charged to districts by the agency for an acre-foot of surface water delivered in year t. A slight complication in this interpretation arises from the fact that λ_t is really the price charged *now* (i.e., at the beginning of the year 1 for water delivered in year t). λ_t is a *futures* price, whereas one ordinarily thinks in terms of *spot* prices. Replace the variable λ_t, the price of a year t surface water future, with p_t, the spot price in year t of surface water delivered in year t. Since we are assuming a world of certainty and a given discount factor R, it must be true that $R^t p_t = \lambda_t$. Substituting in 11

$$h_i(y_{it} + z_{it}) = f_i'(y_{it}) + p_t \quad (11')$$

The rule then for a district decision-maker to follow would be: Buy from the agency that amount of surface water that equates the value of marginal product with the sum of marginal distribution cost and price to the agency. The rule for the agency is: Sell surface water to whatever district will pay the price, and set the price at that level that just clears the market.

For derivative 9 to equal zero

$$h_i(y_{it} + z_{it}) = \frac{\partial}{\partial z} g_i(z_{it}, m_{i,t-1}) + B_i R^{-t} \sum_{s=t}^{\infty} \theta_{is} \quad (12)$$

The first term on the right is the direct marginal cost of pumping at current levels of production and lift. To understand the second term, let us look at derivative 10. Equality there allows substitution for θ_{is} in (12), yielding

$$h_i(y_{it} + z_{it}) = \frac{\partial}{\partial z} g_i(z_{it}, m_{i,t-1}) + B_i \sum_{s=t}^{\infty} R^{s+1-t} \frac{\partial}{\partial m} g_i(z_{i,s+1}, m_{is}) \quad (12')$$

The meaning of the second term is now clear: it is the sum of the discounted marginal effects of a change in z_{it} on future pumping costs via future pumping lifts. (In the case referred to earlier, when some m_{it} is constrained from below, $\leq$ can hold in (10) and hence $\geq$ in (12).)

For a district decision-maker the rule as regards groundwater would therefore be: Pump that amount of groundwater that equates value of marginal product with the sum of direct marginal pumping cost at current lift and discounted marginal effects of current pumping on future pumping costs.

Assuming that the demand curves and the cost functions have the simple linear form stated earlier, by substitution rules (11′) and (12′) become

$$u_i - v_i(y_{it} + z_{it}) = d_i + p_t \qquad (11'')$$

$$u_i - v_i(y_{it} + z_{it}) = c_i m_{i,t-1} + B_i\left[\sum_{s=t}^{\infty} R^{s+1-t}(b_i + c_i z_{i,s+1})\right] \qquad (12'')$$

The steady-state solution. The assumptions of constant demand and constant groundwater recharge mean that under an optimum water policy the system will, as time goes on, approach nearer and nearer to a steady-state operation. In this steady state, groundwater consumption, surface water consumption, and pumping lifts all remain the same from year to year. In this case, $y_{it} = y_i$, $z_{it} = z_i$, $m_{it} = m_i$, and $p_t = p$. Conditions 11″ and 12″ become

$$u_i - v_i(y_i + z_i) = d_i + p \qquad (13)$$

and

$$u_i - v_i(y_i + z_i) = c_i m_i + (1/r)B_i(b_i + c_i z_i) \qquad (14)$$

since

$$\sum_{t=1}^{\infty} R^t = \frac{R}{1-R} = \frac{1/(1+r)}{1 - 1/(1+r)} = \frac{1}{r}$$

Furthermore, if lift m_i is to remain constant, it must be the case that exactly the safe yield is pumped from the aquifer, that is, $z_i = A_i/B_i$.

Hence 14 can be rewritten

$$u_i - v_i(y_i + z_i) = c_i[m_i + (B_i b_i)/rc_i + A_i/r] \qquad (14')$$

If in the solution both $y_i > 0$ and $z > 0$, then equality must hold in both (13) and (14′). It follows that

$$p + d_i = c_i[m_i + (B_i b_i)/rc_i + A_i/r]$$

Solving for m_i, the only variable in this statement, we find

$$m_i = (p + d_i)/c_i - (B_i b_i)/rc_i - A_i/r \qquad (15)$$

This is the level of the optimal lift in the steady state. The first term represents that value of lift at which *current* marginal pumping costs just equal marginal costs to the district of surface water. This would appear to be the optimum lift level to the district decision-maker, who was not aware of the effect on future pumping costs of today's pumping.

Taxes to equate social cost and private cost. The marginal costs discussed in the two preceding sections are *social* costs incurred by the master water service region. However, part of the marginal social cost of pumping does not enter into the individual farmer's calculation of marginal private cost. The part left out consists of two subparts, corresponding to the two rightmost terms in (14′).

The first is the present discounted value of all incremental fixed costs that follow from the increase in lift caused by pumping an additional acre-foot today. The second part is the present discounted value of all increases in direct pumping costs, the variable costs, that follow from the increase in lift caused by pumping an additional acre-foot today.

The individual farmer's choice of pumping intensity is determined only by changes in cost as a result of *his* pumping an additional acre-foot today at today's lift $c_i m_i$. If each farmer does not determine his annual groundwater withdrawals on the basis of the true marginal cost, ultimately pumping lifts and pumping costs will be too high and total social welfare, as defined, will not be maximized.

If a tax T_i just equal to the sum of these two ignored subparts is imposed on each acre-foot of groundwater pumped, marginal private cost will be precisely the same as marginal social cost, and the decisions resulting from each farmer's attempt to maximize his own profit will yield the desired social optimum. The rule, thus, for individual farmers is, in addition to rule 13

$$u_i + v_i(y_i + z_i) = c_i m_i + T_i \qquad (16)$$

where

$$T_i = (1/r)[B_i b_i + A_i c_i] \qquad (17)$$

or equivalently

$$T_i = c_i[(B_i b_i)/rc_i + A_i/r]$$

The last expression shows that the tax is just equal to c_i times the difference between optimal lift and that level to which the lift would go if farmers pumped groundwater until it competed (in *current* cost terms) with surface water.

Profit redistribution. The imposition of a pumping tax induces each farmer to act in the best interest of all. Note that the tax extracts from the farmer an amount just equal to the present value of the costs incurred by him if he were to act in his own best interest in the absence of the tax. It would appear, from any one farmer's point of view, hence from all, that there is little to commend the tax scheme. There is, however, a significant difference between the two situations. The future costs saved by the taxing scheme represent payment for additional resources necessary to pump water from a deeper groundwater table. All of these payments are losses to the system while the tax revenues remain in the system (the taxing agency). These revenues might be redistributed to the farmers, or they might be used to help to cover KCWA's payments to the State if the market price for surface water is inadequate. In this latter case, the tax revenues are still not counted as social losses, because they would be making up for other kinds of taxes that would have to be imposed to cover the KCWA deficit.

If it is felt that the tax payments should be redistributed to the farmers, it is essential that the redistributive pattern adopted does not affect marginal groundwater pumping decisions.

DEMAND AND COST ESTIMATES AND THE APPLICATION OF THE MODEL

Benefits to farmers. In the context of this steady-state model, the measurement of gross benefit to a farmer necessarily entails the estimation of a long-run demand function for water. Ideally, a price for water is posted and the farmer chooses those farm activities and selects that combination of factors, including the choice of a unique quantity of water, that maximizes his net revenue. The experiment is repeated, a different price is posted, and the farmer recalculates his most desirable factor-product combination, regarding land as his only fixed factor. The long-run water demand function is derived by repeating this experiment for all possible water prices.

A farmer's gross benefit will be taken to be the full area under the long-run demand curve. The measure of profit for a given water price is then the sum of the difference between the revenue from and the associated cost of the first annual acre-foot applied and subsequent acre-feet applied. A district annual water demand function is simply the aggregate of the individual water demand relations.

Two demand schedules have been estimated (Table 1, Case 2) for each member district. In the first instance, linear water price-quantity relationships for potential member districts were fitted to the demand curves prepared by the California Department of Water Resources [*Calif. Dept. Water Resources*, 1963]. The data underlying these relationships reflect the customary payment-capacity procedures followed by that agency.

The results of a recent farm budget study provide the basis for an alternative estimate of water demand for the nine probable agricultural water districts in the Kern County Water Agency [*Moore and Hedges*, 1963*a*, *b*].

In general, water demand schedules based on farm budget data are more elastic than the Department's demand estimates based on a crop budget analysis. This is not surprising, given the different estimating procedures of the two studies. The primary response to a change in water price is crop substitution according to the Department's procedure. The substitution of water for other inputs was not permitted. Moreover, a fixed level of water use was assumed for each crop. In contrast, the farm budget analysis permitted crop and factor substitution and the intensity of water use to vary in response to changes in the price of water.

Rarely, if ever, has there been an actual water demand study that fully satisfied the definition of a long-run demand curve. Thus, apart from unavoidable forecasting errors, further inaccuracies are introduced which may or may not be significant, depending on the comprehensiveness of the empirical demand analysis.

TABLE 1. Estimated Annual Water Demand and Distribution Cost Parameters for KCWA Member Districts

	Estimated Number of Farms	CASE 1 Farm Budget Survey Data		CASE 2 Crop Survey Data		Local Distribution Cost: Capital Cost per acre-foot	Local Distribution Cost: Variable Cost per acre-foot	Local Distribution Cost: Transportation Cost per acre-foot
		u_i	v_i	u_i	v_i	d_i^{**}		d_i^*
		dollars						
Belridge W.S.D.	103	42.5	0.0001178	50.0	0.0002174	2	5	0.75
Lost Hills W.D.	73	42.5	0.0001663	42.5	0.0003864	1	3	0.00
Rosedale-Rio Bravo W.S.D.	38	42.5	0.0003194	50.0	0.0005555	3	4	1.70
Semitropic W.S.D.	93	42.5	0.0001305	45.0	0.0001500	4	2	1.20
West Kern W.D.	17	42.5	0.0007142	50.0	0.0001111	4	6	2.00
Antelope Plain W.D.	37	42.5	0.0003282	45.0	0.0004285	2	5	5.70
Wheeler Ridge—Maricopa W.S.D. No. 1	90	42.5	0.0001349	48.3	0.0001667	2	5	5.80
No. 2	45	42.5	0.0002698	45.0	0.0004285	3	4	11.25
Kern River Delta and Others	325	42.5	0.00003736	42.5[1]	0.00003736[1]	2	4	1.50

[1] No data provided in the original sources. It is therefore assumed to be equal to Case 1 estimate.

Estimates of water demand derived from the farm budget analysis (Case 1) are most consistent with the analytical requirements of the steady-state model, because a relatively greater set of critical farm enterprise decisions is regarded as variable.

Surface water cost. The annual cost to the KCWA for surface water from the State system has two components: a fixed and unavoidable unit cost for each acre-foot of the entitlement, whether used or not, and a variable transportation cost for each acre-foot of the annual entitlement actually delivered. Fixed costs play no role in the determination of the best use of water within the KCWA. No decision by the KCWA could alter this part of the water bill.

For present purposes, variable surface water costs also play no significant allocative role, because a condition of demand in excess of the annual entitlement would exist for a price set at this level. The estimated annual fixed and variable cost of surface water, according to unpublished data, was estimated to be $16.7 million.

The cost of surface water to the farmer differs from the cost to KCWA because of local distribution costs. Annual district distribution costs will be of two parts, those that are fixed–interest on the fixed system, maintenance, and depreciation costs—and those that vary with the quantity of water transported. Since district distribution facilities have not been constructed, it is appropriate to regard all such costs as variable.

The cost of surface water to KCWA depends on the location of the diversion of the annual entitlement. During the planning period when the decision about diverting the entitlement is still open, certain costs are variable that later become fixed after this decision has been made. The intra-KCWA transportation cost of surface water is such a cost. For the allocative efficiency problem it is conceptually akin to the district distribution cost and is so treated in the present analysis. Let

$$d_i = d_i^* + d_i^{**}$$

where d_i^* is the unit cost of transporting water within the KCWA, and d_i^{**} is the variable unit cost of the distribution system within district i. Estimates of d_i^* and d_i^{**} in Table 1 are based on unpublished data from the *California Department of Water Resources* [1963].

Groundwater costs and parameters. Present knowledge regarding safe yields, water quality, overdraft, and other important dimensions of groundwater in the Kern County service area is incomplete. Nevertheless, estimates of annual safe yield are available for those districts overlying groundwater basins and are exhibited in Table 2.

TABLE 2. District Groundwater Parameters

	Annual Safe Yield A_i/B_i, acre-feet	Pumping Lift M_{io}, ft	A_i, ft	B_i, ft/million acre-feet	a_i, $	b_i, $/ft	c_i, $/acre-feet
Rosedale-Rio Bravo W.S.D.	3,300	218	0.62	189.0	1,320	42.9	0.025
Semitropic W.S.D.	63,000	260	3.99	63.3	25,200	819.0	0.025
West Kern W.D.	25,200	165	4.00	160.0	10,080	327.6	0.025
Wheeler Ridge—Maricopa W.S.D. #2	22,000	625	3.78	172.0	8,800	286.0	0.025
Kern River Delta and Others	347,000	205	18.50	53.0	138,800	4511.0	0.025

The pumping lift of a particular district varies directly with the quantity of water withdrawn by pumps located in the district. A district's average pumping lift is also affected by water withdrawn from wells located outside a particular district if there is a hydrological interdependence between the two regions. Although such dependence may exist, insufficient information precluded its specification. To simplify the analysis further, it was assumed that the effects of pumping on groundwater tables are slow; this year's pumping has no effect until next year. A linear relationship between the change in lift and annual groundwater withdrawals was estimated from data prepared by *California Department of Water Resources* [1959, 1960*a*, 1960*b*] and *Boyle Engineering* [1963]

$$\Delta m = -A_i + B_i z_{it}$$

where Δm = change in lift. The estimated values of these parameters for each district are given in Table 2.

It will be recalled that the annual cost of pumping z acre-feet of water from one well in the KCWA region is given by

$$g(z, m) = a + bm + cmz$$

The parameters of this equation were estimated on the basis of linear relationships fitted to the empirical data published elsewhere [*Moore and Hedges*, 1962]. To estimate the annual cost of pumping groundwater for a district, assume that one well pumps 1000 acre-feet annually. Thus the annual cost of pumping groundwater for a member district is

$$g_i(z_{it}, m) = a_i + b_i m + c_i m z_{it}$$

where $a_i = az_{it}/1000$; $b_i = bz_{it}/1000$; and $c_i = c$ (see Table 2).

The steady-state calculation. Given estimates for the parameters, a steady-state solution is readily found. From (13)

$$y_i = [(p + d_i - u_i)/-v_i] - z_i \qquad (18)$$

so that

$$\partial/\partial p(\sum y_i) = -\sum 1/v_i$$

If surface water is priced at zero a total amount $\Sigma[u_i - d_i)/v_i - z_i]$ will be demanded. Hence the total quantity demanded at price p will be

$$\sum [(u_i - d_i)/v_i - z_i] - p \sum (1/v_i)$$

If this demand is to be equal to the supply $\bar{Y}$ it must be true that

$$p = \{\sum [(u_i - d_i)/(v_i - z_i)] - \bar{Y}\} / [\sum (1/v_i)] \qquad (19)$$

The market clearing price is calculated by (19) with the safe yield quantity A_i/B_i substituted for z_i. The individual y_i are then found by plugging p into (18). The remaining variables, the m_i, are then found from (15). Steady-state values for the y_i, p_i, m_i for the two alternative water demand estimates are presented in Table 3.

The use of the Department's steeper sloped district demand functions results in a relatively lower equilibrium p, consequently relatively smaller (numerically) m_i's. Different district demand functions result in differences that are small relative to the total surface water allocation, but of course absolute differences do exist.

TABLE 3. District Water Deliveries, Prices, and Lifts under Steady-State Conditions

	Case 1 $p = \$10.50$			Case 2 $p = \$6.85$			Kern County Water Agency[1]		
	Annual Delivery	Annual Charge	Lift	Annual Delivery	Annual Charge	Lift	Annual Delivery	Annual Charge	Lift
	y_i, thousand acre-feet	$p + d_i^*$ $/acre-feet	m_i, ft	y_i, thousand acre-feet	$p + d_i^*$, $/acre-feet	m_i, ft	y_i, thousand acre-feet	$p + d_i^*$, $/acre-feet	m_i, ft
Belridge W.S.D.	206	11.25	...	163	7.60	...	157	15.80	...
Lost Hills W.D.	168	10.50	...	82	6.85	...	95	15.20	...
Rosedale-Rio Bravo W.S.D.	70	12.20	752	59	8.55	606	60	12.00	744
Semitropic W.S.D.	127	11.70	607	143	8.05	461	171	11.10	583
West Kern County W.D.	3	12.50	799	3	8.85	652	30	17.30	990
Antelope Plain W.D.	59	16.20	...	59	12.55	...	60	15.00	...
Wheeler Ridge—Maricopa W.S.D.									
No. 1	142	16.30	...	172	12.65	...	151	17.30	...
No. 2	29	21.75	1054	24	18.10	908	84	24.00	1144
Kern River Delta and others	309	12.00	251	406	8.35	105	150	12.00	251
Total	1111			1111			958		

Note: Individual entries may not sum to the total because of rounding error.
[1] *Leeds, Hill and Jewett, Inc.*, 1963.

For example, Semitropic W.S.D. would take 16,000 acre-feet more per year if the Case 2 demand functions were the more accurate descriptions of actual future water demand.

The value for the optimal lift in each district is given in Table 4. In the absence of a pump tax under Case 1 conditions, pumping lifts would vary between 708 and 1150 feet, depending on the particular district. When the pumping tax is imposed the socially optimum lift is lower, varying between 251 feet and 1054 feet.

The lift effect of the tax is directly related to the 'socialness' of the groundwater basin. The greater the annual safe yield of a basin is or the more numerous the pumping units are, the higher is the aggregated social cost of individual pumping. The difference in lift with and without the tax is about fifteen feet for Rosedale-Rio Bravo W.S.D., whose estimated safe yield equals 3300 acre-feet, whereas the difference is about 468 feet for the Kern River Delta region, whose estimated annual safe yield is 347,000 acre-feet.

TABLE 4. District Lift Level and Tax Rate under Alternative Price Policies and Demand Specifications

					Case 1		Case 2		KCWA	
	$(B_i b_i)/rc_i$, ft	A_i/r, ft	T_i, $/acre-feet	$T_i z_i$, hundred dollars	$(p + d_i)/c_i$, ft	m_i, ft	$(p + d_i)/c_i$, ft	m_i, ft	$(p + d_i)/c_i$, ft	m_i, ft
Rosedale-Rio Bravo W.S.D.	5	10	0.39	13	768	752	622	606	760	744
Semitropic W.S.D.	35	66	2.53	1,593	708	607	562	461	684	583
West Kern County W.D.	35	67	2.54	640	900	799	754	652	1092	990
Wheeler Ridge—Maricopa W.S.D.	33	63	2.40	527	1150	1054	1004	908	1240	1144
Kern River Delta and Others	160	308	11.72	40,670	720	251	574	105	720	251
Total				43,443						

The difference between the optimum lift for a district under Case 1 and Case 2 water demand conditions depends on the cost of surface water at the farm headgate. Thus, when the allocative efficiency price is $3.85 per acre-foot greater for each district, Case 1 versus Case 2, the optimum lift in each district is 146 feet greater. From the foregoing remarks it follows that a district's total tax payment will be high or low, depending on the safe yield of the groundwater basin it overlies. For Rosedale-Rio Bravo W.S.D. the total pumping tax would be $1299; for the Kern River Delta region it is over $4 million annually.

Given a maximum annual surface water entitlement, the solution values for y_i and p that bring about allocative efficiency do not guarantee that annual revenue will equal KCWA's annual obligation. This condition would be met only if KCWA had originally contracted for an efficient quantity of surface water. Table 5 indicates that under either set of demand functions the optimum pricing policy results in an annual deficit. The pumping tax could (but not necessarily should) be used to meet the deficit. This policy could be justified if it was believed that beneficiaries should pay for the water and if it could be shown that the secondary beneficiaries received no gains from water importation that were not offset by equal costs. If the annual obligation still exceeded revenue the problem would become one of designing optimum lump sum charges, perhaps through an assessment tax on unimproved property. This issue is separate and is perhaps best solved by contracting for an optimum quantity of water in the first instance.

TABLE 5. Annual Repayment Obligation and Sources of Revenue under Alternative Pricing Policies

	Socially Optimum Pricing Policy		KCWA Pricing and Tax Policy
	Case 1 Demand	Case 2 Demand	
	million dollars		
Total Annual Repayment Obligation	16.664	16.664	17.496
Total Annual Revenues from Water Charges	14.058	10.236	14.496
Deficit	2.606	6.428	3.000
Total Annual Pumping Tax Revenue	4.344	4.344	...
Total Annual Revenue from Assessments	...	...	3.000

In 1962, the Board of the KCWA searched for a pricing policy that would alleviate overdraft conditions in the groundwater basin and would ensure that its member districts contracted for an annual 1.1 million acre-feet, an amount for which the KCWA had contracted with the State of California [*Public Hearings*, 1964]. To these ends it adopted a discriminatory pricing system, charging a lower price for surface water to districts without groundwater. Water charges were escalated through time. In addition, a property tax will return about $3 million annually. This pricing policy does not alone ensure the stabilization of groundwater supplies. Only if an irrigator were to act voluntarily against his own self-interest would the stabilization goal be achieved, because no strictures prevent prospective irrigators from pumping at overdraft intensities.

The optimum pricing policy would ensure that only the safe yield was actually withdrawn from any given groundwater basin; hence the stability of the groundwater supply is ensured. Moreover, if a pumping tax is not imposed, the KCWA region will lose an estimated $4.344 million annually, less the value added created by only those firms located within this region whose well drilling, maintenance, and operation activities would be expanded.

If the optimum pricing policy is to be of general use, several conditions must be met. First, there is an institutional requirement. A district that wishes to manage efficiently surface and groundwater supplies must possess a legal right to levy a pumping tax. A recent court decision in California upholds the right of agencies such as the KCWA to levy a pumping tax on some or all of its members [Orange County Water District v. Farnsworth]. Not all public water districts have taxing powers broad enough to make a pumping tax a feasible policy option.

Second, in an actual problem setting, estimation must be feasible. Assumptions about the linearity of relationships are convenient, but the physical and economic setting may not be so benign. It is neither difficult nor expensive to perform a sensitivity analysis to test whether either this assumption or error of estimation has a significant effect on the solution values of the variables. If it is clear, for example, that nonlinear demand functions are in order, the steady-state model is not vitiated, but the new algorithm would be more complicated and the solution would be reached most efficiently with the aid of a computer.

Acknowledgments. The research of the first author was supported in part by a grant from the Ford Foundation to the Graduate School of Business Administration, administered through the Center for Research in Management Science. Both authors wish to record their indebtedness for many profitable discussions to Neil Houston and Julius Margolis.

REFERENCES

Boyle Engineering Company, Engineering and economic report on imported water supply project for Rosedale-Rio Bravo water storage district, November, 1963.

Calif. Dept. Water Resources, Report on proposed Rosedale-Rio Bravo water storage district, April, 1959.

Calif. Dept. Water Resources, Office report: Supplement to information and data on proposed program for planning and constructing state water facilities, May, 1960*a*.

Calif. Dept. Water Resources, Office report: Second supplement to information and data on proposed program for financing and constructing state water facilities, June, 1960*b*.

Calif. Dept. Water Resources, Feasibility of serving the Kern County Water Agency from the State Water Project, Bull. 119-8 (September, 1963).

Hedges, Trimble R., and Charles V. Moore, *Economics of On-Farm Irrigation Water Availability and Costs and Related Farm Adjustments: 1.—Enterprise Choices, Resources Allocations, and Earnings on 640-acre General Crop Farms on the San Joaquin Valley Eastside,* Giannini Foundation Research Report No. 257, University of California, Berkeley, 1962.

Leeds, Hill and Jewett, Inc., Letter to board of directors, Kern County Water Agency, 1963.

Moore, Charles V., and Trimble R. Hedges, *Some Characteristics of Farm Irrigation Water Supplies in the San Joaquin Valley,* Giannini Foundation Report No. 258, University of California, 1962.

Moore, Charles V., and Trimble R. Hedges, *Economics of On-Farm Irrigation Water Availability and Costs and Related Farm Adjustments: 2.—Farm Size in Relation to Resource Use, Earnings, and Adjustments on the San Joaquin Valley Eastside,* Giannini Foundation Research Report No. 258, University of California, Berkeley, 1963*a*.

Moore, Charles V., and Trimble R. Hedges, *Economics of On-Farm Irrigation Water Availability and Costs and Related Farm Adjustment: 3.—Some Aggregate Aspects of Farmer Demand for Irrigation Water and Production Response on the San Joaquin Valley Eastside,* Giannini Foundation Research Report No. 261, University of California, Berkeley, 1963*b*.

Orange County Water District v. Farnsworth, 138 Cal. App. 2nd 518, 1956.

Public hearing on proposed zone(s) of benefit in the San Joaquin Valley portion of Kern County, Transcript of proceedings at the meeting of the Kern County Water Agency held in Bakersfield, California, July 13, September 9, September 10, October 12, October 21, October 22, 1964.

(Manuscript received August 15, 1966.)

CHAPTER 19

ECONOMICS OF PRODUCTION FROM NATURAL RESOURCES

By VERNON L. SMITH*

I. *Introduction*

This paper attempts to provide a unified theory of production from natural resources. A single model of an industry is used to describe a dynamic process of recovery from such technologically diverse resources as fish, timber, petroleum, and minerals. Recovery from each of these resources is seen as a special case of a general model, depending upon whether the resource is replenishable, and on whether production exhibits significant externalities. A model of centralized management, with particular reference to "common property" resources, such as fisheries, under stationary conditions, is also discussed and compared with competitive recovery in the stationary state.

The paper builds directly upon, and has been much influenced by, the basic contributions of Gordon [6] and Scott [11] [12].

II. *Environmental Technology*

The economy of man consumes two fundamental kinds of naturally occurring resources: (1) Replenishable resources, such as fish, timber, bison, and the whooping crane, and (2) nonreplenishable resources, such as petroleum, natural gas, and the products of mines. The second category is often called ' exhaustible resources," which is something of a misnomer since both types of resources are capable of exhaustion. The American bison, once of value to the American economy, is such a case, as also were the native trout of Lake Michigan.[1] This particular dichotomy is important analytically in that the first category of resources is capable of regeneration, as man consumes a flow of the resource, while the second represents a fixed stock whose inventory can only be diminished over time.

For purposes of production analysis, one of the most important technological features of a replenishable commercial resource like a fish or

* The author is professor of economics, Brown University. This research was supported by National Science Foundation Grant No. GS-1835 to Brown University. I am indebted to J. A. Crutchfield for several helpful comments, and to Eric L. Smith for assistance in preparing the diagrams.

[1] The two cases are different, however. Neither was exhausted in the physical sense, but in the economic sense. The biotic potential of fish is so large that complete extinction may be very difficult. With the Lake Michigan trout it was invasion by another predator—the sea lamprey —that destroyed the trout harvest. The lamprey have since been brought under control, and with restocking, the lake may again become an important fishery resource if pollution does not win the battle.

timber species is its law of growth. The growth characteristics of a species may be studied in terms of the growth in the number of members, and in the size of individual members [1], or in the aggregate mass of the species [8]. This paper will take a crude macrobiological approach, and deal only with variables which measure the aggregate masses of species. Such an approach is analogous to the aggregate production function hypothesis employed by economists in macroeconomics and growth theory.

The mass growth of a species will depend upon certain internal biological characteristics of the species, and on its environment, i.e., the abundance of food nutrients, and the existence and efficiency of other species which have predator or symbiotic relationships to the given species. We can think of any species to be harvested by man as subject to a 'technological" law of growth governed by the ecological characteristics of the biosystem in which it resides [8].

In the simplest model of the technology of a replenishable resource, we consider a single species population with mass X in pounds, board feet, or other appropriate measure of quantity. The ecological balance between this species and its natural environment is postulated to give rise to a law of mass growth of the form

$$X \equiv \frac{dX}{dt} = f(X). \quad (2.1)$$

From the general ecological descriptions usually given for any species [8] as well as for fish [2, pp. 7–8] [4, p. 209] and timber [7] [9] resources, it is reasonable to assume that $f(X)$ has the inverted "U" properties shown in Figure 1, i.e., $f(\underline{X}) = f(\overline{X}) = 0$, $f'(X^{\circ}) = 0$, $f''(X) < 0$, $0 \leq X \leq \overline{X}$, where $\underline{X}$ and $\overline{X}$ are the minimum and maximum self-sustaining populations, and X° is the population producing the largest sustainable yield or net rate of growth. The yield function $f(X)$ measures the net effect of the birth rate, the growth rate of individual members, and the death rate from natural causes, including predation from nonhuman sources. Populations smaller than $\underline{X} \leq 0$, are assumed not to be viable.

The most frequently postulated form for the yield function is the quadratic, giving

$$X = a_0 + X(a_1 - a_{11}X), \quad (2.1')$$

whose solution, $X(t)$, is the familiar and ubiquitous logistic law of growth [8, pp. 64–76].

In the natural state a replenishable resource, whose law of growth is governed by (2.1), will normally be expected to grow until the stable equilibrium $X = \overline{X}$, $\dot{X} = 0$ is reached. In such circumstances commercial

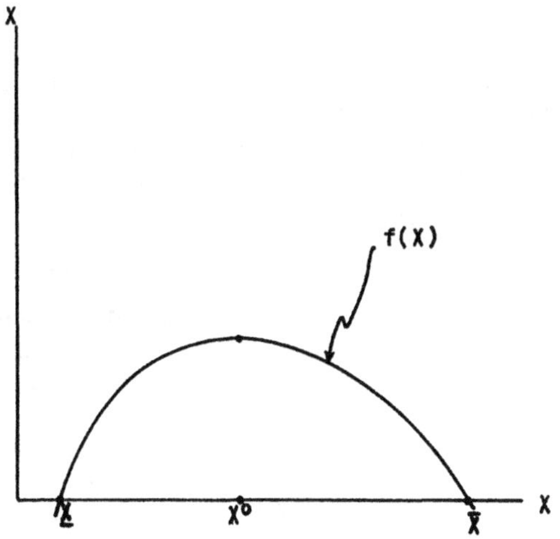

FIGURE 1

production from the resource by man will begin with these as initial conditions. (Note that $\underline{X}$ is unstable.)

With the entry of man as a predator in the form of an extractive industry—commercial fishing, forest products, and so on—equation (2.1) must be modified to serve as a technological restriction on the activities of the industry. Throughout this paper, in order to sharpen the essential features of the theory and simplify the arithmetic we will assume that recovery from a given resource is effected by K homogeneous firms or units of capital, each producing an output rate, x. Total industry output is then Kx, where both K and x are, in general, variables. Hence, the required technological restriction might be written:[2]

$$\dot{X} = f(X) - Kx. \tag{2.2}$$

It is understood that x, K, X are each a function of time. Under our assumptions, K is both the number of firms (e.g., fishing boats) in the

[2] More generally, we should write $\dot{X}=f(X, Kx)$. In (2.2) we assume no interaction between the total harvest and the growth properties of the population mass, as likely will be the case if only restricted portions of the age distribution are harvested. Concerning my formulation of the constraint (2.2), and its use in the models to follow, the reader is urged to refer to [3], especially the mathematical appendix and the references cited there. Unfortunately, I suffered the impoverishment of not having acquired a copy of the important Crutchfield-Zellner book until after the present paper had been written. They work with the quadratic form of (2.2) in the context of a supply and demand industry model (and again in the treatment of the optimization problem of central management, both static and dynamic). Although my treatment was independent, and differs from theirs, the reader should view the present paper as essentially a generalization and explication of this earlier literature.

industry, and a measure of the real capital stock invested by the industry.

Turning now to nonreplenishable resources like petroleum, coal, iron ore, and other products of mines, we note that these form a simple special case of (2.2) in which $f(X) \equiv 0$, i.e., regeneration is assumed to be impossible so that the fixed stock declines at a time rate equal to aggregate industry output.

III. *Cost Behavior—The Technology of Recovery*

The cost structure of the recovery process varies widely among the major commercial natural resources. Recovery cost in fishing, petroleum and natural gas is uniquely influenced by the "common property" character of these resources [6] [11]. No one has exclusively private rights in ocean fishing nor are such rights feasible to grant when commercial species are migrants. Similarly with crude oil extraction the reservoir's physical boundaries are often unknown, and even unknowable except at prohibitive cost. Such resources may therefore be shared by many private firms. An important consequence of this is that there may be direct and very significant external diseconomies in production, with an attending divergence of private and social optima.

On the other hand, forest and mineral resources are relatively divisible into independent productive units and to this extent are relatvelyi free of significant production externalities.[3] Thus, of the two replenishable resources, fisheries and forests, it is assumed that the former shows significant external diseconomies of production while the latter does not. With the two nonreplenishable resources, petroleum and mining, again, the former is assumed to exhibit significant diseconomies, the latter is not.

In industries such as mining and lumbering, the extractive total cost function for the individual firm is assumed to be of the form,

$$C = \phi(x) + \hat{\pi}, \qquad C'(x) > 0, \qquad C''(x) < 0, \tag{3.1}$$

where $\phi(x)$ is total (fixed and variable) operating cost,[4] and $\hat{\pi}$ is the

[3] The specialist will want to take this statement with a grain of salt. In forestry there are obvious externalities with regard to fire control (except remember that we are working with certainty models) and the spread of insects and disease. Also, in mining, one man's shaft may cause cave-ins or water encroachment on another mining property. A general disclaimer is in order: In a paper trying to emphasize the unity of production theory in the natural resource setting, one inevitably does a certain violence to the detailed facts, for there are indeed diverse elements to consider in the various cases of extraction. But the truth of unity, even if partial, is easily obscured by concentrating on more-or-less minor differentiating details.

[4] In (3.1) we somewhat oversimplify the view of mining and forestry production. In mining, cumulative output (or the unrecovered stock remaining) may affect cost; for this and other important considerations in mining see [13]. See footnote 11 for some relevant qualifications applying to appropriated forest resources.

normal profit or return on a unit of capital required to hold the unit (or firm) in the industry.

The most natural general hypothesis about total operating cost for the individual fisherman requires it to be an increasing function of the vessel's catch rate, x, but a decreasing function of fish population, i.e., $\phi=\phi(x,X)$, with $\phi_1\equiv\partial\phi/\partial x>0$, and $\phi_2\equiv\partial\phi/\partial X<0$. The latter specification is implied if it is the case that when there are more fish of a given species they are easier to catch. On the other hand if increases in X cause no change in the density of stocks, as may be the case in some species, then it may be that $\phi_2\equiv 0$. Externalities enter in an interesting and simple manner: *No individual competitive fisherman has control over population size as a private decision variable yet it enters as a parameter in each fisherman's cost function.* Externalities may also enter via crowding phenomena: If the fish population is highly concentrated, the efficiency of each boat may be lowered by congestion over the fishing grounds.[5] In general then the cost function may include K, and our most general cost hypothesis for the fishing firm is:

$$(3.2)\qquad \begin{aligned} C &= \phi(x, X, K) + \pi, & C_1 &\equiv \partial C/\partial x > 0, \\ C_2 &\equiv \partial C/\partial X \leq 0, & C_3 &\equiv \partial C/\partial K \geq 0. \end{aligned}$$

When $C_2<0$, recovery cost exhibits resource *stock externalities*. When $C_3>0$, recovery cost exhibits *crowding externalities*. Each case represents an external diseconomy to the industry. Equation (3.2) will serve as the most general cost function with which we shall be concerned. It includes (3.1) as a special case. Another special case is crude oil production, since oil well drilling, development and operating costs are essentially independent of crude production in primary recovery fields (fields subject to natural drive forces).

IV. *A Model of the Competitive Recovery of Natural Resources*

We propose to characterize the competitive recovery process in any extractive industry by a system of three behavior equations describing the interactions of the resource, individual firms, and the industry. The term "industry" in the case of fishing and petroleum extraction will not necessarily refer to the entire industry, but to the collection of firms exploiting a given fishery or oil reservoir, since in these cases external interdependence is postulated.

[5] A good example is sport fishing for striped bass in San Francisco Bay. The stripers form schools to feed on schools of smaller food fish. The latter are driven to the surface, attempting to escape, and this attracts the gulls to feed. The fishing boats simply motor into the Bay looking for the mass of fighting gulls. The boats congregate around the gulls and then alternate with trolling passes through the concentrated school of stripers. On a busy holiday a considerable waiting line may develop.

The behavior equation for the resource has already been stated in (2.2), and describes the growth or decline of the stock as a function of stock size and industry output.

If we let $\rho\ (Kx)$ be the total revenue rate from the sale of Kx units of the resource, then revenue per firm is $\rho(Kx)/K$, and, using (3.2) the most general form of the firm's pure or excess profit function is

$$\pi = \frac{\rho(Kx)}{K} - C(x, X, K). \tag{4.1}$$

It is assumed that each firm perceives this profit to vary only with its own output and this only because its private cost is variable with output. Thus price, $\rho(Kx)/Kx$, is perceived as a given constant, and $C(x, X, K)$ is treated as a function only of the private control variable x. The behavior equation for firms is a perceived profit maximizing condition (price equals marginal cost), which serves to determine x as a function of capital and resource stocks depending on revenue, cost and externality conditions, *viz*

$$\frac{\rho(Kx)}{Kx} = \phi_1(x, X, K). \tag{4.2}$$

Some modification of the hypothesis (4.2) must be specified in the case of crude oil production where cost is substantially independent of output, and output depends primarily upon the characteristics of the field and its exploitation. In primary producing fields all crude oil is produced at the surface of a well by the action of one or more naturally occurring underground drives or pressures from edge water encroachment, a gas cap, or gas dissolved in the crude [10, pp. 391–93]. Both the rate of recovery and the cumulative recovery reduces the pressure level. So the output, x, of a given well can be regarded as a decreasing function of aggregate current output, Kx, and a decreasing function of cumulative output, $\overline{X}$-X, or[6]

$$x = g(Kx, X), \quad \frac{\partial g}{\partial (Kx)} \equiv g_1 < 0, \quad \frac{\partial g}{\partial X} = g_2 > 0. \tag{4.2a}$$

Finally, new firms (capital) are assumed to be attracted into the industry when $\pi > 0$, while producing firms are driven out of the industry when $\pi < 0$. Specifically, it is supposed that this flow of capital is proportional to pure profit, or

[6] Alternatively we could write $x = h(K, X)$, $h_1 < 0$, $h_2 > 0$. With secondary (water or gas injection) and stripper (mechanical pumping) recovery fields, the cost function will be as in (3.2). We assume in the text that the ultimate cumulative recovery, $\overline{X} - \underline{X}$ is known and is independent of the production path. In fact, the total free-flow recovery may depend upon the extraction rate. See, for example, [5, pp. 91–92], and the references cited there.

$$\dot{K} = \delta\left[\frac{\rho(Kx)}{K} - C(x, X, K)\right], \tag{4.3}$$

where $\delta > 0$ is a behavioral constant for the industry.[7]

In summary, our behavioral equation system is

$$X = f(X) - Kx, \tag{I.1}$$

$$\frac{\rho(Kx)}{Kx} = C_1(x, X, K), \quad \text{or} \quad x = g(Kx, X), \qquad \text{for crude oil,} \tag{I.2}$$

$$\dot{K} = \delta\left[\frac{\rho(Kx)}{K} - C(x, X, K)\right], \tag{I.3}$$

with $f(X) \equiv 0$ for oil, gas and mineral stocks, and $C_2 \equiv C_3 \equiv 0$, for mineral and timber resources.[8] It is further assumed that equation (I.2), whatever its particular form, always provides a unique x for every (X, K) pair (i.e., a mapping $X, K \rightarrow x$). Then the system I provides two first-order differential equations in X and K of the form,

$$X = F(X, K) \tag{II.1}$$

$$K = I(X, K), \tag{II.2}$$

with initial conditions $X(0)$ and $K(0)$. Where recovery requires specialized capital, exploitation begins with $X(0) = \overline{X}$ and $K(0) = 0$, i.e., the resource is in static mass equilibrium with its environment, and an exploiting industry does not exist. If exploitation begins with a direct transfer of capital from other industries (e.g., haddock and cod fishing vessels shift to lobster), then $K(0) > 0$.

V. *The Dynamics of Competitive Recovery*

A. *General*

Equation system II together with the initial conditions describe the velocity of a point in the "phase space" (X, K) i.e., the rates of increase

[7] In (4.3) we assume capital to be equally mobile out as well as into an industry, i.e., there is no problem of irreversibility. More generally we could write

$$\dot{K} = \begin{cases} \delta_1 \pi, & \text{if } \pi \geq 0 \\ \delta_2 \pi, & \text{if } \pi < 0. \end{cases}$$

We later assume $\delta_2 = 0$ in the case of oil wells, which clearly cannot be reduced in quantity once drilled.

[8] Many variations on the particular forms of these behavior equations could be made. In place of (I.3) some variant of the accelerator hypothesis or an adaptive expectations hypothesis about investment could be introduced. In (I.2) any output adjustment hypothesis might be used in place of the classical—price equals marginal cost. If fishing is concentrated in a single season of the year (such as spawning time), then a difference equation expression of growth-harvest behavior could substitute for (I.1).

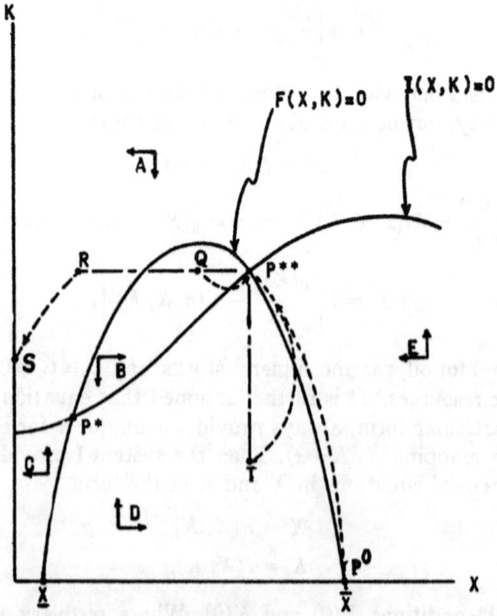

FIGURE 2

or decrease in (i) the resource stock, (ii) the level of capital investment of the industry.

A static equilibrium or singular point (X^*, K^*) is defined by the property that $F(X^*, K^*)=0$, $I(X^*, K^*)=0$. There may be many such points. Two such singular points (P^* and P^{**}) are illustrated in the phase diagram of Figure 2 for a replenishable resource. Points in the set defined by $F(X, K)=0$ correspond to *equilibria between the resource mass and its environment*, while points in the set defined by $I(X, K)=0$ correspond to *equilibria between the exploiting industry and alternative uses of capital in the economy* as a whole. Both equilibrium relations presuppose instantaneous output adjustment in accordance with firm profit maximization (I.2). In Figure 2 it is assumed that $\partial F/\partial K<0$; for any given resource stock, an increase (decrease) in the size of the industry will decrease (increase) the rate of growth of the resource, i.e., production exceeds the rate of replenishment. Also it is assumed that $\partial I/\partial K<0$; for any given resource stock, an increase (decrease) in the size of the industry lowers (raises) profit and reduces (increases) the flow of capital into the industry. Conditions for the validity of these two assumptions are stated in the appendix. The assumptions apply only to the illustration in Figure 2, and not to the model in general.

Under these assumptions the nonnegative quadrant is partitioned into five regions by the F and I curves. In region A, above both curves, both the industry and the resource stock will decline. In region D, below both curves, both the industry and the resource stock will grow. In regions B, C and E the remaining combinations of growth in K and X occur as shown. The perpendicular arrows in each region indicate in the usual way, the directions of motion along a development path in phase space. If initially the resource population is at $\overline{X}$, and $K=0$, then (by hypothesis) $\dot{K}>0$ and capital flows into the new extractive industry reducing the resource mass along the path from P^0 to P^{**} as shown. P^{**} is an equilibrium point for the conditions postulated in the illustration. At P^{**} the industry is in equilibrium with the economy, and the species mass is in ecological equilibrium (total recruitment of new mass equals the harvest rate). The illustration shows P^{**} to be locally, but not globally stable. Thus, suppose having reached P^{**}, there is a sudden reduction in X from natural causes—such as a disease which wipes out the susceptible portion of the species and then disappears. The system is then shifted to the point Q or R. At Q firms suffer losses, and capital starts to leave the industry, while the natural productivity of the resource is increased to a level above harvesting by the industry. The resource mass rises, and the industry declines until the state of the system crosses into region D where the industry is once more profitable. Capital now flows back into the industry, and the resource mass continues to grow until balanced by the industry harvest at P^{**}. If the catastrophe is large, and the system shifts to a point such as R in region A, the resource mass declines, and the yield of the species is lowered. As a result the harvest exceeds the yield, the resource stock falls, and the industry declines until both may be put out of business at S.

The qualitative properties of virtually any conceivable pattern of resource exploitation can be depicted by a phase diagram similar to the illustration of Figure 2. Invasion of the resource domain by a new parasite or predator, which becomes a permanent aspect of the environment, can be represented by a downward shift of the F function. F may fall below I so that the invading parasite or predator together with the industrial harvest wipes out the resource and thence the industry. Such was the course of events when the lamprey invaded Lake Michigan destroying both the lake trout and the lake's fishing industry.

From the above illustration it is clear that commercial production from a replenishable resource need not in time destroy the resource. Exploitation by man *may* disrupt a delicate balance which destroys a resource. But the existence of external diseconomies (though it lead to non-Pareto efficient production states) does provide a built-in mechanism tending to resist annihilation of the resource: harvesting depletes the stock, costs rise and, *ceteris paribus*, discourages harvesting, with the possibility if not a guarantee of an equilibrium such as P^{**} in Figure 2.

We turn next to an analysis of various special applications and examples of the general model.

B. *Selling Price Constant: The Fishery*

Much of the more systematic literature on resource economics has been concerned with the implications of competitive recovery under conditions of constant price, not only to the individual firm, but also to the individual resource deposit, fishing ground, and so on [2] [6]. It is therefore of some interest to explore the implications of the model for this case.

With selling price, $p \equiv \rho(Kx)/Kx \equiv$ constant, system I becomes,

$$\text{(IA.1)} \qquad \dot{X} = f(X) - Kx$$

$$\text{(IA.2)} \qquad p = C_1(x, X, K)$$

$$\text{(IA.3)} \qquad \dot{K} = \delta[px - C(x, X, K)].$$

Writing total differentials of equations (IA.2) and (IA.3), and solving for dK/dX, we get

$$\text{(5.1)} \qquad \left.\frac{dK}{dX}\right|_{\dot{K}=0} = \frac{-C_2}{C_3},$$

which is the slope of the $I(X, K)=0$ function in system II. Hence, if $C_2<0$, $C_3>0$, i.e., we have external diseconomies from both fish shortage and crowding by vessels, then $I(X, K)=0$ defines K as an increasing function of X. Every reduction in the fish mass will increase costs, and force some fishermen out of the industry until a new normal-return equilibrium is established.

In like manner, differentiating (IA.1) and (IA.2), with $\dot{X}=0$, we get

$$\text{(5.2)} \qquad \left.\frac{dK}{dX}\right|_{\dot{X}=0} = \frac{KC_{12} + C_{11}f'}{xC_{11} - KC_{13}}$$

for the slope of $F(X, K)=0$. Since $f' \lesseqgtr 0$, if $C_{12}<0$, $C_{11}>0$, $C_{13}>0$, the sign of this derivative is not determined on the basis of qualitative considerations alone, and may change in the phase space.

Figures 3–5 illustrate some possible effects of different externality assumptions on industry equilibrium, $I(X, K)=0$, and several possible solution paths in phase space. In each case it is assumed that

$$\left.\frac{dK}{dX}\right|_{\dot{X}=0}$$

is positive below some value of X, and negative above that value.

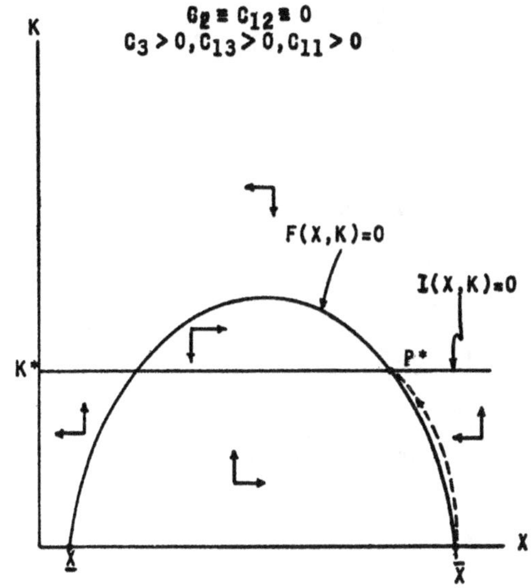

FIGURE 3a

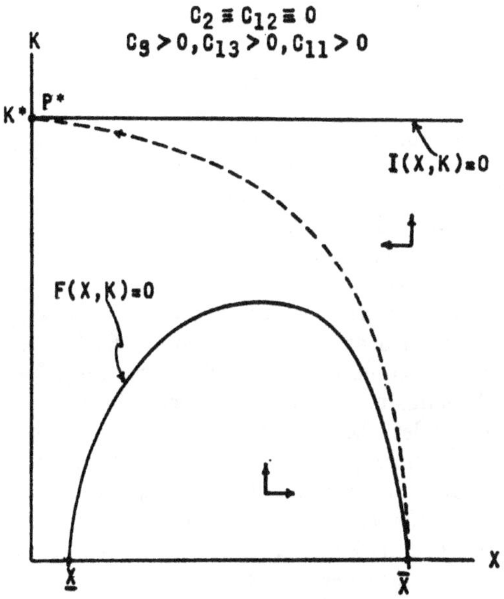

FIGURE 3b

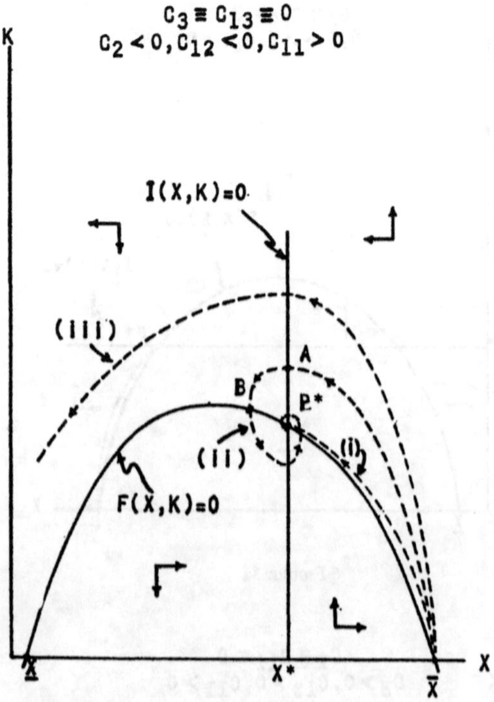

FIGURE 4a

In Figures 3a and 3b, with no resource stock externalities, but with crowding externalities, industry equilibrium occurs at K^* independent of X. A possible path to the equilibrium at P^* is shown. In Figure 3b the resource is so profitable that it is wiped out before crowding externalities limit the industry's growth.

In Figures 4a–c, we assume stock externalities to be significant but no crowding externalities. In contrast to the previous case, industry equilibrium is determined at X^* independent of K. Figure 4a shows three possible paths to equilibrium: (i) a direct path to P^* with monotone growth in the industry and monotone decline in the resource stock to the self-sustaining level X^*; (ii) a cyclical path in which firms respond so quickly to pure profits that when industry equilibrium is reached at A the harvest exceeds the yield of the stock causing the stock to continue falling. But with the stock continuing to fall costs rise, losses are incurred, and firms are forced out of the industry. The declining harvest eventually provides equilibrium of the resource stock, at B but the industry is declining. And so on in a convergent cyclical path

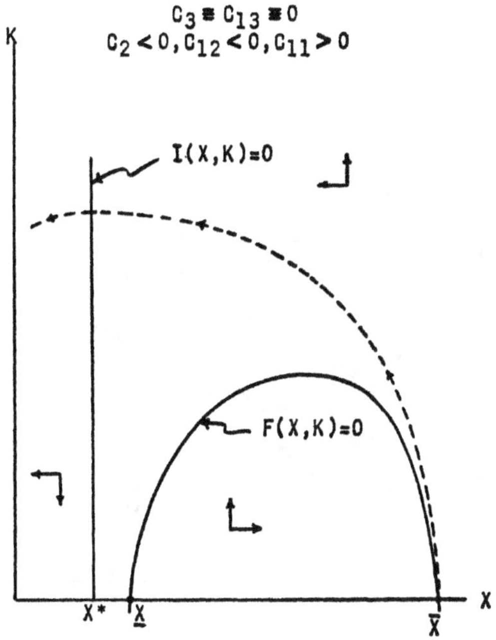

FIGURE 4b

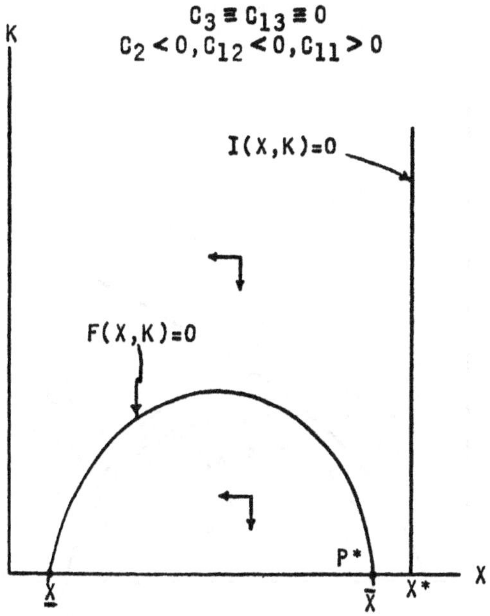

FIGURE 4c

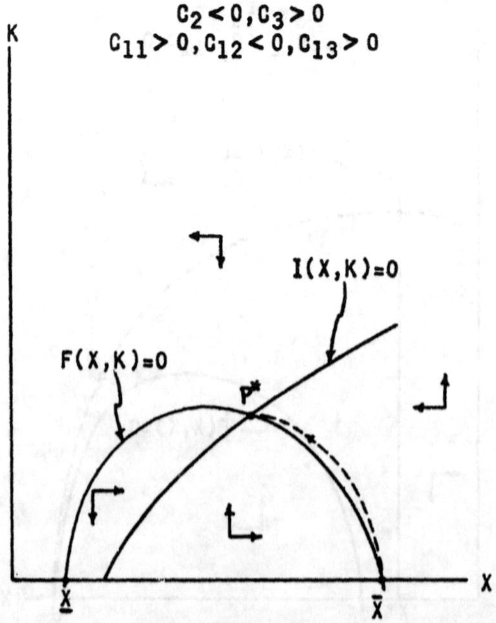

Figure 5a

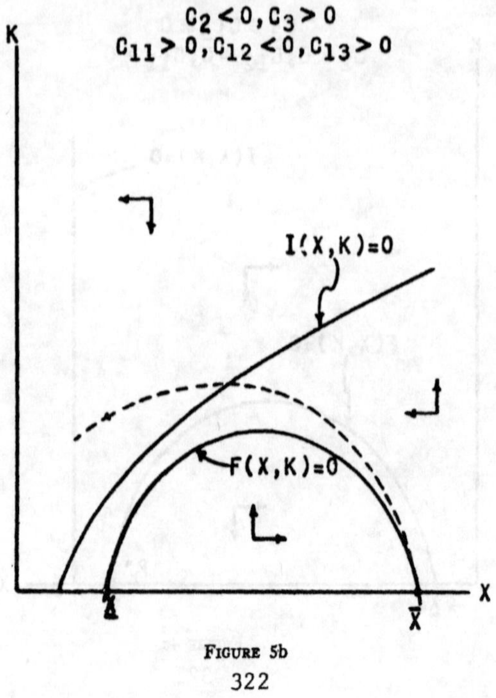

Figure 5b

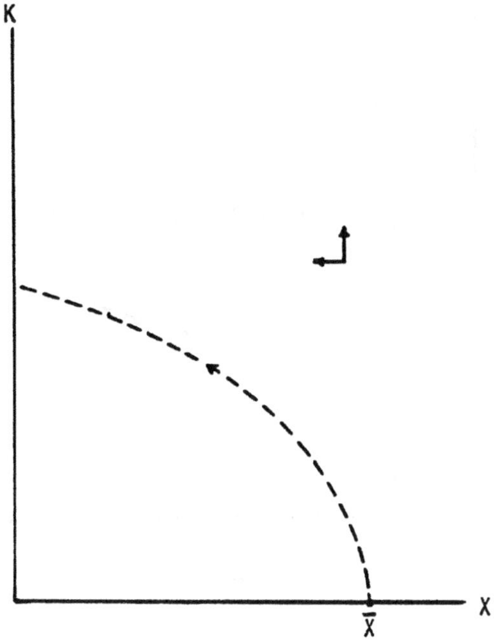

FIGURE 6

with capital flowing in and out in response to cost changes induced by the decline and rise of the stock level; (iii) a path in which the entry speed of new firms is so rapid, and resource stock externalities such, that the stock is depleted before capital outflow due to losses can bring the harvest rate below the yield. Figure 4b illustrates the polar case in which the harvest is so profitable that the resource is sure to be depleted, while 4c shows the opposite pole where it does not pay to harvest any of the resource. Figures 5a and 5b illustrate the more general case in which both kinds of externalities are present.

C. *Mining*

We have assumed mining to be the prototype of a nonreplenishable resource with insignificant externalities due to resource scarcity and crowding. Under these assumptions $f(X)\equiv 0$, and $C_2\equiv C_3\equiv 0$ in system (IA). Hence, if recovery is profitable, $x=x^0$ is determined by equation (IA.2), and $\dot{K}=\delta[px^0-C(x^0)]>0$. Capital flows into the resource at a constant rate, and the depletion rate of the resource is $\dot{X}=-Kx^0$. Figure 6 illustrates the equilibrium path to depletion.

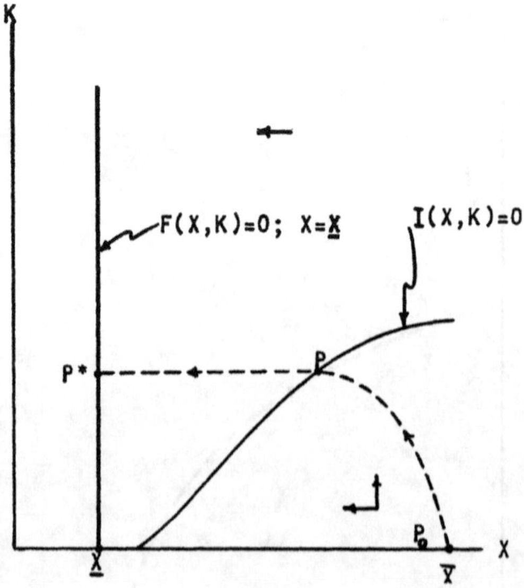

FIGURE 7

D. *Petroleum*

The dynamics of competitive petroleum recovery is slightly more complicated due to externalities. The fixed price equation system is:

(IB.1) $\dot{X} = -Kx$

(IB.2) $x = g(Kx, X), \quad g_1 < 0, \quad g_2 > 0.$

(IB.3) $\dot{K} = \delta[px - C_0], \quad \delta = 0, \quad \text{if } px < C_0, \quad \delta > 0 \text{ otherwise.}$

In equation (IB.3) we impose the condition that $\dot{K} \geq 0$; wells once drilled cannot "flow out" of the resource. With all costs fixed, production continues as long as the natural drive forces persist.

Observe first that if it pays to drill any wells at all, then at some point $K > 0$, and, by (IB.3), K can never fall. Hence, $\dot{X} = 0$ in (IB.1) if and only if $x = 0$, i.e., the resource is not in equilibrium until well output is zero. The resource equilibrium set, defined by $F(X, K) = 0$ in system II is here defined by the condition $g(0, \underline{X}) = 0$, where $X = \underline{X}$ is the depleted level of the oil reservoir (Figure 7). That is, the primary or free-flow stage of recovery ends at $X = \underline{X}$, when $x = 0$. Similarly, equilibrium in the industry, defined by the function $I(X, K) = 0$ in system II, is here defined by (IB.2) and (IB.3) with $\dot{K} = 0$, or $C_0/p = g(KC_0/p, X)$. Writing the total differential of this last equation and solving for

dK/dX, gives the slope of $I(X, K)=0$:

$$\left.\frac{dK}{dX}\right|_{\dot{K}=0} = -\frac{pg_1}{C_0 g_2} > 0. \tag{5.3}$$

Hence, the equilibrium size of the industry is a strictly increasing function of the size of the untapped oil reservoir, X.

The phase diagram for the competitive exploitation of an oil reservoir will therefore appear as in Figure 7. Initially, the system is at $P_0(K=0, X=\overline{X})$, where $\overline{X}$ is the initial level of the oil reservoir stock. Since $I(X, K)=0$ is shown above P_0, it pays for drilling firms to exploit the resource. Hence $\dot{K}>0$, $\dot{X}=-Kx<0$, and the state of the system moves along some path to a point P on $I(X, K)=0$ as shown. Thereafter, $\dot{K}=0$, but the stock decline, $\dot{X}=-Kx<0$, proceeds apace until $x=0$ at P^*. The reservoir is depleted, the wells capped and abandoned (unless pumping is profitable).

E. *Timber*

Timber resources are replenishable, but we assume no significant production externalities either from population scarcity or crowding by producers. These assumptions may also apply to exhausted historical species like the whooping crane and the American bison (if both species were so easily harvested that cost was not influenced by population mass). System (IA) becomes:

$$\dot{X} = f(X) - Kx \tag{IC.1}$$

$$p = C_1(x) \tag{IC.2}$$

$$\dot{K} = \delta[px - C(x)] \tag{C.3}$$

(IC.2) determines x^0. If $px^0 - C(x^0) > 0$ harvesting is profitable, and firms enter the resource. Eventually the entire stand, and all new growth during the exploitation period is exhausted, as illustrated in Figure 8. Such is the demise of an unappropriated replenishable resource which does not exhibit external diseconomies to the industry.

VI. *Centralized Fishery Management: Sole Ownership and Regulated Competition*

In the literature of fishery economics the important papers by H. Gordon [6] and A. Scott [11] have emphasized the advantages of unified management or "sole ownership" of the fishing ground as distinct from the unregulated decentralized exploitation of the resource. Sole ownership permits the social costs of production to be borne privately with the result that the private producer has the incentive to manage the

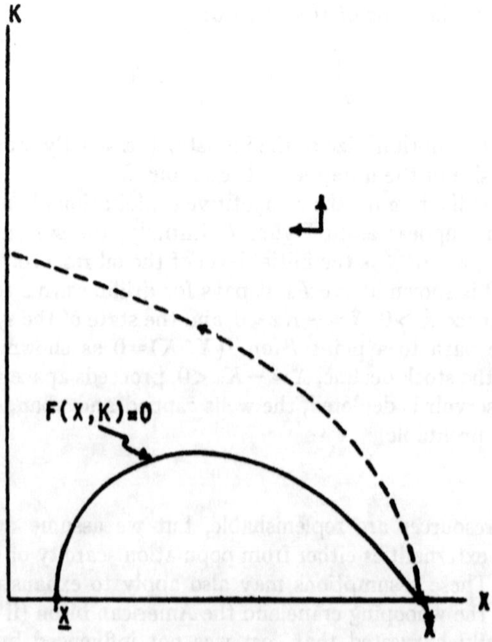

FIGURE 8

resource in the interests of society as well as his own. To see how these results follow using the competitive model of this paper, we must develop the contrasting model of centralized management.

We assume with Gordon and Scott that there are many fishing grounds so that centralizing the ownership (or right of access) of any one does not introduce monopoly elements.[9] We continue to assume steady-state equilibrium, $\dot{X}=0$. Under centralized management x, X and K will all be decision variables subject to control, in the interest of profit, by the sole owner. His profit function will be $\pi = pKx - KC(x, X, K)$ which is to be maximized with respect to (x, X, K), subject to $\dot{X} = f(X) - Kx = 0$. The Lagrangean is thus

$$\Psi = pKx - KC(x, X, K) + \lambda[f(X) - Kx],$$

and the first order conditions for an interior maximum can be written:

[9] This assumption is not essential, but keeps the arithmetic simpler. If sole ownership leads also to monopoly, we might still study the efficiency implication of the former uncontaminated by monopoly effects by imposing as an *additional constraint* upon the sole owner the price control condition $\rho(Kx) \leq Kx\bar{p}$, where $\bar{p}$ is the maximum selling price permitted.

$$\frac{\partial \Psi}{\partial x} = pK - KC_1 - \lambda K = 0$$

$$\frac{\partial \Psi}{\partial X} = - KC_2 + \lambda f'(X) = 0$$

$$\frac{\partial \Psi}{\partial K} = px - KC_3 - C - \lambda x = 0$$

An interior maximum must therefore satisfy the system

$$f(X) = Kx \tag{6.1}$$

$$p - C_1 = \lambda \tag{6.2}$$

$$p - \frac{C}{x} - \frac{KC_3}{x} = \lambda \tag{6.3}$$

$$\lambda = \frac{KC_2}{f'} \tag{6.4}$$

By way of interpreting these conditions, note that total fleet catch, Kx, can be increased either by increasing catch per vessel, x, or by expanding the fleet, K. The Lagrange multiplier λ, in this instance, is the marginal profitability of the total fleet catch (or yield of the fish mass). Condition (6.2) requires the marginal profitability of increasing catch by intensive use of the fleet (i.e., by increasing x) to be equal to the marginal profitability of total fleet catch, λ. Condition (6.3) requires the marginal profitability of the catch from fleet expansion to equal λ. Thus (6.2) and (6.3) state that profitability at the intensive and extensive capital margins must be equal. Finally, KC_2/f' is the marginal external or social cost of the fleet catch. An increase in catch tending to lower the fish mass contributes fishing costs external to the individual boats. Since C_2 is negative while f' may be negative or positive, the question arises as to whether a maximum can occur with negative marginal social cost. It is easy to prove that a global maximum cannot occur at an X^* such that $f'(X^*)>0$. Suppose we have equations (6.1)−(6.4) satisfied by a point (x^*, X^*, K^*), with $f'(X^*)>0$. Then we know from the properties of $f(X)$, that there is an $X^{**}>X^*$ such that $f'(X^{**})<0$, and $K^*x^* = f(X^*) = f(X^{**})$. But since $C_2<0$, $C(x^*, X^*, K^*)>C(x^*, X^{**}, K^*)$ It follows that the point (x^*, X^{**}, K^*) satisfies the constraint, and yields a greater profit. Hence, $f'<0$ and $KC_2/f'>0$ in (6.4).[10]

Under competitive harvesting KC_2/f' is a social cost which does not

[10] Imposing a global maximum criterion is essential here since a "solution" with $X=X^*$ may not only satisfy (6.1)–(6.4) but also the corresponding second-order conditions for a relative interior maximum.

affect firm behavior; but this cost is "privatized" when property rights are vested in a central manager-owner who adjusts his operations according to (6.2) and (6.4) to account for these social costs. Similarly will the central manager adjust for the effects of boat crowding over the fishing ground. Thus in (6.3), multiplying through by x, px is the gross marginal revenue from an additional vessel, C is the long-run direct internal cost, while $KC_3+\lambda x$ is the long-run marginal external social cost of operating an additional vessel. An addition to the fleet produces external crowding cost at the rate KC_3, and external fish scarcity cost at the rate λx.

For the sole owner when $C_2 \equiv C_3 \equiv 0$, we have the conditions which could be postulated to apply to *appropriated* timber resources. With the appropriation of forest property rights comes an incentive to "conserve," and the forest will not be wiped out as in our previous model. The first order conditions become:

$$f(X) = Kx$$

$$p - C_1 = \lambda$$

$$C_1 = \frac{C}{x}$$

$$f'(X) = 0$$

We see that only in the absence of resource stock externalities is it optimal to maintain the resource stock at the level which maximizes recruitment or sustainable yield, where $f'(X^0)=0$.[11]

[11] This result could be misleading in that it conflicts with some of the forestry economics literature [7], which contains valid arguments against the objective of maximizing sustainable yield. I do not argue that forest managers "should" maximize sustainable yield. This is simply a result of the assumptions made above, and I do not have any commitment to the assumptions. In a model of maximization over time and/or in a model in which forest husbanding costs are introduced and assumed to depend upon forest stock, sustainable yield will no longer be maximized in an optimal program.

With maximization over time, the discounting process will associate interest cost with X because forest growth depends upon X. Even in a static model, if husbanding costs depend upon X, we must then write cost as $C(x, X)$, not because of externalities measured by X, as in fishing, but because appropriation brings the incentive to incur costs of cultivating the stock. In such a case, the first order conditions for the sole forest owner are:

$$f(X) = Kx$$

$$p - C_1 = \lambda$$

$$C_1 = \frac{C}{x}$$

$$\lambda = \frac{KC_2}{f'}$$

However, in contrast with the fishing model, $C_2 > 0$ (husbanding costs increase with the stock). Consequently, for a global maximum, $f' > 0$, and the optimally managed stock is lower than the stock corresponding to maximum sustainable yield.

By comparing (6.1)–(6.4) with the system (IA.1)–(IA.3), where $\dot{K}=\dot{X}=0$ in the latter, we contrast sole ownership with decentralized competitive recovery in the stationary state. The two systems differ only in that the sole owner perceives a *unit catch* cost, $\lambda=KC_2/f'$, and an *annual boat* cost $KC_3+\lambda x$, which is not incurred by the decentralized competitive fisherman. Theoretically, then, the problem of regulating competitive recovery can be stated as one of imposing these unperceived social costs on the industry. The partial equilibrium solution to the regulation problem is to levy an extraction fee $\mathsf{U}=KC_2/f'$ per unit of catch unloaded at the wharf, plus an annual license fee $L=KC_3$ on each fishing vessel.[12] As a consequence profit after taxes to each competitive fishing vessel is

$$\pi^* = px - C(x, X, K) - L - \mathsf{U}x.$$

If each fisherman chooses x to maximize π^*, and fishermen, with their boats, enter the industry as long as $\pi^*>0$, the equilibrium conditions become

$$f(X) = Kx \tag{6.5}$$

$$p - C_1 = \mathsf{U} \tag{6.6}$$

$$p - \frac{C}{x} - \frac{L}{x} = \mathsf{U} \tag{6.7}$$

This system is identical with (6.1)–(6.4) for centralized management provided only that the regulating authorities are omniscient enough to fix $\mathsf{U}=\lambda=KC_2/f'$, and $L=KC_3$ at optimizing valves satisfying (6.1)–(6.4).[13]

APPENDIX

In this appendix we consider some qualitative properties of the system (I.1)–(I.3) or (II.1)–(II.2), particularly as the system is illustrated in Figure 2.

The following qualitative restrictions on the cost function will be assumed: $C_1>0$, $C_2<0$, $C_3\geq 0$, $C_{11}>0$, $C_{12}<0$, $C_{13}\geq 0$. Also it is assumed that

[12] Regulatory devices other than taxes or fees could, of course, be used, such as direct controls on entry [4, p. 214]. But the resulting large rents may induce investment in gear improvement, more intense fishing, and other operating changes which invite more detailed controls. In practice, such direct controls have almost invariably taken the form of devices that reduce efficiency [4, p. 207].

[13] There are, of course, other important aspects of the problem of optimal fishery regulation. Of particular importance is the problem of regulating mesh size as a means of selective harvesting [1, 14]. The idea behind mesh control is to limit the harvest to the older, and larger, members of the species whose growth rates are considerably slower than those of the younger members. The present paper has also omitted any explicit analysis of the problem of interspecies equilibrium where more than a single species have commercial value. There is also the interesting problem of optimization over time for centrally managed recovery—a problem in Pontryagin control theory. Such extensions will be treated in separate papers.

the demand (or average revenue) function, $\rho(Kx)/Kx$, is monotone decreasing in Kx. Hence $\rho'<\rho/Kx$, and therefore from (I.2) $\rho'<C_1$.

We first examine the slopes in phase space along the equilibrium sets $\dot{K}=F(X, K)=0$ and $\dot{K}=I(X, K)=0$. Setting $\dot{K}=0$, differentiating the equations (I.1) and (I.2), and eliminating dx/dX by substitution, we solve for

$$\text{(A.1)} \qquad \left.\frac{dK}{dX}\right|_{\dot{X}=0} = \frac{(C_1 + xC_{11} - \rho')f' + KxC_{12}}{x(xC_{11} - KC_{13})}$$

If $C_{13}=0$, or if $KC_{13}<xC_{11}$, the denominator of this expression is positive. Since $C_{12}<0$, $\rho'<C_1$, with $f'\gtreqless 0$ according as $X\lesseqgtr X^0$ it follows that

$$\left.\frac{dK}{dX}\right|_{\dot{X}=0}$$

is either (i) always negative or (ii) nonnegative for all $X\leq\hat{X}<X^0$, and negative for $X>\hat{X}$. The curve for $F(X, K)=0$ in Figure 2 illustrates this second case.

Setting $\dot{K}=0$, differentiating (I.2) and (I.3), and eliminating dx/dX by substitution, we solve for

$$\text{(A.2)} \qquad \left.\frac{dK}{dX}\right|_{\dot{K}=0} = \frac{KxC_2C_{11} + K(\rho' - C_1)(xC_{12} - C_2)}{(\rho' - C_1)KC_3 + (\rho' - C_1)x(xC_{11} - KC_{13}) - KxC_{11}C_3}$$

If $C_{13}=0$, or $KC_{13}<xC_{11}$, the denominator in (A.2) is negative. If $xC_{12}-C_2>0$, the numerator is negative, and

$$\left.\frac{dK}{dX}\right|_{\dot{K}=0}$$

is positive, but if $xC_{12}-C_2<0$,

$$\left.\frac{dK}{dK}\right|_{\dot{K}=0}$$

may change sign. The curve for $I(X, K)=0$ in Figure 2 illustrates a case in which

$$\left.\frac{dK}{dX}\right|_{\dot{K}=0}$$

changes signs once, from positive to negative as X increases from zero. From (A.2) it is clear that many other configurations are compatible with the stated qualitative restrictions.

Now consider the directions of motion in phase space of points in the partitions A–E of Figure 2. Differentiating (II.1), or (I.1) and (I.2), with X fixed, gives

$$\text{(A.3)} \qquad \frac{\partial \dot{X}}{\partial K} = F_K = \frac{x(KC_{13} - xC_{11})}{C_1 + xC_{11} - \rho'} \,.$$

The denominator is strictly positive. If $C_{13}=0$, or $KC_{13}<xC_{11}$ then $F_K<0$. It follows that $\dot{X}<0$ for all points above the $F(X, K)=0$ curve in Figure 2, and $\dot{X}>0$ for all points below this curve.

Differentiating (II. 2), or (I.2) and (I.3), with X fixed, gives

$$\text{(A.4)} \qquad \frac{\partial K}{\partial K} = I_K = -\frac{\delta x}{K}\left\{\frac{(\rho' - C_1)(KC_{13} - xC_{11})}{C_1 + xC_{11} - \rho'} + \frac{KC_3}{x}\right\}$$

Repeating the previous restrictions on C_{13} and C_{11}, we see that $I_K<0$. It follows that $\dot{K}<0$ for all points above $I(X, K)=0$ in Figure 2 and $\dot{K}>0$ for all points below this curve.

In the special case in which price is constant to the exploited resource $p\equiv\rho/Kx$, $\rho'=p=C_1$, and (A.1) reduces to (5.2) in the text, while (A.2) becomes (5.1).

References

1. R. J. H. Beverton and S. V. Holt, *On the Dynamics of Exploited Fish Populations*, Ministry of Agriculture, Fisheries and Food, Fishery Investigations, Ser. II, Vol. XIX, London 1957.
2. F. T. Christy and A. Scott, *The Common Wealth in Ocean Fisheries.* Baltimore 1965.
3. J. A. Crutchfield and A. Zellner, *Economic Aspects of the Pacific Halibut Fishery*, Fishery Industrial Research I, U. S. Department of the Interior, Washington 1962.
4. J. A. Crutchfield, "The Marine Fisheries: A Problem in International Cooperation," *Am. Econ. Rev., Proc.*, May 1964, *54*, 207–18.
5. P. Davidson, "Public Policy Problems of the Domestic Crude Oil Industry," *Am. Econ. Rev.*, March 1963, *53*, 85–108.
6. H. S. Gordon, "The Economic Theory of a Common Property Resource: The Fishery," *Jour. Pol. Econ.*, April 1954, *62*, 124–42.
7. G. K. Goundry, "Forest Management and the Theory of Capital," *Can. Jour. Econ. and Pol. Sci.*, Aug. 1960, 439–51.
8. A. J. Lotka, *Elements of Mathematical Biology*, New York 1956.
9. A. L. MacKinney, F. Schumacher and L. Chaiken, "Construction of Yield Tables for Nonnormal Loblolly Pine Stands," *Jour. Agric. Res.*, April 1937, *54*, 531–45.
10. S. V. Pirson, *Elements of Reservoir Engineering.* New York 1950.
11. A. Scott, "The Fishery: The Objectives of Sole Ownership," *Jour. Pol. Econ.*, April 1955, *63*, 116–24.
12. ———, *Natural Resources: The Economics of Conservation.* Toronto 1955.
13. ———, "The Theory of the Mine Under Conditions of Certainty," Ch. 2 in Mason Gaffney, ed., *Extractive Resources and Taxation*, Madison 1967.
14. R. Turvey, "Optimization in Fishery Regulation," *Am. Econ. Rev.*, March 1964, *54*, 64–76.

CHAPTER 20

Production and Investment in Natural Resource Industries

By OSCAR R. BURT AND RONALD G. CUMMINGS*

There has been a recent tendency for economists to view natural resource scarcity as a diminishing threat to man's existence and his ability to produce an abundant supply of worldly goods (see John V. Krutilla). This change in view has emanated from the world's experience of the last few decades with technological development, and the absence of any evidence that this rapid accumulation of technical knowledge will cease.

In some respects, one might think that modern technology has removed the need for an economic theory of conservation (temporal allocation) of natural resources. On the other hand, conservation of natural resources can now be looked upon with less emotion since the dire consequences of too rapid exploitation are no longer a threat. The question of conservation is thus a cold economic problem removed from many of its older value connotations.

There is indeed, considerable effort taking place in the economics profession to fill this need for a quantitative economic theory of conservation; however, with one exception (Vernon Smith), focus has been limited to *specific* resources. Earlier works by Lewis C. Gray and Harold Hotelling concerning the "Theory of the Mine" have recently been extended in numerous papers (see R. Cummings and O. Burt, Richard L. Gordon, Anthony Scott 1967). Problems associated with petroleum production are considered in Paul Davidson, and the fishery is considered in J. A. Crutchfield and Arnold Zellner, H. Scott Gordon, James Quirk and Vernon Smith, Anthony Scott (1955), and Ralph Turvey. An extensive literature exists on the temporal allocation of groundwater; two recent contributions are Gardner Brown and Charles B. McGuire, and Burt.[1]

A logical problem has been encountered, however, in efforts to examine the optimum allocation of a natural resource over time without explicitly considering the rate of investment associated with resource use. This difficulty stems from the long life of many capital items used in the process of exploiting the natural resource. Earlier studies have either tacitly or explicitly amortized costs of investment associated with resource use and proceeded as though all costs of production were essentially variable. Smith was the first to explicitly bring capital investment into a production model for natural resources, and his work was followed by the authors where only exhaustible resources were considered. More recently, Quirk and Smith have introduced a dynamic model of the fishery in which capital investment is treated explicitly.

It seems then that there is a need for a comprehensive model for simultaneously optimizing the rate of resource use and investment in natural resource industries

* The authors are, respectively, professor of agricultural economics and economics at Montana State University, and economist with Resources for the Future, Inc. This article is a contribution from Montana Agricultural Experiment Station, Journal Series No. 133.

[1] This list is by no means meant to be all inclusive concerning works related to natural resource use. No discussion of conservation economics would be complete without mention of the many contributions of S. V. Ciriacy-Wantrup.

in general. Such a model should be sufficiently general that the functional relations used could be adapted and the results applicable to any specific resource. Earlier reports concerning specific resources would fall out as a special case of a general theory concerning the intertemporal allocation of natural resources.

The purpose of this paper is to attempt to provide such a model. Optimization is viewed from the standpoint of society; however, our "social benefit" function may easily be viewed as a profit function and the results applied to the optimum behavior of the firm. The paper takes the following form: in Section I, a general model for social production and investment in natural resource industries is specified. In Section II, an economic interpretation of the characteristics for optimum time paths of production and investment are discussed under the assumption that society's planning horizon is finite. In Section III, equilibrium conditions under an infinite planning horizon are considered. Finally, in Section IV, our results are generalized to include multiple interrelated resources. The Appendix takes up some technical problems associated with the infinite planning horizon and second-order conditions for optimization.

I. *A General Production Model*

We begin our analysis with the following definitions and assumptions. Let $t=0$ and $t=T$ be the beginning and end, respectively, of society's planning horizon. This period will be taken as finite, but later in our analysis we shall consider the case where $T\rightarrow\infty$. Define u_t as the rate at which the resource is used at time t, x_t as the amount of resource in stock at t, and y_t as capital stocks at t. The variable u_t is assumed subject to the constraints

$$(1)\quad 0 \leq u_t \leq h(x_t, y_t) \quad t = 0, \ldots, T-1$$

where $h(x_t, y_t)$ is assumed concave. The relationship $h(x_t, y_t)$ is such that larger resource and capital stocks allow for larger rates of production, i.e., its first partial derivatives are nonnegative.

In referring to u_t, we use the terms rate of production, rate of extraction, and rate of use as though they were synonymous. One or the other is most appropriate in a particular resource industry, but neither fits all situations. In some applications, the physical and biological nature of the resource may require u_t to be an indirect control. For example, an application to livestock range management is conveniently formulated with u_t defined as the number of animal units per acre, and the resource stock variable might be a composite index of range conditions (instead of a physical stock of an easily quantified natural resource such as groundwater). Another example is found in the discussion of the commercial fishery by Crutchfield and Zellner, where x_t is some measure of stocks of the fish specie in the sea and u_t is a measure of "fishing effort."' However, u_t might be defined in the same units as x_t by using a fixed functional relationship between tons of fish harvested and the pair of variables, fishing effort and specie-stocks. At a given level of stocks, a specific fishing effort would imply a unique amount of harvested fish, and vice versa, so that the choice of a control variable is arbitrary.

At the beginning of any period $t+1$, resource and capital stocks are given by the difference equations,

$$(2)\quad x_{t+1} = x_t + g(u_t, x_t) \qquad x_0 = a$$

$$(3)\quad y_{t+1} = y_t - D(u_t, v_t, y_t) \qquad y_0 = b$$

$$t = 0, 1, \ldots, T-1$$

where v_t is gross addition to capital stocks at t. The only restriction on v_t is nonnegativity; no upper limit is specified. The functions $g(u_t, x_t)$ and $D(u_t, v_t, y_t)$ are assumed concave and convex, respectively.

The function $g(u_t, x_t)$ is net additions

to resource stocks during period t. The relationship $g(u_t, x_t)$ is such that (relatively) larger resource stocks and smaller rates of extraction result in greater additions to resource stocks, i.e., $\partial g/\partial x_t \geq 0$ and $\partial g/\partial u_t \leq 0$. The simplest case where u_t is in the same units as x_t would usually imply $\partial g/\partial u_t = -1$. In the case of groundwater, $g(u_t, x_t)$ is recharge to the groundwater aquifer minus the amount of water pumped. In a mineral industry, $g(u_t, x_t)$ is the difference between new discoveries and quantity extracted during the period t. For the fishery, u_t is usually defined as fishing effort instead of quantity of fish harvested, in which case, $g(u_t, x_t)$ reflects a combination of ecological and technological growth factors associated with the particular species of fish (see Smith).

The function $D(u_t, v_t, y_t)$ is a depreciation function for capital stocks which measures net changes during period t. A non-decreasing relation is assumed between depreciation and the rate of resource use as well as for the level of capital stocks, while a non-increasing relation is assumed for gross investment, i.e., $\partial D/\partial u_t \geq 0$, $\partial D/\partial y_t \geq 0$, $\partial D/\partial v_t \leq 0$. The simplest formulation would define v_t in the same units as y_t, giving $\partial D/\partial v_t = -1$, but it would be advantageous in some applications to have a more subtle relation between y_{t+1} and v_t. The presence of u_t in the depreciation function measures the consumption of capital associated with current production.[2]

If capital stocks, y_t, and capital investment, v_t, are limited in scalar measures, they must be interpreted as indices specific to a particular natural resource industry. At this point, we conceive them as such indices, but will later develop the case where the variables u_t, v_t, x_t, and y_t are vectors.

The functions $g(x_t, u_t)$ and $D(u_t, v_t, y_t)$ could be made explicitly dependent on time to allow for changing technical knowledge, but the same effect can be accomplished by defining capital measures specific to the technology at t=0, and taking changes in technology into account through the social benefit function (introduced below). Advancing technology would then be measured indirectly through fewer inputs used to achieve the same measure of capital investment in units of the index defined for t=0. This approach requires only that the benefit function be made explicitly a function of time.

It is convenient for later discussion to introduce a concave terminal value function for the natural resource and capital stocks, $\psi(x_T, y_T)$. It is difficult to conceive terminal stocks having value to society at the end of its planning horizon. Nevertheless, the function $\psi(x_T, y_T)$ is useful to analyze the implications of an infinite time-horizon.

We assume the existence of a concave social benefit function in the general form $B_t(u_t, v_t, x_t, y_t)$, and further assume that society wishes to maximize the present value of social benefits attributable to resource use during the time interval [0, T].

The rationale for including u_t in the benefit function is quite obvious since u_t is the rate of use of the resource which is assumed to have value in economic production, or as a direct consumption good. Likewise, v_t is a measure of periodic capital investment and has opportunity costs in the economy. The role of x_t and y_t is a little more subtle. Resource stocks, x_t, reflect accessibility of the resource. For example, large stocks of fish permit capture of a given quantity at a lower cost, and large stocks of a mineral are associated with relatively accessible and rich ores.

[2] The authors wish to express their appreciation to Vernon Smith for his comments on the form of the depreciation function during the presentation of an earlier draft of this paper at the University of Massachusetts.

$$(5)\qquad L = \sum_{t=0}^{T-1} \Big\{ B_t(u_t, v_t, x_t, y_t)\beta^t - \lambda_{t+1}\beta^{t+1}[x_{t+1} - x_t - g(u_t, x_t)] - \mu_{t+1}\beta^{t+1}[y_{t+1} - y_t + D(u_t, v_t, y_t)] - \nu_t\beta^t[u_t - h(x_t, y_t)]\Big\} - \lambda_0(x_0 - a) - \mu_0(y_0 - b) + \beta^T\psi(x_T, y_T),$$

Capital stocks, y_t, measure the amount of fixed capital invested in the natural resource industry, and thus higher stocks of capital imply lower costs of production per period.

All of the relationships involved are for a specific situation and the influence of the variables must be interpreted within that context. Relatively high resource stocks merely mean higher stocks at a particular point in time as compared to what the level might be under a different temporal allocation policy.

Let $\beta = 1/(1+r)$, where r is the appropriate positive discount rate. Since analysis of a single natural resource industry is a partial analysis relative to national economic growth, the discount rate should reflect the opportunity cost of capital to the remainder of the economy, and not a social discount rate per se.[3]

Our postulated societal optimization problem, vis-a-vis the use of a particular natural resource, is then given by

$$(4)\quad \operatorname{Max}\left[\sum_{t=0}^{T-1} B_t(u_t, v_t, x_t, y_t)\beta^t + \beta^T\psi(x_T, y_T)\right]$$

subject to

a) $x_{t+1} - x_t - g(u_t, x_t) = 0$

b) $y_{t+1} - y_t + D(u_t, v_t, y_t) = 0$

c) $u_t - h(x_t, y_t) \leq 0,$

d) $u_t, v_t, x_t, y_t \geq 0$

e) $x_0 = a$ and $y_0 = b$

where the variables of optimization are u_t, v_t, $t=0, 1, \ldots, T-1$, and x_t, y_t, $t=1, \ldots, T$.

We assume that the functions in (4) are continuous and possess continuous first partial derivatives with respect to each argument. Following Kuhn and Tucker we form the Lagrangian Expression (5) where the multipliers, λ_t, μ_t, and ν_t are written with a discounting factor for the purpose of economic interpretation. This is also the purpose of including the terms associated with λ_0 and μ_0 which are, in a sense, redundant for the optimization problem.

As a notational device, the subscript t on the functions g, D, and h in the partial derivative of these functions implies that the partial derivative is evaluated with its arguments set equal to their magnitudes in period t. For example, $\partial g_t/\partial x_t$ is the partial derivative of $g(u, x)$ with respect to x, evaluated at $u = u_t$ and $x = x_t$.

Partial derivatives of L are listed below for future reference:

$$(6)\quad \frac{\partial L}{\partial u_t} = \left[\frac{\partial B_t}{\partial u_t} + \beta\lambda_{t+1}\frac{\partial g_t}{\partial u_t} - \beta\mu_{t+1}\frac{\partial D_t}{\partial u_t} - \nu_t\right]\beta^t,$$

$$t = 0, 1, \ldots, T-1$$

[3] For an exceptional treatment of the fishery resource within the framework of General Equilibrium Theory, see Quirk and Smith.

$$(7)\quad \frac{\partial L}{\partial v_t} = \left[\frac{\partial B_t}{\partial v_t} - \beta\mu_{t+1}\frac{\partial D_t}{\partial v_t}\right]\beta^t,$$

$$t = 0, 1, \ldots, T-1$$

$$(8)\quad \frac{\partial L}{\partial x_0} = \frac{\partial B_0}{\partial x_0} + \beta\lambda_1\left(1 + \frac{\partial g_0}{\partial x_0}\right) + \nu_0\frac{\partial h_0}{\partial x_0} - \lambda_0$$

$$\frac{\partial L}{\partial x_t} = \left[\frac{\partial B_t}{\partial x_t} - \lambda_t + \beta\lambda_{t+1}\left(1 + \frac{\partial g_t}{\partial x_t}\right) + \nu_t\frac{\partial h_t}{\partial x_t}\right]\beta^t,$$

$$t = 1, 2, \ldots, T-1$$

$$\frac{\partial L}{\partial x_T} = \left[\frac{\partial \psi}{\partial x_T} - \lambda_T\right]\beta^T$$

$$(9)\quad \frac{\partial L}{\partial y_0} = \frac{\partial B_0}{\partial y_0} + \beta\mu_1\left(1 - \frac{\partial D_0}{\partial y_0}\right) + \nu_0\frac{\partial h_0}{\partial y_0} - \mu_0$$

$$\frac{\partial L}{\partial y_t} = \left[\frac{\partial B_t}{\partial y_t} - \mu_t + \beta\mu_{t+1}\left(1 - \frac{\partial D_t}{\partial y_t}\right) + \nu_t\frac{\partial h_t}{\partial y_t}\right]\beta^t$$

$$t = 1, 2, \ldots, T-1$$

$$\frac{\partial L}{\partial y_T} = \left[\frac{\partial \psi}{\partial y_T} - \mu_T\right]\beta^T$$

We wish to derive values for the multipliers λ_t and μ_t by an iterative process explained below. In order to do this, we must assume that x_t and y_t will be positive for all t, $0 \leq t \leq T$. With but rare exceptions, it seems plausible to expect that stocks of the natural resource will indeed remain at positive levels throughout the period of economic production. In some cases, zero stocks would make it impossible to produce at positive levels of production again; biological resources such as fish and wildlife are examples.

It also seems that capital stocks would be at positive levels throughout the period of economic production. Capital stocks may be zero initially and for some time before production begins, but once production is started, one would expect stocks of capital to remain positive until the resource industry is abandoned. At any rate, we can think of a cycle of production where both natural resources and capital stocks are positive on an interval [0, T], and the terminal value function $\psi(x_T, y_T)$ reflects the future value of the industry for $t > T$.

Necessary conditions for a maximum in (4) are that (6) through (9) be nonpositive. If, at any t, a variable of optimization is positive, the associated partial derivative of L must then be zero. In view of the above discussion on positive levels of natural resource and capital stocks, we set the partial derivatives in (8) and (9) equal to zero as necessary conditions for maximum discounted social benefits within a production cycle.

The result for (8) is a recurrence relation in λ_t,

$$(10)\quad \lambda_t = \frac{\partial B_t}{\partial x_t} + \nu_t\frac{\partial h_t}{\partial x_t} + \beta\lambda_{t+1}\left(1 + \frac{\partial g_t}{\partial x_t}\right)$$

Iterating the above recursion for t, t+1, . . . , T yields equation (11). A comparative derivation from (9) gives equation (12).

At this point, we make a short digression to obtain simplifications in (11) and (12). Differentiating equations (2) and (3) we get

$$(13)\quad \frac{\partial x_{t+1}}{\partial x_t} = 1 + \frac{\partial g_t}{\partial x_t}$$

$$\frac{\partial y_{t+1}}{\partial y_t} = 1 - \frac{\partial D_t}{\partial y_t}$$

$$\lambda_t = \frac{\partial B_t}{\partial x_t} + \nu_t \frac{\partial h_t}{\partial x_t} + \beta\left[\frac{\partial B_{t+1}}{\partial x_{t+1}} + \nu_{t+1}\frac{\partial h_{t+1}}{\partial x_{t+1}} + \beta\lambda_{t+2}\left(1 + \frac{\partial g_{t+1}}{\partial x_{t+1}}\right)\right]\left(1 + \frac{\partial g_t}{\partial x_t}\right) \tag{11}$$

$$\vdots$$

$$= \left(\frac{\partial B_t}{\partial x_t} + \nu_t \frac{\partial h_t}{\partial x_t}\right) + \sum_{j=t+1}^{T-1}\left\{\left(\frac{\partial B_j}{\partial x_j} + \nu_i \frac{\partial g_i}{\partial x_j}\right)\prod_{i=t}^{j-1}\beta\left(1 + \frac{\partial g_i}{\partial x_i}\right)\right\}$$

$$+ \frac{\partial \psi}{\partial x_T}\prod_{i=t}^{T-1}\beta\left(1 + \frac{\partial g_i}{\partial x_i}\right)$$

$$\mu_t = \left(\frac{\partial B_t}{\partial y_t} + \nu_t \frac{\partial h_t}{\partial y_t}\right) + \sum_{j=t+1}^{T-1}\left[\left(\frac{\partial B_j}{\partial y_j} + \nu_i \frac{\partial h_j}{\partial y_i}\right)\prod_{i=t}^{j-1}\beta\left(1 + \frac{\partial D_i}{\partial y_i}\right)\right] \tag{12}$$

$$+ \frac{\partial \psi}{\partial y_T}\prod_{i=t}^{T-1}\beta\left(1 - \frac{\partial D_i}{\partial y_i}\right)$$

$$\lambda_t = \sum_{j=t}^{T-1}\beta^{j-t}\left(\frac{\partial B_j}{\partial x_j} + \nu_j \frac{\partial h_j}{\partial x_j}\right)\frac{\partial x_j}{\partial x_t} + \beta^{T-t}\frac{\partial \psi}{\partial x_T}\frac{\partial x_T}{\partial x_t}, \tag{15}$$

$$\mu_t = \sum_{j=t}^{T-1}\beta^{j-t}\left(\frac{\partial B_j}{\partial y_j} + \nu_j \frac{\partial h_j}{\partial y_i}\right)\frac{\partial y_j}{\partial y_t} + \beta^{T-t}\frac{\partial \psi}{\partial y_T}\frac{\partial y_T}{\partial y_t}, \qquad t = 1, 2, \ldots, T. \tag{16}$$

$$\frac{\partial B_t}{\partial u_t} - \nu_t \leqq \left[\sum_{j=t+1}^{T-1}\beta^{j-t}\left(\frac{\partial B_j}{\partial x_j} + \nu_j \frac{\partial h_j}{\partial x_j}\right)\frac{\partial x_j}{\partial x_{t+1}} + \beta^{T-t}\frac{\partial \psi}{\partial x_T}\frac{\partial x_T}{\partial x_{t+1}}\right]\left(-\frac{\partial g_t}{\partial u_t}\right) \tag{17}$$

$$+ \left[\sum_{j=t+1}^{T-1}\beta^{j-t}\left(\frac{\partial B_j}{\partial y_j} + \nu_j \frac{\partial h_j}{\partial y_j}\right)\frac{\partial y_j}{\partial y_{t+1}} + \beta^{T-t}\frac{\partial \psi}{\partial y_T}\frac{\partial y_T}{\partial y_{t+1}}\right]\left(\frac{\partial D_t}{\partial u_t}\right)$$

$$\frac{\partial B_t}{\partial v_t} \leqq \left[\sum_{j=t+1}^{T-1}\beta^{j-t}\left(\frac{\partial B_j}{\partial y_j} + \nu_j \frac{\partial h_j}{\partial y_j}\right)\frac{\partial y_j}{\partial y_{t+1}} + \beta^{T-t}\frac{\partial \psi}{\partial y_T}\frac{\partial y_T}{\partial y_{t+1}}\right]\left(\frac{\partial D_t}{\partial v_t}\right) \tag{18}$$

Successively applying the chain rule for implicit functions,

$$\frac{\partial x_j}{\partial x_t} = \prod_{i=t}^{j-1}\left(1 + \frac{\partial g_i}{\partial x_i}\right), \qquad j > t \tag{14}$$

$$\frac{\partial y_j}{\partial y_t} = \prod_{i=t}^{j-1}\left(1 - \frac{\partial D_i}{\partial y_i}\right), \qquad j > t$$

Substitution of (14) into (11) and (12) gives the simplified and more intuitive equations[4] (15) and (16).

Substituting (15) and (16), evaluated at t+1, into (6), (16) into (7), and applying the Kuhn-Tucker theorem, we find that necessary conditions for a maximum in (4) are (17) and (18). For u_t or v_t positive, relation (17) or (18) is a strict equality. We also note that ν_t is positive or zero as $u_t = h(x_t, y_t)$ or $u_t < h(x_t, y_t)$.

[4] For (15) and (16) to equal (11) and (12), the following notational adjustment must be made:

$$\prod_{i=t}^{t-1} a_i \equiv 0$$

$$
\begin{aligned}
(19)\qquad \frac{\partial B_0}{\partial u_0} - \nu_0 &= \beta\lambda_1\left(-\frac{\partial g_0}{\partial u_0}\right) + \beta\mu_1\frac{\partial D_0}{\partial u_0} \\
&= \left[\sum_{j=1}^{T-1}\beta^j\left(\frac{\partial B_j}{\partial x_j} + \nu_j\frac{\partial h_j}{\partial x_j}\right)\frac{\partial x_j}{\partial x_1} + \beta^T\frac{\partial \psi}{\partial x_T}\frac{\partial x_T}{\partial x_1}\right]\left(-\frac{\partial g_0}{\partial u_0}\right) \\
&\quad + \left[\sum_{j=1}^{T-1}\beta^j\left(\frac{\partial B_i}{\partial y_j} + \nu_j\frac{\partial h_j}{\partial y_j}\right)\frac{\partial y_j}{\partial y_1} + \beta^T\frac{\partial \psi}{\partial y_T}\frac{\partial y_T}{\partial y_1}\right]\left(\frac{\partial D_0}{\partial u_0}\right)
\end{aligned}
$$

$$
(20)\qquad \frac{\partial B_0}{\partial v_0} = \beta\mu_1\frac{\partial D_0}{\partial v_0} = \left[\sum_{j=1}^{T-1}\beta^j\left(\frac{\partial B_j}{\partial y_j} + \nu_j\frac{\partial h_j}{\partial y_j}\right)\frac{\partial y_j}{\partial y_1} + \beta^T\frac{\partial \psi}{\partial y_T}\frac{\partial y_T}{\partial y_1}\right]\left(\frac{\partial D_0}{\partial v_0}\right)
$$

An immediate conclusion from (17) and (18) is that given x_t and y_t, the optimal levels of u_t and v_t are independent of u_i and v_i, $i<t$. This is essentially a Markovian dependence structure in the decision process (see R. Bellman 1961, p. 54). The resource and capital stock variables completely summarize the impact of all previous decisions upon current and future optimal decisions.

In view of this recursive structure for optimal allocation through time, nothing is lost in generality by focusing on $t=0$ and thinking of any T-period allocation problem with x_0 and y_0 specified. Solution of (8) and (9) for λ_0 and μ_0 shows them to fit (15) and (16) for $t=0$, which justifies the previously questionable notation for these two multipliers associated with initial stocks.

Assume that u_0 and v_0 are positive at $t=0$. Then by (17) and (18), the optimum rates of production and investment are given by equations (19) and (20). Equations (19) and (20) will serve as the basis for the economic interpretations that follow.

II. *Economic Interpretations*

Attention is now focused on an interpretation of the results generated in Section I. While the solutions for u_t and v_t must be determined simultaneously within the model, we shall discuss the characteristics of optimal rates of production and investment separately.

The Optimum Time Path of Resource Use

At $t=0$, the optimum time path for production from the natural resource is given by (19). On the left-hand side of (19) is the measure of marginal social benefits attributable to an increment in resource use at $t=0$, less the imputed value of the constraint (4-c) *if* strict equality should hold at $t=0$ $\{\nu_0=0 \text{ if } u_0<h(x_0,y_0)\}$.

On the right-hand side of (19), the partial derivatives $\partial g_0/\partial u_0$ and $\partial D_0/\partial u_0$ measure the marginal influence of u_0 on resource and capital stocks. Most applications imply $\partial g_0/\partial u_0<0$, and $\partial D_0/\partial u_0=-1$ when resource use is measured in the same units as resource stocks. The latter derivative, $\partial D_0/\partial u_0$, is marginal capital consumption from current production.

The factor $\beta\lambda_1$ is the discounted value of increments to resource stocks in all future periods associated with an increment to stocks in period $t=1$. Likewise, $\beta\mu_1$ is the discounted value of increments to capital stocks in future periods associated with an increment to capital stocks in period one. The right-hand side of (19) is essentially the "user cost" reflecting " . . . the present value of future profit (social benefits) foregone by a decision to produce a unit of output today (at t=0)" (Scott 1967, p. 42) and (19) may be interpreted as the decision rule: increase production at t=0 until net marginal social benefits at t=0 (net of the "boundary cost" μ_0) equal user costs.

This economic interpretation is clarified by analyzing the separate components of $\beta\lambda_1$, as written in (19). An almost identical detailed explanation applies to $\beta\mu_1$, except that the stocks would be capital instead of the natural resource.

The term $\mu_j(\partial h_j/\partial x_j)$ is the implicit value of a marginal unit of the resource available in period j to relax the constraint $u_j \leq h(x_j, y_j)$. Thus, the sum $\partial B_j/\partial x_j + \mu_j(\partial h_j/\partial x_j)$ is the direct marginal value of the resource stock during period j, i.e., the increment to benefits in period j associated with an increment to resource stocks in the same period, *ceteris paribus.* Of course, in the terminal period, t=T, this same measure is $\partial\psi/\partial x_T$. Since no production is permitted by the model in that period, only a lump sum value is assigned to remaining stocks. These marginal values multiplied by $\partial x_j/\partial x_1$ are values which are comparable to an increment to stocks in period one instead of period j. This follows from the implicit function theorem of the calculus.

In summary, the left-hand side of (19) is marginal social value of current production and the right-hand side is our user cost consisting of two terms, 1) the discounted marginal value of a unit of resource retained in stocks instead of used in current production and 2) the discounted marginal value of capital stocks consumed by an increment to current production.

The Optimum Time Path of Social Investment

Equation (20) is most easily interpreted after multiplication by (-1). Then the left-hand side is marginal social cost of investment in the current period, while the right-hand side is the discounted value of the increment to all future capital stocks associated with an increment to current investment. The economic interpretation of the right-hand side of (20) is identical to the second cost term in (19) with the exception that the weight is $\partial D_0/\partial v_0$, the effect on current rates of depreciation of an increment in gross investment, rather than $\partial D_0/\partial u_0$.

Further Ramifications of the Model

Another interesting result is derived by solving for $\beta\mu_1$ in (20) and substituting it into (19) to get

$$(21)\quad \frac{\partial B_0}{\partial u_0} - \nu_0 = \beta\lambda_1\left(-\frac{\partial g_0}{\partial u_0}\right) - \frac{\partial B_0}{\partial v_0}\frac{\partial v_0}{\partial u_0}$$

The last term in (21) measures the capital cost associated with an increment to current production. By holding y_1 constant, total adjustment in capital at the margin must take place through variation in v_0 in order that the net effect on depreciation will be zero. Thus, $-\partial B_0/\partial v_0$ is marginal social cost with respect to current investment, and multiplication by $\partial v_0/\partial u_0$ converts it to marginal social cost with respect to current resource use insofar as associated capital consumption is concerned.

Going back to equation (14), we see that

$$(22)\quad \beta^t \frac{\partial x_t}{\partial x_1} = \beta \prod_{i=1}^{t-1}\left(1 + \frac{\partial g_i}{\partial x_i}\right)/(1 + r)$$

$$(23)\quad \beta^t \frac{\partial y_t}{\partial y_1} = \beta \prod_{i=1}^{t-1}\left(1 - \frac{\partial D_i}{\partial y_i}\right)/(1 + r)$$

The left-hand sides of (22) and (23) represent the discount factors on $(\partial B_t/\partial x_t + \nu_t\partial h_t/\partial x_t)$ and $(\partial B_t/\partial y_t + \nu_t\partial h_t/\partial y_t)$ appearing in the summations of (19) and (20).

The term $\partial g_i/\partial x_i$ measures the effect of

an incremental change in resource stocks on the rate of growth in resource stocks at period i. If resource use at t=0 results in lower resource stocks at t=1, then the product $\prod_{i=1}^{t-1}[1+(\partial g_i/\partial x_i)]$ reflects the fact that the losses in resource stocks at t=1 affect the rates of growth in the resource stock in *all* future time periods. Thus, $[1+(\partial g_i/\partial x_i)]$ may be viewed as an ecological or biological (in some cases) compounding factor. Therefore, (22) essentially represents the ratio of a compounding to a discounting factor, the former relating to productivity of the resource stock in terms of generating *additions* to resource stocks, and the latter reflecting the productivity of social capital in all lines of economic activity. If $\partial g_t/\partial x_t < r$, the net effect is a discounting in the user cost equation.

Looking at (23), the term $\partial D_i/\partial y_i$ is the marginal rate of capital decay representing the effect on the depreciation of capital stocks of an incremental change in the magnitude of capital stocks at t=i. The term $(1-\partial D_i/\partial y_i)$ may then be interpreted as an internalized (to the resource industry from society's point of view) marginal rate of capital survival. Thus, investment at t=0 yields benefits in all future periods which are discounted by the product of the social discount factor and a discount rate emanating from marginal effects on capital decay. The larger is $\partial D/\partial y$, the more severe is this discounting, and the rate of social investment in the natural resource industry at t=0 is diminished. Of course, as the marginal rate of capital decay in the resource industry becomes small, the rate of social investment in the natural resource industry is increased.

III. *Equilibrium Resource and Capital Stocks*

In this section, the implications of equilibrium stocks of the natural resource and capital are pursued. An infinite planning horizon is assumed with the social benefit function invariant through time. Essentially, the assumptions of (A−1) in the Appendix are made, although they seem stronger than is probably necessary. Under these assumptions (combined with earlier specifications of continuity and convexity), either an equilibrium must exist, or resource stocks go to zero in a finite period. An equilibrium of zero is not ruled out. Some of the technical problems associated with an infinite planning horizon are relegated to the Appendix.

The case where resource stocks go to zero in a finite period can be interpreted as a situation where discounting economically overrides maintenance of the resource stock. Of course, exhaustible resources are quite likely to fall in this category, and one would expect that the case where stocks asymptotically approach zero (the only equilibrium possible) would be the exception. From this point, we assume existence of an equilibrium and analyze its implications.

Equilibrium implies $x_t = x_{t-1} = \ldots$ and $y_t = y_{t-1} = \ldots$, which in turn implies

$$(24)\quad \begin{aligned} g(u_t, x_t) &= 0, \\ D(u_t, v_t, y_t) &= 0, \qquad \text{for all t} \end{aligned}$$

But for (24) to hold, $u_t = u_{t+1} = \ldots$ and $v_t = v_{t+1} = \ldots$.

Let us now examine the implications of constancy of these variables on the necessary conditions for maximum discounted social benefit, viz., equations (19) and (20). We drop subscripts on the variables to denote independence through time. The functions appearing in (19) and (20) are then constant over t because all the arguments are fixed at constant values u, v, x, y. Likewise, the Lagrange multipliers υ, λ, and μ will be constant over time t. The multiplier υ will very likely be zero except in the special case where $u = h(x, y)$ at equilibrium.

$$(26)\qquad \frac{\partial B}{\partial u} - \nu = \left[\sum_{j=1}^{\infty} \beta^j \left(\frac{\partial B}{\partial x} + \nu \frac{\partial h}{\partial x} \right) \left(1 + \frac{\partial g}{\partial x} \right)^{j-1} + \lim_{T\to\infty} \beta^T \frac{\partial \psi}{\partial x} \left(1 + \frac{\partial g}{\partial x} \right)^{T-1} \right] \left(- \frac{\partial g}{\partial u} \right)$$
$$+ \left[\sum_{j=1}^{\infty} \beta^j \left(\frac{\partial B}{\partial y} + \nu \frac{\partial h}{\partial y} \right) \left(1 - \frac{\partial D}{\partial y} \right)^{j-1} + \lim_{T\to\infty} \beta^T \frac{\partial \psi}{\partial y} \left(1 - \frac{\partial D}{\partial y} \right)^{T-1} \right] \left(\frac{\partial D}{\partial u} \right)$$
$$= \beta \left(\frac{\partial B}{\partial x} + \nu \frac{\partial h}{\partial x} \right) \left[1 - \beta \left(1 + \frac{\partial g}{\partial x} \right) \right]^{-1} \left(- \frac{\partial g}{\partial u} \right) + \beta \left(\frac{\partial B}{\partial y} + \nu \frac{\partial h}{\partial y} \right) \left[1 - \beta \left(1 - \frac{\partial D}{\partial y} \right) \right]^{-1} \left(\frac{\partial D}{\partial u} \right)$$

With this prelude, we start simplifying equations (19) and (20) under the assumption that the summations are convergent as $T \to \infty$. Since $g(u, x)$ and $D(u, v, x)$ are constant through time in equilibrium (their arguments are at fixed values), the partial derivatives of (14) at $t=1$ can be written

$$(25)\qquad \frac{\partial x_j}{\partial x_1} = \prod_{i=1}^{j-1} \left(1 + \frac{\partial g}{\partial x} \right) = \left(1 + \frac{\partial g}{\partial x} \right)^{j-1}$$
$$\frac{\partial y_i}{\partial y_1} \quad \prod_{i=1}^{j-1} \left(1 - \frac{\partial D}{\partial y} \right) = \left(1 - \frac{\partial D}{\partial y} \right)^{j-1}$$

Substitution of (25) into (19), and letting $T \to \infty$, we have equation (26). The corresponding derivation in (20) yields

$$(27)\qquad \frac{\partial B}{\partial v} = \beta \left(\frac{\partial B}{\partial y} + \nu \frac{\partial h}{\partial y} \right) \cdot \left[1 - \beta \left(1 - \frac{\partial D}{\partial y} \right) \right]^{-1} \left(\frac{\partial D}{\partial v} \right)$$

Convergence of the infinite sums requires that[5]

$$(28)\qquad |1 + \partial g/\partial x| < 1 + r$$
$$|1 - \partial D/\partial y| < 1 + r$$

Assumptions (A-1-b) and (A-1-c) indirectly force these conditions, but a direct examination of the implications of (28) is instructive. We would expect $\partial g/\partial x > 0$ throughout the economically relevant range of resource stocks. If the resource is fish or wildlife, $\partial g/\partial x < 0$ would imply such large populations that an increment to the population causes a net decrease for next year (starvation, disease hazards, etc., could be the cause). Logically, $\partial D/\partial y > 0$ and $|\partial D/\partial y| < 1$ since $D(u, v, y)$ is a depreciation function and y is an index of capital stocks. It is hard to imagine a case where an increment to capital stocks would be associated with a

[5] This result is similar to that obtained by Quirk and Smith. In their dynamic model of the fishery, they show that necessary and sufficient conditions for user costs to be positive (under an infinite planning horizon) is that the productivity of the fish stock in producing *additional* stocks be less than the social rate of discount (p. 16).

decrement in stocks a year later that exceeded the initial increment, *ceteris paribus*. The one reasonable possibility that could cause divergence is $\partial g/\partial x > r$, but this case also is extremely unlikely since the natural resource stocks would ultimately reach such high levels that natural phenomena would limit their unbounded growth, and ultimately $\partial g/\partial x$ would drop below r. Therefore, assumptions (A-1-b) and (A-1-c) seem quite plausible for any conceivable application.

Economic interpretation of (26) and (27) is the same as for (19) and (20). The left side of (26) is marginal social benefits with respect to resource use in the current period, while the right-hand side is the sum of two terms: 1) "capitalized value" of an increment to resource stocks multiplied by the marginal effect that current production has on next year's stocks and 2) capitalized value of an increment to capital stocks multiplied by the marginal effect that current production has on next year's capital stocks. We are using capitalized value to describe reduction of a perpetual flow to a present value measure when the "discount factor" is $\beta(1+\partial g/\partial x)$ or $\beta(1-\partial D/\partial y)$. These latter discount factors are a combination of an economic factor, β, and a stock compounding (discounting) factor, $1+\partial g/\partial x$ (or $1-\partial D/\partial y$). The analogous interpretation for (27) is obvious.

Dividing (27) by $\partial D/\partial v$ and making a substitution into (26), we get the equilibrium counterpart of (21), i.e.,

$$(29)\quad \frac{\partial B}{\partial u} - \nu = \beta\left(\frac{\partial B}{\partial x} + \nu\frac{\partial h}{\partial x}\right) \cdot \left[1 - \beta\left(1 + \frac{\partial g}{\partial x}\right)\right]^{-1}\left(-\frac{\partial g}{\partial w}\right) - \frac{\partial B}{\partial v}\frac{\partial v}{\partial u}$$

The last term is an alternative expression for the implicit cost in capital consumption associated with an increment to resource use in the current period. This cost is expressed as the cost of current investment required to maintain capital stocks, while in (26) this same cost is expressed as the implicit cost of having incrementally less capital stock in future periods.

If the constraint, $u \leq h(x, y)$, is not binding at equilibrium, solution of the system of four equations, (24), (26), and (27) in the variables u, v, x, and y will provide the equilibrium solution. Should the upper constraint on u be binding $u = h(x, y)$ is a fifth equation and v is the fifth variable of equilibrium. This straightforward solution to determine equilibrium stocks and rates of resource use and investment is attractive for easy analysis in applications. A good deal can be learned about optimal production and investment in a resource industry from knowledge of equilibrium under an optimal policy.

IV. *A Generalization to Multiple Interrelated Resources*

The preceding analysis is now generalized to N, interrelated natural resources and M, interrelated indices of capital stocks. Fortunately, all of the preceding analysis is applicable after defining certain vector and matrix relationships. The functions $B_t(u_t, v_t, x_t, y_t)$ and $\psi(x_T, y_T)$ are kept as scalars, while $g(u_t, x_t)$ and $h(x_t, y_t)$ are vectors of N components each and $D(u_t, v_t, y_t)$ has M components. The variables u_t and x_t are N component vectors, and v_t and y_t are vectors of M components each. The above vectors are all column vectors.

In the Lagrangian relationship, the multipliers λ_t, μ_t, and v_t are defined as row vectors of N, M, and N components. These definitions make the partial derivatives of L in equations (6) through (9) row vectors, and also imply that the partial derivatives of B_t and ψ are row vectors. The partial derviatives of D, g, and h are matrices with rows equal in number to the dimension of the vector function, and number of columns equal to the number of components in the vector variables of differentiation. Also, in expressions like $(1+\partial g_t/\partial x_t)$. the scalar 1 is replaced by the identity matrix I. With these conventions, all the derivations and equations presented for scalar relationships are valid. Ordering of factors in multiplication were kept consistent with the vector-matrix generalization, and divisions were even indicated by the inverse notation for easy transition.

In the derivation of equation (26), there arises the infinite sum

$$\sum_{j=0}^{\infty} \beta^j \left(I + \frac{\partial g}{\partial x}\right)^j = \sum_{j=0}^{\infty} A^j, \tag{30}$$

where it is assumed that

$$\lim_{t\to\infty} A^j = 0 \tag{31}$$

The limiting behavior of A in (31) is the analogue of $\beta(1+\partial g/\partial x)<1$ (cf (28)) in the case of a single resource. The limiting sum in (30) with condition (31) met is

$$[I - A]^{-1} = \left[I - \beta\left(I + \frac{\partial g}{\partial x}\right)\right]^{-1} \tag{32}$$

The same relationship exists for the depreciation function, i.e.,

$$\sum_{j=0}^{\infty} \beta^j \left(I - \frac{\partial D}{\partial y}\right)^j = \left[I - \beta\left(I - \frac{\partial D}{\partial y}\right)\right]^{-1} \tag{33}$$

Therefore, equations (26) and (27) are also applicable in our generalized framework.

Applications may often call for a model capable of handling several interrelated natural resources. Biologically interacting species of fish in a commercial fishery is an economically important area of application. Another common situation is interrelated groundwater aquifers. In fact, many single groundwater basins can be advantageously partitioned into highly interrelated sub-basins for more detailed analysis, both from the point of view of withdrawal rates and investment in pumping capacity. In many respects the number of separate resources would be arbitrarily determined vis-à-vis the number of sub-basins specified.

Appendix

In this Appendix, we take a brief look at sufficient conditions for a maximum in relation (4), consider existence of the Lagrange multipliers in the Kuhn-Tucker Theorem, and examine some problems arising under an infinite planning horizon.

We begin under the assumptions of a finite planning horizon and existence of the Lagrange multipliers in the Kuhn-Tucker Theorem, and specify a set of conditions that are sufficient for (4) to be a maximum. The assumptions that $g(u_t, x_t)$ and $h(x_t, y_t)$ are concave and that $D(u_t, v_t, y_t)$ is convex imply convexity for the constraint equations in (4-a) through (4-c). We have also assumed a concave criterion function by the assumed concavity of $B_t(u_t, v_t, x_t, y_t)$, $t=0, 1, \ldots, T-1$, and $\psi(x_T, y_T)$.

We note that the multipliers, $\{\mu_t\}$ and $\{\lambda_t\}$, can be negative in the formulation depicted by (4) because of the equalities in constraints (4-a) and (4-b). If these equations were replaced by inequalities,

$$x_{t+1} \leq x_t + g(u_t, x_t),$$
$$y_{t+1} \leq y_t - D(u_t, v_t, y_t),$$
$$t = 0, 1, \ldots, T-1,$$

all the multipliers would be nonnegative by the necessary conditions of Kuhn and Tucker. But the implication of inequalities replacing the equalities of (4-a) and (4-b) is costless disposal of any redundant resource or capital stocks. Of course, costless disposal of surplus resource or capital stocks may be extremely restrictive in some cases. For example, surplus groundwater stocks would usually imply a drainage problem. Therefore, an additional restriction must be imposed before the Kuhn-Tucker conditions imply sufficiency as well as necessity, even with our assumptions of concavity and convexity on the functions of (4). This restriction is that the multipliers $\{\lambda_t\}$ and $\{\mu_t\}$ be positive (see Garland Hadley, pp. 192–93), which may imply free disposal. In other words, free disposal is a sufficient, but not a necessary, condition for $\{\lambda_t\}$ and $\{\mu_t\}$ positive.

Necessary and sufficient conditions for existence of the Lagrange multipliers and thus application of the Kuhn-Tucker theorem, were proved by David Gale. Let w be a vector of variables added to the right-hand side of the constraints (4-a) through (4-c) replacing the zeros. We define $\phi(w)$ as the supremum of the criterion function in (4) for this modification in the constraints. In other words, $\phi(w)$ is the criterion function at its supremum for the family of optimization problems obtained by substitution of the vector w for the null vector in the right-hand side of the constraints (4-a) through (4-c).

Gale's main result for our purposes is that the Lagrange multipliers in (5) exist if, and only if, $\phi(w)$ has bounded steepness at $w=0$. Bounded steepness is defined as a finite value for

$$s = \sup_{w \in W}[\phi(w) - \phi(0)]/\|w\|,$$

where $\|w\|$ is some arbitrary norm of the vector w. The set W is all vectors w that are consistent with the modified constraint set on $\{u_t, v_t, x_t, y_t\}$ after replacing the null vector in (4-a) through (4-c) with w.

It would seem that violation of this condition for existence would imply a logical error in the specification of the economic model. If the steepness, s, is unbounded, discounted social benefits per unit of input (in some aggregated measure of the natural resource and capital) can be increased without limit. Therefore, it seems appropriate to assume existence of the multipliers, and should difficulty be encountered in applications, the problem is almost certainly a wrong specification of the constraint set.

The case of an infinite planning horizon raises problems of considerable difficulty. We come to grips with them in only a superficial manner by exploiting previous analyses that are applicable, viz., the dynamic programming approach of Bellman (1957). Bellman proved existence and uniqueness for our criterion function under conditions more restrictive, in some ways, then we have assumed thus far. Also, a method of successive approximations is provided by his analysis that gives uniform convergence for the criterion function. This method of successive approximations can be applied to a sequence of models identical to (4).

At this point, let us define a function $f_T(x_0, y_0)$ which is the value of the objective function in (4) at its maximum value, given that initial stocks are x_0 and y_0, viz., $f_T(x_0, y_0)$ is the solution of a family of optimization problems defined by (4). The following more restrictive assumptions are made with respect to this optimization problem:

(A-1) a) $B(u, v, x, y)$ is not explicitly a function of time (subscript t removed);
b) x and y are confined to a bounded region, say R;
c) The difference equations (4-a) and (4-b) are consistent with $(x, y) \in R$;
d) $B(u, v, x, y)$ is uniformly bounded for all values of its arguments belonging to the constraint set specified in (4) and $(x, y) \in R$.

The theorem of interest to us states that under our new assumptions, $f_T(x_0, y_0)$ converges as $T \to \infty$ to the functional equation,

$$\text{(A-2)} \quad f(x, y) = \max_{u,v}[B(u, v, x, y) + \beta f(x + g(u, x), y - D(u, v, y))],$$

which has a unique solution (Bellman 1957, p. 121). Further, the solution may be obtained as the limit of a sequence $\{f_n(x, y)\}$, defined as (A-3), shown below. Also, the sequence converges uniformly to its limit. As a result of our more restrictive assumptions (continuity and the bounded region R), we were able to dispense with the supremum in Bellman's an alysis and use a maximum.

The reader may be disturbed that we dropped the terminal function $\psi(x, y)$ by our definition of $f_0(x, y)$ in (A-3). This is of

$$\text{(A-3)} \quad f_0(x, y) = \underset{u,v}{\text{Max}}\, B(u, v, x, y)$$

$$\vdots$$

$$f_n(x, y) = \underset{u,v}{\text{Max}}\, [B(u, v, x, y) + \beta f_{n-1}(x + g(u, x), y - D(u, v, y))], \qquad n = 1, 2, \ldots.$$

no consequence, however, since the final value of resource and capital stocks are ultimately of infinitesimal importance as $T \to \infty$. We could just as well have used $f_0(x, y) = \psi(x, y)$ with suitable boundedness constraints on ψ.

With the additional restrictions in (A-1) appended to the optimization model in (4), a sequence of solutions can be used to approximate the infinite horizon solution to any desired degree of accuracy. The method is to solve the T-horizon model for *many* initial stocks (x_0, y_0), which permits an estimate of $f_T(x, y)$. The magnitude of T is arbitrary and in applications would be determined to considerable extent by computer capacity required in non-linear programming algorithms. The next step is to set $\psi(x, y) = f_T(x, y)$ in the T-period horizon model and solve the problem again for many pairs (x_0, y_0), which will yield an estimate of $f_{2T}(x, y)$. The next iteration uses $\psi(x, y) = f_{2T}(x, y)$ to generate an estimate of $f_{3T}(x, y)$ etc. Thereby, approximation to $f(x, y)$ is achieved to any degree desired by virtue of the uniform convergence of $f_n(x, y)$ to $f(x, y)$ as $n \to \infty$.

The restriction (A-1a) is not very burdensome because projections of the future become so nebulous after about 50 years that the best guess is to assume $B(u, v, x, y)$ constant for $t > M$, where M is some finite year in the future after which changes are too vague to project. After getting a sufficiently accurate estimate of $f(x, y)$ using the invarient function $B(u, v, x, y)$, set $\psi(x, y) = f(x, y)$, then solve the model exemplified by (4) with $T = M$, where time enters the social benefit function explicitly. If necessary for computational purposes, two or more steps could be used in solving this M-period problem.

In Section III we are concerned with the necessary conditions for a maximum of social benefits as the planning horizon becomes infinite. Therefore, we need to show that the necessary conditions of (19) and (20) hold for the limiting case where $T \to \infty$, which would imply an infinite number of variables in (4). This result follows almost directly from Bellman's theorem and the function, $f(x, y)$, in (A-2). We know that $f(x, y)$ exists and is unique under the additional constraints of (A-1). Let us think of the optimization problem in (4), modified by the additional constraints of (A-1), as that associated with an infinite planning horizon where the terminal value function $\psi(x_T, y_T)$ measures value for $t \geq T$. Then obviously, the terminal value function is $f(x, y)$, viz.,

$$\psi(x_T, y_T) = f(x_T, y_T).$$

Going to the necessary conditions for (4) to be a maximum (under the assumption $x_t, y_t > 0$, $t = 0, 1, \ldots$), equations (19) and (20), it is clear that we can approximate the necessary conditions under an infinite planning horizon as closely as we please by taking T arbitrarily large, as long as the terms of the summations in (19) and (20) ultimately converge to zero. The discount factor, $0 < \beta < 1$, in conjunction with boundedness assumptions, etc., imposed in (4) and (A-1) assure such convergence.

REFERENCES

R. E. Bellman, *Dynamic Programming*, Princeton 1957.

———, *Adaptive Control Processes: A Guided Tour*, Princeton 1961.

G. Brown, Jr. and C. B. McGuire, "A Socially Optimum Pricing Policy for a Public Water Agency," *Water Resources Research*, 1st quarter 1967, *3*, 33–43.

O. R. Burt, "Groundwater Management Under

Quadratic Criterion Functions," *Water Resources Research*, 3d quarter 1967, *3*, 673–82.

J. A. Crutchfield and A. Zellner, *Economic Aspects of the Pacific Halibut Industry*, Fishery Industrial Research I, U.S. Department of the Interior, Washington 1962.

R. Cummings and O. Burt, "The Economics of Production from Natural Resources: Note," *Amer. Econ. Rev.*, Dec. 1969, *59*, 985–90.

P. Davidson, "Public Policy Problems of the Domestic Crude Oil Industry," *Amer. Econ. Rev.*, Mar. 1963, *53*, 85–108.

D. Gale, "On Optimal Development in a Multi-sector Economy," *Rev. Econ. Stud.*, Jan. 1967, *34*, 1–18.

H. S. Gordon, "The Economic Theory of a Common Property Resource: The Fishery," *J. Polit. Econ.*, Apr. 1954, *62*, 124–42.

R. L. Gordon, "A Reinterpretation of the Pure Theory of Exhaustion," *J. Polit. Econ.*, June 1967, *75*, 274–86.

L. C. Gray, "Rent Under the Assumption of Exhaustibility," *Quart. J. Econ.*, May 1914, *28*, 466–89.

G. Hadley, *Nonlinear and Dynamic Programming*, Reading 1964.

H. Hotelling, "The Economics of Exhaustible Resources," *J. Polit. Econ.*, Apr. 1931, *39*, 137–75.

J. V. Krutilla, "Conservation Reconsidered," *Amer. Econ. Rev.*, Sept. 1967, *57*, 777–86.

H. W. Kuhn and A. W. Tucker, "Nonlinear Programming," in J. Neyman, ed., *Proceedings of the Second Berkeley Symposium On Mathematical Statistics and Probability*, Berkeley 1951, pp. 481–92.

J. Quirk and V. Smith, "Dynamic Economic Models of Fishing," in A. Scott, ed., *Proceedings of the H. R. MacMillan Fisheries Economics Symposium*, Vancouver 1969.

A. Scott, "The Fishery: The Objectives of Sole Ownership," *J. Polit. Econ.*, Apr. 1955, *63*, 116–24.

———, "The Theory of the Mine under Conditions of Certainty," in M. Gaffney, ed., *Extraction Resources and Taxation*, Madison 1967.

V. Smith, "Economics of Production from Natural Resources," *Amer. Econ. Rev.*, June 1968, *58*, 409–31.

R. Turvey, "Optimization in Fishery Regulation," *Amer. Econ. Rev.*, Mar. 1964, *54*, 64–76.

CHAPTER 21

Production, Consumption, and Externalities

By ROBERT U. AYRES AND ALLEN V. KNEESE*

"For all that, welfare economics can no more reach conclusions applicable to the real world without some knowledge of the real world than can positive economics" [21].

Despite tremendous public and governmental concern with problems such as environmental pollution, there has been a tendency in the economics literature to view externalities as exceptional cases. They may distort the allocation of resources but can be dealt with adequately through simple *ad hoc* arrangements. To quote Pigou:

> When it was urged above, that in certain industries a wrong amount of resources is being invested because the value of the marginal social net product there differs from the value of the marginal private net product, it was tacitly assumed that in the main body of industries these two values are equal [22][1].

And Scitovsky, after having described his cases two and four which deal with technological externalities affecting consumers and producers respectively, says:

> The second case seems exceptional, because most instances of it can be and usually are eliminated by zoning ordnances and industrial regulations concerned with public health and safety. The fourth case seems unimportant, simply because examples of it seem to be few and exceptional [25].

We believe that at least one class of externalities—those associated with the disposal of residuals resulting from the consumption and production process—must be viewed quite differently.[2] They are a normal, indeed, inevitable part of these processes. Their economic significance tends to increase as economic development proceeds, and the ability of the ambient environment to receive and assimilate them is an important natural resource of increasing value.[3] We will argue below that

* The authors are respectively visiting scholar and director, Quality of the Environment Program, Resources for the Future, Inc. We are indebted to our colleagues Blair Bower, Orris Herfindahl, Charles Howe, John Krutilla, and Robert Steinberg for comments on an earlier draft. We have also benefited from comments by James Buchanan, Paul Davidson, Robert Dorfman, Otto Eckstein, Myrick Freeman, Mason Gaffney, Lester Lave, Herbert Mohring, and Gordon Tullock.

[1] Even Baumol who saw externalities as a rather pervasive feature of the economy tends to discuss external diseconomies like "smoke nuisance" entirely in terms of particular examples [3]. A perspective more like that of the present paper is found in Kapp [16].

[2] We by no means wish to imply that this is the only important class of externalities associated with production and consumption. Also, we do not wish to imply that there has been a lack of theoretical attention to the externalities problem. In fact, the past few years have seen the publication of several excellent articles which have gone far toward systematizing definitions and illuminating certain policy issues. Of special note are Coase [9], Davis and Whinston [12], Buchanan and Stubblebine [6], and Turvey [27]. However, all these contributions deal with externality as a comparatively minor aberration from Pareto optimality in competitive markets and focus upon externalities between two parties. Mishan, after a careful review of the literature, has commented on this as follows: "The form in which external effects have been presented in the literature is that of partial equilibrium analysis; a situation in which a single industry produces an equilibrium output, usually under conditions of perfect competition, some form of intervention being required in order to induce the industry to produce an "ideal" or "optimal" output. If the point is not made explicitly, it is tacitly understood that unless the rest of the economy remains organized in conformity with optimum conditions, one runs smack into Second Best problems" [21].

[3] That external diseconomies are integrally related to economic development and increasing congestion has been noted in passing in the literature. Mishan has commented: "The attention given to external effects in

the common failure to recognize these facts may result from viewing the production and consumption processes in a manner that is somewhat at variance with the fundamental law of conservation of mass.

Modern welfare economics concludes that if (1) preference orderings of consumers and production functions of producers are independent and their shapes appropriately constrained, (2) consumers maximize utility subject to given income and price parameters, and (3) producers maximize profits subject to the price parameters; a set of prices exists such that no individual can be made better off without making some other individual worse off. For a given distribution of income this is an efficient state. Given certain further assumptions concerning the structure of markets, this "Pareto optimum" can be achieved via a pricing mechanism and voluntary decentralized exchange.

If waste assimilative capacity of the environment is scarce, the decentralized voluntary exchange process cannot be free of uncompensated technological external diseconomies unless (1) all inputs are fully converted into outputs, with no unwanted material residuals along the way,[4] and all final outputs are utterly destroyed in the process of consumption, or (2) property rights are so arranged that all relevant environmental attributes are in private ownership and these rights are exchanged in competitive markets. Neither of these conditions can be expected to hold in an actual economy and they do not.

Nature does not permit the destruction of matter except by annihilation with antimatter, and the means of disposal of unwanted residuals which maximizes the internal return of decentralized decision units is by discharge to the environment, principally, watercourses and the atmosphere. Water and air are traditionally examples of free goods in economics. But in reality, in developed economies they are common property resources of great and increasing value presenting society with important and difficult allocation problems which exchange in private markets cannot resolve. These problems loom larger as increased population and industrial production put more pressure on the environment's ability to dilute and chemically degrade waste products. Only the crudest estimates of present external costs associated with residuals discharge exist but it would not be surprising if these costs were in the tens of billions of dollars annually.[5] Moreover, as we shall emphasize again, technological means for processing or purifying one or another type of waste discharge do not destroy the residuals but only alter their form. Thus, given the level, patterns, and technology of production and consumption, recycle of materials into productive uses or discharge into an alternative medium are the only general options for protecting a particular environmental medium such as water. Residual problems must be seen in a broad regional or economy-wide context rather

the recent literature is, I think, fully justified by the unfortunate, albeit inescapable, fact that as societies grow in material wealth, the incidence of these effects grows rapidly . . . " [21]; and Buchanan and Tullock have stated that as economic development proceeds, "congestion" tends to replace "co-operation" as the underlying motive force behind collective action, i.e., controlling external diseconomies tends to become more important than cooperation to realize external economies [7].

[4] Or any residuals which occur must be stored on the producer's premises.

[5] It is interesting to compare this with estimates of the cost of another well known misallocation of resources that has occupied a central place in economic theory and research. In 1954, Harberger published an estimate of the welfare cost of monopoly which indicated that it amounted to about .07 percent of GNP [15]. In a later study, Schwartzman calculated the allocative cost at only .01 percent of GNP [24]. Leibenstein generalized studies such as these to the statement that " . . . in a great many instances the amount to be gained by increasing allocative efficiency is trivial . . . " [19]. But Leibenstein did not consider the allocative costs associated with environmental pollution.

than as separate and isolated problems of disposal of gas, liquid, and solid wastes.

Frank Knight perhaps provides a key to why these elementary facts have played so small a role in economic theorizing and empirical research.

> The next heading to be mentioned ties up with the question of dimensions from another angle, and relates to the second main error mentioned earlier as connected with taking food and eating as the type of economic activity. The basic economic magnitude (value or utility) is service, not good. It is inherently a stream or flow in time . . . [18].[6]

Almost all of standard economic theory is in reality concerned with services. Material objects are merely the vehicles which carry some of these services, and they are exchanged because of consumer preferences for the services associated with their use or because they can help to add value in the manufacturing process. Yet we persist in referring to the "final consumption" of goods as though material objects such as fuels, materials, and finished goods somehow disappeared into the void—a practice which was comparatively harmless so long as air and water were almost literally free goods.[7] Of course, residuals from both the production and consumption processes remain and they usually render disservices (like killing fish, increasing the difficulty of water treatment, reducing public health, soiling and deteriorating buildings, etc.) rather than services. Control efforts are aimed at eliminating or reducing those disservices which flow to consumers and producers whether they want them or not and which, except in unusual cases, they cannot control by engaging in individual exchanges.[8]

I. *The Flow of Materials*

To elaborate on these points, we find it useful initially to view environmental pollution and its control as a materials balance problem for the entire economy.[9] The inputs to the system are fuels, foods, and raw materials which are partly converted into final goods and partly become waste residuals. Except for increases in inventory, final goods also ultimately enter the waste stream. Thus goods which are "consumed" really only render certain services. Their material substance remains in existence and must either be reused or discharged to the ambient environment.

In an economy which is closed (no imports or exports) and where there is no net accumulation of stocks (plant, equipment, inventories, consumer durables, or residential buildings), the amount of residuals inserted into the natural environment must be approximately equal to the weight of basic fuels, food, and raw materials entering the processing and production system, plus oxygen taken from the atmosphere.[10] This result, while obvious

[6] The point was also clearly made by Fisher: "The only true method, in our view, is to regard uniformly as income the *service* of a dwelling to its owner (shelter or money rental), the *service* of a piano (music), and the *service* of food (nourishment) . . . " (emphasis in original) [14].

[7] We are tempted to suggest that the word consumption be dropped entirely from the economist's vocabulary as being basically deceptive. It is difficult to think of a suitable substitute, however. At least, the word consumption should not be used in connection with goods, but only with regard to services or flows of "utility."

[8] There is a substantial literature dealing with the question of under what conditions individual exchanges can optimally control technological external diseconomies. A discussion of this literature, as it relates to waterborne residuals, is found in Kneese and Bower [17].

[9] As far as we know, the idea of applying materials balance concepts to waste disposal problems was first expressed by Smith [26]. We also benefitted from an unpublished paper by Joseph Headley in which a pollution "matrix" is suggested. We have also found references by Boulding to a "spaceship economy" suggestive [4]. One of the authors has previously used a similar approach in ecological studies of nutrient interchange among plants and animals; see [1].

[10] To simplify our language, we will not repeat this essential qualification at each opportunity, but assume it applies throughout the following discussion. In addition, we must include residuals such as NO and NO_2 arising from reactions between components of the air itself but occurring as combustion by-products.

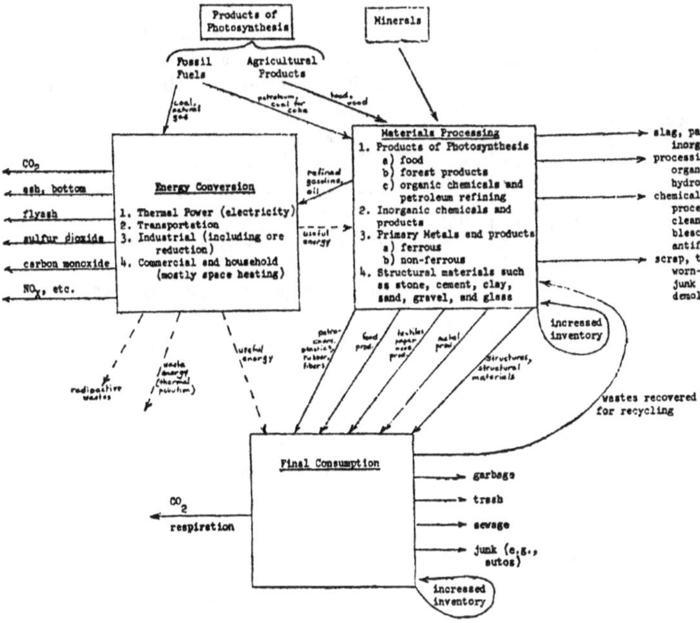

FIGURE 1.—MATERIALS FLOW

upon reflection, leads to the, at first rather surprising, corollary that residuals disposal involves a greater tonnage of materials than basic materials processing, although many of the residuals, being gaseous, require no physical "handling."

Figure 1 shows a materials flow of the type we have in mind in greater detail and relates it to a broad classification of economic sectors for convenience in our later discussion, and for general consistency with the Standard Industrial Classification. In an open (regional or national) economy, it would be necessary to add flows representing imports and exports. In an economy undergoing stock or capital accumulation, the production of residuals in any given year would be less by that amount than the basic inputs. In the entire U.S. economy, accumulation accounts for about 10–15 percent of basic annual inputs, mostly in the form of construction materials, and there is some net importation of raw and partially processed materials amounting to 4 or 5 percent of domestic production. Table 1 shows estimates of the weight of raw materials produced in the United States in several recent years, plus net imports of raw and partially processed materials.

Of the active inputs,[11] perhaps three-quarters of the overall weight is eventually discharged to the atmosphere as carbon (combined with atmospheric oxygen in the form of CO or CO_2) and hydrogen (combined with atmospheric oxygen as H_2O) under current conditions. This results from combustion of fossil fuels and from animal respiration. Discharge of carbon dioxide can be considered harmless in the short run. There are large "sinks" (in the form of vegetation and large water bodies,

[11] See footnote to Table 1.

TABLE 1—WEIGHT OF BASIC MATERIALS PRODUCTION IN THE UNITED STATES PLUS NET IMPORTS, 1963 (10^6 tons)

	1963	1964	1965
Agricultural (incl. fishery and wildlife and forest) products			
Food: Crops (excl. livestock feed)	125	128	130
Food: Livestock	100	103	102
Other products	5	6	6
Fishery	3	3	3
Forestry products (85 per cent dry wt. basis)			
Sawlogs	53	55	56
Pulpwood	107	116	120
Other	41	41	42
Total	434	452	459
Mineral fuels	1,337	1,399	1,448
Other minerals			
Iron ore	204	237	245
Other metal ores	161	171	191
Other nonmetals	125	133	149
Total	490	541	585
Grand total[a]	2,261	2,392	2,492

[a] Excluding construction materials, stone, sand, gravel, and other minerals used for structural purposes, ballast, fillers, insulation, etc. Gangue and mine tailings are also excluded from this total. These materials account for enormous tonnages but undergo essentially no chemical change. Hence, their use is more or less tantamount to physically moving them from one location to another. If this were to be included, there is no logical reason to exclude material shifted in highway cut and fill operations, harbor dredging, land-fill, plowing, and even silt moved by rivers. Since a line must be drawn somewhere, we chose to draw it as indicated above.

Source: R. U. Ayres and A. V. Kneese [2, p. 630].

mainly the oceans) which reabsorb this gas, although there is evidence of net accumulation of CO_2 in the atmosphere. Some experts believe that the latter is likely to show a large relative increase, as much as 50 per cent by the end of the century, possibly giving rise to significant—and probably, on balance, adverse—weather changes.[12] Thus continued combustion of fossil fuels at a high rate could produce externalities affecting the entire world. The effects associated with most residuals will normally be more confined, however, usually limited to regional air and water sheds.

The remaining residuals are either gases (like carbon monoxide, nitrogen dioxide, and sulfur dioxide—all potentially harmful even in the short run), dry solids (like rubbish and scrap), or wet solids (like garbage, sewage, and industrial wastes suspended or dissolved in water). In a sense, the dry solids are an irreducible, limiting form of waste. By the application of appropriate equipment and energy, most undesirable substances can, in principle, be removed from water and air streams[13]—but what is left must be disposed of in solid form, transformed, or reused. Looking at the matter in this way clearly reveals a primary interdependence between the various waste streams which casts into doubt the traditional classification of air, water, and land pollution as individual categories for purposes of planning and control policy.

Residuals do not necessarily have to be discharged to the environment. In many instances, it is possible to recycle them back into the productive system. The materials balance view underlines the fact that the throughput of new materials necessary to maintain a given level of production and consumption decreases as the technical efficiency of energy conversion and materials utilization increases. Similarly, other things being equal, the longer that cars, buildings, machinery, and other durables remain in service, the fewer new materials are required to compensate for loss, wear, and obsolescence—although the use of old or worn machinery (e.g., automobiles) tends to increase other residuals problems. Technically efficient combustion of (desulfurized) fossil fuels

[12] See [30]. There is strong evidence that discharge of residuals has already affected the climate of individual cities; see Lowry [20].

[13] Except CO_2, which may be harmful in the long run, as noted.

would leave only water, ash, and carbon dioxide as residuals, while nuclear energy conversion need leave only negligible quantities of material residuals (although thermal pollution and radiation hazards cannot be dismissed by any means).

Given the population, industrial production, and transport service in an economy (a regional rather than a national economy would normally be the relevant unit), it is possible to visualize combinations of social policy which could lead to quite different relative burdens placed on the various residuals-receiving environmental media; or, given the possibilities for recycle and less residual-generating production processes, the overall burden to be placed upon the environment as a whole. To take one extreme, a region which went in heavily for electric space heating and wet scrubbing of stack gases (from steam plants and industries), which ground up its garbage and delivered it to the sewers and then discharged the raw sewage to watercourses, would protect its air resources to an exceptional degree. But this would come at the sacrifice of placing a heavy residuals load upon water resources. On the other hand, a region which treated municipal and industrial waste water streams to a high level and relied heavily on the incineration of sludges and solid wastes would protect its water and land resources at the expense of discharging waste residuals predominantly to the air. Finally, a region which practiced high level recovery and recycle of waste materials and fostered low residual production processes to a far reaching extent in each of the economic sectors might discharge very little residual waste to any of the environmental media.

Further complexities are added by the fact that sometimes it is possible to modify an environmental medium through investment in control facilities so as to improve its assimilative capacity. The clearest, but far from only, example is with respect to watercourses where reservoir storage can be used to augment low river flows that ordinarily are associated with critical pollution (high external cost situations).[14] Thus internalization of external costs associated with particular discharges, by means of taxes or other restrictions, even if done perfectly, cannot guarantee Pareto optimality. Investments involving public good aspects must enter into an optimal solution.[15]

To recapitulate our main points briefly: (1) Technological external diseconomies are not freakish anomalies in the processes of production and consumption but an inherent and normal part of them. (2) These external diseconomies are quantitatively negligible in a low-population or economically undeveloped setting, but they become progressively (nonlinearly) more important as the population rises and the level of output increases (i.e., as the natural reservoirs of dilution and assimilative capacity become exhausted).[16] (3) They cannot be properly dealt with by considering environmental media such as air and water in isolation. (4) Isolated and *ad hoc* taxes and other restrictions are not sufficient for their optimum control, although they are essential elements in a more systematic and coherent program of environmental quality management. (5) Public investment programs, particularly including transportation systems, sewage disposal, and river flow regulation, are intimately related to the amounts and

[14] Careful empirical work has shown that this technique can fit efficiently into water quality management systems. See Davis [11].

[15] A discussion of the theory of such public investments with respect to water quality management is found in Boyd [5].

[16] Externalities associated with residuals discharge may appear only at certain threshold values which are relevant only at some stage of economic development and industrial and population concentrations. This may account for their general treatment as "exceptional" cases in the economics literature. These threshold values truly were exceptional cases for less developed economies.

effects of residuals and must be planned in light of them.

It is important to develop not only improved measures of the external costs resulting from differing concentrations and duration of residuals in the environment but more systematic methods for forecasting emissions of external-cost-producing residuals, technical and economic trade-offs between them, and the effects of recycle on environmental quality.

In the hope of contributing to this effort and of revealing more clearly the types of information which would be needed to implement such a program, we set forth a more formal model of the materials balance approach in the following sections and relate it to some conventional economic models of production and consumption. The main objective is to make some progress toward defining a system in which flows of services and materials are simultaneously accounted for and related to welfare.

II. *Basic Model*

The take off point for our discussion is the Walras-Cassel general equilibrium model,[17] extended to include intermediate consumption, which involve the following quantities:

$$\overbrace{r_1, \cdots\cdots, r_M}^{\text{resources and services}}$$

$$\overbrace{X_1, \cdots\cdots, X_N}^{\text{products or commodities}}$$

$$\overbrace{v_1, \cdots\cdots, v_M}^{\text{resource prices}}$$

$$\overbrace{p_1, \cdots\cdots, p_N}^{\text{product or commodity prices}}$$

$$\overbrace{Y_1, \cdots\cdots, Y_N}^{\text{final demands}}$$

[17] The original references are Walras [28] and Cassel [8]. Our own treatment is largely based on Dorfman *et al.* [13].

The M basic resources are allocated among the N sectors as follows:

$$\begin{aligned} r_1 &= a_{11}X_1 + a_{12}X_2 + \cdots + a_{1N}X_N \\ r_2 &= a_{21}X_1 + a_{22}X_2 + \cdots + a_{2N}X_N \\ &\vdots \\ r_M &= a_{M1}X_1 + a_{M2}X_2 + \cdots + a_{MN}X_N \end{aligned}$$

(1a) or

$$r_j = \sum_{k=1}^{N} a_{jk}X_k \qquad j = 1, \cdots, M$$

In (1a) we have implicitly assumed that there is no possibility of factor or process substitution and no joint production. These conditions will be discussed later. In matrix notation we can write:

$$\text{(1b)} \qquad [r_{j1}]_{M,1} = [a_{jk}]_{M,N} \cdot [X_{k1}]_{N,1}$$

where $[a]$ is an $M \times N$ matrix.

A similar set of equations describes the relations between commodity production and final demand:

$$\text{(2a)} \qquad X_k = \sum_{l=1}^{N} A_{kl}Y_l \qquad k = 1, \cdots, N$$

$$\text{(2b)} \qquad [X_{k1}]_{N,1} = [A_{kl}]_{N,N} \cdot [Y_{l1}]_{N,1}$$

and the matrix $[A]$ is given by

$$\text{(3)} \qquad [A] = [I - C]^{-1}$$

where $[I]$ is the unit diagonal matrix and the elements C_{ij} of the matrix $[C]$ are essentially the well known Leontief input coefficients. In principle these are functions of the existing technology and, therefore, are fixed for any given situation.

By combining (1) and (2), we obtain a set of equations relating resource inputs directly to final demand, viz.,

$$\text{(4a)} \qquad \begin{aligned} r_j &= \sum_{k=1}^{N} a_{jk} \sum_{l=1}^{N} A_{kl}Y_l = \sum_{k,l=1}^{N} a_{jk}A_{kl}Y_l \\ &= \sum_{l=1}^{N} b_{jl}Y_l \qquad j = 1, \cdots, M \end{aligned}$$

or, of course, in matrix notation (4b).

$$(4b)\quad \begin{aligned}[r_{j1}]_{M,1} &= [a_{jk}]_{M,N}\cdot[A_{kl}]_{N,N}\cdot[Y_{l1}]_{N,1}\\ &= [b_{jl}]_{M,N}\cdot[Y_{l1}]_{N,1}\end{aligned}$$

We can also impute the prices of N intermediate goods and commodities to the prices of the M basic resources, as follows:

$$(5a)\quad p_k = \sum_{j=1}^{M} v_j b_{jk} \qquad k = 1, \cdots, N$$

$$(5b)\quad [p_{1k}]_{1,N} = [v_{1j}]_{1,M}\cdot[b_{jk}]_{M,N}$$

To complete the system, it may be supposed that demand and supply relationships are given, a priori, by Pareto-type preference functions:

$$(6)\quad \text{Demand:} \quad Y_k = F_k(p_1, \cdots, p_N) \qquad k = 1, \cdots, N$$

$$(7)\quad \text{Supply:} \quad r_k = G_k(v_1, \cdots, v_M) \qquad k = 1, \cdots, M$$

where, of course, the p_j are functions of the v_j as in (5b).

In order to interpret the X's as physical production, it is necessary for the sake of consistency to arrange that outputs and inputs always balance, which implies that the C_{ij} must comprise *all* materials exchanges including residuals. To complete the system so that there is no net gain or loss of physical substances, it is also convenient to introduce two additional sectors, viz., an "environmental" sector whose (physical) output is X_0 and a "final consumption" sector whose output is denoted X_f. The system is then easily balanced by explicitly including flows both to and from these sectors.

To implement this further modification of the Walras-Cassel model, it is convenient to subdivide and relabel the resource category into tangible raw materials $\{r^m\}$ and services $\{r^s\}$:

$$\begin{bmatrix} r_1 \\ r_2 \\ \vdots \\ r_L \end{bmatrix} \text{ becomes } \left.\begin{bmatrix} r^m_1 \\ r^m_2 \\ \vdots \\ r^m_L \end{bmatrix}\right\} \text{raw materials (units)}$$

$$\begin{bmatrix} r_{L+1} \\ \vdots \\ r_M \end{bmatrix} \text{ becomes } \left.\begin{bmatrix} r^s_1 \\ \vdots \\ r^s_p \end{bmatrix}\right\} \text{service (units)}$$

where, of course,

$$(8)\quad L + P = M$$

It is understood that services, while not counted in tons, can be measured in meaningful units, such as man-days, with well defined prices. Thus, we similarly relabel the price variables as follows:

$$\begin{bmatrix} V_1 \\ \vdots \\ V_L \end{bmatrix} \text{ becomes } \left.\begin{bmatrix} V^m_1 \\ \vdots \\ V^m_L \end{bmatrix}\right\} \text{raw material (prices)}$$

$$\begin{bmatrix} V_{L+1} \\ \vdots \\ V_M \end{bmatrix} \text{ becomes } \left.\begin{bmatrix} V^s_1 \\ \vdots \\ V^s_p \end{bmatrix}\right\} \text{labor and service (prices)}$$

The coefficients $\{a_{ij}\}$, $\{b_{ij}\}$ are similarly partitioned into two groups,

$$\text{e.g.,}\quad \begin{matrix} b_{1j} \\ \vdots \\ b_{Lj} \\ b_{L+1,j} \\ \vdots \\ b_{Mj} \end{matrix} \quad \text{becomes} \quad \begin{matrix} b^m_{1j} \\ \vdots \\ b^m_{Lj} \\ b^s_{1j} \\ \vdots \\ b^s_{pj} \end{matrix}$$

These notational changes have no effect whatever on the substance of the model, although the equations become somewhat more cumbersome. The partitioned matrix notation simplifies the restatement of the basic equations. Thus (1b) becomes (9), while (5b) becomes (10).

$$M\left\{\begin{bmatrix} \vdots \\ r \\ \vdots \end{bmatrix}\right. \equiv \begin{bmatrix} r^m \\ \cdots \\ r^s \end{bmatrix}\begin{matrix} \}L \\ \\ \}P \end{matrix} = M\left\{\overbrace{\begin{bmatrix} \}L & b^m \\ & \cdots \\ \}P & b^s \end{bmatrix}}^{N}\right.\begin{bmatrix} \\ Y \\ \\ \end{bmatrix}\Big\}N \tag{9}$$

$$\underbrace{[p_1, \cdots, p_N]}_{N} = \underbrace{[\overset{L}{v^m} : \overset{P}{v^s}]}_{M}\underbrace{\begin{bmatrix} b^m \\ \cdots \\ b^s \end{bmatrix}}_{N}\Big\}M \tag{10}$$

$$= [\cdots v^m \cdots]\begin{bmatrix} \vdots & b^m & \vdots \\ \cdot & \cdots & \cdot \end{bmatrix} + [\cdots v^s \cdots]\begin{bmatrix} \vdots & b^s & \vdots \\ \cdot & \cdots & \cdot \end{bmatrix}$$

The equivalent of (5a) is:

$$p_k = \underbrace{\sum_{j=1}^{L} b_{jk}^{m} v_j^{m}}_{\substack{\text{prices imputed} \\ \text{to cost of raw} \\ \text{materials}}} + \underbrace{\sum_{j=1}^{P} b_{jk}^{s} v_j^{s}}_{\substack{\text{prices imputed} \\ \text{to cost of} \\ \text{services}}} \tag{11}$$

where $k = 1, \cdots, N$

We wish to focus attention explicitly on the flow of materials through the economy. By definition of the Leontief input coefficients (now related to materials flow), we have:

$C_{kj}X_j$ (physical) quantity transferred from k to j

$C_{jk}X_k$ quantity transferred from j to k

Hence, material flows *from* the environment to all other sectors are given by:

$$\sum_{k=1}^{N} C_{0k}X_k = \sum_{j=1}^{L} r_j^m = \sum_{j=1}^{L}\sum_{k=1}^{N} a_{jk}^m X_k = \sum_{j=1}^{L}\sum_{k=1}^{N} b_{jk}^m Y_k \tag{12}$$

using equation (1), as modified.[18] Obviously, comparing the first and third terms,

$$\underbrace{C_{0k}}_{\substack{\text{total material} \\ \text{flow (0 to } k)}} = \underbrace{\sum_{j=1}^{L} a_{jk}^m}_{\substack{\text{all raw materials} \\ \text{(0 to } k)}} \tag{13}$$

Flows into and out of the environmental sector must be in balance:

$$\underbrace{\sum_{k=1}^{N} C_{0k}X_k}_{\substack{\text{sum of all raw} \\ \text{material flows}}} = \underbrace{\sum_{k=1}^{N} C_{k0}X_0 + C_{f0}X_0}_{\substack{\text{sum of all return} \\ \text{(waste) flows}}} \tag{14}$$

Material flows to and from the final sector must also balance:

$$\underbrace{\sum_{k=1}^{N} C_{kf}X_f}_{\substack{\text{sum of all} \\ \text{final goods}}} = \underbrace{\sum_{k=1}^{N} C_{fk}X_k}_{\substack{\text{sum of all} \\ \text{materials} \\ \text{recycled}}} + \underbrace{C_{f0}X_0}_{\substack{\text{waste residuals} \\ \text{(plus accumulation[19])}}} \tag{15}$$

[18] Ignoring, for convenience, any materials flow from the environment *directly* to the final consumption sector.

[19] For convenience, we can treat accumulation in the final sector as a return flow to the environment. In truth, structures actually *become* part of our environment, although certain disposal costs may be deferred.

Of course, by definition, X_f is the sum of the final demands:

$$(16) \qquad X_f = \sum_{j=1}^{N} Y_j$$

Substituting (16) into the left side of (15) and (2a) into the right side of (15), we obtain an expression for the waste flow in terms of final demands:

$$(17) \quad C_{f0}X_0 = \sum_{j=1}^{N} \sum_{k=1}^{N} (C_{if} - C_{fj}A_{jk}) Y_k$$

The treatment could be simplified slightly if we assumed that there is no recycling per se. Thus, in the context of the model, we could suppose that all residuals return to the environmental sector,[20] where some of them (e.g., waste paper) become "raw materials." They would then be indistinguishable from new raw materials, however, and price differentials between the two would be washed out. In principle, this is an important distinction to retain.

III. *Inclusion of Externalities*

The physical flow of materials between various intermediate (production) sectors and the final (consumption) sector tends to be accompanied by, and correlated with, a (reverse) flow of dollars.[21] However, the physical flow of materials from and back to the environment is only partly reflected by actual dollar flows, namely, land rents and payments for raw materials. There are three classes of physical exchange for which there exist no counterpart economic transactions. These are: (1) private use for production inputs of "common property" resources, notably air, streams, lakes, and the ocean; (2) private use of the assimilative capacity of the environment to "dispose of" or dilute wastes and residuals; (3) inadvertent or unwanted material inputs to productive processes—diluents and pollutants.

All these goods (or "bads") are physically transferred at zero price, not because they are not scarce relative to demand—they often are in developed economies—or because they confer no service or disservice on the user—since they demonstrably do so—but because there exist no social institutions that permit the resources in question to be "owned," and exchanged in the market.

The allocation of resources corresponding to a Pareto optimum cannot be attained without subjecting the above-mentioned nonmarket and involuntary exchanges to the moderation of a market or a surrogate thereof. In principle, the influence of a market might be simulated, to a first approximation, by introducing a set of shadow (or virtual) prices.[22] These may well be zero, where supply truly exceeds demand, or negative (i.e., costs) in some instances; they will be positive in others. The exchanges are, of course, real.

The Walras-Cassel model can be generalized to handle these effects in the following way:

1. One can introduce a set of R common-property resources or services of raw materials $\{r_1^{cp}, \cdots, r_R^{cp}\}$ as a subset of the set $\{r_j\}$; these will have corresponding virtual prices $\{v_j^{cp}\}$, which would constitute an "income" from the environment. Such resources include the atmosphere; streams, lakes, and oceans; landscape; wildlife and biological diversity; and the indispensable assimilative capacity of the environment (its ability to accept and neutralize or recycle residuals).[23]

[20] In calculating actual quantities, we would (by convention) ignore the weight of oxygen taken free from the atmosphere in combustion and return as CO^2. However, such inputs will be treated explicitly later.

[21] To be precise, the dollar flow governs and is governed by a combined flow of materials and services (value added).

[22] A similar concept exists in mechanics where the forces producing "reaction" (to balance action and reaction) are commonly described as "virtual forces."

[23] Economists have previously suggested generalization of the Walras-Cassel model to take account of public goods. One of the earliest appears to be Schles-

2. One can introduce a set of S environmental *disservices* imposed on consumers of material resources, by forcing them to accept unwanted inputs $\{r_1^u, \cdots, r_s^u\}$ (pollutants, contaminants, etc.); these disservices would have negative value, giving rise to *negative* virtual prices $\{u_j\}$.[24]

The matrix coefficients $\{a_{ij}\}$ and $\{b_{ij}\}$ can be further partitioned to take account of this additional refinement, and equations analogous to (9), (10), and (11) can be generalized in the obvious way. Equation (6) carries over unchanged, but (7) must be appropriately generalized to take account of the altered situation. Actually, (7) breaks up into several groups of equations:

$$r_k^m = G_k^m(p_1, \cdots, p_N) \qquad k = 1, \cdots, L \tag{18}$$

$$r_k^s = G_k^s(p_1, \cdots, p_N) \qquad k = 1, \cdots, P \tag{19}$$

However, as we have noted at the outset, the supplies of common-property resources and environmental services or disservices are *not* regulated directly by market prices of other goods and services. In the case of common-property resources, the supplies are simply constants fixed by nature or otherwise determined by accident or noneconomic factors.

The total value of these services performed by the environment cannot be calculated but it is suggestive to consider the situation if the natural reservoir of air, water, minerals, etc., were very much smaller, as if the earth were a submarine or "spaceship" (i.e., a vehicle with no assimilative and/or regenerative capacity). In such a case, all material resources would have to be recycled,[25] and the cost of all goods would necessarily reflect the cost of reprocessing residuals and wastes for reuse. In this case, incidentally, the ambient level of unrecovered wastes continuously circulating through the resource inventory of the system (i.e., the spaceship) would in general be nonzero because of the difficulty of 100 percent efficient waste-removal of air and water. However, although the quantitity of waste products in constant circulation may fluctuate within limits, it cannot be allowed to increase monotonically with time, which means that as much material must be recycled, on the average, as is discarded. The value of common resources plus the assimilation services performed by the environment, then, is only indirectly a function of the ambient level of untreated residuals per se, or the disutility caused thereby, which depend on the cost efficiency of the available treatment technology. Be this as it may, of course, the bill of goods produced in a spaceship economy would certainly be radically different from that we are familiar with. For this reason, no standard economic comparison between the two situations is meaningful. The measure of worth we are seeking is actually the difference between the total welfare "produced" by a spaceship economy, where 100 percent of all residuals are promptly recycled, vis-à-vis the existing welfare output on earth, where resource inventories are substantial and

inger [23]. We are indebted to Otto Eckstein for calling our attention to this key reference.

[24] The notion of introducing the possibility of negative prices in general equilibrium theory has apparently been discussed before, although we are not aware of any systematic development of the idea in the published literature. In this connection, it is worth pointing out the underlying similarity of negative prices and effluent taxes—which have been, and still are being considered as an attractive alternative to subsidies and federal standard-setting as a means of controlling air and water pollution. Such taxes would, of course, be an explicit attempt to rectify an imbalance caused by a market failure.

[25] Any consistent deviation from this 100 per cent rule implies an accumulation of waste products, on the average, which, by definition, is inconsistent with maintaining an equilibrium.

complete recycling need not be contemplated for a very long time to come.

This welfare difference might well be very large, although we possess no methodological tools for quantifying it. In any case, the resource inventory and assimilative capacity of the environment probably contribute very considerably to our standard of living.

If these environmental contributions were paid for, the overall effect on prices would presumably to be push them generally upward. However, the major *differential* effect of undervaluing the environmental contribution is that goods produced by high residual-producing processes, such as papermaking, are substantially underpriced vis-à-vis goods which involve more economical uses of basic resources. This is, however, not socially disadvantageous per se: that is, it causes no misallocation of resources unless, or until, the large resource inventory and/or the assimilative capacity of the environment are used up. When this happens, however, as it now has in most highly industrialized regions, either a market must be allowed to operate or some other form of decision rule must be introduced to permit a rational choice to be made, e.g., between curtailing or controlling the production of residuals or tolerating the effects (disservice) thereof.

It appears that the natural inventory of most common resources used as inputs (e.g., air as an input to combustion and respiratory processes) is still ample,[26] but the assimilative capacity of the environment has already been exceeded in many areas, with important external costs resulting. This suggests a compromise treatment. If an appropriate price could be charged to the producers of the residuals and used to compensate the inadvertent recipients—with the price determined by appropriate Pareto preference criteria—there would be no particular analytic purpose in keeping books on the exchange of the other environmental benefits mentioned, although they are quantitatively massive. We will, therefore, in the remainder of the discussion omit the common-property variables $\{r_j^{cp}\}$ and the corresponding virtual-price variables $\{v_j^{cp}\}$ defined previously, retaining only the terms $\{r_j^u\}$ and $\{u_{jk}\}$. The variable $\{r_j^u\}$ represents a physical quantity of the jth unwanted input. There are S such terms, by assumption, whose magnitudes are proportional to the levels of consumption of basic raw materials, subject to the existing technology. However, residuals production is not immutable: it can be increased or decreased by investment, changes in materials processing technology, raw material substitutions, and so forth.

At first glance it might seem entirely reasonable to assert that the *supplies* of unwanted residuals received will be functions of the (negative) prices (i.e., compensation) paid for them, in analogy with (7). Unfortunately, this assertion immediately introduces a theoretical difficulty, since the assumption of unique coefficients $\{a_{ij}\}$ and $\{C_{ij}\}$[27] is not consistent with the possibility of factor or process substitution or joint-production, as stated earlier. To permit such substitutions, one would have to envision a very large collection of alternative sets of coefficients: one complete set of a's and C's for each specific combination of factors and processes. Maximization of any objective function (such as GNP) would involve solving the entire system of equations as many times as there are combinations of factors and pro-

[26] Water is an exception in arid regions; in humid regions, however, water "shortages" are misnomers: they are really consequences of excessive use of watercourses as cheap means of waste disposal. But some ecologists have claimed that oxygen depletion may be a very serious long-run problem; see Cole [10].

[27] Or $\{b_{ij}\}$ and $\{A_{ij}\}$.

$$(21)\qquad [r]=\begin{bmatrix} r^m \\ r^s \\ r^u \end{bmatrix} = M\left\{\underbrace{\begin{bmatrix} a^m \\ \cdots \\ a^s \\ \cdots \\ a^u \end{bmatrix}}_{N}\begin{bmatrix} \\ X \\ \\ \end{bmatrix}\right\} N = \begin{bmatrix} b^m \\ \cdots \\ b^s \\ \cdots \\ b^u \end{bmatrix}\begin{bmatrix} \\ Y \\ \\ \end{bmatrix}$$

---

cesses, and picking out that set of solutions which yields the largest value. Alternatively, if the a's and C's are assumed to be continuously variable functions (of each other), the objective function could also, presumably, be parameterized. However, as long as the a's and C's are uniquely given, the supply of the kth unwanted residual is only marginally under the control of the producer, since it will be produced in strict relationship to the composition of the bill of final goods $\{Y_j\}$.

Hence, for the present model it is only correct to assume

$$(20)\qquad r^u_k = G^u_k(Y_1, \cdots, Y_N)$$

This limitation does not affect the existence of an equilibrium solution for the system of equations; it merely means that the shadow prices $\{u_{jk}\}$ which would emerge from such a solution for given coefficients $\{a_{ij}\}$, $\{b_{ij}\}$, and $\{C_{ij}\}$ might be considerably higher than the real economic optimum, since the latter could only be achieved by introducing factor and process changes.

Of course, the physical inputs are also related to the physical outputs of goods, as in (21).

Written out in full detail (21) is equivalent to:

$$(22)\quad \text{raw materials}\qquad r^m_k = \sum_{j=1}^{N} a^m_{kj} X_j = \sum_{j=1}^{N} b^m_{kj} Y_j \qquad k = 1, \cdots, L$$

$$(23)\quad \text{labor and technical services}\qquad r^s_k = \sum_{j=1}^{N} a^s_{kj} X_j = \sum_{j=1}^{N} b^s_{kj} Y_j \qquad k = 1, \cdots, P$$

$$(24)\quad \text{unwanted inputs}\qquad r^u_k = \sum_{j=1}^{N} a^u_{kj} X_j = \sum_{j=1}^{N} b^u_{kj} Y_j \qquad k = 1, \cdots, S$$

where, of course,

$$(25)\qquad L + P + S = M$$

The corresponding matrix equation for the prices of goods, in terms of production costs, is

$$(26)\qquad [p_1, \cdots, p_N] = [v^m : v^s : u]\begin{bmatrix} b^m \\ \cdots \\ b^s \\ \cdots \\ b^u \end{bmatrix}$$

Written out in the standard form, we obtain

$$(27)\qquad p_k = \underbrace{\sum_{j=1}^{L} b^m_{jk} v^m_j}_{\text{cost of raw materials}} + \underbrace{\sum_{j=1}^{P} b^s_{jk} v^s_j}_{\text{cost of labor and technical services}} + \underbrace{\sum_{j=1}^{S} b^u_{jk} v^u_j}_{\text{cost (compensation) for providing environmental disservices}} \qquad k = 1, \cdots, N$$

Evidently, the coefficients b_{jk}^{u} are empirically determined by the structure of the regional economy and its geography. It is assumed that a single overall (negative) price for each residual has meaning, even though each productive sector—and even each consumer—has his own individual utility function. Much the same assumption is conventionally made, and accepted, in the case of positive real prices.

All of the additional variables now fit into the general framework of the original Walras-Cassel analysis. Indeed, we have $2N+2M-1$ variables (r_i, Y_i, p_i, v_i) (allowing an arbitrary normalization factor for the price level) and $2N+2M-1$ independent equations.[28] If solutions exist for the Walras-Cassel system of equations, the arguments presumably continue to hold true for the generalized model. In any case, a discussion of such mathematical questions would carry us too far from our main theme.

IV. *Concluding Comments*

The limited economics literature currently available which is devoted to environmental pollution problems has generally taken a partial equilibrium view of the matter, as well as treated the pollution of particular environmental media, such as air and water, as separate problems.[29] This no doubt reflects the propensity of the theoretical literature to view externalities as exceptional and minor. Clearly, the partial equilibrium approach in particular is very convenient theoretically and empirically for it permits external damage and control cost functions to be defined for each particular case without reference to broader interrelationships and adjustments in the economy.

We have argued in this paper that the production of residuals is an inherent and general part of the production and consumption process and, moreover, that there are important trade-offs between the gaseous, liquid, or solid forms that these residuals may take. Further, we have argued that under conditions of intensive economic and population development the environmental media which can receive and assimilate residual wastes are not free goods but natural resources of great value with respect to which voluntary exchange cannot operate because of their common property characteristics. We have also noted, in passing, that the assimilative capacity of environmental media can sometimes be altered and that therefore the problem of achieving Pareto optimality reaches beyond devising appropriate shadow prices and involves the planning and execution of investments with public goods aspects.

We have exhibited a formal mathematical framework for tracing residuals flows in the economy and related it to the general equilibrium model of resources allocation, altered to accommodate recycle and containing unpriced sectors to represent the environment. This formulation, in contrast to the usual partial equilibrium treatments, implies knowledge of all preference and production functions including relations between residuals discharge and external cost and all possible factor and process substitutions. While we feel that it represents reality with greater fidelity than the usual view, it also implies a central planning problem of impossible difficulty, both from the standpoint of data collection and computation.

What, if any, help can the general interdependency approach we have outlined offer in dealing with pollution problems effectively and reasonably efficiently? A minimal contribution is its warning that partial equilibrium approaches, while more

[28] There is one redundant equation in the system, which expresses the identity between gross product and gross income for the system as a whole (sometimes called "Walras law").

[29] See, for example, the essays in Wolozin [29].

tractable, may lead to serious errors. Second, in projecting waste residuals for an economy—a regional economy would usually be the most relevant for planning and control—the inter-industry materials flow model can provide a much more conceptually satisfying and accurate tool for projecting future residuals production than the normal aggregative extrapolations.[30] The latter not only treat gaseous, liquid, and solid wastes separately, but do not take account of input-output relations and the fact that the materials account for the region must balance.

We think that in the next few years it will be possible to make improved regional projections of residuals along the lines sketched above. Undoubtedly, there will also be further progress in empirically estimating external costs associated with residuals discharge and in estimating control costs via various alternative measures. On the basis of this kind of information, a control policy can be devised. However, this approach will still be partial. Interrelations between the regional and national economy must be treated simplistically and to be manageable, the analysis must confine itself to a specific projected bill of goods.

The basic practical question which remains to be answered is whether an iterated series of partial equilibrium treatments—e.g., focusing on one industry or region at a time, *ceteris paribus*—would converge toward the general equilibrium solution, or not. We know of no theoretical test of convergence which would be applicable in this case but, in the absence of such a criterion, would be willing to admit the possible relevance of an empirical sensitivity test more or less along the following lines: take a major residuals-producing industry (such as electric power) and parametrize its cost structure in terms of emission control levels, allowing all technically feasible permutations of factor (fuel) inputs and processes. It would be a straightforward, but complicated, operations research problem to determine the minimum cost solution as a function of the assumed (negative) price of the residuals produced. If possible industry patterns—factor and process combinations—exist which would permit a high level of emission control at only a small increase in power production cost, then it might be possible to conclude that for a significant range of (negative) residuals prices the effect on power prices —and therefore on the rest of the economy —would not be great. Such a conclusion would support the convergence hypothesis. If, on the other hand, electric power prices are very sensitive to residuals prices, then one would at least have to undertake a deeper study of consumer preference functions to try to determine what residuals prices would actually be if a market mechanism existed. If people prove to have a strong antipathy to soot and sulfur dioxide, for instance, resulting in a high (negative) price for these unwanted inputs, then one would be forced to suspect that the partial equilibrium approach is probably not convergent to the general equilibrium solution and that much more elaborate forms of analysis will be required.

[30] Some efforts to implement these concepts are already underway. Walter Isard and his associates have prepared an input-output table for Philadelphia which includes coefficients representing waterborne wastes (unpublished). The recent study of waste management in the New York Metropolitan region by the Regional Plan Association took a relatively broad view of the waste residuals problem [31]. Relevant data on several industries are being gathered. Richard Frankel's not yet published study of thermal power in which the range of technical options for controlling residuals, and their costs, is being explored is notable in this regard. His and other salient studies are described in Ayres and Kneese [2].

References

1. R. U. Ayres, "Stability of Biosystems in Sea Water," Tech. Rept. No. 142, Hudson Laboratories, Columbia University, New York 1967.

2. ——— AND A. V. KNEESE, "Environmental Pollution," in U.S. Congress, Joint Economic Committee, *Federal Programs for the Development of Human Resources*, Vol. 2, Washington 1968.
3. W. J. BAUMOL, *Welfare Economics and the Theory of the State*. Cambridge 1967.
4. K. E. BOULDING, "The Economics of the Coming Spaceship Earth," in H. Jarrett, ed., *Environmental Quality in a Growing Economy*, Baltimore 1966, pp. 3–14.
5. J. H. BOYD, "Collective Facilities in Water Quality Management," Appendix to Kneese and Bower [17].
6. J. W. BUCHANAN AND WM. C. STUBBLEBINE, "Externality," *Economica*, Nov. 1962, *29*, 371–84.
7. ——— AND G. TULLOCK, "Public and Private Interaction under Reciprocal Externality," in J. Margolis, ed., *The Public Economy of Urban Communities*, Baltimore 1965, pp. 52–73.
8. G. CASSEL, *The Theory of Social Economy*. New York 1932.
9. R. H. COASE, "The Problem of Social Cost," *Jour. Law and Econ.*, Oct. 1960, *3*, 1–44.
10. L. COLE, "Can the World be Saved?" Paper presented at the 134th Meeting of the American Association for the Advancement of Science, December 27, 1967.
11. R. K. DAVIS, *The Range of Choice in Water Management*. Baltimore 1968.
12. O. A. DAVIS AND A. WHINSTON, "Externalities, Welfare, and the Theory of Games," *Jour. Pol. Econ.*, June 1962, *70*, 241–62.
13. R. DORFMAN, P. SAMUELSON AND R. M. SOLOW, *Linear Programming and Economic Analysis*. New York 1958.
14. I. FISHER, *Nature of Capital and Income*. New York 1906.
15. A. C. HARBERGER, "Monopoly and Resources Allocation," *Am. Econ. Rev.*, Proc., May 1954, *44*, 77–87.
16. K. W. KAPP, *The Social Costs of Private Enterprise*. Cambridge 1950.
17. A. V. KNEESE AND B. T. BOWER, *Managing Water Quality: Economics, Technology, Institutions*. Baltimore 1968.
18. F. H. KNIGHT, *Risk, Uncertainty, and Profit*. Boston and New York 1921.
19. H. LEIBENSTEIN, "Allocative Efficiency vs. 'X-Efficiency,'" *Am. Econ. Rev.*, June 1966, *56*, 392–415.
20. W. P. LOWRY, "The Climate of Cities," *Sci. Am.*, Aug. 1967, *217*, 15–23.
21. E. J. MISHAN, "Reflections on Recent Developments in the Concept of External Effects," *Canadian Jour. Econ. Pol. Sci.*, Feb. 1965, *31*, 1–34.
22. A. C. PIGOU, *Economics of Welfare*. London 1952.
23. K. SCHLESINGER, "Über die Produktionsgleichungen der ökonomischen Wertlehre," *Ergebnisse eines mathematischen Kolloquiums*, No. 6. Vienna, F. Denticke, 1933.
24. D. SCHWARTZMAN, "The Burden of Monopoly," *Jour. Pol. Econ.*, Dec. 1960, *68*, 627–30.
25. T. SCITOVSKY, "Two Concepts of External Economies," *Jour. Pol. Econ.*, Apr. 1954, *62*, 143–51.
26. F. SMITH, *The Economic Theory of Industrial Waste Production and Disposal*, draft of a doctoral dissertation, Northwestern Univ. 1967.
27. R. TURVEY, "On Divergencies between Social Cost and Private Cost," *Economica*, Nov. 1962, *30*, 309–13.
28. L. WALRAS, *Elements d'economie politique pure*, Jaffé translation. London 1954.
29. H. WOLOZIN, ed., *The Economics of Air Pollution*. New York 1966.
30. CONSERVATION FOUNDATION, *Implications of Rising Carbon Dioxide Content of the Atmosphere*. New York 1963.
31. REGIONAL PLAN ASSOCIATION, *Waste Management*, a Report of the Second Regional Plan. New York 1968.

CHAPTER 22

LITTERING, DERELICTS AND THE PRICING SYSTEM*

VERNON L. SMITH

Nothing is more essential to the understanding of the socio-economics of littering, waste disposal and environmental pollution than to realize that consumer and producer decision makers only discard items of zero or negative net value, i.e., "bads". Furthermore, a vast number of producer and consumer goods leave an undesirable residue or container after use, or emit such residues as joint products in the process of consumption or use. After eating a banana, there is the peeling; after consuming beer, milk or coca cola, there is the container; when an automobile is worn out one is left with as much as two tons of junk; and a hearth fire, or the generation of electricity from fuel combustion must inevitably produce smoke. It is in the individual self-interest, usually, to heave the banana peel or beer can out the window, to abandon the old car on the parkway, and let the smoke go up the chimney.

The dominating power of the self-interest in these matters is revealed by the trash in New York City streets, the beer cans in the woods of suburbia, the smoke-choked skies of the Gary-East Chicago industrial complex, and virtually every conceivable form of litter in such unlikely places as rural Alaska, and along the highway right-of-ways in the relatively isolated Hopi and Navaho Indian reservations. Who litters? Everybody litters in some form, including even the ardent and devoted conservationist who may drive an internal combustion powered automobile to meetings of his local society, buy beer in no deposit, no return, bottles, and verily complain that the city dump (where his bottles and fat copies of the *New York Times* are laid to rest) is an eyesore.

It is futile to implore people to voluntarily give up "littering" in all its forms. Intensive campaigns and demonstrations can yield temporary cooperation. A few may heed the call — Leonard Bernstein drives an electric car — but only those who do must pay the penalty of higher costs for their social concerns.

Nor can a system of fines and punishments be a general solution to the littering-pollution problem. Most if not all states have for many years imposed stiff littering fines. "One should not get caught," rather than "One should not litter," seems to be the practical interpretation put upon such fines. Any attempt to enforce such fines on an effective scale would almost surely be prohibitively expensive, and in any case would not solve the problem of ultimate disposal of commodity wastes.

As it is manifest in littering, "the system" is nothing more insidious or subtle than everybody simply "doing his thing".

An alternative approach to the littering-pollution problem is to increase private incentives, through the pricing system, to recycle containers and commodity or process residues [1]. The pricing system was used in this manner (until recently) with beverages by requiring a deposit fee for the return of containers [2]. Anyone over forty can remember when the five-cent soft drink came in a reusable bottle on which there was a two-cent deposit fee. With a 40% deposit such containers were either carefully returned or, if thrown away by one, were salvaged and redeemed by another. The private and the social interest were not in conflict. The deposit approach has been suggested in connection with solving the problem of abandoned automobiles, and the closely related concept of environmental "user charges" may have an important role in raising the incentive to recycle waste gases and liquids in industry. Generally, with present technology, private values alone are too low to justify a significant volume of recycling. In periods of high demand for steel, the recycling of scrap steel is encouraged by its higher value as raw material. This raises scrap prices and increases the return of scrap to the furnaces, but in other periods scrap prices are too low to cover the private costs of assembling and shipping scrap steel to distant mills. Gradually, the recycling of beverage bottles has given away to the lower private cost, no deposit, no return, bottle, and the distressingly durable aluminum can.

But in all these cases, deposit fees and scrap values to not reflect the social costs of littering, abandonment, and city dump disposal. These social costs do not appear in the calculations of producers, when they make decisions concerning the design of products and their containers, when they select the raw materials to be used, and when they make choices between recycling and non-recycling technologies. It is not known what might be the extent of recycling if container and other scrap values reflected these social costs, but there can be little doubt that recycling would be more commonplace.

In what follows we explore the economics of littering by means of a static model which associates a discommodious container or residue with the consumption of a commodity. We examine first the consumer choice problem assuming no littering (or pollution) externalities in consumption. Then we introduce externality by assuming that the aggregate of all commodity residues which are not recycled is an external diseconomy to each consumer. We then add a producer's market and derive the general equilibrium condition for consumption, production and recycling. These conditions are then compared with those of Pareto optimal littering. It is shown that a system of "social deposit" fees or scrap values, will produce the Pareto optimal amount of littering. These values converge to a single public value independent of the individual if the littering disutility for any one individual is negligible compared to the sum of the disutilities (suitably normalized) of all other individuals. Finally, it is shown that a tax or "disposal charge" on the production of new units or a subsidy on the reprocessing of recycled units is equivalent to the social deposit fee as a means of reflecting to each individual the social cost of his littering activity.

1. THE CONSUMER RECYCLING DECISION

We begin with an analysis of consumer's choice as applied to the decision to return container units, or the residue of commodity consumption, for reprocessing and reuse. The entirely appropriate paradigm is the "coke" or beer bottle, for this represents the general case. What is important is that after consumption (production, use) there is something left which is discommodious troublesome and "costly" for the decision maker to recycle, but which has a marketable reuse value. In the case of a reuseable container the manufacturer of the commodity may institute a deposit fee on the container to be refunded upon return. But this is an artifice of product differentiation [3] to insure the return of particular containers to particular sources. In a competitive market, with container standardization, one would simply observe a market for containers, just as there is a market for scrap steel, copper, aluminum and paper.

Thus, the empty container, old newspaper, or junk automobile, is discommodious to return for recycling, but we assume it can be discarded, abandoned, or "littered" at zero cost (both private and social in this section). Depending on the utility function, prices and income, some, all or no containers or scrap units may be returned by a given consumer.

We model this behaviour below, assuming a single commodity which comes in a reuseable container or leaves a scrap residue. (The general case is described by interpreting all prices and quantities as vectors). Let

I = income of consumer
x = commodity units purchased
y = container (or residual scrap) units returned
z = x - y container units discarded
p = net price of x excluding its container
r = price of container (refund or "deposit"), or scrap residue
P = p + r = gross price of x including its container

(You cannot avoid buying a container or residue unit when you buy a commodity unit).

The utility function is

$$U = \Phi(x,y),\ \Phi_1 \equiv \frac{\delta\Phi}{\delta x} > 0,$$

$$\Phi_2 \equiv \frac{\delta\Phi}{\delta y} < 0,\ \left.\frac{d^2y}{dx^2}\right|_{\Phi = \text{constant}} < 0. \tag{1}$$

That is we assume that x and y have positive and negative marginal utilities respectively with strictly concave indifference curves. The budget constraint is

$$I \geq Px - ry = px + r(x - y) = px + rz \tag{2}$$

and if each consumer returns only his own waste, then

$$x \geq y \geq 0. \tag{3}$$

The Lagrange criterion is then to maximize
$L = \Phi(x,y) + \lambda(I - Px + ry) + \mu(x - y)$.

The solutions of greatest economic interest to the littering problem are those in which the consumer always buys some of the commodity ($x^\circ > 0$); may return all, some, or none of the container ($x^\circ - y^\circ \geq 0$, $y^\circ \geq 0$, $\mu^\circ \geq 0$), and is nonsatiated ($\lambda^\circ > 0$). The Kuhn-Tucker first order conditions for this set of maxima are

$$\Phi_1^\circ - \lambda^\circ P + \mu^\circ = 0,\ x^\circ > 0 \qquad (4)$$

$$y^\circ[\Phi_2^\circ + \lambda^\circ r - \mu^\circ] = 0,\ y^\circ \geq 0,\ \Phi_2^\circ + \lambda^\circ r - \mu^\circ \leq 0 \qquad (5)$$

$$\mu^\circ(x^\circ - y^\circ) = 0,\ \mu^\circ \geq 0,\ (x^\circ - y^\circ) \geq 0 \qquad (6)$$

$$\lambda^\circ(I - Px^\circ + ry^\circ) = 0,\ I - Px^\circ + ry^\circ \geq 0,\ \lambda^\circ > 0. \qquad (7)$$

The constraint set defined by (2) and (3) is illustrated in Figs. 1-3.

Three different solutions (x°, y°, λ°, μ°), corresponding to the return of all, none, or some containers as scrap are shown in Figs. 1-3.

Case (i) $x^\circ = y^\circ > 0$. Conditions (4) - (7) for this case are

$$\Phi_1^\circ - \lambda^\circ P + \mu^\circ = 0$$

$$\Phi_2^\circ + \lambda^\circ r - \mu^\circ = 0$$

$$\left.\begin{array}{l} x^\circ - y^\circ = 0,\ \mu^\circ \geq 0 \\ I - Px^\circ + ry^\circ = 0,\ \lambda^\circ > 0 \end{array}\right\}\ x^\circ = y^\circ = I/(P - r)$$

Therefore, $0 \leq \mu^\circ = (r\Phi_1^\circ + P\Phi_2^\circ)/(P - 3)$ or $-(\Phi_1^\circ/\Phi_2^\circ) \geq (P/r)$.

At the corner solution $x^\circ = y^\circ$, the slope of the indifference curve must not be less than the slope of the budget line.

Case (ii) $x^\circ > 0$ $y^\circ = 0$. From (4) - (7),

$$\Phi_1^\circ - \lambda^\circ P + \mu^\circ = 0$$

$$\Phi_2^\circ + \lambda^\circ r - \mu^\circ \leq 0$$

$$\left.\begin{array}{l} x^\circ - y^\circ > 0,\ y^\circ = 0,\ \mu^\circ = 0 \\ I - Px^\circ + ry^\circ = 0,\ \lambda^\circ > 0 \end{array}\right\}\ x^\circ = I/P$$

With $\mu^\circ = 0$, we have

$$-(\Phi_1^\circ/\Phi_2^\circ) \leq (P/r).$$

At the corner solution $x^\circ > 0$, $y^\circ = 0$, the slope of an indifference curve cannot exceed that of the budget line. Since $\mu^\circ = 0$, one would pay nothing to return more containers or scrap since the container constraint is not binding.

Case (iii) $x^\circ > y^\circ > 0$. From (4) - (7)

$$\Phi_1^\circ - \lambda^\circ P + \mu^\circ = 0$$

$$\Phi_2^\circ + \lambda^\circ r - \mu^\circ = 0$$

$$x^\circ - y^\circ > 0, \mu^\circ = 0$$

$$I - Px^\circ + ry^\circ = 0, \lambda^\circ > 0$$

Hence, we have a tangency solution on the budget line where

$$-(\Phi_1^\circ/\Phi_2^\circ) = (P/r)$$

Two propositions stating conditions under which all or no commodity waste will be returned for recycling, are basic to the economic theory of littering.

> *Proposition 1:* If the scrap value, r, is small enough, no waste units will be returned.

This is proved by noting that the limiting value of the slope of a budget line is $\lim_{r\to o} (p + r)/r = \infty$. Therefore, since the slope of the indifference curves are assumed to be positive everywhere, we can always find an r small enough to give the "maximum litter" corner solution such as is illustrated in Fig. 2. This proposition covers the limiting case of banana peels and aluminum cans, that is no deposit, no return!

> *Proposition 2:* If the marginal utility of an additional unit of commodity net of the disutility of returning its residue $(\Phi_1 + \Phi_2)$ is positive for all (x,y), then there exists a deposit fee large enough to induce the return of all such waste units.

Again taking the limit of the slope of the budget line, $\lim_{r\to\infty}(p + r)/r = 1$. But since $\Phi_1 + \Phi_2 > 0$, $\Phi_1 > 0$, $\Phi_2 < 0$, the slope of an indifference curve is $-(\Phi_1/\Phi_2) > 1$. Therefore we can always find an r large enough to yield the "no littering" corner solution such as that in Fig. 1.

It is reasonable to assume that at high utility levels the indifference curves are not as steep as at low levels of utility. Thus, at low levels of utility, along a given indifference curve, one might be willing to return a relatively large increment of containers in compensation for an additional increment of commodity. But this substitution rate could be expected to decline with increases in the utility level. The income-consumption curve corresponding to these considerations is shown in Fig. 4. At low levels of income, the consumer returns all his commodity waste, while at high levels of income he returns a smaller quanity (perhaps none) of his commodity waste.

2. CONSUMER'S MARKET WITH EXTERNALITIES

We next introduce littering or "pollution" externalities in a simple and obvious way. It is assumed that the aggregate commodity waste of all consumers that is *not* recycled appears as an external diseconomy in each consumer's utility function. This is because all disposed waste is assumed to appear as litter, city dump eyesores, or air or water "contamination".

The utility functions for n consumers are

$$U^i = \Phi^i\,[x_i,\ y_i,\ \Sigma_k(x_k - y_k)],\ i = 1, 2, \ldots, n,$$

where the first two arguments of the utility function are assumed, as before, to yield positive and negative marginal utilities respectively. Since disposed waste is discommodious, $\Phi^i_3 < 0$. We assume that $\Phi^i_1 + \Phi^i_3 > 0$, i.e. an additional unit consumed yields positive marginal utility net of its "littering" disutility; also that $\Phi^i_2 < \Phi^i_3$ i.e. the self-interest is better served by littering than recycling!

If there are m firms in the economy, and consumer i owns the fraction α_{ij} of firm j's profit, π_j, then the ith consumer's profit (rent) income is $\pi_i = \Sigma_j\alpha_{ij}\pi_j$. Letting L_i be the ith consumer's fixed endowment of (scarce) labour, commanding the wage, w, his budget equation is

$$\pi_i + wL_i = Px_i - ry_i.$$

Maximizing utility subject to this budget constraint, and $x_i - y_i \geq 0$, $y_i > 0$, where the Lagrangian is

$$\Phi^i + \lambda^i(\pi_i + wL_i - Px_i + ry_i) + \mu^i(x_i - y_i), \text{ gives}$$

$$\Phi^i_1 + \Phi^i_3 - \lambda^i P + \mu^i = 0,\ x^\circ_1 > 0,\ \lambda^i > 0. \tag{8}$$

$$y^\circ_1[\Phi^i_2 - \Phi^i_3 + \lambda^i r - \mu^i] = 0,\ \Phi^i_2 - \Phi^i_3 + \lambda^i r - \mu^i \leq 0,\ y^\circ_i \geq 0 \tag{9}$$

$$\mu^i(x^\circ_i - y^\circ_i) = 0,\ x^\circ_i - y^\circ_i \geq 0,\ \mu^i \geq 0 \tag{10}$$

3. PRODUCER'S MARKET

The producer's market is assumed to consist of firms engaged in one or more of the three activities: (i) commodity production, (ii) the reprocessing of commodity containers, derelicts or other waste, and (iii) the production of new containers or commodity materials (from free raw material, as an alternative to recycling).

For firm j, let

L^j_x, labour used in commodity production.

L^j_y, labour used in reprocessing containers or waste.

L^j_z, labour used in producing new containers or commodity material.

$x_j = f_j(L^j_x)$, output of commodity.

$y_j = g_j(L^j_y)$, output of reprocessed containers or waste.

$z_j = h_j(L^j_z)$, output of new containers or materials.

If R is the price of a new or reprocessed container and w the wage of labour, the jth firm's profit from each of the three activities is

$$\pi^j_x = (p + r - R)f_j(L^j_x) - wL^j_x$$

$$\pi^j_y = (R - r)g_j(L^j_y) - wL^j_y$$

$$\pi^j_z = Rh_j(L^j_z) - wL^j_z$$

The Kuhn-Tucker conditions for maximizing $\pi^j = \pi^j_x + \pi^j_y + \pi^j_z$, setting w = 1 as numeraire, are

$$[(P - R)f'_j(L^j_x) - 1]\, L^j_x = 0, \qquad (p + r - R)f'_j(L^j_x) \leq 1,\ L^j_x \geq 0 \tag{11}$$

$$[(R - r)g'_j(L^j_y) - 1]\, L^j_y = 0, \qquad (R - r)g'_j(L^j_y) \leq 1,\ L^j_y \geq 0 \tag{12}$$

$$[Rh'_j(L^j_z) - 1]\, L^j_z = 0,\ Rh'_j(L^j_z) \leq 1,\ L^j_z \geq 0 \tag{13}$$

Each of these conditions simply state that, at a profit maximum, price cannot exceed marginal cost, e.g. $(p + r - R) \leq 1/f'_j(L^j_x)$, and if net price is less than marginal cost for any activity the firm does not perform that activity. Hence, we could have complete specialization of firms among the three activities, or some firms could perform two or all three of the activities.

From (12) and (13), if $L^a_y > 0$, $L^b_z > 0$, for any firms a and b, then $r = (1/h'_b) - (1/g'_a)$. The deposit fee r (or commodity scrap value) must equal the difference between the marginal cost of a new unit and the marginal cost of reprocessing a unit. If this difference is negative or zero, then the commodity or container has no recycling value.

4. GENERAL EQUILIBRIUM

By adding the following closure conditions, we complete the general equilibrium system of decentralized competitive production, consumption, and "littering."

$$\Sigma_j \alpha_{ij} \pi^j + L_i = Px_i - ry_i,\ i = 1, 2, \ldots, n \tag{14}$$

$$\Sigma_i L_i = \Sigma_j (L^j_x + L^j_y + L^j_z) \tag{15}$$

$$\Sigma_i x_i = \Sigma_j f_j(L^j_x) \tag{16}$$

$$\Sigma_i y_i = \Sigma_j g_j(L^j_y) \tag{17}$$

$$\Sigma_i (x_i - y_i) = \Sigma_j h_j(L^j_z) \tag{18}$$

$$\pi^j = (P - R)f_j(L^j_x) + (R - r)g_j(L^j_y) + Rh_j(L^j_z) - (L^j_x + L^j_y + L^j_z),\ j = 1, 2, \ldots, n \tag{19}$$

5. PARETO OPTIMAL LITTERING

Suppose the above general equilibrium problem is formulated as a control problem using the Pareto criterion. The objective is to maximize one consumer's utility (say, number 1) subject to given utility levels for the other n - 1 consumers, and subject to the resource and technological restrictions on the general equilibrium model. This is equivalent to maximizing $\Sigma_{i=1}^{n} k_i \Phi^i[x_i, y_i, \Sigma_k(x_k - y_k)]$ ($k_1 = 1$) subject to $x_i - y_i \geq 0$, and the conservation conditions (15) through (18). The problem of a central manager is to choose nonnegative vectors x, y, L_x, L_y, L_z so as to maximize

$$\Sigma_i k_i \Phi^i + \Sigma_i \alpha^i(x_i - y_i) + \lambda_0[\Sigma_i L_i - \Sigma_j(L_x^j + L_y^j + L_z^j)]$$
$$+ \lambda_1[\Sigma_j f_j(L_x^j) - \Sigma_i x_i] + \lambda_2[\Sigma_j g_j(L_y^j) - \Sigma_i y_i]$$
$$+ \lambda_3[\Sigma_j h_j(L_z^j) - \Sigma_i(x_i - y_i)],$$

where the k_i, α^i, and λ's are Lagrange multipliers.

Since λ_0 is the central planner's implicit shadow wage of labour, we set $\lambda_0 = 1$ in what follows. The first order Kuhn-Tucker conditions are then:

$$k_i(\Phi_1^i + \Phi_3^i) + \Sigma_{s \neq i} k_s \Phi_3^s + \alpha^i - \lambda_1 - \lambda_3 = 0, \quad x_i^\circ > 0,\ i = 1, 2, \ldots, n \tag{8'}$$

$$y_i^\circ[k_i(\Phi_2^i - \Phi_3^i) - \Sigma_{s \neq i} k_s \Phi_3^s - \alpha^i - \lambda_2 + \lambda_3] = 0,$$
$$y_i^\circ \geq 0,\ k_i(\Phi_2^i - \Phi_3^i) - \Sigma_{s \neq i} k_s \Phi_3^s - \alpha^i - \lambda_2 + \lambda_3 \leq 0, \tag{9'}$$
$$i = 1, 2, \ldots, n$$

$$\alpha^i(x_i^\circ - y_i^\circ) = 0,\ x_i^\circ - y_i^\circ \geq 0,\ \alpha^i \geq 0, \tag{10'}$$

$$[\lambda_1 f_j'(L_x^j) - 1]L_x^j = 0,\ \lambda_1 f_j'(L_x^j) \leq 1,\ L_x^j \geq 0 \tag{11'}$$

$$[\lambda_2 g_j'(L_y^j) - 1]L_y^j = 0,\ \lambda_2 g_j'(L_y^j) \leq 1,\ L_y^j \geq 0 \tag{12'}$$

$$[\lambda_3 h_j'(L_z^j) - 1]L_z^j = 0,\ \lambda_3 h_j'(L_z^j) \leq 1,\ L_z^j \geq 0 \tag{13'}$$

These conditions correspond to conditions (8) - (13) for competitive decentralized general equilibrium. Since there are no postulated externalities in the production activities conditions (11') - (13') are identical with (11) - (13) for general equilibrium where the λ's are related to the free market prices by the transformations,

$$\left.\begin{aligned} \lambda_1 &= p + r - R \\ \lambda_2 &= R - r \\ \lambda_3 &= R \end{aligned}\right\} \qquad (20)$$

In conditions (8') and (9') note that we have separated the private disutility of "own" disposal or littering, $k_i\Phi_3^i$, from the social disutility of such activity, $\sum_{s\neq i} k_s\Phi_3^s$. By combining the marginal consumption conditions (8) and (9) into the familiar substitution form we have

$$\frac{\Phi_2^i - \Phi_3^i - \mu^i}{\Phi_1^i + \Phi_3^i + \mu^i} \leq - \frac{r}{p + r}, \qquad (21)$$

where if < holds, $y_i^\circ = 0$

If we perform the same operation on the Pareto consumption conditions (8') and (9'), we can write

$$\frac{\Phi_2^i - \Phi_3^i - (\alpha^i/k_i)}{\Phi_1^i + \Phi_3^i + (\alpha^i/k_i)} \leq - \frac{(\lambda_3 - \lambda_2 - \sum_{s\neq i} k_s\Phi_3^s)}{\lambda_1 + \lambda_3 - \sum_{s\neq i} k_s\Phi_3^s}.$$

Using the transformations (20), and letting $\mu^i = \alpha^i/k_i$, this becomes

$$\frac{\Phi_2^i - \Phi_3^i - \mu^i}{\Phi_1^i + \Phi_3^i + \mu^i} \leq - \frac{(r - \sum_{s\neq i} k_s\Phi_3^s)}{p + r - \sum_{s\neq i} k_s\Phi_3}, \qquad (22)$$

where if < holds, $y_i^\circ = 0$.

Comparing (21) and (22) it is seen that the general equilibrium conditions on consumption will correspond to those of Pareto optimality if a system of *social* deposit fees or scrap values, r_i' are incorporated into the price structure, where

$$r_i' = r - \Sigma_{s \neq i} k_s \Phi_3^s > r.$$

These social fees or prices exceed the free market values, r, by the social costs of littering $\Sigma_{s \neq i} k_s \Phi_3^s < 0$. That is, the value of a unit of commodity waste for recycling purposes must reflect to consumer i the disutility of the units disposed to the other n - 1 consumers. Furthermore, it is reasonable to assume that each indivisual's "own" littering disutility is negligible in comparison with the aggregate of the other n - 1 consumers. That is we assume

$$\Sigma_s k_s \Phi_3^s \cong \Sigma_{s \neq i} k_s \Phi_3^s, \text{ for all i.}$$

Operationally, this assumption means that the amount that any one individual would pay to see one more beer bottle reused rather than disposed is as nothing compared with the total amount that the rest of the population would pay. Using this assumption, we can write

$r_i' = r - \Sigma_{s \neq i} k_s \Phi_3^s \cong r - \Sigma_s k_s \Phi_3^s = r'$, for all i, and the "social deposit fee", r' becomes a uniform fee or price independent of i. For Pareto optimality the recycling value of commodity waste must include the social opportunity cost of waste disposal.

In general it is clear that the decentralized competitive system will not produce Pareto optimal disposal activities. However, there is one situation in which the competitive solution is Pareto optimal. Suppose, in (22) that the inequality holds for all i. Then $y_i^\circ = 0$, $\mu^i = 0$, for all i. But since $k_s \Phi_3^s < 0$ we have

$$-\frac{r - \Sigma_{s \neq i} k_s \Phi_3^s}{p + r - \Sigma_{s \neq i} k_s \Phi^s} < -\frac{r}{p + r}.$$

Therefore the inequality holds in (21) for all i, and (21)

and (22) are equivalent conditions. The competitive model yields Pareto optimal disposal if it does not pay to recycle commodity waste after taking full account of the social opportunity cost of disposal. This condition no doubt held somewhat more universally in earlier ages when the population was small, the volume of refuse small, and the capacity of air, water and soil to dissolve, absorb, purify or simply "hide" pollutants was large. The condition no doubt holds today for some forms of commodity waste. For example, it is doubtful that it would pay to recycle toothpicks in any form. The social cost of toothpick litter is surely so low, that accounting for such social costs would yield the same corner solution as that of the competitive economy.

6. DISPOSAL CHARGES, RECYCLING SUBSIDIES AND PARETO OPTIMALITY

It is not difficult to show that the social cost of littering can be internalized in other ways than by a system of social deposit or waste values. An appropriate "disposal charge" levied on the production of net new containers (or commodity material net of recycled waste) or a recycle subsidy paid to producers for the reuse of containers or waste, are alternative ways of inducing Pareto optimality in the competitive model.

Consider first the use of a disposal charge T levied on each unit of *newly* manufactured container (e.g. beer bottles) or commodity material (e.g. steel). The profit of the jth firm is now

$$\pi^j = (P - R)f_j(L_x^j) + (R - r)g_j(L_y^j) + (R - T)h_j(L_z^j) - (L_x^j + L_y^j + L_z^j)$$

giving the maximizing conditions (11), (12) and

$$[(R - T)h_j'(L_z^j) - 1]L_z^j = 0, \qquad (R - T)h_j'(L_z^j) \leq 1, \; L_z^j = 0. \tag{13''}$$

Now assume that at least some new container or material units are produced. Then $(R - T)h_j' = 1$, for some j, in (13"), and from the second inequality in (12),

$$r \geq R - (1/g_j') = (1/h_j') - (1/g_j') + T.$$

Substituting into the free market conditions (21),

$$\frac{\Phi_2^i - \Phi_3^i - \mu^i}{\Phi_1^i + \Phi_3^i + \mu^i} \leq -\frac{r}{p+r} \leq -\frac{[(1/h_j') - (1/g_j') + T]}{p + (1/h_j') - (1/g_j') + T}. \quad (21')$$

Similarly, from the Pareto conditions (12') and (13'), we have

$$\lambda_3 - \lambda_2 \geq (1/h_j') - (1/g_j'),$$

and, using (20), we can write the Pareto conditions (22) in the form

$$\frac{\Phi_2^i - \Phi_3^i - \mu^i}{\Phi_1 + \Phi_3 + \mu^i} \leq -\frac{[(1/h_j') - (1/g_j') - \sum_{s\neq i} k_s\Phi_3^s]}{p + (1/h_j') - (1/g_j') - \sum_{s\neq i} k_s\Phi_3^s}. \quad (22')$$

Comparing (21') and (22') it is clear that (21') corresponds to Pareto optimality if $T = -\sum_{s\neq i} k_s\Phi_3^s$, i.e. if the disposal charge T is equal to the social cost of littering.

The reader may easily verify that if a subsidy S is given for each container or commodity waste material unit that is recycled, then the profit maximizing condition (12) is replaced by $(R - r + S)g_j' \leq 1$. Therefore, if $Rh_j' = 1$ for some j, $r \geq R + S - (1/g_j') = S + (1h_j') - (1/g_j')$, and the condition (21) becomes

$$\frac{\Phi_2^i - \Phi_3^i - \mu^i}{\Phi_1^i + \Phi_3^i + \mu^i} \leq -\frac{r}{p+r} \leq -\frac{[(1/h_j') - (1/g_j') + S]}{p + (1/h_j') - (1/g_j') + S}. \quad (21'')$$

Consequently, we have Pareto optimal littering if $S = -\sum_{s\neq i} k_s\Phi_3^s$.

7. DISCUSSION

In the above model, waste disposal, littering, or pollution enters the economic system as a "public bad" in each consumer's utility function. In principle, the use of Pigou-Hotelling disposal charges or recycling subsidies will yield efficient competitive solutions. But choosing the "right" charges requires decision makers to reveal their distaste for litter [cf. 4]. Since waste disposal and litter clean-up are usually public enterprises voted into existence indirectly if not directly by consumers whose purchase choices have created the disposal problem, an operational approach might be to take such disposal and clean-up costs as a measure of the "revealed" social disutility of commodity waste. But the real problem of implementation is the allocation of such costs to specific types of waste which vary in decomposability, ugliness and toxicity.

In principle public intervention through a charge system is not the only alternative. Decentralized alternatives are available through the legal system [cf. 2]. Damage suits brought by consumer classes (e.g. non-beer drinkers) against consumer or producer decision makers (beer drinkers or bottlers) are an entirely appropriate avenue. Such suits are popularly interpreted as punitive, but their economic function is (or should be) to internalize cost at key points in the inter-industry decision tree.

The problem of best choice between public policies — direct administration of a pollution charge (or subsidy) system, or establishment of a legal system more favorable to pollution damage suits — is primarily a problem of choosing a system with lowest administrative, or transactions cost. For certain kinds of littering-pollution activities, such as offshore oil spillage, the full-cost damage suit approach may be much the lower cost means of internalizing social cost to the appropriate decision makers in the appropriate amounts. Uniform government precautionary drilling rules, in the absence of damage responsibility, may simply invite technical compliance with the rules in a situation where drilling conditions and spillage risk are widely variable. Damage responsibility might more effectively induce self-imposed drilling rules which vary with conditions that only decentralized decision makers can judge, given the incentive to do so.

But court costs are high, and it is questionable whether the damage suit approach can be a general solution to all forms of the littering problem. The charge or subsidy systems have the potential of inducing positive value upon a host of waste items which no one now has the incentive to recycle. To the extent that such a charge system can be administered at lower cost than the court costs of processing thousands of small scale damage suits, the former is to be preferred.

FOOTNOTES

* I am grateful to the National Science Foundation for research support. I have had the benefit of numerous discussions with members of the faculty-student graduate seminar at the University of Massachusetts, and with Charles Holt who posed to me the question of the equivalence of disposal charges and deposit fees.

[1] Implicit in our utility hypothesis is the assumption that an additional unit of disposed commodity waste yields the same disutility regardless of who disposed of the unit. If however some consumers carry a sense of "guilt" caused by their own littering, then it would be necessary to write

$$U^i = \Phi^i[x_i \; y_i \; x_i - y_i \; , \sum_{k \neq i} (x_k - y_k)],$$

where $\Phi^i_3 \neq \Phi^i_4$ i.e. we would distinguish the disutility of "own" versus "other" littering activity. Any consumer for whom $\Phi^i_2 > \Phi^i_3$ would then refrain from littering out of a sense of "social responsibility".

[2] The models of this and the previous section can be generalized in various ways. Besides the routine generalization to multiple commodities, alternative or additional assumptions can be made about technology. For example, one could introduce waste collection and clean-up activities which could include the sorting out of marketable scrap so that such activities become part of production rather than household decision making. But littering proper, as distinct from waste disposal, would still be essentially a consumer activity, and for this reason the present paper has focused on the littering paradigm of the pollution problem. A general model should include as constraints on the economy the ultimate physical laws governing the conservation of mass and energy in the conversion of inputs into outputs, where "inputs and outputs" include all physical objects and energy

(electricity, smoke, airline service, noise etc). Some subset of such objects and energy emissions appear in utility functions as goods or bads, with bads being recycled, disposed or absorbed by nature depending on the corner solutions in firm and household decisions.

REFERENCES

[1] AYRES, R.U. and A.V. KNEESE, "Production, Consumption and Externalities", *American Economic Review*, June 1969, 59, 282-297.

[2] COASE, RONALD H. "The Problem of Social Cost", *Journal of Law and Economics*, Oct. 1960, pp. 1-44.

[3] MASSELL, BENTON F. and ROSS M. PARISH, "Empty Bottles", *Journal of Political Economy*, Nov/Dec. 1968, 76, 1224-33.

[4] SAMUELSON, PAUL A. "The Pure Theory of Public Expenditure", *Review of Economics and Statistics*, Nov. 1954, 36, pp. 387-9.

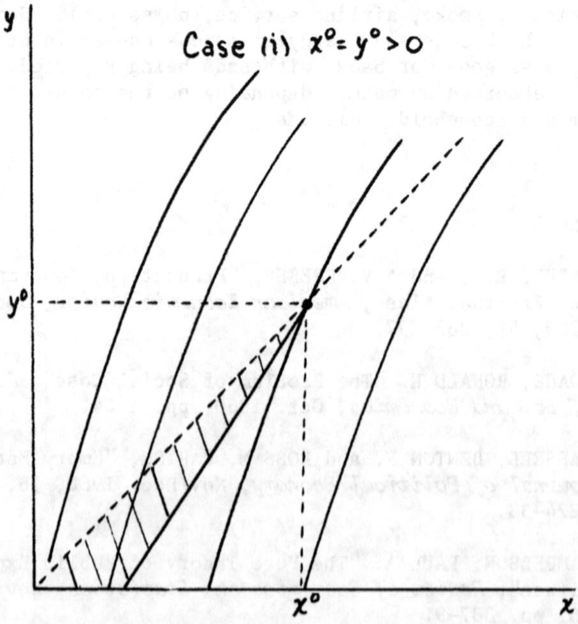

FIGURE 1

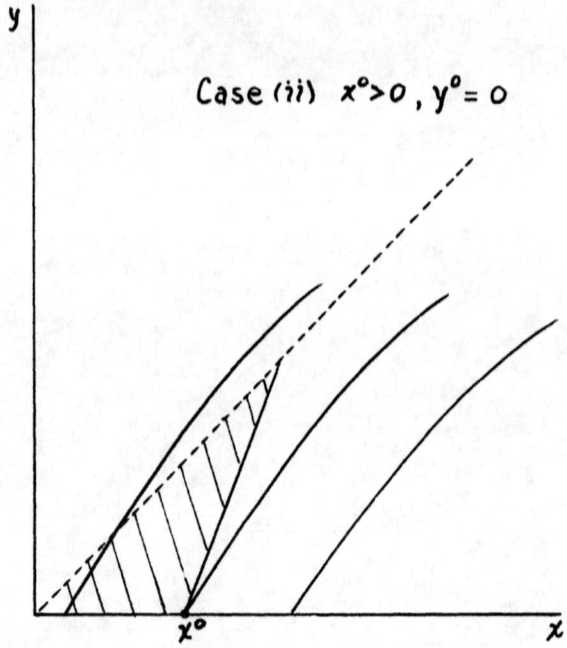

FIGURE 2

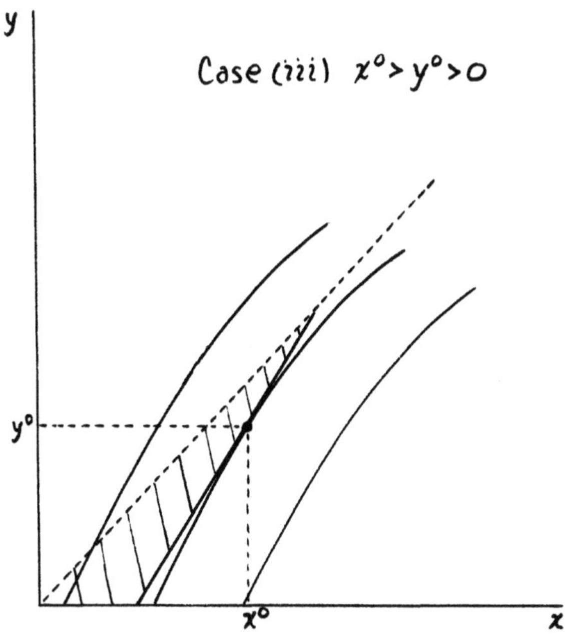

FIGURE 3

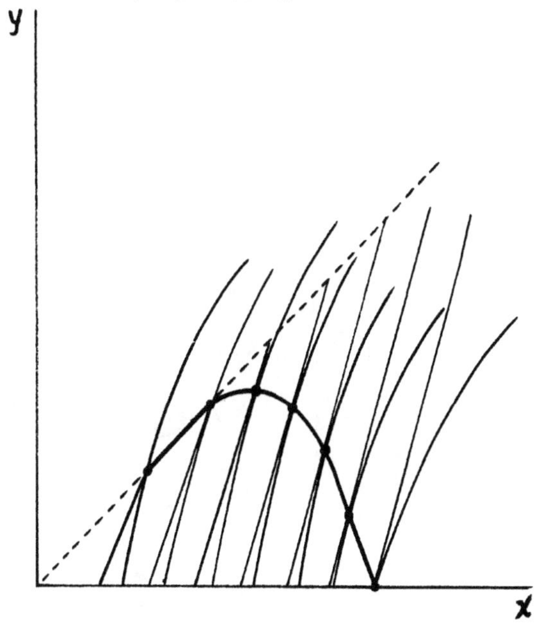

FIGURE 4

CHAPTER 23

DYNAMICS OF WASTE ACCUMULATION: DISPOSAL VERSUS RECYCLING*

VERNON L. SMITH

INTRODUCTION

Several authors have explored recently the problem of pollution or waste disposal with models of social optimization over time.[1] The general hypothesis underlying these models is that waste, which is a public "bad", is created as a by-product of producing private goods. The classic example is of course smoke produced in the generation of electricity.

This paper focuses on the dynamics of recycling, using a rudimentary model emphasizing only those elements essential to the recycling problem.[2] The problem of waste accumulation is viewed as the joint result of household and firm decisions to "litter", i.e., let waste degrade by natural biological and chemical processes, instead of recycling waste into production. Consumption of the typical private good is assumed to leave a waste residue that is a consumer "bad", although it may have scrap value for recycling purposes. One paradigm is the beverage container, while another is the derelict automobile. If the container is of the non-deposit-no-return variety it has no recycling value (no "deposit" fee) and households have no incentive to do other than dispose of such waste either by littering or by city dump deposit, the latter alternative being merely a form of concentrated littering. The same applies to the junk automobile. In the absence of scrap values sufficient to pay for the return of junk automobiles to the steel furnaces, the self-interest is served by abandonment on the parkway, the vacant lot, or the river bank.

Almost everybody litters or pollutes in some form because the incentive structure favours waste discharge activities. Essentially the environment is viewed by each decision maker as a free resource for discharge purposes. Each individual's litter contributes marginally to the general discomfort, but in the aggregate may produce severe disruption of the environment. Since environmental quality is actually a scarce resource which has value, and since no one must pay for the right to discharge, the implicit effect is to subsidize pollution activities.

Underlying recent proposals to institute disposal charges or deposit fees on packaging materials and commodity materials is a desire to alter the incentive structure of the "system" in which everybody in some sense litters or pollutes, yet everybody protests that littering is a public bad. The final section of the paper discusses some of the features of a Senate bill designed to introduce "package pollution" charges.

A MODEL OF WASTE REUSE

Assume an economy of n households each with identical, strictly concave, utility function $u(q_1, q_2, Q)$ having continuous partial derivatives. The instantaneous quantity of commodity units consumed is q_1 (a "good") with $\partial u/\partial q_1 > 0$, but q_1 is equal also to the instantaneous quantity of waste units (a "bad") resulting as a by-product of consumption. The commodity is assumed to produce an undesirable residue following consumption or use, such as banana peels, junk automobiles, and newspaper trash, or else the commodity comes in a container that is a "bad," such as milk cartons, hamburger wrappers, and beer cans. In general it is assumed that such waste units can be reprocessed or recycled into the productive system, but not without utility losses to households. Thus, to households (in the absence of incentives to do otherwise), it is in the individual self-interest to litter beer cans and abandon junk automobiles. In the context of this model we do not distinguish between littering and disposal. Thus, "to litter" is also "to dispose" of waste in rivers, the ocean, or even city dumps since city dumps are an eyesore, and ultimately "disposal" by such means must spoil land or water or directly pollute the air by burning. Due to the law of conservation of mass, we make the reasonable assumption that, ultimately, there is *no* escape except by recycling.[3] That is, material commodity waste may be compacted, burned, or chemically treated for disposal, but there remains a physical mass of undesirable material that yields disutility. Only by recycling can the material again be embodied in service, yielding commodities. The quantity of recycled waste is $q_2 \leq q_1$, and since it may be more troublesome for households to retain and return waste for recycling than to litter or dispose of such waste, we have $\partial u/\partial q_2 \leq 0$.

The quantity of container units that are disposed, and that must be replaced by newly produced units, is $q_3 = q_1 - q_2$.

Therefore new materials, such as glass, paper or steel must be manufactured in order to replace the beer bottles, newspapers and automobiles that are not recycled.

The stock of waste, Q, accumulates at a gross rate $n(q_1 - q_2)$, but as in Plourde and Brock we assume that waste degrades at a percentage rate γ applied to Q. Hence, the net accumulation rate of waste is $\dot{Q} = n(q_1 - q_2) - \gamma Q$, and the accumulated stock of waste enters utility functions as a "bad," $\partial u/\partial Q \leq 0$.

We assume n identical firms that can perform any or all of three productive activities: the production of commodity (complete with container in the case, say, of beer or milk), according to the production function, $f_1(L_1)$; the reprocessing of waste residue into new containers or commodity materials, with production function $f_2(L_2)$; and the production of new containers or materials to replace waste units not recycled, $f_3(L_3)$. L_i is the quantity of some homogeneous, non-produced resource, such as labour, used in productive activity i, and L is the total quantity of such a resource that is available for allocation. Each $f_i(L_i)$ is concave with continuous derivatives, and $f_i' > 0$, $f_i(0) = 0$.

These assumptions about technology and tastes imply that the cost of recycling is reflected in private utility losses ($\partial u/\partial q_2 \leq 0$) and in the labour ($L_2$) required for reprocessing. The opportunity cost of recycling arises from the public utility losses ($\partial u/\partial Q \leq 0$) of waste accumulation and the labour (L_3) required to produce new commodity materials or containers. The cost of raw material itself is zero, and there is a zero technological cost of disposal. Later sections will show how the model can be amended to deal explicitly with natural resources that can be saved by recycling, and how the model can be interpreted in terms of a pure waste or pollution reduction model.

For pedagogical purposes it will be assumed initially that some, but not all, waste material is recycled, i.e., $q_1 > 0$, $q_2 > 0$, $q_3 = q_1 - q_2 > 0$. This allows the problem to be formulated entirely in terms of equality constraints with interior solutions. The development will be interpreted graphically by means of the usual phase diagram. Then the important boundary solutions will be introduced with a graphical exposition. The boundary solutions are of immense economic significance, and are not a technical curiosity, for they constitute the cases in which there is total recycling and no recycling.[4]

For the interior case, substituting $q_i = f_i(L_i)$, the social welfare problem is to choose the L_i (as functions of time) so as to maximize

$$\int_0^\infty u[f_1(L_1), f_2(L_2), Q]e^{-\delta t}dt \quad \text{subject to } L - L_1 - L_2 - L_3$$

$= 0$, $f_3(L_3) - f_1(L_1) + f_2(L_2) = 0$, and the differential equation $\dot{Q} = nf_3(L_3) - \gamma Q$, where δ is the continuous rate of discount. The Hamiltonian for this autonomous system (L fixed in time) is[5]

$$H = u[f_1(L_1), f_2(L_2), Q] + \xi[n(f_1(L_1) - f_2(L_2)) - \gamma Q] + \lambda(L - L_1 - L_2 - L_3) + \mu[f_3(L_3) - f_1(L_1) + f_2(L_2)],$$

where the state variable (Q), control variables (L_1, L_2, L_3) and auxiliary shadow price variables (ξ, λ, μ) are understood to be functions of time.

The following first order conditions must be satisfied along a maximal (interior) time path:

$$\frac{\partial H}{\partial L_1} = \left[\frac{\partial u}{\partial q_1}\right] f_1' + n\xi f_1' - \lambda - \mu f_1' = 0 \qquad (1)$$

$$\frac{\partial H}{\partial L_2} = \left[\frac{\partial u}{\partial q_2}\right] f_2' - n\xi f_2' - \lambda + \mu f_2' = 0 \qquad (2)$$

$$\frac{\partial H}{\partial L_3} = -\lambda + \mu f_3' = 0 \qquad (3)$$

$$\dot{\xi} = \xi\delta - \frac{\partial H}{\partial Q} = (\delta+\gamma)\xi - \frac{\partial u}{\partial Q} \qquad (4)$$

$$\lim_{t\to\infty} e^{-\delta t}\xi(t) \geq 0, \quad \lim_{t\to\infty} e^{-\delta t}\xi(t)Q(t) = 0.$$

This solution is particularly simple and easy to illustrate where the utility function is additively separable, or

$$u(q_1, q_2, Q) \equiv u_1(q_1) + u_2(q_2) + u_3(Q), \qquad (5)$$

with $\lim_{Q \to \bar{Q}} u_3'(Q) \to -\infty$, where Q is an intolerable level of litter pollution.

It is instructive to begin by interpreting the auxiliary variables (ξ, λ, μ), all of which are measured in utility (welfare) units per head. ($-n\xi$) is the unit implicit social cost of the stock of waste, Q. λ is the implicit wage of the resource, while μ is the implicit price of new containers or commodity material. Therefore condition (3) states that the price of new containers must equal their marginal cost, $\mu = \lambda/f_3'$. Substituting from (5) and (3), condition (1) can be put in the form

$$u_1' = (\lambda/f_1') + (\lambda/f_3') - n\xi \tag{6}$$

where u_1' is the marginal utility of commodity, and $(\lambda/f_1') + (\lambda/f_3') + (-n\xi)$ is the marginal private cost of producing the commodity and its container or fabrication material, plus the public litter-pollution cost resulting from its production. Condition (2) can be written

$$-u_2' + \lambda/f_2' = (\lambda/f_3') - n\xi \ , \tag{7}$$

where $-u_2' + (\lambda/f_2')$ is the marginal cost of recycling to both households and firms, and $(\lambda/f_3') + (-n\xi)$ is the marginal private plus public litter-pollution cost of producing a new unit of container or commodity material.

Equations (6) and (7) together with the labour constraint $L = L_1 + L_2 + L_3$ and the joint production constraint $f_3(L_3) = f_1(L_1) - f_2(L_2)$ determine (L_1, L_2, L_3) as functions of $n\xi$, given L, say $L_1(n\xi)$, $L_2(n\xi)$, $L_3(n\xi)$. Therefore the motion of the system in the phase space (ξ,Q) is governed by the differential equations,

$$\dot{Q} = nf_3[L_3(n\xi)] - \gamma Q \tag{8}$$

$$\dot{\xi} = (\delta+\gamma)\xi - u_3'(Q) \ . \tag{9}$$

Figure 1 illustrates the locus of points $Q = nf_3[L_3(n\xi)]/\gamma$ such that $\dot{Q} = 0$, i.e. the production of waste net of production recycling is just balanced by the rate at which waste is degraded by nature so that net accumulation is zero. Since it is shown in the appendix that $\partial L_3/\partial\xi > 0$, this locus will be increasing. At any point above this locus, the social charge for waste disposal to the environment, ($-n\xi$), is lowered, waste recycling is discouraged and the net stock of waste will increase ($\dot{Q} > 0$). At any point below this locus, the waste disposal charge is increased, recycling is encouraged, and the net stock of waste will decrease.

Also in Fig. 1 is illustrated the locus of points $\xi = u_3'(Q)/(\delta+\gamma)$ defined by $\dot{\xi} = 0$, i.e. the price of waste discharge is stationary. At any point to the right of this locus the discounted marginal disutility of the stock of waste, $-u_3'(Q)/(\delta+\gamma)$, exceeds the price $(-\xi)$ associated with that stock of waste, and optimality requires this price to be decreasing, $(-\dot{\xi}) < 0$. In like manner, at any point to the left of this locus, optimality necessitates increasing the social charge for waste emission. An optimal path, starting at some initial state (Q_0, ξ_0), and passing through the stationary state equilibrium at $P_2(Q_2^*, \xi_2^*)$, is shown in Fig. 1.

PRICES IN THE CONTROL MODEL

If p_1 is the price of a unit of commodity net of the recycling value of its container or material residue, s, then $P_1 = p_1 + s$ is the gross price of the commodity as sold. Thus P_1 is the price of a "coke" including the bottle, or the price of a car including its residual scrap value, and in equilibrium cannot differ from the marginal cost of producing the commodity plus its container or material, $P_1 = p_1 + s = (\lambda/f_1') + (\lambda/f_3')$. Under the condition that some but not all waste material is recycled, the marginal cost of producing new containers or commodity materials cannot differ from the scrap value of waste material plus the marginal cost of recycling it, i.e. $(\lambda/f_3') = s + (\lambda/f_2')$. Hence, (6) and (7) can be interpreted in terms of the scrap and net commodity prices (s, p_1):

$$u_1' = p_1 + s - n\xi \ , \tag{6'}$$

$$-u_2' = s - n\xi \ . \tag{7'}$$

In these equations s is a private, technological, scrap or "deposit" fee, while $(-n\xi)$, the public cost of accumulated waste, represents the social (opportunity) cost of *not* recycling. Equilibrium requires scrap value to be $s - n\xi > s$ so that the recycling decision of firms can include this social opportunity cost.

CONDITIONS FOR COMPLETE AND ZERO RECYCLING

Polar cases of the above analysis occur when there is recycling of all or no waste material. If the charge for waste disposal to the environment is sufficiently small, it may be the case that no waste material will be recycled. Then $L_2 = 0$, $f_2(0) = 0$, and $f_1(L_1) = f_2(L_3)$, $L = L_1 + L_3$, i.e. container or material production is determined jointly with commodity output. Under such conditions L_1 and L_3 will be independent of ξ, and the locus of points $Q = nf_3(L_3)/\gamma = Q_1$, a constant independent of ξ. If $L_2 = 0$ at $\xi = \xi_1$, say, then we have $Q = Q_1$ for all $\xi \geq \xi_1$ as shown in Fig. 1, segment I. An optimal path yielding a stationary equilibrium with no recycling is shown in Fig. 2a.

If the charge $(-n\xi)$ is sufficiently large, we may have all waste material recycled, with $L_3 = 0$, $f_3(0) = 0$, and $f_1(L_1) = f_2(L_2)$, $L = L_1 + L_2$ so that the volume of recycling is determined jointly with commodity output. Then $Q = nf_3(0)/\gamma = 0$. In Figs. 1-3 this case is assumed to occur for all $\xi \leq \xi_3$. An equilibrium path yielding a stationary equilibrium with complete recycling is shown in Fig. 2b.

POLLUTION UNDER FREE COMPETITION

In a decentralized competitive economic organization no market will exist to reflect the social cost $(-n\xi)$ of public pollution to household and firm decision makers. Each household and each firm will view waste disposal as a free activity. The stationary competitive solution is therefore obtained very simply by setting $\xi \equiv 0$ in the control model.

In Fig. 1, starting at the initial level Q_0, the decentralized competitive stock of waste will grow at the rate $\dot{Q} = nf_3[L_3(0)] - \gamma Q > 0$ until $Q = Q_1$ as shown. In Figs. 1, 2a and 2b three different optimal control solutions are illustrated for comparison with the competitive solution. In each case, the disutility of waste function is $u_3(Q)$ which yields the discounted marginal disutility of waste solution set $\xi = u_3'(Q)/(\gamma+\delta)$, for which $\dot{\xi} = 0$.

If the discounted marginal disutility of waste is sufficiently low, as illustrated in Fig. 2a, the control solution is at P_1, with $Q = Q_1$ and the competitive solution is also optimal.

In Fig. 1, representing a more odious level of discounted disutility of waste, the control equilibrium tends to P_2 at which the optimal waste stock Q_2^*, is less than its competitively produced level, Q_1. Finally, in Fig. 2b, waste is so odious, and the corresponding social cost $-\xi$ is so large that at the stationary control equilibrium, P_3, all waste will be recycled. In such an equilibrium the social "deposit fee" on containers is large enough to induce 100% recycling of all such materials by firms and households. We have a "spotless" environment, and such a result, under the assumed conditions, is unattainable except through some mechanism for internalizing the public opportunity cost of waste production.

Figure 3 illustrates a configuration in which the private costs of recycling are sufficiently low to yield some recycling even when the social charge $\xi = 0$. Consequently the locus $Q = nf_3[L_3(n\xi)]/\gamma$ intersects the Q axis at some $Q = Q_2$. But $Q_2 = nf_3[L_3(0)]/\gamma$ now corresponds to the competitive stationary equilibrium stock of waste that involves some positive level of recycling based on private costs and incentives only. However, Q_2 is not a social optimum. For a social optimum still more recycling is necessary, and this occurs ultimately at the point R_2 with an appropriate waste charge ξ_2^*. An example of this configuration is to be found in the returnable milk, beer and soft drink bottle. Until recently the private costs of recycling were low enough to induce partial recycling. But since deposit fees were modest one can conclude that the advantages of recycling were slight. Many units were discarded at these low deposit fees and recycling was incomplete. Eventually the returnable container gave way to the no-deposit-no-return unit with no recycling. One can speculate that recycling would have continued, if not increased, if deposit fees had reflected the social costs of container litter.

In Fig. 4 we assume that recycling cost is so much lower than the production of new units that the solution $L_3 = 0$ holds with zero disposal charge. Consequently, the stationary equilibrium is at $Q = 0$, and this is achieved under decentralization competition.

EFFECTS OF POPULATION

The effects of a change in the population level, n, on the steady-state equilibrium can be determined from the resulting shift in the locus $Q = nf_3[L_3(n\xi)]/\gamma$. For the three types of solutions we have $\partial Q/\partial n \geq 0$, as shown in the appendix (omitted). Consequently this locus shifts to the right as shown in Fig. 5. An increase in the population from n_1 to n_2 shifts the steady-state equilibrium from P_1 to P_2, for solutions in segment II, and from P_1' to P_2' for solutions in segment I. As expected, an increase in population increases the equilibrium stock level of waste residues, and increases the optimal equilibrium pollution charge.

INTERPRETATION AS A WASTE REDUCTION MODEL

A pure waste or pollution reduction model is obtained as a special case of the model expressed in conditions (1) - (5). For each unit of commodity produced and consumed let a unit of pollution be produced. The waste could be an industrial by-product instead of a household by-product. Pollution reduction can be obtained at a rate given by $q_2 = f_2(L_2)$ which now represents a control, or clean-up technology. An example would be the industrial pollution of a river or lake that could be reduced by prefiltering of waste or by application of cleaning technology to the water resource itself. The resulting model is represented in (1) - (5) by setting $L_3 \equiv 0$ and removing condition (3). If only prefiltering were feasible, the constraint $q_1 \geq q_2$ would apply, but if the pollution stock can be reduced at any desired rate determined by $f_2(L_2)$, then $q_1 \gtreqless q_2$.

MATERIAL PRODUCTION FROM NATURAL RESOURCES

The assumption that the raw material cost of containers and commodities is zero will now be relaxed by introducing explicitly a natural extractive resource from which the material for commodities and containers is produced. The incentive for recycling will then depend not only on savings in labour and public waste reduction, but also on savings in extractive resources. We assume that material is recovered from the earth without despoiling it so that the only source of litter-pollution activity is in the accumulation of unrecycled waste residues. If the mining or harvesting activity itself spoils the environment then of course this becomes another public "bad" and a source of saving by recycling.

If the natural resource that provides the source of raw material is a nonreplenishable resource occuring in fixed initial amount, M_0, then the stock of unrecovered material at time t is $M(t) = M_0 - \int_0^t q_3(\tau)d\tau$ where the resource is measured in terms of commodity or container units, e.g. one automobile's worth of iron ore, or one newspaper's worth of wood. This adds a new state variable M to the system, and a new differential equation side condition $\dot{M} = -q_3 = -(q_1 - q_2)$. If the resource (such as a forest) is replenishable through a natural growth process yielding new mass at the rate f(M)[6], the differential equation side constraint is $\dot{M} = f(M) - (q_1 - q_2)$.

It is also reasonable to assume that the material output of mines or forests depends not only on the labour input, but also on the stock of the resource, or $q_3 = q_1 - q_2 = f_3(L_3, M)$. Consequently, the production constraint becomes

$$f_3(L_3, M) - f_1(L_1) + f_2(L_2) = 0.$$

The Hamiltonian is now

$$H = u[f_1(L_1), f_2(L_2), Q] + \xi[n(f_1(L_1) - f_2(L_2)) - \gamma Q]$$
$$+ \nu[f(M) - f_1(L_1) + f_2(L_2)] + \lambda(L - L_1 - L_2 - L_3)$$
$$+ \mu[f_3(L_3, M) - f_1(L_1) + f_2(L_2)],$$

where $f(M) \equiv 0$ in the case of a nonreplenishable resource like iron ore.

The motion of the system for the interior case must now satisfy the conditions:

$$u_1' = (\lambda/f_1') - \lambda/(\partial f_3/\partial L_3) - n\xi + \nu \quad (10)$$

$$-u_2' + (\lambda/f_2') = \lambda/(\partial f_3/\partial L_3) - n\xi + \nu \quad (11)$$

$$\dot{\xi} = (\delta+\gamma)\xi - u_3'. \quad (12)$$

$$\dot{\nu} = (\delta - f')\nu - \mu(\partial f_3/\partial M) \quad (13)$$

$$\dot{Q} = nf_3(L_3, M) - \gamma Q \quad (14)$$

$$M = f(M) - f_3(L_3) \qquad (15)$$

Equations (10) and (11) together with the labour and production constraints determine $L_1(n\xi, \nu, M)$, $L_2(n\xi, \nu, M)$, and $L_3(n\xi, \nu, M)$. The state of the system is then described by the four differential equations in (ξ, ν, Q, M). The shadow price of the natural resource stock, ν, now appears on the right side of (10) as a component of the marginal cost of a unit of commodity, and on the right side of (11) as a component of the marginal opportunity cost of recycling a unit of waste material. The right side of (11) now yields the three sources of marginal opportunity cost savings from recycling: labour cost, $\lambda/(\partial f_3/\partial L_3)$, public littering cost $(-n\xi)$, and material cost, ν.

SUMMARY AND DISCUSSION OF POLICY

This paper has provided a simple control model of the economics of waste recycling. Pollution, litter or waste disposal is assumed to enter the economic system as a public bad in household utility functions. The resulting subjective cost of using the environment for discharge is not borne directly by those whose decisions result in environmental degradation. The optimal control solution requires a price to be associated with waste discharge, depending upon the accumulated stock of waste, the interest rate and the rate at which waste decomposes in nature. A competitive decentralized economy is generated by the model when the waste discharge price is indentically zero. This corresponds to an unappropriated environment available to all as a free resource for waste discharge purposes. The control solution and the decentralized competitive solution approach the same stationary state equilibrium in two special cases: (1) the private costs of recycling are so high relative to the public disutility of waste that no recycling is economical either privately or socially. (2) The private costs of recycling are so low relative to the public disutility of waste that the decentralized economy will recycle all waste. Adding in the public cost of disposal cannot therefore increase recycling.

To economists the natural control device is a Pigouvian system of charges. The idea behind environmental "user" charges is to employ the pricing system to redirect resources in accordance with the reality of public costs associated with environmental use. A bill designed to implement this objective has been proposed in the United States Senate.[7]

The bill has two principal provisions on which the present paper has a direct bearing.

1. To establish a schedule of national packaging disposal charges that will reflect "the quantity of solid wastes which result from such packaging, the ultimate costs of disposal of such packaging, the toxicity and health effects of such packaging, the degradability of such packaging, and the likelihood that such packaging will be returned, reused, or recycled into the economy."[8]

2. The Treasury is instructed to place the revenues collected into a fund to be distributed "in each fiscal year in the form of grants to any State, municipality or interstate or intermunicipal agency for the construction of solid waste disposal and resource recovery facilities..."[9]

The intent of this bill represents an effort to be commended. However, as is clear from the theory discussed in this paper, it is important that the charges be levied on packaging materials *net* of reprocessed material rather than that the charges merely take account of the "likelihood" that packaging materials will be recycled. It is essential for an effective reordering of incentives that the charge system raise the value of scrap materials relative to that of newly manufactured materials. There may be a great many circumstances in which it is economical to recycle packaging materials or commodity residue into an entirely different use.

To use the beverage container example once again, suppose reprocessing costs are such that even with a sizable charge on net new container units it does not pay to reuse old bottles. But with a little added incentive suppose it does pay the producers of concrete or asphalt road paving to pulverize old bottles and include such material in their output recipe. If the charge on glass containers is, say, one cent per ounce with an equivalent credit for each ounce recycled, then it is the paving material manufacturer who must receive this incentive credit. But if he produces no waste item subject to charge, his credit should be taken in the form of a direct subsidy from revenue generated by the charge system. The basic function of the bill should be to employ charges to impose the cost of waste disposal on *all* production and consumption activities that create waste, and to use the resulting revenues to subsidize *all* waste *using*, as well as disposal, activities. In those cases in which the waste producing and using decisions are made by the same manufacturer (the beverage producer who can recycle used bottles, or the steel maker who can use scrap input), he will incur a charge liability, but also a subsidy credit and should only pay on the difference. In those cases in which the waste producing and using decisions are made by different manufacturers, then charge funds collected from the waste producer must be transferred as subsidy funds to the waste user. Finally, and this is explicit in the bill, in cases where the waste is not used by anyone and the cost of disposal falls on states and municipalities, the charge funds are transferred to the states and municipalities to finance waste disposal.

Based on these considerations the bill should be broadened to permit payments to *any waste user* whose recycling credit exceeds any charge liability. If such a provision is not added, the bill is in danger of artificially stimulating high cost waste disposal activities as a substitute for lower cost waste-using activities.

Also, the bill deals only with "package pollution", and leaves open the problem of waste created by commodity residuals such as old newspapers and magazines, derelict cars, and virtually all household durables. Charges on commodity residue would be most effectively levied on the manufacturer (and therefore also his customers) of the basic refined material (steel, copper, aluminum, paper). In each case the charge is levied on output net of scrap input. In one stroke this raises the manufacturer's incentive to bid for junk autos, refrigerators, pots and pans, cans or whatever can be remelted into new material for fabrication into products. In the short run the effect is to decrease the profitability of plant technologies oriented to the refining of ore, relative to the profitability of plants capable of handling scrap input. In the long-run it encourages development and investment in scrap-using technologies.

Discussion has centered on the use of "taxes" to internalize the costs of public waste discharge, but other devices, which are theoretically equivalent to a charge system, are possible and perhaps desirable in some cases.

One device, popular with legislatures, is the pollution quota, which is equivalent to a pollution charge when the quota is such that its shadow price is equal to the optimal public disposal charge. Under this condition the quota imposes a compliance cost on producer and household decision makers that is the equivalent of a user charge. This result, like the results generally in this paper, depends on the assumption that households share a common disutility of accumulated waste. Otherwise we have the public "bad" problem with implicit prices differing among individuals.

A decentralized alternative is that of the full-cost damage lawsuit the use of which has been expanded by the legal institution of the class suit wherein representatives of a class such as the victims of oil spillage or "coke" bottle litter bring suit against oil companies or bottlers to recover damages. This would be equivalent to the user charge system provided that the damage payments equal the discounted value of accumulated waste disutilities.

APPENDIX

A complete statement of the model of development over time is to

$$\underset{q_1,q_2,L_1,L_2,L_3}{\text{maximize}} \int_0^{\infty} u(q_1, q_2, Q)e^{-\delta t}dt$$

subject to

$$L - L_1 - L_2 - L_3 = 0 \qquad (1)$$

$$q_1 - q_2 \geq 0 \qquad (2)$$

$$f_1(L_1) - q_1 = 0,\ q_1 > 0 \qquad (3)$$

$$f_2(L_2) - q_2 = 0,\ q_2 \geq 0 \qquad (4)$$

$$f_3(L_3) - (q_1 - q_2) = 0,\ (q_1 - q_2) \geq 0 \qquad (5)$$

$$\dot{Q} = n(q_1 - q_2) - \gamma Q. \qquad (6)$$

The Hamiltonian for this autonomous system is

$$H = u(q_1, q_2, Q) + \xi[n(q_1 - q_2) - \gamma Q] + \lambda_1(L - L_1 - L_2 - L_3) + \lambda_2(q_1 - q_2) + \mu_1[f_1(L_1) - q_1] + \mu_2[f_2(L_2) - q_2] + \mu_3[f_3(L_3) - (q_1 - q_2)]$$

with the following first order conditions applying along a maximal path

$[q_1^0(t),\ q_2^0(t),\ Q^0(t),\ L_1^0(t),\ L_2^0(t),\ L_3^0(t),\ \xi^0(t),\ \lambda_1^0(t),$

$\lambda_2^0(t),\ \mu_1^0(t),\ \mu_2^0(t),\ \mu_3^0(t)]$:

$$\frac{\partial H}{\partial q_1} = \frac{\partial u}{\partial q_2} + n\xi + \lambda_2 - \mu_1 - \mu_3 = 0, \qquad q_1 > 0,\ \lambda_2(q_1 - q_2) = 0. \tag{7}$$

$$\frac{\partial H}{\partial q_2} \quad \frac{\partial u}{\partial q_2} - n\xi - \lambda_2 - \mu_2 + \mu_3 \leq 0, \qquad q_2 \geq 0,\ q_2 \frac{\partial H}{\partial q_2} = 0. \tag{8}$$

$$\frac{\partial H}{\partial L_1} = -\lambda_1 + \mu_1 f_1' = 0,\ L_1 > 0,\ \mu_1 > 0,\ \lambda_1 > 0. \tag{9}$$

$$\frac{\partial H}{\partial L_2} = -\lambda_1 + \mu_2 f_2' \leq 0,\ L_2 \geq 0,\ L_2 \frac{\partial H}{\partial L_2} = 0,\ \mu_2 > 0. \tag{10}$$

$$\frac{\partial H}{\partial L_3} = -\lambda_1 + \mu_3 f_3' \leq 0,\ L_3 \geq 0,\ L_3 \frac{\partial H}{\partial L_3} = 0,\ \mu_3 > 0. \tag{11}$$

$$\dot{\xi} = \xi\delta - \frac{\partial H}{\partial Q} = \xi\delta - \left(\frac{\partial u}{\partial Q} - \gamma\xi \right). \qquad \lim_{t\to\infty} e^{-\delta t}\xi(t) \geq 0,\quad \lim_{t\to\infty} e^{-\delta t}\xi(t)Q(t) = 0\ . \tag{12}$$

In (7) and (9) we rule out the uninteresting case in which no commodity is produced and consumed. In (8), (10) and (11) we allow for the possibility of no recycling, $q_2^0 = f_2(0) = 0$, and its polar alternative, complete recycling, $q_3^0 = q_1^0 - q_2^0 = f_3(0) = 0$. In what follows the superscript zero on all the state and control variables will be omitted, but it should be understood that we are dealing with extremal paths for these variables.

Three solution cases are distinguishable:

Case I. The pollution solution, where there is zero recycling of waste, with

$$q_1 = f_1(L_1) > 0,\ q_2 = f_2(0) = 0,\ q_1 - q_2 = f_3(L_3) > 0,\ \lambda_2 = 0.$$

Case II. The partial-pollution solution, where there is recycling of some, but not all waste, with $q_1 = f_1(L_1) > 0$, $q_2 = f_2(L_2) > 0$, $q_1 - q_2 = f_3(L_3) > 0$, $\lambda_2 = 0$.

Case III. The no-pollution solution, where there is recycling of all waste, with $q_1 = f_1(L_1) > 0$, $q_2 = f_2(L_2) > 0$, $q_1 - q_2 = f_3(0) = 0$, $\lambda_2 \geq 0$.

These various solutions are illustrated by means of the usual phase diagram, on the assumption that

$$u(q_1, q_2, Q) \equiv u_1(q_1) + u_2(q_2) + u_3(Q), \text{ with}$$

$$\lim_{Q \to \bar{Q}} u_3'(Q) \to -\infty;\ u_1' > 0,\ u_1'' < 0; \tag{13}$$

$$u_j' \leq 0,\ u_j'' < 0,\ j = 2, 3.$$

Consequently under all three solution classes one of the equations of motion of the system will be the differential equation (12), which becomes, from (13),

$$\dot{\xi} = (\gamma+\delta)\xi - u_3'(Q). \tag{14}$$

Under conditions of stationary equilibrium $\dot{\xi} = 0$ defines a set of potential equilibria $\{(Q, \xi) | \dot{\xi} = 0\}$ or $\xi = u_3'(Q)/(\gamma+\delta) < 0$. Assume $u_3'(Q)$ is decreasing, then $\left.\frac{d\xi}{dQ}\right|_{\dot{\xi}=0} = u_3''(Q)/(\gamma+\delta) < 0$ as shown in Fig. 1. From (14)

$$\frac{\partial \dot{\xi}}{\partial Q} = -u_3''(Q) > 0. \tag{15}$$

Hence, for points to the right of the set $\{(Q, \xi) | \dot{\xi} = 0\}$ the social price of waste ξ must be rising, while at points to the left of this set, ξ must be falling, as shown by the arrows in Fig. 1.

Similarly, under conditions of stationary equilibrium, $\dot{Q} = 0$ in (6) defines the set of potential equilibria $\{(Q, \xi) | \dot{Q} = 0\}$. However, the characteristics of this set differ among the above three solution classes.

Case I. Setting $L_2 = q_2 = \lambda_2 = 0$, for this case, and substituting from (3), (9), (11), the equations of motion for the system (1) - (12) reduce to (14) and the system

$$u_1'[f_1(L_1)] + n\xi - \lambda_1/f_1'(L_1) - \lambda_1/f_3'(L_3) = 0 \qquad \text{(I.1)}$$

$$u_2'(0) - n\xi - \lambda_1/f_2'(0) + \lambda_1/f_3'(L_3) \leq 0 \qquad \text{(I.2)}$$

$$L - L_1 - L_3 = 0 \qquad \text{(I.3)}$$

$$f_1(L_1) - f_3(L_3) = 0 \qquad \text{(I.4)}$$

$$\dot{Q} = nf_1(L_1) - \gamma Q = nf_3(L_3) - \gamma Q\,. \qquad \text{(I.5)}$$

At a stationary equilibrium in this case the stock of waste will have grown until its degradation rate equals the production rate of commodity.

Equations (I.3) - (I.4) determine $L_1 = L_1^1$, $L_3 = L_3^1$ and therefore from (I.5)

$$Q\Big|_{\dot{Q}=0} = Q_1 = nf_3(L_3^1)/\gamma\,. \qquad (16)$$

Let $\xi \geq \xi_1 = \{u_2'(0)[(1/f_1') + (1/f_3')] - u_1'(f_1)[(1/f_2') - (1/f_3')]\}/n[(1/f_1') + (1/f_2')]$ satisfy (I.1) - (I.4). Then a stationary solution in case I must be in the set $(Q = Q_1, \xi \geq \xi_1)$, as shown in Fig. 1.

Case II. Setting $\lambda_2 = 0$ for this case and substituting as above, the equations of motion reduce to (14) and the system

$$u_1'[f_1(L_1)] + n\xi - \lambda_1/f_1'(L_1) - \lambda_1/f_3'(L_3) = 0 \qquad \text{(II.1)}$$

$$u_2'[f_2(L_2)] - n\xi - \lambda_1/f_2'(L_2) + \lambda_1/f_3'(L_3) = 0 \qquad \text{(II.2)}$$

$$L - L_1 - L_2 - L_3 = 0 \qquad \text{(II.3)}$$

$$f_1(L_1) - f_2(L_2) - f_3(L_3) = 0 \qquad \text{(II.4)}$$

$$\dot{Q} = n[f_1(L_1) - f_2(L_2)] - \gamma Q = nf_3(L_3) - \gamma Q\,. \qquad \text{(II.5)}$$

In stationary equilibrium, for this case, the stock of

waste will be such that the degradation rate plus the recycling rate equals the production rate of commodity.

Since $u_j'' < 0$, $f_j'' < 0$, $j = 1, 2, 3$, the Jacobian of (II.1) - (II.4) is

$$\begin{aligned} J = &-(1/f_1')\{f_3'[u_2''f_2' + \lambda_1 f_2''/(f_2')^2] \\ &+ (f_1' + f_2')\lambda_1 f_3''/(f_3')^2 + f_1'[u_2''f_2' + \lambda_1 f_2''/(f_2')^2]\} \\ &-(1/f_3')\{f_3'[u_2''f_2' + \lambda_1 f_2''/(f_2')^2] + f_1'[u_2''f_2' + \lambda_1 f_2''/(f_2')^2]\} \\ &-\{[u_1''f_1' + \lambda_1 f_1''/(f_1')^2][(f_3' - f_2')^2/f_2'f_3'] \\ &+ [\lambda_1 f_3''/(f_3')^2](f_1' + f_2')\} > 0 \end{aligned} \quad (17)$$

Differentiation (II.1) - (II.4), gives

$$\frac{\partial L_3}{\partial \xi} = (f_1' + f_2')^2 n/f_1'f_2'J > 0. \quad (18)$$

Hence, from (II.5)

$$\left.\frac{\partial Q}{\partial \xi}\right|_{\dot{Q}=0} = nf_3' \frac{\partial L_3}{\partial \xi} /\gamma > 0 \quad (19)$$

gives the slope of the set $\{(Q, \xi)|\dot{Q} = 0\}$ for Case II, as shown in Fig. 1.

Case III. Setting $q_1 - q_2 = L_3 = 0$, $\lambda_2 \geq 0$, the system (1) - (12) reduces to (14) and

$$\begin{aligned} u_1'[f_1(L_1)] + n\xi = \mu_1 + \mu_3 - \lambda_2 \leq [\lambda_1/f_1'(L_1)] \\ + [\lambda_1/f_3'(0)] - \lambda_2 \end{aligned} \quad (III.1)$$

$$\begin{aligned} u_2'[f_2(L_2)] - n\xi = \mu_2 - \mu_3 + \lambda_2 \geq [\lambda_1/f_2'(L_2)] \\ - [\lambda_1/f_3'(0)] + \lambda_2 \end{aligned} \quad (III.2)$$

$$L - L_1 - L_2 = 0 \quad (III.3)$$

$$f_1(L_1) - f_2(L_2) = 0 \quad (III.4)$$

$$\dot{Q} = -\gamma Q. \quad (III.5)$$

If $\xi = \xi_3$, $\lambda_1 = \lambda_1^3$ satisfies (III.1) - (III.4) when $\lambda_2 = 0$ and the equality holds in (III.1) and (III.2), then a stationary solution in Case III must be in the line set $Q = 0$, $\xi \leq \xi_3$, as shown in Fig. 1.

In all three solution cases represented by (I.5), (II.5) and (III.5), we have $\partial\dot{Q}/\partial Q < 0$, and at points to the right of the set $\{(Q, \xi) | \dot{Q} = 0\}$ the stock of waste must be falling, while to the left it must be rising. An optimal path starting from some initial (Q_0, ξ_0) is shown in Fig. 1.

If p_1 is the price of a unit of commodity net of its recycling value, s, then $P_1 = p_1 + s$ is the gross price of the commodity. We also define p_3 as the market price of a new (or reprocessed) container or commodity material unit. Then the Lagrange multipliers (μ_1, μ_2, μ_3) can be interpreted in terms of these prices, as follows:

$$\begin{aligned} \mu_1 &= p_1 + s - p_3 = P_1 - p_3 \\ \mu_2 &= p_3 - s \\ \mu_3 &= p_3 \\ (\mu_3 - \mu_2) &= s \\ (\mu_1 + \mu_3) &= P_1 \end{aligned} \tag{20}$$

Thus μ_1 is the price (value added) of a unit of commodity, *net* of the container or material cost. Similarly, the producers of recycled units receive a price $\mu_2 = p_3 - s$ which is net of their out-of-pocket cost of purchasing commodity residues for recycling. Finally, $\mu_3 = p_3$ is the price of new containers or commodity materials.

Using these price transformations, conditions (7) and (8) for consumer equilibrium can be written in the marginal rate of substitution form:

$$\frac{u_2' - \lambda_2}{u_1' + \lambda_2} \leq \frac{\mu_2 - \mu_3 + n\xi}{\mu_1 + \mu_3 - n\xi} = -\frac{s - n\xi}{P_1 + s - n\xi} . \tag{21}$$

Note that $\lambda_2 = 0$ in cases I and II.

The effects of a change in population level, n, on the steady-state equilibrium can be determined from its effect on the set $\{(Q, \xi)|\dot{Q} = 0\}$. From (16), for case I,

$$\left.\frac{\partial Q_1}{\partial n}\right|_{\dot{Q}=0} = f_3(L_3^1)/\gamma > 0 \qquad (22)$$

Differentiating (II.1) - (II.4), for Case II, gives

$$\frac{\partial L_3}{\partial n} = (f_1' + f_2')^2\xi/f_1'f_2'J > 0. \qquad (23)$$

and from (II.5)

$$\left.\frac{\partial Q}{\partial n}\right|_{\dot{Q}=0} = (f_3/\gamma) + nf_3'\frac{\partial L_3}{\partial n}\Big/\gamma > 0\,. \qquad (24)$$

FOOTNOTES

*Support by the National Science Foundation is gratefully acknowledged.

[1]For example, W.A. Brock, "A Polluted Golden Age," unpublished, University of Rochester, 1970. C.G. Plourde, "A Simple Model of Waste Disposal," unpublished, University of Western Ontario, 1970. R. Wong, "Optimal Growth with Production Inhibited by Pollution Generation," unpublished, University of Southern California, 1970. R. Zeckhauser, M. Spence, and E. Keeler, "The Optimal Control of Pollution," Discussion Paper, Kennedy School of Government, Harvard University, June 1970.

[2]The model abstracts from a capital goods sector, and population growth which have been the subjects of thorough study in the neoclassical growth literature.

[3]See R.U. Ayres and A.V. Kneese, "Production, Consumption and Externalities," *American Economic Review*, Vol. 59, No. 3, June 1969.

[4]See the mathematical appendix that derives characteristics of these boundary solutions more rigorously.

[5]See K.J. Arrow, "Applications of Control Theory to Economic Growth," *Lectures in Applied Mathematics*, Vol. 22 (Mathematics of the Decision Sciences — Part 2) 1968 , pp. 335-345.

[6]See V.L. Smith, "Economics of Production from Natural Resources," *American Economic Review*, Vol. 58, No. 3, June 1968, pp. 409-31; and J.P. Quirk and V.L. Smith, "Dynamic Economic Models of Fishing," *Economics of Fisheries Management* (Ed. A. Scott), Vancouver: University of British Columbia, Institute of Animal Resource Ecology, 1970.

[7]Senate bill S. 3665, cited as the "Package Pollution Control Act of 1970," introduced April 1, 1970 by the Honorable Gaylord Nelson, 91st Congress, 2nd session.

[8]Senate bill S. 3665, p.3.

[9]Senate bill S. 3665, p.4.

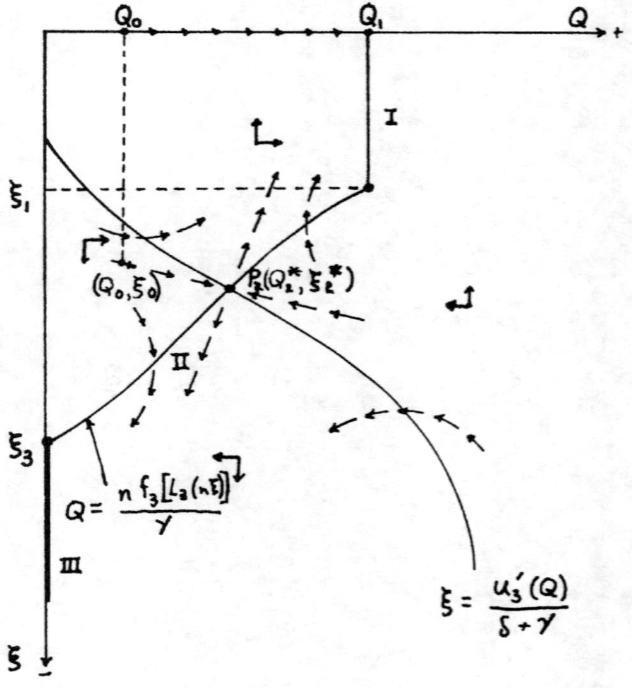

FIGURE 1

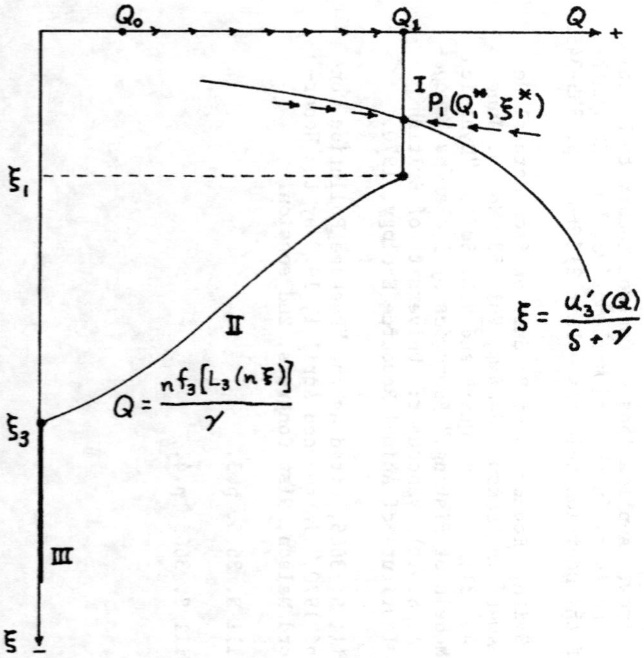

FIGURE 2a

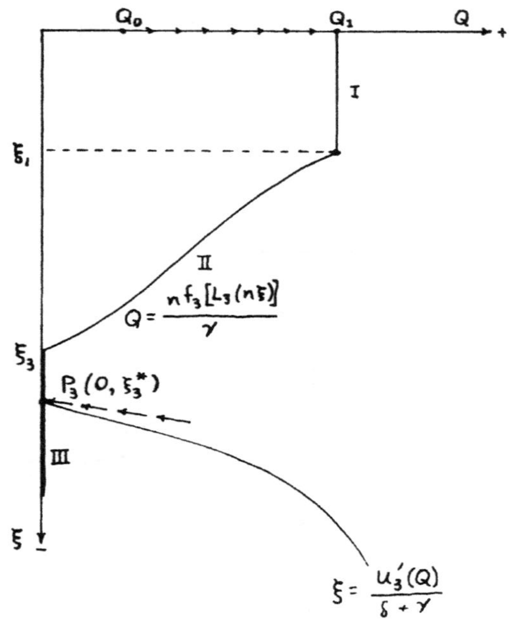

FIGURE 2b

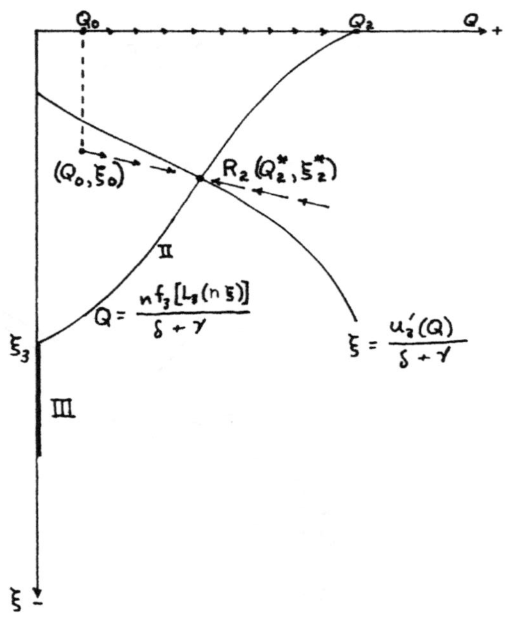

FIGURE 3

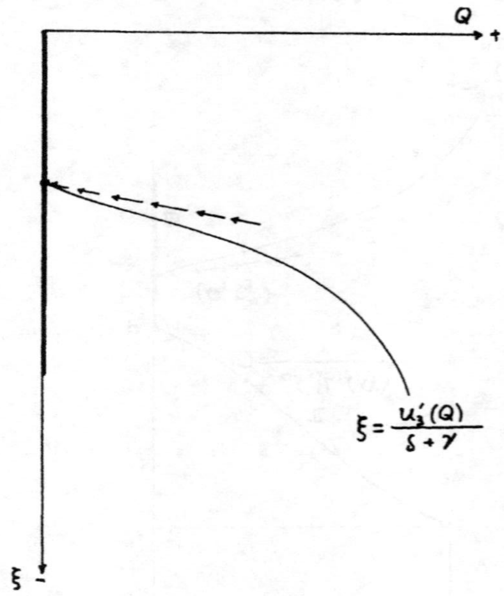

FIGURE 4

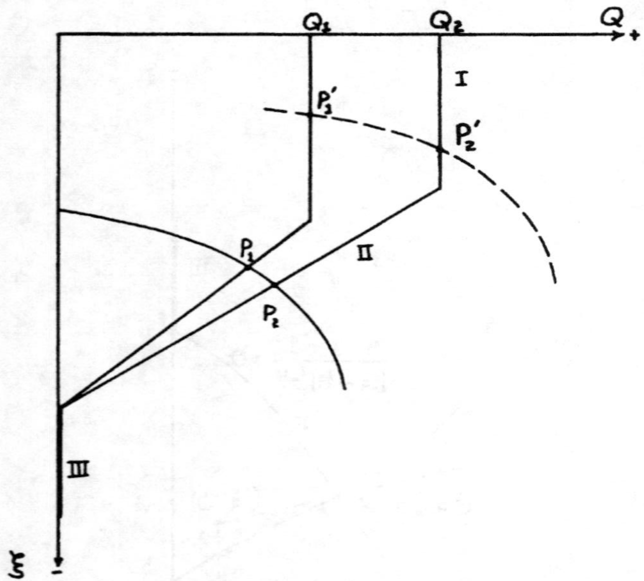

FIGURE 5

CHAPTER 24

THE OPTIMAL CONTROL OF POLLUTION*

EMMETT KEELER, MICHAEL SPENCE, and RICHARD ZECKHAUSER

Pollution we define to be any stock or flow of physical substances that impairs man's capacity to enjoy life. So defined, pollution is a pervasive phenomenon. Physical garbage; air and water pollution, soil exhaustion via excessive use, D.D.T., radiation, and the running down of any natural resource faster than it can rejuvenate itself (if it can rejuvenate itself), are all problems of pollution in this extended sense. By operating at such an all inclusive level we may miss some of the interesting aspects of particular pollutants. We hope to gain in return by illuminating the conceptual similarities among apparently diverse problems.

From the time of Professor Pigou, economists have regarded pollution as a problem of externalities. It is not our purpose to suggest that his view of the problem is in error. On the other hand, it is increasingly evident that the traditional remedies proposed for simple cases of market failure may be inadequate to achieve desirable outcomes where matters of pollution are involved. To deal with these complex and intractable matters may require some form of centralized coordination and control. An approach beyond the usual externalities analysis seems called for.

The framework of control theory provides us with insights

---

*Research support for this project was provided by the Analytic Methods Seminar of the Public Policy Program, John F. Kennedy School of Government, Harvard University.

Professors Henry Jacoby, Thomas Schelling and a referee provided us with helpful comments.

An abridged version of this chapter appeared in the *Journal of Economic Theory*. This Journal kindly gave us reprint permission.

on the use of mechanisms to direct patterns of consumption and production. The optimal control of pollution may require curtailing certain types of consumption, limiting the use of some productive processes and perhaps even restricting the growth of population. There are strong intertemporal aspects of the pollution problem. They reinforce the relevance of the dynamic approach of control theory.

Before proceeding to a formal model, we shall mention three important distinctions that relate to the economic effects of pollutants. The first is whether the pollutant has its major impact on consumption, on production, or possibly on both. The pollutant enters directly into the societal utility function with a negative marginal utility. Its presence may have an adverse effect on production as well. However, in many instances, as we shall elaborate later, pollutants will have positive marginal products.

The second distinction is whether the pollutant has its impact as a stock or a flow. Frequently a pollutant will have an impact as both. D.D.T. as a flow has a positive marginal product in the agricultural production function. As a stock it confers a negative marginal utility. This is a fairly typical pattern for pollutants. The stock is detrimental, either because of its direct effect on consumption or because it impairs production; while the flow is beneficial, either because it has a positive marginal product, or because it is an unfortunate by-product which can only be removed with the expenditure of resources. A pollutant of this sort is the conceptual opposite of a capital stock; the latter has a positive marginal product as a stock, and a negative marginal utility as a flow (because its accumulation reduces present consumption).

The central problem of pollution, that its presence impairs man's capacity to enjoy life, we believe to be a stock control problem. However, if the pollutant has a very high rate of depreciation or decay, the stock notion loses its significance. With a special case of this sort, the magnitude of the stock becomes proportional to the size of the flow, and the policy problem can be more appropriately thought of as one of controlling a flow. Noise pollution is the limiting example of such a situation, although the air pollution problem can conveniently be regarded as a flow problem as well.

The distinction we have emphasized between stocks and flows relates directly to our third distinction, the traditional one made in control theory between state and control variables. We suggest that the only reasonable definition of a stock is that it could not, in any conceivable world, be regarded as an instrument. It follows that there is no formal distinction between what are traditionally regarded as instruments of policy and variables which are functionally related to them. The important thing about pollution as a social problem is that we frequently are not capable of exercising direct control over the undesired quantity. Planning becomes imperative. By ignoring the problem or by over-reacting to it, enormous quantities of resources are wasted.[1]

MODELS OF POLLUTION CONTROL

In what follows we discuss optimal equilibria and approach paths for each of two related models in which it is desirable to control the stock of pollution. The models differ in the structure of their production functions and in the way in which they allow pollution to be controlled. They can be thought of as specific formulations of a less tractable, general model presented in an appendix.

The objective function for the two models is the same. It is defined from the standpoint of the total society, but it could equally well be defined on an individual basis. To avoid difficulties in assessing the appropriate structure for the objective function, we will assume that the supply of labour is fixed over time.[2]

The welfare of the society at any point in time is a function of the flow of consumption, c, and the stock of pollution, P. The time invariant utility function can be indicated

$$u(c,P)\ . \qquad (1)$$

The first argument is valued positively, the second negatively. The utility function has continuous first and second derivatives with the signs $u_c > 0$, $u_{cc} < 0$, $u_P < 0$, $u_{PP} < 0$. It is assumed that for $c = 0$, $u_c = \infty$. Indifference curves curve the right way. Neither consumption, nor (what is in effect) the reduction of pollution is an inferior good.[3]

The subjective discount rate, r, is applied to the flow of utility. The total welfare, W, associated with any particular time path for c and P is derived by summing the discounted flow. Total welfare can thus be indicated

$$W = \int_0^\infty u(c,P)e^{-rt}dt. \tag{2}$$

MODEL I — POLLUTION CONTROL THROUGH A POLLUTION REDUCTION PROCESS

Model I has labour and a single capital good as the two factors of production. It has the additional special characteristic that output may be devoted not only to capital accumulation and consumption, but also to reduce the stock of pollution. Advantageous pollution reduction expenditures are available to combat a wide variety of pollutants. Many forms of water pollution control, for example, fit the Model I paradigm.

The production function is assumed to exhibit the customary concavity properties. Given the fixed labour supply, this means that output, y, can be represented as an increasing and concave function of the capital stock, K. Thus we have

$$y = f(K), \tag{3}$$

where $f' > 0$ and $f'' < 0$. The capital stock depreciates at the positive rate a.

The pollutant serves no useful or productive purpose in this model. Its flow is assumed to be a fixed proportion by-product of production; they are joint products. Whey from dairies, offal from meat-packing plants, and the organic residues from paper making are among the many pollutants that fit this characterization.

The joint product relationship of pollution and production enables us to adopt the convenience of measuring pollution in the same units as those with which production is measured. Appropriate adjustments are made, of course, so that the utility function is consistent. Our units of measurement technique is equivalent, for example, to measuring wool in terms of the pounds of accompanying mutton.

Fortunately, as we observe empirically, the stock of pollution deteriorates naturally. Its depreciation rate, b, is assumed to be non-negative. (In situations such as bacterial contamination, b may be negative.) There is another way to reduce pollution, through pollution control expenditures. It is assumed that there are constant returns to depollution efforts. An expenditure of one unit of production will reduce pollution (measured in units of production, its joint product) by d units.

Let α and β represent the non-negative fractions of output expended respectively on consumption and pollution control, so that, for example, $c = \alpha f(K)$. The growth rate of the capital stock can be represented

$$\dot{K} = (1 - \alpha - \beta)\cdot f(K) - aK \quad . \tag{4}$$

The growth rate of the pollution stock will be

$$\dot{P} = (1 - \beta d)\cdot f(K) - bP \ . \tag{5}$$

It is assumed that the stocks of both capital and pollution must be non-negative.

All output must be allocated to one of three areas: capital accumulation, consumption, or pollution control. The allocations to two areas determine the one to the third. The model is effectively one with two control variables; we will work with α and β. By logic, neither one of them can be negative.

NECESSARY CONDITIONS FOR AN OPTIMAL PATH

The formulated problem is one of optimal control. To deal with it let us represent the shadow price for capital at any point in time as κ, and that for pollution as π. The Hamiltonian, H, can be defined

$$H = e^{-rt}\Big[u(c,P) + \kappa[(1 - \alpha - \beta)f - aK] + \\ + \pi[(1 - \beta d)f - bP]\Big] \ . \tag{6}$$

Applying Pontryagin's maximum principle, we know a maximum will be achieved if we maximize H, provided that the shadow prices obey the perfect foresight conditions

$$\dot{\kappa} = -H_\kappa + \kappa r = -u_c\alpha f' + \kappa[r + a - (1 - \alpha - \beta)f'] - \\ - \pi(1 - \beta d)f' \ , \tag{7a}$$

$$\dot{\pi} = -H_\pi + \pi r = - u_P + (r + b)\pi \quad , \qquad (7b)$$

and that the initial prices, $\kappa(0)$, $\pi(0)$ are properly set. The question then becomes what assignment of α and β maximizes H. Taking partial derivatives we get

$$H_\alpha = e^{-rt}(u_c - \kappa)f \ , \ \text{and} \qquad (8a)$$

$$H_\beta = e^{-rt}(-\kappa - d\pi)f. \qquad (8b)$$

Since H is linear in β, along the optimal path α must be chosen so that $H_\alpha = \max\ (H_\beta, 0)$.

There may be a constraint, however, on the proportion of output that can be spent on consumption plus pollution control: $\alpha + \beta \leq M$. In this case, there is a non-negative time-dependent parameter, $\lambda(t)$, such that

$$H_\alpha = H_\beta + \lambda(t) \ ,$$

with $\lambda(t) \cdot (\alpha - M) \equiv 0$, for all t.

STEADY STATE EQUILIBRIA

Are there values of K and P, which trace out an optimal path when they are held constant? We shall show that there are at most two such pairs of values. At one of these steady states, no money is spent on pollution control. We shall call such a state the Murky Age Equilibrium. It is characterized by an abundance of capital, a high consumption level, and an extreme pollution level that is controlled solely by natural processes of amelioration (depreciation). A steady state at which expenditures are made on both consumption and pollution control will be called a Golden Age Equilibrium. It will offer lower capital, consumption and pollution levels than the Murky Age.[4]

At either such equilibrium $\dot{K}$ and $\dot{P}$ must be zero. This implies that

$$f(K)(1 - \alpha - \beta) = aK \ , \ \text{and} \qquad (9a)$$

$$f(K)(1 - \beta d) = bP \quad . \qquad (9b)$$

Multiply (9a) by d and subtract from (9b) to get

$$d\alpha f(K) = dc = bP - adK + (d - 1)f(K) \quad . \tag{10}$$

Since K is fixed, and a is positive, $\alpha + \beta$ is constant and less than one. Thus, $H_\alpha = 0$, which means that $H_\beta \leq 0$, and that

$$u_c(\alpha f(K),P) = \kappa \quad . \tag{11}$$

This last equation implies that κ and hence π is constant. Equation (7a) becomes on substitution of (11)

$$\dot{\kappa} = \kappa(r + a - f') - \pi f' + \beta(\pi d - \kappa)f' \quad . \tag{12}$$

Let us now consider the two cases of equilibrium. The Golden Age Equilibrium will be one for which $H_\beta = 0$. The Murky Age Equilibrium will be one for which $H_\beta < 0$.

Case 1 — The Golden Age

If $H_\beta = 0$, $\pi = -\kappa/d$ and we have

$$\dot{\kappa} = 0 = \kappa(r + a - (1 - 1/d)f') \, , \tag{13}$$

which is only satisfied when

$$f'(K) = \frac{r + a}{1 - 1/d} \quad . \tag{14}$$

Since $f'' < 0$, the K satisfying (14) is unique (if it exists). But $\dot{\pi} = 0$, so

$$u_P = (r + b)\pi = -u_c\frac{(r + b)}{d} \tag{15}$$

By the assumption of non-inferiority, the curve in c,P space satisfying (15) is downward sloping, so that (10) and (15) together can have at most one solution.

Case 2 — The Murky Age

If $H_\beta < 0$, $\beta = 0$ and we can solve (12) to get

$$f'(K) = \frac{r + a}{1 + \pi/\kappa} = \frac{r + a}{1 + \dfrac{u_P}{u_c(r + b)}} \tag{16}$$

This defines P implicitly as a function of K. We can solve

for $P'(K)$:

$$P'(K) = \frac{C_1 f'' - C_2 \alpha f' [u_{cc} u_P - u_c u_{cP}]}{u_{cP} u_P - u_c u_{PP}} \;, \tag{17}$$

where C_1 and C_2 are factors which are always positive.

By our assumption of non-inferiority $P' < 0$. Since (9b) is upward sloping and (17) is downward sloping, once again there can be at most one solution.

The diagram below is drawn to illustrate the Golden Age Equilibrium for the case where $u(c,P) = c^{\frac{1}{2}} - \frac{P^{1.1}}{5,000}$ and $f(K) = 10 \cdot K^{\frac{1}{2}}$. The parameters of the model are a = .06, b = .1, d = 10, and r = .05.

The K which satisfies (14) is 1673.6. Total output, y = f(K), will be 409.09. At the Golden Age Equilibrium, the value of α, the portion of total output going to consumption, is .68462. Consumption, c, is thus 280.07. The stock of pollution, P, will equal 1230.4. The value of β, the portion of output going to pollution control, is .06992. The remaining output, roughly one quarter of the total, goes to replace depreciating capital. The utility u(c,P) = 16.234. At the Murky Age Equilibrium, for this same set of parameters, K = 2080.3, f(K) = 456.1, P = 4561, α = .7264, β = 0, and c = 331.3. Here utility, u(c,P) = 16.08, is less than it is at the Golden Age. In other situations this ordering could be reversed.

To summarize, there can be no more than two K,P equilibrium pairs that satisfy the necessary conditions for optimality. The no-depollution-expenditure equilibrium will exist if the K value satisfying (9b) and (17) is greater than the K defined in (14), the Golden Age Equilibrium K. The Golden Age Equilibrium will exist if (14) can be satisfied and if the c simultaneously solving (10) and (15) lies between 0 and f(K) - aK. Further, if capital is fixed at K, the optimal path is going directly from P(0) to the P of the Golden Age Equilibrium. This last result can be generalized. For any choice of fixed K, the optimal path is going directly to the level of P for which

$$u_P = -u_c \cdot \left(\frac{r + b}{d} \right) .$$

Figure 1

The Golden Age Equilibrium

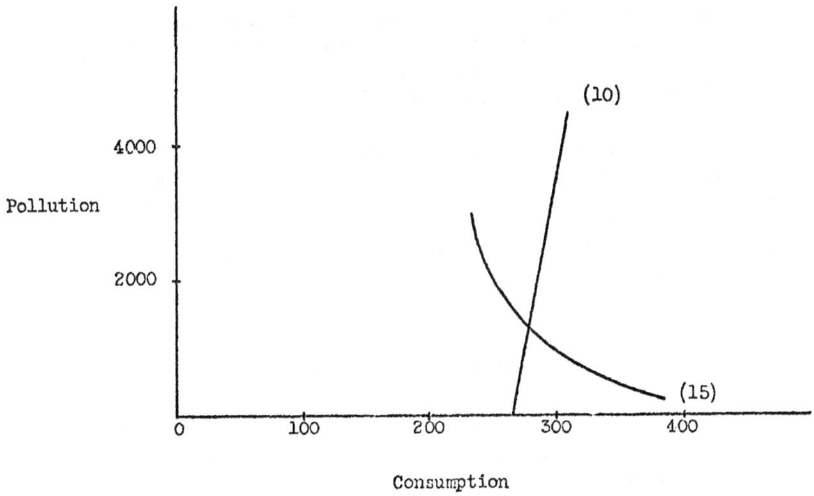

We conjecture, although we have not yet been able to prove, that starting with any initial stocks for K and P the optimal path will in time get arbitrarily close to an equilibrium. The analysis of optimal paths from arbitrary K(0),P(0) is extremely complicated.

What follows is a proof of our conjecture for a simple example in which the disutility of pollution is linear and separable.[5] Thus we are assuming

$$u(c,P) = g(c) - mP \quad , \text{ where} \tag{18}$$

m is small enough so that $P > 0$ throughout all the paths we consider. The solution we derive here requires that the shadow price for pollution be constant. When $P = 0$ at some point along the optimal path, the shadow price may vary.[6] In addition we assume that $\alpha + \beta \leq 1$.[7]

Let us return to consider the properties of the Hamiltonian along an optimal path. There are six possibilities depending on the values of H_α and H_β. Since $u_c(0,P) = \infty$, H_α can never be negative and c must be greater than 0. Table I shows the assignments of α and β which define the optimal path.

TABLE I

Optimal Assignments of α and β

	$H_\alpha = \max(0,H_\beta)$	$H_\alpha(1) > \max(0,H_\beta)$
$H_\beta < 0$	$\beta = 0,\ 0 < \alpha \leq 1$	$\alpha = 1$
$H_\beta = 0$	$0 < \alpha + \beta \leq 1$	$\alpha = 1$
$H_\beta > 0$	$\alpha + \beta = 1$	$\alpha = 1$

Equation (7b) becomes

$$\dot{\pi} = m + (r + b)\pi \quad . \tag{19}$$

Solving (19) we get

$$\pi = \frac{-m}{r + b} + Ae^{(r + b)t} \qquad (20)$$

If $A > 0$, then π eventually will be positive. If $A < 0$, then $u_c = \max(-\pi d, \kappa)$ would imply that consumption eventually approaches zero. Since both possibilities are absurd, $A = 0$, and π is constant.

To determine the optimal $\kappa(0)$, we shall construct a snapshot of the K,κ phase space. Since the rate of discount is constant, the optimal α,β decision does not depend on time; it is a pure function of K and P.

Since $u(c,P)$ is less concave than before, there can be no more than the two previously discussed equilibria which satisfy the optimality conditions. In fact, as we shall show in this case, there will be either a Murky Age or a Golden Age Equilibrium, but not both.

To understand the behaviour of the system, we shall compute the lines $\dot{K} = 0$ and $\dot{\kappa} = 0$.

We know $\dot{K}$ can never equal zero when $\kappa < -\pi d$, for then $H_\beta > 0$ and $\alpha + \beta = 1$. If $\kappa > -\pi d$, optimality requires that

$$g'(\alpha f(K)) = \kappa . \qquad (21)$$

However, $\dot{K} = 0$ when

$$f(K) - aK = \alpha f(K) . \qquad (22)$$

Thus, on the line $\dot{K} = 0$,

$$\kappa'(K) = \frac{1}{(f' - a)g''(\alpha f(K))} . \qquad (23)$$

Let us now consider the lines $\dot{\kappa} = 0$. If $\kappa > -\pi d$, from equation (16) $\dot{\kappa} = 0$ when

$$f'(K) = \frac{r + a}{1 + \pi/\kappa} . \qquad (24)$$

Thus $\kappa'(K) > 0$ and as $f' \rightarrow r + a$, $\kappa \rightarrow \infty$. If $\kappa < -\pi d$, $g' = -\pi d$, $\alpha + \beta = 1$, and $\dot{\kappa} = 0$ when

$$\kappa(r + a) + (d - 1)\pi f' = 0 . \qquad (25)$$

Figure 2a

The Golden Age Equilibrium

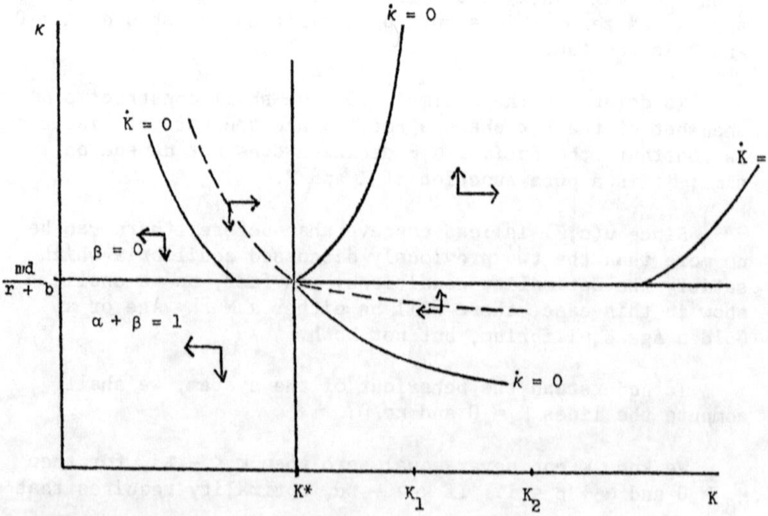

Figure 2b

The Murky Age Equilibrium

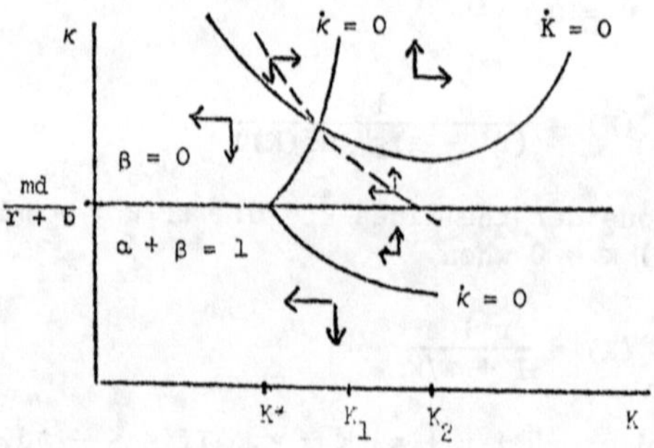

On this line,

$$\kappa'(K) = \frac{-\pi(d - 1)}{r + a} f'' < 0. \qquad (26)$$

At this point it will be convenient to introduce some notation. Let K^*, P^* and κ^* represent the Golden Age Equilibrium values of K, P and κ. To complete the analysis of the K,κ phase space observe that if $\kappa = -d\pi$, that is if $H_\beta = 0$, is to be sustained, $\dot{\kappa}$ must be zero, so K must equal K^*. Also κ must be zero, so K must be zero, which determines β. On the singular arc $K = K^*$; $\frac{\partial}{\partial\beta}(\ddot{K}) \leq 0$, so the Legendre-Clebsch necessary condition is satisfied.

As Figs. 2a and 2b show, depending on whether the point $(K^*, -\pi d)$ lies above or below the line $\dot{K} = 0$, there is a Golden Age or Murky Age Equilibrium. In either case, the equilibrium is a saddle-point and only one value of $\kappa(0)$ will lead to the equilibrium.

Figure 3 shows the computed optimal paths in the K,P phase space for the case where $g(c) = c^{\frac{1}{2}}$ and $m = .00298769$. These values produce a Golden Age Equilibrium with the same K and P we found in Fig. 1. The line $K = K^*$ is a singular arc corresponding to the equilibrium point (K^*, κ^*) in Fig. 2. Each path goes to K^* and then to K^*,P^*.

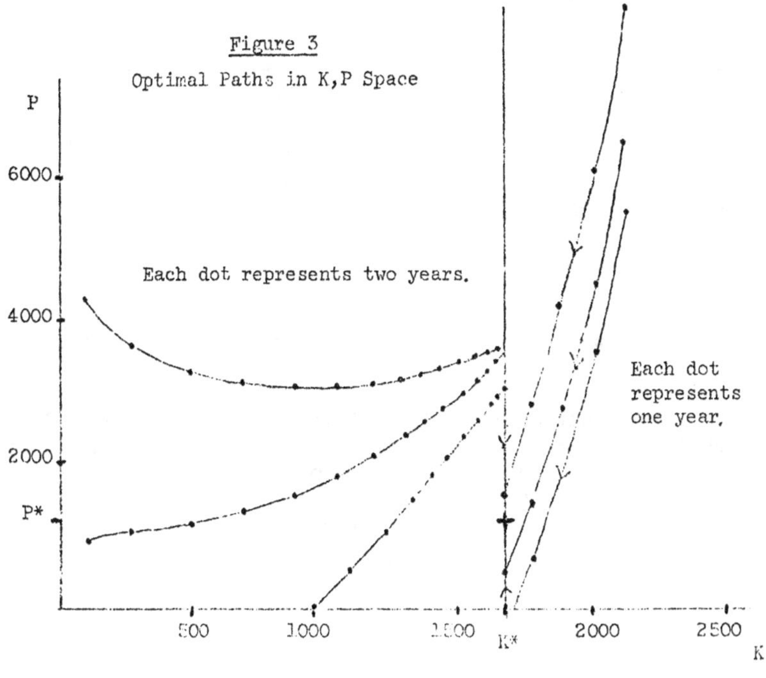

Figure 3

Optimal Paths in K,P Space

Since the disutility of pollution is linear in this example, the amount spent is independent of P. Thus, when capital is low, pollution may rise higher than P* while capital is accumulating. Conversely, when capital is high, pollution may go below P* while capital is decumulating. This whole analysis suggests that there is a luxury aspect to pollution control, and that in general capital buildup takes precedence.

THE OPTIMAL PATH COMPARED TO AN ALTERNATE CONTROL SCHEME

How much is gained by using the optimal, rather than some other path? A reasonable alternative would be to fix consumption and pollution control at their Golden Age Equilibrium proportions. Such a policy would not be so sensitive to miscalculation. It would result in convergence to the Golden Age Equilibrium though at a slower rate. Table II shows the results for the two schemes for two different cases.

TABLE II

A Comparison of the Two Paths

Initial Values	Through Time Period	Accumulated Utilities: Golden Age Proportions Path	Accumulated Utilities: Optimal Path
Case I K = 955, P = 1000	50	279.061	280.177
	75	298.117	299.597
Case II K = 100, P = 1000	50	210.250	225.668
	75	228.462	245.042

Figure 4 displays the optimal paths for the two schemes for case I.

If the initial capital level is very low, the optimal path is significantly better, primarily because capital grows so slowly using the Golden Age proportions. However, for more intermediate values of initial capital, the improvement is less than one half of one percent.[8]

Figure 4

Optimal and Golden Age Proportions Paths

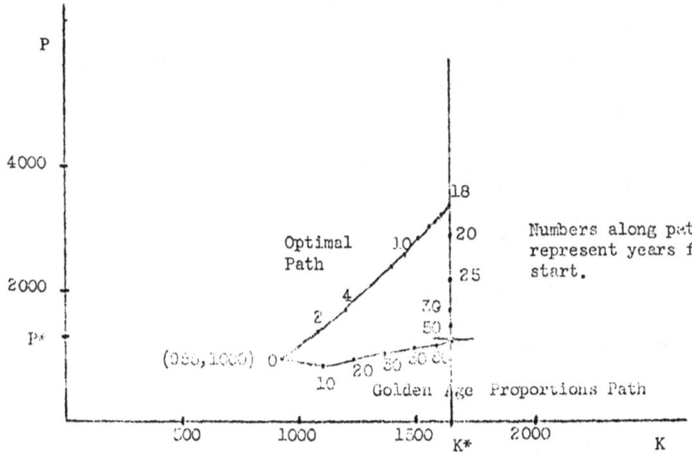

This suggests that: (1) The exact computation of the optimal growth path in this model, as well as in others, will be of greater import for a developing economy than it is for a mature economy. (2) An economy that wishes to approach the Golden Age Equilibrium might find it advisable to employ a two part scheme. First, prices for capital and pollution could be employed to drive the capital stock to an approximately appropriate level. Then, once the equilibrium is in sight, the less sensitive proportional controls could be employed to do fine tuning.

MODEL II — POLLUTION CONTROL THROUGH CHOICE OF PRODUCTION PROCESS

We now present a model for a pollutant which as a stock enters the welfare function with a negative marginal utility, but as a flow enters the production function with a positive marginal product. The insecticide D.D.T. is a good real-life example of a dual-roled pollutant of this type.

For simplicity, we assume that once the pollutant has been created, it can only be reduced by natural decay. To avoid irrelevant complications, we take labour to be the single scarce productive resource. Thus the policy problem in this model is the choice of production procedures — this choice is exercised by dividing labour between the consumption good sector and the pollutant sector.

The objective function is the same as before. To facilitate exposition, we shall assume that the utility function has a specific form, that it is separable in consumption and pollution, so that

$$u(c,P) = g(c) - h(P) \tag{27}$$

We assume that $g'(0) = +\infty$, $g' \geq 0$, $g'' < 0$, $h'(0) = 0$, $h' \geq 0$, and $h'' > 0$.

Labour, the only factor of production, is in fixed supply, L. Some labour, L_1, is allocated to the production of the pollutant through its production function $j(L_1)$. We assume that $j'(L_1) > 0$, $j''(L_1) < 0$ and $0 \leq L_1 \leq L$.

The rest of the labour supply, $L-L_1$, is allocated to the production of the consumption good. The pollutant, serving as an intermediate good, is the other input to the consumption good's production function. That function is

$$c = F(L-L_1, j(L_1)) \quad , \tag{28}$$

where $j(L_1)$ gives the primary flow of the produced pollutant. A positive amount of the labour input, but not of the pollutant input, is needed for any production of the good. It is clear that this function can be reduced to $c = f(L_1)$, with L an unspecified parameter lurking in the background. The shape of $f(L_1)$ is shown in Fig. 5.[9]

Figure 5

Production as A Function of Labor Allocated to Pollutant Production

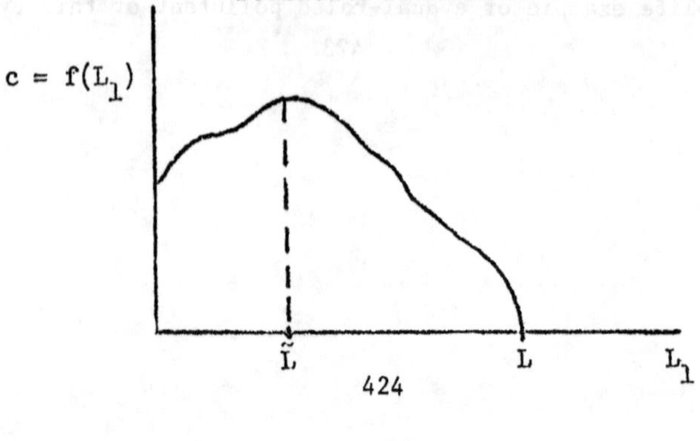

Beyond the point $\tilde{L}$ of maximum production, increased labour to pollutant production reduces the output of the consumption good, because the loss from the reduced direct labour input outweighs the gain from increased pollutant input.

NECESSARY CONDITIONS FOR OPTIMALITY

The modified Hamiltonian expression, with the e^{-rt} dropped, is

$$H = g(f(L_1)) - h(P) + \pi(a(L_1) - bP) + q(L-L_1) + sL_1 \ . \quad (29)$$

Here q and s are time dependent non-negative multipliers corresponding to the constraints on L_1. It is clearly inefficient to devote more than $\tilde{L}$ to pollutant production, since pollution is valued non-positively. Hence, $L_1 < L$, and q will be identically zero. That the multiplier, s, may be positive is an important aspect of the problem.

The instantaneous optimal value for L_1, given the shadow price π, can be derived from

$$H_{L_1} = g'f' + \pi j' + s = 0, \text{ with } s \geq 0 \text{ and } sL_1 = 0 \ . \quad (30)$$

Consider first the case where $L_1 > 0$ and hence s = 0. If $\pi = 0$, clearly L = L.

We can differentiate (21) to obtain

$$\frac{dL_1}{d\pi} = - \frac{j'}{(g''f'^2 + g'f'' + j''\pi)} \quad (31)$$

This will be positive whenever j" is "small" relative to g" and f". In what follows we assume

$$\frac{dL_1}{d\pi} > 0 \ . \quad (32)$$

[10]

Since $f(L_1) > 0$ at $L_1 = 0$, $g'(f(0))$ is finite. Thus, for s = 0, there is a lower bound on π given by

$$\tilde{\pi} = - \frac{g'(f(0))\ f'(0)}{j'(0)} \quad (33)$$

For $\pi < \tilde{\pi}$, equation (21) defines s, which becomes positive. In this region, L_1 is zero.

The perfect foresight condition is

$$\dot{\pi} = (q + b)\,\pi + h' \quad . \tag{34}$$

As before, we adopt the phase-diagram approach to solution. The line $\pi = 0$ passes through the origin and the negative slope, $-(q + b)/h''(P)$. The line $\dot{P} = 0$ is defined by $P = j(L_1(\pi))/b$. Since $b > 0$, and $j' > 0$, the slope of $\dot{P} = 0$ is positive. Thus the two lines have a unique intersection, and there exists an optimal path through the point of intersection. For a proof of this kind of result, see Arrow [1]. As before, the optimal initial level of π is the value on the optimal path corresponding to the initial level, P_0, of the pollutant.

Figure 6

Phase Diagram for Model 2

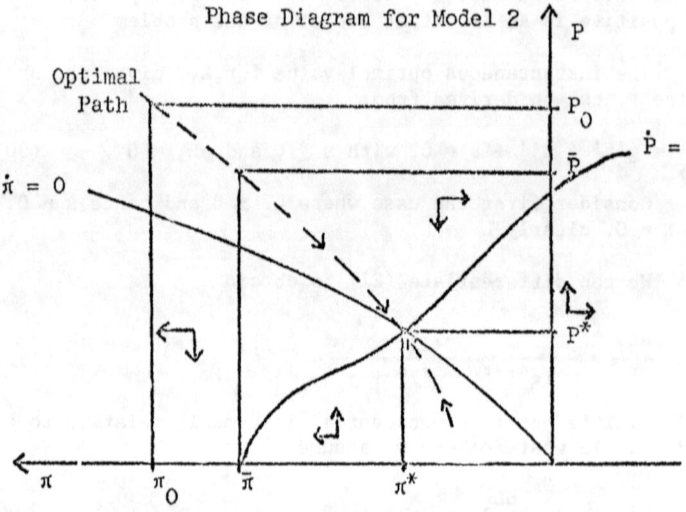

The interesting aspects of this problem may now be examined. Let $\bar{P}$ be the abscissa of the point of intersection of the optimal path with the line $\pi = \bar{\pi}$. If $P_0 > \bar{P}$, the optimal policy consists of setting $L_1 = 0$, and leaving it there until the natural decay of P reduces the level of the pollutant to $\bar{P}$. Then it gradually increases L_1 while maintaining $\dot{P} < 0$, until the optimal stationary point (π^*, P^*) is approached. At the stationary point (which will never quite be reached), $L_1 < \tilde{L}$.

The model points out that just as it is not optimal to ignore the pollution problem, neither is it optimal to ban the flow of the pollutant forever. It may not even be optimal to ban its use now; whether it is depends on the current level of the stock of the pollutant. There are at least two policy problems here. One is to determine the critical level, $\bar{P}$, below which production of the pollutant should be allowed. The second is one of implementation — limiting the use of the pollutant to the required amount. In general, simple policies like complete permissiveness and complete abolition are easiest to administer. But the economic losses from opting for a simple policy, when others are feasible, may be large.

The rate of decay, b, is the crucial factor in determining the level $\bar{P}$ beyond which the use of the pollutant should be banned. In the case of D.D.T., b is very small, so that banning its use altogether might not be far from the optimal policy. As an experiment, let us allow b to rise.[11] On the optimal path in (π,P) space, the direction of motion is $(\dot{\pi},\dot{P})$. The derivative $\frac{d}{db}(\dot{\pi},\dot{P}) = (\pi,-P)$. On the upper part of the path, this represents a clockwise twist as b increases. Even if the optimal stationary point (π^*,P^*) were the same, $\bar{P}$ would have to rise. But, in addition, the line $\dot{\pi} = 0$ is steeper and the line $\dot{P} = 0$ is flattened out. Hence the stationary π^* rises which makes the stationary L_1^* rise. If b is raised far enough, P^* must fall, but for small increases in intermediate values of b, the value of P^* may rise or fall. To sum up, the higher the rate of decay, the higher is the level at which the pollutant's use is banned, and the less likely is the policy of banning to be optimal.

RESULTS AND EXTENSIONS

The two models we discussed produced quite different results. The differences suggest that there are no general rules for dealing with the pollution problem, and that there is no single model that is sufficiently well defined to give results of interest without further specification. Nevertheless, we believe that our models can be extended to relate to a variety of pollution problems that maintain the spirit of the assumptions set out below.

		Flow of Pollution Controlled Through	
		Pollution Reduction Process	Choice of Production Process
Pollutant Enters Model	As By-product of Production	Model I	—
	Produced as Intermediate Good	—	Model II

Consider river pollution. If factories treat their own effluents, they will be adopting a more expensive production process. Pollutant flow reduction is achieved at a cost in productivity; the tools of Model II apply. On the other hand, if the pollutants are dumped but the river is treated, say through aeration, then the logical structure is that of Model I.

The paper-making industry affords a good illustration of the upper right-hand box of the table. That industry offers a choice of productive processes, the less organic residue that is dumped for a particular process, the less efficient it is in terms of cost per unit of paper produced. The tools of Model II can be applied to this, or any, situation in which a choice must be made among productive processes, the ones which are more productive producing as well greater pollutant by-product.

The models can be applied to problems involving more than pure production processes. With non-returnable bottles, the "producers" of drinks in the consumers' refrigerators have lower costs (recognizing convenience as a cost) than with the returnable bottle production process, but the latter process causes less pollution. Although the costs of disposing of non-littered bottles is low, littered bottles are expensive to remove, in many cases prohibitively so. Thus, applying Model II (to them) may be reasonable. A ban on littered bottles may be appropriate depending on the aesthetic costs.[12] Another example is traffic congestion; it can be viewed as a by-product of transportation.

Future investigations should relax three assumptions of our models. (1) Capital should be employed in the pollution reduction sector. (2) Technological progress should be considered, particularly in the pollutant-removal sector where progress can and should be anticipated over the short-term future. (3) The labour supply should be treated as an endogenous variable to acknowledge explicitly the relationship between population growth and pollution, and to illustrate the possible need for methods of population control.

CONCLUSION

If strongly expressed social and political concerns reflect non-optimal situations, our society is currently functioning with a pollution level well in excess of the optimal equilibrium. Too much emphasis, it is believed, has been placed on building the capital stock and on maintaining a high level of consumption. The overwhelming presence of external diseconomies in an unhindered market situation has led to a non-optimal outcome. What is needed is some form of centralized coordination to correct a situation which presents inappropriate incentives. Such coordination might be carried out through effluent charges, a market for pollution rights, or perhaps through direct control.

Our models point out that, in general, drastic measures are not called for. In many situations over reaction is a significant danger. What is called for is a controlled movement toward optimal paths. Unfortunately, political realities may proscribe policies which call for incremental changes in behaviour. Banning may be possible in places where reducing would require an infeasible amount of administration. The radical policy, or perhaps no policy at all, may be best among those that can be implemented.

The real-life role of the economist is not only to identify paths of optimality, as we have done, but also to suggest practical ways in which these paths might be approached. It is in this "but also" area where our contributions have been traditionally the weakest.

APPENDIX I

Other Models of Pollution Control

Purely for the purpose of avoiding duplication of research effort, we append the following brief description of models which we have examined. The results are not startling, but serve to round out the picture painted in the essay, and to demonstrate that the results derived there are not atypical.

Model III — Pollutant Has Utility Impact as a Flow

We mentioned, but did not examine in detail, the possibility that pollution could have its major impact on utility as a flow. We now take up that suggestion. The objective in this model is to maximize

$$\int_0^\infty u(c,\dot{P})e^{-rt}dt$$

subject to

$$\dot{P} = g(K_1) - h(K_2) \ ,$$

$$K = K_1 + K_2 \ , \text{ and}$$

$$\dot{K} = f(K_1) - c - aK \ .$$

Substituting the expression for $\dot{P}$ in the utility function gives a maximand of

$$\int_0^\infty u(c,g(K_1) - h(K_2))e^{-rt}dt \ .$$

This problem is equivalent to one in which the capital stock must be divided between the public and private sectors, the division appearing as well in the utility function.[13] This problem, with but one structural difference, has been solved by Professors Arrow and Kurz [2]. The difference is that capital in the public sector, K_2, does not appear in the utility function in their model. It should be said that they were not dealing directly with a pollution problem, but rather with the general problem of the optimal accumulation of capital in the public sector.

An interesting variant of Model III, which has not been studied, would have the same maximand but the dynamic equations,

$$\dot{K} = f(K) - I - c - aK \quad ,$$

$$\dot{K}_2 = I \quad , \quad \text{and}$$

$$\dot{P} = g(K) - h(K_2) \quad .$$

This variant represents pollution control through capital investment, such as reducing traffic congestion, $\dot{P}$, through the construction of new highways, K_2. The earlier variant better represents short run control measures such as programs of traffic expedition, (e.g. by enforced doubling up, public transportation fare subsidies, etc.).

Next we show that if pollution, P, appears in separable and linear form in the utility function, and if the discount factor remains constant, then the complex stock control problem considered in Model I reduces formally to the flow control problem of Model III. This reduction affords a substantial gain in simplicity. The proof requires straightforward manipulation of the maximand. We have

$$\int_0^\infty (u(c) - mP)e^{-rt}dt$$

$$= \int_0^\infty e^{-rt}u(c)dt - m\int_0^\infty e^{-rt}\left[\int_0^t \dot{P}(j)dj + P_0\right]dt$$

$$= \int_0^\infty e^{-rt}u(c)dt - mP_0\int_0^\infty e^{-rt} - m\int_0^\infty \dot{P}(j)\int_t^\infty e^{-rj}djdt$$

$$= \frac{P_0}{r} + \int_0^\infty e^{-rt}u(c)dt - \frac{m}{r}\int_0^\infty e^{-rt}\,\dot{P}(t)dt$$

$$= \text{constant} + \int_0^\infty \left[u(c) - \frac{m}{r}\dot{P}(t)\right]e^{-rt}dt \quad .$$

The second term gives the modified objective function. Since only c and $\dot{P}$ appear in the modified objective function, it follows that policy can operate solely on the flow of the pollutant, without any loss of optimality. Admittedly, this case is very special. But if the linear approximation can be made plausibly in given circumstances, then considerable simplification can be achieved. The choice of the constant marginal disutility of pollution, m, might be made to depend on the initial level of pollution; the higher the initial level, the larger one would take m to be.

We considered three more models. We comment here on their relevance and area of application.

Model IV — Pollution Model Analogous to the Ramsey Model

The problem is to maximize

$$\int_0^\infty u(c,P)e^{-rt}dt$$

subject to

$$c = F(L_1) \quad ,$$

$$L = L_1 + L_2 \quad , \text{ and}$$

$$\dot{P} = g(L_1) - h(L_2) \quad .$$

Here L is the constant labour supply and L_1 and L_2 its allocation between production of the consumption good, and reduction of the pollutant. The problem is of some interest because the formal solution is the exact analogue of the simple Ramsey problem, only pollution rather than capital is the one-state variable. The solution of the problem is formally the same as the solution to the Ramsey problem.

Model V — Exogenous Population Growth

This is a slight variant of Model I, with the population of size L growing at a constant rate, n, and utility a function of per capita consumption and total pollution. Let $c = C/L$, $k = K/L$.

The maximand is $c - v(P)$ subject to

$$\dot{k} = (1 - \alpha - \beta)f(k) - (a + n)K, \quad \text{and}$$

$$\dot{P} = f(K)(1 - \beta d) - bP \ .$$

In this case, there is no steady state equilibrium. Because there are decreasing returns to production, as well as positive depreciation, per capita consumption is bounded. Since paths of zero utility are feasible, total pollution must be bounded on any optimal path and hence pollution cannot increase proportionally with population. Of course, indefinite exponential population growth leads to more serious problems than mathematical intractability.

Model VI — Generalized Model Presenting Two-State Variable Problem

The last is a full-blown two-state variable problem in capital and pollution, in which both the stock and flow of pollution appear in both the production and utility functions, and both capital and current income can be used to reduce the level of flow of the pollutant.

Let K_1 represent the part of the capital stock which is devoted to the production of the good, with K_2 devoted to the reduction of the flow of the pollutant. The fraction of current income devoted to pollution control is β; its constant productivity is given by d. The problem then is to maximize

$$\int_0^\infty e^{-rt} u(c,\dot{P},P)dt$$

subject to

$$\dot{K} = F(K_1,\dot{P},P) - c - \beta F - aK \quad ,$$

$$\dot{P} = g(K_1) - h(K_2) - d\beta F - bP \quad ,$$

$$K = K_1 + K_2 \quad , \text{ and}$$

$$c \geq 0, \ \beta \geq 0 \quad .$$

We have had limited success dealing with this general problem at an abstract level. The problem is that with two state variables, P and K, the optimal paths are defined by four differential equations in four dimensional space, and hence, unlike the Ramsey problem, are hard to visualize.[14] Progress in analyzing such two-state variable problems would be a significant step forward. The quantities in the model deserve some attention. Situations which fit the general model or any one of its many possible specializations will undoubtedly occur to the reader. We have mentioned several in the paper. In particular, Model I is obtained by setting $\frac{\partial u}{\partial \dot{P}} \equiv 0$, $K_2 \equiv 0$, $\frac{\partial F}{\partial \dot{P}} \equiv 0$, $\frac{\partial F}{\partial \dot{P}} \equiv 0$.

APPENDIX II

Analysis of the Case P = 0 Along Part of the Optimal Path

If we consider initial values of K,P from which P may be zero along the optimal path, the analysis is somewhat more complicated.

In the expression for the Hamiltonian, H, π is replaced by $\pi + \eta$ where

$$\eta = 0 \quad \text{if } P > 0$$
$$\geq 0 \quad \text{if } P = 0 \text{ .[15]} \tag{35}$$

The only possible case where $P = 0$ is when $K \geq K^*$, since when $K < K^*$, the optimal choice of β is 0. While $P = 0$ is sustained, $\dot{P} = 0$ so $\beta = 1/d$, and $\pi + \eta$ is set so that $H_\beta = 0$. Hence $-d(\pi + \eta) = \kappa$, and thus from equation (12)

$$\dot{\kappa} = (r + a - (1 - 1/d)f')\kappa \quad , \tag{36a}$$

$$\dot{\pi} = m - (r + b)\kappa/d \quad \text{, and} \tag{36b}$$

$$\dot{K} = (1 - 1/d - \alpha)f(K) - aK \quad . \tag{36c}$$

Once again K^*,κ^* is a saddle-point in the phase space, so at the time t_1, when P becomes 0, $\kappa(t_1)$ must be set so that when $K(t_2) = K^*$, $\kappa(t_2) = \kappa^*$. Whenever $P > 0$ for the remainder of the optimal path, $-d\pi = \kappa^*$. Thus, since when $K = K^*$, P rising to P* is optimal; $-\pi d = \kappa^*$ at t_2.

We can integrate equations (36) backwards from $K(t_2) = K^*$, $\kappa(t_2) = \kappa^*$, $\pi(t_2) = -\kappa^*/d$, until either $u_c^{-1}(\kappa) + 1/d \geq 1$, (where pollution control is less valuable than consumption), or $-\pi d \leq \kappa$, (where pollution control is the same as capital replacement).[16] This gives us the curve of the optimal path starting from P = 0.

A path on which P = 0, must hook up with this curve at some point. If this occurs at t_1, the corner conditions imply

$$\kappa(t_1^-) = \kappa(t_1^+),\ K(t_1^-) = K(t_1^+),\ \pi(t_1^-) = \pi(t_1^+) \quad , \tag{37}$$

and η represents the drop in the value of depollution from $-\pi$ to κ/d. This drop may be zero, but is never positive since if the value of depollution were less than κ/d, $\beta = 0$ and $P > 0$.

Thus from initial $K(0), P(0)$, we must set $\kappa(0), \pi(0)$ so that when P becomes 0, equations (37) are satisfied. To complete the analysis, we now show that P can become positive only at $K = K^*$ on any optimal path. From equations (12) and (36a), whenever $K > K^*$, κ is increasing and hence $\kappa < \kappa^*$. At the time, t_2, when P becomes positive, $-\pi d \leq \kappa$, and hence $-\pi d \leq \kappa \leq \kappa^*$. If $-\pi d < \kappa^*$ at t_2, then by equation (20), $-\pi d$ is decreasing, so β is zero and P is positive for the rest of the path. But, on this remaining path, $-\pi d$ must be constant by the argument following equation (20). This contradiction implies $-\pi d \geq \kappa^*$ at t_2. Thus, at t_2, $-\pi d = \kappa = \kappa^*$, and the only possible value for K is K*. Figure 7 shows the optimal trajectories in K,κ phase space.

Figure 7

Optimal Initial Values of κ

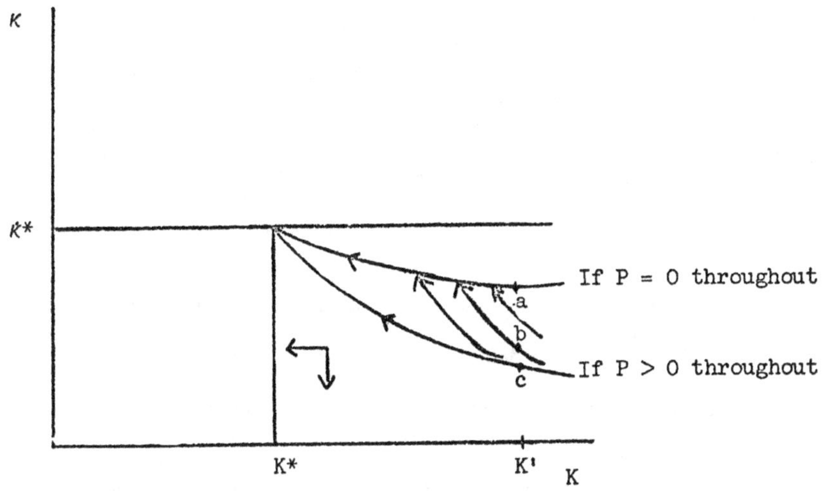

Starting with initial capital K', the appropriate initial value for κ depends upon the pollution level. If the initial value of $P = 0$, κ should be set at its value at a and should follow the upper path throughout. If the initial value of P is so great that P never equals 0 along the optimal path, the value of κ should follow the lower path starting at c. (This is the optimal path shown in Fig. 2a.) If P, though positive at the outset, goes to 0 along the optimal path, the value of the optimal κ will start on and follow one of the in between arrows, e.g. the one through b. The chosen in between arrow is the one that just meets the upper path when P = 0. The value of κ then follows the upper path to K^*,κ^*.

FOOTNOTES

[1]Other analysts may employ different terminology in making the types of distinctions we draw here. Thomas Schelling suggests that a "term like, 'anti-commodity,' or 'dis-commodity,' or 'bad,' might better reflect the broad meaning we attach to the term pollutant. Then you can say that this category includes things like 'pollution,' 'noise,' and maybe even 'negative production.'"

Matthew Edel classifies methods of environmental contamination in the categories contamination, overdurability, and depletion. The first two mentioned relate closely to our flow-stock distinction. "If the continued existence of a capital good which may not be removed (except perhaps at a high cost) causes damage after the capital ceases to be used, this is overdurability, whereas in contamination as defined here, the causing of new damage is dependent on continued use of the capital in production." The control theory equivalent of his depletion concept is a stock-control problem.

> The depletion of natural resources, so that they are not available for later production, takes different forms depending upon whether the resources are renewable if used at less than some critical rate (as are soils, forests, or animal species), or nonrenewable, as are fossil fuels and nonrecuperable minerals. Destruction of renewable resources always may be described in terms of a flow of benefits which is positive at first, but becomes highly negative over time.

See [6, pp. 3-9].

[2]Matters would not be difficult if all arguments of the welfare function were appropriately measured on a per capita basis. The pollution level, unfortunately, is a public good (bad) and is therefore not allocable on an individual basis.

[3]The appropriate shape for indifference curves is guaranteed if $u_{cc}u_{PP}-u_{cP}^2>0$. Non-inferiority requires that $u_{cc}-u_{cP}u_c/u_P<0$ and $u_{PP}u_c/u_P-u_{cP}>0$. (This will trivially be the case if $u_{cP}<0$. If consumption expenditures such as air conditioning are thought of as ways of reducing the effects of pollution, then this cross-product term may be positive.)

[4]Kurz pointed out the possible existence of multiple equilibria in another model in which both a stock (capital) and a flow (consumption) were arguments of the utility function. See Kurz [7].

[5]A linear model replaces the strict inequality $u_{PP}<0$ with $u_{PP}\leq 0$.

[6]The analysis of optimal paths on which P = 0 at some point is presented in Appendix II.

[7]We need only the assumption that $\alpha + \beta$ is bounded. The more restrictive assumption taken here might represent a situation in which capital once emplaced is no longer available for either consumption or pollution control.

[8]Mr. J. Budelis suggested to us the comparison with the Golden Age proportions path.

[9]If $F_{12}\geq 0$, then $f''<0$ throughout.

[10]This seems reasonable for D.D.T., since the resources devoted to its production are so small relative to total agricultural production resources.

[11]This might be accomplished by the development of biodegradable pesticides. The research on juvenile hormone pesticides has a different impetus. These are more specific, i.e. only damaging to particular insects, and are effective in smaller quantities. In terms of our model, h(P) is reduced by their first property, and $\tilde{L}$ is reduced by the second, because of the increase in F_1.

[12]The marginal disutility of litter may be decreasing, $h''(P)<0$, in which case, rather than our marginal approach, zero or total removal strategies may be appropriate.

[13]There may be a problem with the loss of concavity when the substitution is made for $\dot{P}$.

[14]Additional complications arise if the realistic irreversibility conditions $\dot{K}_1 \geq -aK_1$ and $\dot{K}_2 \geq -aK_2$ are imposed.

[15]This is the approach given in Dobell and Ho [5].

[16]If $u_c^{-1}(\kappa^*)+1/d \geq 1$, then P=0 at the Golden Age Equilibrium. We might call this special case a Pristine Age Equilibrium. For the rest of the appendix we shall assume that $u_c^{-1}(\kappa^*)+1/d<1$.

REFERENCES

1. K.J. ARROW, "Applications of Control Theory to Economic Growth," Reprint No. 95, Institute for Mathematical Studies in the Social Sciences, Stanford University, 1968.

2. K.J. ARROW and M. KURZ, "Public Investment, the Rate of Return, and Optimal Fiscal Policy," Institute for Mathematical Studies in the Social Sciences, Stanford University, 1968.

3. A.E. BRYSON and Y.C. HO, "Applied Optimal Control," (preliminary text), Blaisdell Publishing Co., 1968.

4. R. COURANT, "Differential and Integral Calculus," Blackie and Son Ltd., New York, 1936.

5. A.R. DOBELL and Y.C. HO, Optimal Investment Policy: An Example of a Control Problem in Economic Theory, *IEEE Transactions on Automatic Control*, Vol. AC-12 (February 1967), 4-14.

6. M.D. EDEL, "On Silent Spring and Multiple Roots: Cost-Benefit Methods and Environmental Damage," Working Paper No. 48, Department of Economics, Massachusetts Institute of Technology, January 1970.

7. M. KURZ, Optimal Economic Growth and Wealth Effects, *International Economic Review*, Vol. 9 (October 1968), 348-357.

8. H.E. RYDER, Jr., "Optimal Accumulation in a Two Sector Economy with Nonshiftable Capital," (mimeographed).

9. H.E. RYDER, Jr., "Optimal Allocation in a Listian Model," (mimeographed).

10. H. UZAWA, Optimal Growth in a Two-Sector Model of Capital Accumulation, *Review of Economic Studies*, Vol. 31 (1964).

CHAPTER 25

A POLLUTED GOLDEN AGE

WILLIAM A. BROCK[1]

University of Chicago and *University of Rochester*

September 1973

I. INTRODUCTION

Received growth theory is biased. It neglects to take into account the pollution costs of economic growth. It generates a language that lulls one into believing that all is well so long as one steams toward the golden age or modified golden rule of capital accumulation. After reading a book like E.J. Mishan's, *The Costs of Economic Growth*, the numbing nirvana induced by the happy language generated by our received theory is quickly disturbed.

Recently several attempts have been made to introduce pollution costs into the theory of optimal growth. Among these are Pitchford [14], Forster [10], Wong [20], Zeckhauser, Spence and Keeler [21].

These authors introduce pollution into growth models and study the impact of pollution on the accumulation of capital. These studies are quite technical and make little attempt to use the models as an aid for an intelligent discussion of current economic issues.

For a book of this type we feel that it is necessary not only to conduct a technical exercise in a growth model but also to use that model to discuss current issues of the day. The layout of this paper follows.

We shall first present a model and analyze it. Second we shall show how growth theory relates to equilibrium theory and discuss externality taxes in this framework. Third, we shall discuss biases in the observed market rate of interest when pollution is accounted for. This has important implications for the issue of using the market rate of interest in discounting future benefits in cost-benefit analysis. Fourth, we shall discuss how models of this type could be used to build a theoretical apparatus that will allow us to discuss the issues raised by the "doomsday theorists" (Forrester, Meadows, et al. in the famous Club of Rome report), whether free enterprise has a self-corrective mechanism to avert the crunch predicted by the Club of Rome. As the reader probably knows most economists have been hostile to the Club of Rome. See for example Solow [17]. We hope to convince the reader that much theoretical work needs to be done before the case is closed, and that growth models will be a useful tool in doing this theoretical work.

Our task in this paper, as we see it, is to show readers of this book how growth models may be used to discuss the vital environmental issues of the day. We hope the following pages accomplish that end.

2. A MODEL

In this section we will put down a growth model and discuss existence and convergence of optimal paths. This is quite technical and may be skipped by the reader if he is not technically inclined.

Consider the problem I:

$$\text{Maximize} \quad \sum_{t=0}^{\infty} \delta^t u(C_t, P_t)$$

$$\text{s.t.} \quad C_0 + K_0 = S, \tag{1}$$

$$C_t + K_t = F(K_{t-1}, W_{t-1})$$

$$t = 1, 2, \ldots$$

$$P_1 = mP_0 + W_0 \tag{2}$$

$$P_t = mP_{t-1} + W_{t-1}$$

$$t = 1, 2 \ldots$$

where C_t, K_t, P_t, W_t, S, δ, u, F, m are consumption, capital stock, pollution stock, waste generated by production (all at t), initial capital stock, discount factor, utility of consumption and pollution level, production function, and decay factor, respectively.

Waste is treated as a joint product in this model. F is assumed to be a usual textbook production function of the two factor inputs K, W. The idea that we are trying to capture is that techniques of production are less costly in terms of capital input if more[2] pollution is allowed - which seems to crudely correspond to observation in the real world. The problems of constructing an index to measure waste output are quite similar, as far as we can see, to those involved in constructing an index for K - except that for K we could use market valuation, whereas, for W there are no markets - due to the public goods character of "bads". Nevertheless we write F(K,W) for our stylized economy. We have suppressed labour because assuming exponential labour force growth merely clutters the picture and what we want to do here is concentrate on any aspects of the model that have promise of not being trivial variations on the theme of received theory. Since labour is suppressed in F it must be kept in mind that F is not homogeneous of degree one.

Waste is a joint product. It acts as an input to production. It also is discharged into the environment where it is assumed to decay exponentially as in (2) with factor, $0 < m < 1$. Actually m will probably depend on the stock of pollution, P_t, but, for simplicity, assume that it is constant. Although different contaminants decay at different rates a large number of contaminants in approximately steady state proportions will have approximately constant decay rate as a composite entity - we think. One further word on F. We are assuming reversible investment so that we may write the capital accumulation equations in the form (1). The utility function u is concave, increasing in C - decreasing in P. What kind of results would one hope to get from I? One would hope that optimal programs exist, that a "modified golden rule" of capital stock and pollution level exists, that optimal paths converge to this modified golden rule, and that "decentralizing" or, to use another name, competitive (Gale [9]) prices exist. For the discounted case ($0 < \delta < 1$) examples have been constructed by Sutherland [18] in the Gale [9] model where optimal paths oscillate and never converge. This qualitative departure of multisector theory from the one sector theory is fairly well known. Since we have not yet sorted out (in an economically interesting manner) the various possibilities for $0 < \delta < 1$; here we shall assume $\delta = 1$ and save $0 < \delta < 1$ for another piece. The assumption $\delta = 1$ rules out Sutherland-type oscillatory phenomena in the Gale model.

For simplicity let us assume that F,u are differentiable as many times as needed. This is not necessary but avoids concern with essentially side track issues.

Suppose a pollution level, $\hat{P}$ exists that is intolerable, i.e., $u(C,\hat{P}) = -\infty$ for all $C > 0$. We make a change of variable $E = \hat{P}-P$ and rewrite (2) as follows.

$$E_t = mE_{t-1} - W_{t-1} + (1-m)\hat{P} \qquad t = 1,2,\ldots \quad (3)$$

Think of E as "environmental goods". $u(C,P)$ becomes $u(C,P-\hat{E})$ which we also denote $u(C,E)$. Notice that the "new" u is concave and increasing in both C,E and $u(C,0) = -\infty$. Assume that u is strictly concave and that F is strictly concave so that solving the problem

$$\text{maximize} \quad u(C,E) \quad (4)$$

$$\text{s.t.} \quad C = F(K,W) - K \ ,$$
$$E = mE - W + (1-m)\hat{P}$$

gives us a unique stationary path $(\bar{C}, \bar{E})$ which we shall call the optimal stationary path (Gale). We shall sometimes call it the polluted golden age or polluted turnpike. From here on we drop the bars on C,E. Problem (4) gives the necessary conditions

$$F_1 = 1, \ u_1F_2 = u_2\frac{1}{1-m} \quad (5)$$

where u_i, F_i denote partial derivatives in the usual way.

It may be worthwhile to expand on the meaning of equations (5). Look at the equations of capital accumulation (1): If capital geometrically decays at rate η then a more illuminating way to write (1) is

$$C_t + K_t - K_{t-1} = G(K_{t-1}, W_{t-1}) - \eta K_{t-1}$$

where $G(K_{t-1}, W_{t-1})$ is gross output at a function of capital services K_{t-1} and environmental services W_{t-1}. Net output $G - \eta K_{t-1}$ is gross output minus depreciation. Put $F(K,W) \equiv G(K,W) + (1-\eta)K$ to reduce the problem to the form (1).

What do the steady state equations (5) mean? This is the case where the discount on future utility is zero i.e. $F_1 = 1$, which boils down to

$$\partial G/\partial K = \eta$$

In other words, the gross marginal product of capital is equal to the depreciation rate. This result is standard in optimal growth theory [4].

The second equation equates the marginal benefit u_1F_2 from a unit increase in W to the marginal cost $u_2/(1-m)$. In other words consider a unit increase in W. This creates $F_2 = G_2$ extra units of produce. The produce may be consumed to yield u_1F_2 extra utils. The cost of this maneuver is that an extra unit of pollution is discharged into the environment. That extra unit decays to m^t units by period t. Hence u_2m^t disutilities are expected at t. The total cost is the present value of the stream of disutilities u_2, u_2m, u_2m^2,... Since the rate of discount on future utility is zero, the present value is

$$\sum_{t=0}^{\infty} u_2 m^t$$

But u_2 is independent of t so that this becomes

$$u_2\left(\sum_{t=0}^{\infty} m^t\right) = u_2/(1-m)$$

Following [1] we find $\{\delta_t\}_{t=0}^{\infty}$ associated with a path $\{C_t, E_t\}_{t=0}^{\infty}$ starting from initial levels S, E_0 so that

$$\sum_{t=0}^{T} [u(C_t,E_t) - u(C,E)] = a_T - \sum_{t=0}^{\infty} \delta_t \qquad (6)$$

where $\{a_T\}_{T=0}^{\infty}$ is an appropriately defined sequence which converges to 0 for paths $\{C_t,E_t\}$ that converge to C,E and $\{\delta_t\}_{t=0}^{\infty}$ is a non-negative sequence. Then we show that a path with minimum associated $\{\delta_t\}$ exists and that it converges to C,E which gives existence and stability of the optimum path. The details are appropriately banished to the appendix. A full discussion of stability and existence is given there.

For $\delta = 1$ the optimal path exists, is unique, and

converges to the same steady state independent of initial K_0, P_0. This is important because it gives the theoretical underpinning for long run stability and long run comparative statics.

It says that regardless of the starting point the economy will converge to a state where the net of depreciation marginal product of capital is zero and the utility marginal value product of pollution equals the present value of disutilities generated by a unit of pollution.

The case $\delta = 1$ was brought into prominence by the philosopher Frank Ramsey when he argued that it was "unethical" to discount the future generation's utility. In our model it would seem likely that the smaller the δ the larger the steady state stock of pollution for "reasonable" conditions on technology and utility. The Ramsey case $\delta = 1$ is useful to highlight the inherent trade-off between production and pollution regardless of people's disdain for the future. Let us now turn to a discussion of market schemes to realize the optimum path.

3. INTERTEMPORAL EQUILIBRIUM AND EXTERNALITY TAXES

At this point we switch to continuous time for convenience.

Consider

$$\begin{aligned} &\underset{C,P}{\text{maximize}} \quad \int_0^\infty e^{-\rho t} u(C,P)dt \\ &\text{s.f.} \quad C + \dot{K} = F(K,W,L) \quad , K(0) = K_0 \\ &\qquad \dot{P} = -mP + W \qquad , P(0) = P_0 \end{aligned} \tag{7}$$

Here $\dot{K}$ is dK/dt, $\rho \geqq 0$, $m > 0$. We will treat the special case of perfectly inelastic supply of labour. Thus we set $L = 1$ for all moments of time.

The growth problem (7) yields the same solution as the general equilibrium problem with externalities:

(a) Representative Consumer: $\underset{C}{\text{maximize}} \int_0^\infty e^{-\rho t} u(C,P)dt$

$$\text{s.t.} \qquad qC + q\dot{K} = \pi + rK + wL = T$$

$$K(0) = K_0$$

(b) Representative Firm: $\underset{K,W,L}{\text{maximize}}\ \pi = qF(K,W,L) - rK - \tau W - WL$

$$\begin{aligned} &\text{(c) Government:} && T = \tau W \\ &\text{(d) Environment:} && \dot{P} = -mP + W, \quad P(0) = P_0 \end{aligned} \tag{8}$$

The logic of this latter problem works thus. Each period the representative parametric price-taking consumer expects to receive total income, $\pi + rK + wL + T$, which consists of profits π, rents on capital loaned out, rK, wages, wL, and lump sum externality taxes redistributed to the consumer, T. He can spend this income on consumption qC or addition to capital stock $q\dot{K}$. Note that the consumption good is identical to the capital good. The consumer facing q, π, r, w, T solves his problem 8(a) to lay out his demands for consumption C, additions to capital $\dot{K}$, stock supply of capital, K, and inelastically supplied labour $L = 1$. The firm solves its problem 8(b) to lay out demand for services of capital K, supply of goods, $F(K,W,L)$, demand for labour L, demand for environment W. The government collects the externality taxes, τW, from the firms and redistributes them to the representative consumer. For each value of the tax, τ, there will be an equilibrium where all markets clear. Corresponding to τ there will be a flow of waste W and pollution in the environment will accumulate according to $\dot{P} = -mP + W$, $P(0) = P_0$. Now there is no market to set τ. It must be set by the political process. A logical place to set τ is to set it to solve

$$\underset{\tau}{\text{maximize}} \int_0^{\infty} e^{-\rho t} u(C_\tau, P_\tau)dt \equiv U(\tau) \tag{9}$$

where C_τ, P_τ are equilibrium paths corresponding to τ.

We will sketch a proof that welfare $U(\tau)$ is optimum when $\tau(t) = \lambda(t)$ where $\lambda(t)$ is the shadow price of pollution calculated from (7). Furthermore, the equilibrium quantities of K, C, etc. are the same as the optimum ones calculated from (7).

Let us solve (7). Doing the usual Pontryagin [4], routine write

$$\begin{aligned} H(C,P;\, q_1, q_2) &= \underset{C,W}{\text{maximum}} \\ &\{u(C,P) + q_1(F-C) + q_2(-mP + W)\} \end{aligned} \tag{10}$$

H is called the current value Hamiltonian. From the Maximum Principle necessary conditions for an optimum are

$$\begin{aligned}
&\text{(a)} \quad q_1 = \partial u/\partial C, \quad q_2 = -q_1 \; \partial F/\partial W, \quad \lambda \equiv -q_1^{-1} q_2 \\
&\text{(b)} \quad \dot{q}_1 = \rho q_1 = -\frac{\partial H}{\partial K} = -q_1 \frac{\partial F}{\partial K} \\
&\text{(c)} \quad \dot{q}_2 - \rho q_2 = -\frac{\partial H}{\partial P} = m\, q_2 - \partial u/\partial P \\
&\text{(d)} \quad C + \dot{K} = F(K,W,1), \; K(0) = K_0, \; \dot{P} = -mP + W, \; P(0) = P_0
\end{aligned} \tag{11}$$

Note that L = 1 for all moments of time.

Economic interpretation of these follow the standard line from capital theory (e.g. Burmeister and Dobell [4]), viz. (11) b,c, state that capital gains on K, $\dot{q}_1/q_1$, plus yield on K, $(q_1 \partial F/\partial K)/q_1$, equals "capital gains" on P, plus "yield" on P, $\left(\frac{\partial u}{\partial P} - m\, q_2\right)/q_2$, equals a common rate of return, ρ. Here we are treating P as "negative" capital to facilitate the interpretation.

Let us write out necessary conditions for the equilibrium problem and compare the two sets of conditions: The representative consumer solves the calculus of variations problem

$$\underset{K}{\text{maximize}} \int_0^\infty e^{-\rho t} u[(\pi + rK + wL + T - q\dot{K})q^{-1}, P]dt \tag{12}$$

$$\text{s.t. } K(0) = K_0$$

This yields the Euler equation

$$\frac{d}{dt}\left(\frac{\partial u}{\partial C}\right) = \frac{\partial u}{\partial C}\left(\rho - rq^{-1}\right) \tag{13}$$

The representative firm maximizes profits to give

$$\partial F/\partial K = r, \; \frac{\partial F}{\partial W} = \tau, \; \frac{\partial F}{\partial L} = w \tag{14}$$

Now set $\tau \equiv \lambda$ where λ is the shadow "rental value" of polution from (11a). It is now straightforward to check that the equilibrium problem with $\tau \equiv \lambda$ generates exactly the same set of equations as (11). Thus the solutions must be identical.

The intuition is this: If one sets the tax on polluting, τ, equal to the marginal social cost of polluting then the competitive equilibrium internalizes the externality and produces the optimal amount of goods and pollution.

The result that optimal taxes on pollution are set equal to marginal social cost is not very surprising. It is, however, worthwhile to have a precise framework in which to discuss such issues. Let us use our framework to discuss the issue of the proper discount rate in cost benefit analysis. From this point on our discussion will not be rigorous. We will indicate how to make it rigorous, however.

Cost Benefit Analysis and the Market Rate of Interest

Suppose that firms were not being charged a τ equal to the marginal social cost of polluting. In a competitive market the observed marginal product of capital corresponding to the competitive equilibrium associated with τ would be the market rate of interest, $r_\tau \equiv \partial F/\partial K\ (K_\tau, W_\tau, 1)$ and for each τ there would be a different market interest rate observed.

The use of the market rate of interest to discount future net benefits in cost benefit analysis has been debated intensively in the literature (Harberger [11], Marglin [13], for example). Our model allows us to focus on another problem with the market rate of interest viz., if τ is not set at social optimum then r_τ will be biased. If the reader believes, as many environmentalists do, that τ is set too low, and if $\partial^2 F/\partial K \partial W > 0$ (the "normal" case) then at each point in time the observed equilibrium interest rate $r_\tau \equiv \partial F/\partial K(K,W,1)$ is likely to be larger than the socially optimum interest rate. Thus future net benefits will be discounted too heavily by analysts using the observed market rate of interest as a discount rate. It is clear, then, that projects that yield a small stream of benefits over a long period are biased against. Many projects dear to environmentalists have a better chance with a small discount rate. (So also may the SST!) Let us discuss this bias issue with more precision.

Suppose, to simplify matters, that instead of taxes there is a law that forbids more than $\bar{W}$ units of pollution by firms each period. Here $\bar{W}$ is a constant independent of time. Then the optimal growth problem with W(t) fixed at $\bar{W}$, generates the same solution as the equilibrium problem when $W(t) = \bar{W}$. Now if P(t) were constant we would have a standard one-sector growth problem.

$$\underset{C}{\text{maximize}} \quad \int_0^\infty e^{-\rho t} u(C,\bar{P})\,dt \tag{15}$$

$$C + \dot{K} = F(K,\bar{W},1)$$
$$K(0) = K_0$$

It is a classic result ([5], [12]) that for each value of $\bar{W},\bar{P}$ the optimal path $\{C,K\}$ of (15) converges to a unique steady state $\bar{K}$ independent of K_0. Furthermore, if $K_0 < \bar{K}$ the marginal product of capital $\frac{\partial F}{\partial K}(K,\bar{W},1)$ falls to ρ as $t \to \infty$. If $K_0 > \bar{K}$ $\frac{\partial F}{\partial K}(K,\bar{W},1)$ rises to ρ as K falls to $\bar{K}$.

To study the interest rate bias question we need to examine the behaviour of $\frac{\partial F}{\partial K}(K,\bar{W},1)$ along optimal solutions of (15) for different values of $\bar{W}$. Obviously since $\{K\}$ is a time path this gets complicated. For this paper we just indicate what is likely to be a theorem.[4] *Conjecture*: If K_0 is small and $\partial F/\partial K \partial W > 0$ then increased $\bar{W}$ will increase $\frac{\partial F}{\partial K}(K,\bar{W},1)$ at each point in time along the optimum path. Here K_0 "small" means to $K_0 < \bar{K}$ before the increase, where $\bar{K}$ is associated with $\bar{W},\bar{P}$.

In words a loose argument goes thus. Let it be permitted for firms to pollute more at no extra cost. Since the marginal product of capital increases with W there is a rightward shift in the demand for capital at each point in time. Thus the market clearing interest rate must increase if the supply effect is smaller than the demand effect. It seems unlikely that the supply curve for capital will shift in any particular way. Hence it is likely that the rate of interest will rise at each point in time and more capital will be accumulated.

Now back to the issue of discount rates in cost benefit analysis. If one believes that the economy is "growing" i.e. $(K_0 < \bar{K})$ and the current $\bar{W}$ is greater than the optimum W then our conjecture says that it is quite likely that C-B analysts, using the market rate of interest as a discount rate are discounting future net benefits too heavily in favour of present net benefits.

Of course we have not *proved* anything, but we have shown that there is a serious conceptual problem in the use of the market rate of interest as a discount rate in C-B analysis above and beyond the objections of, for example, Marglin [13], and others. It seems to us that there is a promising line of research in studying bias caused by using equilibrium prices generated by economies with[5] distortions to price net benefits. Now that growth models with externalities have proved useful in the discussion of one important question, let us turn to a second.

4. THE CLUB OF ROME REPORT

The Club of Rome Report generated a hot debate. Needless to say, economists gave it a hostile reception. See Solow [17] for a list of critical remarks. A caricature of the Club of Rome argument is that population growth, production of pollution and consumption of energy - if allowed to continue at rates even quite a bit smaller than present rates - will cause a "crunch" where society essentially collapses. A caricature of the critics' argument is that the Club of Rome people ignored the important role of the price system in choking off the high rate of energy usage and thus avoiding catastrophe. Can growth models with externalities be used to shed any light on this controversy?

Externality Prices on Pollution

Suppose population is constant, for the moment. Then, in such a world the Club of Rome argument amounts to saying that we are not putting a correct price on the environment. In fact it is easy to see that if there is a satiation level of pollution $\hat{P}$ beyond which society perishes then a market economy with a small tax on pollution may perish if the private marginal product of pollution, $\frac{\partial F}{\partial W}$, is larger than the tax at a flow rate of pollution W that sustains a steady state P larger than $\hat{P}$. This is a simple problem to take care of in the theoretical world of economic models but what about the real world where τ is set by political pressures rather than by optimal control theory? It is hard to say whether there are natural pressures in the system to push

τ away from a doomsday value. A positive theory of political action is needed to intelligently discuss this issue. It seems easy to believe that if the burden of pollution gets bad enough that even diffuse groups will surmount the inherent public goods problems of forming an anti-pollution lobby and win legislation against the more typically heavily concentrated industrial pollutors. But will this process work fast enough? That is an empirical question for political scientists to answer.

Slowly Adapting Expectations

Another direction that the Club of Rome argument may have force is incorrect expectations as to the future value of natural resources. Economic logic suggests that if speculators foresaw a sharp rise in the price of tin, in the year 1984 that they would bid up the current price of tin. Thus tin would be expensive today. This would cause substitution away from tin. Thus the "scarce" tin would be conserved.

Now if market expectations on the future price of tin were incorrect then there may be something to the Club of Rome argument. Thinking about intertemporal general equilibrium models of the type studied above leads to the following verbiage. Let people form expectations on the future price of tin. Current market price is the present value of the stream of services from a ton of tin evaluated at time t. If tin decays at rate δ, the rate of profit is ρ, the expected rental rate at time s based at time t is $R(s,t)$ then the current price is

$$q(t) = \int_t^\infty e^{-(\rho+\delta)(s-t)} R(s,t)\, ds. \qquad (16)$$

Note that if $R(s,t) \equiv q_1 \partial F/\partial K$ in (11b) then (16) is the same type of equation as (11b). Differentiate (16) w•r•t t to see this. Thus as common sense and formal capital theory dictate: The asset price of tin, q, is equal to the expected present value of its stream of services discounted at the rate of profit ρ and the rate of depreciation.

With this background out of the way we will sketch a model of a capital market with imperfect foresight. We speak in period language to ease the presentation. At time t people have expectations concerning the value of the stream of services of each asset for times t+1, t+2,... The market sets a current price, p_t^a, determined by market clearing.

p_t^a will be some sort of "average" of the "subjective present values" held by each agent in the market. p_t^a will be compared by each agent with expectations held in the previous period t-1 and then expectations based at t+1 on prices in t+2, t+3 will be revised according to some adaptive scheme. Now for "reasonable" expectation revision mechanisms such a process should converge to the happy situation of perfect foresight where the market is placing correct evaluation on assets. But what about the speed of such convergence? In such markets where the demand for tin is rising at a rapid rate but expectations are adjusting slowly upward then the tin would be "used up" too rapidly from a social point of view.

In our opinion the correct way to debate the Club of Rome on the expectations issue is to set up a rigorous model of expectations revision and asset pricing along the lines sketched above, and attempt to get an empirical handle on the "coefficient" of expectations adjustment. Then we can rationally discuss if the asset market is working well enough that no state interference is called for by economic theory.

OTHER ISSUES

We could mention the issue of population growth. Also there is the fact that unborn generations do not cast the dollar votes that determine the prices that dictate the rate of utilization of our natural resources. The private market may have serious faults in both of these areas. It still remains for economics to produce a macro growth theory where population is determined endogenously. See Pitchford [14] for a beginning on such a theory.

It still remains for economists to face the intergenerational income distribution problem underlying the free market allocation of resources across generations. It should be true in most cases that this distribution is Pareto efficient in the sense that one generation can't be made better off without another being made worse off. See Samuelson [16], Diamond [7], Gale [8], Wilson [19] for cases where the free market distribution is *not* Pareto efficient.

Apart from Pareto efficiency there is the question of justice. Following current policy, are future generations expected to become better off over time? Does the individual bequest motive generate savings behaviour in these days of environmental concern that is strong enough to conserve enough resources so that "average" welfare will not fall over future generations if the free market is allowed to set the rate of resource utilization? Will the effect of technical change be strong enough to cancel the effect of inherent impatience of current generations for consumption today over consumption tomorrow? Even though the market distribution of consumption may be Pareto efficient across generations there may be many other Pareto efficient distributions that are more "just". Growth models and capital theory are at the heart of these issues. We hope that we have convinced the reader of the usefulness of growth theory as a tool for discussing these issues.

CONCLUSION

In this paper we set up a growth model with accumulation of pollution. We related it to market equilibrium theory with a tax on externalities. This relationship was used to discuss biases in the market rate of interest for use as a discount factor on future net benefits in cost benefit analysis. Using this analysis we argued that the market rate was probably higher than the "current" rate.

We then launched a loose verbal discussion of points raised by the Club of Rome and how growth models may be used to shed light on these issues.

FOOTNOTES

[1]Ralph D'Arge and Lionel McKenzie have influenced my thinking on this subject. Rudi Dornbusch gave me many useful comments. The NSF helped support this research. Needless to say, none of the above are responsible for errors.

[2]Let us expand upon this point. First, when we refer to waste we are talking about effluent, smoke, unsightly factory buildings, etc. We are not talking about excess capacity, poorly allocated resources, etc. Second, as far as pollution is concerned, what is in the individual interest is not necessarily in the social interest. For example, polluting by firms may raise the production cost for all firms (loss of paint on buildings, impairment of working conditions, etc.) but, nevertheless, due to the publicness character of pollution, individual firms will choose the cheaper pollution

intensive technique provided it costs less. Since our model is a planning model these externalities are "internalized" by the planning authority. Hence our model captures only the unavoidable pollution costs of economic growth. The real cost (that which includes the externalities) will be much greater due to the difficulty of internalizing externalities and constructing public goods through the market mechanism.

[3]It is not necessary to assume strict concavity of u,F. It suffices to assume that C,E;K,W is unique to get convergence.

[4]We should point out to the reader that there is work to do to get a rigorous statement and proof of this conjecture. The trouble is that P(t) follows a difference equation so that P(t) is independent of t *only at steady state*. Now if $\bar{W}$ is changed from $\bar{W}_1$ to $\bar{W}_2$ then it will take time for P(t) to adjust from $\bar{P}_1$ to $\bar{P}_2$. In fact, for $P_0 = \bar{P}_1$, $P_t = mP_{t-1} + \bar{W}_2$ we have $\lim_{t\to\infty} P(t) = \bar{P}_2$, where $(1-m)\bar{P}_i = \bar{W}_i$, $i = 1,2$. Since P(t) is changing with t therefore the utility function is changing with t which renders the classical one sector theory ([5], [12]) inapplicable. Thus we state the conjecture in a loose way.

Now if P_0 is adjusted from $\bar{P}_1$ to $\bar{P}_2$ when $\bar{W}_1$ is changed to $\bar{W}_2$ then P(t) is constant, the one sector theory is valid, and for small $K_0 < \min\{\bar{K}_1, \bar{K}_2\}$ the optimal capital accumulation path will rise to $\bar{K}_2$ instead of $\bar{K}_1$. Here $\bar{K}_i$ solves $F_1(\bar{K}_i, \bar{W}_i, 1) = \rho$. Furthermore $F_1(K_t, \bar{W}, 1)$ increases in $\bar{W}$ for all t along the optimal path $\{K_t\}$. Thus if P_0 is simultaneously adjusted with W we obtain a precise result with little difficulty. But the economic meaning of such simultaneous adjustment is dubious at best.

[5]Harberger emphasizes that the market rate of interest must be "adjusted" for distortions that are present. He focuses on distortions due to taxes and subsidies of various kinds. Here we deal with an implicit "subsidy" to capital accumulation via free use of the environment. Incorrect pricing of the environment leads to distortion problems that could be analyzed by a dynamic generalization of Harberger's methods.

APPENDIX: EXISTENCE AND CONVERGENCE OF OPTIMAL PATHS

Before going into the details we remind the reader that $\{\bar{C}_t, \bar{E}_t\}$ *overtakes* $\{C_t, E_t\}$ if

$$\underline{\lim}_{T\to\infty} \sum_{t=0}^{T} [u(\bar{C}_t,\bar{E}_t) - u(C_t,E_t)] \geqq 0 \qquad \text{(a)}$$

where $\underline{\lim}_{T\to\infty} x_t$ denotes the smallest limit point of the sequence $\{x_t\}$. By concavity of u we have

$$\sum_{t=0}^{T} [u(C_t,E_t) - u(C,E)] = u_1 \sum_{t=0}^{T} (C_t-C) \qquad \text{(b)}$$

$$+ u_2 \sum_{t=0}^{T} (E_t-E) - \sum_{t=0}^{T} \alpha_{1t}$$

where $-\alpha_{1t} \equiv u(C_t,E_t) - u(C,E) - u_1(C_t-C) - u_2(E_t-E) \leqq 0.$

By using concavity of the production function the term $\sum_{t=0}^{T} (C_t-C)$ may be put into the form

$$\sum_{t=0}^{T} (C_t-C) = S - F(K,W) + K-K_0 + F_1(K_0-K) + \qquad (9)$$

$$F_2(W_0-W) + K-K_1 - \alpha_{21} +\ldots+ F_1(K_{T-1}-K) + F_2(W_{T-1}-W)$$

$$+ K-K_T - \alpha_{2T}$$

where $-\alpha_{2t} \equiv F(K_{t-1},W_{t-1}) - F(K,W) - F_1(K_{t-1}-K) - F_2(W_{t-1}-W)$

Since $F_1=1$ from the necessary condition (5), (9) reduces to

$$\sum_{t=0}^{T} (C_t-C) = S-F(K,W) + F_2\Big(\sum_{t=0}^{T-1} W_t-W\Big) + K-K_T - \sum_{t=1}^{T} \alpha_{2t} \qquad (10)$$

Using the second part of (5) the expression

$$u_1 \sum_{t=0}^{T} (C_t - C) + u_2 \sum_{t=0}^{T} (E_t - E) \qquad \text{becomes}$$

$$u_1[(S-F(K,W)) + K-K_T - \sum_{t=1}^{T} \alpha_{2t}] + E_0(u_2 + mu_1F_2) + E_T(u_2-u_1F_2) \tag{11}$$

Putting it all together we get the fundamental equation

$$\sum_{t=0}^{T} [u(C_t,E_t) - u(C,E)]$$

$$= u_1(S-F(K,W)) + E_0(u_2+mu_1F_2) + u_1(K-K_T) + E_T(u_2-u_1F_2) - \sum_{t=0}^{T} \delta_t \tag{12}$$

where $\delta_t \equiv \alpha_{1t} + u_1\alpha_{2t}$, $t = 0,1,\ldots;\ \alpha_{20} \equiv 0$.

Let us look closely at (12). When is (12) bounded above? Since $\delta_t \geqq 0$, $t = 0,1,\ldots$ this amounts to boundedness of $\{K_t\}$ and $\{E_t\}$. Now it is trivial to check that $\{E_t\}$ is bounded. Just check (3) to note that $\overline{\lim}_{t\to\infty} E_t \leqq \hat{P}$. As far as $\{K_t\}$ is concerned it is reasonable to assume that $F(K,W)$ considered as a function of K cuts the 45° line for each W. In fact we are just assuming for each W that $F(\cdot,W)$ is a standard one sector growth theory production function. Given this and given that $F(K,W)$ is increasing in W it follows that $\{K_t\}_{t=0}^{\infty}$ is bounded above. This follows because from (3) $\{W_t\}$ is bounded above by $\hat{W}$, say. Then $\{K_t\}$ is bounded above the path of pure accumulation $\{K_t\}_{t=0}^{\infty}$ generated by $\hat{K}_{t+1} = F(\hat{K}_t,\hat{W})$, $t = 0,1,\ldots$ so that $\overline{\lim}_{t\to\infty} \hat{K}_t \leqq \hat{K}$ where $\hat{K} = F(\hat{K},\hat{W})$.

We are now in a position to apply the results in [1]. Much of the technique of [1] is based on that contained in the well known paper by Gale [9]. Gale defines a program to be *good* if the partial sums defined by (12) are bounded below. Gale shows that all programs are either *good* or the partial sums defined by (12) converge to $-\infty$. He uses the fact that they are bounded above to establish this. He then shows that for good programs $\{C_t,E_t\}$, that $C_t \to C$, $E_t \to E$. This is trivial to show for our model because for good programs, $\delta_t \to 0, t \to \infty$ but $\delta_t = \alpha_{1t} + u_1\alpha_{2t}$. Hence $\alpha_{1t} \to 0$, $\alpha_{2t} \to 0$, $t \to \infty$. But $-\alpha_{1t}$, $-\alpha_{2t}$ are strictly concave[3] functions of C_t,E_t; K_{t-1}, W_{t-1} respectively both of which take unique maxima at C,E; K,W. Consult Equations (9), (10) for definitions of α_{1t},α_{2t}. Thus any limit points of $\{C_t,E_t\}$, $\{K_t,W_t\}$ must be maximizers. Hence any limit points must be C,E; K,W respectively - which proves convergence.

If we can show that a good program exists then we can use the technique of [1] to prove existence of an optimal program. It is easy to see that a good program exists for our simple model. If initial stock S is below the golden age level, F(K,W) then build it up to this level by "tightening the belt" for several periods. But don't increase it so fast that the stock of pollution rises to the intolerable level $\hat{P}$. Since the environment "biodegrades" the pollution with factor m, $0 < m < 1$ in a finite amount of time we can reach F(K,W). Now consume F(K,W) - K each period and waste W each period. Environmental goods E_t will rise to E exponentially fast because the excess of pollutants created by the period of "industrial development" disappears from the environment with exponential speed. It is straightforward to show that the partial sums of (12) are bounded below for the above kind of program. The situation where $S < F(K,W)$ presents no problem. Hence a good program exists. We may now copy the argument in [1] to show that an optimum exists.

Look upon $(1,u_1,u_2)$ as "golden age prices" of utils, consumption goods, and environmental goods, respectively. Then the term $-\sum_{t=0}^{T} \delta_t$ in (12) may be looked upon as the value at golden age prices of the T period program $\{C_t,E_t\}_{t=0}^{T}$. The procedure in [1] constructs an infinite program $\{\bar{C}_t,\bar{E}_t\}$ that has maximum value, $-\sum_{t=0}^{\infty} \delta_t$, at golden prices.

We briefly describe the procedure in [1], leaving the full detail to that paper. Look at the set

$$\Sigma \equiv \{\sigma \equiv \sum_{t=0}^{\infty} \delta_t \mid \{\delta_t\}_{t=0}^{\infty}$$

is the sequence associated with a program $\{C_t,E_t\}$ starting from $S,E_0\}$. Let $\underline{\sigma} = \inf \{\sigma \mid \sigma\varepsilon\Sigma\}$. Then construct minimizing sequence $\{\{C_t^n,E_t^n\}_{t=0}^{\infty}\}_{n=0}^{\infty}$ such that $\sigma_n \to \underline{\sigma}$, $n \to \infty$.

By the usual diagonal process, pick a convergent subsequence of $\{\{C_t^n,E_t^n\}_{t=0}^{\infty}\}_{n=1}^{\infty}$, i.e., pick $\{n_j\} \subseteq \{n\}$ such that for all t, $C_t^{n_j},E_t^{n_j} \to \bar{C}_t,\bar{E}_t$, $j \to \infty$. $\{\bar{C}_t,\bar{E}_t\}$ is a program and its associated series $\sum_{t=0}^{\infty} \delta_t = \underline{\sigma}$ because

$$\underline{\sigma} = \lim_{j\to\infty} \sum_{t=0}^{\infty} \delta_t^{n_j} \leqq \sum_{t=0}^{\infty} \lim_{j\to\infty} \delta_t^{n_j} = \sum_{t=0}^{\infty} \lim \delta_t^{n_j} = \sum_{t=0}^{\infty} \bar{\delta}_t \leqq \underline{\sigma}$$

because $\underline{\sigma}$ is the infinum over Σ. Hence a program $\{\bar{C}_t,\bar{E}_t\}_{t=0}^{\infty}$ that attains maximum value at golden age prices $(1,u_1,u_2)$ exists.

We have, now, a fairly complete picture of the qualitative behaviour of optimal paths in the no discounting case. Recent work of Brock-Scheinkman [3], Cass-Shell [6], Rockafellar [15] can be applied to the stability problem in the discounted case. Also it appears that one could prove the following for the discounted case using the results of Brock [2]: If E,C are normal goods and F(K,W,L) is concave, constant returns then there is at most one steady state. Time does not permit, in a paper of this type, to explore any more technical issues here.

REFERENCES

[1] BROCK,W., "On Existence of Weakly Maximal Programs in a Multi-Sector Economy"

[2] BROCK, W., Some Results on the Uniqueness of Steady States In Multi-Sector Models of Optimum Growth When Future Utilities Are Discounted., I.E.R. Oct. 1973 (forthcoming)

[3] BROCK, W. and SCHEINKMAN, J. "Work in Progress" Department of Economics, University of Chicago and University of Rochester, Work in Progress, September 1973

[4] BURMEISTER, E. and DOBELD R. Mathematical Theories of Economic Growth, The Macmillan Co., New York, 1970

[5] CASS, D., "Optimal Growth in an Aggregative Model of Capital Accumulation: A Turnpike Theorem," Econometrica, 1966

[6] CASS, D. and SHELL, K. "Work in Progress" Graduate School of Industrial Administration, Carnegie Mellon University and Department of Economics, University of Pennsylvania

[7] DIAMOND, P., "National Debt in a Neoclassical Growth Model," *A.E.R.* (December, 1965) 1126-50

[8] GALE, D., "Pure Exchange Equilibrium of Dynamic Economic Models", University of California, Berkeley, Department of Industrial Engineering, Unpublished, November, 1971

[9] GALE, D., "On Optimal Development in a Multi-Sector Economy," *RES*, 1967

[10] FORSTER, B., A Note on the Optimal Control of Pollution *Journal of Economic Theory*, Vol. 5, November 3, December 1972, 537-539

[11] HARBERGER, A. *Project Evaluation: Collected Papers.* Markham Publishing Co., Chicago

[12] KOOPMANS, T., "On the Concept of Optimal Economic Growth" in *The Econometric Approach to Development Planning*, Rand McNally, Chicago, 1966

[13] MARGLIN, S., "The Social Rate of Discount and the Optimal Rate of Saving," Q.J.E. February, 1963

[14] PITCHFORD, J., Population and Optimal Growth. Econometrica, Vol. 40, No. 1, January 1972, 109-136

[15] ROCKAFELLAR, R.T., "Work in Progress", Department of Mathematics, University of Washington, Seattle, Washington

[16] SAMUELSON, P., "An Exact Consumption-Loan Model with or without the Contrivance of Money," J.P.E. 1972, 39-55.

[17] SOLOW, R., "Is the End of the World at Hand?" *Challenge*, March-April, 1973, 39-50

[18] SUTHERLAND, R., "On Optimal Development Programs When Future Utilities are Discounted" *RES*, Vol. XXXVII (4), October 1970, 585-589

[19] WILSON C., "An Analysis of A One-Sector Dynamic General Equilibrium Model with Capital." Second year paper, Department of Economics, University of Rochester, November 1972

[20] WONG, R., "Optimal Growth with Production Inhibited by Pollution Generation," in unpublished PhD Thesis, Department of Economics, University of Southern California, Los Angeles, 1970

[21] ZECKHAUSER, R., SPENCE, M. and KEELER, E., "The Optimal Control of Pollution," *Journal of Economic Theory*, 4 (1972), 19-34

CHAPTER 26

The Economics of Environmental Preservation: A Theoretical and Empirical Analysis

By ANTHONY C. FISHER, JOHN V. KRUTILLA, AND CHARLES J. CICCHETTI*

Concern over the adequacy of nature's endowments has been reflected in economic literature at least from the time of Malthus. For Malthus, the natural environment was essentially a source of increasingly scarce resources to sustain economic activity. Recent theoretical contributions in this framework have sought to develop programs for the optimal intertemporal consumption of fixed and renewable natural resource stocks.[1] Some evidence, on the other hand, suggests that technological progress has so broadened the resource base that the scarcity foreseen by Malthus and assumed, for example, in the stationary utility function postulated by Plourde, has not in fact been realized.[2] Yet, though the statistical evidence is that the direct costs of production from natural resources have fallen (relatively) over time, it seems likely that some of the environmental costs have risen.

It is desirable to distinguish two kinds of environmental costs. One is pollution, concerning which there is a relatively large and growing literature,[3] which we do not address in this paper. The other is the transformation and loss of whole environments as would result, for example, from clear cutting a redwood forest, or developing a hydroelectric project in the Grand Canyon. Surely there are important economic issues here, yet although there is a vast literature dating back to the 1930's on benefit-cost criteria for water resource projects, economists have said virtually nothing about the environmental opportunity costs of these projects. Where reference is made to the despoliation of natural environments, note is made only in passing to "extra-economic" considerations.[4] Similarly in the texts on land economics no mention is made of the economic issues involved in the allocation of wildlands and scenic resources, nor do the costs of land development include the opportunity returns foregone as a result of destroying natural areas.

More recently Krutilla has argued that private market allocations are likely to preserve less than the socially optimal

* Fisher's work was done at Brown University and Resources for the Future, Inc. Krutilla and Cicchetti are at Resources for the Future, Inc. This paper represents work done in the Natural Environments Program, Resources for the Future, Inc. Fisher's work was additionally supported partially by NSF Grant GS2530 to the Institute for Mathematical Studies in the Social Sciences, Stanford University. We are indebted to George Borts, John Brown, and Harl Ryder for many perceptive comments and suggestions. We are also grateful to our colleagues at Resources for the Future; to faculty and students of the Natural Resources Institute, Oregon State University 1969, and to Darwin Nelson, Arnold Quint, and Donald Sander of the Federal Power Commission for many constructive suggestions. We wish to acknowledge as well comments on an earlier draft of this paper from Gardner Brown, Ronald Cummings, A. Myrick Freeman III, Richard Judy, Clifford Russell, V. Kerry Smith, and an anonymous reviewer.

[1] See for example, studies by Vernon Smith, Charles Plourde, Oscar Burt and Ronald Cummings.

[2] See the studies by Neal Potter and Francis Christy, and Harold Barnett and Chandler Morse.

[3] For a summary of this literature, see E. J. Mishan.

[4] See for example, *Proposed Practices for Economic Analysis of River Basin Projects*, p. 44, Krutilla and Otto Eckstein, p. 265, Roland McKean, p. 61, and Maynard Hufschmidt, Krutilla, and Julius Margolis, pp. 52–53.

amount of natural environments. Moreover, he concludes that the optimal amount is likely to be increasing over time—a particularly serious problem in view of the irreversibility of many environmental transformations.

In this paper we extend Krutilla's discussion in two ways. First, in Sections I and II we develop a model for the allocation of natural environments between preservation and development. Then, in Section III, we apply the model to a currently debated issue: Should the Hells Canyon of the Snake River, the deepest gorge on the North American continent, be preserved in its current state for wilderness recreation and other activities,[5] or further developed as a hydroelectric facility?

I

Before proceeding with the discussion of allocation between preservation and development, we observe that a natural area may have not just one, but several uses in each state. For the development alternative, we abstract from this problem by assuming allocation to the highest valued use or combination of uses via the market, or some appropriate mix of market, government intervention and bargaining.[6] Similarly for an area reserved from development, we make the same assumption; i.e., the area is used optimally for recreation.[7] Our objective at this stage, then, is to formulate a model for guiding choice between the two broad alternatives of preservation and development.

We begin in this section with a rather general model for the optimum use of natural environments. In succeeding sections a more specific methodology will be developed and used to evaluate the Hells Canyon alternatives.

As a defensible definition of optimum use we propose that use which maximizes the present value of net social returns, or benefits, from an area. In symbols, we wish to maximize

$$(1) \quad \int_0^\infty e^{-\rho t}[B^P(P(t), t) + B^D(D(t), t) - I(t)]dt$$

where B^P and B^D are expected net social benefits (benefits minus costs) at time t, from P units of preserved area, and D units of developed; I is the "social overhead" capital investment cost at time t of transforming from preserved into developed; and ρ is the social discount rate. Note that the opportunity costs of development, the benefits B^P from preservation, generally ignored in benefit-cost calculations, here enter explicitly into the expression to be maximized.

There are several constraints, imposed by nature and past development, on the maximization of (1). We recognize, first, that the amount of any given area developed, residually determines the amount preserved. In symbols,

$$(2) \qquad P + D = L$$

where L is the fixed amount of land in the area.[8] Second, current and future choice is

[5] For a discussion of some of the uses of a preserved natural environment, including some suggestions as to how benefits might be evaluated, see Krutilla.

[6] At least two types of externality, pollution and crowding, are likely to be significant in the commercial exploitation of a natural area, making an efficient allocation in general unattainable in the absence of some form of government intervention or private bargaining to internalize. For a summary discussion of the general externality problem, see Mishan. For an interesting treatment of the crowding problem in particular, see Smith.

[7] The problem is that beyond some point, expanding recreation activity can result in congestion disutility to recreationists, or ecological damage, or both. For a detailed discussion, see Fisher and Krutilla.

[8] For sufficient flexibility in application, we think of D as the number of units affected by the development activity, adjusted perhaps for the character of the activity.

constrained by the results of past choices. In symbols,

$$(3) \quad P(0) = P_0 \text{ and, } D(0) = D_0,$$

i.e., initial values for preserved and developed portions of the area are given. The dynamic and irreversibility constraints are:

$$(4) \quad \dot{D} = \sigma I,$$

where σ is a positive constant of transformation with dimensions area/money,[9] and

$$(5) \quad I \geq 0$$

Clearly, were the converse true, i.e., were the transformation reversible, much of the conflict between preservation and development would vanish. It seems to us that it is precisely because the losses of certain natural environments would be losses virtually in perpetuity that they are significant.

Finally, we assume concave benefit functions B^P and B^D, so that returns to increasing preservation or development are positive but diminishing; in symbols,

$$(6) \quad B_P^P, B_D^D > 0 \text{ and, } B_{PP}^P, B_{DD}^D < 0$$

It is conceivable that initial stages of water resource development may be characterized by increasing returns. This will not in general be true of river systems in advanced stages of development, such as the Columbia River system, of which the Hells Canyon reach of the Snake River is a part. Accordingly, while the larger High Mountain Sheep project is more profitable than the smaller Pleasant Valley-Low Mountain Sheep, any increase in scale beyond High Mountain Sheep runs into severely diminishing returns, as the higher pool reduces the existing developed head upstream. Moreover, though this anticipates the analysis just a bit, what really matters is the behavior of development benefits *net* of opportunity costs. And the marginal opportunity costs of development, the benefits from preservation, are *increasing* as *development* increases.[10]

We now proceed with a control-theoretic solution of this problem in the general case, in which no restrictions are placed on the time paths of the benefit functions.[11] The Hamiltonian is

$$(7) \quad H = e^{-\rho t}[B^P(P, t) + B^D(D, t) - I(t)] + p(t)\sigma I(t)$$

where the first term on the right-hand side, $e^{-\rho t}[B^P(P, t)+B^D(D, t)-I(t)]$, is the (discounted) flow of net benefits at time t, and $p(t)$ is the (discounted) shadow price (value of future benefits) of development. Setting $q(t)=p(t)\sigma - e^{-\rho t}$, H can be simplified to

$$(8) \quad H = e^{-\rho t}[B^P(P, t) + B^D(D, t)] + q(t)I(t)$$

Note the relationship of q to p. If technology or demand relationships are changing, then p and hence q will be affected.

Applying the maximum principle of Pontryagin, et al., I is chosen to maximize H subject to the irreversibility restriction (5):

$$(9) \quad H \text{ is maximized by } \begin{array}{ll} I = 0 & q < 0 \\ I \geq 0 & q = 0 \end{array}$$

For $q>0$, investment would have to be infinite over an interval. Quite apart from its impracticality, this possibility can be ruled out because it leads to a contradic-

[9] In specifying the constraint in this fashion we are assuming "constant returns" to increasing investment. This seems at least as plausible, in the general case, as either increasing or decreasing returns, as would be implied by some more complicated functional form for the relationship between investment and development.

[10] This follows from the other half of equation (6), namely that $B_P^P>0$ and $B_{PP}^P<0$.

[11] Problems similar in form to (1)-(6) have recently been studied by Arrow and Kurz and by Arrow. In the remainder of this section we draw heavily on their work.

tion. Obviously, past development could not have been optimal; more should have been invested earlier.

Since, from (2) P and D are not independent, H can also be written

$$H = e^{-\rho t}[B^P(L - D, \mathrm{t}) + B^D(D, \mathrm{t})] + q(\mathrm{t})I(\mathrm{t}) \tag{10}$$

Again applying the maximum principle,

$$\dot{P} = -\frac{\partial H_{\max}}{\partial D} = -e^{-\rho t}(-B^P_P + B^D_D) \tag{11}$$

Since equation (9) is written in q, not p, let us write

$$\begin{aligned} \dot{q} &= \sigma\dot{P} + \rho e^{-\rho t} \\ &= \sigma e^{-\rho t}(B^P_P - B^D_D) + \rho e^{-\rho t} \\ &= e^{-\rho t}[\rho - \sigma(B^D_D - B^P_P)], \end{aligned} \tag{12}$$

and,

$$q(\mathrm{t}_1) - q(\mathrm{t}_0) = \int_{\mathrm{t}_0}^{\mathrm{t}_1} e^{-\rho t}[\rho - \sigma(B^D_D - B^P_P)]dt \tag{13}$$

From (9), the optimal development path is a sequence of intervals satisfying alternately the conditions $q(\mathrm{t}) = 0$ and $q(\mathrm{t}) < 0$. Following Kenneth Arrow, define intervals in which $q(\mathrm{t}) = 0$ as free intervals, intervals in which $q(\mathrm{t}) < 0$ as blocked (no investment) intervals. In a free interval, $\dot{q} = 0$, so

$$\rho = \sigma(B^D_D - B^P_P) \tag{14}$$

Assume, however unrealistically, that investment were costlessly reversible, except for prior interest charges. This would be equivalent to renting the area for this period, at a rate equal to the rate of interest. As in the related capital accumulation problem, optimal investment policy would then have the myopic property

$$\frac{\rho}{\sigma} = B^D_D(D^*, \mathrm{t}) - B^P_P(P^*, \mathrm{t}), \tag{15}$$

or

$$B^D_D(D^*, \mathrm{t}) = \frac{\rho}{\sigma} + B^P_P(P^*, \mathrm{t}),$$

which may be interpreted to mean that optimal investment policy equates the marginal benefits from development B^D_D to the sum of direct and marginal opportunity costs $(\rho/\sigma + B^P_P)$ at any point in time.

Combining (14) and (15), we have

(16) $D(\mathrm{t}) = D^*(\mathrm{t})$ on a free interval

Again, following Arrow, define a rising segment of $D^*(\mathrm{t})$ as a riser. Then, since $D(\mathrm{t})$ is increasing on a free interval, $D^*(\mathrm{t})$ is increasing, and a free interval lies within a single riser.

On a blocked interval $(\mathrm{t}_0, \mathrm{t}_1)$, $0 < \mathrm{t}_0 < \mathrm{t}_1 < \infty$, it follows that $D(\mathrm{t}_0) = D^*(\mathrm{t}_0)$ and $q(\mathrm{t}_0) = 0$, since t_0 is also the end of a free interval. Since $I = 0$, $D(\mathrm{t})$ is constant, so $D(\mathrm{t}) = D^*(\mathrm{t}_0)$, $\mathrm{t}_0 \leq \mathrm{t} \leq \mathrm{t}_1$. Similarly, since t_1 is the start of a free interval, $D(\mathrm{t}) = D^*(\mathrm{t}_1)$, $\mathrm{t}_0 \leq \mathrm{t} \leq \mathrm{t}_1$ and $q(\mathrm{t}_1) = 0$. Summarizing, on a blocked interval $(\mathrm{t}_0, \mathrm{t}_1)$, $0 < \mathrm{t}_0 < \mathrm{t}_1 < \infty$,

$$D^*(\mathrm{t}_0) = D^*(\mathrm{t}_1), \tag{17}$$

$$\int_{\mathrm{t}_0}^{\mathrm{t}_1} e^{-\rho t} r[D^*(\mathrm{t}_0), \mathrm{t}]dt = 0 \tag{18}$$

where

$$r(D, \mathrm{t}) = \rho - \sigma[B^D_D(D, \mathrm{t}) - B^P_P(P, \mathrm{t})],$$

$$\int_{\mathrm{t}_0}^{\mathrm{t}} e^{-\rho t} r[D^*(\mathrm{t}_0), \mathrm{t}]dt < 0, \ \mathrm{t}_0 < \mathrm{t} < \mathrm{t}_1, \tag{19}$$

and

$$\int_{\mathrm{t}}^{\mathrm{t}_1} e^{-\rho t} r[D^*(\mathrm{t}_0), \mathrm{t}]dt > 0, \ \mathrm{t}_0 < \mathrm{t} < \mathrm{t}_1 \tag{20}$$

Equations (18)–(20) can be given economic interpretations. Holding $D(t) = D^*(t_0)$, net marginal benefits $(B_D^D - B_P^D)$ first exceed (constant) marginal costs, since we do not invest, or push development, to the point $(D^*(t))$ at which they are equal. As short-run optimal development $(D^*(t))$ begins to fall, however, beyond some point there is too much development, i.e., $D(t) = D^*(t_0) > D^*(t)$. From this point, marginal benefits are less than marginal costs. Equation (18) then says that over the full interval (t_0, t_1) the sum of (discounted) marginal costs just equals the sum of (discounted) marginal benefits. Equation (19) says that, over an interval starting at t_0 and ending at any time t short of t_1, marginal benefits exceed marginal costs. Equation (20) is, of course, not independent of (18) and (19), and says that, over an interval starting at any time t beyond t_0 and ending at t_1, marginal benefits are less than marginal costs.

Myopic (D^*) and "corrected" (D) optimal development paths are shown in Figure 1. Note that at a point such as

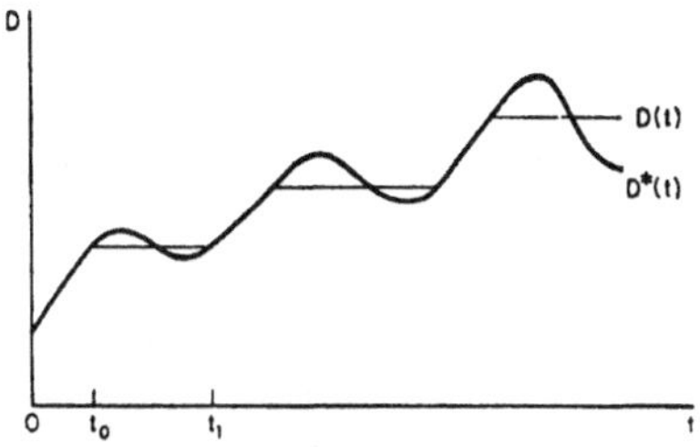

FIGURE 1

t_0 at which D^* is rising, if it will be falling in the relatively near future, then the present value of benefits may be sufficiently low for $q < 0$, and investment should cease (equation (9))—until t_1 (equation (17)). We should observe, then, an alternating sequence of rising segments and plateaus in the path of optimal growth over time of the stock of developed land. The divergence of this corrected path from the myopic is a crucially important result. It says that it will in general be optimal to refrain from development even when indicated by a comparison of current benefits and costs if, in the relatively near future, "undevelopment" or disinvestment, which are impossible, would be indicated.[12]

II

In the foregoing analysis no restrictions were placed on the patterns of time variation of the benefit functions. But when we come to consider the Hells Canyon project, and quite probably other similar proposals, both theoretical and empirical considerations suggest that benefits from development are likely to be decreasing, whereas benefits from preservation are likely to be increasing. The former, at least, may seem implausible. After all, shouldn't the demands of a growing economy increase the benefits from development of a natural area such as a hydroelectric power site? In this section we first explore this question, and the related one concerning the time pattern of benefits from preservation, then go on to show how the suggested restrictions affect optimal policy.

The traditional measure of the benefits of a hydroelectric power project, at any point in time, is simply the difference in costs between the most economic alternative source and the hydro project. This assumes, of course, that the amount of power provided by the project will be provided in any event, so that gross benefits are equal and the net benefit of the project is the saving in costs.[13] However, over the relatively long life of a hydro

[12] This result was anticipated by Krutilla, who noted ". . . our problem is akin to the dynamic programming problem which requires a present action (which may violate conventional benefit-cost criteria) to be compatible with the attainment of future states of affairs" (p. 785).

[13] For a fuller discussion of this point, see Peter Steiner.

project, costs of the (best) alternative source of energy will be decreasing as plants embodying new technologies replace the shorter-lived obsolete plants in the alternative system. This means that the benefits from developing the hydro project are correspondingly decreasing over the life of the project. In the traditional benefit-cost analysis this adjustment is not made. Benefits are calculated as of the construction date, implicitly assuming that the technology of alternative sources is fixed over the entire life of the project. For purposes of discussion in this section, a simplified process of technical change and replacement involving some constant rate of decrease of benefits is considered. The implications of a more complicated and realistic process are derived in the Appendix, and applied in our computations in the next section.

Benefits from not developing, on the other hand, appear to be increasing over time. The benefit from a nonpriced service such as wilderness recreation in the Hells Canyon, at any point in time, is the aggregate consumer surplus or area under the aggregate demand curve for the service. Much evidence suggests that demand for wilderness recreation in general, and for the Hells Canyon area in particular, is growing rapidly. This growth is due perhaps to growing population and per capita income, with the extra income used by consumers in part to "purchase" more leisure for themselves. Rising education levels, which seem to be associated with increasing preferences for taking this leisure in a natural environment doubtless also account for the rapidly growing demands.[14] Growth in demand can be broken down into two components: a quantity and a price shift. The effect of population growth, for example, given unchanging distributions of preferences and income, would be to increase the quantity demanded by the same percentage at any given "price," or willingness-to-pay.

On the other hand, for any fixed quantity, assuming growth of incomes, a set of conditions which will guarantee an increase in price to occur can be summarized as follows: if (a) present services of the environmental resource have no good substitutes among produced goods, (b) income and initial price elasticities of demand for such services are larger than for produced goods in general, and (c) the fraction of the budget spent on the environmental services in fixed supply is smaller than for produced goods in general, then the relative "price" or value of the environmental services in fixed supply will increase over time relative to the price of the produced goods at those levels of use short of the point at which congestion externalities occur.[15] Additionally, changes in consumer preferences clearly can affect both the quantity and the price shift parameters.

Suppose, now, that the demand for wilderness recreation in the Hells Canyon is expanding at some rate in the quantity dimension, due perhaps to changes in population and preferences, and at some other rate in the price dimension, due perhaps to changes in income and technology. Then total benefits will be increasing at a rate equal to the sum of these rates, assuming a linear imputed demand function.[16]

[14] For an illustration of the rapid growth in wilderness recreation, see the figures for National Forest wilderness, wild and primitive area recreation, reported by Irving Hoch.

[15] These conditions can be derived from the Hicks-Allen two-good general equilibrium model. Details can be furnished by the authors on request.

[16] Let P_t = the vertical intercept at time t

Q_t = the horizontal intercept at time t

r_y = rate of growth in willingness to pay (vertical shift)

γ = rate of growth in quantity (horizontal shift)

B_t = benefits at time t

Then

It is easily seen that as benefits from preservation increase relative to benefits from development, the optimal short-run level of development $D^*(t)$ decreases.[17]

We can now show, in the analytical framework of the preceding section, the effect of this trend on optimal policy. If $D^*(t)$ is monotone decreasing, then there is in effect an infinite blocked interval. Development is either frozen at the initial level $D(0)$, or jumps, at $t=0$, to some higher level $\overline{D}$, and is then frozen. If there is some initial investment, obviously $q(0)=0$. Also, $\lim_{t\to\infty} q(t)=0$, because

$$(21) \quad -e^{-\rho t} \leq q(t) = \sigma p(t) - e^{-\rho t} \leq 0,$$

and

$$(22) \quad \lim_{t\to\infty} - e^{-\rho t} = 0$$

On the blocked interval $(0, \infty)$ then, $D(t)=\overline{D}$, with

$$(23) \quad D(0) \leq \overline{D},$$

$$(24) \quad \int_0^\infty e^{-\rho t} r(\overline{D}, t)dt \geq 0$$

(but the strict inequality cannot hold in both) and

$$(25) \quad \int_t^\infty e^{-\rho t} r(\overline{D}, t)dt > 0 \quad 0 < t < \infty$$

For the projected development in the Hells Canyon, the interpretation of the analytical results is that it should be undertaken immediately, if at all. In symbols, if

$$(26) \quad \int_0^\infty [B^P(L - \overline{D}, t) + B^D(\overline{D}, t) - I(t)]e^{-\rho t}dt > \int_0^\infty [B^P(L - D(0), t) - I(t)]e^{-\rho t}dt,$$

where $\overline{D} > D(0)$, then some initial development, to a level of $\overline{D}$, will be optimal. If the inequality is reversed, then no further development beyond $D(0)$ should be undertaken. In the next section, a partial and approximate evaluation of these present value integrals is attempted, with $\overline{D}$ corresponding to the most profitable level of development, the High Mountain Sheep project.

Before proceeding with the evaluation, a few qualifying remarks about the analytical results may be made. First, although a particular program, in this case nondevelopment, may be indicated given current anticipations, it can be revised (in the direction of further development) at any time following the emergence of new and unanticipated relationships in the econ-

---

$$\text{(a)} \quad B_t = (1/2)P_tQ_t = 1/2\,(P_0e^{r_v t})(Q_0e^{\gamma t}) = 1/2\,P_0Q_0e^{(r_v+\gamma)t}$$

The increment over an infinitesimal period is

$$\text{(b)} \quad \frac{dB_t}{dt} = 1/2P_0Q_0e^{(r_v+\gamma)t}(r_v + \gamma),$$

and the percent rate of increase is

$$\text{(c)} \quad \frac{\frac{dB_t}{dt}}{B_t} = \frac{1/2P_0Q_0e^{(r_v+\gamma)t}(r_v+\gamma)}{1/2P_0Q_0e^{(r_v+\gamma)t}} = r_v + \gamma$$

[17] Ignoring investment, total benefits at any time t from an area of size L, where $L=P+D$, and benefits B^P from the preserved area P are increasing relative to benefits B^D from developed area D at a rate of α', are

$$\text{(a)} \quad B = B^P(P, t)e^{\alpha' t} + B^D(D, t) = B^P(L - D, t)e^{\alpha' t} + B^D(D, t)$$

Optimal D, D^*, is found by differentiating with respect to D and setting equal to zero.

$$\text{(b)} \quad \frac{\partial B}{\partial D} = -B_P^P e^{\alpha' t} + B_D^D = 0$$

or

$$B_D^D = B_P^P e^{\alpha' t}$$

As t increases, $e^{\alpha' t}$ increases, so that B_P^P (the marginal benefits of preservation) must be decreasing, implying that P^* is increasing—and D^* decreasing.

omy, as for example, a reversal of the historic decline in energy costs. Or, though a particular level of development, corresponding say to High Mountain Sheep in the Hells Canyon, may be optimal for the purposes of power generation, a more intensive level may be indicated by the inclusion of another purpose, for example, flat water recreation. In fact, this is not now true for development in the Hells Canyon, because the separable costs of high density recreation facilities would exceed their benefits.[18]

Second, the somewhat abstract nature of the development measure D might be noted. D can increase, for example, by developing additional sites along the river, the construction of facilities to accommodate larger numbers of flat water recreation seekers, the penetration by roads of virgin sections, etc.

Third, to what extent, if any, has the case for preservation been overstated by the absolute restriction on reversibility, and can the restriction be relaxed? Our view, as stated earlier, is that the irreversibility of development is fundamental to the problem. This does not, however, mean that it must be absolute. Two kinds of reversal are possible, or at least conceivable. One is the restoration of an area by a program of direct investment. This would seem to have little relevance, however, for the sorts of phenomena with which we are mainly concerned: an extinct species or ecological community that cannot be resurrected, a flooded canyon that cannot be replicated, an old-growth redwood forest that cannot be restored, etc.[19]

The other kind of reversal is the natural reversion to the wild, which, though also seemingly of little relevance to our main concerns, is easily fit into the analytical framework. Suppose some (constant, though this is not necessary) nonzero rate of reversion, δ. Then $D'(t) = D(t)\ e^{-\delta t}$, where $D'(t)$ is development subject to reversion. It is not clear how much additional flexibility this gives to investment policy. Even in situations in which δ is significantly different from zero, it may be much smaller than the desired rate of decrease as determined by changing technology and demand and unconstrained by nature.

III

In this section we present estimates of the costs and benefits associated with the alternatives for Hells Canyon. There are various services which the canyon can provide if preserved in its natural state. The value of some have become measurable through recent advances in economic analysis, for example, outdoor recreation, while the value of others are still intractable to economic measurement, for example, preservation of rare scientific research materials. Since we cannot measure the benefits in toto, we ask, rather, what would the present value of preserving the area need to be to equal or exceed the present value of the developmental alternative. Owing to the inverse relationship between π and α_t (see below) the initial year's preservation benefit may need to be only very modest in comparison with the development benefit. This is illustrated in simplified, discrete form in equation (27) below.

$$b_p^m = \sum_{t=1}^{T} \frac{b_0/(1+\pi)^t}{(1+i)^t} \div \sum_{t=1}^{T'} \frac{S1(1+\alpha_t)^t}{(1+i)^t} \tag{27}$$

where:

b_p^m = the minimum initial year's benefit

[18] See testimony of Krutilla, *FPC* hearings, R-5840 and R-6494-6499.

[19] This is not to deny its relevance in some contexts, as shown for example in the clean-up and revegetation of certain former coal mining areas.

required to make the present value of benefits from preserving the area equal to the present value of the development benefits,

b_0 = the initial year's development benefit,

π = the simplified representation of technological change for the development alternative and is defined in the Appendix

T = the relevant terminal year for the development alternative,

T′ = the relevant terminal year for the preservation alternative,

i = the discount rate,

α_t = the percent rate of growth in annual benefits as described in footnote 16.

This is the required initial year's benefit from preservation which makes the two alternatives equivalent and relation (26) an equality.

The terminal years for each choice, T and T′, are determined by the years in which the discounted annual benefit falls to zero. They need not and probably would not be the same. Any change in the relative annual values of the incompatible alternatives would result in different relevant time horizons.[20] For convenience in computation, we select T and T′ as the years in which the increment to the present value of net benefits of each alternative falls to \$0.01 per \$1.00 of initial year's benefits.

Now π in the numerator of equation (27) is derived from our technical change model (see the Appendix). The value of π depends on a) investment per unit of thermal capacity, b) cost per kilowatt hour of thermal energy, and c) the rate of advance in technical efficiency. We have relied on construction cost data provided by Federal Power Commission (*FPC*) staff witnesses;[21] taken energy costs to be increasing from 0.98 mills per kilowatt hour in the early stage to 1.28 mills per kilowatt hour in the later period of analysis owing to projected increases in cost of processing nuclear materials;[22] and selected rates of technological progress of 3 to 5 percent, believed to bracket the relevant range.[23] Using such data in our technological change model we find that gross hydroelectric benefits will be overstated between 5 and 11 percent when technological change is not introduced into the analysis.[24] While the difference in *gross* benefits may not be very large, if the two alternatives are close cost competitors, such small differences can make a large difference in *net* benefits. In short, using a medium value for all of the parameters tested results in a reduction in the net present value by approximately a half in the Hells Canyon hydroelectric evaluation.[25]

[20] Since control theory has not previously been applied in public sector benefit-cost studies, the time horizons have been selected arbitrarily.

[21] See testimony of *FPC* witness Joseph J. A. Jessell, *FPC* hearings, and Exhibit No. R-54-B.

[22] See testimony of *FPC* witness I. Paul Chavez, "In the Matter of . . . , " and Exhibit No. R-107-B.

[23] The rate of technological change was computed from data presented in the biennial reports of *Electrical World* over a period representing a consistent method of reporting, 1950–68. It must be acknowledged that the model used for computational purposes is applicable to the period of the past, dominated by use of fossil fuels and not specifically relevant to the yet unspecified changes in technology of the future, doubtless to be tied closely to nuclear reactors. The argument, however, is that while the relevant models would differ, the effects of technological change on costs of generation will be of the same or greater order of magnitude and should not be ignored. (See testimony of Krutilla, *FPC* hearings, R-5838.) Although, as noted earlier, at least some of the reduction in costs may be balanced by a rise in environmental pollution from the more efficient fossil fuel plants, estimated costs of dealing with the thermal pollution from a nuclear plant *are* included in our calculations (though not the possible but unknown costs of radioactive waste disposal).

[24] See Table 1, Exhibit R-670, *FPC* hearings, for the complete range of values resulting from the computational model given in the Appendix.

[25] See testimony of John V. Krutilla, *FPC* hearings, R-5842-3 and Exhibit Nos. R-669 and R-671.

In our discussion of benefits from preservation in the last section, especially in footnote 16, we took α_t to be constant. This is plausible, however, only so long as the capacity of the area for recreation activity is not reached. If demand for the wilderness recreation services of the area is growing, congestion externalities eventually will arise. That is, a point will be reached beyond which use of the area by one more individual per unit time will result in a diminution of the utility obtained by others using the area. For purposes of this analysis, this point is taken as the "carrying capacity" of the area. If the benefits of additional use exceeded the congestion costs, total benefits could be increased by relaxing this constraint.[26] But we seek here to define a quantity of constant quality services, the value of which will be a lower bound for preservation benefits. Counting from the base year, let k be the year in which use of the area reaches capacity, m the year in which γ falls to the rate of growth of population, and d the rate of decay of γ.

Beyond some point, then, annual benefits do not grow at a uniform rate over time but depend upon the values taken by γ, r_y, k, d, and m. The particular values taken, i.e., γ of 10 percent and k of 20 years, with alternative assumptions for purposes of sensitivity analyses, were chosen for reasons given elsewhere.[27] A discount rate of 9 percent with alternatives of 8 and 10 percent was the result of independent study.[28] The selection of the value of m for 50 years, with alternative assumptions of 40 and 60, was governed by both the rate of growth of general demand for wilderness or primitive area recreation, and the estimated "saturation level" for such recreational participation for the population as a whole. Finally, the range of values for r_y was taken from what we know about the conventional income elasticity of demand[29] as related to the special case of a unique resource in fixed supply and growth in per capita income over the past two or three decades.[30]

To contrast the results of our analysis with traditional benefit-cost analysis, consider the computed initial year's preservation benefit (Table 1) corresponding to i of 9 percent, r of 0.04, γ of 10 percent and k of 20 years, m of 50 years and r_y of 0.05; namely, \$80,122. This sum compares with the sum of \$2.9 million, which represents the "levelized" annual benefit from the hydro-electric development, when neither adjustments for technological progress have been made in hydroelectric power value computations, nor any site value (i.e., present value of opportunity benefits foreclosed by altering the present use of Hells Canyon) is imputed to costs. Typically then, the question would be raised whether or not the preservation value is equal to or greater than the \$2.9 million annual benefits from development.

Let us now consider the readily quantifiable opportunity benefits which would be foreclosed by development of the canyon. These are based on studies conducted by the Oregon and Idaho fish and game commissions in cooperation with the U.S. Forest Service and monitored by an observer representing the applicants for the *FPC* license. Presented in summarized form they appear in Table 2.[31]

While systematic demand studies of the several different recreational activities were not conducted in connection with the imputed values, given what is known about prices paid for fishing and hunting rights where such rights are vested in

[26] For a detailed discussion of this and other considerations in determining the capacity of a natural area for recreation activity, see Fisher and Krutilla.

[27] See testimony of John V. Krutilla, *FPC* hearings, R-5859-73.

[28] See Eckstein and Arnold Harberger, and also James Seagraves.

[29] See Cicchetti, Joseph Seneca and Paul Davidson.

[30] See footnote 15.

[31] See testimony of John V. Krutilla, *FPC* hearings, R-5877-, Table 3 R-5878-9, R-5880-4.

TABLE 1—INITIAL YEAR'S PRESERVATION BENEFITS, b_p^m, (GROWING AT THE RATE α_t) REQUIRED IN ORDER TO HAVE PRESENT VALUE EQUAL TO DEVELOPMENT

r_v	$\gamma=7.5$ Percent k=25 years	$\gamma=10$ Percent k=20 years	$\gamma=12.5$ Percent k=15 years
$i=8$ Percent,	m=50 years,	$r=0.04$,	$PVC_{1...T}$ = $18,540,000
0.04	$138,276	$109,149	$106,613
0.05	87,568	70,363	70,731
0.06	48,143	39,674	41,292
$i=9$ Percent,	m=50 years,	$r=0.04$,	$PVC_{1...T}$ = $13,809,000
0.04	$147,422	$115,008	$109,691
0.05	101,447	80,122	78,336
0.06	64,300	51,700	52,210
$i=10$ Percent,	m=50 years,	$r=0.04$,	$PVC_{1...T}$ = $ 9,861,000
0.04	$142,335	$110,240	$103,030
0.05	103,626	80,888	77,232
0.06	71,369	56,397	55,194

Sources: Exhibit No. R-671, R-672, *FPC* hearings, and Transcript R-5869-5873.
Where:
i = discount rate
r_v = annual rate of growth in price for a given quantity
γ = annual rate of growth of quantity demanded at given price
k = number of years following initial year upon which carrying capacity constraint becomes effective
m = number of years after initial year upon which γ falls to rate of growth of population
$PVC_{1...T}$ = present value of development (adjusted)
r = annual rate of technological progress in the development case

private parties, we feel our estimates are rather conservative.[32]

[32] See also William Brown, Ajmer Singh and Emery Castle; Stephen Mathews and Gardiner Brown; and Peter Pearse for more systematic evaluation of the Oregon and Washington Steelhead-Salmon Fisheries and other big game resource values, and the estimated willingness to pay. On the basis of all the evidence available to us the imputation of values in the Hells Canyon case appear to be most conservative. It should be noted, however, that two assumptions are made in order that the values appearing in Table 2 represent net benefits, consistent with the benefits estimated for the hydro development. One assumption is that there are no adequate substitutes of like quality, i.e., other primitive scenic areas are either congested or being rationed, conditions which are widely encountered in national parks and over much of the wilderness system. Secondly, it is assumed that the demand unsatisfied by virtue of the transformation of the Hells Canyon would impinge on the margin in other sectors of the economy characterized by free entry and feasibility of augmenting supplies, i.e., incremental costs will equal incremental benefits.

Considering the estimates one might argue, for example, that the preservation benefits shown are roughly only a third ($.9 to $2.9 million) as large as would be

TABLE 2—ESTIMATED INITIAL YEAR'S QUANTIFIABLE PRESERVATION BENEFITS

Recreation Activity	Visitor Days Initial Year	Unit Value	Imputed Benefits
Streamside Use			
Angling	84,000	$ 5.00	$420,000
Canyon Area Hunting			
Big game	7,000	25.00	175,000
Upland bird	1,000	10.00	10,000
Increased value of remaining hunting experience	29,000	10.00	290,000
Total Quantifiable Opportunity Benefits			$895,000

required in comparisons based on traditional analysis of similar cases. By introducing the differential incidence of technological progress on, and growth in demand for, the mutually exclusive alternative uses of the Hells Canyon, we reach quite a different conclusion. The initial year's preservation benefit, subject to reevaluation on the basis of sensitivity tests, appears to be an order of magnitude ($900,000 to $80,000) larger than it needs to be to have a present value equaling or exceeding the present value of the development alternative. Thus we get results significantly different from traditional analysis.

What about the sensitivity of these conclusions to the particular values the variables used in our two simulation models are given? Sensitivity tests can be performed with the data contained in Table 1, along with additional information available from computer runs performed. Some of these checks are displayed in Table 3.

TABLE 3—SENSIVITIY OF ESTIMATED INITIAL YEAR'S REQUIRED PRESERVATION BENEFITS TO CHANGES IN VALUE OF VARIABLES AND PARAMETERS (at $i=9$ percent)

Variable	Variation in Variable From	To	Percent Change	Percent Change in Preservation Benefit
r_y	0.04	0.05	25	39–49
r	0.04	0.05	25	25
k[a] (years)	20	25	25	30–40
γ (percent)	10	12.5	25	−4 to +7
m (years)	40	50	25	3

[a] The 25 percent change in years before carrying capacity is reached translates into a 40 percent change in carrying capacity at the growth rate of 10 percent used here.

Given the estimated user days and imputed value per user day, the conclusion regarding the relative economic merit of the two alternatives is not sensitive within a reasonable range, to the particular values chosen for the variables and parameters used in the computation models.

There is need, however, for another set of tests when geometric growth rates are being used. We might regard these as "plausibility analyses." For example, the ratio of the implicit price to the projected per capita income in the terminal year was examined and found to equal $2.5\text{x}10^{-3}$. At today's per capita income level this is comparable to a user fee of approximately $10.00. Similarly, the ratio of the terminal year's preservation benefit to the *GNP* in the terminal year is found to be $4.0\text{x}10^{-7}$. This value compares with a ratio of the total revenue of the applicants in 1968 to *GNP* of $5.0\text{x}10^{-4}$. The year at which the growth rate in quantity of wilderness-type outdoor recreation services demanded falls to the rate of growth of the population must also be checked to ensure that the implicit population participation rate is something one would regard as plausible. Such tests were performed in order to avoid problems which otherwise would stem from use of unbounded estimates. We found our assumed initial rate of 10 percent, appropriately damped over time, was a realistic value.

Finally, since the readily observed initial year's benefits appear to be in excess of the minimum which would be required to have their present value exceed the present value of development, the computation is concluded at this point. Note, however, that since the analysis relies implicitly on the price compensating measure of consumer surplus, the resulting estimate of preservation value would be for this reason, as well as the restricted carrying capacity, a lower bound. Moreover, in seeking maximum expected benefits, we have implicitly assumed a neutral attitude toward risk. In fact, some preliminary findings as to the effect of uncertainty on optimal environmental policy suggest that there may be a kind of risk premium, or other adjustment, in the direction of reducing benefits from development relative to preservation.[33]

IV

In Section I of this study we propose a model for the allocation of natural environments between preservation and development, and show that it will in general be optimal to refrain from some development indicated by current benefits and costs if, in the relatively near future, "undevelopment," which is impossible, would be indicated. In Section II we show that if, as in the case of the proposed development in the Hells Canyon, benefits from development are decreasing over time relative to benefits from preservation, it will be optimal to proceed with the development immediately, if at all.[34] In Section III we consider this question in detail for the case of the Hells Canyon, and show that it will not, in fact, be optimal to undertake even the most profitable development project there. Rather the area is likely to yield greater benefits if left in its natural state.

Appendix

Over the first 30-year period, taken as the useful life of a thermal facility, let PVC_t represent the present value of annual costs per kilowatt of the thermal alternative in year t:

$$PVC_1 = C_1 + E(8760F)$$

$$PVC_2 = \left\{C_1 + [E8760(F - k)] + \frac{E}{(1+r)}(8760k)\right\}\left(\frac{1}{(1+i)}\right)$$

$$PVC_n = \left\{C_1 + E[8760(F - (n-1)k)] + \frac{E}{(1+r)^{n-1}}[8760(n-1)k]\right\} \cdot \left(\frac{1}{1+i}\right)^{n-1} \quad \text{for } 1 < n < 30$$

where

C_1 = Capacity Cost/KW/yr during first 30-year perlod
E = Energy Cost/KWh
F = The plant factor; (.90)
k = a constant representing the time decay of the plant factor (.03)
i = the discount rate
r = the annual rate of technological progress

Writing out the nth term yields:

$$PVC_n = \frac{C_I}{(1+i)^{n-1}} + \frac{8760EF}{(1+i)^{n-1}} - \frac{8760Ek(n-1)}{(1+i)^{n-1}} + \frac{8760Ek(n-1)}{[(1+r)(1+i)]^{n-1}}$$

These terms can be summed individually using standard formulas for geometric progressions and then factored to form:

$$PVC_{1,\ldots,30} = \sum_{n=1}^{30} PVC_n = (C_I + 8760EF) \cdot \left[\frac{1-a^{30}}{1-a}\right] - \frac{8760Ek}{i} \cdot \left\{\frac{1-a^{29}}{1-a} - 29a^{29}\right\} + \frac{8760Ek}{(1+r)(1+i)-1}\left\{\frac{1-b^{29}}{1-b} - 29b^{29}\right\}$$

where

$$a = \left(\frac{1}{1+i}\right)$$

$$b = \frac{1}{(1+r)(1+i)}$$

[33] See Cicchetti and A. Myrick Freeman, and Fisher. This is an important question and one which bears on the design of optimal policies for pollution control as well, but further consideration is beyond the scope of this paper.

[34] This is consistent with the obvious differences in views held by members of affluent societies and less developed countries on these and related environmental issues.

Over years 31, . . . , T the cost expressions are similar except that we are dealing with only T−30 additional years and all terms thus get discounted by a factor of $(1/1+i)^{30}$. Hence, using similar formulas for the sum of geometric series the present value of annual costs per kilowatt from this later period is determined to be:

$$PVC_{31,\ldots,T} = \sum_{p=31}^{T} PVC_p = \left(\frac{1}{1+i}\right)^{30}$$

$$\cdot \left\{ C_{II} + 8760E'F) \left[\frac{1-a^{(T-30)}}{1-a}\right] - \frac{8760E'k}{i}\left[\frac{1-a^{(T-31)}}{1-a} - 19a^{(T-31)}\right] + \frac{8760E'k}{(1+r)(1+i)-1}\left[\frac{1-b^{(T-31)}}{1-b} - 19b^{(T-31)}\right]\right\}$$

where

$$C_{II} = \frac{C_I}{(1+r)^{30}}$$

$$E' = \frac{E}{(1+r)^{30}}$$

The overall present value is:

$$PVC_{1,\ldots,T} = PVC_1 + \ldots + PVC_{30} + PVC_{31} + \ldots + PVC_T$$

Traditional analyses are based essentially on the model given below.

$$K = \sum_{n=1}^{T} \frac{[C_I + E(8760F)]}{(1+i)^{n-1}}$$

or, which is equivalent,

$$= [C_I + E(8760F)]\left[\frac{1-a^T}{1-a}\right]$$

We can therefore determine a relationship between the traditional measure of development benefit (K) and the measure outlined in this appendix ($PVC_{1,\ldots,T}$) in order to define the simplified measure of technological change (π) utilized in the text above.

$$\frac{K}{PVC_{1,\ldots,T}} = \sum_{t=1}^{T} \frac{b_0}{(1+i)^t} \div \sum_{t=1}^{T} \frac{b_0/(1+\pi)^t}{(1+i)^t} = T \Big/ \sum_{t=1}^{T} \frac{1}{(1+\pi)_t}$$

REFERENCES

K. J. Arrow, "Optimal Capital Policy with Irreversible Investment," in J. N. Wolfe, ed., *Value, Capital and Growth*, Chicago 1968, pp. 1–20.

——— and M. Kurz, "Optimal Growth with Irreversible Investment in a Ramsey Model," *Econometrica*, Mar. 1970, *38*, 331–44.

——— and A. C. Fisher, "Environmental Preservation, Uncertainty, and Irreversibility," *Quart. J. Econ.*, forthcoming.

H. J. Barnett and C. Morse, *Scarcity and Growth*, Baltimore 1963.

W. G. Brown, A. Singh, and E. N. Castle, "Net Economic Value of the Oregon Salmon-Steelhead Sport Fishery," *J. Wildlife Manage.*, Apr. 1965, *29*, 66–79.

O. R. Burt and R. Cummings, "Production and Investment in Natural Resource Industries," *Amer. Econ. Rev.*, Sept. 1970, *60*, 576–90.

C. J. Cicchetti, J. Seneca, and P. Davidson, *The Demand and Supply of Outdoor Recreation*, Washington 1969.

C. J. Cicchetti and A. M. Freeman, III, "Option Demand and Consumer Surplus," *Quart. J. Econ.*, Aug. 1971, *85*, 528–39.

O. Eckstein, *Water Resource Development*, Cambridge 1958.

———, in *Economic Analysis of Public Investment Decisions: Interest Rate Policy and Discounting Analysis*, Hearings, Joint Economic Committee, 90th Congress, 2d Sess., Washington 1968.

A. C. Fisher and J. V. Krutilla, "Determination of Optimal Capacity for Resource-Based Recreation Facilities," *Natur. Resources J.*, forthcoming.

A. **Harberger**, in *Economic Analysis of Public Investment Decisions: Interest Rate Policy and Discounting Analysis*, Hearings, Joint Economic Committee, 90th Congress, 2d Sess., Washington 1968.

J. R. **Hicks and R. G. D. Allen**, "A Reconsideration of the Theory of Value," Part I, II, *Economica*, Feb., May 1934, *1*, 52–76; 196–219.

I. **Hoch**, "Economic Analysis of Wilderness Areas," in *Wilderness and Recreation—a Report on Resources, Values and Problems, ORRRC Study Report No. 3*, Washington 1962, pp. 203–64.

M. M. **Hufschmidt, J. V. Krutilla, and J. Margolis**, *Standards and Criteria for Formulating and Evaluating Federal Water Resources Development. Report to the Bureau of the Budget*, Washington 1961.

J. V. **Krutilla**, "Conservation Reconsidered," *Amer. Econ. Rev.*, Sept. 1967, *57*, 777–86.

——— and O. **Eckstein**, *Multiple Purpose River Development*, Baltimore 1958.

S. B. **Mathews and G. S. Brown**, *Economic Evaluation of the 1967 Sport Salmon Fisheries of Washington*, Washington Dept. of Fisheries Technical Report 2, Olympia 1970.

R. N. **McKean**, *Efficiency in Government Through Systems Analysis*, New York 1958.

E. J. **Mishan**, "The Postwar Literature on Externalities: An Interpretive Essay," *J. Econ. Lit.*, Mar. 1971, *9*, 1–28.

P. H. **Pearse**. "A New Approach to the Evaluation of Non-Priced Recreation Resources," *Land Econ.*, Feb. 1968, *44*, 87–99.

C. G. **Plourde**, "A Simple Model of Replenishable Natural Resource Exploitation," *Amer. Econ. Rev.*, June 1970, *60*, 518–22.

N. **Potter and F. T. Christy, Jr.**, *Trends in Natural Resource Commodities*, Baltimore 1962.

J. A. **Seagraves**, "More on the Social Rate of Discount," *Quart. J. Econ.*, Aug. 1970, *84*, 430–50.

V. L. **Smith**, "Economics of Production from Natural Resources," *Amer. Econ. Rev.*, June 1968, *58*, 409–31.

P. O. **Steiner**, "The Role of Alternative Cost in Project Design and Selection," *Quart. J. Econ.*, Aug. 1965, *79*, 417–30.

H. **Wold and L. Jureen**, *Demand Analysis*, New York 1953.

Federal Power Commission (*FPC*), "In the Matter of: Pacific Northwest Power Company and Washington Public Power Supply System," hearings, Washington 1970.

Policies, Standards, and Procedures in the Formulation, Evaluation, and Review of Plans for Use and Development of Water and Related Land Resources, prepared under the direction of the President's Water Resources Council, Senate Document no. 97, 87th Cong., 2d sess., Washington 1964.

———, Supp. no. 1, "Evaluation Standards for Primary Outdoor Recreation Benefits," Ad Hoc Resources Council, Washington 1964.

Proposed Practices for Economic Analysis of River Basin Projects, report to the Inter-Agency Committee on Water Resources, prepared by the Subcommittee on Evaluation Standards, Washington 1958.

"Steam Station Cost Survey," *Electrical World*, Nov. 3, 1969.

CHAPTER 27

ENVIRONMENTAL PRESERVATION, UNCERTAINTY, AND IRREVERSIBILITY

KENNETH J. ARROW* and ANTHONY C. FISHER**

I

A number of recent contributions by economists have provided a clear insight into the causes of the varied forms of environmental quality deterioration, and have also suggested, implicitly or explicitly, policies for more efficient management of environmental as well as other resources.[1] Yet, as Allen Kneese has pointed out in a review of empirical studies of pollution damages, "a general shortcoming of [these studies] has been that they have treated a stochastic or probabilistic phenomenon as being deterministic.[2] The purpose of this paper is to explore the implications of uncertainty surrounding estimates of the environmental costs of some economic activities. It is shown in particular that the existence of uncertainty will, in certain important cases, lead to a reduction in net benefits from an activity with environmental costs. In such cases the implication for an efficient control policy will generally involve some restriction of the activity.

Any discussion of public policy in the face of uncertainty must come to grips with the problem of determining an appropriate attitude towards risk on the part of the policy-maker. Thus in the essay quoted above, Kneese asks, "is the concept of mathematical expectation applicable here or must we give attention to higher moments of the probability distribution...?"[3] Although the question has not, to our knowledge, received consideration in just this form in the environmental literature, received theory does shed some light on the issue it poses.

Weisbrod first suggested that where there is uncertainty in demand for a publicly provided good or service, there may be some benefit ("option value") to the individual in addition to the conventional price-compensating consumer surplus.[4] More recently Cicchetti and Freeman have shown that, where there is uncertainty in either demand or supply, Weisbrod's option value will be positive for risk-averse individuals.[5] In the Cicchetti-Freeman analysis this extra benefit from the public good is in fact equivalent to a premium for risk-bearing. Examples of such goods in the environmental sector (to which we will return) might be the preservation of certain valuable natural phenomena, or the abatement of pollution.

At this point a very interesting corollary question arises. It is that, even assuming a non-neutral attitude toward risk, hence the need for some adjustment of expected benefits and costs *to the individual*, as demonstrated by Cicchetti and Freeman, does it necessarily follow that the social calculus should properly make the same adjustment? It does seem plausible, but a challenge to this point of view has been put forward in an analysis of the evaluation of benefits from more traditional public investments by Arrow and Lind.[6] They show that, as the net returns to an investment of given size are shared by increasingly many individuals, the individual risk premium, and more importantly, and perhaps unexpectedly, the aggregate of all such premiums, goes to zero. Only expected returns, then, should be taken into account in evaluating the investment.

This is the approach taken in the next section, in which the discussion focuses on a decision as to whether or not, or how far, to proceed with some form of commercial development of an unspoiled natural area that is also capable of yielding benefits in its preserved state. In particular, the question considered is, does the introduction of uncertainty as to the costs or benefits of a proposed development have any effect on an appropriately formulated investment criterion beyond the replacement of known values with their expectations? It turns out that if the development involves some irreversible transformation of the environment, hence a loss in perpetuity of the benefits from preservation, and if information about the costs and benefits of both alternatives realized in one period results in a change in their expected values for the next, the answer is yes — net benefits from developing the area are reduced and, broadly speaking, less of the area should be developed.

II

In this section we are concerned primarily with the effect of uncertainty on the criteria for choice between two broadly alternative uses of a natural environment — preservation and development. As an example of the type of problem to which the analysis might be applied, consider the choice, at each moment in time, between preserving (part of) a virgin redwood forest for wilderness recreation, on the one hand, or opening (part of) it up to clear-cut logging, on the other. Although this sort of transformation may be technically reversible, the length of time required for regeneration of the forest for purposes of wilderness recreation is so great that, given some positive rate of time preference, it might as well be irreversible.

A problem having just these characteristics has in fact been studied by Fisher, Krutilla and Cicchetti.[7] Without going into the structure of the problem in more detail, their results, following results obtained by Arrow[8] and by Arrow and Kurz[9] in dynamic optimization theory, can be summarized as follows. First, it will in general be optimal to refrain from some development that is currently profitable if, in the near future, "undevelopment," which is impossible, would be indicated. Second, if net benefits from development are in fact decreasing over time relative to benefits from preservation, as shown in an empirical application to proposed further development of hydroelectric capacity along the Hells Canyon reach of the Snake River, it will be optimal to develop either immediately or not at all. It is then shown that even the most profitable of current development projects there can be expected at this time to yield a smaller return than the preservation-recreation alternative.

The notion of "irreversibility" underlying these results might be spelled out a bit further. Ordinarily, it would be technical. Thus the construction of a major dam or series of dams in the Hells Canyon clearly could not be undone in such a way as to make possible the enjoyment of the recreational and other services currently provided by the free-flowing stream through the deepest canyon on the North American continent.

Conceivably, construction of an alternative power source could preclude development of the hydroelectric potential there. This would however be an economic decision, and one that might in any case be reversed — although this would not be indicated by a continuation of present trends in benefits from wilderness preservation vs. power development there, as assumed in the Fisher-Krutilla-Cicchetti study.

Of course, what looks like a technically irreversible development could be characterized as one that would be infinitely costly to reverse. This suggests the possibility of the cost of reversal more generally taking intermediate values that would vary with the alternative chosen. For the remainder of this section, however, it may be helpful to rely on the intuitive notion of a technically irreversible development such as the placing of a dam.

As the Fisher-Krutilla-Cicchetti study adopts the risk-neutral approach in its specificaiton of only expected costs and gains in the investment criterion, with no adjustment, for example, for option value in preserving, the bias against development is due solely to the restriction on reversibility. By joining to this restriction the additional and plausible assumption that realizations in one period affect expectations in the next, as spelled out in the following simple model, we discover, consistent with the continuing assumption of risk neutrality, a "quasi-option value" having an effect in the same direction as risk aversion, namely, a reduction in net benefits from development.

Consider, now, the development of an area, d, over a two-period time horizon consisting in a first period followed by all future intervals compressed into a single second period. Though not particularly elegant, this seems sufficient to capture the essential features of the process described above.

Let d = unity (a normalized unit of land)

d_1 = the amount of land developed in the first period

d_2 = the amount of land developed in the second period

b_p = benefits from preservation of d in first period

b_d = benefits from development of d in first period

β_p = expected benefits, conditional on b_p and b_d, from preservation of d in second period

β_d = expected benefits, conditional on b_p and b_d, from development of d in second period

c_1 = investment costs in first period

c_2 = investment costs in second period

Several remarks can be made concerning structure of this model.

1. Though explicitly dynamic, it need not deal with time discounting in any meaningful way. Thus the second period benefits and costs β_p, β_d and c_2 can be viewed as present values, and the results are not affected.

2. It is assumed that development entails investment costs but preservation does not. Costs of preservation could easily be introduced (where meaningful) but again, results would not be affected, and extra terms would clutter the model. The real difference between the alternatives is that one is assumed to be reversible, and the other not.

3. Note that second period expectations are conditional on first period realizations. Some amount of development is planned at the start of the first period, but the plan can be revised (at least in the direction of additional development) at the start of the second period, based upon information that has accumulated concerning benefits in the first period.

4. Note, finally, that all benefits are specified as coefficients, so that constant returns to any level of development or preservation are assumed. Later on this assumption is relaxed.

Let us focus, now, on the decision at the start of the second period. If $\beta_d - \beta_p > c_2$, then $d_2 = 1 - d_1$. If $\beta_d - \beta_p < c_2$, then $d_2 = 0$. Define $z = \beta_d - \beta_p$, $w = b_d - b_p - c_1$, and event E as $z > c_2$. If E occurs, total benefits from the area are

$$\begin{aligned} &b_p(1-d_1) + b_d d_1 - c_1 d_1 + \beta_d - c_2\ (1-d_1) = \\ &wd_1 + c_2 d_1 + b_p + \beta_d - c_2 \end{aligned} \quad (1)$$

If E does not occur, then benefits are

$$\begin{aligned} &b_p(1-d_1) + b_d d_1 - c_1 d_1 + \beta_p(1-d_1) + \beta_d d_1 = \\ &wd_1 + zd_1 + b_p + \beta_p \end{aligned} \quad (2)$$

The expected benefits from developing $d_1 > 0$ in the first period are

$$E[(w + \min(c_2, z))\, d_1 + b_p + \max(\beta_d - c_2, \beta_p)] \qquad (3)$$

Now suppose $d_1 = 0$. If E occurs, total benefits from the area are $b_p + \beta_d - c_2$; if E does not occur, benefits are $b_p + \beta_p$; and expected benefits are $E[b_p + \max(\beta_d - c_2, \beta_p)]$. Then the difference (in expected benefits) between developing $d_1 > 0$ and $d_1 = 0$ is

$$E[(w + \min(c_2, z))\, d_1 + b_p + \max(\beta_d - c_2, \beta_p)] - E[b_p + \max(\beta_d - c_2, \beta_p)] = E[(w + \min(c_2, z))\, d_1]. \qquad (4)$$

We are interested in the sign of the expression $E[w + \min(c_2, z)]$. If it is positive, it will be optimal to develop in the first period.

Now suppose that the decision-maker ignores uncertainty, i.e., he lets z and w be replaced by known numbers E[z] and E[w], so that the criterion is $E[w] + \min(c_2, E[z])$. Either $c_2 < E[z]$ or $c_2 > E[z]$. Consider the case in which $c_2 < E[z]$, so that the criterion is $E[w] + c_2$. Clearly,

$$\min(c_2, z) \leq c_2 \qquad (5)$$

with

$$P[\min(c_2, z) < c_2] > 0 \qquad (6)$$

where P[ ] represents the probability of occurrence of the expression in brackets. Thus

$$E[\min(c_2, z)] < c_2 \qquad (7)$$

and

$$E[w + \min(c_2, z)] < E[w] + c_2.$$

The expected value of benefits under uncertainty is seen to be less than the value of benefits under certainty. There exists a range of values for z and w for which development should not, then, take place under uncertainty, but should under certainty. An interpretation of this result might be, if we are uncertain about the payoff to investment in development, we should err on the side of under-investment, rather than over-investment, since development is irreversible. Given an ability to learn from experience, under-investment can be remedied before the second period, whereas mistaken over-investment cannot, the consequences persisting in effect for all time.

Similarly, for the case in which $c_2 > E[z]$,

$$\min (c_2, z) \leq z \tag{8}$$

with

$$P [\min (c_2, z) < z] > 0. \tag{9}$$

Thus

$$E [\min (c_2, z)] < E[z]. \tag{10}$$

Note that the assumed rigidity of the benefit (and cost) coefficients requires that, if the criterion is positive, the entire area be developed. Our result then states that the entire area is less likely to be developed under uncertainty. It might be desirable to have a result of this type in more flexible form, in particular that less of a given area be developed under uncertainty — rather than less chance of the entire area being developed.

Let (as yet) undeveloped area d be divided into n units, $\mu_1, \mu_2, \ldots \mu_n$, each with fixed coefficients. Suppose, now, we consider development of d on a unit-by-unit basis, proceeding exactly as above, but with the benefit and cost coefficients referring respectively to the first unit considered, then the second, etc. Under the plausible assumption of diminishing returns to both development and preservation, it is easily verified that, if it does not pay to develop the first unit considered then it does not pay to develop any of the others. If, on the other hand, it pays to develop the first unit then the second must be considered, and so on. Corner solutions are possible, as before, but so are interior solutions of part preserved and part developed.

In order to avoid confusion over the terms "constant returns" and "diminishing returns" we can define them more precisely. Let each of the n units μ_i, i = 1, ... n be further divided into m subunits μ_{ij}, i = 1, ... n, j = 1, ... m, each with fixed coefficients. Constant returns to, say, first period development within any unit μ_i can be represented as ${}^{b}di_1 = {}^{b}di_2 = \ldots = {}^{b}dim$, with ${}^{b}di_1 + {}^{b}di_2 + \ldots + {}^{b}dim = {}^{b}di$, where ${}^{b}di_1$ = benefits from development in the first period of unit ${}^{\mu}i_1$, etc. Diminishing returns to development across units μ_i can be represented as $\frac{db_{di}}{di} < 0$. (Note that $\frac{db_{pi}}{di} > 0$, as benefits from preserving the marginal unit increase with the number of units already developed.) In this formulation the size and number of units μ_i are defined by the condition that returns are constant within each.

III

The foregoing analysis indicates that, even where it is not appropriate to postulate risk aversion in evaluating an activity, something of the "feel" of risk aversion is produced by a restriction on reversibility. If one takes the view that some means of spreading the risk associated with the uncertain environmental costs of the activity is likely to be feasible in most cases, then there are clear policy implications to this result, as it sharply distinguishes between reversible and irreversible changes in the environment.

One such implication however is *not* the overthrow of marginal analysis. Just because an action is irreversible does not mean that it should not be undertaken. Rather, the effect of irreversibility is to reduce the benefits, which are then balanced against costs in the usual way.

The analysis can be applied to problems of pollution control as well. Let b_d and β_d represent the benefits from an investment, and c_1 and c_2 the direct costs, as before. Then b_p and β_p can be taken to represent the benefits (reduced losses) from the cleaner or less toxic air, or water, that would be enjoyed were the investment not made.

Of course, the dynamic model is relevant only if the pollution is in some sense irreversible, as is the extinction of a form of life, or the destruction of a unique geomorphological phenomenon. This is an empirical matter. Clearly, much pollution is shortlived; sufficiently diffused or degraded by the assimilative medium to render it negligible in concentration and harmless in effect beyond some point in time. To this type of pollution the model does not apply.

On the other hand, there is evidence that some pollution does accumulate in the environment, perhaps sufficiently to be considered irreversible. Recent research has shed light on the toxicity and the persistence, indeed the increasing concentration, of the "hard" or non-degradable pesticides such as DDT, for example, and of industrial substances such as lead. A decision on a project involving discharge into the ambient environment of any of these or other potentially harmful and persistent substances should then take into account the continuing effect, as in the analysis of the preceding section. The same reasoning would apply to cumulative "macro" environmental effects such as the increasing concentration of carbon dioxide in the global atmosphere, with its attendant climatic changes, as predicted by some ecologists.

The point about uncertainty, information and irreversibility might be made still more generally, i.e., without reference to environmental effects. Essentially, the point is that the expected benefits of an irreversible decision should be adjusted to reflect the loss of options it entails.[10]

FOOTNOTES

* Harvard University

** Brown University and Resources for the Future, Inc.

Research reported in this paper has been supported by a grant from the Natural Environments Program at RFF and also in part by NSF Grant GS 2530 to the Institute for Mathematical Studies in the Social Sciences, Stanford University. Comments and suggestions by Harl Ryder and a referee are gratefully acknowledged.

[1]Also some not so recent, as in the classic work of Pigou. For a review of some more recent contributions, see E.J. Mishan, "The Postwar Literature on Externalities: An Interpretative Essay," *Journal of Economic Literature*, Vol. 9 (March 1971), pp. 1-28.

[2]A.V. Kneese, *Economics and the Quality of the Environment—Some Empirical Experiences*, Reprint Number 71, Resources for the Future, 1968, p. 172.

[3]*Ibid.*, p. 172.

[4]B.A. Weisbrod, "Collective-Consumption Services of Individual-Consumption Goods," *Quarterly Journal of Economics*, Vol. 78 (Aug. 1964), pp. 471-7.

[5]C.J. Cicchetti and A.M. Freeman III, "Option Demand and Consumer Surplus: Further Comment," *Quarterly Journal of Economics*, Vol. 85 (Aug. 1971), pp. 528-39.

[6]K.J. Arrow and R.C. Lind, "Uncertainty and the Evaluation of Public Investment Decisions," *American Economic Review*, Vol. 60 (June 1970), pp. 364-78.

[7]A.C. Fisher, J.V. Krutilla, and C.J. Cicchetti, "The Economics of Environmental Preservation: A Theoretical and Empirical Analysis," *American Economic Review*, forthcoming.

[8]K.J. Arrow, "Optimal Capital Policy and Irreversible Investment," in J.N. Wolfe, ed., *Value, Capital and Growth*, Chicago, 1968, pp. 1-20.

[9]K.J. Arrow and M. Kurz, "Optimal Growth with Irreversible Investment in a Ramsey Model," *Econometrica*, Vol. 38 (March 1970), pp. 331-44.

[10]For an earlier statement see A.G. Hart, "Risk, Uncertainty, and the Unprofitability of Compounding Probabilities," in *Studies in Mathematical Economics and Econometrics*, ed. by O. Lange, F. McIntyre and T.O. Yntema, Chicago, 1942.

CHAPTER 28

ECONOMICS OF WILDERNESS RESOURCES

VERNON L. SMITH

In 1972 over 16,400 commercial and private users sought the supreme "white water" experience by traversing the Grand Canyon, or a portion of it, by means of inflatable rubber boats. This compares with 372 in 1962 and 70 in 1955. Although Grand Canyon represents one of the most spectacular wilderness experiences, similar explosions in visitor use are reported in the High Sierra, the Salmon and Snake Rivers of Idaho, and hundreds of miles of wilderness trails and rivers in the National Park and National Forest systems. This trend is causing considerable distress for naturalists and environmentalists interested in wilderness preservation, and for National Park and Forest Service administrators caught in the cross currents of political pressure to make public lands freely available to the citizenry while attempting to maintain such lands in some approximation to their natural state.

Visitor use of the National Parks in general, although increasing, has not kept pace with growth in the use of the more primitive areas, as mountain climbing, backpacking and river running have become popular activities that engage remote public lands never previously used for recreational purposes by more than an insignificant segment of the population. The contrast between growth in visits to developed park centers and to more rugged areas is illustrated in Chart 1 for visitor use of Grand Canyon. While total visits to Grand Canyon nearly doubled, 1960-1970, Colorado River excursions increased about 50 times.

Economic analysis of recreational lands has been concerned primarily with the principles (Krutilla, 1967) and techniques (Carlin, 1968; Fisher, Krutilla and Cicchetti, 1972; Hearse, 1968; Hoch, 1962) of allocating and valuing land for recreational or preservational as against developed industrial uses. For example, should Hells Canyon or Grand Canyon be flooded behind hydroelectric dams or preserved as scenic resources? Formal treatments of the dynamic and uncertainty aspects of this allocation problem with particular emphasis on the relative irreversibility of decisions to flood or otherwise destroy whole ecosystems through industrial development, have been provided by Fisher, Krutilla, and Cicchetti (1972) and by Arrow and Fisher (1973). These contributions do not deal with the problem of managing, developing, and rationing the use of resources already allocated to recreational uses, although there are informal studies of the problem (for example, Hoch, 1962, discusses and recommends license fees for park users).

In what follows, the familiar tools of control theory and stationary general equilibrium theory will be used to study a model that captures certain stylized characteristics of public recreational resources. These characteristics include external crowding diseconomies in consumption, deterioration effects of resource use, the capacity of the resource for ecological adjustment to (or recovery from) use, and the public good aspect of the quality, beauty, or "naturalness" of the resource. Several types of equilibria will be illustrated and compared: An optimal control solution, with and without administrative cost, and a corresponding free use competitive solution; and stationary state competitive solutions for undeveloped and developed access technologies, and an optimal solution with administrative cost. An illustration is given whereby investment in an easier-access technology produces crowding and resource deterioration to the point where all users are made worse off. The administrative cost of overlaying direct controls as a remedy may cause further social losses, or, in any case, be worse than leaving the resource in its original state of high-cost access. This suggests the possibility that rationing by deliberately increasing (or not decreasing) the cost of access to scenic resources may be society's best option. Although this appears somewhat counterintuitive there are many institutional examples of a scarce resource being rationed by the imposition of artificial costs. Public toilet facilities nearly always ration tissue paper and towels through dispensers designed to raise the cost of transacting for each unit. One imagines this design evolving from a great deal of experience with excessive waste from simple, more convenient dispensing devices. Similarly, the problem of overfishing for Pacific salmon has been alleviated in part by prohibiting the use of traps that clearly represent the most efficient capture technology. Requirements that oars rather than motors be used on wild river floats, that jeeps and trail bikes be prohibited in wilderness areas, and that certain park roads be left unpaved or restricted to four-wheel drive vehicles, may represent relatively efficient rationing techniques. Such rationing devices not only reduce crowding, and ecosystem damage; they also restrict use to those whose preferences are strong enough to overcome substantial cost of transacting, and in this sense the scarce resource is allocated to its more highly valued uses.

CONCEPTS AND ASSUMPTIONS

Consider a scenic or wilderness recreational resource to be represented in the abstract by a stock, Q, of pleasurable homogeneous services. Real world prototypes would be the Grand Canyon, Yosemite and Glacial National Parks or any of the Wild Areas contained in the National Forest system. In the "natural" state, i.e. "undisturbed" by man, Q is generated by an ecosystem which is boldly assumed to be governed by a differential equation

$$dQ/dt = g(Q) \ , \ g'(Q) < 0, \ g''(Q) < 0 \ , \ \text{for } Q \geq 0, \ g(\bar{Q}) = 0 \quad (1)$$

where $\bar{Q}$ is the natural state equilibrium. This borders on an offensive oversimplification of reality, but serves to capture the idea that there exist natural biological and geological forces by which a scenic resource develops in the "undisturbed" state. Also, the stage is set for the beauty or wildness of the resource to be modified by man's utilization of it. In particular, if the stock is reduced to some $Q < \bar{Q}$, natural forces will generate recovery so long as the utilization (consumption) rate is below $g(Q)$. Figure 1 illustrates the natural state equilibrium, $\bar{Q}$. At $Q < \bar{Q}$ if the resource is consumed at a rate $q < g(Q)$, it will recover at the net rate $g(Q) - q$ until $dQ/dt = g(Q) - q = 0$.

It is assumed that the natural resource resides in an economy which produces two goods. There is a normal or ordinary good (like corn or meat) produced and consumed at the rate q_1, while consumer exposure to the natural resource is produced at the rate q_2. Exposure to the natural resource affects consumer taste in three distinct ways: (1) q_2 enters the utility function as an ordinary private good just as does q_1. Consumer use of the resource (as measured, for example, in visitor-use days) is variable, controllable, and excludable so that intensity of use is a private activity. (2) Total consumption by all users enters the utility function of each consumer on the assumption that crowding, or merely the presence of other users, even in modest numbers, detracts from the pleasure of scenic or wilderness resources. A dramatic example of external diseconomy on Colorado River excursions is the recent epidemic of dysentery (*New York Times*, 1972). Thus if q_2^k is the kth individual's consumption $\sum_{k=1}^{n} q_2^k$ enters the utility function of each of n consumers. Assuming, as we shall, identical utility functions, q_2 is the common consumption rate, and nq_2 is total consumption. (3) The stock of services (Q) represented by the resource enters each utility function as a public good measure of the quality or character of the resource. This is the case whether or not one assumes identical utility functions.

The utility function is then of the form $u^m = u^m (q_1^m, q_2^m, \sum_{k=1}^{n} q_2^k, Q)$ for consumer m,[1] or $u = u(q_1, q_2, nq_2, Q)$ when an economy of n identical individuals is postulated.[2] In the analysis of this paper, u will be assumed to be concave and additively separable,[3]

$$u = u_1(q_1) + u_2(q_2) + u_3(nq_2) + u_4(Q), \tag{2}$$

$$u_1' > 0,\ u_2' > 0,\ u_3' < 0,\ u_4' > 0, \tag{2}$$

$$u_j'' < 0,\ j = 1, 2, 3, 4.$$

A simple homogeneous productive input, available in the amount L, is allocated L_1 units to producing q_1 and L_2 to producing q_2, i.e.

$$L = L_1 + L_2 \tag{3}$$

$$q_i = f_i(L_i),\ i = 1,2, \tag{4}$$

where the production functions f_i are assumed increasing and concave,

$$f_i' > 0,\ f_i'' \leq 0,\ i = 1,2.$$

The effect of using the resource is assumed to cause deterioration at a time rate which is an increasing convex function of total consumption, $h(nq_2)$, $h' > 0$, $h'' \geq 0$. Hence changes in the net stock of services provided by the resource are described by the differential equation,

$$dQ/dt = g(Q) - h(nq_2) \tag{5}$$

It may be instructive to relate the technology functions, $g(Q)$, $h(nq_2)$ to particular types of recreational resources. A "pure" scenic resource such as Monument Valley, as viewed from U.S. 163, or the Grand Canyon as viewed from the North or South rims (insofar as they are merely resources viewed at a distance) would not be subject to deterioration, and would therefore be characterized by specifying $h(nq_2) \equiv 0$, and $g'(\bar{Q}) = -\infty$, i.e., $Q \equiv \bar{Q}$. The specification $g'(Q) = -\infty$ merely states that geological change in these resources is negligible in contemporary time, and Q is fixed and independent of resource utilization. But note that crowding, nq_2, is still in the utility function, and such considerations may detract from the viewing pleasure of a fixed landscape.

The Grand Canyon as viewed from the inner gorge, as part of a Colorado River experience (and similarly Desolation Canyon on the Green River), is a scenic resource requiring direct physical contact. One has only to imagine over 16,000 people floating 225 miles of the Colorado River from Lees Ferry to Diamond Creek in 1972 — an area totally without sleeping or sanitary facilities — to appreciate the effect of such use on the terrain, flora and fauna of the River and its immediate environs. Clearly a deterioration function $h(nq_2)$, perhaps with high inelasticity, may apply. Furthermore, the growth or restoration function, $g(Q)$, might be highly elastic for the arid ecosystem of the inner gorge so that recovery from a disturbed state may be very slow. On the other hand, the more lush Allagash region of Northern Maine or parts of the New York State Forest Preserve may recover more quickly from disturbances in their wilderness ecosystem.

A CONVENTIONAL CONTROL THEORY ANALYSIS

If u measures instantaneous social welfare and δ is the social rate of time preference the standard control problem is to choose $[L_1(t), L_2(t)]$ so as to maximize $\int_0^\infty ue^{-\delta t}dt$ subject to (3)-(5).

The current value Hamilton-Lagrange criterion is

$$H = u_1[f_1(L_1)] + u_2[f_2(L_2)] + u_3[nf_2(L_2)] + u_4(Q) + \mu\left(g(Q) - h[nf_2(L_2)]\right) + \lambda(L - L_1 - L_2)$$

and along a maximizing path the conditions

$\frac{\partial H}{\partial L_i} = 0$, i = 1, 2, and $\dot{\mu} = \delta\mu - \frac{\partial H}{\partial Q}$ must be satisfied.

By substitution from (3) and (4), the state of the system is described by

$$\left\{ u_2' \, [f_2(L_2)] + nu_3' \, [nf_2(L_2)] - n\mu h'[nf_2(L_2)] \right\} / u_1' \, [f_1(L - L_2)] = f_1' \, (L - L_2) \; / \; f_2' \, (L_2) \tag{6a}$$

$$\dot{\mu} = \mu[\delta - g'(Q)] - u_4'(Q) \tag{6b}$$

$$\dot{Q} = g(Q) - h[nf_2(L_2)] \tag{6c}$$

and $\lim_{t \to \infty} e^{-\delta t} \mu(t) \geq 0$, $\lim_{t \to \infty} e^{-\delta t} \mu(t) \, Q(t) = 0$.

Equation (6a) defines a function $L_2 = L_2(\mu)$ with

$$dL_2 \; / \; d\mu = nf_2' \, h' / \, J < 0 \tag{7}$$

where $J = u_1' \, f_1'' + u_1''(f_2')^2 + (u_2' + nu_3' - n\mu h') \, f_2'' - \mu h'' \, (nf_2')^2 + u_2'' \, (f_2')^2 + u_3'' \, (nf_2')^2 < 0$,

since $f_i'' \leq 0$, $u_1' > 0$, $u_j'' < 0$, $h'' \geq 0$, and from (6a), $(u_2' + nu_3' - n\mu h') = u_1' \, f_1'/f_2' > 0$. Then the differential equations (6b) and (6c), with $L_2 = L_2(\mu)$, describe time paths $Q = Q^*(t)$, $\mu = \mu^*(t)$. The motion of the system in state space (Q,μ) is characterized by the usual phase diagram of Fig. 2.

From (6c), the set of points $\{(Q,\mu) \mid \dot{Q} = 0\}$, with the property that the stock of resource services is stationary, is given by

$$Q = g^{-1}(h\{nf_2[L_2(\mu)]\}). \tag{8}$$

This function is strictly increasing since

$d\mu/dQ \mid_{\dot{Q}=0} = g'/nh'f_2' \, (dL_2/d\mu) > 0$, as shown in Fig. 2. Also from (6c) , $\partial\dot{Q} \; / \; \partial Q = g'(Q) \lessgtr 0$. At any point to the right (left) of the set $\{(Q,\mu) \mid \dot{Q} = 0\}$ the recovery rate of the resource is below (above) its deterioration rate and the stock of resource services will decline (increase).

Along an optimizing path, (6b) requires the subjective instantaneous unit value of the resource stock, $u_4'(Q)$, to equal total interest on the market value of a unit of the stock, $\mu[\delta - g'(Q)]$, less capital gains on the stock, $\dot{\mu}$. Total interest includes the time preference rate, δ, and $-g'(Q)$, an "own" ecological rate of interest which measures the marginal cost, in terms of reduced natural growth, of consuming the resource stock. The set of points $\{(Q,\mu) \mid \dot{\mu}=0\}$, with the property that the implicit price of the resource stock is stationary, is given by

$$\mu = \frac{u_4'(Q)}{\delta - g'(Q)} \qquad (9)$$

a strictly decreasing function since

$d\mu / dQ \,\big|_{\dot{\mu}=0} = (u_4'' + \mu g'') / (\delta - g') < 0$, as shown in Fig. 2. Also $\partial\dot{\mu} / \partial\mu = \delta - g' > 0$ and for points above (below) the set $\{(Q,\mu) \mid \dot{\mu} = 0\}$, the price of the resource stock must be increasing (decreasing).

A stationary state equilibrium point (Q^*,μ^*) is shown in Fig. 2. If the initial rsource stock is $\bar{Q}$, the corresponding optimal initial price is $\bar{\mu}$ and the equilibrium path is along the dashed line passing through $(\bar{Q},\bar{\mu})$ and (Q^*,μ^*).

If we assume that $\lim_{\mu \to \infty} L_2(\mu) = 0$ in (6a), $\lim_{L_i \to 0} f_i(L_i) = 0$, $\lim_{q \to 0} h(q) = 0$, and $\lim_{\dot{Q} \to 0} g^{-1}(\dot{Q}) = \bar{Q}$, then from (8) $\lim_{\mu \to \infty} g^{-1}(h\{nf_2[L_2(\mu)]\}) \longrightarrow \bar{Q}$ as shown in Fig. 2. If we let $L_2^\dagger = L_2(0)$, where $0 < L_2^\dagger < L$, be the amount of input L_2 used when there is free access to the resource, then we must have

$$Q^\dagger = g^{-1}\,(h\{nf_2[L_2^\dagger]\}) < \bar{Q}\ ,$$

as shown. From (9) if $\lim_{Q \to \infty} u_4'(Q) = 0$, and since $g''(Q) < 0$ for all $Q \geq 0$, we must have $\mu \to 0$ as $Q \to \infty$; and if $\lim_{Q \to 0} u_4'(Q) = \infty$, then we must have $\mu \to \infty$ as $Q \to 0$, as shown in Fig. 2. Thus an intersection point at Q^*, where $Q^\dagger < Q^* < \bar{Q}$, will exist.

REDUCTION TO A MODEL OF DECENTRALIZED COMPETITION

The control model reduces to a model of decentralized competition if we set $\mu \equiv 0$, $nu_3' \equiv 0$ in equations (6a) - (6c). That is there exists no free market price for using the free-access natural resource and each consumer, following his own self-interest, fails to take account of the crowding diseconomies produced by his own consumption of the natural resource.

The competitive time path is then defined by (6c) and

$$\frac{u_2'[f_2(L_2)]}{u_1'[f_1(L - L_2)]} = \frac{f_1'(L - L_2)}{f_2'(L_2)} \tag{10}$$

At a stationary competitive equilibrium $\hat{Q}$, $\hat{L}_2$, $\mu \equiv 0$, we will have

$$\hat{Q} = g^{-1}\left\{h\{nf_2[\hat{L}_2]\}\right\} \tag{11}$$

with $\hat{Q} < Q^{\dagger}$.

FURTHER ANALYSIS OF THE STATIONARY STATE

The stationary state is defined by (6a)-(6c) when $\dot{Q} = \dot{\mu} = 0$. The state of the economy can then be represented in (q_1, q_2) space in the usual manner of static general equilibrium. This is accomplished by noting that (6b) and (6c) can be combined in the form

$$\mu = \frac{u_4'(Q)}{\delta - g'(Q)} = \frac{u_4'\{g^{-1}[h(nq_2)]\}}{\delta - g'\{g^{-1}[h(nq_2)]\}} .$$

In (q_1, q_2) space, using (3) and (4), and transforming (6a), equilibrium is defined by

$$\frac{-u_1'(q_1^*)}{u_2'(q_2^*)+nu_3'(nq_2^*) - \dfrac{nh'(nq_2^*)u_4'\{g^{-1}[h(nq_2^*)]\}}{\delta - g'\{g^{-1}[h(nq_2^*)]\}}} \tag{12}$$

$$= -\frac{f_1'[f_1^{-1}(q_1^*)]}{f_2'[f_2^{-1}(q_2^*)]}$$

$$f_1^{-1}(q_1^*) + f_2^{-1}(q_2^*) = L. \tag{13}$$

Condition (12) states the familiar requirement that the social marginal rate of substitution equal the marginal rate of transformation, while (13) requires the economy to operate on its production possibility frontier. The left side of (12) is the slope of an indifference curve adjusted for the external effect of Q and nq_2. This is seen most directly by letting the time preference rate $\delta = 0$. Then the left side of (12) is the slope of an indifference curve defined by

$$u_1(q_1) + u_2(q_2) + u_3(nq_2) + u_4\{g^{-1}[h(nq_2)]\} = \text{constant},$$

where $Q = g^{-1}[h(nq_2)]$ is determined by equilibrium of the resource stock.

However, decentralized competitive consumers of the natural resource do not have private incentive to consider the components u_3 and u_4 when making their consumption decisions. They perceive a substitution rate u_1'/u_2', and therefore the competitive equilibrium $(\hat{q}_1, \hat{q}_2)$ as defined by

$$-\frac{u_1'(\hat{q}_1)}{u_2'(\hat{q}_2)} = -\frac{f_1'[f_1^{-1}(\hat{q}_1)]}{f_2'[f_2^{-1}(\hat{q}_2)]} \tag{12'}$$

$$f_1^{-1}(\hat{q}_1) + f_2^{-}(\hat{q}_2) = L. \tag{13'}$$

In Fig. 3 the point C represents a competitive equilibrium, while P represents the social optimum. The indifference curve J_p corresponds to maximum utility taking full account of all social opportunity costs. At P, the indifference curve I_p corresponds to the set of substitutions perceived by the individual as he views the free access natural resource. At any point in the commodity space, I will have a greater algebraic slope than J, since $g' < 0$. $h' < 0$, $u'_3 < 0$, $u'_4 < 0$ implies

$$\frac{-u'_1}{u'_2} > -\frac{u'_1}{u'_2 + nu'_3 - \dfrac{nh'u'_4}{\delta - g'}}$$

In a free market q_1 would exchange for q_2 at the rate $-f'_1/f'_2 < -u'_1/u'_2$ at P, and each consumer would substitute q_1 for q_2 — in the myopic belief that his position would be improved — until the point C was reached. But at C everyone is worse off than at P.

OPTIMAL CONTROL AND THE COST OF ADMINISTRATION

Society's choice between P and C in Fig. 3, or between stocks Q^* and Q^+ in Fig. 2, would be simple if there were no costs associated with achieving the control solution. Everyone would benefit from, and would favour, intervention to impose the allocation represented by P in Fig. 3.

But suppose there is a cost to administering this locally efficient allocation. This cost may arise from the need to compute and charge the resource price $\mu^*(t)$ and the congestion charge[4], or to compute and enforce an optimal quota $q_2^*(t)$ for rationing access to the natural resource. In particular, suppose the administrative machinery requires the fixed expenditure of L_a units of the productive input, leaving $L - L_a$ available for direct productive allocation. This will shift the resource stock equilibrium set to the right, say to $\{(Q,\mu) \mid \dot{Q} = Q\}_a$, as indicated by the broken curve in Fig. 2. An equilibrium path will now pass through the intersection at Q^a, the stationary state equilibrium optimal stock taking into account administrative cost. In Fig. 3, the effect of administrative cost is to lower the production possibility frontier from S to S_a, and the optimal stationary state solution is at A. This *may* occur, as illustrated in Fig. 3, at a utility level J_a below J_c. Hence the competitive free access solution might be superior to the control solution net of administrative cost. In this interpretation L_a represents cost in excess of any similar cost, such as transactions cost, required to support or maintain free markets.

RATIONING BY COSTLY ACCESS OR NON-DEVELOPMENT

National Park (Forest, Monument) administrators are not normally confronted with a simple choice between optimal controlled access versus free competitive access to a scenic or wilderness resource. Decisions usually take the form of how to permit development or which access technologies are to be permitted. Typically there is the question of whether or not roads to a scenic area are to be paved, or whether trails in a wilderness area are to be closed to motorized traffic. Such decisions can be stylized in our model by asking if it pays society to invest in an easier-access technology. Should a road be built across the Escalante River to Lake Powell permitting automobile access to a hitherto isolated scenic area accessible only by backpacking or horseback? Should jeep trails be closed to all motorized traffic in the Manti La Sal National Forest? Should the use of outboard motors be prohibited on Colorado River excursions through Cataract Canyon or Grand Canyon? These are typical policy decisions facing public lands administrators.

Phrasing the question in this way rather than as a problem concerned only with controlling access is particularly appropriate since the need for limiting access is frequently a consequence of an earlier decision to develop a natural resource by making it more accessible. This raises the question of whether costly forms of primitive access, or non-development in general, are not preferable to overlaying administrative controls upon investment in an easier-access technology as a means of undoing with the left hand that which the right hand has already done.

Suppose that by incurring a fixed input cost equal to L_2° units per period, the production technology $q_2 = \max\,[0, F_2(L_2 - L_2^\circ)]$ can be substituted for the technology $q_2 = f_2(L_2)$, where $F_2(0) = 0$, $F_2' > 0$, $F_2'' \leq 0$ and $f_2(L_2) < F_2(L_2 - L_2^\circ)$ beyond some level of L_2 (see Fig. 4). In terms of production possibilities society can increase its opportunity set over some region by producing less q_1 and investing the input savings in a substitute means of producing q_2. In Fig. 5 the frontier of this substitute set is represented by S'.

A possible effect of the investment of L_2° units of input, or the foregone output, $f_1(L) - f_1(L - L_2^\circ)$ units of q_1, in developing the natural resource is illustrated in Fig. 5. Initially the free access equilibrium is at C.

Then society invests in a motorized technology yielding the frontier S'. The resulting sacrifice of q_1 output permits an enlarged set of q_2 consumption opportunities, and society moves to the new stationary state C'. If at C utility net of external effects is represented by an indifference curve J_C passing to the northeast (southwest) of C' as shown, then society is unambiguously worse (better) off as a result of the development expenditure.[5] Note, however, that at C each consumer perceives that an increase in production possibilities from S to S' will permit him to improve his position by moving to indifference curves above I_C. Myopic consumers may thus press for a change in public land policy that will permit the technological change, but the consequent crowding and deterioration in resource quality may lead to disappointing long-run levels of satisfaction. Such a process seems to portray actual experience in many instances of recreational land development.

After the movement from C to C', if the public authorities are pressured to intervene and set up the administrative bureaucracy to ration access, this will lower the production possibility set and society ends up at a point such as O'_a which might represent a still lower level of satisfaction even though the point is allocatively efficient. If such be the case it would be preferable, if somewhat paradoxical, to do nothing, and "ration" access with the higher cost technology, S, and let competition result in the state represented by C.

FOOTNOTES

*I am grateful to the National Science Foundation for research support.

[1]It should be noted that $\sum_{k-1}^{n} q_2^k$ and Q may enter the utility function of consumer m as externality variables with nonzero marginal effects even if $q_2^m = 0$. Thie Sierra Club member who never climbs Mt. McKinley may derive satisfaction from the knowledge that the largest North American mountain is relatively unspoiled, with few climbers littering its slopes. (He should, of course, also be willing to pay for these satisfactions.)

[2]Alternatively, one could think of u as a welfare function depending on the per capita consumption rates (q_1, q_2), and

wilderness quality, Q. In either case, as in most of the growth economics literature, we dodge the whole set of complications introduced by conflicting subjective evaluations of the arguments of u.

[3]Additivity is neither very realistic nor strictly necessary to the analysis, but it very much simplifies the arithmetic by permitting us to deduce that the phase curves of Fig. 2 are monotone. Alternatively we could postulate the more general utility function in the text, and then postulate monotonicity for the more general equilibrium state equations corresponding to (8) and (9) and illustrated in Fig. 2.

[4]If consumers are required to pay a visitor-use charge, θ_2 per day or other unit of use, then from (6a) and (10') free market allocations will be optimal if

$$\theta_2 = -\frac{nu'_3}{u'_1} + \frac{n\mu h'}{u'_1}, \text{ where } -\frac{nu'_3}{u'_1} > 0 \text{ is the congestion}$$

or crowding toll, and $\frac{n\mu h'}{u'_1} > 0$ is the rental rate for the resource services provided by the stock, Q. In Fig. 3, θ_2 is measured by the difference between the slopes of I_p and J_p, or between I_p and S, at P, so that for the consumer

$$\frac{u'_2}{u'_1} = \theta_2 + \frac{f'_1}{f'_2}, \text{ yielding budget equilibrium at P.}$$

[5]This judgment ignores the time path of utility between equilibria and is based entirely on the comparative statics in Fig. 5.

REFERENCES

1. ARROW, K.J. and A.C. FISHER, "Environmental Preservation, Uncertainty, and Irreversibility," *Quarterly Journal of Economics, 88*, May 1974, 312-319.

2. CARLIN, ALAN, "The Grand Canyon Controversy: Lessons for Federal Cost Benefit Practices," *Land Economics, 44*, May 1968, 219-227.

3. FISHER, A.C., J.V. KRUTILLA and C.J. CICCHETTI, "The

Economics of Environmental Preservation: A Theoretical and Empirical Analysis," *Amer. Econ. Rev.*, Sept. 1972, *62*, 605-619.

4. KRUTILLA, J.V., "Conservation Reconsidered," *Amer. Econ. Rev.*, Sept. 1967, *57*, 777-786.

5. HEARSE, P.H., "A New Approach to the Evaluation of Non-Priced Recreation Resources," *Land Economics*, Feb. 1968, *44*, 87-99.

6. HOCH, I., "Economic Analysis of Wilderness Areas," in *Wilderness and Recreation - A Report on Resources, Values and Problems*, *ORRRC Study Report No. 3*, Washington 1962, 203-264.

7. *New York Times*, "Epidemic of Dysentery Affected Excursions on Colorado Rapids," October 10, 1972.

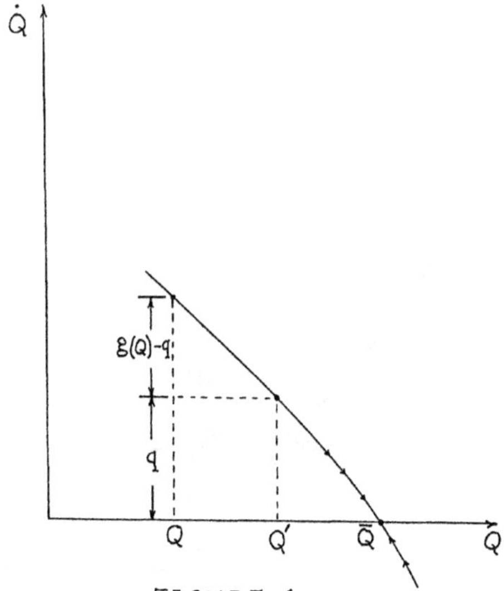

FIGURE 1

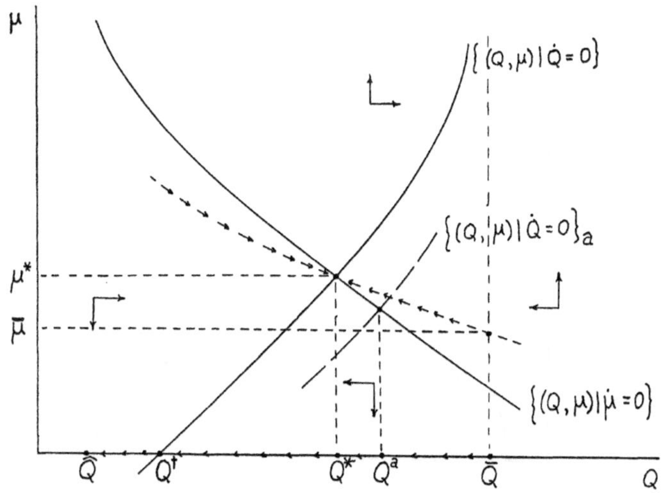

FIGURE 2

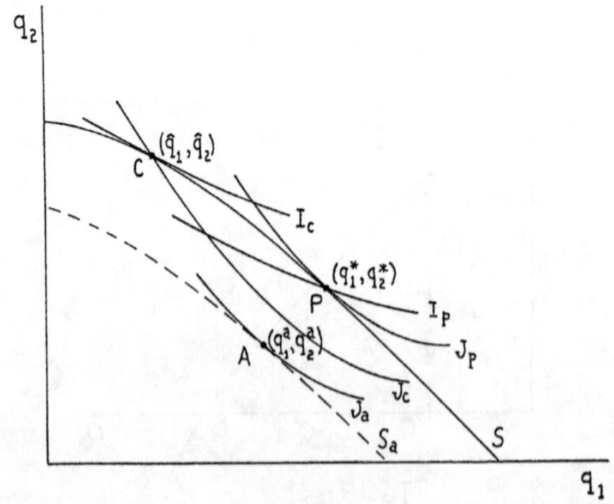

FIGURE 3

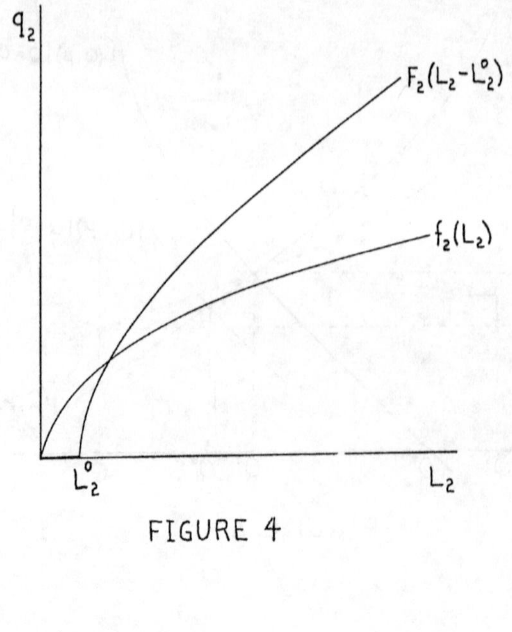

FIGURE 4

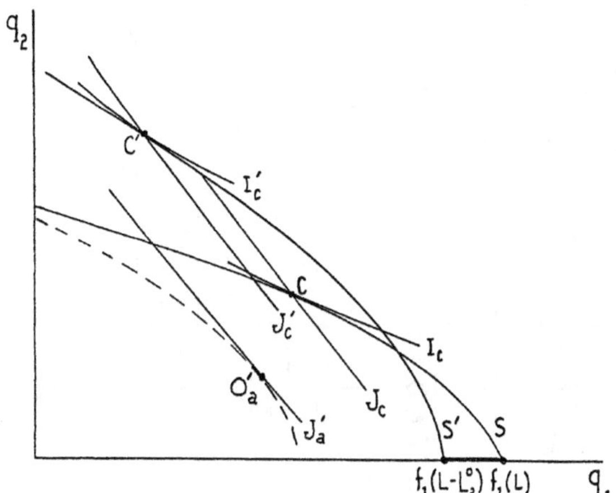

FIGURE 5

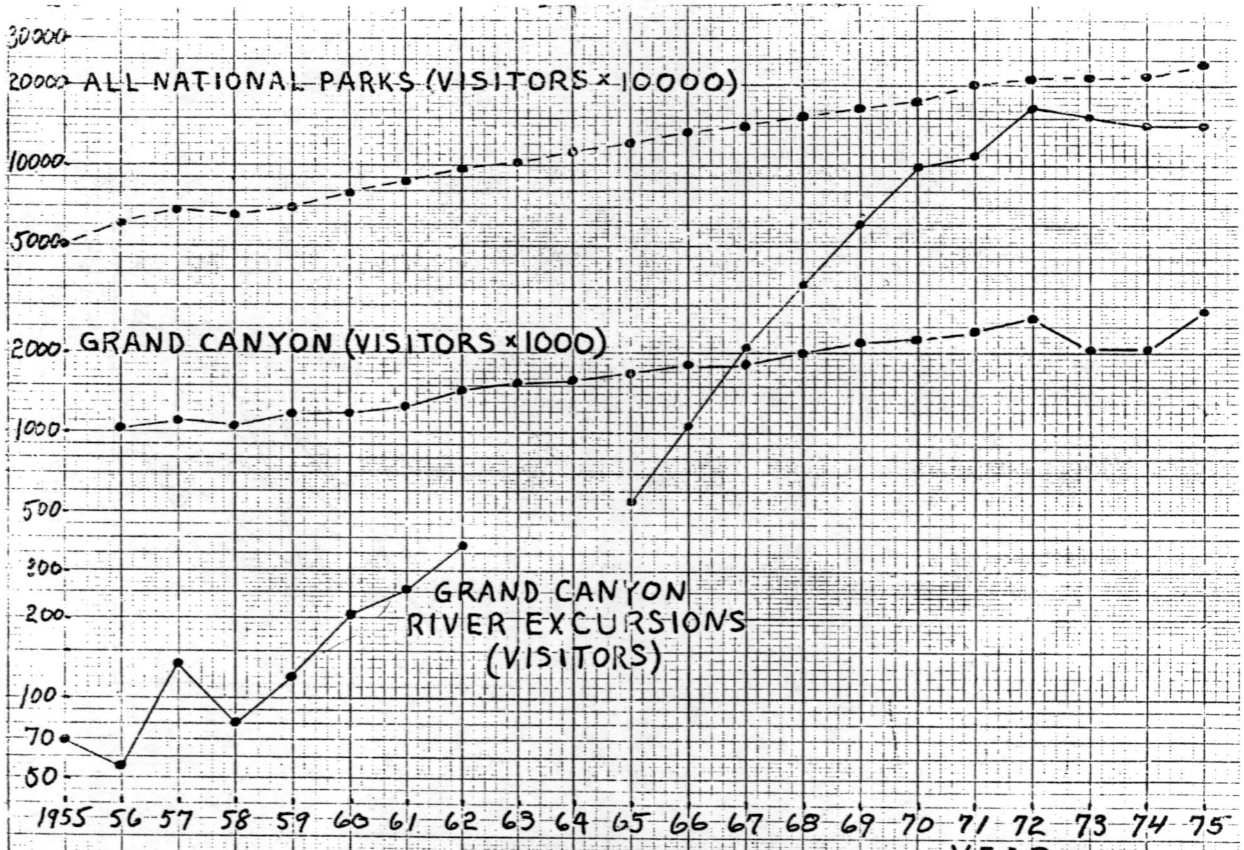

30000
20000
10000
5000
2000
1000
500
300
200
100
70
50
ALL NATIONAL PARKS (VISITORS × 10000)
GRAND CANYON (VISITORS × 1000)
GRAND CANYON
RIVER EXCURSIONS
(VISITORS)
1955 56 57 58 59 60 61 62 63 64 65 66 67 68 69 70 71 72 73 74 75
YEAR

CHART 1

For Product Safety Concerns and Information please contact our EU representative GPSR@taylorandfrancis.com
Taylor & Francis Verlag GmbH, Kaufingerstraße 24, 80331 München, Germany

www.ingramcontent.com/pod-product-compliance
Lightning Source LLC
LaVergne TN
LVHW011101300926
849160LV00008B/249

* 9 7 8 0 4 1 5 8 4 2 2 8 0 *